GEORGIA

The History of an American State

GEORGIA

The History of an American State

By

BONITA BULLARD LONDON

CLAIRMONT PRESS
Selma, Alabama

BONITA BULLARD LONDON is a graduate of Sullins College, The University of Georgia, and Georgia State University. She has taught in grades K-12, with a concentration in eighth-grade Georgia History in the Atlanta City Schools. She has also been an instructor with the Governor's Summer Honors Program. In addition, Bonnie has served as an elementary principal in the Atlanta City Schools and in the Clarke County School District. She has worked as a consultant for the Northeast Georgia RESA and for the Georgia State Department of Education. Presently, Bonnie is president of London Limited, an education consulting firm. She has authored a number of articles and student workbooks in the areas of Georgia Studies and Language Arts.

ACKNOWLEDGMENTS Like any textbook, *Georgia: The History of an American State,* is the result of the collaborative efforts of many people. Special recognition is given to Barbara Mathis, who spent countless hours keying the hundreds of pages of manuscript; to Sandra Nichols, who culled materials and provided constant support; and to Patricia VanGorder, who searched for and found exemplary resource materials. In addition, thanks is given to Dr. Ron Ridgley of Coastal Georgia Community College; to the computer site *Serevitus*; to the Clarke County Regional Library; and to the Georgia Department of Trade, Industry, and Tourism for their vital information. I also appreciate the many comments and suggestions concerning the previous edition of this text that were received from students and teachers throughout the state.

Editor in Chief: Ralph M. Holmes

Editor: Georges Carpentier

Editor: Kathy Conway

Associate Editor: Billie Holmes

Photo Research: Robin McDonald

Design: Robin McDonald

ISBN 1-56733-994-8 Third Printing Printed in U.S.A.

INTRODUCTION

THE AMERICAN HISTORIAN AND PHILOSOPHER George Santayana wrote that "Those who cannot remember the past are condemned to repeat it." That is why the study of history is so essential to the development of a well-rounded and educated person. To me, history is far more than a list of boring dates and events. It allows one to reflect on economics, geography, political science, anthropology, sociology, psychology—in other words, the sum total of the human experience. It influences who you are and who your children will be. Enjoy the experience.

—*Bonita Bullard London*

***Above:** One of Georgia's most famous citizens is memorialized at the Martin Luther King, Jr., Center. **Cover:** Georgia's state capitol dome is covered with sixty ounces of Dahlonega gold. **Page i:** Savannah's statue of James Oglethorpe. **Pages ii-iii:** Relaxing on Little St. Simons Island. **Pages iv-v:** Recreating Georgia's colonial history at Fort King George in Darien.*

TABLE OF CONTENTS

Top: *Spanish moss decorates cypress trees in the Okefenokee Swamp, the largest national wildlife refuge in the eastern United States.* ***Above:*** *Springer Mountain marks one end of the Appalachian Trail, which stretches all the way to Maine.*

Top: *A Civil War cannon contrasts with the modern skyline of downtown Atlanta.* ***Above:*** *Diners are dwarfed by the massive columns of the Peachtree Plaza Hotel.*

UNIT I

A STATE AND ITS BEGINNING

Geography is the study of the earth as home for man.
—Grammar School Geography, Alexis Frye, 1902

LONG BEFORE MAN LIVED in the state of Georgia, the sun, wind, rain, snow, and ocean currents were preparing the land to receive its first inhabitants. It was a long process and continues today. Had you lived in Macon millions of years ago, you could have enjoyed swimming and picking up sea shells right from your back door, for all of the area south of Macon was under water. Volcanic eruptions deep within the earth's core changed the surface above, and as the ice age ended, the oceans began to recede. This enabled the rest of our state to emerge slowly. Because of this past history, we can assume that changes in our *topography*, or landforms, so familiar to us today will be quite different thousands of years from now.

An awareness of the geography of an area is essential to understanding how our state was settled and has continued to grow and prosper through the years. As you will learn, it was, in large part, the geography of the region that enticed prehistoric Indians to settle here and become part of Georgia's ancient history. This location also appealed to early explorers such as Hernando de Soto and later to other Europeans who sailed from England to establish a colony in the land we proudly call home.

This salt marsh on Little St. Simons Island provides a haven for a wide variety of water life. Georgia's fertile coastal plain was the first part of the state to be colonized by settlers from Europe.

CHAPTER ONE

GEORGIA: SOMETHING FOR EVERYONE

To be short, it is a thing unspeakable to consider the things that bee seene there, and shal be founde more and more in this incomparable land, which never yet broken with plough yrons, bringeth forth all things according to his first nature wherewith the eternall God indued it. . . . [It is] the fairest, fruit fullest, and plesantest of all the world.

—French explorer Captain Jean Ribault, 1562

CAPTAIN JEAN RIBAULT praised the area many call the "Empire State of the South." He described a place with mild weather, many natural resources, and different kinds of land regions from the mountains to the coast. Ribault had traveled along the Georgia coast seeking a new home for his shipload of French Huguenots. Despite the kind words in his description of our state's geography, Ribault did not settle in Georgia.

To understand the history of Georgia, one needs to know its geography. The term **geography** comes from the Greek word *geographia* and means "earth's description." Geography is the science of studying the earth as the home of humans. It helps answer such questions as why Indians lived in certain places, why early settlers moved to particular areas, how the location of a town affects its economy, and why department stores carry certain kinds of clothing.

Opposite page, left: *Downtown Atlanta's skyscrapers.*
Left: *The old style beauty of Savannah with azaleas in bloom.*
Right: *The St. Simons Island lighthouse, built in 1872.*

If you were writing to a friend from Japan, which is located in the eastern hemisphere on the continent of Asia, trying to explain where you live, you would first write that you lived in the *western hemisphere* on the *continent* of North America. To define your location even further, you would write that your *country* is called the United States and the *state* in which you live is Georgia. If your pen pal needed specific directions to your home, you could add that, for example, you live in *Clarke county* in the *city* of Athens and even provide an exact street address.

Located in the southeastern part of the United States, Georgia extends from 30° 21' to 35° north **latitude.** (Latitude is the distance north or south of the equator.) The state also extends from 80° 50' to 85° 36' west **longitude**. (Longitude is a measure of the distance east or west of the **prime meridian,** an imaginary line located at Greenwich, England.) Another way to describe Georgia's location is to say that along straight lines Honolulu, Hawaii; Rio de Janeiro, Brazil; and Berlin, Germany are all equal distances from Atlanta.

Georgia is one of the ten fastest growing states in the country, and there is room enough for that growth. The best estimate of the size of our state is 58,910 square miles. In land area, it is the largest state east of the Mississippi River. In comparison of size with the rest of the states, Georgia ranks twenty-first in terms of land area. Its greatest length is 315 miles, and its greatest width is 250 miles. Georgia has almost as much land as all the New England states combined and is larger than England and Wales together. The elevation of the state begins at sea level along the eastern coastline and rises to 4,784 feet at Brasstown Bald in Towns County in northeast Georgia.

There are 159 counties in the state. The largest is Ware County with 907 square miles, and the smallest is Clarke County with

GEORGIA'S LATITUDE AND LONGITUDE

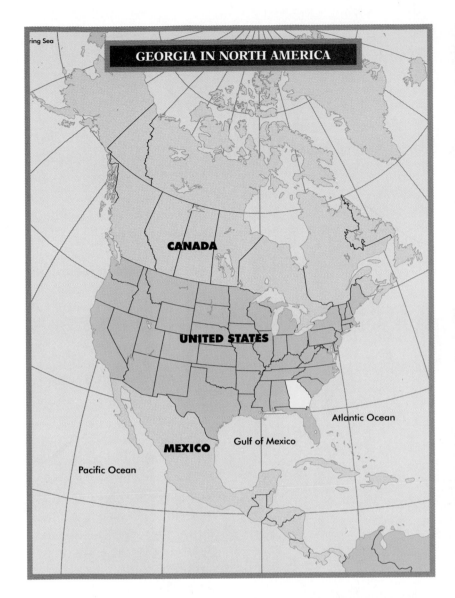

GEORGIA IN NORTH AMERICA

CANADA

UNITED STATES

MEXICO

Pacific Ocean

Gulf of Mexico

Atlantic Ocean

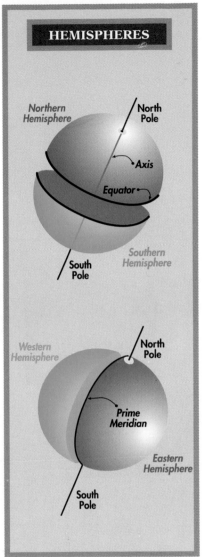

HEMISPHERES

Northern Hemisphere

North Pole

Axis

Equator

South Pole

Southern Hemisphere

Western Hemisphere

North Pole

Prime Meridian

Eastern Hemisphere

South Pole

122 square miles. Georgia is bordered by the Atlantic Ocean on the east, Florida on the south, Tennessee and North Carolina on the north, South Carolina along the Savannah River, and Alabama on the west. The geographic center of Georgia is located in Twiggs County, about 18 miles southeast of Macon.

Do You Remember?

1. List at least five of the words Captain Jean Ribault used to describe Georgia.
2. What is latitude? Longitude?
3. List three ways in which the size of Georgia is described.
4. Which states border Georgia?
5. Where is the geographic center of Georgia?

GEOGRAPHY'S EFFECT ON HISTORY

Geography has played an important role in American history. In early days, the Atlantic Ocean was a great "highway" that brought Europeans and Africans to America. That highway was also an important trade route among the three continents.

The Appalachian Mountains were a barrier to early westward movement. But that barrier gave the young British colonies time to grow and prosper before settlers pushed over the mountains.

The great inland river systems —the Ohio, Mississippi, Missouri, Red, and Arkansas—carried farm products to New Orleans for export. The need to protect those river routes led the United States to seek control of the mouth of the Mississippi.

America's geography also helped determine the types of economies that arose. For example, New England's narrow, rocky coast fostered an economy based on manufacturing, trade, fishing, shipbuilding, and small-farm agriculture. The wide coastal plain and subtropical climate of the South led to plantations, slavery, and agriculture for export. The treeless plains beginning in Illinois were perfect for grain and livestock production. The geography of the Midwest provided not only the raw materials for industry—coal deposits in Pennsylvania, iron ore in Minnesota, limestone in the Ohio Valley—but also lakes and river systems for cheap transportation for both raw materials and finished products.

The flat land, rich soil, and subtropical climate of Georgia's coastal plain led to an economy based on large plantations that depended on slaves for labor.

GEOGRAPHIC DIVISIONS

The people who call Georgia home can enjoy a wide range of geographic areas. There are twenty-four physiographic patterns (natural characteristics of the earth's surface) in Georgia. These natural divisions differ both in area and in their land base, which may be limestone, clay sediment, shale, or marsh. There are enough similarities among the twenty-four patterns however; that they can be combined into five major physiographic regions: (1) the Appalachian Plateau Region; (2) the Blue Ridge Region; (3) the Ridge and Valley Region; (4) the Piedmont Region; and (5) the Coastal Plain Region.

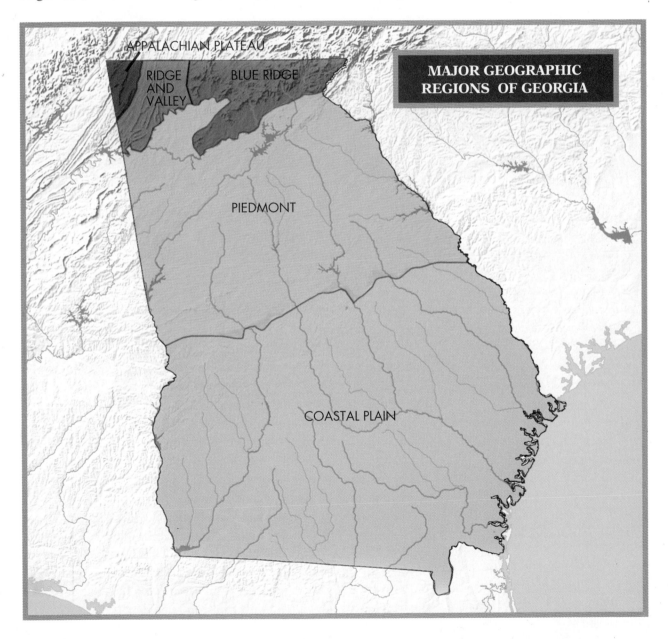

Above: The Appalachian Plateau, also known as Lookout and Sand mountain plateaus, is a small region in the north-western corner of the state and includes Dade County and part of Walker County. The plateau is made up of two flat-topped mountains that drop into Lookout and Chickamauga valleys. At the base of both mountains are almost vertical cliffs 200 to 300 feet in height.

Opposite page: *Sometimes called the "Grand Canyon of North Georgia," Cloudland Canyon is located on the west side of Lookout Mountain.*

THE APPALACHIAN PLATEAU REGION

Although the smallest of the physiographic areas, the Appalachian Plateau Region, which is in the far northwest corner of the state, is a maze of limestone caves, deep canyons, and interesting rock formations. Many people refer to this as the TAG Corner because it is the point at which Tennessee, Alabama, and Georgia meet. The region, sometimes referred to as the Cumberland Plateau, has the broad, flat-topped, 100-mile-long Lookout Mountain on one side and Sand Mountain on the other. In between these two mountains is a long, narrow valley. With an elevation of up to two thousand feet, this region is one of the most scenic but least traveled parts of the state. Civil War buffs throughout the nation frequent the Chickamauga and Chattanooga National Military Park, the site of historic Civil War battles. Cloudland Canyon, located between Trenton and Lafayette, has two beautiful waterfalls that cascade over layers of sandstone and shale millions of years old.

The area between the Appalachian Plateau Region and the adjoining Ridge and Valley Region marks the beginning of the Appalachian Trail at Springer Mountain, northeast of Dahlonega. Every year, outdoor adventurers begin the 2,144-mile hike, hoping to arrive at its end in Maine. Although over a million people hike some part of the trail each year, few actually make the entire trip.

THE BLUE RIDGE REGION

The Blue Ridge Region of Georgia is known for its rugged beauty. Located in the northeast part of the state, it is part of the Appalachian Highlands that stretch from New York to Alabama. The Blue Ridge Region is a hundred miles wide and has an area of about two thousand square miles. The highest and largest group of mountains in Georgia is in this region. These mountains are important to the rest of the state because they are the first barrier to warm, moist air rising from the Gulf of Mexico. When that air makes contact with the high mountains, it cools. The **precipitation** (rain, hail, sleet, or snow) that results provides water for the entire state. Here, precipitation can exceed 80 inches per year. Brasstown Bald, the highest peak in the state, is located in this region. The peak is almost five thousand feet high, and if you climb to the top of the observation

Above: *Hundreds of trails along Georgia's Blue Ridge Mountains lure hikers from all over the state.* *Above left:* *Peaks rising from 2,000 to almost 5,000 feet above sea level provide a picturesque view of the tree-covered mountains.* ***Opposite page:*** *Located in Union County, Brasstown Bald is the highest peak in Georgia at 4,784 feet. It was formerly known as the Summit of Mount Enotah.*

tower, you can catch a glimpse of three surrounding states: North Carolina, South Carolina, and Tennessee. Travelers to this region can also visit other well-known Georgia landmarks including Tallulah Gorge in Rabun County and the alpine community of Helen in White County. The roads that wind around the mountains lead to much of Georgia's state-owned forest land. In addition, this region is known for its many recreational opportunities.

THE RIDGE AND VALLEY REGION

Between the Blue Ridge Mountains and the Appalachian Mountains lies the Ridge and Valley Region. This area of the state looks just like its name suggests: it has low open valleys and narrow ridges that run parallel to the valleys. There are flat and fertile farmlands with fields of grain, pastures for cattle, and rows of apple orchards near Ellijay. Elevation ranges from 700 to 1,600 feet above sea level. The valleys are divided by steep and narrow ridges capped with limestone.

The region runs from Polk and Bartow counties northward to Chattanooga, Tennessee. It is known for its industry, particularly textile and carpet manufacturing, with Dalton, known as the "carpet capital of the world," leading the way.

Below: *The Ridge and Valley land region is a heavily forested area with rich fertile soil.*
Opposite page, top: *This old grist mill is in Dalton, the "carpet capital of the world."*

Above: Once a sleepy little community called Terminus, Atlanta is the business center of the Piedmont Region, the most heavily populated area in Georgia. Opposite page: Containing thirty-one percent of the state's land area, the rich red earth of the Piedmont Region provides acres of fertile farmland.

THE PIEDMONT REGION

The Piedmont Region begins in the mountain foothills of northern Georgia and goes to the central part of the state. It has gently sloping hills and valleys in the north and flatlands in the south.

Some Georgians refer to the gently rolling hills and the southern flatlands as the "heartland" of the state. The term *Piedmont* means "foot of the mountain," but the plateau is so long that it actually runs from Alabama northward to Delaware. The granite-based landform makes up about one-third of the state's land area. In addition to the granite base, there is another familiar type of soil: clay. People new to the region often seem perplexed after a heavy rain and ask, "What is that red stuff?" Long-term residents usually simply smile and respond, "Well, that is our famous Georgia red clay."

About one-half of the state's population is in the Piedmont Region. It was the cotton belt of antebellum days, the period before the Civil War. Today it is known for the production of wheat, soybeans, corn, poultry, and cattle. Business and industry also flourish throughout the area. Cities such as Atlanta, Athens, Madison, and Milledgeville are among some of the densely populated areas crisscrossed by the Chattahoochee, Flint, Ocmulgee, and Oconee rivers.

THE COASTAL PLAIN REGION

The Coastal Plain Region, which occupies about three-fifths of the state, is the largest of the physiographic regions. It is divided into the Inner Coastal Plain and the Outer Coastal Plain. The Inner Coastal Plain has a mild climate and a good supply of underground water. It is the major agricultural region of the state, with soil that varies from limestone to clay. The Vidalia Upland has become world famous because of the unique sweet onions that grow there. The southwestern corner around Bainbridge and Albany is called the Dougherty Plain, a rich soil sector for peanuts, corn, and pecan trees.

The Outer Coastal Plain does not have drained soil to provide fertile farmlands, but it is the center of naval stores and pulp production in the state. As you travel along the flat coastline area, which in some places is fairly swampy and marshy, you are in the territory first visited by early explorers. One of the major features of the Outer Coastal Plain is the 681-square-mile Okefenokee Swamp, located south of Waycross. Along the coast, the deep harbors and barrier islands offer

Above: Sunset marks the end of another day along the beach on St. Simons Island—one of Georgia's "Golden Isles." ***Left:*** Tree farms can be seen throughout the Inner Coastal Plain. ***Opposite page, right:*** Shrimpers use heavy nets to harvest the state's most valuable catch.

recreational facilities, seafood gathering and processing industries, and major shipyard ports. Here, for example, are cities such as Savannah, Darien, and Brunswick with their enduring, genteel beauty.

The coast is an interlocking chain of marshes, rivers, and tributaries that eventually flow into the Atlantic Ocean. Along the one-hundred-mile shoreline is a group of *barrier islands*, so called because they protect the beaches by blocking much of the wind, sand, and water that could erode the mainland. The Spanish explorers called this subtropical region "Islands of Gold." Even today, this chain of islands, which includes Tybee, St. Simons, Jekyll, and Cumberland islands, offers much in terms of beauty, recreation, and tourism. Nevertheless, perhaps the greatest legacy of the barrier island group is that two-thirds of the land remain wilderness sanctuaries.

"LAND OF THE TREMBLING EARTH"

In the southeastern part of our state, near Folkston and Waycross, is the *Okefenokee Swamp*. The area, which was once part of the Atlantic Ocean floor, comes from the Indian word *"o-wa-qua-phenoga,"* which means the "land of the trembling earth."

As you drive into the National Park area, you step back millions of years into a world of giant, 80-foot cypress trees draped with moss and with hordes of alligators peering up out of the murky dark water. Hundreds of water waders, including herons, egrets, and cranes, stand statue-still waiting for one of the many fish swimming by. Black bears up to 300 pounds lumber along the thick foliage in search of the many small animals scurrying about or stopping to eat berries and succulent plants. The shy but graceful whitetail deer dine on green plant shoots or watch the otters cavorting, or playing, in one of the numerous ponds around the swamp.

The Okefenokee Swamp covers a half million acres, about seven hundred square miles. This primitive wetland is a haven for hundreds of species of plants, animals, and reptiles, many of whom are endangered. For thousands of years, Indians hunted and fished in the Swamp and used it as a pharmacy. Many of the plants were used for medicines to combat everything from snake bites to pneumonia.

Perhaps the most famous "resident" of the swamp was a character named Pogo. In 1943, cartoonist Walt Kelly introduced *Pogo Possum*, a comic-strip character who was a wise observer to national events. Pogo and his "swamp critter" friends would sit back and comment on political and social situations in the country. They remained popular for twenty-six years.

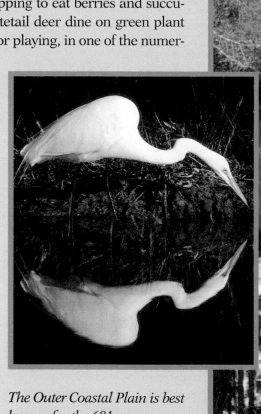

The Outer Coastal Plain is best known for the 681-square-mile Okefenokee Swamp (right), home to alligators, and hundreds of bird species like the great egret (above).

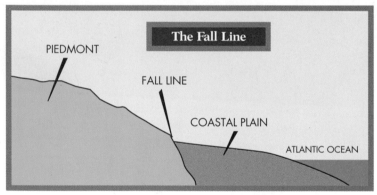

*Above: The fall line separates the Piedmont Region from the Coastal Plain. **Top:** Fall line waterfalls provide a source of power for numerous textile mills like this one in Columbus.*

THE FALL LINE

The Coastal Plain Region is separated from the Piedmont Region by a natural boundary known as the fall line. The fall line is the point at which hilly or mountainous lands meet the coastal plain. This line runs from Columbus on the western side of the state, through Macon and into Augusta on the eastern side. Other cities located on the fall line are Milledgeville, Roberta, Thomson, and Warrenton. Rivers and creeks flowing from the rocky hill country cut deep channels in the softer soil of the plains. This drops the elevation and creates waterfalls. As early settlers began to leave the coastal regions and explore inland, many were forced to stop at the fall line because they could not travel over the steep and rushing falls. These early settlers, as well as Indians and traders, found the waterfalls an excellent power source and built settlements there.

Do You Remember?
1. Which of Georgia's physiographic regions is the smallest? The largest?
2. What does TAG mean?
3. In which region is the Okefenokee Swamp located?
4. Name at least three cities that are located on the fall line.

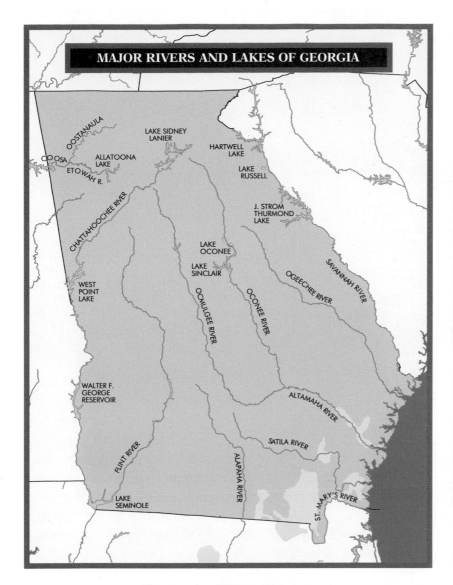

MAJOR RIVERS AND LAKES OF GEORGIA

GEORGIA WATERWAYS

Georgia's waterways provided transportation to trading posts for the Indians and landing sites for the early settlers. Today, the Atlantic Ocean and inland rivers, lakes, and streams are used for recreation, to make electricity, and as ports for trade and tourism.

THE ATLANTIC OCEAN

Georgia has more than one hundred miles of coastline on the Atlantic Ocean, beginning at the Savannah River and going to the St. Mary's River. Some parts of the coastline serve as wildlife refuges and others as commercial fishing and shrimping centers. There are harbors for the coming and going of luxury cruise ships, as well as miles of recreational beaches that draw tourists from far and near.

Above left: Over 20,000 miles of rivers and streams crisscross the state providing navigable water routes, hydroelectric power, and numerous recreation areas for Georgians. **Top right:** Beautiful shells can be found on Georgia's Atlantic beaches. **Above right:** Georgia's 100 miles of coastline are a center of tourism and recreation.

WATER TRANSPORTATION AND CITIES

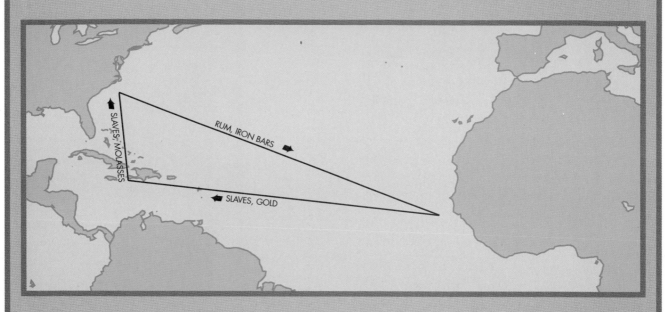

RUM, IRON BARS

SLAVES, MOLASSES

SLAVES, GOLD

The route used by merchants to keep rum, molasses, iron, gold, spices, and slaves flowing between America, the West Indies, and Africa was known as the Triangular Trade Route.

During the seventeenth and early eighteenth centuries, the most notable cities to arise in America were New York, Boston, Charles Town, Savannah, and Philadelphia. Their growth into major cities happened in part because of their geographical locations near deep water.

These cities became important trading centers, exporting local commodities and importing goods from many points around the Atlantic basin. All had deep water to accommodate large ocean-going ships and smaller coastal vessels. All had harbors protected from wind and wave. All developed wharves for loading and unloading cargo. All were located on rivers, which encouraged trade with the back country: Savannah on the Savannah River, Charles Town at the junction of the Ashley and Cooper rivers; Philadelphia on the Delaware; New York on the Hudson; and Boston on the Charles.

Farmers and other workers produced more goods than could be used locally. They sold their goods to city merchants. The merchants sold the goods mainly to the West Indies to get money, slaves, sugar, spices, and molasses to make into rum. Profits from this trade were used to import manufactured goods from Great Britain.

Trade increased the wealth of these cities. That wealth enabled them to become important economic, cultural, and political centers.

Between the barrier islands and the mainland is a four- to six-mile band of salt water marshes covering a total of 450,000 acres. At least one-third of the salt marshes along the Atlantic coastline are in Georgia. The marshes, protected by the government, are home to many kinds of water life. A marine biology laboratory sponsored by the National Science Foundation is located there. Sidney Lanier pictured the beauty of the area in his poem "The Marshes of Glynn" when he wrote, "Ye marshes, how candid and simple, and nothing-withholding and free."

Many inlets and creeks lead inland from the ocean and provide excellent fishing and crabbing. They were a hiding place for pirates during the eighteenth century when Spanish and English trading ships traveled along the coast. Pirates, such as the infamous Blackbeard, attacked the ships and took goods for their own use or for resale.

There are also sand ridges along the coast. These ridges were formed by the continuous beating of ocean waves. Coastal Indians used them as trails. Those trails became the routes of present-day highways within the coastal plain. Seaport bluffs and ridges were the sites of early towns, including Savannah and Darien.

Top: *The marshes of Glynn.*
Above: *The Sidney Lanier Bridge spans the major entrance into the port city of Brunswick.*

RIVERS

Georgia has twelve principal river systems. The Savannah, Ogeechee, Altamaha (which combines the Oconee and Ocmulgee rivers), and Satilla rivers flow directly into the Atlantic Ocean. Western rivers, including the Chattahoochee and Flint, become a part of the Gulf of Mexico. In the northern part of the state, the Etowah and Oostanaula rivers form the Coosa River, which flows through Alabama into the Gulf. The Alapaha and the St. Mary's, located in south Georgia, flow across the Georgia-Florida border.

The Savannah River

By the time Hernando de Soto reached the Savannah River in 1540, Indians had traveled the 314-mile-long waterway for many years. They called it the "Isondega," meaning "blue water." Many of their villages were located along its banks. Along the border of South Carolina, it spreads into three lakes: J. Strom Thurmond Lake (formerly called Clark Hill Lake), Lake Russell, and Hartwell Lake.

Today the state has two major seaports in its eastern basin: Savannah and Brunswick. Savannah also holds the distinction of being one of the larger port cities in the country. Goods that come into the port include steel and iron, wood pulp, foodstuffs, machinery, ammonia, and oil products along with other items that are then shipped to markets across the United States. Cargoes that leave the port of Savannah include our native kaolin (clay), wood pulp, oil products, wheat, soybeans, and a host of other commodities.

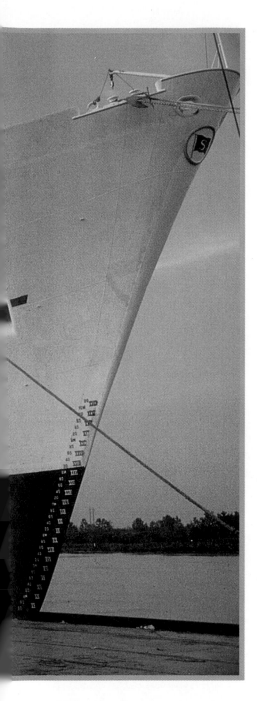

Above: As the gateway to the Atlantic, Savannah is Georgia's largest seaport. Ships from around the world stop here.
Right: The Eagle and Phenix Cotton Mill in Columbus dwarfs a fisherman on the Chattahoochee River.

The Chattahoochee River

The name of the Chattahoochee comes from the Cherokee and means the "river of the painted rock." It was so named because of the colorful stones that lay across the riverbed. The river itself flows 436 miles from the foothills of the Blue Ridge Mountains to the Gulf of Mexico. Part of the southern section forms the natural border between Georgia and Alabama. The chief cities along its banks include Gainesville, Atlanta, and Columbus. Major lakes, including Lake Lanier, West Point Lake, and the Walter F. George Reservoir, are

Above: *The ninety-mile-long Altamaha River was claimed by France, Spain, and England during the days of exploration in the early 1700s.* **Right:** *The 150-mile-long Ocmulgee River begins where the South, Yellow, and Alcovy rivers join at Lake Jackson. It joins the Little Ocmulgee and Oconee rivers to become the Altamaha River.*

Opposite page, below: *Named for the Etowah Indians who once lived along its banks, the Etowah River flows from the Blue Ridge Mountains in Lumpkin County to Rome.*

part of the Chattahoochee's winding path. In addition to supplying water to Atlanta and Columbus, the river is a water source for Helen, Buford, LaGrange, and West Point.

All is not well, however, along this picturesque, or attractive, river. Years of farm and urban runoff, including industrial waste and sewage, is polluting the river so much that some conservation groups list it as one of the ten most endangered rivers in the United States.

Other Rivers

The 265-mile-long Flint River runs parallel to the Chattahoochee from College Park, near Atlanta, until it empties into Lake Seminole at Bainbridge. In northwestern Georgia, the Cherokee traveled the Oostanaula and the Etowah rivers to the Indian village of Chiaha, the site of present-day Rome. Chiaha, known as the "Head of the Coosa," had a trading post and post office.

The Ocmulgee and Oconee rivers meet near Hazlehurst and Lumber City. They then flow into one of Georgia's most powerful rivers, the Altamaha. This muddy river is rich in fish and fertile swamps. It empties into the Atlantic Ocean near the coastal city of Darien.

These major waterways have been important to the social, political, and economic growth of Georgia. In looking at a map of Georgia's river systems, it is notable that more than half show an Indian influence such as Ocmulgee, Altamaha, and Coosa. The Coosa River gets its name from the Choctaw. It means "kusha," or cane. Cane was used to make arrows, spears, and knives. It also was used as a container for storing fragile pieces of clothing. *Altamaha* is believed to mean "Chief's Lodge." Other smaller river systems also have Indian names, including Apalachee, Towaliga, and Coosawatee. But the American influence can certainly be seen in river names like Rottenwood Creek, Settingdown, Potato Creek, and Mud Creek. All of these rivers play important roles in recreation for such uses as fishing and white-water rafting and canoeing along with the roles they play in providing water sources for towns and cities.

LAKES

Although Georgia does not have any large natural lakes, the state is fortunate to have excellent lakes created by the U.S. Corps of Engineers and Georgia Power Company. There is also a network of lakes that is formed from Georgia's massive river systems. Whether artificial or natural, the state's lake system provides recreational areas, reservoirs, and hydroelectric power. Allatoona, Carter Lake, Lake Lanier, Walter George, West Point, and Seminole all generate hydroelectric power, which provides us with the electricity we use in our homes. In addition, J. Strom Thurmond Lake, Hartwell Lake, Oconee Lake, and others offer enjoyable fishing, camping, boating, and recreational shorelines. Some of the smaller lakes also act as reservoirs, or holding tanks, to meet our water needs.

Do You Remember?

1. Across which state border does the Alapaha flow?
2. What three cities are located along the borders of the Chattahoochee River?
3. List three ways in which Georgia's rivers are important to its citizens.

*Above: One of six lakes managed by the United States Army Corps of Engineers, Hartwell Lake is located on the Savannah River seven miles east of the city of Hartwell. The lake boasts a 960-mile shoreline, four marinas, and three state parks, making it a favorite recreational area. **Opposite page, below:** Located in the southwestern corner of the state where Georgia, Florida, and Alabama meet, 5,000-acre Lake Seminole is known throughout the region as a prize lake where the state fish of Georgia, the largemouth bass, can be caught.*

CLIMATE

Geography influences where people live, what crops are grown, and which industries develop. Climate is equally important. **Climate** refers to the kind of weather a region has over a period of time. **Weather** refers to the day-to-day changes in temperature, precipitation, wind, and so on.

TEMPERATURE

As a result of Georgia's latitude and longitude, the climate is usually humid and moist. In most places, summers are hot and winters are mild. There is a narrow band across the north Georgia mountain area, however, that has warm summers and moderately cold winters.

The highest temperatures in the state usually occur in July, and the coldest readings are normally in January. The average temperature for the year is 65°F (Fahrenheit). However, the mercury can fall below 0°F in the northern sections and rise above 100°F in the middle and southern regions of the state.

Several unlikely records have been set in the state. For example, on July 24, 1952, the town of Louisville, which was once a capital of Georgia, had a temperature of 112°F. At the other end of the scale, Floyd County shivered on January 27, 1940, when the temperature plunged to -17°F. Generally, though, temperatures are relatively comfortable through most of the year, which is one of the reasons so many companies move into our state.

PRECIPITATION

Precipitation, usually in the form of rain, ice, or snow, is vital to Georgia's economy. Snow, which generally falls only in the mountain regions, melts to provide a water runoff into streams and lakes. Rainfall aids the growth of crops and forests. In a normal year, Georgia receives an average of 40 to 52 inches of rain in central and southern regions and 65 to 76 inches in the northern mountains. July is the wettest month of the year, and October is the driest.

During the last half of the 1980s, Georgia, like many other parts of the country, experienced a severe drought, with rainfall far below average. Scientists disagree about the exact causes of Georgia's drought conditions, but the results concern everyone. Lack of rain lowers lake levels and underground water tables. There is not as much water to use in the production of hydroelectric power. Businesses, industries, and home users are all affected by having less water. Shortages of rainfall also mean fewer water-related recreational opportunities.

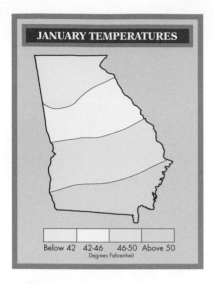

JANUARY TEMPERATURES

Below 42 42-46 46-50 Above 50
Degrees Fahrenheit

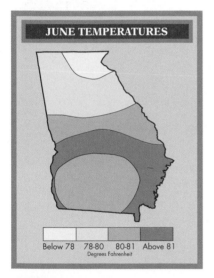

JUNE TEMPERATURES

Below 78 78-80 80-81 Above 81
Degrees Fahrenheit

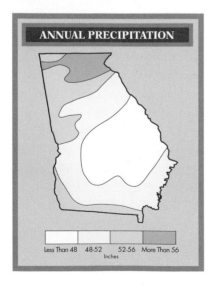

ANNUAL PRECIPITATION

Less Than 48 48-52 52-56 More Than 56
Inches

Drought periods limit agricultural production, so there is less harvest to sell to farmers' markets, food production companies, and grocery stores. Droughts also cut back the growth of grain for livestock. This affects beef, dairy, and poultry farms.

To Georgia's economy, snow means much more than a day out of school for students. Rain means more than carrying an umbrella. Rain and snow mean economic survival. Sometimes, however, too much of a good thing can be troublesome. In 1994, for example, all Georgia precipitation records were broken in most of the region from Bainbridge to Macon as the "Great Flood" dumped over 23 inches of rain within a week's time. Thirty-two counties were declared disaster areas by the federal government. Officials in Albany, one of the hardest-hit areas, had to find shelter and food for 15,000 people trying to escape the dangerous flood conditions. In Macon, 150,000 people were without water, while the town of Montezuma was virtually under water. Caring people along with various state and federal governmental agencies came to the aid of these Georgia citizens, many of whom lost everything they had worked so hard to attain. The flooding was so devastating, or ruinous, that in some areas, coffins buried long ago came floating to the top of the flood waters. The task of re-identifying and reburying the bodies was a sad and stressful time for everyone. As a result, today coffins have a capsule inserted into the casket identifying the deceased person. Despite all the human and property losses, health hazards, and bewildering inconveniences, residents nevertheless showed courage and an admirable spirit throughout the ordeal.

The winter months in the northwest Georgia mountains not only provide beautiful natural sculptures, but are also essential in providing water runoff into lakes and streams as winter turns to spring.

WINDS

Winds influence the overall weather pattern of Georgia. Air masses that begin over the Gulf of Mexico and the Atlantic Ocean control summer's warm months. The winter months are controlled by air masses that start in the polar regions of Alaska and Canada. Wind patterns can bring moderate weather or intense storms in the forms of tornadoes and hurricanes.

Wind Currents

The early explorers who traveled to Georgia and the rest of the southeastern area sought favorable wind currents to shorten their trip and to make for smoother sailing. A **wind current** is a continuous movement or flow of air. Surface winds from the equator to around latitude 30° south of the equator flow from the southeast. Winds from the equator to around latitude 30° north of the equator generally flow from the northeast. These winds are known as *trade winds*. The early navigators used the trade winds to sail westward to the New World. Depending on the winds and currents, the average trip to the New World took approximately nine to fifteen weeks.

Islands off the Atlantic shore, like St. Catherine's Island, are constantly reshaped by wind and ocean currents.

Winds from around 30° to 60° latitude north and south of the equator generally blow from the west to the east. These winds, often called *westerlies*, were the winds used by explorers on their homebound trips, usually traveling a route slightly north of the trade winds. These areas are known as the *middle latitudes* and are prone to produce cyclones, which can bring winds from any direction as they pass. These westerly winds carry storms across the Atlantic, creating dangerous gales and heavy winds that are severe hazards to shipping.

Ocean Currents

About seventy-one percent of the earth is covered with water. Most of that water is in the oceans—the Atlantic, the Pacific, the Indian, the Arctic, and the Antarctic. The water in these oceans is constantly moving, and some of this movement forms rivers in the ocean. *Oceanographers*, scientists who study oceans, call these rivers of ocean water **ocean currents**. Strong ocean currents, especially the Canary Current and the Atlantic Equatorial Current, combined with the trade winds to push the explorers' ships south and west to the new world. On their homeward voyage, the ships were pushed to the east by the Gulf Stream.

Ocean currents are caused by the uneven heating of the earth's surface by the sun. The earth is hottest at the equator, where the sun shines most directly on the earth. The earth is coldest at the poles, where the sun shines less directly. Ocean currents contribute to the movement of heat from the equator to the poles, thus helping equalize the earth's surface temperatures. Ocean currents affect not only the routes chosen by ships carrying people and goods across the sea to the New World; they also influence climate and living conditions for the plants and animals on land.

HURRICANES

Hurricanes are spawned when waters of 80°F or more transform the heat energy of tropical waters into strong winds and heavy waves. In our section of the world, the beginnings of these storms occur off the coast of Africa as depressions. It may take several weeks for the depression to turn into a tropical storm and eventually a hurricane. The season for these fierce storms is from the beginning of June to the end of November, and their devastation can be frightening. In September 1996, Hurricane Fran struck the coast of North Carolina. It drove inland, left thousands of homes in ruin, and caused twenty-two deaths. The storm caused heavy damage to the coastline in four states as a result of driving winds and storm-surge tides. Costs are still being determined. Georgia's most damaging hurricane-like storm, in terms of loss of life, came ashore in Savannah on August 27, 1893. Although the winds were not strong, a thousand people died from flying debris and other storm-related causes. During that period, weather alerts were not nearly as effective as

THE PATHS OF HURRICANES

Scale Number or Class	Kilometers/Hour	Miles/Hour	Storm Surge		Expected Damage
			Meters	Feet	
1	119-153	74-95	1.2-1.5	4.0-4.9	minimal
2	154-177	96-110	1.6-2.4	5.0-7.9	moderate
3	178-209	111-130	2.5-3.6	8.0-11.9	extensive
4	210-250	131-155	3.7-5.4	12.0-18.0	extreme
5	greater than 250	greater than 155	greater than 5.4	greater than 18.0	catastrophic

SAFFIR-SIMPSON HURRICANE SCALE

they are today. Many people were simply unaware and unprepared for the 72-mile-per-hour storm.

Hurricane strength is registered on a scale from one to five. A category-one hurricane has top winds of 74 to 94 miles per hour. A category-five hurricane has winds of over 155 miles per hour and a water surge of more than 18 feet. Hurricanes are given names by the National Hurricane Center in Miami, Florida. The center usually chooses one name, either male or female, from each letter of the alphabet, although occasionally a letter is skipped. The costliest hurricane to hit the East Coast was Hurricane Andrew in 1992, in Dade County, Florida. This category-four hurricane cost over $25 billion in damages. Through years of experience, residents along the coast of the eastern United States have learned to pay close heed to tropical storm reports.

FUJITA INTENSITY SCALE FOR TORNADOES

Rating	Miles/Hour	Expected Damage
F-0	40-72	Light: Loose Debris
F-1	73-112	Moderate: Broken Windows and Doors
F-2	113-157	Considerable: Trees Broken
F-3	158-206	Severe: Outer Walls Collapse
F-4	207-260	Devastating: Structure Damage
F-5	261-318	Incredible

TORNADOES

When we see action movies or read about the excitement of storm chasers, we sometimes forget that these are dangerous and life-threatening cyclones. The word **tornado** comes from the Spanish word *tornada*, which means "thunderstorm." When warm moist air mixes with a rapidly moving cold front, severe thunderstorms are possible. In the southeastern United States, these storms can produce tornadoes. Georgia has an average of nineteen tornadoes a year, with most of them occurring from March to July. Tornadoes are swirling cyclonic winds that in our hemisphere move in from southwest to northeast and spin in a counterclockwise motion. A tornado can last for a few minutes and travel as little as one-half mile with wind speeds up to 100 miles per hour. Larger tornadoes, called *maxis*, may travel over 200 miles during a three-hour period, with wind speeds of a shattering 250 miles per hour.

Tornadoes can cause extensive property damage, injuries, and loss of life. And, they are unpredictable. Both large and small tornadoes seem to have minds of their own. They can move in a straight line, loop, hop over places, and even double-back on themselves. If you have seen pictures of damage after a tornado, you know that a line of houses can be totally crushed—with the single exception of one house in the middle of the storm path that stands without so much as a cracked window.

Do You Remember?
1. In what month does the state's highest temperature usually occur? The coldest?
2. What is the average annual temperature in Georgia?
3. List three ways in which the amount of precipitation affects our state.
4. When do we have the most hurricanes? The most tornadoes?

Springtime in Georgia not only means budding flowers, it also means tornado weather. These funnel clouds can move up to 300 miles per hour and cause substantial destruction to life and property.

GEORGIA WILDLIFE

With enough land, different physiographic features, and a moderate climate, Georgia is a natural home for wildlife. Among its **fauna**, a term that refers to the animal life of a particular area, are mammals, birds, reptiles and amphibians, and fish.

MAMMALS

Over forty *species*, or kinds, of mammals are found in Georgia. One of them, prized by hunters and naturalists alike, is the whitetail deer. It was almost extinct by the early 1900s but, because of careful management, whitetail deer can now be found in all 159 Georgia counties.

Squirrels, chipmunks, opossums, raccoons, and rabbits live all over the state, and foxes can be seen in most sections. Bobcats are usually found in the forest mountain regions or in swamps. Wild hogs make their home in coastal plain river swamps, along with beavers, otters, and minks.

BIRDS

Georgia is a year-round home for 170 species of birds, including robins, cardinals, blue jays, thrashers, and woodpeckers. Two hundred other species feed and nest in the state during spring and fall migrations. One of the most popular visitors is the ruby-throated hummingbird. Thousands of people place feeders of sugar water in their yards each year hoping to attract the shy, tiny visitors as they migrate to South America.

There are also many game birds in Georgia. Quail, doves, ducks, and wild turkeys are the most popular with hunters. Georgia has joined at least forty-two other states in classifying the bald eagle as an endangered species. Hunting eagles is strictly forbidden by law. The state funds a program to feed the young eaglets until they are ready to live on their own. Extensive federal and state programs, along with caring private citizens, have resulted in a significant increase in the number of nesting bald eagles. It is heartening to note that for now the well-being of Georgia's bald eagle population seems secure.

*Opposite page, above: Foxes, like this red fox, can be found in most parts of the state. **Opposite page, below:** The whitetail deer was almost extinct by the early 1900s but, because of careful management, can now be found all over Georgia. **Left:** The national emblem of the United States, the bald eagle, generally nests near water. **Above:** The northern cardinal is one of the most common birds in Georgia gardens.*

Top: The alligator is Georgia's largest reptile. ***Above:*** *The copperhead is one of Georgia's six species of poisonous snakes.*

REPTILES AND AMPHIBIANS

Forty species of snakes live in Georgia. All but six are harmless. These are valuable to the state's agriculture because they eat undesirable rodents. Poisonous snakes include the copperhead, cottonmouth, coral, and three types of rattlesnakes.

The Coastal Plain Region, particularly swampy areas such as Okefenokee, is home to the American alligator. Alligators grow to an adult length of six to twelve feet. They are protected by the federal government from unauthorized killing.

There are twenty-seven varieties of turtles in Georgia. The famous loggerhead sea turtles live on the barrier islands off Georgia's coast. Visitors to a stream, marsh, or pond can easily find some of Georgia's other amphibians. The state is a natural home for twenty-four types of frogs, four species of toads, and thirty-six kinds of salamanders.

FISH

If you ask Georgia fishers, "What do you like to catch?," you can almost guess the part of the state in which they fish by the answer given. If they like trout, chances are they are from north Georgia. On April 1, they join scores of fishers, equipped with handmade fishing flies or cans of corn, wading into the cold mountain streams. The state boasts four thousand miles of public and private trout streams. To Georgians in the middle and southern part of the state, nothing can match the fun of bringing in a largemouth bass from one of the thousands of ponds and lakes that dot the region. Two fish hatcheries are maintained, the Chattahoochee National Forest and the Warm

Springs National Fish Hatchery, to ensure that our lakes and streams are always full of the hundreds of fish species available to sportspersons. Coastal fishers enjoy the challenge of bringing in red drum, spotted sea trout, sheepshead, and croaker. Locals along the Golden Isles frequently catch their dinner of blue crabs or pink shrimp. Offshore artificial reefs are being constructed to ensure an abundance of fish off the coastal shores for future generations to enjoy. The Grays Reef National Marine Sanctuary, off Sapelo Island, is one of the largest bottom reefs in the southeastern United States.

One other fish deserves recognition: shad. The Ogeechee River near Savannah is the home of this special delicacy. The season for shad runs from January 1 to March 31, and restaurants throughout the country call in orders for the tasty and expensive luxury.

One final interesting addition to Georgia waters is not a fish but a mammal—whales, who use the coastal waters of our state and Florida as calving grounds. Of forty species of whales, the right whale is considered to be one of the most endangered species in the world. Weighing up to seventy tons, the seventy-foot right whale is actually a baleen whale. It earned the name "right" during long-ago whaling days. Whalers claimed this species was "just right" in terms of weight, amount of oil, and whalebone. Instead of teeth, this whale has plates, which are a fingernail-type material used to filter out food. These plates may be as long as eight feet. The black upper body has wart-like patches on the head and a pale underbelly. Its most distinctive characteristic is the production of a V-shape blow. Unfortunately, unless we take care of this species, which is millions of years old, it will have no future at all.

Georgia's state fish, the largemouth bass, is one of the most popular game fish in the South.

Do You Remember?

1. What animal, once almost extinct, can be found in all Georgia counties?
2. What poisonous snakes are native to Georgia?
3. What is Georgia's largest reptile?
4. Which kind of fish would you most likely find in north Georgia?
5. What mammal uses the coastal waters of our state as a calving ground?

TREES AND PLANTS

Although every locale has its unique beauty, it is hard to imagine Georgia without its rich assortment of **flora**, the natural vegetation of the land. Regardless of the time of year, there are trees and plants on display for residents and visitors to enjoy.

TREES

Georgia has over 36 million acres of land. Sixty-three percent of that area is forested, which is twice the national average. With over two hundred species of trees in Georgia and the southeastern United States, the variety seems endless. For example, in the northern part of the state there are hardwoods such as hickory, red spruce, beech, and maple. Loblolly and other pines are abundant in the Piedmont and parts of the Coastal Plain, while bald cypress and cedar cover large areas of the Okefenokee Swamp.

Some of our cities are known for their trees. Magnolias line many of the neighborhood streets in Augusta, while dogwoods abound in Atlanta. In the fall, downtown Athens turns bright gold with fan-shaped leaves of the gingko trees, and in the spring, thousands of visitors pour into Macon as the Yoshino cherry trees blossom. It is also difficult to imagine Savannah without thinking of the moss-laden, giant live oaks and palmetto, both of which are seen through-out the city. Then, of course, there are the two trees that are synonymous with Georgia: the peach tree and the pecan tree. Both contribute significantly to Georgia's economy. Interestingly, although Atlanta has fifty-five streets with the name of Peachtree, there are no peach groves within miles of the city.

PLANTS

As the result of a 180-day growing period in the northern section of our state and a 270-day season along the coast, Georgia is home to hundreds of species of plants. There are the hearty purple verbena found throughout the state to the rare and delicate trillium found only in the Tallulah Gorge.

Few places can equal the beauty of Georgia's springtime with azaleas, wild dogwood, iris, and daffodils. Native plants, however, are not just for beauty. Some can be fun and useful. Most people have, at one time or another, picked a dandelion and blown the soft, feathery fuzz into the air. But did you know some families use the dandelion leaves for salad?

The grand and stately live oak, seen here among the azaleas in Reynolds Square, Savannah, is the official state tree of Georgia.

Rare plum-leaf azaleas are found at Providence Canyon. While the Cherokee rose is the state flower, azaleas have the distinction of being Georgia's official wildflower.

Plants also serve medicinal purposes. Aloe plants, for example, are a mainstay in many kitchens as an immediate healing agent for burns. Indians used meadows and forests as open-air pharmacies to make salve and syrups. They used purple cornflowers as an insect repellant; they crushed goldenrod to use against snake bites; and they made wort, a type of moss, into an ointment to ease the discomfort of cuts and bruises. Jewelweed took away the itch of poison ivy, while tobacco juice rid the body of worms or cured a headache. Over two hundred medicines from plants were passed down from generation to generation and are still used today.

Not all of our plants are popular. During the summer, you need not drive far to see a species of greenery that frustrates all farmers, gardeners, and Department of Transportation work crews. Kudzu has a long but less-than-distinguished career. In 1876, one hundred years after our nation's first birthday, a Centennial Industrial Exposition was held in Philadelphia. One hit of the fair was a bed of thick, green growth on display at the Japanese Exposition. The Japanese used the plant as both medicine and food flavoring. Because of its reputation as an agent in stopping soil erosion, plants were introduced into Georgia in 1930. Today, our state's neighbors to the north and south are finding out what Georgians quickly discovered. Not only does kudzu fail to stop soil erosion, the multi-leafed, cascading plant can grow up to one hundred feet during the summer months and is almost impossible to kill. But, the news is not all bad. Recently, research scientists have found the leaves can be crushed into a powder that is used as a cooking starch. It is also found in health foods and even made into kudzu candy.

Besides kudzu, there are other botanical invaders in our state. Botanists think that approximately 20 percent of plants found in the wild are foreign to Georgia soil, including privet, Japanese honeysuckle, chinaberry, and tallow trees.

Do You Remember?
1. What percent of Georgia is forested?
2. What two trees are most closely identified with Georgia?
3. How long a growing season does the part of Georgia along the coast have?
4. What percent of Georgia plants found in the wild are native to the state?

SUMMARY

A type of daisy, the black-eyed susan is common along roadsides throughout the state.

To understand Georgia's history, one needs to know its geography.
- There are 58,910 square miles of land in the state.
- There are 159 counties in Georgia.
- The five physiographic regions of Georgia are the Appalachian Plateau Region, the Blue Ridge Region, the Ridge and Valley Region, the Piedmont Region, and the Coastal Plain Region.
- Besides the hundred miles of water on its eastern coast, Georgia has twelve main river systems. Important rivers in Georgia include the Savannah, Ogeechee, Altamaha, Chattahoochee, and Flint.
- Georgia's climate is humid and moist. Summers are hot and winters are usually mild, except in the mountain areas, which tend to have warm summers and fairly cold winters.
- Rain and snowfall is 40 to 52 inches in central and south Georgia and 65 to 76 inches in north Georgia.
- Hurricanes can affect the coast between June and November.
- Georgia has many wild mammals, birds, snakes, turtles, and fish. It also has a great variety of plants and trees.

CHAPTER REVIEW

Reviewing People, Places, and Terms

Define, identify, or explain the importance of the following:

1. Appalachian Plateau Region
2. Blue Ridge Region
3. climate
4. Coastal Plain Region
5. fall line
6. fauna
7. flora
8. geography
9. hurricane
10. Inner Coastal Plain
11. latitude
12. longitude
13. ocean current
14. Outer Coastal Plain
15. Piedmont Region
16. precipitation
17. prime meridian
18. Ridge and Valley Region
19. tornado
20. weather
21. wind current

Understanding the Facts

1. How do the barrier islands protect the mainland of Georgia?
2. In what ways did the fall line affect Georgia settlement locations?
3. Name three Georgia rivers that flow directly into the Atlantic Ocean.
4. What effect does a drought period have on Georgia's agricultural production?
5. How did wind and ocean currents affect explorers' ships on their way to the New World?
6. What is the average number of tornadoes that Georgia has in a year?
7. Name two game birds found in Georgia.
8. What species of greenery, introduced to Georgia in 1930 to stop soil erosion, has proved a problem to farmers, gardeners, and transportation work crews?

Developing Critical Thinking

1. Why is geography important to your understanding of history? How does geography relate to your daily life?
2. Georgia has approximately 5 million acres of wetlands. Each year, experts estimate a loss of over three thousand acres. Why is this fact important and what can we do about it?
3. How does the average rainfall in the state affect you and your family?
4. If Georgia could be moved to the present location of Iowa, list specific ways your life would be different as the result of this geographic change.

Applying Your Skills

1. Using a globe, locate England and Georgia. Compare the size of these two areas and describe their specific location using at least three different indicators.
2. Make a map that shows the topographical features (rivers, plains, and so on) of the county in which you live.
3. If you were traveling from Dalton to Savannah at an average speed of sixty miles per hour, how long would the trip take? In what specific ways does a map of Georgia help you with your computations?
4. Take hourly readings of the temperature on an outside thermometer to see how the temperature changes during the day. Determine the high and low temperatures and the average temperature for the day.

Making Connections

1. After reading the feature on page 6, why do

you think the study of geography is important to the study of history?

2. Select a highway, river, or body of water in your area. Try to find out—in the library, from the Internet, or from a local historian—what part it played in the settlement of your area. Write your findings in a brief report.

3. Identify the two largest Georgia ports in terms of tonnage shipped through the port facilities.

Did You Know?

• According to folklore, you can tell if it is going to be a cold winter by examining the covering of an onion skin: "Onion skins very thin, mild winter coming in. Onion skins very tough, winter's coming cold and rough."

• On Sea Island, the endangered leatherback turtle can weigh up to two thousand pounds.

• The Spanish moss that drapes over the limbs of live oaks has no roots. This epiphyte lives on moisture in the atmosphere and can grow to be as long as twenty-five feet. Believe it or not, these gray, thready tendrils are kin to the pineapple family.

BUILDING SKILLS: USING YOUR TEXTBOOK

Making proper use of your textbook is different from reading a novel or science fiction story. Your textbook could be thought of as having two parts: the narrative, which tells the story of the state of Georgia, and the visual information, which makes the narrative come alive. The visual information—photographs, cartoons, illustrations, maps, charts, graphs, and captions (copy printed below or alongside illustrations)—is an important part of the study of Georgia.

The narrative is divided into sections by headings. The major headings are large, boldfaced, centered, and underlined. Lower-level headings are set in boldface capital letters and boldface italics. These headings are like an outline of the chapter. They help you organize the information in the chapter. If you scan these headings before you begin to read, you may better understand the overall plan of the chapter.

Look over the terms, people, and places listed in the "Chapter Preview" before you begin reading. If you do not know the meaning of some of the terms, locate them in the glossary at the back of the book or in a dictionary. The terms appear in boldface type the first time they appear in the narrative. They are often defined there, or you may be able to determine the meanings by the way they are used in the sentences.

Once you begin to read the chapter, read the narrative straight through without interruption. Answer the questions labeled "Do You Remember?" This will help you check your understanding of what you have read. After you have read the narrative, study the photographs and their captions and any maps and charts in the chapter. Photographs help you visualize some of the people, places, and events in the chapter. The captions may point out the important information about the photograph or provide more information about the subject or events. Maps and charts help you summarize information provided in the chapter.

Try the following activities to help you make use of these suggestions.

1. Prepare an outline of Chapter 1 using the headings in the chapter.

2. Look at the maps in the chapter. What information do the maps provide? How do they help you understand the narrative?

3. Find two captions that provide information not in the narrative. What is that information?

4. Find and list the photographs that illustrate the geographic region in which you live. Choose your favorite photograph from the list. Why did you choose that photograph?

Be sure to follow these suggestions as you read the rest of the chapters in the textbook.

This engraving of Indians at Towaliga Falls in Butts County presents an idealized view of Georgia before the coming of the Europeans.

CHAPTER TWO

THE LAND AND ITS EARLY PEOPLE

There were . . . many very magnificent monuments of the power and industry of the ancient inhabitants of these lands. . . . I observed a stupendous conical pyramid, or artificial mound of earth, vast tetragon terraces, and a large sunken area, of a cubic form, encompassed with banks of earth; and certain traces of a larger Indian town, the work of a powerful nation, whose period of grandeur perhaps long preceded the discovery of this continent.

—William Bartram

ANY STUDY OF HISTORY depends primarily on written and oral records that have been passed down over the years. Systems of writing, which began in Africa, are only 6,000 years old. Prior to that time, early civilizations depended on oral traditions. *Oral tradition* is a system in which older persons in a family or other members of a group repeated narratives of events over and over until the younger generations learned them by heart. In turn, these younger generations told their children. As the succeeding generations grew up, the traditions, beliefs, and folklore were passed down. Later civilizations used cave walls, animal hides, or bark to record stories of past events.

GEORGIA'S EARLIEST PEOPLE

When Christopher Columbus explored the New World in the late 1400s, he found people with dark eyes, straight black hair, and light brown to reddish-brown skin. Their faces were large, with jaws that stuck out and small chins. Columbus, thinking he was in the East Indies, called the natives Indians. Columbus was wrong on two counts. First, he was not in the East Indies. He was on the North American continent, probably in the area of the Bahamas. Second, the Indians he thought native to the New World are believed to have come from Asia to North America some 20,000 to 40,000 years earlier.

HOW WE LEARN ABOUT GEORGIA'S EARLY PEOPLE

In the preceding chapter, you found how we learn from geographers about Georgia's landforms, rivers, climate, and plant or wild life. To learn about Georgia's early people and their cultures, we depend on archaeologists and anthropologists. **Culture** is a term that describes the beliefs, traditions, music, art, and social institutions of a group of people.

Archaeologists study artifacts to learn about the life, people, and customs of early times. **Artifacts** are things, such as pottery, tools, or weapons, that were made by humans. Archaeologists dig into the earth and remove such items with great care in order to preserve as much of them as possible. These artifacts, as well as rocks and *fossils* (the traces or remains of once living things), can tell us much about the land and animals during prehistoric times.

Sometimes archaeologists can tell how old a prehistoric site is because they know when particular tools, weapons, or pottery found there were used. They may also choose to use the Carbon 14 test to help date things they find. This test, discovered by Dr. W. F. Libby, is quite complicated, but the idea behind it is simple. Radioactive carbon is in all living things. When an animal or plant dies, it begins to lose this carbon at a known rate. By learning how much carbon is left in the remains, scientists can tell, within about two hundred years, when it lived. The Carbon 14 test can also be used to date artifacts such as clothing or written records.

Anthropologists study how human culture began and developed. Anthropologists may also study artifacts and fossils to find out how groups of people lived. There are, for example, many types of projectile points. By studying a particular point, looking at its type, size, markings, and what it is made of, anthropologists can guess what size animals were killed with the point. Working together, geographers, archaeologists, anthropologists, and other scientists help us understand prehistoric cultures.

Scientists think that during the Ice Age the sea level was much lower than it is today. There is evidence that a land bridge connected Asia and America across what is now the Bering Strait, the narrow

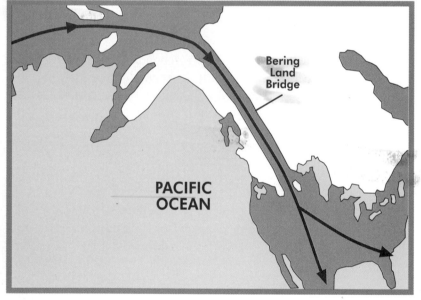
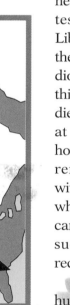

Bering Land Bridge

PACIFIC OCEAN

body of water that separates Alaska and Russia. It is thought that bands of people crossed the land bridge in search of game for food. Projectile points, remains of camp sites, and other evidence indicate that, when the food was gone in one area, the people moved to another. In this way, some of them came to what is now Georgia.

What archaeologists have learned about prehistoric times is not identified by the names of the groups of Indians we know today, such as Cherokee or Creek. Instead, early Indians are identified by cultural periods. No two cultures were exactly alike, and changes took place slowly. People learned from those who lived before, discovered new things, and taught what they knew to their children. Although cultural periods in history overlap, archaeologists have grouped prehistoric people in the following cultures: Paleo Indians, Archaic Indians, Woodland Indians, and Mississippian Indians.

Plants, animals and, later, man (above) used the Bering land bridge (map, opposite page) to cross over from Asia to North America. This crossing continued until about 10,000 years ago when the glaciers began to melt, flooding the land bridge.

PALEO INDIANS

The earliest known Indian culture is that of the Paleo Indians, whose culture lasted until 10,000 years ago. The word *Paleo* comes from the Greek and means "very old" or "long ago." As you learned above, early people sometimes can be identified by the material they used to make knives, scrapers, and points for spears. Because most tools and spear points used by the people of this culture were made of stone, the period is referred to as the *paleolithic* (old stone) age.

The Paleo Indians were *nomadic* (roaming) hunters who wandered from place to place following herds of large animals. Hunters used long wooden spears to kill large animals such as mammoths, bison, ground sloths, and mastodons, which they would then use for food. Archaeologists have also found large numbers of animal bones at the bases of cliffs. This leads them to believe that, at times, Indians chased the animals over the cliffs to kill them.

Large mammals like the wooly mammoth were one of the Paleo Indians' major sources of food.

Remains of their dwelling places indicate that Paleo Indians lived in groups of twenty-five to fifty people. Because these Indians moved around, however, they did not leave many artifacts in any one place.

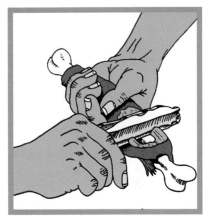

Left: Using bone and stone tools, Paleo Indians would chip flintstone to make the precise spear points used to kill large game. Below: The unifacial knife was used to cut meat.

Only a few Paleo sites have been found in Georgia. Archaeologists have uncovered artifacts from the Paleo period in the Savannah River area, in the Ocmulgee River area, and in the Flint River at Albany.

ARCHAIC INDIANS

The period of the Archaic Indians (from the word *archaic*, or old) included three distinct time spans: early, middle, and late.

Early Archaic Period

During the early Archaic period, from about 8000 B.C. to about 5000 B.C., Indians still hunted large game. These animals, however, slowly became extinct either because the climate grew warmer or because too many of them were killed. Whatever the reason, early Archaic Indians began hunting smaller game, including deer, bear, turkey, and rabbit. Hunters made their spears and points smaller. The people also began to eat reptiles, game birds, and fish.

The early Archaic Indians invented useful items, such as choppers, drills, and chipping tools made from deer antlers. Some of the stone artifacts found in Georgia are made from rock not often found in this state, but common in other parts of the country. This has led archaeologists to think there was some trading among different groups of Indians.

Archaeological evidence also indicates that the early Archaic Indians moved each season to look for food. During the fall they lived where berries, nuts, and fruits were plentiful. In summer they moved

Archaic Indians hunted smaller game such as deer and bear. When spear points were broken during a hunt, they were chipped into smaller points and used again.

to good fishing locations. They also migrated during spring and winter. The moves, however, were always for the same reason: to find food for their people.

Middle Archaic Period

Geographers tell us that by 5000 B.C., when the middle Archaic period began, the area had grown warm and dry. Water levels along rivers and the coastal areas moved back, and the Indians began to eat shellfish, such as mussels and clams. Scientists have found hooks made from animal bones that came from this period. These hooks were sometimes on the ends of long spears that were weighted in the middle with polished stones. Because hunters could throw the weighted spears long distances, food became easier to get. Finding more food meant the people did not need to move as often as they once did. Evidence also suggests that several small groups joined together to establish camps.

Late Archaic Period

A common artifact from the late Archaic period (4000 B.C. to 1000 B.C.) is the grooved axe. Indians made this tool by putting a stone axe head on a wooden handle. *Excavations* (archaeological diggings) of late Archaic settlements indicate that axes were used to clear trees and bushes around the camp. The Indians also saved seed to plant in the next growing season. It is thought that *horticulture*, the science of cultivating plants and trees, began in the late Archaic period.

By 2500 B.C., the climate had become cooler and wetter, much like the climate of Georgia today. Water filled rivers, streams, and lakes, and the Archaic Indians of this period depended on shellfish for most of their food. On Stallings Island, a few miles above Augusta on the Savannah River, archaeologists discovered a mound of mussel and clam shells. The mound was 512 feet long, 300 feet wide, and 23 feet higher than the depth of the river. Also at the Stallings site were remains of burial grounds, fire hearths, pipes, axes, shell beads, bone pins and needles, bone hooks, and many different spear points. Because of these discoveries, historians think late Archaic Indian villages were more permanent than those of any group before them.

The way food was prepared also changed. Pottery *shards*, or pieces, dating from the Archaic period indicate that clay containers were used for storing, cooking, and serving food. Archaeologists think learning to make and use pottery may be one of the greatest contributions the Archaic Indians made to Indian culture.

Other archaeological finds help us understand the lives of Archaic Indians. A grinding stone found in Fayette County, for example, may

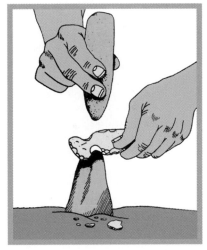

Left and above: *Points made by Archaic Indians had notches on the side which were attached to smaller spears than those used by the Paleo Indians.*

have been used to crush nuts into a type of flour. A nutting stone found in Coweta County is believed by scientists to have been used by Indians to hammer nuts in order to get the meat and oil from them.

WOODLAND INDIANS

Evidence suggests that during the period of the Woodland Indians, a culture that developed about 1000 B.C. and lasted until about 1000 A.D., several hundred families began banding together to form tribes. A **tribe** is a group of people who share a common ancestry, name, and way of living. The tribes lived in villages and built huts in which to house themselves.

The Woodland Indians used small trees and bark to build the dome-shaped huts. They stuck the trees into the ground on one end, then bent them forward and tied them together at the top. They then wove sticks in and out between the trees to form walls. Sometimes the Woodland Indians covered the sides of their huts with cane mats or tree bark. They made roofs of grass or pieces of bark and left a small opening in the top of the hut so smoke from cooking fires could get out. They also put fiber mats on the dirt floors for sleeping and sitting.

Hunting became easier in the time of the Woodland Indians, a period during which the bow and arrow came into use. Arrow points were made out of stone, shark teeth, or deer antlers. Fishing, hunting, and gathering nuts and berries remained important ways of getting food. The people also grew such things as squash, wild greens, and sunflowers.

Top: Pottery appeared during the Archaic Period, probably between 3000 and 2500 B.C. ***Bottom:*** *Woodland Indians decorated pots by scratching designs around the sides and by stamping the pottery with carved paddles.* ***Right:*** *Compare these Woodland projectile points with the Archaic points on page 53. How are they alike? How are they different?*

The Woodland Indians learned to make pottery last longer. They found clay along river banks and mixed it with sand. They rolled the mixture into strips and coiled the strips on top of each other into the shape they wanted. The Indians then made the clay smooth with a rock and water. They used wooden paddles to make designs on the pottery. After the clay containers dried in the sun, they were baked in a hot fire to make them hard enough to use for cooking.

Elaborate religious ceremonies were introduced during the period of the Woodland Indians. These ceremonies were spread through trade among different tribes. The Hopewell culture in Ohio, for example, had many of the same ceremonies used by the Indians in Georgia..

During this period, the Woodland Indians built cone-shaped burial mounds for the dead. They adorned bodies with necklaces, bracelets, rings, and copper or bone combs. When Woodland Indians were buried, their families and friends put special funeral pottery, tools, tobacco pipes, and weapons in the graves with them. These artifacts cause archaeologists and anthropologists to think this group of people believed in some type of life after death.

The expansion of farming allowed more stable settlements and free time for the Woodland peoples. Circular houses, probably of pole, wickerwork, and bark construction, characterized Woodland settlements.

ROCK EAGLE MOUND

During the period in which the Woodland Indians lived, from about 1000 B.C. to 1000 A.D., many mounds were built. Some of these were used as burying grounds, while others served different ceremonial purposes. The mounds were built in different sizes and shapes. Some were cone-shaped, some had flat tops, and some were built in the shapes of birds or animals.

Georgia has several examples of these mounds, but perhaps the one whose original purposes archaeologists and anthropologists are least sure of is Rock Eagle Mound. Located in Putnam County, between Eatonton and Madison, the mound is made of quartz and is the shape of a bird—either an eagle or a turkey buzzard. Because there were few Indian artifacts close to the mound to provide clues, no one can fully explain its significance.

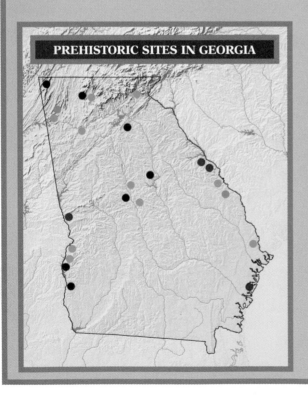

PREHISTORIC SITES IN GEORGIA

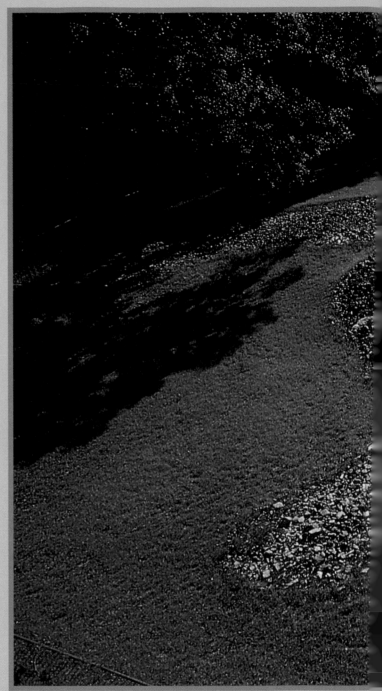

Above: *Rock Eagle Mound is made of quartz and is the shape of a bird, with a body 102 feet long and a wing span of 120 feet.* **Left:** *This map shows prehistoric Indian sites in Georgia (green dots represent Paleo sites, red dots are Archaic sites, black dots are Woodland sites and blue dots are Mississippian sites).*

Above: The Etowah Indian Mounds located three miles from Cartersville were home to the Etowah Indians from 1000 A.D. to 1500 A.D. during the Mississippian period. ***Opposite page, below:*** The Ocmulgee ceremonial earthlodge used for meetings and religious activities is considered to be one of the oldest buildings in the country.

MISSISSIPPIAN INDIANS

The culture of the Mississippian Indians is considered to be the highest prehistoric civilization in Georgia. The culture, which started about 700 A.D., is so called because the first things learned about it were from villages excavated along the Mississippi River. The Mississippian Indian age, sometimes called the *Temple Mound* period, was a time when the people lived in villages, farmed, and practiced religion.

There are ten major Mississippian Indian archaeological sites in Georgia. From them we learn much about how the Indians lived. We know, for example, that the people grew most of their food. Maize (corn), beans, pumpkins, and squash were all planted together in hills. They also grew tobacco to use in ceremonies. The Mississippian Indi-

ans planted in different fields each year so the soil would stay fertile. The land was prepared with stone or bone hoes and digging sticks.

Mississippian Indians began to dress and fix their hair differently. Their clothes were less simple, and they wore beads and ear ornaments. Sometimes they painted or tattooed their bodies. They also began wearing feather headdresses.

Villages grew, and several thousand families might live in a single settlement. They built centers for religious ceremonies and as a home for the priest-chief, who was the head of the village. The villages were often protected by moats and palisades (wooden fences). In some Georgia villages, guard towers have been found a hundred feet apart along the palisades, indicating the need for defense against tribal enemies.

Excavations at Ocmulgee National Monument near Macon led to the discovery of a large ceremonial lodge built of red clay in the shape of a circle. It is about 45 feet across, and has a 6-inch-high bench around the inner wall. The bench, which is divided into forty-seven sections, is believed to have been for seating tribal nobles. There is a large eagle-shaped clay platform with seats for the priest-chief and two assistants. A fire pit is in the center of the floor. Archaeologists and anthropologists think the lodge was probably used for both religious and village ceremonies and for other meetings.

At Etowah, near Cartersville, and at Kolomoki in Early County, excavations have uncovered elaborate flat-topped mounds. The 40-acre Etowah Indian Mounds site has seven of these pyramid-shaped mounds. One is 53 feet high and has steps leading to the top. Graves have been found along the base of a single mound, and bodies have been discovered in the tops of the mounds. The bodies were dressed in fine clothes, and beads and feather or copper headdresses were placed on them. Some of the intricately designed copper headdresses weighed almost 100 pounds. Carved marble statues also have been found at some burial sites.

The Kolomoki Indian Mounds site in Early County covers over three hundred acres. One of the temple mounds is about 50 feet high, 320 feet long, and 200 feet wide. With the tools available to the Mississippian Indians, it took a long time and many workers to build a mound of this size.

About 1600 A.D., something mysterious happened. The people left the villages, and there is nothing to tell us where they went. Did disease wipe out whole settlements? Did tribal enemies kill all the people in the villages? Did family units decide to migrate to other areas and become part of a new tribe? Because this was in the prehistoric period before written history, we may never learn what happened to the Mississippian Indians.

Above: Small arrow points like this one were used by the Etowah tribe. They were made from stone, wood, or deer antlers. Opposite page: These stone statues belonging to the Etowah Indian tribe were believed to represent their images of god and were treated with great reverence.

At the time of the first European exploration of what we now know as Georgia, there were small bands of Shawnee and Chickasaw in the area. However, the two largest Indian tribes were the Creek and Cherokee.

THE CREEK

Fourteen tribes with names such as Yamacraw, Yamasee, Ocmulgee, Oconee, Chiaha, and Apalachiee made up the Creek *confederacy*, or nation. Even though the tribes had different names, their language and way of living were much the same.

The true name for the Creek was Muscogee, and they were known for being brave and for carrying on the ways of their fathers. During the early days of exploration, Europeans discovered a tribe living on the banks of the Ocheese Creek, known today as the Ocmulgee River. The explorers did not know the Indians' tribal name, so they called them Creek.

There were two main groups of Creek: the Upper Creek and the Lower Creek. The Upper Creek lived along the Coosa, Tallapoosa, and Alabama rivers. The Lower Creek in Georgia made their homes along the banks of the Flint and Chattahoochee rivers. One of the largest of the Lower Creek towns was Coweta, which was a "war town." It was across the Chattahoochee River from the present-day city of Columbus. Cusseta, the "peace town," stood on the land where Fort Benning is now.

THE CHEROKEE

The Cherokee were the other large tribe in Georgia. They lived in the northwestern mountain region of the state. There were about 22,000 Cherokee in the southeastern United States, and they were all loyal to each other. They called themselves "Awi-yum-wija," which meant "real people" or "principal people." The Cherokee learned more from the life and government of settlers than did any other group of Indians.

Do You Remember?

1. What do archaeologists study?
2. What is the difference between artifacts and fossils?
3. Which important hunting tool was developed during the period of the Woodland Indians?
4. Which cultural period is considered the highest stage of prehistoric Indian civilization?
5. How many tribes were in the Creek nation?

Opposite page: Yoholo-Micco, who was born about 1788 and died in 1838, was the chieftain of an Upper Creek village located on the Tallapoosa River in what is now Alabama. He was a White Stick, fighting with the United States Army against the British and the Red Sticks. He later served as the Speaker of the Creek Nation. ***Above:*** *Menewa was a member of the anti-American Red Sticks. He led the Red Sticks at the Battle at Horseshoe Bend. Menewa was one of only 70 Red Sticks to survive the battle.*

Above: Swimmer, a Cherokee priest, was born about 1835. He related much of his knowledge of Cherokee lore to ethnologist James Mooney about 1887.
Above right: Today's Cherokee practice Christianity and sometimes engage in ancient religious rites.

INDIAN CULTURE

Even though there were differences in each tribe's way of life, much of the culture of the Creek and Cherokee was alike. Most of them built their villages on high banks or hills along rivers and streams. This gave them rich soil, enough water, fish for food, and a good place from which to defend themselves. The ways they built their houses, carried out religious ceremonies, and played were much the same. Describing the culture of one, therefore, serves to describe the culture of both. Because Cherokee still live in the Southeast, their civilization will be used to illustrate the developments of Indian life in the early historic period, the period of written history.

BELIEF SYSTEMS

Although the Indians belonged to different tribes and spoke different languages, they had many common beliefs. All Indians believed, for example, that many gods and spirits affected people on earth. They believed that they must cleanse themselves inside and out to purify the spirits. They believed in an afterlife where brave warriors and faithful women were rewarded and cowards and thieves were punished.

Many beliefs were recorded by anthropologists who interviewed Indians, mainly Cherokee, over a hundred years ago. Many of the following beliefs, for example, were related by a Cherokee medicine man named Swimmer in the 1800s. In the 1700s, early explorers recorded similar stories.

This World

The Cherokee believed that the earth was a large island resting on the waters. It hung from the sky by four cords, one each from the north, south, east, and west. The four directions were sacred, as was the number 4. Each direction had a special color. East was red, which represented life and success. West was black, which stood for death. North was blue and indicated cold, trouble, and defeat. South was white, which meant warmth, happiness, and peace. Each tribe thought that it was at the center of the earth, which it called "This World."

The Upper World

Above This World was the "Upper World," which represented order and expectation. Cleaner and purer than This World, the Upper World lay above a sky vault of solid rock. Twice a day, the vault rose to let the sun and the moon pass below it. At night the sun returned to its starting point by passing over the sky vault so that it would not be seen. When the moon darkened from an eclipse, the Indians believed that a giant frog was trying to swallow the moon. They made noises to scare the frog into releasing the moon. It always worked.

The Under World

Below the waters on which the earth rested was the "Under World," a place of disorder and change. The Under World was the opposite of This World. When it was summer in This World, for example, it was winter in the Under World. The Under World was home to cannibals, ghosts, man-killing witches, and monsters. This World lay between the order of the Upper World and the confusion of the Under World. One could pass from This World into the Under World by entering deep water, guided by a friendly spirit.

Gods and Spirits

The chief gods, who were found in the Upper World, were the Sun and the Moon. The Sun was the main god, and she had the power of night and day, of life and breath. As a symbol of the Sun, the Indians kept a sacred fire burning. The Indians believed that the Sun was kindhearted and watched over This World. In darkness, however, she was not watching and bad things could happen. The Moon was also a god, the Sun's brother. He represented rain and fertility.

The Cherokee had two other gods. One was Kanati, or the "red man who lived above the sky vault in the east." Kanati's voice was thunder. The Cherokee believed Kanati was a friend and spoke of him with respect. The other god was Long Man, the river. His head rested in the hills and his feet in the lowlands. His voice could be heard in the rippling waters, and priests could interpret what he said.

This "buffalo man" mask was worn in ceremonies to depict the existence of ghosts, witches, and evil spirits.

Besides the chief gods, there were also lesser beings in the Under World who often helped the Indians. All of these lesser spirits had to be treated with honor so they would not become resentful and spread disease.

The Cherokee also believed in the Immortals and the Little People. The Immortals lived in the mountains, especially inside bald mountains. They were invisible, except when they wanted to be seen. On one occasion, say the Cherokee, the Immortals came out from under the mound and helped to drive away an attacking tribe. The Little People were very short (about eighteen inches high) and had long hair. While they usually helped people, they were sometimes very mischievous, causing bewilderment and insanity.

According to their beliefs, ghosts were the spirits of dead persons. When a person died, if the person's ghost was not frightened away, it might stay and cause illness and death. The ghosts of murdered people, however, could not be frightened away. They remained until their murders were avenged.

There were two monsters in which the Indians placed great store. One was the Tlanuwa, the great hawk. The other was the Uktena, a dragon-like being. The Uktena had the body of a snake, the antlers of a deer, the wings of a bird, and sometimes the teeth and claws of a cougar. The Tlanuwa and the Uktena were mortal enemies. They usually ignored humans, but did sometimes kill them. The Cherokee believed that, just after the creation of the earth, a priest tricked the Tlanuwa into destroying the Uktena.

Beings

The Cherokee believed that there were three types of beings in This World. These were human beings, animals, and plants. Human beings and animals opposed one another. There were three kinds of animals: four-footed animals, birds, and vermin. The greatest of the four-footed animals was the deer.

Birds were important animals because they came in contact with the Upper World. Their feathers were often used in ceremonies. The most important bird was the eagle, which stood for peace and order. Its tail feathers were highly prized, and it was an honor to wear them. Falcon feathers were used to improve eyesight. Turkey buzzard feathers helped healing. The Indians associated the turkey and the red-bellied woodpecker with war.

Vermin included snakes, lizards, frogs, fish, and perhaps insects that were harmful to man, like fleas and hornets. Indians associated vermin with the Under World because many of them lived in water. They were afraid to kill a snake because it might want revenge. The rattlesnake, however, was different. The Cherokee believed it was

Indians avoided most snakes, regarding them as vermin, but they found ceremonial uses for the fangs and rattles of the rattlesnake.

once a man sent to This World to save humans from disease caused by the Sun. Eating its meat would make one fierce. Its rattles were used to scare enemies, its oil was good for sore joints, its fangs were used to draw blood during healing, and its bones were made into necklaces.

Some animals did not fit neatly into these three groups. The Cherokee believed that the owl was a witch because its eyes were spaced like a human's and it could see in the dark, unlike other birds. The bat and flying squirrel were four-footed but could also fly. The cougar was special because it could see in the dark and had claws like a bird. The frog and the turtle had four legs but lived in the water.

The bear was also a special case, for it stood on two legs like a man. The Cherokee believed that bears were once men who failed to avenge wrongs done to their people. Because this was a great crime, the men were turned into bears. Before the Indians killed any animal, they asked the animal's spirit to forgive them. But not the bear. Bear-men who would not avenge wrongs did not deserve respect.

PLANTS

Being the friends of humans, plants were used for food and to fight disease and bring healing. The most important plant and main source of food was corn.

The Indians had over two hundred plants they used for medicine. Priests or medicine men often made a ceremony of giving out medicines. The root of bear grass was used against snakebite and rheumatism. To ease shortness of breath and to stop bleeding, the Cherokee drank a potion containing ginseng. Angelica root was good for back pain, while spicebush tea cleaned the blood. Horsemint tea brought on sweating and reduced swelling in the legs. The roots of the Venus's flytrap and the pitcher plant were thought to have unusual powers because the plants fed on dead insects.

Tobacco was a special plant. When smoked in a pipe, its pure, white smoke rose up to the Upper World. As a result, the Cherokee, and most other tribes, used tobacco on ceremonial occasions when asking for blessings from the gods.

PURIFICATION

The Indians believed This World was usually orderly and predictable. As long as people stayed pure and behaved themselves and kept nature in balance, the spirits treated them justly. But illness and bad luck could come to people who misbehaved and polluted This World, especially by mixing things from the Upper World and the Under World. The body then had to be purified, inside and out. To cleanse the inside of the body, the person drank a black tea, usually yaupon

Tobacco was a special plant, used on ceremonial occasions when asking for blessings from the gods.

(a type of holly). To cleanse the outside of the body, the person first spent time in a sweat house and then washed in a cold stream.

People in the tribe came from near and far to take part in the Green Corn Ceremony. The main purpose of the ceremony was to give thanks for the corn that would feed them for another year. It usually took place at the first full moon after the late corn ripened. The first day was spent feasting, cleaning all the buildings, and putting out all fires. The second day was a day of fasting. The men drank tea to cleanse themselves. During the second day, the men would forgive wrongs done to them. Murder, however, was not forgiven. On the morning of the third day, everyone feasted again. That afternoon, the priest lit a new fire and carried it to the ceremonial center. From that fire the village fires were restarted. All wrongs were forgiven and the priest urged the people to remain pure so they would have good luck. Then the women joined the men in dancing. On the fourth day they feasted, danced, painted themselves with white clay, and took a ceremonial bath in a stream. Some Native Americans still practice this ceremony.

LAW OF RETALIATION

The Indians had few laws. The most important was the law of retaliation. *Retaliation* means "the act of striking back or getting even." According to this law, if one person injured another, the person harmed had the right to harm the first in a similar manner. If one person killed another, the spirit or ghost of the person who had been killed would not rest until relatives avenged the death.

When one tribe killed people from another tribe, war often resulted. The Cherokee looked upon war as a way to avenge deaths. Indians did not often go to war to gain territory or property. Raiding the enemy was a way to win honor. Warriors prepared for it by purifying themselves. Then, in small groups, they crept up on and attacked their enemies, taking trophies to show their people that the deaths were avenged.

Some tribes were mortal enemies, and they might travel hundreds of miles to make war. For some tribes, war was a way of life, a way to prove manhood and win glory. When tribes wanted to make peace, they asked a neutral tribe to arrange peace talks.

As they developed agriculture, corn became the Indians' most important crop, a symbol of life. The Green Corn Ceremony was one of the most important of the year.

Do You Remember?
1. In the Cherokee belief system, what did the Upper World and the Under World represent?
2. What were the four major gods of the Cherokee?
3. What were three uses of plants by the Indians?
4. What was the purpose of the law of retaliation?

How Native Americans Lived

Most tribes had a mother-centered family system. Within a tribe were **clans**, groups of people who believed themselves related by blood. A clan was usually represented by a totem animal like a wolf. Women were at the center of these clans. As a result, women had a considerable voice in matters affecting the clan and the tribe.

THE FAMILY

Within the family system, a child was related by blood only to the mother, not to the father or the father's family. The parents and grandparents, brothers and sisters, aunts and uncles, nieces and nephews, and other children of an Indian mother were her children's closest relatives. Therefore, her children could not marry any of them. Nor could they marry close relatives in their natural father's clan.

This lithograph of an early Cherokee village shows the change from a migratory lifestyle to established, permanent settlements.

This model of a Cherokee brave shows us how the Cherokee appeared in the mid-1500s before the arrival of Europeans. During that time, Indian clothing was made of animal skins. Weapons were fashioned from wood, stone, or antlers. This brave is carrying a blow gun.

The mother's brothers were responsible for raising her children. Indian parents were loving and easy going and disciplined their children very little. An early English explorer reported that a Catawba boy who almost hit him with an arrow was not even scolded.

In some tribes, mothers bound their babies to a board. This made it easier to care for the baby as the mother worked around the house or in the fields. To the Indians, a flattened head was a mark of beauty. An Indian mother would bind her baby's head tightly to the board, flattening the back of the head.

Children played at games that helped them learn their adult roles. Boys learned to use the bow and arrow and girls learned to cook and tend small children. Special ceremonies marked the time when girls became women and boys became men. Men and women married at different ages. Women just past the age of puberty were ready for marriage. Men were usually older, having had to prove themselves at hunting and war. A man and a woman who wanted to marry usually asked permission of the woman's family. After a small ceremony, the husband went to live with his wife's family and clan. Husbands and wives could divorce one another if they both agreed, and divorce was common.

GOVERNMENT

On the local level, Native Americans were governed by the clans. Each clan took care of its own affairs, deciding who could marry and who should be punished for wrongs.

A village was ruled by a headman. The village headman and other respected elders made up a council, which advised the tribal chief. The chief rarely made an important decision without talking to the council. Decisions at council meetings were reached by agreement rather than by a majority vote. At some point in the discussions, the council simply agreed on the best thing to do. Some tribes had two chiefs, one for making war and one for making peaceful decisions.

FOOD

All of the Native Americans fished and hunted animals to obtain meat. Deer was their main meat, but they also ate rabbit, squirrel, bear, turkey, raccoon, and small birds. Meat was often cooked by roasting it over an open fire. Fat from bear meat made a grease that was used in many ways.

Fish was also an important part of the Native Americans' diet. They used various methods to catch fish: hook and line, traps, spearing, and nets. On inland streams, they built V-shaped rock dams with traps at the pointed end of the V. The remains of some of these dams may still be seen in mountain rivers. At night, they would build fires on piles of sand in their canoes. The firelight attracted fish like flounder and sea trout, which they then speared.

The tribes also grew a number of crops. Their chief crop was corn. Corn was prepared in many ways: ground into meal for bread, cooked in wood-ash water to make hominy, or roasted by the ear over a fire. During the winter, dried corn was stored in an airtight crib built high above the ground.

Other crops included squash, pumpkins, beans, and sunflowers. The main fruit tree they grew was the peach. Honey and berries, fruits, and nuts gathered from the wild rounded out their diet. The Indians made a delicious vegetable oil for cooking and seasoning by boiling crushed hickory nuts.

CLOTHING

The Native Americans wore little clothing. Tanned deerskins provided breechcloths for men and apron-skirts for women. Small children often wore no clothes. During warm weather, no one wore shoes. During cold weather, the Indians wore moccasins, leggings, and match-coats for warmth. Match-coats were long, very warm capes made of furs or feathers. An early explorer who lived among the Indians for several years was amazed that they could sleep on the ground at night with no match-coat or other cover.

SHELTER

Indian shelters were made from materials at hand. They first built a framework of poles or saplings, which they then covered with bark or tree branches. Some houses were round, others rectangular. Inside were benches for sleeping and sitting. Because fleas were numerous, the benches were built higher than a flea could jump. Other furnishings included woven mats, pottery, baskets, and wooden utensils. Fires were built in the middle of the dirt floors. During the summer, the sides were opened to let in cool air. During the winter, the sides were closed to hold in the heat.

The Cherokee built log houses for winter living. A small fire kept the house very warm but filled it with smoke. This was useful when they wanted to make the body sweat out impurities. The Indians also built council houses for meetings. These council houses were larger versions of their dwellings.

Do You Remember?

1. What is meant by a mother-centered family system?
2. How were Indian children raised?
3. What were the three levels of Indian government?
4. Name three foods eaten by Native Americans.

Notice the differences in Indian dress from the 1500s as compared with the picture of the brave shown here in the 1830s. The influence of European settlers was reflected in both dress and lifestyle.

NATIVE AMERICAN GAMES

Scholars estimate that in 1492 there were about 2.5 million North American Indians in hundreds of tribes. Although they had different cultures and spoke over three hundred languages, certain practices united them all. These practices were play, games, and sport.

Ball games were most popular among all tribes, and lacrosse was the most common game. Both men and women played it, and the number of people on a side could be fifty to a hundred. The game was very rough, and players sometimes broke bones. Shinny and double ball were two other popular ball games.

Foot racing was another universal and popular sport, especially in the Southwest. There, long distance runners excelled. One Cree Indian is recorded as running 125 miles in 25 hours. The Zunis could easily run 25 miles in 2 hours while kicking a ball! Speed and stamina were important because tribes communicated with one another by sending runners.

Games that children played helped prepare them for adult roles. Mud ball fights were common, and children were taught not to cry when hit. Hide-and-seek taught the skills of searching and evading. Children also played archery games, wrestled, sledded, and raced on foot and on ponies.

These games and sports were common to all tribes, much as the Olympic sports are common to many nations.

Above: The Choctaw Indians played ball games as a form of recreation. Games also helped them improve their skills for hunting and war. *Left:* Teams carried out elaborate ceremonies before and after the game.

Above: *Many tribes made dugout canoes from a single log by burning and scraping out the middle.* **Left:** *This log house in the Oconoluftee Village in Cherokee, North Carolina, is typical of eighteenth century Cherokee dwellings.* **Opposite page:** *This replica of a Cherokee council house, also at Oconoluftee Village, provides seating for representatives of the seven clans. It was in the council house that village problems were discussed, arguments settled, and religious ceremonies practiced.*

GEORGIA PLACE NAMES

Native Americans have left their mark on Georgia. The state is full of communities, rivers, and attractions that bear descriptive Indian names. Among the communities whose names are based on Indian words are Dahlonega, in Lumpkin County, from the Cherokee *ateladalaniger*, meaning "yellow money"; Chiaha, in Floyd County, from the Creek, meaning "where the others live"; and Nahunta, from the Tuscarora, meaning "tall trees."

Many rivers in Georgia also take their names from Indian terms. The Chickamauga River, which flows through Catoosa, Walker, and Whitfield counties, comes from the Muskogean *Tchiskamaga* and means "sluggish or dead water." The Ocmulgee River, which begins at Lake Jackson, is from the Hitchiti *oki mulgia*, or "bubbling water." The Chatooga River, which flows through Walker and Chatooga counties, gets its name from the Cherokee *t satu 'gi*, meaning "He has crossed the stream and come out on the other side."

In Towns County, the Nantahala Mountains come from the Cherokee *nan-tah-ee-yah-heh-lik*, or "sun in the middle noon." Tallulah Falls and Tallulah Gorge in Rabun County get their names from a Cherokee word that means "awesome."

These and many more beautiful Native American place names have added a lyrical richness to our language.

The name of the Chattahoochee River (above) comes from the Cherokee and means the "river of the painted rock." It was so named because of the colorful stones that lay on the riverbed.

SUMMARY

- To learn about prehistoric people, we depend on the findings of archaeologists and anthropologists.
- The first settlers in our country are believed to be Asians who came to North America over a land bridge across what is now the Bering Strait.
- Scientists group prehistoric people into four cultures and time periods: Paleo Indians, Archaic Indians, Woodland Indians, and Mississippian Indians.
- The Mississippian was the most advanced of the four cultures.
- The two largest Indian tribes in what is now Georgia were the Cherokee and the Creek.
- The Cherokee and the Creek had a rich culture with strong belief, family, and government systems.

Opposite page: The Cherokee still make baskets of split oak, cane, and honeysuckle vines. They dye the baskets with natural dyes like walnut and bloodroot.

CHAPTER REVIEW

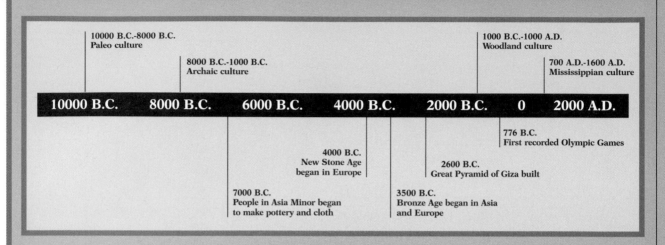

10000 B.C.-8000 B.C.
Paleo culture

8000 B.C.-1000 B.C.
Archaic culture

1000 B.C.-1000 A.D.
Woodland culture

700 A.D.-1600 A.D.
Mississippian culture

| 10000 B.C. | 8000 B.C. | 6000 B.C. | 4000 B.C. | 2000 B.C. | 0 | 2000 A.D. |

776 B.C.
First recorded Olympic Games

4000 B.C.
New Stone Age
began in Europe

2600 B.C.
Great Pyramid of Giza built

7000 B.C.
People in Asia Minor began
to make pottery and cloth

3500 B.C.
Bronze Age began in Asia
and Europe

Reviewing People, Places, and Terms

Match each of the following words with the definitions that follow:

anthropologist
archaeologist
artifacts
clans
culture
tribe

1. A scientist who studies how human cultures began and developed.
2. A group of people who share a common ancestry, name, and way of living.
3. A scientist who studies the items left behind by ancient people to determine how they lived.
4. A term that describes the beliefs, traditions, music, art, and social institutions of a group of people.
5. Groups of people who believe themselves related by blood.
6. Things, such as pottery, tools, or weapons, that were made by humans.

Understanding the Facts

1. How do scientists use artifacts to find out how people lived?
2. What is the Carbon 14 test?

3. Where is the Bering Strait? Why was this strait important in understanding how some of the earliest people came to America?
4. Which was the older Indian culture, the Archaic Indian or the Paleo Indian?
5. In what period do scientists believe horticulture began?
6. During which period did the bow and arrow come into use?
7. What did the Cherokee name for themselves mean?
8. What did the Cherokee call earth?
9. What was the Green Corn Ceremony?

Developing Critical Thinking

1. How can archaeologists tell about early cultures? What items do they study to learn about the past?
2. How did changes in climate affect the migration (moving) of early people from one part of the world to another?
3. What could have happened to cause some of the Mississippian Indian tribes to disappear?
4. Compare and contrast the methods of obtaining food in each of the four prehistoric cultural groups.
5. In what ways do you think "civilized" society

has demonstrated the Indians' law of retaliation?

6. How are the games played by today's boys and girls different from those played by the Cherokee children? How are they the same?

Applying Your Skills

1. Using poster board and color markers, draw a detailed diagram of the Cherokee belief system showing the earth, the four cords, the Upper World, and the Lower World.
2. Sign language was important to Native American culture and is still a method of communication between people who cannot hear or who do not speak the same language. Develop a short story to present to your class; and create signs with your hands that will represent the major people, places, and things in your story.
3. What do you think archaeologists and anthropologists of future centuries will think about today's eighth graders and their schools? What artifacts do you think might be used as evidence to describe your social and tribal life?

BUILDING SKILLS: FINDING THE MAIN IDEA

When you read about a topic, do not try to remember every detail. Identifying the main idea of a paragraph will help you organize information and remember more of what you read.

The main idea of a whole paragraph is often stated in the first sentence of the paragraph, although it may also appear in the second or third sentence. The other sentences in the paragraph provide supporting details. For example, the main ideas of the following paragraphs are stated in the first sentence. The other sentences in the paragraph provide the supporting details. Read again the following selection from this chapter.

The Indians had over two hundred plants they used for medicine. Priests or medicine men often made a ceremony of giving out medicines. The root of bear grass was used against snakebite and rheumatism. To ease shortness of breath and to stop bleeding, the Cherokee drank a potion containing ginseng. Angelica root was good for back pain, while spicebush tea cleaned the blood. Horsemint tea brought on sweating and reduced swelling in the legs. The roots of the Venus's flytrap and the pitcher plant were thought to have unusual powers because the plants fed on dead insects.

Tobacco was a special plant. When smoked in a pipe, its pure, white smoke rose up to the Upper World. As a result, the Cherokee, and most other tribes, used tobacco on ceremonial occasions when asking for blessings from the gods.

What are some of the details provided by the other sentences? You are correct if you answered the names of the plants that were used for specific ailments, the unusual powers of those plants that ate insects, and the special place given to the tobacco plant.

Do you think it is necessary to remember all the details in the paragraphs? If not, which are most important? You can probably remember that certain plants were considered to be helpful against specific ills or that the tobacco plant was considered special. But it would be difficult to remember the names of each of the plants and the ailments they were believed to help. It is not necessary to remember all details, but try to pick out the major facts from a paragraph.

Read the first paragraph under the heading "Belief Systems" on page 65, and answer the following questions.

1. What is the main idea of the paragraph?
2. Which sentence in the paragraph states the main idea?
3. Which sentences provide supporting details?

UNIT II

ALTHOUGH SEVERAL EUROPEAN NATIONS HAD earlier explored and made attempts at starting colonies in Georgia, the actual settlement period in the state lasted only fifty years. It began in 1733 when the first English colonist set foot on Georgia soil and lasted until 1783 when the Treaty of Paris was signed ending the American Revolution. During that period, Georgians found and built new homes in the wilderness; fought in a war against former friends, neighbors, and relatives; and started the process of building a new government called the United States of America.

It was an adventure filled with excitement, danger, disappointment, and hope for a better tomorrow.

Hernando de Soto (mounted on horseback) was the first European explorer to travel through Georgia. After winding their way through much of the Southeast, the expedition discovered the Mississippi River, as depicted in this mural in the U.S. Capitol.

CHAPTER THREE

THE THIRTEENTH COLONY

The air is always serene, pleasant and temperate, never subject to excessive Heat or Cold. [The soil] is impregnated with such a fertile Mixture which will . . . produce almost every Thing in Wonderful Quantities with very little Culture.

—James Edward Oglethorpe

F OR CENTURIES, EUROPEANS had traded with Asia through such Mediterranean ports as Venice and Constantinople and along a land route known as the Silk Road. Many middlemen took part in the Far Eastern trade. A **middleman** is a trader who buys goods from producers and sells them to other traders and consumers. The middlemen drove up the prices of such luxury items as dyes, silk, perfumes, drugs, gold, jewels, and spices such as pepper, cinnamon, nutmeg, and cloves.

In 1477, the publication of Marco Polo's *Travels* led many Europeans to believe that China's fabulous riches could be reached by ship.

Left: Marco Polo reached the Orient by land in the thirteenth century. His writings inspired Columbus. Above: This mural in the U.S. Capitol commemorates Christopher Columbus' first voyage to the New World.

Terms: middlemen, monarchs, Northwest Passage, mercantilism, indentured servant, slave, charter, regulation, artisan, militia

People: Hernando de Soto, James Edward Oglethorpe, Robert Castell, Chief Tomochichi, Mary Musgrove, Dr. Samuel Nunis, Salzburgers, John Wesley, George Whitfield

Places: Gaule, The Lost Colony, Jamestown, Battle of Bloody Marsh

The riches of the East Indies, Polo said, were "something wonderful, whether in gold or precious stones, or in all manner of spicery." First, however, Europeans would have to find a shorter trade route to the Orient before they could make these items more available to the people.

THE SEARCH FOR NEW TRADE ROUTES

Among those looking for a trade route to the Far East was Prince Henry the Navigator of Portugal. During the early to mid-1400s, Prince Henry sent ships along the south coast of Africa in search of an eastern passage to the Indian Ocean. But it was not until 1488, long after Prince Henry's death, that Bartholomew Diaz rounded the southern tip of Africa at the Cape of Good Hope.

Another European sea captain, Christopher Columbus, believed that the route to the Far East lay to the west. Like other experienced navigators of his day, Columbus believed the earth was round. Columbus thought that the distance from Portugal to Japan was less than 3,000 miles. (It was really 12,000 miles.) He also believed that no land mass would bar his way to the Orient. For years, Columbus tried to get support for his plan from the **monarchs** (kings and queens) of France, Portugal, and England. Finally, Queen Isabella and King Ferdinand of Spain agreed to finance his voyage.

On August 3, 1492, Columbus, a 41-year-old Italian, set sail from Palos, Spain, hoping to reach China and the East Indies. His ships were named the *Pinta*, the *Nina*, and the *Santa Maria*. On one of the best-known dates in American history—October 12, 1492—Columbus landed on a Caribbean island he named San Salvador (now one of the Bahama Islands).

Columbus believed that the islands he had found lay off the coast of India. As you learned in a previous chapter, he even called the friendly and gentle natives he met "Indians." He believed that they could easily be converted to Christianity and hoped to make them faithful subjects of the Spanish monarchs.

In all, Columbus made four voyages to the western hemisphere (1492, 1493, 1498, and 1502). In his later voyages, he explored along the coasts of Central and South America and was the first European to visit Puerto Rico, Jamaica, and the Virgin Islands. In his reports he described the extraordinary beauty of the "New World" he found. (Europe was the "Old World.") When he died in 1506, Columbus still believed that he had discovered a westward route to the Far East's riches. Vast stores of gold and spices, he insisted, lay close at hand.

John Cabot, who like Columbus was from Genoa, Italy, also sailed west. In 1497, sailing under an English flag, he discovered Newfoundland in present-day Canada. Actually, however, he rediscovered it.

Norsemen led by Leif Ericsson had landed in Labrador in the year 1001. They established a settlement in a region they called *Vinland*. After trying several times to colonize the area, the Norsemen fled back to Greenland. Unfriendly natives helped hasten their departure.

In 1498, Vasco de Gama sailed around Africa and reached India. An ocean trade route to the Orient had finally been found.

Amerigo Vespucci, an Italian navigator, had the honor of giving his name to the New World. In 1499, Vespucci sailed along the coast of South America. His writings caught the attention of a mapmaker who, in 1507, named the new land *America*.

In 1522, Ferdinand Magellan succeeded in reaching Asia by sailing west. However, his route around the southern tip of South America was long and hard. Europeans wanted an easier route to China and India. They were looking for the so-called **Northwest Passage,** an all-water route to Asia through the North American continent.

Do You Remember?
1. On what date did Columbus land at San Salvador?
2. What explorer tried to establish a settlement in Labrador in 1001?
3. For whom was the New World named?
4. What is the Northwest Passage?

EARLY EXPLORATION OF THE NEW WORLD

In the fifty years after Columbus's first voyage, European explorers continued to search for a shorter and easier route to the East Indies. King Francis I of France backed Giovanni Verrazano, who sighted land in March 1524, near what is now Cape Fear, North Carolina. He followed the coastline south for about 150 miles before turning to the north again. Verrazano did not continue farther south because he was afraid he would run into the Spanish.

Spanish explorers searched the Caribbean for wealth. In 1513, Juan Ponce de León discovered Florida, and Vasco Nuñez de Balboa crossed the Isthmus of Panama to reach the Pacific Ocean. (An *isthmus* is a narrow strip of land bordered on both sides by water and connecting larger pieces of land.)

Another Spanish explorer, Hernando Cortés, was the first to live up to Spanish dreams of tremendous wealth. In 1519, he landed in what is now Mexico. Within two years, Cortés had conquered the native Aztec Indians, killed their ruler Montezuma, and won a treasure in gold and silver. Hearing of the wealth of the Incas in Peru, Francisco Pizarro set out for the western coast of South America. In 1535, in the Andes, Pizarro defeated the Incas. In doing so, he captured the richest silver mines in the world.

Top: *America was named for the explorer Amerigo Vespucci.*
Above: *In 1498 Vasco da Gama reached India by sailing to the east, around Africa.*

SPANISH EXPLORATION OF GEORGIA

In 1539, the Spanish explorer Hernando de Soto left Havana, Cuba, with a huge group: over 600 men; 200 horses; and a number of other animals, including mules, dogs, and pigs. They landed in Florida and marched north. In 1540, they entered the southwestern part of Georgia, close to present-day Albany.

De Soto and his army wanted one thing as they moved across the state: to find gold. When De Soto arrived in Georgia, the Indians saw white men and horses for the first time. De Soto had only a small number of men to face thousands of Indians, but his weapons were better. His army had guns and crossbows, and his soldiers were mounted on horses. The Spanish also wore plated armor, which Indian arrows could not pierce.

During De Soto's search for gold in Georgia, thousands of Indians were killed by his soldiers. Many more Indians died from diseases brought to the New World by the Spanish and other explorers. Some historians believe almost half the Indian population died from measles, smallpox, influenza, and whooping cough.

De Soto's expedition into North America was a failure. He found no gold or treasure. Most of his army was lost to starvation and disease, and De Soto himself died somewhere along the Mississippi River. However, his march through Georgia changed the lives and culture of the Indians forever.

Above: *A skilled swordsman, horseman, and explorer, Hernando de Soto had little trouble enlisting young Spaniards to travel with him to Florida in search of gold.* **Right:** *De Soto's soldiers, called "Conquistadores" or "Conquerors," along with eight priests, a large number of slaves, horses, and battle-trained dogs, made up the expedition that traveled through Georgia in 1540.*

De Soto was followed by many other European explorers, most of them from Spain, France, and England. These nations established settlements in Georgia and competed with each other and with the Indian tribes for control of the land.

In 1565, Spain sent Captain General Pedro Menendez to begin a colony in St. Augustine, Florida. The following year, the Spaniards moved up the coast to St. Catherine's and Cumberland islands. They named the region Gaule (pronounced *Wallie*) for the Creek Indians living in the area. About thirty men were left to establish the first Spanish post on Georgia soil. Missions were later established on St. Simons Island and at Sapelo at the mouth of the Altamaha River.

For most of the 1500s, Spain's hold over the missions and colonies it established made it an important player in the race for control of the New World. As a result of the gold it took from the New World, Spain became rich and powerful. But this wealth also brought with it the resentment of other European nations. During the coming years, as Spain fought to hold on to its gains, the English and French fought to gain a share of the treasures.

DE SOTO'S EXPLORATION ROUTE

Maubila

Historians are still finding new information about De Soto's travels and do not always agree on the exact route. The map above shows one of several suggested routes.

At sea, the conflict between Spain and England had already turned into an undeclared war by the end of the 1500s. English sea captains, men such as John Hawkins, Francis Drake, and Richard Greenville, captured Spanish treasure ships filled with gold, silver, and other valuable goods. These sailors were really pirates sailing with the approval of Queen Elizabeth I. They also attacked and burned Spanish settlements in the New World.

To counter these attacks, Spanish King Phillip II plotted to invade England, using a huge fleet of ships that the Spanish called the "Invincible Armada." The plot failed as the British, who had superior seamen and faster ships, destroyed or ran off much of the Armada, which was also heavily damaged by fierce storms.

Do You Remember?
1. What was De Soto searching for in Georgia?
2. Where was the region called Gaule located?
3. Who was Francis Drake?
4. What was the "Invincible Armada"?

HENRY VIII, THE PROTESTANT REFORMATION, AND THE SEARCH FOR RELIGIOUS FREEDOM

In the early 1550s, King Henry VIII of England broke with the Catholic Church and established the Church of England.

During the 1500s, the Catholic Church was under attack from many quarters. Martin Luther began the Protestant Reformation with his demands for reform. His reforms became established beliefs in almost all Protestant religions.

In England, however, Luther's views met with stern disapproval in *Defense of the Seven Sacraments*, written by King Henry VIII. The king had studied theology, and no one questioned his strong religious views. In gratitude, the pope named Henry "Defender of the Faith."

Unfortunately, Henry had no male heir. Henry asked the pope in 1527 to annul his marriage to Catherine of Aragon. When the pope refused, Henry took a step that was sure to lead to a break with the Catholic Church: he pressured English church officials to grant him an annulment. They did, and Henry married Anne Boleyn. Their daughter became Queen Elizabeth I.

Henry VIII's break with the Catholic Church was completed in 1534 with the Act of Supremacy, which made the king the head of the Church of England. Henry's actions made it possible for even more radical forms of Protestantism to enter England and to find even freer expression in the New World. Thus the Protestant Reformation helped to unsettle the Old World and to lead colonists searching for religious liberty to the New World.

ENGLISH EXPLORATION OF THE NEW WORLD

After England defeated the Spanish Armada in 1588, it gained undisputed control of the seas and was ready to pursue its interest in the New World. Like most Europeans, the English believed there were large amounts of gold, silver, and exotic foods in the New World. They thought the country who claimed this new land would become even more powerful.

THE LOST COLONY

English explorers made several attempts to establish a colony on Roanoke Island in North Carolina's Outer Banks. In 1584, English ships reached the Outer Banks and claimed the area in the name of Queen Elizabeth. After spending six weeks on or around Roanoke Island, the ships returned to England, taking with them some samples of local crops and maps of the area. Queen Elizabeth was pleased with the expedition. On January 6, 1585, she named the land *Virginia*, after herself, the Virgin Queen.

Other expeditions to the area followed in 1585 and 1586. On July 22, 1587, a colony of 117 people was established. The colonists, however, arrived too late to plant crops, so their leader, Governor John White, returned to England

In 1584, English ships reached the Outer Banks of North Carolina and claimed the area in the name of Queen Elizabeth (above). Queen Elizabeth was pleased with the expedition. On January 6, 1585, she named the land Virginia, *after herself, the Virgin Queen.*

for supplies. Because of the war between England and Spain, no ships were allowed to leave England for some time. It was not until 1590 that White was able to return to Roanoke with two ships. When they got close to the shore, White sounded a trumpet and made other noises to get the colonists' attention. There was no answer. No one was there.

The settlement was overgrown with grass and weeds, and the houses were no longer standing. Iron bars, ammunition, and guns lay on the ground. Books, papers, pictures, and other items once buried in chests had been dug up and exposed to rain and weather.

Governor John White of the Roanoke Island colony was a superb artist whose paintings provide much information on the early Indians.

Even White's property was ruined. Clearly, the colonists had not been there for some time. At the fort's entrance, White found a carved message. Five feet above the ground on a tree trunk stripped of its bark, the letters *CROATOAN* had been carved.

To this day, Roanoke Island is known as the "Lost Colony." Many historians have offered theories to explain what happened to the Lost Colony. Some believe, as did White himself, that the colonists moved south to Croatoan Island (present-day Cape Hatteras). Croatoan Island was the home of the tribe to which a local Indian, Manteo, belonged. Together with another Indian, Manteo had been taken several years earlier to England, but both returned on the same ship that carried members of the ill-fated colony. Other historians believe that the colonists either went north to the Chesapeake Bay or split into two groups. Some believe the Indians killed the colonists. Still others think that the Spanish sailed up from Florida and destroyed the colonists. To this day, no one really knows what happened to them.

PERMANENT ENGLISH SETTLEMENTS

In the 1600s, the English began permanent settlements along the coast of the New World. They founded colonies at Jamestown and Massachusetts, as well as others in both the North and the South. Some were begun by refugees from religious persecution while others were primarily settled for economic gain. By the close of the 1600s, England had established twelve colonies along the Atlantic coastline.

Among the colonists, the reasons for moving to the New World were as different as the people. Some came to Maryland, Rhode Island, and Massachusetts so they could have religious freedom. A few felt a spiritual "calling" to bring Christianity to the Indians. Others wanted adventure and the chance to make a new start. Almost everyone thought that with hard work, they could have a better life. Most of the settlers did, indeed, face a variety of hardships before they succeeded.

For its part, England hoped to establish a system of **mercantilism,** a part of which was a trade policy that England should export more than it imported. Among the things it had to buy from other countries were cotton, forest products, tobacco, and some foods. Under the system of mercantilism, its colonies would produce such raw materials and ship them to England. There, English citizens could use the raw materials to make finished goods, such as furniture, clothing, tools, and sugar. England could then sell these items to other nations and strengthen its own economy.

England was also interested in defense. As each colony was settled, it had to be protected from the French, Spanish, and Indians. This need for protection eventually led to the settlement of the area we know as Georgia.

MERCANTILISM

England began establishing colonies in America during a period of world history known for exploration and colonization. All of the European countries wanted colonies so they could be more powerful.

During the 1500s-1700s, England—and the other nations of Europe—followed policies that came to be known as *mercantilism*. An important goal was to make England largely self-sufficient. To do that, the monarchy needed to create a "favorable balance of trade" by exporting more goods than were imported. A favorable balance of trade would bring gold and silver into England and make it militarily and economically strong. Laws were enacted to regulate trade. They made it difficult for foreign merchants to import goods into England; English merchants were told to export goods only in English ships.

Colonies were to help England gain that favorable balance of trade. They were sources of such raw materials and foods as sugar, timber, rice, tobacco, and cotton, thus ending any need to import these goods from other countries. Colonies were also markets for goods manufactured in England.

Captain John Smith, a founder of the Virginia colony, clearly understood the purpose of mercantilism. He viewed the colony as "a nurse for soldiers, a practice for mariners, [and] a trade for merchants."

Tobacco produced at manufactories as shown above ended England's need to import it from other countries. Thus, the colonies contributed to a favorable trade balance.

On April 26, 1607, about 104 hearty English settlers sailed down a river they named the James River, after King James I. A few days later they chose a piece of land by the river to build the first permanent English colony in the New World, called Jamestown.

Jamestown

Permanent colonization in the New World began in 1607 with the English settlement of Jamestown, which is located in what we now call Virginia. From the beginning, Jamestown, which was named after King James I, had its troubles. Like the Lost Colony, the 104 settlers that survived the transatlantic crossing arrived too late to plant crops. Moreover, Jamestown was located beside a swamp, and malaria swept through the village during the colonists' first year. By the end of that year, only 38 settlers remained alive. The colony survived, however, and flourished, especially after the settlers discovered that tobacco grew well in the land. Soon other settlers were attracted to Jamestown.

The cultivation of tobacco created a need for labor, a need that was met by Dutch traders. In 1619, these traders introduced Africans into Virginia, most of whom were indentured servants. **Indentured servants** agreed to work for someone for a set period of time (usually 4 to 7 years) in return for passage to the New World. At the end of that time, indentured servants were free to do anything they wished. As the seventeenth century wore on, however, Africans more and more were treated as slaves. **Slaves** had few rights and spent their entire lives in service to others.

Massachusetts Bay Colony

In 1620, another group of settlers disembarked from the *Mayflower* onto Plymouth Rock near Cape Cod and founded the colony that became known as the Massachusetts Bay Colony. Some of the settlers

HOW MASSACHUSETTS CREATED THE FIRST BICAMERAL LEGISLATURE

In 1640, about twenty thousand colonists scratched out a living in New England. They lived in twelve scattered communities, the largest of which was the Massachusetts Bay Colony.

The Bay Colony was founded by religious dissenters known as Puritans, who tried to govern the colony by religious principles. Many settlers, however, demanded rule by law. The battle for government of laws came to a head in the colony's General Court (legislature), which consisted of eight magistrates and twenty deputies. The magistrates served as assistants to the governor. The deputies represented the towns, each of which sent two representatives.

A disagreement over a pig turned into a challenge of the magistrates' power. The pig was claimed by both a wealthy, unpopular merchant and a widow who ran a boardinghouse. The deputies sided with the widow. The magistrates, who could veto the deputies' decisions, sided with the merchant. The issue of who owned the pig was lost in the political struggle that followed. The deputies protested the right of a few magistrates to overturn the decisions of the people's representatives. A 1644 law resolved the matter. Deputies and magistrates would sit as separate bodies. To pass any measure, both bodies had to agree. Thus, a dispute over a pig led to the establishment of the first bicameral legislature.

In 1644, a dispute over the ownership of a pig led to the establishment of the first bicameral legislature.

belonged to a religious group called "Pilgrims," who had spoken out against the practices and beliefs of the Church of England. They were coming to the New World to find a place where they could worship according to their own beliefs. The rest of the settlers, however, were members of different churches who did not want to be associated with the Pilgrims. The disagreement between the two groups was settled by a document called the "Mayflower Compact," which was the first written constitution in North America. Later, another large group, called the Puritans, left England and also settled in Massachusetts.

Spain moved out of the region called Gaule by 1686. However, more than one country claimed the land. Among those who tried to lay claim to the land was England.

England first claimed Georgia in 1663, but it was not until 1717 that the English made plans to settle there. Sir Robert Montgomery, a nobleman from Skelmony, Scotland, and two partners, poet Aaron Hill and merchant Amos Kettleby, wanted to create the "Margravate of Azilia," a new colony. Montgomery's dream was to have "the most delightful country of the universe [where] coffee, tea, figs, currants, olives, rice, almonds and silk" would be produced for English markets. Montgomery proposed to settle an area that lay west of the Savannah River and ran to the Altamaha River. He promised to give land, gold, silver, and precious stones to those who would move to this "paradise."

Montgomery's plan seemed good, but there was not enough financial backing to carry it out. After a few years, Montgomery's dream of a "future Eden" died.

In the years that followed, there were several other proposals to settle the area for England. None was successful until the late 1720s, when James Edward Oglethorpe began to talk of a colony for the "working poor."

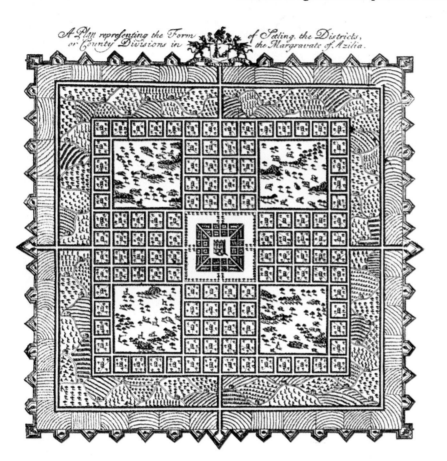

Above: Sir Robert Montgomery proposed a Georgia settlement called Margravate of Azilia, envisioning a heavily fortified settlement with intricate homesteads and pasture land.

Opposite page: As a man who possessed the virtues of kindness, compassion, and leadership, James Oglethorpe was a commendable choice to lead the settlers to their new home.

JAMES EDWARD OGLETHORPE

James Edward Oglethorpe, born in London in 1696, was a member of an influential family. He was well educated and wealthy. He cared greatly about people in trouble and tried to find ways to help them. Oglethorpe became a member of Parliament's House of Commons in 1722.

During that time, England was faced with many problems. There were more people than there were jobs. Many citizens, including

some well-known ones, could not pay their debts. Laws concerning debtors were strict and harsh, and those who could not pay went to jail. Among those jailed was Oglethorpe's friend, architect Robert Castell.

Oglethorpe was on a committee studying prison reform when he learned that Castell had died of smallpox. Oglethorpe was angry because he believed debtors should not have to go to jail. He felt, therefore, that his friend had died needlessly in a dirty prison. Stirred into action, Oglethorpe worked to get laws passed that both improved the conditions in prison and let thousands of prisoners go free.

Unfortunately, just letting people out of prison did not help them. There were no jobs for them, and without work, they still could not pay their debts. Dr. Thomas Bray, a clergyman and active humanitarian, proposed that a colony be founded to help these people.

Bray died before his proposal was acted on. However, James Oglethorpe, Lord John Percival, and nineteen other men outlined a plan that promised a fresh start in the New World to "unfortunate but worthy individuals."

Oglethorpe was shocked at the inhumane treatment of debtors he visited in prison and wanted to pass laws to help them. Not only were thousands arrested each year for not paying their debts, but many were charged a fee for being in jail. The death of his friend, Robert Castell, while in debtor's prison led Oglethorpe to demand reforms.

Do You Remember?

1. What was the "Lost Colony"?
2. How many coastal colonies were established?
3. Why did England want to establish colonies in North America?
4. Where was the first permanent English settlement in North America?
5. What crop led to the need for new sources of labor?
6. What was the first written constitution in North America?
7. When did England first claim the land we now call Georgia?
8. What was the "Margravate of Azilia"?
9. Who first proposed a colony for debtors?

A DREAM BECOMES A REALITY

In the summer of 1730, Oglethorpe's group of twenty-one men asked King George II for a tract of land on the "southwest of Carolina for settling poor persons of London." The group knew England's reasons for beginning new colonies, so they proposed ways to carry out England's goals. The new settlement could defend the southern Carolinas from Spanish Florida. It could also provide protection from the French, who were pushing east from the Mississippi.

Oglethorpe's group listed economic reasons for the proposed settlement. France and Spain made money trading with the Indians who lived between the Atlantic Ocean and the Mississippi River. England could share in this. Oglethorpe and his supporters also said the new colony could produce silk, cotton dyes, and wine—three items England was importing from France, Russia, and Spain. They promised to send spices and semi-tropical fruit to England. English merchants were pleased with the idea of getting a good supply of raw materials while, at the same time, having a new market for their manufactured goods.

Georgia, like other American colonies, would offer religious freedom to Protestants who were being mistreated by the Catholic Church in Europe. Too, the King liked the idea of more land and greater power for England.

On June 7, 1732, King George II granted a charter making Oglethorpe's group of twenty-one trustees responsible for establishing the colony of Georgia and for managing it for twenty-one years.

Left: *This 1733 map was the first map of Georgia. It was used as part of the advertising campaign to entice settlers to seek a new home in the colony.* **Above:** *King George II was anxious to settle the region named in his honor in order to add wealth to England and as a defensive buffer for the South Carolina colony.*

Trustees are people who hold responsibility on the behalf of others. The **charter,** which is a legal document that grants special rights and privileges, noted that the grant covered an area of "all vacant land between the Savannah and the Altamaha rivers extending from the Atlantic Ocean westward indefinitely to the South Seas" (the Pacific Ocean).

GEORGIA'S CHARTER

The charter had six thousand words and many limits. The King stated that the trustees could not own land, hold political office, or be given money for their work. "Papists" (Catholics), blacks, liquor dealers, and lawyers could not become colonists. Catholics were excluded because of a longstanding division between the Catholic Church and the Church of England. Blacks were not admitted so as not to introduce slavery to the colony. The trustees feared settlers would not work if liquor was permitted. They wanted colonists to settle their differences out of court and did not think lawyers would allow them to do this.

The colony belonged to the Crown, so the trustees were to get instructions from King George II. They could pass no laws unless the king agreed. The trustees worked around some of the rules by not having a governor and by using **regulations,** or government orders, instead of laws.

In allowing settlement of the colony, King George limited the trustees' authority, made them managers for a definite period of time, and said they could make no profit. In spite of the limits, excitement grew as the trustees developed the "Georgia Plan for Colonization."

PREPARATION FOR THE VOYAGE

A search began to find settlers for the newest colony. Newspapers told of a land with mild temperatures and rich soil. They offered those who were chosen a new start in life. Sir Robert Montgomery's description as the "most delightful Country of the Universe" was widely accepted as fact. Clergymen preached sermons, wrote religious books, and raised a great deal of money by talking about the goodness of the proposed colony.

The trustees talked with applicants and planned for the voyage and settlement. Unfortunately, debtors and former prisoners did not get to go. This meant the humanitarian reasons for the proposal were all but forgotten. Only a few of those chosen had ever been in debtors' prison, and no one got out of jail to make the trip. All who applied were carefully investigated. Those chosen were promised fifty acres of land, tools, and enough food for one year. Potential colonists who could pay their own way were given five hundred acres of land and could take ten indentured servants.

The seal of the Trustees of Georgia. The cornucopia stands for "plenty" and was used to indicate that money would be made from the settlement of Georgia. The figures with water jars represent the Savannah and Altamaha rivers.

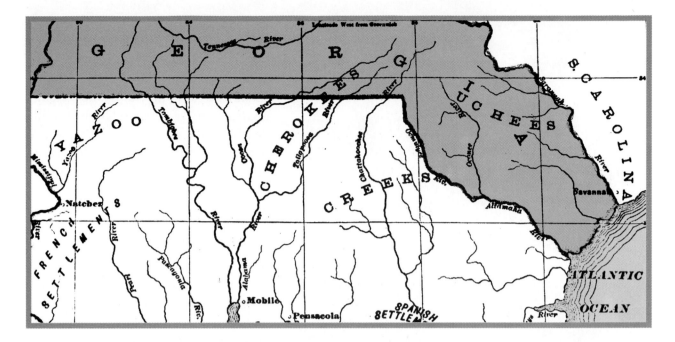

This nineteenth century map shows the area covered by the original charter.

In exchange, colonists had to agree to the following: (a) each man was to defend the new colony against all enemies; (b) land given to colonists could not be sold, and no money could be borrowed on it, but it could be passed on to a male heir; (c) each colonist was to receive seeds and agricultural tools and was to use them in cultivating the lands of the new settlement; (d) colonists were to use a portion of their land to grow mulberry trees so that silkworms would eat the leaves and make cocoons for the production of silk; and (e) each colonist was to obey all regulations established by the trustees.

Even though the agreement was strict, the fever of settling in the new colony grew. On October 24, 1732, the chosen settlers met to receive instructions for their voyage to Georgia.

THE VOYAGE ON THE SHIP *ANN*

When the settlers gathered on the London docks, they were both excited and a little afraid of the adventure ahead. Historians do not agree on the exact number of men, women, and children who traveled from England to Georgia, but between 114 and 125 people left London on November 17, 1732. Their voyage to the New World took eighty-eight days.

Besides its passengers and crew, the *Ann* carried sheep, hogs, ducks, geese, and several dogs. There is no record of the ship being uncomfortable, but it was probably crowded with people and their belongings. Food was simple, mostly salted pork and peas or dried beef and sweet pudding. Bread and hard cider were served with meals. There were few fresh vegetables other than carrots and on-

ions. Fish were caught and cooked whenever possible.

Only two deaths were reported on the trip, both of them infants. The passengers spent their days playing games, talking together, and planning what they would do when the voyage was over. Finally, land was sighted and the *Ann* docked at Charleston, South Carolina. She stayed in Charleston one day, then put in at Beaufort, South Carolina.

Before the *Ann* could set anchor, Oglethorpe had to make friends with the Yamacraw Indians through their chief, Tomochichi. Oglethorpe went to the trading post in the Yamacraw village to find an interpreter. The trading post was operated by John Musgrove and his wife Mary, who was part Indian and part English. Oglethorpe offered John Musgrove about 100 English pounds a year to interpret for the Indians and settlers. John agreed to act as interpreter, but Mary soon took over for him. With Mary's help, Oglethorpe and Chief Tomochichi established a close friendship that lasted until the chief's death in 1739.

The passengers waited on board the *Ann* while Oglethorpe and his staff searched for a permanent settlement site. The place decided on was about eighteen miles from the mouth of the Savannah River.

On February 12, 1733, Chief Tomochichi allowed the *Ann's* passengers to land on sandy Yamacraw Bluff overlooking the Savannah River. The settlement they established was the thirteenth English colony in the New World. Georgia's citizens were added to about 654,950 other colonists spread from Massachusetts through the southern Carolinas.

Above: When Tomochichi, Chief of the Yamacraws, met James Oglethorpe, leader of the settlement, little did they know they were to become life long friends. *Opposite page:* Chief Tomochichi with his nephew, who was probably the chief's sister's son. Notice the intricate designs on the chest of the chief.

Do You Remember?

1. What were some reasons England wanted to settle Georgia?
2. What land was included in the original Georgia charter?
3. What were some of the rules to which the first colonists had to agree?
4. What Indian chief was a friend to the Georgia settlers?

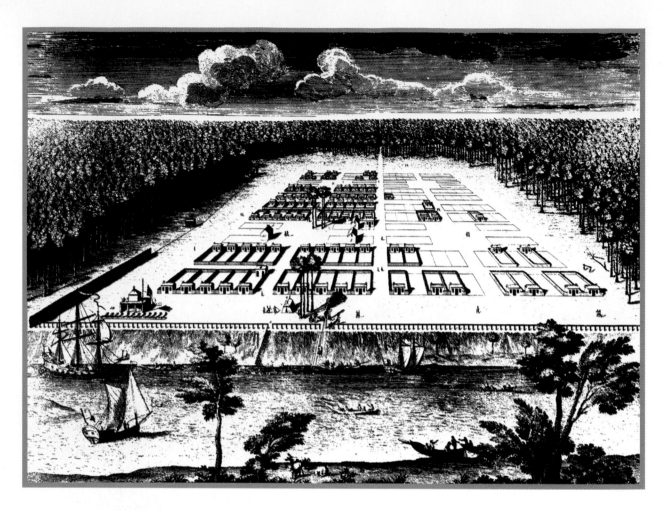

Peter Gordon, an upholsterer by trade, kept a journal describing the crossing of the Atlantic on the Ann *and providing us with the earliest view of the layout of Savannah.*

BUILDING A NEW HOME

The group put up four large tents for shelter. After that, they began getting the land ready for planting and preparing timber to build permanent homes. Most of the settlers had lived in the city and were **artisans,** or craftspeople. They were not used to hard physical labor. Within two weeks, however, the first permanent homes were being built. The settlers were welcomed with gifts of food and farm animals from their Carolina neighbors.

Oglethorpe had no title and limited power, but he was accepted as leader of the colony. During the early months, he got grants of land and made treaties with the Indians. He had a small fort built on the bank of the river, and trained a **militia,** or citizen army, to defend the settlement. Oglethorpe gave advice to local leaders and encouraged the colonists. He also worked with Colonel William Bull and surveyor Noble Jones to design the future city of Savannah. The basic pattern of this first planned city in the colonies was after a design by Robert Castell, Oglethorpe's friend who had died in a British debtors' prison.

The plan was for Savannah to have four squares. On the north and south sides of each square were twenty lots sixty by ninety feet. On the east and west sides, four larger lots were set aside for buildings such as churches or stores. The center of each square was for social, political, and religious gatherings. The squares were divided into blocks, which were called *tithings*, and wards. There were ten houses in each block and four blocks in each ward.

An examination of a present-day map of Savannah shows the influence of Jones, Bull, Castell, and Oglethorpe. Modern Savannah, with a population of over 146,000, is built much the same as the city that was planned over 255 years ago.

Each settler was expected to care for his house in Savannah, his five-acre garden plot on the edge of town, and his forty-five farm acres in the country. During the first months, the colonists cultivated mulberry trees to feed silkworms. They also built a sundial for telling time, a *gristmill* for grinding corn into meal, a courthouse, a water well, and a bakery.

Work was done in spite of growing medical problems. Oglethorpe thought the use of rum caused the people to be sick. However, the scurvy, dysentery, and fever were more likely caused by a lack of fresh vegetables, changes in the climate, poor sanitation, and hard physical labor. Forty settlers died in the first year. That number might have been greater if new colonists had not arrived to help.

THE ARRIVAL OF NEW COLONISTS

In July 1733, when the sickness was the worst, a ship carrying forty-two Jews landed in Savannah's harbor. The passengers asked to join the settlement. Because Catholics were the only religious group not allowed by the charter, Oglethorpe agreed. He needed to replace the colony's only doctor, who had died earlier. He also needed more able-bodied men in the militia. Because of the services of Dr. Samuel Nunis, the newly arrived doctor, Georgia's first medical crisis passed.

In March 1734, Oglethorpe was planning to leave for England to report to the colony's trustees when more new settlers arrived. A group of German Protestants had been made to leave Salzburg, which was then controlled by Catholics. They were led by John Martin Bolzius, and they asked to live in Georgia. Oglethorpe carried the Salzburgers to a place twenty-five miles from Sa-

Fifty German Protestant families received an offer from the Trustees of the Georgia colony to come to the colony in 1734 to escape the religious persecution in their own country. By 1741, close to 1,000 Salzburgers had built homes in the new colony.

Above: *Reverend John Martin Bolzius was the leader of the German Protestants from Salzburg.* **Right:** *On June 28, 1734, Oglethorpe and his party of nine Indian guests, including Chief Tomochichi, reached London. The British wanted the assistance of the Indians in developing their enterprises in the colony, and entertained them with numerous parties and dinners during their stay. King George II even granted Oglethorpe's Indian guests a meeting at Kensington Palace. This group portrait commemorating the meeting of the Indians and the Trustees of Georgia was painted by Willem Verelst in 1736.*

vannah. There they began a town called Ebenezer, which means "the Rock of Help." They spoke a different language from the other settlers, so they stayed mostly to themselves. However, they worked hard and were busy colonists. Because the land was marshy with poor soil for crops, the Salzburgers asked Oglethorpe for a better site. In

1736, they moved to Red Bluff on the Savannah River. There they built another town, which they called New Ebenezer.

When the Salzburgers were settled, Oglethorpe left for England. He took with him Chief Tomochichi, as well as the Chief's wife, grand-nephew, and five other members of the tribe. The English liked the

Ebenezer, located upriver from Savannah, was the first home of the hardworking Salzburgers.

Yamacraws and held parties and receptions in their honor. The Indians were presented to King George II and the Archbishop of Canterbury. His countrymen thought Oglethorpe was a hero, and excitement about the newest English colony grew. The visit strengthened Indian-British relationships, and Oglethorpe went back to Georgia with the full support of the trustees.

When Oglethorpe reached Savannah in early February 1736, there were three hundred new colonists with him. Included were another group of Salzburgers, some Moravians (Protestants who banded together in Saxony, Germany, in 1722), and two religious leaders, John and Charles Wesley.

During his visit to England, Oglethorpe was given a large amount of money from the trustees to use in making the frontier borders stronger. They also agreed with three new regulations Oglethorpe wanted to introduce. Upon his return, Oglethorpe first helped the Salzburgers move to Frederica on St. Simons Island. Then he began to present the three new regulations to Georgia's settlers.

DISCONTENTMENT AMONG THE SETTLERS

Oglethorpe's new regulations were not popular. Buying rum was against the law, and alcohol could not be used in trading with the Indians. Slavery was not allowed because Oglethorpe thought it caused landowners to be idle while, at the same time, made them want more land. Trade with the Indians was to be watched carefully.

These regulations, added to an earlier one which said land could be passed on only through male heirs, began to divide the colonists. They were already facing economic hardships. Their mulberry trees were the wrong kind for producing large amounts of silk. The colonists were not able to grow hemp, flax, indigo, or grapes for wine. To make the discontent worse, their South Carolina neighbors, who had large amounts of land, slaves, and rum, were doing well. They were growing rice, cotton, and tobacco, and their success was due, in part, to the use of slave labor.

Scottish Highlanders, who had settled in Darien in 1735, and the Salzburgers opposed slavery. However, growing numbers of English settlers wanted slaves. There was less and less support for trustees' regulations. Many Georgia settlers moved to places where they could live more nearly as they wished. When Oglethorpe returned to Georgia after a trip to England, he found people upset all over the colony.

Oglethorpe, however, had little time to listen to the colonists. In the fall of 1739, a war broke out between England and Spain. England controlled Georgia's borders, and Spain controlled Florida's. There seemed to be no way to keep the two groups from fighting.

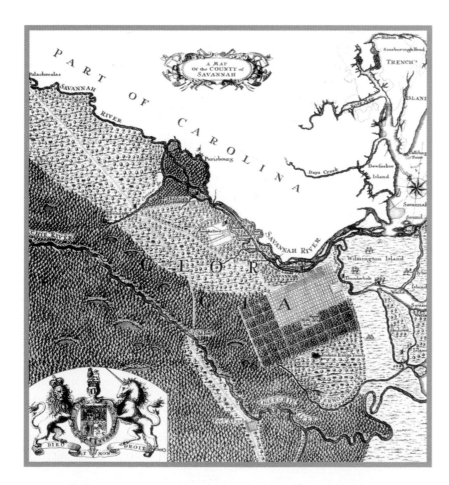

This map, drawn in about 1735, shows the colony of Georgia in its first year. Notice the number of settlements that had grown outside the planned community of Savannah.

The Battle of Bloody Marsh was fought between the St. Simons lighthouse and Fort Frederica (top). A stately man, James Oglethorpe (above) inspired his often ill-trained troops to follow him in battle.

THE SPANISH INVASION

Oglethorpe welcomed the war. (The war was given the name the "War of Jenkins' Ear," because several years earlier Spanish sailors were said to have cut off the ear of Robert Jenkins, an English seaman, to serve as a warning to British ship captains smuggling goods off the Florida coast.) Oglethorpe wanted a reason to invade neighboring Florida. A troop of about 2,000 men, mostly Indians and settlers from Georgia and South Carolina, was quickly organized. They tried to take major Spanish forts in Florida, particularly St. Augustine. However, a well-organized Spanish militia met Oglethorpe and his soldiers with a surprise attack on June 15, 1740. The Spanish won, and Oglethorpe's forces had to retreat to St. Simons Island.

During the next two years, there were numerous attacks and counterattacks between the Spanish and the English settlers, with neither side gaining much ground. In July 1742, Oglethorpe got the opportunity he needed. His forces, assisted by the Scottish Highlanders, waited in the dense woods along the marshes on St. Simons Island. Spanish troops who came that way were caught completely by surprise and, in a minor skirmish, were beaten back across the Florida border. Even though the action was known as the Battle of Bloody Marsh, it was neither big nor very bloody. It did, however, mark the beginning of a safe southern frontier for the English.

After that battle, Oglethorpe tried a plan that worked. One of his soldiers had deserted and gone to the Spanish. Oglethorpe sent a note to the deserter by way of a released Spanish prisoner. The note, which was taken away from the prisoner by Spanish troops, said that British warships were on their way to begin a great battle against the Spanish settlers. These "warships" were really trading vessels that moved quickly to safe waters the first time they met the Spanish Navy. However, the Spanish troops did not know this and, because they thought they were outnumbered, chose to leave the area for good.

THE END OF THE DREAM

In 1743, Oglethorpe was called to England to answer charges that he had not acted correctly when he failed to capture Spanish-held St. Augustine. Oglethorpe was cleared of the charges, but he did not return to Georgia. Instead, he remained in England, married a young heiress, and settled down to life as a patron of the arts.

William Stephens, the trustees' secretary, was named president of a colony filled with disagreement. Efforts to keep rum from being sold had been stopped in 1742. However, the people still wanted to own more land and have slaves. By 1750, this was allowed. The regulation against slavery was repealed, along with the one that allowed a colonist to own only five hundred acres of land. When President Stephens retired in 1751, he was replaced by his assistant, Henry Parker. President Parker died a year later. In the next three years (1752-1754), Georgia was led by President Patrick Graham. During his tenure, many settlers who had left under the rule of the trustees returned to the colony. At about this same time, the English Parliament decided not to set aside enough money to take care of the colony's needs. In 1752, one year before the charter's end, the trustees returned Georgia to the authority of King George II. A new era was about to begin.

The English victory in the Battle of Bloody Marsh on July 7, 1742, helped secure the frontier boundaries against future Spanish invasions.

A FINAL LOOK AT THE CHARTER COLONY

The idealistic vision of society that had been shared by the trustees of the colony was never fulfilled. Few debtors reached Georgia's shores, and the colony was an economic failure. Many unhappy settlers moved elsewhere, but the dissension in the colony continued. Rum was freely

imported, and slavery was introduced. Nearly one-third of the population of three thousand were slaves by the time the Georgia charter ended. Finally, the colony suffered from a lack of continuity in leadership. However, with all its failures, the colony had made progress.

During the twenty years under the original charter, 5,500 people had settled in Georgia. They had built new homes and started new lives. Although some left the colony to go elsewhere, they still made an imprint on Georgia society and culture.

A large number of settlers were European Protestants who came to the colony to escape religious persecution. In Georgia, they were able to practice their beliefs without fear of punishment.

Treaties with the Indians and the elimination of the threat of Spanish invasion ended the necessity for British military protection. Georgia was a safe haven on the southern frontier.

There were also noteworthy religious, social, and political accomplishments in the colony's short his-

After serving Georgia for ten years, Oglethorpe left in 1743 to return to England. Until his death in 1785, at the age of 88, Oglethorpe continued to work in many charities while living the life of a country gentleman.

tory. Evangelist George Whitfield established the Bethesda Orphans Home in Ebenezer. The home served as a refuge for children without parents. Later the home was expanded into a school and renamed Bethesda House. The school provided a basic education for many of Georgia's future leaders. In Savannah, John and Charles Wesley established the first Sunday School in America. They were also founders of the Methodist Church.

The court system, established during the early days of the settlement, was still functioning. By 1750, when the colonists gained outright ownership of the land, women were able to inherit property.

Perhaps the greatest accomplishment of the trustees of the charter colony had been their ability to enable the Georgia colony to survive the many hardships encountered during the first twenty years. The survival set the stage for Georgia to become a successful and profitable royal colony.

SUMMARY

- For years, European explorers searched for the Northwest Passage, an all-water route to reach the riches of the East Indies.
- Spain, France, and England supported the exploration of lands along the coast of the New World.
- In 1732, King George II granted twenty-one trustees, including James Oglethorpe, the right to settle a colony in what is now called Georgia.
- England hoped that the new colony would defend its other colonies from the attacks of the French, Spanish, and Indians. England also planned for the colony to produce and ship to it raw materials it had to buy from other countries.
- Led by James Oglethorpe, a group of settlers landed on a site near the mouth of the Savannah River. Some of the settlers were looking for religious freedom, while others wanted adventure and the opportunity to make a fresh start in life.
- The charter contained many limits on the freedom of the colonists, who were expected to defend the colony and obey all regulations.
- Land was given to the colonists; however, they could not sell it, borrow money on it, or pass it on to anyone other than a male heir.
- Later regulations, including a ban on slavery, caused discontent among the settlers, who needed more help to work their properties.
- Although the original ideals for the colony were never fulfilled, the colony made progress and survived.

Chief Tomochichi asked Oglethorpe to bring a minister to the colonies to serve his tribe. John Wesley (above), a young Church of England minister, volunteered. During his brief one-year stay, Wesley preached to the Indians and colonists. He conducted Bible study classes for the children every Sunday. Those classes are believed to be the first "Sunday School" held in the colonies.

CHAPTER REVIEW

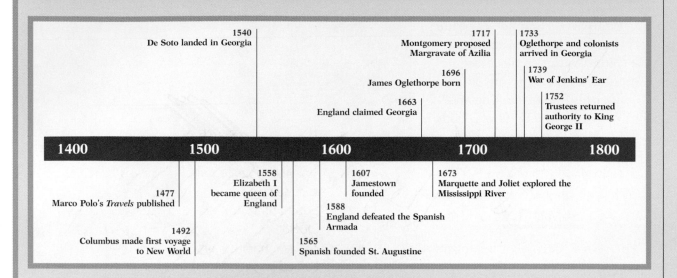

| 1400 | 1500 | 1600 | 1700 | 1800 |

1540 De Soto landed in Georgia

1717 Montgomery proposed Margravate of Azilia

1733 Oglethorpe and colonists arrived in Georgia

1696 James Oglethorpe born

1739 War of Jenkins' Ear

1663 England claimed Georgia

1752 Trustees returned authority to King George II

1558 Elizabeth I became queen of England

1607 Jamestown founded

1673 Marquette and Joliet explored the Mississippi River

1477 Marco Polo's *Travels* published

1588 England defeated the Spanish Armada

1492 Columbus made first voyage to New World

1565 Spanish founded St. Augustine

Reviewing People, Places, and Terms

Define, identify, or explain the importance of the following.

1. artisan
2. charter
3. Gaule
4. indentured servant
5. mercantilism
6. middlemen
7. militia
8. monarch
9. Mary Musgrove
10. Northwest Passage
11. Dr. Samuel Nunis
12. James Edward Oglethorpe
13. regulation
14. slave

Understanding the Facts

1. How did Marco Polo help encourage exploration?
2. Where did Christopher Columbus land on October 12, 1492?
3. Where was slavery first introduced into North America?
4. When did England first claim Georgia?
5. Why did King George II want to establish the thirteenth colony?
6. Why did many Georgia settlers want to introduce slavery into the colony?
7. How many trustees were responsible for establishing and managing the colony of Georgia? For how many years were the trustees supposed to manage the colony?
8. What was the purpose for planting mulberry trees?
9. In what year were the people in the colony allowed to own more land and have slaves?

Developing Critical Thinking

1. If you had been a citizen of London when Oglethorpe brought the first colonists to Georgia, would you have been willing to travel to a new land? Why or why not? What parts of the trip would have been the most exciting for you? What parts of the settlement process would have been the most frightening for you?
2. Suppose the initial regulations governing the colonies had been upheld. How would life in the colonies have been different? Explain.

Applying Your Skills

1. Using a United States map, outline the original land area granted to Oglethorpe and the other trustees.

2. Using a current map of Savannah, Georgia, examine the layout of the early colony and compare it to modern Savannah. How are the maps similar and different? How do current street names indicate a sense of the history of the early settlement?

3. On a blank Georgia county map, locate Savannah, Ebenezer, Darien, and St. Simons.

4. Draw what you think would be a good layout for Savannah. How does your design differ from that used by Oglethorpe?

Making Connections

1. Are countries still worried about their "balance of trade"?

2. The United States has become the world's largest debtor nation. What does this mean, and how do you suppose it happened?

3. The bicameral legislature that developed in the Massachusetts Bay Colony was an attempt to balance the power of two opposing groups.

Can you think of other ways that power is balanced in our national government today?

Did You Know?

• Spanish explorer Christopher Columbus maintained two sets of official logbooks on his voyage to the New World. One logbook was public, the other was private. Columbus felt that the crew would panic if they knew how far they were actually sailing.

• Hernando de Soto brought swine with him to the New World as he moved north from Florida with Spanish hogs to breed along his way. Although the men were often hungry because they weren't good at foraging (hunting and fishing) for food, De Soto would not allow the slaughter of the pigs. In less than a year, there were 300 swine who served to protect the men from poisonous reptiles.

• A Yamacraw Bluff monument is located in front of the Savannah Hyatt Regency Hotel on the riverfront.

• During early colonial days, many settlers only bathed two or three times a year. More than that was thought to be dangerous.

BUILDING SKILLS: UNDERSTANDING TIMELINES

Keeping track of all the events you read about can be difficult. Timelines can help you remember events in the order that they happened. Although a timeline can show events over a short period of time, most often it covers years. Making a timeline is a useful way to organize the events that took place during a given period of time. Sometimes, it is not possible to include all events in a timeline. Only the most important ones can be included. These important events then provide reference points for other events that occurred during the period covered by a timeline.

In your textbook, timelines appear in the Chapter Review section of the chapter, where they help you remember the events in the order they occurred during the chapter. They also help you place other events within the time frame of the timeline. You may want to expand these timelines and add other events to help you in your study of the chapter.

Look at the timeline for this chapter. It covers a period of about 400 years. On a separate sheet of paper, expand the timeline to include at least two other events you read about in the chapter that were not included in the timeline.

Try This! Make a timeline of your life or that of one of your older relatives (mother, father, grandmother, grandfather, uncle, or aunt). Start the timeline with the year you (or they) were born. Then write in the present year. Show at least eight events in the order they occurred.

CHAPTER FOUR

GEORGIA IN TRANSITION

What is it that gentlemen wish? What would they have? Is life so dear, or peace so sweet, as to be purchased at the price of chains and slavery? Forbid it, Almighty God! I know not what course others may take; but as for me, Give me liberty or give me death!

—Patrick Henry

MUCH OF THE PERIOD from the mid-1700s until the outbreak of the Revolutionary War was overshadowed by the political events that led to the break between England and its former colonies. Nevertheless, for most of the people in the thirteen colonies, their concerns centered on the problems of everyday living.

LIFE IN THE COLONIES

In the years before the Revolutionary War, everyday life in the colonies continued to remain challenging and difficult, although there were differences from one colony to another. The economy still was largely based on agriculture. Settlers still had to work hard to plant and keep up their farms. Transportation and communication still were primitive and time consuming. The teachings of the various religions were strictly and sometimes sternly observed. Little time was available for education and even less for leisure.

THE COLONIAL ECONOMY

Because all of the colonies had to raise food for survival, farming was essential in all three regions—the New England colonies of Massachusetts, Rhode Island, Connecticut, and New Hampshire; the middle colonies of New York, New Jersey, Pennsylvania, and Delaware; and the southern colonies of Maryland, Virginia, North Carolina, South Carolina, and Georgia. In addition to agriculture, other industries grew up in several of the colonies.

This painting depicts a happy ending to a day of hunting. Wild turkey was a popular food source for the early settlers.

Colonial life in Georgia can be seen at Wormsloe, below Savannah, the 750-acre estate of surveyor Noble Jones. Purchased in 1733, it is thought to be the oldest estate in Georgia. It is now a state historical site.

The land in the New England colonies was rocky and the soil poor. Most farms in the region were small and difficult to work. However, there were abundant trees, and the colonists of New England were known for their fine craftsmanship in making furniture. Shipbuilding, fishing, and whaling became profitable industries in the region.

The middle colonies were often known as the "bread" colonies because their primary crop was wheat. Farmers in the region also raised cattle, sheep, and hogs. For the most part, their farms were small, but the land was easier to work than the land in New England. Besides agriculture, other important industries in the middle colonies were shipbuilding, manufacturing, mining, and textiles.

Due to its mild climate and rich soil, the South had many large plantations where tobacco, rice, and indigo were grown. Forest products were a large part of the southern economy. Casks and barrels for shipping goods, as well as *naval stores* such as tar, pitch, rosin, and turpentine, were produced from the abundant longleaf pine forests.

TRANSPORTATION AND COMMUNICATION

Transportation had improved very little since the days of the early settlers. Indian paths still guided colonists on foot or horseback, while boats delivered passengers and trade goods from port to port. Stage-coaches offered quick transportation among the colonies. Quick, that is, if you call the week it took to travel the 90 miles from New York to Philadelphia speedy.

By the mid-1700s, most cities had cobblestone streets; however, citizens walked at their own peril because many streets were used as garbage dumps as were the streets of the typical European cities of the time. While watching where they stepped, the city dwellers also had to stay out of the way of hogs and the occasional chickens that roamed about.

Communication was equally primitive. People in the cities relied on newspapers for information. Those in the rural areas had to wait for newspapers, often as long as several weeks or months. Trading posts were sources of information, and bulletins and announcements were placed at the posts and in whatever local shops there were. This, of course, was still in the period when those who could write wrote long letters and wrote them often. Mail was slow in the country, but in the larger cities it was not unusual for citizens to dispatch couriers with messages several times a day. Sometimes, the messages were simply to tell someone that they could expect a visitor later that day.

EDUCATION

For most children, schooling was something that occurred between daily chores at home. Seasonal agricultural needs, such as the planting or harvesting of crops, took precedence. In the early days, most schooling took place either in the home or in the church. Not everyone was given a formal education. Boys were taught practical skills, such as farming or horseshoeing. If they lived in or near cities, they might be sent away to *apprentice* in a trade; that is, learn a particular skill from a master craftsman. Girls learned homemaking skills, either to use in their own homes or working for others as "hired" hands.

Punishment in colonial schools could be very harsh. Students could be caned for not knowing their lessons.

Midway Church was located in St. John's Parish, which included the settlements of Midway and Sunbury. This church building was completed in 1792, replacing one burned by the British during the Revolutionary War.

When public schools first began in the New England colonies, only boys attended. They studied the "3 Rs": reading, 'riting, and 'rithmetic. In some towns, both boys and girls could attend "dame schools" in which a woman who was knowledgeable in the "3 Rs" opened her home as a school. Students carved their writing pens from goose quills and used ink made from boiled bark.

Discipline in early schools was very rigid. In many of the colonies, students were *caned* (whipped with a thick rod) if they could not show that they knew their lessons. Like many other things in their lives, going to school was not something to be treated lightly.

In the South, boys from wealthy families either had a tutor or were sent overseas to be educated in England or France. In some communities, parents banded together to pay someone, almost always a man, to teach the basics to their children.

RELIGION

Depending on the colony, church was generally both a place of worship and the center of community activity. In the stricter New England colonies, church services often lasted three hours in the morning and three more in the afternoon. Most of that time was spent listening to sermons from such "Great Awakening" preachers as Jonathan Edwards and George Whitfield. The Puritans were especially demanding of their followers. **Puritans** were a group of people who had broken away from the Church of England because of religious differences. Those who did not observe the Puritan beliefs to the letter often received punishment ranging from caning to banishment from the area.

In the southern colonies, although church attendance was expected, services tended to have more singing and shorter sermons. After-church socials were times for women to visit and chat while girls played hopscotch and boys played hoop ring or kite flying.

Georgia was a haven for such varied religions as the Moravians and the Jewish, yet the Anglican Church, or Church of England, was the major faith. Indeed, in 1758 it was made the official church of the colony of Georgia.

LEISURE TIME

Even recreation differed among the three regions of the New World. In the New England and the middle colonies, most of the recreation centered around work and included such activities as barn raisings, quilting bees, and corn huskings. As they were in other aspects of their lives, the Puritans were quite strict. People in their colonies were not allowed to gamble, dance, play cards, or wear frilly clothes. Punishment for engaging in these activities included public whippings, having one's legs locked in stocks, and dunking into a pond or river while sitting in what was called the dunking chair.

Weddings were major events on the southern frontier. Dancing was an important part of the festivities that often lasted until the early hours of the morning.

In the southern colonies, fox hunting, horse races, and week-long parties with friends and relatives were a welcome change from the drudgery and isolation of farming or running a plantation. Food was always central to any large social gathering. Tables were laden with roasted pigs, pheasant, chicken, venison, wild turkeys, oysters, and fish. Vegetables included steamed pumpkin pudding, squash, corn, and succotash. Desserts included such treats as shoofly pie, a spice pie with molasses; slump, a fruit cobbler; and sweetmeats, which were candied nuts, fruits, or flowers.

Do You Remember?
1. On what was the economy of the thirteen colonies primarily based in the years before the Revolutionary War?
2. Into what three regions were the thirteen original colonies grouped?
3. Why did people in the cities have to be careful when walking in the streets?

Benjamin Bannaker's
PENNSYLVANIA, DELAWARE, MARY-
LAND, AND VIRGINIA
ALMANAC,
FOR THE
YEAR of our LORD 1795;
Being the Third after Leap-Year.

PHILADELPHIA:
Printed for WILLIAM GIBBONS, Cherry Street

Above: A free black, Benjamin Banneker gained recognition as a farmer, mathematician, astronomer, and surveyor. He put together the first clock made completely in America and also published a well-known almanac. Opposite page: Georgia's third royal governor, Sir James Wright, was responsible for defense of the colony and for maintaining friendly relations with the Indians.

The last part of the eighteenth century was a time of growth and development in all the colonies. New Jersey imported the first steam engine; in Philadelphia, Pennsylvania, the Liberty Bell was hung. Benjamin Banneker, a thirty-year-old black man, put together the first clock made completely in America; and Benjamin Franklin invented bifocals. Transportation became easier as roads started to be paved in the northeastern colonies. Georgia, the youngest and poorest of the colonies, was ready for some of the prosperity enjoyed by the others.

In 1752, Georgia ceased to be a proprietary colony and became a royal colony. A **proprietary colony** was one directed by those to whom a charter had been granted. A **royal colony** was one directly governed by the king.

During the two years before the first royal governor was appointed, some of the people who had left Georgia under the trustees began to return. In 1752, Puritans from South Carolina bought 32,000 acres of land at Midway in present-day Liberty County. They moved there, bringing with them slaves; and soon they began growing rice and *indigo*, a plant from which a blue dye is produced. A port was built nearby at Sunbury so the planters could ship their crops.

GEORGIA'S FIRST GOVERNOR AND FIRST GOVERNMENT

Because the trustees had felt that the first Georgia settlers were not able to govern themselves, they had not given them the right to vote, hold elections, or collect taxes. As a result, the Georgians cheered when on October 1, 1754, John Reynolds, their first royal governor, arrived. Reynolds, a navy captain, introduced an idea that had not been tried before in the colony: self-government. Unlike the trustees, Governor Reynolds wanted the colonists to help run the government.

A bicameral, or two-chamber, legislature was set up to represent the eight parishes of the colony. A **parish** was both a church and a British government district. The two chambers of the legislature were a lower house, called the Commons House of Assembly, and an upper house, called the Governor's Council. In order to vote, a settler had to own at least 50 acres of land. Those wishing to become a member of the lower house, however, had to own no less than 500 acres of land. Members of the lower house could write and vote on bills before they became laws.

The king of England appointed the members of the upper house. The men selected were wealthy, influential landowners. They were to advise the governor, approve land grants, make laws, and, sometimes, act as judges in legal cases. Governor Reynolds also set up a court system. When the colonists had differences with each other,

Top: Beginning in 1754, Georgia had a new seal as a royal province. The front side of the seal depicted the province giving the King of England silk spun in the colony. **Above:** *The coat of arms of King George II was engraved on the back side of the silver seal marking Georgia as a royal province.*

they went before the Court of Conscience, which was presided over by a local justice of the peace. Cases that could not be settled in the Court of Conscience could be carried to the Governor's Council.

GEORGIA'S FIRST ASSEMBLY

The new government met for the first time in 1755 in Savannah, the colony's capital and largest city. They reorganized the state militia and passed bills so roads could be built and repaired. The new legislature also drew up codes that restricted the rights of slaves.

For a while, Governor Reynolds and the legislature worked well together. However, during one legislative session, members of the upper house could not come to an agreement on how much was needed to improve the military defenses of the colony. Governor Reynolds became so angry at their failure to agree that he stopped the meeting and sent the legislators home.

During the months that followed, Reynolds tried to govern Georgia by himself to the despair of the colonists. There were arguments between those who thought Reynolds should leave and those who wanted him to remain. Many Georgians did not like having their right to self-government taken away and wrote to King George II to complain. Other Georgians liked Governor Reynolds. Finally, after two years, the group who wanted self-government won, and Georgia's first royal governor was replaced.

GOVERNOR HENRY ELLIS

In February 1757, the king chose Henry Ellis to take John Reynolds' place as governor. Governor Ellis was a naturalist and a scientist who had been to many different parts of the world. According to reports, he walked the streets of Savannah checking a thermometer that hung around his neck and taking notes of its readings. Ellis believed that Savannah was one of the hottest places in the world, and he often carried an umbrella to protect himself from the sun.

Ellis learned quickly from Reynolds' mistakes. He sought the advice of the governor of the neighboring colony of South Carolina. During his three years as governor, Ellis brought together people of many different political groups. He also depended on well-known and wealthy citizens to lead the colony.

While Ellis was governor, additional numbers of colonists came to Georgia from South Carolina and the West Indies. Many of these new settlers brought slaves with them, and the governor granted the newcomers large amounts of land. By 1759, the population of the colony had grown from about 6,000 to 10,000, including 3,600 slaves.

Not all Georgians wanted slaves in the state. The Highland Scots at Darien and the Salzburgers at Ebenezer believed that hard work by the white settlers would allow the same economic growth as would a system of slave labor. Although there were not many large plantations in the colony at that time, the wealthy kept getting more land and talking about the need for more slaves.

In 1759, Governor Ellis became ill and was allowed to return to England. Ellis had been a popular governor, under whose direction the colony had made economic gains. There were more profitable farms, and because there were many more merchants with a greater variety of items to sell, the colonists could buy the things they could not grow, such as cloth, sugar, farming tools, and seeds for planting.

GOVERNOR JAMES WRIGHT

In 1760, King George III appointed James Wright as Georgia's new governor. Wright had grown up in America and was at one time attorney general of South Carolina. He was loyal to the king, but he also wanted the colonies to do well. He believed that Georgia would continue to grow if large farms were even bigger, if more trading was done, and if the western lands of the colony were opened to settlers. Wright agreed with the self-government program Governor Reynolds had started, and the colonists were pleased with him at first.

The French and Indian War

Some of Georgia's growth during Wright's term of office took place after the **French and Indian War** ended in 1763. In that war, the British fought the French and the American Indians for control of land. After years of fighting, the British won. Under the terms of the Treaty of Paris of 1763, Canada and all lands claimed by France east of the Mississippi River except New Orleans were given over to Great Britain. Equally important, because Spain joined France in the later years of the war, Florida also became part of British territories.

Georgia did not take part in the war, but it was helped by the war. The state's southern boundary was moved to the St. Mary's River. At the same time, the Indians gave up all lands between the Ogeechee and Savannah rivers north to Augusta, which was Georgia's second oldest city and later would become its capital for ten years. The Indians also gave up the coastal land south of

George Washington, a young officer in the Virginia militia, was defeated by the French at Great Meadows in 1754. That clash ignited a war in both America and Europe. In America, it was known as the French and Indian War.

the Altamaha River. All this land came under Georgia's control, and settlers began to migrate to the colony. The new boundaries would be important to Georgia's growth. Not only did they provide water access for future shipping, but they also provided fertile farm acreage and dense forests with timber and naval stores resources.

The end of the French and Indian War also ended the danger of French and Spanish attacks along Georgia's land borders. Colonists could then start to settle inland instead of only along the coast. While the Georgia colonists saw the end of the war as an opportunity to expand, the Indians saw it very differently. As the greed for land became stronger, the Indians slowly found themselves being pushed farther and farther to the west.

Ultimately Great Britain was victorious in the French and Indian War. As a result, in 1763, King George III extended Georgia's boundaries, almost doubling the territory. The southern boundary of the province was now the St. Mary's River (above), which separated Georgia from Florida.

GEORGIA CONTINUES TO GROW AND CHANGE

There were many other changes during James Wright's early years as governor. The town of Sunbury grew and became the colony's official port of entry for ships arriving from other countries and colonies. Both houses of the legislature worked together to promote Georgia's economic growth. Farmers were allowed to borrow more money, so they bought more land. The amount of owned land grew from one million to seven million acres.

Rice and indigo had become profitable crops. Enough silk was being produced so that, by 1767, almost a ton of it was exported to England each year. There were more schools, and more and more people were reading. Many books were sold, and in 1763, the colony's first newspaper, *The Georgia Gazette*, was started. Many of the small frame houses were taken down and, in their place, two-story houses were built of wood or tabby which was a mixture of lime, crushed shells, sand, and water.

There was, however, another side to Georgia during these early years. Many mothers died giving birth to children. School was mostly for children in the upper economic class. Also, a group of what plantation owners called "undesirable people" moved from Virginia and the Carolinas to settle in the middle and western parts of the colony.

These people became known as **crackers**. Historians do not know why they were called that. The term may have come from the cracking sounds of whips used on oxen or horses as these new settlers went to market to sell their goods. It may have come from the cracking of corn as they prepared corn meal. Some say the term came from a Scottish word that meant "boasters." No matter how it started, the term was intended as an insult. These settlers were thought of as people who did not obey the law and were not welcome in the colony.

During this time, Governor Wright had other things that took his attention. There was no plan for defending the colony. Also, a growing number of Georgians who were not wealthy began to ask for a greater voice in government. They were not alone. Shortly, their voices joined with others as the colonies began trying to gain **independence** (political or economic freedom) from Great Britain.

The fortifications of Fort Morris are long overgrown with grass and trees. Fort Morris was built in 1776 to protect the seaport at Sunbury.

Do You Remember?
1. Who was Georgia's first royal governor?
2. What was the lower house of the legislature called?
3. When did Georgia's first legislature meet?
4. What did both the Highland Scots and the Salzburgers believe would allow the same growth as slavery?

DISCONTENT IN THE COLONIES

During the fifteen years before the American Revolution, many colonists began to tire of British rule and resent many of its policies. Although Great Britain had been victorious in the French and Indian War, the war had cost a great deal of money. Moreover, Great Britain had to pay soldiers to protect the colonies from any other aggressors. To the British, it seemed only logical to levy additional taxes on the colonies to cover these expenses. After all, the colonists no longer had to worry about French or Indian invasions.

Owned by Peter Tondee, Tondee's Tavern was a favorite meeting place of the Liberty Boys. Some of the citizens called them "Liberty Brawlers."

GREAT BRITAIN IMPOSES STRICT LAWS

When the American colonists complained about the unfairness of the new taxes, Great Britain passed some strict laws. The **Navigation Act** of 1763 said the colonies could use only British vessels to ship their goods. This was not a problem for Georgia. Most of its trade was still with Great Britain, and British ships often sailed to and from Georgia. However, the act meant that colonies who traded with several countries were no longer allowed to do so.

In 1764, Great Britain's increased tax on wine and imported goods received very little opposition in Georgia. Most of the money Georgia needed for its government was provided by Parliament, so the colony paid little tax to Great Britain. This was not true in the older colonies, and they became very angry about the new tax.

It is important to remember that in 1763 Georgia was only 30 years old. Virginia, on the other hand, had been a colony for 156 years. As a royal colony, Georgia was enjoying economic, political, and social growth. It still needed financial and military help from Great Britain and did not want to damage its standing with the British.

In 1765, Parliament passed the **Stamp Act** in an attempt to raise enough money to pay for the French and Indian War. This act placed a tax on newspapers, legal documents, and licenses. Throughout the colonies the reaction to the act was swift and sometimes violent.

SPREADING THE REVOLUTION

During the Revolutionary period, orators and pamphleteers gave purpose and reason to the Revolution. Many people could not read or write. They depended on political debates to *hear* about important issues. The most famous orator of the day was probably Patrick Henry of Virginia. In 1775, he stirred patriotic blood with his famous declaration "I know not what course others may take, but as for me, give me liberty or give me death."

The Revolutionary period was also a great age of pamphlets. Short, inexpensive to produce, and full of passion and opinion, pamphlets spread the agitation for liberty from house to house, town to town, and colony to colony. Most pamphlets, however, were written by lawyers for educated readers.

In January 1776, a new pamphlet appeared in Philadelphia. In *Common Sense*, Thomas Paine urged America to separate from Great Britain in language all people could understand. The pamphlet was a sensation and sold 120,000 copies in less than three months. Paine quickly followed *Common Sense* with a series of pamphlets called *The Crisis*. The first opened with these inspiring words: "These are the times that try men's souls. The summer soldier and sunshine patriot will, in this crisis, shrink from the service of their country; but he that stands it now, deserves the love and thanks of man and woman."

A Stamp Act Congress met in Boston, Massachusetts, to speak against British taxes. The Georgia legislature was not in session at the time, so it did not send a representative to the Stamp Act Congress. A few Georgia citizens, nevertheless, showed their dislike of the act on the day before it went into effect by burning an *effigy* (a likeness) of the stamp master in the streets of Savannah.

On November 6, a group of Georgians came together to oppose the Stamp Act. They called themselves the **Liberty Boys**. Older Georgians called them the "Liberty Brawlers" because they met in local taverns. Tondee's Tavern in Savannah was a favorite meeting spot. The Liberty Boys were part of a larger group, the Sons of Liberty, whose daring acts came to represent the spirit of the Revolution.

Although the taxes did not bother the average Georgian very much, the colony felt their effect. Georgia was the only colony that ever sold the stamps. Only a few were sold, but Georgia's neighbors in South Carolina, who were more directly affected, spoke out with anger against it. Also, Georgia's only newspaper, *The Georgia Gazette*, had to stop printing until the Stamp Act was repealed a year later.

GEORGIANS BEGIN TO REACT

During the next four years, many Georgians talked openly about their dislike of the strict new British laws. Georgia was divided into two groups: the **Tories**, who remained loyal to Great Britain, and the patriots, also known as **Whigs**, who joined others in the colonies to seek freedom from British rule. Between 1768 and 1772, members of the Georgia General Assembly spoke against the **Townshend Acts of 1767**, which placed import taxes on tea, paper, glass, and coloring for paints. Later, without the approval of the governor, they elected Noble Wimberly Jones as speaker of the general assembly. Jones, a Whig, was a second-generation colonist who came from Savannah. Unlike his father, who was a Tory as were many first-generation colonists, Noble Jones was an outspoken leader of the discontented Georgians.

Governor Wright became upset with the growing discontent and particularly with the idea of having as the speaker of the assembly someone whose ideas ran counter to those of the king. Wright tried to end the protests by doing away with the assembly. However, the people were not so easily silenced.

Noble Wimberly Jones, the son of Noble Jones, was only ten when Georgia was settled. He openly supported the Patriots' cause and was an active participant in the raid on the powder magazine in Savannah in 1775.

Protests Increase

Georgia did not want to damage its standing with Great Britain, but protests against British taxes soon were more open in the other twelve colonies. The slogan "No taxation without representation" became a pre-Revolutionary war cry. Because the Townshend Acts had placed a tax on coloring for paints, the people stopped painting their homes. Because of the tax on tea, they quit drinking tea and turned to coffee.

On a cold day in March 1770, some people in Boston threw snowballs at British soldiers and called them names. The soldiers fired into the crowd, killing five civilians, including a freed slave named Crispus Attucks. Two years later, a group of northern colonists attacked and burned the British cutter *Gaspee* in Rhode Island.

By 1773, the British Parliament had repealed the Townshend Acts, except for the tax on tea. In December of that year, to protest the remaining tax, a group of patriots dressed as Mohawk Indians boarded a British ship anchored in Boston harbor and dumped 340 chests of tea into the Boston bay. This action against British authority is remembered as "the Boston Tea Party."

The Intolerable Acts

To punish the colonists of Massachusetts for the actions of the patriots, Parliament enacted four laws, which because of their harshness became known as the *Intolerable Acts*. Under one of the laws, the British closed the port of Boston until the citizens of Massachusetts paid for the tea. Under another, Massachusetts colonists were not allowed to have a town meeting without the agreement of their governor, who was also commander of the British troops. The operation of the court system was changed so that any British officials who committed capital crimes would be tried in Great Britain rather than by a court in the colonies. As a final punishment, the **Quartering Act** was passed. Under this act, the citizens of all colonies had to house and feed British soldiers at their own expense.

Patriots at the Boston Tea Party crudely disguised themselves as Mohawk Indians. In fact, they were farmers, merchants, artisans, and apprentices.

The laws were aimed at Massachusetts, but, after they were passed, representatives of all the colonies except Georgia gathered in Philadelphia to protest them. On September 5, 1774, the delegates organized the First Continental Congress. At this Congress, there were two major groups. One group wanted to pull away from Great Britain and seek independence. The other wanted to make changes but still remain under British rule. The colonists may not have been sure which group was right, but they agreed on one thing: Something had to be done, and it had to be done soon!

The Congress agreed to stop all trade with Britain and urged each colony to set up *committees of safety*. These committees would enforce the *boycott*, a protest in which people refuse to buy certain items until specific conditions are met. Because its actions would have been called treason by the crown, the Congress carried on its work in secret.

A COLONY DIVIDED

Anti-British feelings were growing in Georgia, but the people still seemed to care more about which parish would have the most power in the Georgia General Assembly. Because the colony still depended on Great Britain, the Assembly chose not to send a delegate to the First Continental Congress. However, one month before the Congress, a group of Georgians met to discuss their reaction to the Intolerable Acts. After talking for a long time, they decided to send a resolution to Parliament demanding that citizens of the thirteen colonies have the same rights as British citizens living in Great Britain. They insisted that the Intolerable Acts did not agree with the "Rights and Privileges of an Englishman."

The General Assembly also decided to have a meeting in Georgia to talk about the growing unhappiness over their ties with Great Britain. This meeting, called the *Provincial Congress*, was held in Savannah in January 1775. Less than one-half of the parishes of Georgia were represented, and the meeting ended without much being done.

Do You Remember?
1. What items were taxed under the Stamp Act?
2. Who were the "Liberty Boys"?
3. Who were the Tories?
4. What was the colonists' slogan about British taxes?
5. What was the Quartering Act?

THE REVOLUTIONARY PERIOD

The Georgia colonists were about to enter into a period of conflict that would require them to take a stand and make commitments. They would emerge from this period as part of a new nation.

WAR PLANS

It took a long time for news to get around the colonies, so it was May before word reached Georgia that the battles of Lexington and Concord had been fought in Massachusetts on April 19, 1775. Those battles, which marked the beginning of the Revolutionary War, forced Georgians to take a stand. In just a few days, a group of radicals broke into the royal arms storehouse in Savannah and stole 600 pounds of gunpowder.

Other protests followed quickly. Gunpowder for cannon used to fire salutes on the king's birthday was tampered with and would not explode. A liberty pole was put up in Savannah's public square. Tories, who were in favor of the king, were openly harassed. Guns were

The first battles of the Revolutionary War took place in Massachusetts on April 19, 1775, at Lexington and Concord (above). The news did not reach Georgia until May.

Georgia's three signers of the Declaration of Independence: **Top:** *Button Gwinnett was a merchant, politician, and, after the war, he served a two-month term as acting governor.* **Above:** *George Walton was the youngest signer, at age 26. Walton served as Georgia's governor twice.* **Opposite page:** *The third Georgia signer of the Declaration of Independence, Lyman Hall, became governor in 1783.*

stolen from public warehouses, and no one paid any attention to what the governor said.

Three weeks after the battles at Lexington and Concord, the **Second Continental Congress** opened in Philadelphia. One of the early decisions made by the Congress was to send a petition to King George III, asking him to not take further unfriendly steps against the colonies. The king refused the petition. At the same time, the Congress also called for the creation of an army, which was to be led by George Washington of Virginia.

Georgia was absent for the first few days, but on May 13, 1775, Lyman Hall, from Midway, arrived in an unofficial capacity. Because it did not seem completely supportive, the other colonies were furious with Georgia, and some members of the Congress called for punishing the youngest colony.

Very shortly, however, Georgia was ready to act. In July 1775, a second Georgia Provincial Congress was held at Tondee's Tavern in Savannah. Unlike the First Provincial Congress, this group was prepared to take positive steps. In addition to Lyman Hall, four others, all from Savannah, were chosen to go to Philadelphia. In the group were Archibald Bulloch, John Houstoun, Noble Wimberly Jones, and Reverend John Zubly. The delegates were given no specific instructions to relay to the Continental Congress. Instead, they were asked to vote as they thought best for the common good of all Georgians. Finally Georgia was ready to join ranks with the other colonies.

Earlier, shortly after the first shots had been fired at the battles of Lexington and Concord, a Council of Safety made up of patriots had met and prepared to form a new government. To show they meant what they said, the group officially *seceded*, or withdrew, from Great Britain. In so doing, the patriots had left Governor Wright without power. Wright was arrested in mid-January of 1776 by the Liberty Boys when he asked the Council of Safety to allow British vessels to purchase supplies from the colony. A month later, Wright escaped and fled to a waiting British warship, leaving the Council of Safety to govern the colony. In the following April, the Georgia Provincial Congress set forth a series of guidelines, called "Rules and Regulations," which were to be used in governing Georgia until a more permanent document could be drawn up

THE DECLARATION OF INDEPENDENCE

On July 4, 1776, the **Declaration of Independence** was approved by the Second Continental Congress. When it was officially signed on August 2, 1776, the names of three Georgians—Lyman Hall, George Walton, and Button Gwinnett—appeared on the left side of the document, right below the signature of John Hancock.

THE DECLARATION OF INDEPENDENCE

On the night of July 4, 1776, John Dunlap printed an unknown number of copies of the Declaration of Independence. Each document was about 14 inches by 18 inches, and the legend "Philadelphia: Printed by John Dunlap" appeared at the bottom of each sheet. Only two dozen of those copies are known to exist.

On July 19, 1776, the Continental Congress ordered another printer, Timothy Matlack, to *engross* (print in final, legal form) the Declaration of Independence. Members of Congress who were present in Philadelphia signed the engrossed copy on August 2, 1776. Other members of Congress signed later. The signed, engrossed copy of the Declaration of Independence, which is 24½ inches by 29¾ inches, is on permanent exhibit at the National Archives in Washington, D.C.

In the 1970s, a copy of the John Dunlap *broadside* (a printed sheet) was discovered in Edenton, North Carolina. It was the personal copy of Joseph Hewes, one of North Carolina's three signers of the Declaration of Independence. At that time, it was the twenty-second known copy of the Dunlap document. In 1983, Williams College in Massachusetts bought the Hewes copy at auction for $412,500. A twenty-fourth copy later sold for $2.4 million.

The engrossed copy of the Declaration of Independence, signed on August 2, 1776, is on permanent exhibit at the National Archives.

The 1,458 words of this powerful document can be divided into three parts. The introduction, or Preamble, told how the colonists felt about democracy. The second part, or body, listed twenty-seven grievances against King George III and his government that caused the colonists to seek independence from Great Britain. The third part, the conclusion, declared the colonies to be an independent nation for all future times.

Those who signed the Declaration of Independence took great risks. Had the colonists lost the war, each man who signed could have been shot for treason. When the Declaration of Independence was read in Georgia, it produced great excitement. Georgians began to make preparations for war. They sent food and ammunition to the Continental Army and began to strengthen the home militia.

POLITICAL CHANGES IN GEORGIA

Georgia joined the other colonies in celebrating the decision to be independent from Great Britain. The new goal of each of the colonies was statehood. Each new state was to develop its own method of governance and pass laws that met its needs. The former colonies were tired of being governed and living under laws made by Great Britain, which they believed was both out of touch and too far away to understand their needs.

Work was begun on a state constitution to replace the earlier "Rules and Regulations." Writing the new constitution was not easy. Some citizens wanted a government like the one already in place, with most of the power in the hands of a few wealthy landowners and merchants. The Whigs, a more extreme group, wanted sweep-

Born in Austria, John Adam Treutlen, a Salzburger, was a member of the Georgia Council of Safety and the Georgia Provincial Congress. He defeated acting governor Button Gwinnett in 1777 and served as governor until 1778. Treutlen County is named in his honor.

ing changes that would give all the people of Georgia a chance to govern themselves. The Whigs won, and Georgia decided on a government that would be based on the separation of powers and the rights of citizens to agree with how they were governed.

By May 1777, Georgia adopted its first state constitution at a constitutional convention held in Savannah. The parish system was done away with, and eight counties were formed. Chatham, Effingham, Burke, Richmond, Wilkes, Glynn, and Camden were named for British subjects who had been in favor of the Revolution; Liberty County was named in honor of American independence.

However well-meaning the lawmakers were in developing the 1777 constitution, there were problems. Rather than a bicameral legislature, the constitution of 1777 provided for a unicameral, or one-house, legislature. This single legislative body had very broad powers, including the ability to make appointments for the judicial branch (the courts) as well as for the executive branch (the governor).

Stung by the loyalty of former governors to the king, the members of the constitutional convention wanted to severely limit the influence and power of the governor. They proposed a one-year term for the governor. The governor was to be selected by the legislature rather than voted on by the people. The actual power, therefore, was in the hands of twelve lawmakers from the legislature who served as an executive council. The executive council could accept or reject any proposals initiated by the governor. The constitutional convention adopted a new state seal. It also selected John Treutlen, a Salzburger, as the first state governor over Button Gwinnett.

Although the constitution of 1777 was changed in 1789, this first endeavor in providing for state's rights was an important step in Georgia's development.

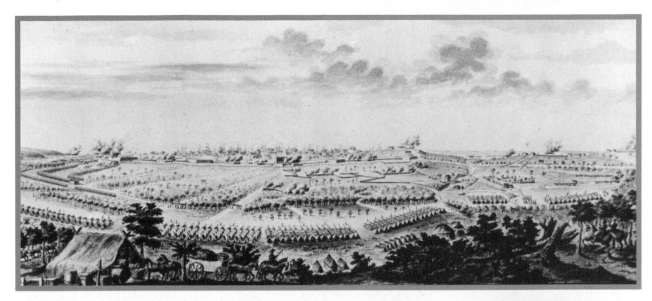

On July 4, 1778, Georgians **ratified**, or approved, the **Articles of Confederation**, which was the first constitution of the United States of America. The Articles did not go into effect until January 1781, when Virginia and Maryland ratified them.

THE REVOLUTION IN GEORGIA

During 1777 and 1778, except for several unsuccessful attempts by Georgian members of the Continental Army to capture British-held St. Augustine and parts of east Florida, little fighting took place in Georgia. In December 1778, however, British troops attacked Savannah. A month later they took the port of Sunbury. Before long, Augusta was under fire from British guns.

In all three cases, the poorly armed and understaffed Georgia militia could do little to stop the British. Georgia fell again under British military rule, and Governor Wright returned to Georgia to take charge of the government.

The Battle of Kettle Creek

Finally, in February 1779, Georgia had a victory. A rebel militia group led by Colonel Elijah Clarke (after whom Clarke County is named) defeated a force of more than eight hundred British troops at the Battle of Kettle Creek, about eight miles from Washington, Georgia.

The Battle of Kettle Creek was minor when compared to those fought in other parts of the country. It was, however, important to Georgia. The militia was able to take badly needed weapons and horses from the British soldiers, and the spirits of the Georgia militia were lifted by their victory. Georgia's success was short-lived, because the British won a major battle a month later at Briar Creek.

Top: British troops laid siege to Savannah in December 1778. Governor James Wright returned to Georgia after the fall of Savannah. **Above:** *Colonel Elijah Clarke distinguished himself in the Revolutionary War by defending Wilkes County against the British, Tories, and Indians in fighting so intense that the area became known as "The Hornets' Nest."*

NANCY HART

Above: Called "the war woman" by the Indians, Nancy Hart is seen here on the Hart County Seal, with her rifle, in recognition of her brave stand against the Tories. Hart County is the only county in Georgia named for a woman. ***Opposite page:*** *According to legend, Nancy Hart captured the British soldiers who had boasted of killing Colonel John Dooley.*

During any wartime period, the exploits of heroes and heroines become part of the ongoing folklore of a nation. The Revolutionary War was no exception, and among those that emerged from it was a woman known as Georgia's most famous war heroine.

Around 1771, Nancy Hart, her husband Benjamin, and their eight children settled twelve miles outside of what we now call Elberton. Even as the war escalated and Tories began harassing the backwoods' citizens, Nancy refused to move from her home.

Several legends surround Nancy Hart, but probably the most repeated one concerns Colonel John Dooley, who commanded a regiment at the Battle of Kettle Creek and was killed by British soldiers. A few days after Dooley's murder, five of these soldiers stopped by Nancy's home and demanded that she cook dinner for them. As the men talked, Nancy overheard them bragging about the murder.

Thinking quickly, Nancy brought out a jug of whiskey and offered it to the soldiers. As they drank, they did not notice Nancy motioning to her daughters to go to the woods and sound the alarm for help. Enjoying their drink and food, they also did not realize that Nancy was quietly taking their rifles as she served them.

When Nancy pulled the third rifle away, one of the soldiers looked up and yelled. As the men rushed her, Nancy calmly pulled the trigger and killed one of them. She grabbed a second rifle and held the other soldiers at gunpoint until help arrived. Some reports say she may have killed two of the soldiers; in any event, the rest were soon put to trial and hanged.

We may never know if the stories of Nancy Hart's courage are true. However, the legend of Nancy Hart remains as an example of the revolutionary spirit of Georgia. Hart County and its county seat, Hartwell, located in northeast Georgia, are named for her. Hart is the only county in Georgia named for a woman.

Blacks in the American Revolution

Although the militia was outmatched in both numbers and weapons at Kettle Creek, it showed fierce spirit. Clarke proved to be an able commander, and among those who followed him was a Revolutionary War hero named Austin Dabney.

Dabney was a freeborn *mulatto*, a child of mixed parentage. He arrived in Georgia just before the war with a man named Richard Aycock. Aycock, a white North Carolinian, was not known for his bravery. Instead of joining the Georgia militia himself, Aycock proposed that Austin Dabney take his place. After much discussion, some of

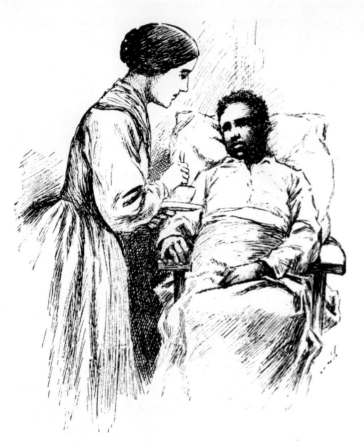

which centered on whether he was freeborn or a slave, Dabney was accepted. He proved to be a good soldier at Kettle Creek and was wounded in action. A family named Harris cared for him while his wounds healed.

After the Revolutionary War, veterans were given plots of land as part of the payment for military service. Many did not want Dabney to get his veteran's share of land. However, Governor George Gilmer and some members of the Georgia legislature did not agree with them. They praised Dabney as a patriot. After months of debate, he was given a valuable piece of land in Madison County. When he moved to his new home, he took the Harris family with him. Together, they made the property profitable. Austin Dabney died in 1834, fifty-five years after the Battle of Kettle Creek.

Dabney was just one of the many people of color who fought in the Revolutionary War. While there are no exact figures on the participation of blacks in the Continental Army, it has been estimated that about 5,000 blacks served. As early as the battles of Lexington and Concord, blacks took up arms against Great Britain in search of freedom. Among the black minutemen who participated in those famous battles were Peter Salem, Cato Stedman, Cuff Whittemore, Cato Wood, Lemuel Haynes, and Prince Estabrook. Peter Salem, an ex-slave from Massachusetts, fired the shot that killed Major John Pitcairn of the Royal Marines, who was second in command of the British force at Lexington. Another black, Salem Poor, was cited for bravery by the Continental Congress.

During his heroic fighting at the Battle of Kettle Creek, Austin Dabney was hit by a rifle ball that passed through his thigh. Dabney is given credit for saving the life of Elijah Clarke by giving the colonel a horse at Kettle Creek after his had been shot out from under him.

Support for Black Troops Varies

Although many blacks distinguished themselves in the Revolutionary War, support for their enlistment in the army varied. Southern colonies did not want to use slaves or freemen as soldiers because the notion of recruiting and arming slaves raised fears of slaves revolting against southern slave owners.

The British both actively recruited blacks to serve with the royal soldiers and captured slaves for use by the British Army. In November 1775, the British governor of Virginia offered freedom to all slaves willing to bear arms against the rebelling colonists. His proclamation led American leaders to accept blacks into the Continental Army, promising that they would receive freedom at the end of their enlistment. The government also made provisions to pay slave owners for all slaves freed in this way.

General George Washington, himself a fourth-generation slave owner, questioned the wisdom of using black troops, but most of the former colonies began to enlist both slaves and free blacks in the armies. Georgia and South Carolina were the only two states to refuse to legalize slave enlistments in their militias.

Anti-slavery sentiment mounted after the war, and in most states public opinion turned strongly against slavery. In many states, blacks were given both their freedom and land at the end of the war. In the South, however, the decline of such staple crops as tobacco, indigo, and rice made the farmers reluctant to free their black slaves.

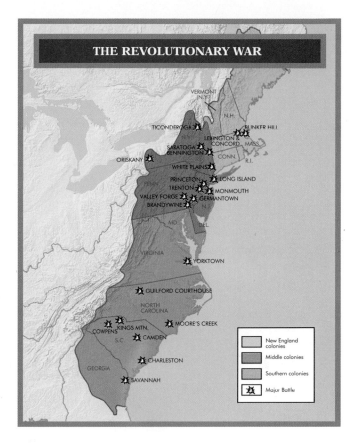

THE REVOLUTIONARY WAR

TWO GOVERNMENTS

As the fighting continued, Savannah remained in British hands. In October, a French fleet of over 4,000 sailors commanded by Charles Henri Comte d'Estaing, tried to help Georgia retake Savannah from the British. The attempt failed, and, after a four-day battle, the French fleet gave up the attack.

Georgia was left in the hands of two governments, one royal and one rebel. Each government tried to take charge of the state, but neither was very effective. Some Georgians openly supported the king, while others just as openly supported the cause of independence. The major battles of the war were over, but guerrilla warfare—both political and military—was still going on in the back country of Georgia.

THE BATTLE OF YORKTOWN

In June 1781, Georgia's militia was again under the command of Colonel Clarke. With the help of Continental troops, Clarke took Augusta from the British. General George Washington, the commander of the Continental Army, was assisted by French forces when he faced British General Lord Cornwallis in October 1781, at the Battle of Yorktown, Virginia. The American forces won that battle, forcing Cornwallis to surrender.

Cornwallis did not know that British ships carrying 6,000 men were on their way to help him. They arrived just six days after his surrender. Had the French not delayed the landing of the British ships, the results of the American Revolution might have been different. By the spring of 1782, British forces in Georgia believed they could not defeat the Americans. They left Savannah, marking an end to 3½ years of occupation.

The **Treaty of Paris** was signed by Great Britain, France, and the United States in September 1783. Independence was finally a reality. There were only eleven battles and skirmishes on Georgia's soil. However, Georgians could be proud of their part in the Revolutionary War as the work of building a new country began.

Do You Remember?
1. Name the Georgia signers of the Declaration of Independence.
2. What was the purpose of the second part of the Declaration of Independence?
3. For whom were the original parishes of Georgia renamed as counties?
4. What was our country's first constitution called?

SUMMARY

- In the years before the Revolutionary War, everyday life in the thirteen colonies remained difficult.
- Georgia became a royal colony in 1752, and as such was governed directly by the king of England.
- Georgia continued to prosper, and many people who had left the colony when it was under the rule of the trustees returned to the royal colony.
- A new group of settlers from South Carolina and the West Indies bought land and moved to Midway, bringing slaves with them.
- Governor John Reynolds was the first royal governor and was followed as governor by Henry Ellis and then James Wright.
- A series of laws imposed by the British on the colonies increased resentment against British rule.
- In 1775, the first shots of the Revolutionary War were fired during the Battles of Lexington and Concord.
- In July 1776, Georgia joined the other twelve colonies in declaring independence from Great Britain.
- Georgia was occupied by British forces for most of the war.
- Several battles were fought on Georgia soil, including the Battle of Kettle Creek.
- People of color, including Austin Dabney, fought in the Continental Army.
- The final battle of the Revolutionary War took place at Yorktown, Virginia.
- The official end of the war came with the signing of the Treaty of Paris in 1783.

By September 1781, combined American and French forces had trapped the British army at Yorktown. Unaware that reinforcements were on the way, British General Cornwallis surrendered on October 18, 1781.

CHAPTER REVIEW

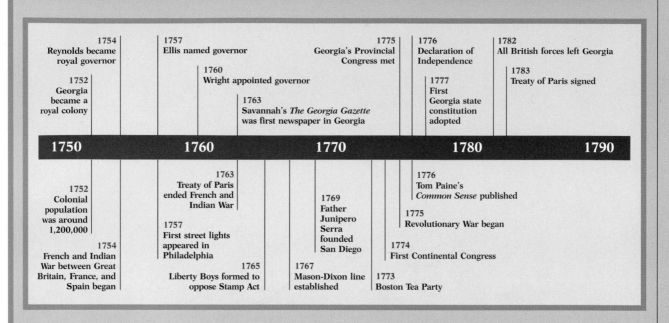

1754
Reynolds became
royal governor

1757
Ellis named governor

1760
Wright appointed governor

1775
Georgia's Provincial
Congress met

1776
Declaration of
Independence

1782
All British forces left Georgia

1752
Georgia
became a
royal colony

1763
Savannah's *The Georgia Gazette*
was first newspaper in Georgia

1777
First
Georgia state
constitution
adopted

1783
Treaty of Paris signed

1750   1760   1770   1780   1790

1752
Colonial
population
was around
1,200,000

1763
Treaty of Paris
ended French and
Indian War

1769
Father
Junipero
Serra
founded
San Diego

1776
Tom Paine's
Common Sense published

1757
First street lights
appeared in
Philadelphia

1775
Revolutionary War began

1754
French and Indian
War between Great
Britain, France, and
Spain began

1765
Liberty Boys formed to
oppose Stamp Act

1767
Mason-Dixon line
established

1774
First Continental Congress

1773
Boston Tea Party

Reviewing People, Places, and Terms

Identify, define, or explain the importance of each of the following.

1. Elijah Clarke
2. Henry Ellis
3. Button Gwinnett
4. the Intolerable Acts
5. Stamp Act
6. Tories
7. Whigs
8. James Wright

Understanding the Facts

1. Why did the South, unlike the other regions, have so many large plantations?
2. What was the difference between a royal colony and a proprietary colony?
3. What were the two chambers of Georgia's first legislature?
4. In what city did Georgia's first legislature meet?
5. What areas of the New World did Great Britain gain as a result of the French and Indian War?

6. What was Georgia's first newspaper?
7. Why were the Liberty Boys sometimes called the "Liberty Brawlers"?
8. What two things did the First Continental Congress agree to do?
9. What were the "Rules and Regulations" set forth by the Georgia Provincial Congress?
10. When was the Declaration of Independence officially signed?

Developing Critical Thinking

1. If you had lived in Georgia in 1772, would you have been a Whig or a Tory? Why?
2. What does the slogan "No taxation without representation" mean? Can you think of some instances in the 1900s where this may have also been used?
3. Why do you think so few battles were fought on Georgia soil?
4. Suppose the British ships had broken through the French lines before Cornwallis surrendered at Yorktown. What might have happened and how would it have affected you today?

Applying Your Skills

1. Which members of Georgia's delegation to the Second Continental Congress have counties named after them? Using a blank map on which the counties of Georgia are outlined, shade each of these counties. Then label the county seats.
2. Rewrite the preamble to the Declaration of Independence in language that would be more understandable to today's teenagers. Use standard English and punctuation and avoid slang.
3. All five of Georgia's delegates to the Second Continental Congress either lived or worked in Savannah. On a modern-day map of the eastern United States, trace a land route from Savannah to Philadelphia and determine the number of miles. Also research the land routes that were available to the delegates at the time the Congress met.

Making Connections

1. Where do you think most Americans today get their information about political or economic issues?
2. Write a one-page "Common Sense" pamphlet calling for students to avoid drugs, stop smoking, start recycling, or support some other cause.
3. What were some of the methods the colonists used to oppose British policies?

Did You Know?

- *The Georgia Gazette* was in publication for only two years because of the Stamp Act.
- An autograph of Button Gwinnett is one of the most sought-after collector's autographs in the world and is valued at over $250,000.
- All three signers of the Declaration of Independence from Georgia have counties named in their honor. Other Georgia counties named after Revolutionary War heroes include Greene, Jasper, Lincoln, Newton, Paulding, Pulaski, Washington, Wayne, and Hart.
- George Walton, at age twenty-six, was the youngest signer of the Declaration of Independence.
- Patriots in Massachusetts were called "Minutemen" because they could be ready to fight in a minute.
- Fort Frederica on St. Simons Island was the most costly British fort built in North America.
- Out of 282,000 men in the thirteen colonies, George Washington never had an army numbering over 25,000.

BUILDING SKILLS: READING FOR DETAILS

Reading for details often requires different techniques than reading for an overview or the big picture. To read for details, do the following:

A. Slow down in your reading. Use a ruler or a guide of colored paper or cardboard to help you read line by line, concentrating on a few words at a time.
B. Look for verbal clues. The first sentence usually gives an idea of what the paragraph is about. Details and examples follow this topic sentence. Look for words such as *for example*, *such as*, and *that is*.
C. Look for visual "tricks" in the text and in the design of the page. Numbers, dashes, and other graphic devices are sometimes used to mark major points or details.

Re-read the section on Nancy Hart on page 140. Answer the following questions based on the details in this section.

1. Where did Nancy and her family settle?
2. Who was Colonel John Dooley?
3. How many British soldiers do some reports say Nancy Hart killed?
4. What county is named after Georgia's Revolutionary War heroine? Where in the state is the county located?

UNIT III

THE NATION BECOMES UNITED

We the People of the United States, in Order to form a more perfect Union, establish Justice, insure domestic Tranquility, provide for the common defense, promote the general Welfare, and secure the Blessings of Liberty to ourselves and our Posterity, do ordain and establish this Constitution for the United States of America.
—Preamble to the Constitution of the United States

HE FIGHTING WAS OVER, and the United States was a free country. However, the common interests that united them against the British were showing signs of weakening. The Articles of Confederation were not strong enough to hold the new states together. A new document and a greater commitment would be needed if the nation were to survive. A great deal of give and take would be required before the conflicting demands of the various states could be brought into agreement.

This mural of the signing of the United States Constitution can be seen in the Capitol in Washington, D.C. Abraham Baldwin and William Few signed the Constitution for Georgia.

CHAPTER FIVE

GEORGIA AS PART OF A NEW COUNTRY

> I believe there are more instances of the abridgement of the freedom of the people by gradual and silent encroachments of those in power than by violent and sudden usurpations.
>
> —James Madison

I N GEORGIA, YEARS OF HARDSHIP and change followed the Revolutionary War. The war ruined the state's economy and divided its people. Many of Georgia's men had left their farms to fight, and because of this, not much food had been grown. The new state government had to see that families in need were provided with such basic items as flour and corn meal until they could plant and harvest a crop. The state also had to honor its commitments to those who had served in the war by making good on its promise to provide them with land.

The war showed that many Georgians were willing to unite for their freedom from foreign rule. At the same time, the war showed that the state government was poorly equipped to deal with many of its problems. It was years before Georgia recovered from the Revolution. However, by 1787, Georgians had joined citizens of the other colonies in working toward founding a new nation.

Above: *The newly formed state of Georgia also boasted a new seal. On the front was a scroll of the Georgia Constitution. At the top were the Latin words,* Pro bono publico, *which meant "for the good of the public." On the reverse side of the seal the images signified the agricultural and commercial endeavors set forth for the state.* **Opposite page:** *James Madison, called the "Father of the Constitution." He became our fourth president.*

GOVERNMENT IN THE NEW NATION

The thirteen states fought hard to become independent from Great Britain, but they were still not a united nation. The country was governed by the Second Continental Congress during the war years. In 1781, the Articles of Confederation and Perpetual Union were ratified. The Articles were a set of rules that attempted to bring about the union of the new states, but the government it set up was weak and inadequate for the task.

CHAPTER PREVIEW

Terms: levy, tariffs, judiciary, states' rights, compromise, U.S. Constitution, amend, General Assembly, Louisiana Purchase, embargo, Treaty of Ghent, headright system, Yazoo Land Fraud

People: Alexander Hamilton, James Madison, William Few, Abraham Baldwin, William Pierce, William Houstoun, Thomas Jefferson, Andrew Jackson

Places: Annapolis, Horseshoe Bend, Louisville, Athens, Brunswick, Macon, Terminus, Atlanta, Milledgeville

THE ARTICLES OF CONFEDERATION

The Articles of Confederation provided for the states to enter "into a firm league of friendship with each other, for their common defense, the security of their liberties, and their mutual general welfare." The Articles created a one-house legislature—the Confederation Congress—in which each state, no matter what its size or population, had only one vote. Delegates from nine states had to approve any important decision the Congress made.

Congress, however, had little power. It could declare war, coin money, establish post offices, and send or recall ambassadors to other nations. Unfortunately, there was much that it could not do. Most importantly, it could not **levy** (impose) taxes to fund a national government. Instead, it had to ask states for money. The states had spent a lot of money to pay soldiers, buy weapons, and feed troops during the war. They had little left to give the national government, and Congress had no power to force the states to do so.

Congress also could not regulate, or control, the trade of goods between one state and another or between a state and other countries. Each state set its own **tariffs** (taxes on imported items) for goods they shipped, and state tariffs often were unfair. The young nation had neither a president nor a **judiciary** (court system). Congress was in the sad position of being able to pass laws without the means of enforcing them through a national system of courts.

The Articles created a loose union where each state retained "its sovereignty, freedom, and independence." Any power not clearly given to the Congress belonged to the states. This emphasis on **states' rights** weakened the Confederation from the start. The Articles of Confederation were not strong enough to make the thirteen separate states into one nation.

THE CONSTITUTIONAL CONVENTION

Upset because Congress was not able to handle trade among states, Virginia, which was having problems with Maryland, invited the other states to a convention at Annapolis, Maryland, in 1786. Only five states sent delegates, who discussed not only trade but also the other problems of the Confederation. The major outcome of the Annapolis meeting was a call by Alexander Hamilton and James Madison for another convention to be held in Philadelphia in 1787 to consider revising the "constitution of the federal government."

In the summer of 1787, fifty-five delegates, representing every state except Rhode Island, met in Philadelphia to revise the Articles of Confederation. The constitutional convention was a secret, "closed-door" meeting; even the windows were closed, which made the room stifling hot. After several delegates almost fainted, the convention

Left: *The first name on the new Constitution was that of George Washington. His leadership prompted his peers to elect him as the first United States President.* **Top:** *Alexander Hamilton served on Washington's staff during the war. From 1789-1795, he served the new nation as secretary of the treasury.* **Above:** *Eighty-one-year-old Benjamin Franklin was the oldest and most famous member of the Constitutional Convention.*

Virginia governor Edmund Randolph proposed a plan at the convention that provided three separate branches of government. He also proposed that the number of representatives in Congress would be based on the population of each state. His proposal led to the system of checks and balances in our government.

moved upstairs to ensure both secrecy and comfort. Even so, some people passing by the open windows reported hearing raised, angry voices among the delegates.

Most of these delegates were wealthy and well thought of in their states. Merchants, planters, physicians, generals, governors, and especially lawyers (twenty-three in all) made up the convention. Among the most prominent were people like Benjamin Franklin, James Madison, John Adams, and George Washington. Georgia sent four representatives: William Few, Abraham Baldwin, William Pierce, and William Houstoun. Several delegates went home before the convention completed its work. In the end, only thirty-nine men decided on the document that would form the final constitution of the new government.

The delegates soon decided that the Articles of Confederation could not be revised. An entirely new plan of government had to be created. For four months, men who had led the nation during the Revolution were again called on to lead. George Washington was chairman of the convention. Alexander Hamilton and eighty-one-year-old Benjamin Franklin worked for government that was both strong and fair. James Madison, later called the "Father of the Constitution," drafted much of the final document. Delegates presented more than one plan. The group narrowed their choices to the Virginia Plan and the New Jersey Plan.

The Virginia Plan

Governor Edmund Randolph of Virginia proposed what became known as the Virginia, or large-state, plan. The so-called *Virginia Plan* reflected the thinking of James Madison. Madison had prepared for the convention by studying more than two hundred books on history and government. He believed that a national government should have three branches of government: legislative, judicial, and executive. At the same time, because he felt that no one branch should be able to control the entire government, he proposed a system of checks and balances among the three branches.

The Virginia Plan provided for a bicameral, or two-house, national legislature. Membership in the legislature would be based on the free population of each state. Members of the lower house would be elected by qualified voters. State legislatures would select members of the upper house. The legislature, or Congress, would choose the chief executive, make laws that affected all the states, and set up a system of courts. Because the plan would give the national government more power than that given to the individual states, representatives of the smaller states objected. They thought the plan would give states with the largest populations control of Congress.

The New Jersey Plan

Some small states, therefore, supported the *New Jersey Plan*, which would keep the government much as it had been under the Articles of Confederation. Under this plan, the legislature would be unicameral, and each state would have the same number of representatives in Congress. The plan was different from the Articles of Confederation in that it allowed Congress to tax the nation's citizens and the national government would be able to regulate interstate and international trade.

THE GREAT COMPROMISE

For a while, it looked as though the convention would not be able to settle on a constitution. Finally, delegates from Connecticut took ideas from both plans and put them together in what was later called the *Great Compromise*. A **compromise** is a way to settle disagreements in which each side gives way a little in its demands. According to the compromise plan, there would be two houses. The upper house of the legislature, the Senate, would have two elected members from each state in the Union. Senators from a given state could vote either as a unit or as individuals. The lower house, the House of Representatives, would have members who were elected to it by each state based on the state's population.

Delegates to the convention agreed to this compromise, and the foundation of the new central government was in place. Differences among the delegates did not, however, end with the Great Compromise. They still had to settle many details before the work of the convention was finished.

OTHER ISSUES OF THE CONVENTION

A major issue centered on slaves. Southerners wanted to know how slaves would affect a state's population. They wanted to include slaves when counting population for the purpose of determining representation in the lower house. Northerners, on the other hand, felt strongly that because slaves could not vote, they should not be counted. After much debate, the delegates agreed to the *Three-Fifths Compromise*. Under this compromise, three-fifths of the slaves could be counted. For example, Georgia had about 29,500 slaves in 1790, so it could count 17,700 slaves in the state's official population. This increased the number of Georgians in the House of Representatives and gave the state a greater voice in the selection of the president.

The issue of slavery was never specifically mentioned in the final document that set up our current framework of government, the **U.S. Constitution**; nevertheless, it was protected. The Constitution would not allow Congress to stop "the importation of such persons as any of the states should think proper to admit" for twenty years. The

Abraham Baldwin was one of Georgia's delegates to the Constitutional Convention and a signer of the Constitution.

fugitive workers' clause ordered that runaway slaves be returned to their masters.

The convention delegates also had to settle the question of how states would select members of Congress. The convention agreed that states would choose members of the House of Representatives by popular vote, and that the state legislatures would select its senators. The president would be chosen by electoral votes. Each state would select the same number of electors as it had members of Congress.

The convention made the president commander-in-chief of the armed forces and made him responsible for relations with other countries. The president was also given the power to appoint judges and other federal officials. The delegates agreed on a four-year term for the president and the possibility of re-election.

One major matter the delegates worked on was how to divide power in the government. They decided to organize three separate branches of government: *executive* (the president and his cabinet, or official staff), *legislative* (the Congress), and *judicial* (the court system). They also agreed on a system of checks and balances. Each branch would have its own job to do and would have a way to keep the other two from having too much power.

A PLAN FOR THE FUTURE

The delegates knew that, as the United States grew, the Constitution would need some changes. They made a way to **amend**, or change, the Constitution without having to rewrite it. Only a few years after the Constitution was written, the first ten amendments, called the *Bill of Rights*, were added to it.

With the work finished, the remaining thirty-nine delegates signed the document that is today the world's oldest written national constitution. Among the signers were Abraham Baldwin and William Few from Georgia.

Only nine states had to ratify the Constitution for it to become official. By the end of 1788, eleven of the states had ratified it. North Carolina in 1789 and Rhode Island in 1790 were the last two states to ratify the Constitution. Georgia was the fourth state to ratify it and did so on a cold Wednesday, January 2, 1788. It was an important beginning to a new year.

In the following year, the new government was in place. On August 30, 1789, George Washington became the first president of the United States of America.

GEORGIA ADOPTS A NEW STATE CONSTITUTION

In 1785, the capital of Georgia was moved from Savannah to Augusta. During 1788 and 1789, delegates met there to make changes

Another of Georgia's delegates to the Constitutional Convention in Philadelphia was William Few. He, too, was a signer of the Constitution.

in the state constitution. After they were made, the Georgia Constitution was very much like the one for the United States. The state would have a bicameral legislature, now called the **General Assembly**, that included a senate and a house of representatives. Members would be elected by popular vote, and those members would select the state's governor. To ensure the separation of power, the state, as it did before, would have three branches of government: legislative, executive, and judicial. But power, although separated, was not equally balanced. Legislators in the General Assembly selected the governor and other state officials, including the judges. More important, the legislators determined both how money was to be raised and how it was to be spent.

Do You Remember?
1. Emphasis on what issue weakened the government from the first under the Articles of Confederation?
2. Who was called the "Father of the Constitution"?
3. What kind of national legislature was called for in the Virginia Plan?
4. Did the U.S. Constitution specifically mention slavery?

THE WAR OF 1812

At the same time that people were moving into the frontier areas of Georgia, the rest of the new nation was also growing. Thomas Jefferson became the country's third president in 1800, succeeding John Adams. In 1803, the Louisiana Territory was bought from France for $15 million. This transaction, which was known as the **Louisiana Purchase**, doubled the size of the country. The United States now extended west to the Rocky Mountains.

INCREASING TENSIONS

In his first inaugural speech, Thomas Jefferson declared: "Peace, commerce, and honest friendship with all nations, entangling alliances with none." Unfortunately, the United States found it very difficult to remain neutral while much of the world around it was at war.

An undeclared naval war with France that had broken out in 1798 was only one of the problems that tested the young nation's ability to survive. Between 1793 and 1815, France and Great Britain were almost always at war. American merchants were caught in the middle as both France and Great Britain tried to block the United States from trading with the other. Great Britain, which had the world's largest navy, even "impressed" American sailors; that is, it took the sailors off American ships and made them serve in the British Navy.

Thomas Jefferson, author of the Declaration of Independence, continued to serve his country as Vice President under John Adams and as the nation's President in 1801. Jefferson was also an inventor, scientist, musician, and architect.

THE LOUISIANA PURCHASE

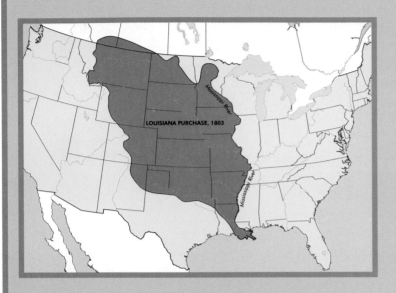

By 1800, the United States was bursting its boundaries. Hundreds of thousands of Americans had poured into western territories in search of rich lands and fresh opportunities. The Ohio and Mississippi rivers became highways of commerce as farmers floated their produce to the port of New Orleans.

Whoever owned Louisiana controlled the destiny of the United States. In 1763, Spain had received Louisiana from France. Spain's transfer of Louisiana back to France in 1802 greatly alarmed Americans. France's leader, Napoleon, wanted to spread French influence throughout Europe. Would he also try to re-establish the French empire in the New World?

In 1803, President Thomas Jefferson sent James Monroe to France to join the negotiations to purchase New Orleans. When Monroe arrived, he learned to his astonishment that France was ready to sell *all* of Louisiana (827,000 square miles) to the United States for $15 million. Monroe and Robert Livingston signed a treaty for a vast uncharted region stretching from the Gulf of Mexico to present-day Minnesota.

The Louisiana Purchase doubled the size of the United States and opened the way for westward expansion across the continent. Ironically, the Constitution contained no clear language about acquiring new territory and attaching it to the nation. Jefferson, who in previous times had argued for a strict interpretation of the Constitution, now took a broader view. He said that he had exercised the president's implied powers to safeguard the nation.

Finally, in 1807, President Jefferson began an **embargo**, which stopped all trade with foreign countries. Jefferson hoped to stop Great Britain and France from seizing American ships. However, the embargo was very unpopular among the American traders and shippers. In the end, it was ignored.

Americans were angrier at Great Britain than at France. The British Navy controlled the Atlantic Ocean. Americans also believed that Great Britain was stirring up the Indians in the states and territories beyond the Appalachian Mountains. In Congress, a group of land-hungry southerners and westerners known as *War Hawks* wanted the United States to declare war on Great Britain. They hoped to capture Canada and eliminate the British and Indian menace in the West. In June 1812, President James Madison asked Congress to declare war on Great Britain. By a narrow vote, Congress agreed.

Most citizens were not sure that Madison's decision was a good one. They thought war at this time was unwise. They felt the country was not prepared to fight against a major power such as Great Britain. The war lasted about two years, with neither side making any headway. In 1814, however, British forces invaded the Chesapeake Bay and worked their way to Washington, which had become the young nation's capital. They burned much of the city, including the Capitol and the White House, the president's residence. Later the British were turned back as they tried to take control of the Baltimore harbor.

One earlier battle came much closer to the soil of present-day Georgia. In March 1814, troops led by Andrew Jackson defeated a band of Upper Creek Indians, known as Red Sticks, in the Battle of Horseshoe Bend on the Tallapoosa River in what is now eastern Alabama. Fortunately, the war had more skirmishes (minor fights) than battles. Both sides grew weary of the war and were glad to make peace. The **Treaty of Ghent** (in Belgium), which was signed in 1814, ended the war and restored everything to what it had been before the war.

The United States got no new land from the War of 1812, but it gained in other ways. The war showed that the United States was willing to fight for its continued independence. Older nations started to pay attention to the young country. At the same time, the experience convinced the U.S. to stay away from European politics.

The war had other effects as well. The separate states truly began to feel united into one nation. The economy of the country started to change. When Americans could not get goods from abroad during the war, they were forced to make them. Industry grew and, by 1815, the United States could supply many of its own needs, including such things as iron, textiles, wood, glassware, leather, and pottery.

The Battle of New Orleans was a stunning victory for the United States. Unknown to the two armies, the treaty to end the War of 1812 had been signed in Paris two weeks earlier. In this depiction, General Andrew Jackson commands American troops from his white charger.

LAND FEVER IN GEORGIA

Like most previous wars, the War of 1812 was very hard on Native Americans. The Indians had been defeated and pushed out of the northwest and southwest territories. This left the national frontier open for future growth. Indeed, towards the middle of the century, fever for land was widespread throughout America. In this respect, Georgians were no different from others in the country.

EARLY WAYS OF OBTAINING LAND

Along with their hunger for independence from Great Britain, many Georgians of the late 1700s and early 1800s developed a huge appetite for increasing their land holdings. During the settlement of the colony, much of the land east of the Oconee River belonging to the Indians was given to settlers by means of the **headright system**. Under this system, each white male counted as a "head" and could receive up to 1,000 acres. Although parts of this system lasted until the early twentieth century, it was largely replaced by a land lottery.

When *public domain* lands (land that belonged to the state or federal government) were opened for settlement, Georgia surveyed land lots of different sizes. This so-called lottery land was located west of the Oconee River. For a small fee, any white male twenty-one years of age or older could buy a chance and, on the spin of a wheel, win land. Heads of households with children, war veterans, and widows were given extra chances in the land lotteries. Other states also had lotteries, and about 30 million acres of land were given away through them.

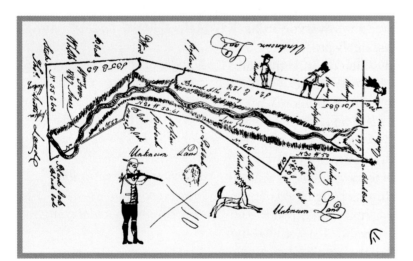

Top: A survey plan of lottery lots in the portion of Baldwin County where Milledgeville is located. Above: This plat (map of the land area) is a layout of a headright grant. Boundaries were shown by naming the types of trees on the property.

THE YAZOO LAND FRAUD

Georgians' growing hunger for land reached a peak in 1795 with the **Yazoo Land Fraud**. At that time, Georgia's western borders were the Mississippi River and one of its *tributaries* (branches), the Yazoo River, which was named for an Indian tribe. Included in this territory were the present states of Mississippi and Alabama. Both South Carolina and Spain also laid claim to some of the same land, and the matter was carried to court for settlement.

Before any settlement was made, however, four land companies approached members of the Georgia General Assembly and Governor George Matthews and bribed them to sell the disputed areas to

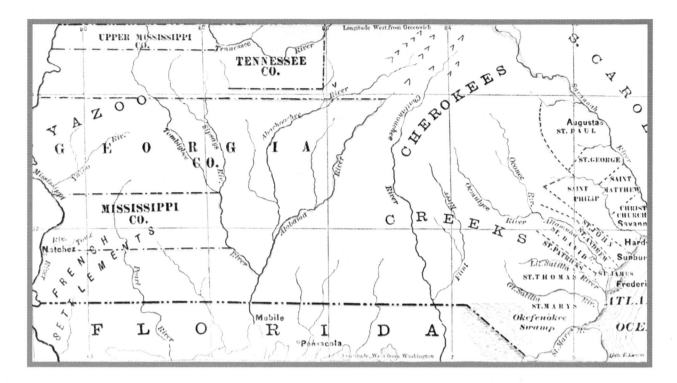

the land companies. The companies offered the governor and key legislators stock and pieces of land if the assembly passed a bill that would allow the western lands to be sold. When the governor and enough members of the assembly accepted the offer and enacted the bill, the land companies bought between 35 and 50 million acres of land for a half million dollars—about 1½ cents an acre.

This map shows the disputed Yazoo lands in what are now the states of Alabama and Mississippi.

The public quickly learned of this bargain sale, and there were protests all over the state. Newspapers printed articles telling what the legislators had done. Grand juries met to look into both the law and the land sales. Many citizens called for the resignations of the legislators involved in what became known as the Yazoo Land Fraud.

As a result of public anger and pressure, the bill that had allowed the land to be sold was repealed by the legislature. The legislators involved were thrown out of office. All records of these land sales were burned in public at Louisville, which had become the state capital of Georgia in 1796.

Money from the land sales was returned to the state treasury. However, there were people who were not part of the original scheme but who had bought some of the land in the hopes of making money from it. These citizens wanted to keep the land that they had purchased for so little and went to court. In 1814, the claims finally were settled by the federal government. Despite all the publicity and furor surrounding the Yazoo Land Fraud, there was little mention of the various Indian tribes that had been forced out of their homes and communities.

GEORGIA CEDES WESTERN LAND

Contrary to their initial hopes, Georgians lost rather than gained from the Yazoo land scheme. Georgia lost a large part of its land and a lot of money as a result of the initial fallout from the failed plan. Further, after Spain renounced its claims to the area, the federal government contested Georgia's right to it. The long aftermath of the Yazoo affair created bad feelings among many of the state's citizenry, and they appealed to the legislature to give in to the federal government. Therefore, in 1802 Georgia *ceded* (gave up) its land west of the Chatta-hoochee River to the government of the United States for $1.25 million, making the river Georgia's western boundary.

By 1814 Congress had also agreed to pay over $400,000 to settle the Yazoo land claims. The government later agreed to remove Indians who still lived in Georgia to places still further west of their hereditary lands. This agreement led to the tragedy now known as the "Trail of Tears," which will be discussed in a later chapter.

Do You Remember?

1. What 1803 transaction between France and the United States doubled the land area of our country?
2. Why were Americans more angry with the British than with the French at the beginning of the War of 1812?
3. What document signed in Belgium in 1814 officially ended the War of 1812?
4. What two methods were used in Georgia to distribute land in the late 1700s and early 1800s?
5. What happened to the members of the Georgia legislature involved in the Yazoo Land Fraud?
6. When was present-day Georgia's western boundary established?
7. How much did it cost the federal government to settle the Yazoo land claims?

ECONOMIC DEVELOPMENTS IN GEORGIA

As it had elsewhere in the new nation, the Revolutionary War brought financial chaos to Georgia. The paper money issued during the war years by Congress and the state was worth almost nothing. Prices of goods went up all over the United States. In some parts of the country, a pound of tea cost a hundred dollars. Soldiers, who had been promised twenty-two cents a day to fight in the Revolution, were not paid. Some sold their farms to try to settle debts.

At the same time, the period following the war also brought some developments that perhaps might make the future a little brighter for both Georgia and the rest of the nation. New improvements in farming and transportation would bring about lasting changes.

FARMING

Many of Georgia's rice and indigo plantations that had done well before the war were in ruins when it was over. When the British left Savannah toward the end of the war, 1,000 Tories went with them.

*Opposite page, above: On February 15, 1796, citizens enraged by news of the Yazoo Land Fraud seized and burned land sale documents. **Opposite page, below:** George Matthews served twice as governor of Georgia. During his second term, he became embroiled in the Yazoo Land Fraud. **Below:** This engraving shows the blossom of a cotton plant. In the next thirty years, cotton would become "king" in the South, aided by Eli Whitney's invention of the cotton gin.*

Together, they took the equivalent of thousands of dollars, along with 4,000 to 6,000 slaves and indentured servants. The state had no money to pay its huge war debts, and few citizens had money to pay taxes.

There were questions about who owned land. Tories, who had remained loyal to England, had their lands taken away during the pre-Revolutionary period. When the British were in charge of the state during the war, they returned land to the Tories. After the war, lands were again taken from the Tories and given to former soldiers. In some cases, two or three families said they owned the same piece of land. It took time to decide which family would keep the land.

Georgia at least had land and enough people to work it. It also had two agricultural crops that would soon be in great demand: cotton and tobacco. In the next thirty years, cotton would become "king" in the south. This development would greatly change the lives of all Georgians, white and black.

*Above: The cotton gin was cheap and easy to make, but it revolutionized the farming of cotton in the South. **Opposite page:** In addition to building the first cotton gin, Eli Whitney also established the first factory to assemble muskets, or guns, with interchangeable parts. This was the first known example of mass production in America.*

Cotton Gin Invented in Georgia

In 1793, Eli Whitney, a New Englander from Westborough, Massachusetts, visited the home of Mrs. Catherine Greene Miller at Mulberry Grove Plantation near Savannah. Whitney, a friend of the family, was a schoolteacher and an inventor.

As the story goes, Mrs. Miller asked Whitney to repair a broken watch, which he agreed to do. Not long afterward, a caller at the Miller home wished aloud for a machine to separate cotton fiber from its seed. Mrs. Miller, remembering the watch repair, asked Whitney if he could make a machine that might be able to speed up the work done so slowly by hand.

After several weeks, Whitney presented a model of his cotton machine. He made the machine with wire teeth on a turning cylinder. It did separate cotton seed, but the lint got caught in the wire teeth and stopped the machine from working. Several legends say that Mrs. Miller saw the machine's problem, took a clothes brush, and brushed the lint off the teeth. No one knows how much help Mrs. Miller really gave Whitney. In any event, before long, he built a factory near Augusta and had a working cotton gin (from the word *engine*).

Cotton growers welcomed Whitney's gin. Before the invention, a worker might have been able to separate six or seven pounds of cotton seed a day by hand. After the cotton gin's development and introduction, farmers were able to separate about fifty pounds a day.

The Mechanical Reaper

Another agricultural invention, the mechanical reaper, further revolutionized the way work was done on a farm. Its inventor, Cyrus McCormick, demonstrated how to use the mechanical grain reaper in Virginia, and its popularity soon spread throughout the nation. McCormick's reaper had wooden paddles fastened to the harness of a horse. As a farmer guided the horse through his fields, the paddles turned and cut the grain. Using it, a farmer could cut six times more grain in a day than he could with a hand-held scythe. Time- and labor-saving devices such as the cotton gin and grain reaper enabled Georgians to work larger and more profitable farms.

The Panic of 1837

Improved ways of farming helped Georgia's economy become strong after the Revolution. However, a brief boom-period of *inflation* (a rapid increase in prices) suddenly ended, causing the Panic of 1837. This was followed by a *depression* (a period of sharp economic downturn) that lasted into the early 1840s. During the depression years, many businesses failed, and many farmers and planters lost their land. Most banks did not have enough cash to pay out money that had been deposited with them. These banks failed and were forced to close for good. At the height of the depression, only eleven banks remained open in Georgia.

TRANSPORTATION

A major economic development during the early 1800s was the building of railroads. Before the railroads were built, people rode on horses, boats, or stagecoaches. Freight was sent to market by riverboats, ferries, or wagon trains. Passengers could go to most Georgia towns from Savannah by stagecoach. Stagecoaches ran regularly from Savannah to Athens in the north and Brunswick in the south. A main stage line connected Augusta and Columbus by way of Macon, but the coaches could cover only thirty to forty miles a day.

Many of Georgia's roads were stage trails cut where Indian footpaths had been. Roads in wet, swampy places had logs across them

Before the railroads were built, passengers endured long, slow, bumpy journeys by stagecoach.

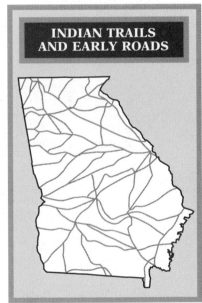

Left: An early locomotive.
Below: This map of Indian trails shows which became roads used by settlers.

INDIAN TRAILS AND EARLY ROADS

and were known as "plank roads." The federal government had some major highways built in the early 1800s. These roads were called turnpikes because they had tollgates, or "pikes." Travelers had to pay a fee at each pike to remain on the road, much like present-day toll roads. Among these turnpikes was the Old Federal Road, built in 1815 to run from Athens northward through Cherokee territory into Tennessee. However, even the "good" roads were poor until the late 1800s.

At first, rail travel was, perhaps, the least favored means of transportation. In 1830, there were only 13 miles of laid track, and these belonged to the Baltimore and Ohio Railroad. By 1840, however, there were 3,300 miles of track. Most of this track belonged to the first railroad owned by the state of Georgia, the Western and Atlantic. The Western and Atlantic ran from Chattanooga, Tennessee, to a point at its southern end, which was called Terminus at first, but is now called Atlanta. The improved railways dramatically shortened travel time for both passengers and freight, reducing to hours trips that had previously taken days.

Do You Remember?
1. What two crops produced in Georgia were in great demand?
2. What was Eli Whitney's invention? How did it affect the preparation of cotton?
3. Who demonstrated the first mechanical grain reaper?
4. What was the original name of the city of Atlanta?

LIFE IN GEORGIA AT THE TURN OF THE CENTURY

At the turn of the century, how you lived in Georgia differed depending on where you lived. There were two different styles of life in Georgia in the late 1700s and early 1800s: the adventurous life of the frontier and the settled life of growing towns. It was a period of social growth. Membership in organized religions increased, and churches and synagogues played major roles in communities. There was more opportunity for formal education for more people, and in 1785, the University of Georgia was chartered.

LIFE ON THE GEORGIA FRONTIER

Frontier Georgia was undeveloped land in the central and western parts of the state, areas that had few settlers. Most of this land had been given away through the lottery system. Some of the people attracted to the frontier were adventurers from settled towns in Georgia, such as Savannah and Augusta, who wanted the excitement of frontier life. Some settlers migrated to the Georgia frontier from other states. They came over rough ground on roads that were little more than trails cut through thick brush and forests. Many of these roads had been cleared by Indian tribes who once lived in the area. Indeed, a comparison of maps of Georgia's present-day roads to maps of early Indian trails shows how much alike they are.

During the early days on the frontier, trading posts located many miles apart were the only stores. Men were known for fighting, hard drinking, and hunting. Women were hardworking and just as handy with a rifle as with a frying pan. Children were younger versions of their parents, and they learned skills that were helpful around the homestead. The homestead itself was often under the threat of attack from Indians, discontented Tories, or British soldiers.

Thirty years later, the frontier was dotted with farms, trading posts, taverns, and sometimes one-room schools. While everyday life continued to be rather difficult, improvements in agriculture and other aspects of life eased things considerably. Then, too, with the removal of British forces and the unrepentant Tories, threats to the settlements were less frequent.

LIFE IN GEORGIA'S TOWNS

Life in Georgia's towns was quite different from life on the frontier. Cultural refinements were everywhere. The *Augusta Herald* and Savannah's *Gazette of the State of Georgia* were the two leading newspapers in the state. Newspapers were also published in Louisville, Athens, Sparta, and Milledgeville. Savannah had a theater where citizens could see plays by Shakespeare, as well as those by more

As the frontier expanded, so did the number of settlements. This drawing by a traveller, done in the 1820s, shows an early view of Columbus, on the Chattahoochee River.

contemporary writers. People joined debating societies, went to concerts, or became members of a library society. They attended fancy dress balls and more informal gatherings such as barbecues and camp meetings. Horse racing drew large crowds in Augusta. *Purses*, or winnings, were as high as $500, a large amount of money in 1785.

Foods served to guests were simple. Beef, pork, and wild game were popular, and seafood, including shrimp, oysters, and fish, was a favorite. Garden vegetables and sweet potatoes were served as side dishes. Many of the recipes used in southern homes today are the same as those enjoyed during the early 1800s.

Communities provided for citizens with special needs. Orphanages cared for children without parents. A hospital for the mentally ill was opened in Milledgeville; a school for the deaf was started at Cave Springs; and the Georgia Academy for the Blind was founded in Macon.

The William Woodward House was typical of the homes of the wealthier families of Savannah in the 1830s.

RELIGION

After the war, many ministers loyal to England went there to live. Still, churches in Georgia grew, both in size and in importance to their communities. There were still many members of the Church of England, or Anglican Church. In addition to them and the already established Quakers and Baptists, Methodist *circuit riders* (ministers who went from district to district) founded churches in the frontier region. Sometimes these ministers could have only one service a month for each church. However, they stayed in touch with the members and visited them as often as possible.

In 1787, the Springfield Baptist Church was founded by free blacks. It is still located on the original site. The First African Baptist Church in Savannah was founded in 1788 under the leadership of Andrew

Bryan. Church and social activities provided members of the black community with opportunities to share news and openly discuss problems and concerns.

In Savannah, a Jewish synagogue was established. In 1796, Georgia's first Roman Catholic church was established in Wilkes County. In 1801, a second parish was formed in Savannah.

During the first decade of the 1800s, towns such as Athens, Monroe, Monticello, Jefferson, Madison, and Milledgeville were established. As in Savannah and Augusta, churches in these new communities were an essential part of town life. There were Sunday and weekday worship services, and church buildings were often used for town meetings and social events.

EDUCATION

Educational growth was slow during the post-Revolutionary War period. Governor Lyman Hall recommended that the state set aside land for schools, but few were built. Some people received only a few years of education. Often even the best farmers knew little, if anything, about reading or mathematics. Many of Georgia's citizens had not been to school at all.

Even though the building of schools was slow, people believed in the value of education. In 1784, the government set aside twenty thousand acres of land and named trustees to establish a state college for Georgia. In 1785, the University of Georgia was chartered as a *land grant university* (a school for which the federal government gave public land) and is the oldest school of its kind in the nation. The university, which was to oversee all public schools in the state, did not open for classes until 1801. The first building for the all-male, all-white student body was Franklin College, and for many years, the University of Georgia was frequently called Franklin College.

Rainy weather had little effect on Methodist preachers who traveled a circuit which could easily cover 500 miles.

Founded in 1783 in Augusta, the Richmond Academy was Georgia's first public school. When President George Washington spent a week visiting Georgia in 1791, he was so impressed with the welcoming speeches made by students from Richmond Academy that he sent every child a book after he had returned to the nation's capital.

In 1786, the Georgia legislature passed a law requiring each county to open *academies,* or schools. However, the lawmakers did not set aside money to build them. In 1820, there were only forty academies in the state. In 1822, some members of the legislature tried to get money for public schools but failed. However, money was placed in a special "state fund" to pay for the education of poor children.

In the early schools, such as the Academy of Richmond County founded in 1783, male students studied Greek, Latin, grammar, and mathematics. Females were taught the arts and music. The Georgia Female College, later known as Wesleyan College, opened in Macon in 1836. There the girls had classes in French, literature, and science education. Tuition was $50 a year, unless a student also wanted to study piano, art, or foreign languages. Piano lessons cost $17 a quarter, art lessons $3 a year, and foreign languages, such as Greek, Latin, Spanish, or Italian, $5 each. Room and board was $15 a quarter, and there were extra charges for laundry and candles.

NOAH WEBSTER AND THE BLUE-BACKED SPELLER

Noah Webster came from an average colonial family in Connecticut. His father farmed and worked as a weaver; his mother worked at home.

Webster loved learning, so his parents sent him to Yale, Connecticut's only college at the time. He graduated in 1778, taught school, and studied law. Webster had some rather strong opinions about American schools. He disliked the crowded one-room school houses, the untrained teachers, and the textbooks that had been published in Great Britain.

In 1783, Webster wrote the first of three textbooks, *The American Spelling Book*. Because of its blue cover, it became known as the "Blue-Backed Speller." For one hundred years, American children learned to read, spell, and pronounce words using Webster's textbook. It was the most popular book of its time; by 1850 more than 15 million copies had been sold.

Noah Webster, a passionate nationalist, spent twenty-seven years putting together the first American dictionary. He believed that "a national language is a bond of national union."

Webster also prepared the first American dictionary. He labored twenty-seven years to publish the 70,000-word, 2-volume dictionary in 1828. A passionate nationalist, Webster used his dictionary to introduce American spellings and words. For example, Webster included American spellings such as *color* instead of the English *colour* and *music* instead of *musick*. He added American words such as *skunk* and *squash*, which were not in English dictionaries.

More than any other person, Noah Webster shaped modern American usage of the English language.

GEORGIAN DISCOVERS MEDICAL USE FOR ETHER

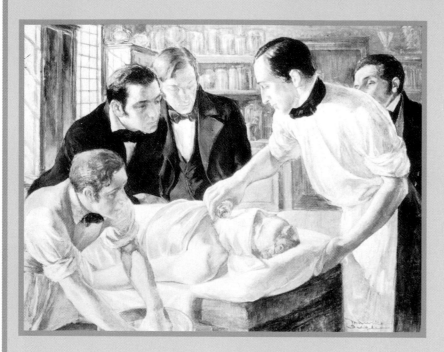

After conducting experiments with sulfuric ether, Dr. Crawford Williamson Long began using the mixture during surgery at his office in Jefferson, Georgia. The resulting "painless operations" revolutionized medicine.

On Wednesday, March 30, 1842, an event occurred in Georgia that changed medicine forever. Dr. Crawford W. Long, a physician in Jefferson, used ether as anesthesia for the first time during surgery to ease the pain of a patient from whom he was removing tumors. Not only did the ether ease the patient's pain, the patient reportedly felt no pain at all.

Before the use of ether, patients who needed surgery basically had two choices. They could die from not having the operation or they could drink large amounts of alcohol in an attempt to numb their senses. Many times, the alcohol was more dangerous than the surgery. Sometimes doctors simply knocked their patients unconscious to do surgery.

Word spread quickly that Dr. Long could offer his patients surgery without pain. Dr. Long, unfortunately, did not write about his discovery. As a result, it was some time before he received credit for his innovative medical procedure.

Four years later, Dr. William Morton, a Boston surgeon, also began using ether on his patients. Dr. Morton wrote about the results of his use of ether in medical journals; because he did, he is known as the discoverer of surgical anesthesia. However, Dr. Crawford actually was the first to demonstrate the practical use of ether, and Georgia is the state where it was first used during a surgical procedure.

The cost does not seem great by today's standards, but only wealthier merchants and large landowners had enough money to send their daughters to Wesleyan. Many Georgia citizens saw no value in teaching females academic subjects, no matter what it cost. Instead, many young girls were taught sewing, cooking, child care, and music.

Do You Remember?
1. In what parts of Georgia was the frontier located?
2. What were the two leading newspapers in Georgia at the turn of the eighteenth century?
3. When was the Springfield Baptist Church founded?
4. What was the University of Georgia often called in its early days?

The University of Georgia was chartered in 1785 as the nation's first land grant university.

SUMMARY

- In the summer of 1787, fifty-five delegates from all states except Rhode Island met to revise the Articles of Confederation.
- After months of looking at various plans and compromises, the delegates agreed on a final document, the U.S. Constitution.
- Georgia revised its state constitution.
- The Louisiana Purchase doubled the land area of the new nation.
- A fever for land gripped the people of Georgia and other parts of the country.
- Inventions such as the cotton gin and the mechanical reaper changed farming.
- At the end of the 1700s, life in Georgia was sharply different depending on whether one lived in the cities and towns or on the frontier.

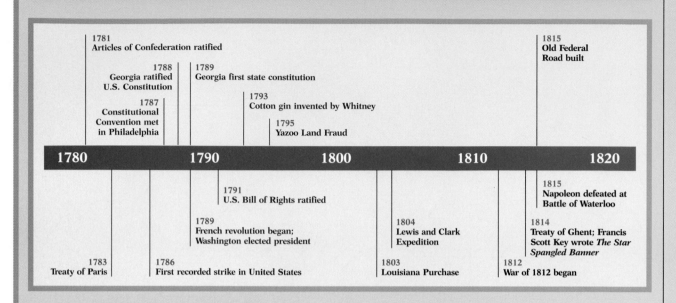

1781
Articles of Confederation ratified

1788
Georgia ratified
U.S. Constitution

1789
Georgia first state constitution

1787
Constitutional
Convention met
in Philadelphia

1793
Cotton gin invented by Whitney

1795
Yazoo Land Fraud

1815
Old Federal
Road built

1780   **1790**   **1800**   **1810**   **1820**

1791
U.S. Bill of Rights ratified

1789
French revolution began;
Washington elected president

1804
Lewis and Clark
Expedition

1815
Napoleon defeated at
Battle of Waterloo

1814
Treaty of Ghent; Francis
Scott Key wrote *The Star
Spangled Banner*

1783
Treaty of Paris

1786
First recorded strike in United States

1803
Louisiana Purchase

1812
War of 1812 began

Reviewing People, Places, and Terms

Use each of the following terms in a sentence.

amend

compromise

embargo

headright system

judiciary

levy

states' rights

tariffs

Yazoo Land Fraud

Understanding the Facts

1. In what year were the Articles of Confederation finally ratified?
2. Under the Articles of Confederation, what four things could Congress do?
3. What important thing could Congress *not* do?
4. Which four men represented Georgia at the Constitutional Convention in 1787?
5. How many houses would Congress have had under the New Jersey Plan?
6. What are the first ten amendments to the U.S. Constitution called?

7. What was the capital of Georgia in 1789?
8. How long did the War of 1812 last?
9. What river became Georgia's western boundary after the settlement of the Yazoo Land Fraud?
10. Under what name is the Georgia Female College known today?

Developing Critical Thinking

1. Why do you think the economy of Georgia was in ruins after the Revolutionary War?
2. What were some of the problems with the Articles of Confederation that were corrected with the passage of the U.S. Constitution?
3. Why do you think the smaller states were politically afraid of the larger states?
4. Why do you believe many of today's roads follow former Indian trails?

Applying Your Skills

1. At various times the capital of Georgia was moved from Savannah to Augusta, then to Louisville, Milledgeville, and, finally, to Atlanta. If distance from most parts of the state

was the most important reason in choosing the site of a capital, in which of these locations should the capital be located? Why do you think it is not?

2. Prepare a report on the first ten amendments to the U.S. Constitution—the Bill of Rights. Discuss how these ten rights affect our society's everyday life.

3. Assume that you are a citizen of Georgia in 1787. Write a "letter to the editor" of a local newspaper telling why Georgia should (or should not) ratify the new federal Constitution.

Making Connections

1. Our language is constantly changing. Make a list of at least twenty-five words that have been added to our language over the past ten years.

2. How did Noah Webster's *Blue-Backed Speller* contribute to the growth of nationalism in the United States?

3. President Jefferson paid about $15 million for the Louisiana territory, which was about 827,000 square miles. How much did he pay per square mile? What states came in total or in part from the Louisiana Purchase territory?

Did You Know?

- Because he suffered from rheumatism and also felt he needed to stay home to manage his plantation, George Washington almost refused to attend the Constitutional Convention.
- The Constitutional Convention in Philadelphia was so secret that a full account of what went on there was not made public until almost sixty years later.
- In 1785, a stagecoach trip from New York to Boston took six days.
- Women were not admitted to the University of Georgia until 1918, 117 years after the college was opened to men.

BUILDING SKILLS: REACHING COMPROMISES

Americans have always had a knack for compromising between tough choices and almost impossible deadlocks between opposing points of view. The alternatives to not being able to reach a compromise can be lack of progress, indecision, and, in some cases, violent action.

America has sometimes been referred to as a "great melting pot" containing nationalities, social and political viewpoints, and religions from around the world. Certainly, the ability and willingness of Americans to reach compromises have helped our country survive and grow.

This chapter contains references to several compromises that took place at the Constitutional Convention in 1787. As the nation's founders were working on creating the Constitution, many plans were proposed to settle differences of opinion.

Do additional research on the Virginia Plan and on the New Jersey Plan. Make careful notes on all the issues. Be prepared to present each point of view and the give-and-take that allowed people with differing opinions to reach an agreement. Did any of the compromises cause a problem? Could conflict have been avoided? Do compromises leave basic problems unresolved?

As citizens of the United States, we all must make compromises. Almost daily, we must give and take with our fellow citizens in order to live together. It is important, though, that we recognize that there are some areas of our lives—our basic values—that cannot be compromised. As citizens, we realize that there are parts of our constitutional democracy that we cannot compromise. What issues are not open to compromise in our society? What types of compromises are necessary for us to be able to exist in society? Would life as we know it be possible without compromise? Are there times when compromise is just not possible? Why are respect, open-mindedness, tolerance, and patience important qualities to have when making compromises?

CHAPTER SIX

THE INDIAN REMOVAL

In 1838, the United States government forced thousands of Cherokee to leave their ancestral homes in the Southeast and march west to what is now Oklahoma. Many died on the trip, which has come to be known as the "Trail of Tears."

The choice now is before you. May the Great Spirit teach you how to choose. The fate of your women and children, the fate of your people to the remotest generation, depend upon the issue. Deceive yourselves no longer. Do not cherish the belief that you can ever resume your former political situation, while you continue in your present residence. As certain as the sun shines to guide you in your path, so certain is it that you cannot drive back the laws of Georgia from among you. Every year will increase your difficulties.

—Andrew Jackson

DURING THE LATE 1700s and early 1800s, white Georgians were working on a state government that would put them in good standing in the Union. They wanted to improve the state's economy and add more land to what they already owned. However, there were thousands of Indians who had hunted in Georgia's forests and fished in its streams and rivers for ten thousand years. The fifty-five years from 1783 to 1838 was one of the darkest periods in the history of these Native Americans. During this period they were forced out of their traditional lands and moved to unknown territories.

GEORGIA'S INDIANS AT THE TURN OF THE CENTURY

At the turn of the century, most Indians in Georgia still made their living in the traditional ways—by hunting and farming. Some, however, owned large plantations. The Cherokee, in particular, were quick to learn from white settlers, who considered them to be the most advanced of the Indian tribes. A few Cherokee, like Chief James Vann, lived in large houses. Vann's home, which was large even by today's standards, was located east of what is now Chatsworth in Murray County. In addition to the main house, the homestead contained forty-two cabins, six barns, five smokehouses, a gristmill, a blacksmith shop, a foundry, a trading post, and a still.

Above: Sequoyah's invention of the syllabary eventually united Cherokee tribes with one written language. In 1819, Sequoyah, who spoke no English, developed an alphabet of symbols to represent the 80 sounds of the Cherokees' spoken language.

SEQUOYAH'S SYLLABARY

One of the most important contributions to the advancement of Cherokee culture was made by George Gist who was born around 1760. Gist's father was a Virginia scout and soldier, and his mother was a Cherokee princess. Gist's Indian name was Sequoyah, which meant "Lonely Lame One." Sequoyah was crippled, from either a childhood illness or a hunting accident, so he could not hunt or farm. Instead, he learned to work with silver; he also became a blacksmith.

Sequoyah was very interested in what were called the white men's "talking leaves," pieces of paper with marks on them. He noticed that the papers could be carried many miles, and the people who used them understood the meaning of the various marks. In 1809, Sequoyah began to make a syllabary. Unlike an alphabet of the letters *A* through *Z*, a **syllabary** is a group of symbols that stand for whole syllables. With Sequoyah's syllabary, all sounds in the Cherokee language except those containing *M* could be spoken without closing the lips.

It took twelve years for Sequoyah to decide on the eighty-five symbols in his syllabary. According to legend, Sequoyah's wife, fearing that the white government would not like what he was doing, once burned all his work. Sequoyah spent more than a year reconstructing the syllabary, so dedicated was he to the task.

When he completed it, members of the tribal council at first made fun of Sequoyah's syllabary. However, after Sequoyah was able to teach his daughter and some young chiefs to write and understand the symbols within a few days, the council members changed their minds. They sent Sequoyah all over the territory to teach his method to other Cherokee. In about six months, most of the tribes could write and read the new symbols. As a result, the Cherokee were the first Indian tribe to have their language in written form. Equally important, it demonstrated that Indians could communicate with each other without using the language of the white settlers.

People in the United States and Europe praised Sequoyah for his work. The Cherokee gave him a medal that he wore as long as he lived. The Cherokee Nation also rewarded him with a gift of about five hundred dollars a year for the remaining years of his life. This gift, by the way, is the first record of a literary prize in America.

THE *CHEROKEE PHOENIX*

By 1828, Elias Boudinot, another Indian leader, became editor of the first Indian newspaper. The paper, **Cherokee Phoenix**, took its name from the fabled bird that rose from ashes. The newspaper was printed in both Cherokee and English. Perhaps its greatest achievement was how it was able to draw together the various tribes of the Cherokee Nation. These tribes were scattered in such far-flung places as Virginia, North Carolina, northeast Alabama, and Georgia; but the newspaper made it possible to spread news among all of them.

The Cherokee Phoenix *newspaper became possible after the development of a written alphabet for the Cherokee language. The newspaper was published in both English and Cherokee languages. Publication began in 1828 and continued until Georgia politicians ordered the editor to stop publication in 1835.*

CHEROKEE CAPITAL MOVES TO NEW ECHOTA

At one time, the capital of the Cherokee Nation was wherever the principal chief lived. In 1715, for example, it was in Stephens County, Georgia. At other times, the capital was in Tennessee or South Carolina. However, by 1825, the Cherokee had established a permanent capital at New Echota, near the present-day city of Calhoun.

New Echota was a thriving, bustling community. One of the twenty Cherokee government buildings in it was a print shop where the *Cherokee Phoenix* and textbooks for Indian schools were published and distributed. Other buildings included a Cherokee national library and a courthouse.

The Cherokee adopted a constitution similar to that of the United States. Their government also was organized along the lines of that of the United States and consisted of three branches: executive, legislative, and judicial. The principal chief and second chief were elected to their offices. Each October, Cherokee leaders, including those in the bicameral legislature and the superior court, met in New Echota to deal with tribal matters.

Do You Remember?
1. What was the name of the Cherokee chief who built a large homestead in Murray County?
2. What was Sequoyah's great contribution to the Cherokee and other Indians?
3. After what fabled bird was the first Cherokee newspaper named?
4. Where was the Cherokee capital located in 1825?

*Above: New Echota became the permanent Cherokee capital in 1825. **Above left:** You can see the restored* Phoenix *office looking much the same as it did in the 1830s when the newspaper was being published.*

CHIEF VANN HOUSE

Located on the outskirts of Chatsworth, Georgia, is the palatial home of Chief James Vann. The two-story classic brick mansion was built by Vann in 1804 and has been called the "Showcase of the Cherokee Nation." The house is decorated with rich Cherokee hand carvings in blue, green, red, and yellow. In it are many examples of fine furniture and other antiques.

Vann was said to be "feared by many and loved by few." Nevertheless, he made numerous contributions to Cherokee culture. He believed that Christianity meant progress for the Cherokee and brought in Moravian missionaries to teach his children and people.

Chief Vann was killed in 1809, and his son Joseph inherited the house and the surrounding businesses. While there, Joseph entertained such notables as President Monroe and John C. Calhoun. His neighbors called him "Rich Joe." However, this also came to an end. Joseph lost his properties when he violated state law by hiring a white man to work for him. All his holdings were seized by the government, and in 1834 the house was auctioned off in a land lottery.

Right: The stately brick home was built by Cherokee leader James Vann in 1804. It remains as a reminder of the Cherokees' wealth and culture. Above: The brightly painted walls of the Vann House dining room are the same colors that were originally in the home.

INDIAN RELATIONSHIPS WITH SETTLERS

To understand why the Creek and Cherokee were pushed out of Georgia, it is helpful to know what happened before that time. Many years of encounters between the settlers and the Indians had created bad feelings between them. The bad feelings grew even worse and flared into armed conflicts when land became a major factor.

You may recall from your reading that Indians first met white men in 1540 when Spanish explorer Hernando de Soto and his band of soldiers went through Georgia in their search for gold. Other Europeans followed De Soto. Some of them began religious missions, and a few opened trading posts. Slowly the Indians came to know some of the ways and weapons of white men. There were times when they used this knowledge to defend themselves against the settlers. At other times, the Indians used the knowledge to attack settlers in Georgia, Alabama, and South Carolina.

For years, a few white traders had cheated, tricked, and enslaved the Indians. At one point, traders said the Indians owed them 100,000 deerskins, the equal to two years of work for every adult male Indian. Finally, one group of Indians decided to defend themselves.

THE YAMASEE WAR

In 1715, the Yamasee, a Creek tribe, killed South Carolina Indian agent Thomas Nairne and some traders. In the skirmishes that followed, in what became known as the **Yamasee War**, the tribe attacked plantations along the South Carolina coast and killed traders in Creek or Choctaw towns. As there were more Indians than whites, the Carolina settlers tried to turn the Indians against each other. They convinced the Cherokee that it would be better for them not to take part in the attacks. The settlers' scheme to divide the Indians soon paid off. Once, when some of the Lower Creek were to meet with the Cherokee to talk about war plans, the Cherokee ambushed and killed them. This led to trouble between the two tribes—trouble that lasted for years.

The divide-and-conquer plan continued to work well for the settlers. After the split between the Creek and Cherokee, it was relatively easy for the settlers and English forces to defeat each of them separately. Some of the Creek became afraid of what might be ahead and, foreseeing a grim future, moved west.

During the years that followed the Yamasee War, life changed little for the remaining Creek until the ship *Ann* arrived. When James Oglethorpe came in 1733, the Yamacraw, a Creek tribe that lived along the Georgia coast, helped the settlers, and the two groups got along well together. However, because of Creek involvement in some of the wars of the eighteenth century, Georgians began to mistrust them.

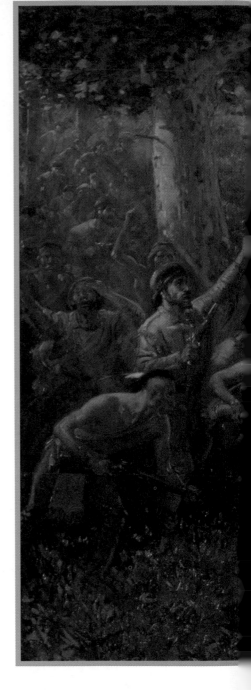

The death of General Braddock (above) was a low point for the British in the French and Indian War. The war was the result of the rival land claims of the French and British. Indians sided with the French.

THE FRENCH AND INDIAN WAR

Beginning in 1689, a series of four wars broke out between France and Great Britain for control of the New World. Three of these conflicts were mainly fought in Europe, but one, known in Europe as the *Seven Years' War* (1756-1763), began in North America. Americans call this war the French and Indian War. This war was briefly mentioned earlier in Chapter Four.

Both France and Great Britain laid claim to the Ohio and Mississippi rivers. In 1747, a group of Virginia colonists formed a company to settle the lands in the Ohio River Valley and control the fur trade. In 1749, King George II gave the Ohio Land Company, as it was called, a grant of 500,000 acres. To strengthen its own claims and slow down British expeditions in the area, France built forts at key points in the Ohio country. Among the forts built by the French was Fort Duquesne (present-day Pittsburgh), located at the junction of the Allegheny and Monongahela rivers, which form the Ohio River.

Governor Dinwiddie of Virginia thought that Fort Duquesne was much too close to the western portions of Virginia, which at that time ran as far as the Ohio River in what is now West Virginia. The governor sent the young, twenty-one-year-old George Washington to give the French an *ultimatum* (a threat to take action if a demand is not met): Leave the area of the Ohio Valley at once or face the consequences. The French commandant, Captain Legardeur de Saint Pierre, read the governor's message with contempt and sent back a resounding "no." The French would not leave the area.

The following year, Washington, now a lieutenant colonel, was once again sent to Fort Duquesne—this time with a force of 150 troops. Raised against him, however, was a French force of 600 men. Washington and his Virginia militia were defeated at Great Meadows (in Pennsylvania).

During this period, a few Indian tribes joined with the British and colonists. The Iroquois spent the war siding with the British, but they did not actively join the British forces. The majority of Indian tribes allied themselves with the French. These tribes included the Cherokee, Delaware, Shawnee, Ottawa, and Chippewa.

Between 1754 and 1763, fighting was mean and savage, with the French and Indian allies fighting under the cover of the forest, hiding behind trees, and attacking and scalping settlers. The British forces, dressed in uniforms and moving with drums resounding, were an easily visible target and suffered a series of defeats.

Georgia was spared warfare during the French and Indian War, although battles were fought as close as South Carolina. In 1759, the war began to wear down after the spectacular capture of Quebec by the British. That battle signaled the end of French power in

Governor Robert Dinwiddie of Virginia (above) sent the young George Washington to Fort Duquesne with an ultimatum for the French to leave the area.

the New World territories. By 1762, most of the hostilities had ended and talk of treaty agreements began.

In November 1763, peace came to the southern colonies with the **Congress of Augusta**. The governors of Georgia, South Carolina, North Carolina, and Virginia met in Augusta, Georgia, with representatives of the Indian nations of the Chickasaw, Choctaw, Creek, and Cherokee. The Indian chiefs promised to live in peace. They also gave up much of their land, including an additional 2.5 million acres in Georgia that the state took from the Creek.

George Washington (above center) finally captured Fort Duquesne in 1758 without a shot being fired.

Treaty of Paris of 1763

The **Treaty of Paris of 1763**, signed on February 10, 1763, formally ended the French and Indian War. Under the terms of the treaty, France gave up all her territory in North America east of the Mississippi (except for New Orleans), and Spain lost Florida. The treaty left Great Britain in control of all land east of the Mississippi.

The Proclamation of 1763

Although the Treaty of Paris settled some problems, it brought about others. Great Britain now had to juggle managing 2 million colonists, taking on 600,000 inhabitants of Canada, and maintaining peace between the colonists and the Indians.

Great Britain felt that the easiest way to manage was to break the country into two parts and, in the **Proclamation of 1763**, established certain boundaries. Colonists could settle in all areas east of the Appalachian Mountains. The rest of the land was left to the Indians. For Georgia, the southern boundary was extended to the St. Mary's River, and the Florida Panhandle fell under British control.

In the following year, Georgia's boundaries were extended westward to include what we now call Alabama and Mississippi. That expansion of land eliminated, for all practical purposes, the home of the Creek Nation.

THE OCONEE WAR

Bad feelings between the Creek and the settlers grew during the late 1700s. Pioneers kept pushing into Creek lands along the Oconee River. Tribes led by Chief Alexander McGillivray sent warriors against some of the pioneer settlements. The Indians burned houses, stole horses and cattle, and killed or captured over two hundred settlers. Georgia colonists got some men together and told them to kill on sight any Creek who were not members of friendly tribes. Although it was not quite a full-scale conflict, these skirmishes and attacks became known as the **Oconee War**.

Fighting between the settlers and the Creek went on for several years. In 1790, President Washington called Chief McGillivray to New York. The chief went, accompanied by twenty-three men of his tribe. President Washington and the chief talked and exchanged presents, which may have included money. McGillivray then signed the **Treaty of New York**, which stated that the Creek would give up all their land east of the Oconee River. They would also honor an earlier treaty in which they gave up lands through the Currahee Mountains to Tugaloo. In return, the United States government promised that no whites would go into land west of the boundary. The government also agreed to help the Creek start farms by giving them tools and farm animals.

When word of the treaty reached Georgians, they were very angry because it appeared to them that the federal government had taken the side of the Indians. During the next few years, neither the Creek nor the Georgians paid any attention to the Treaty of New York. At one point, Governor Edward Telfair was ready to raise an army of 5,000 men to make war against the Creek, but President Washington talked him out of it. However, there were bad feelings between the tribes and the whites until both groups accepted other treaties. This "peace" would last from 1797 until 1812.

It was during this time that the Yazoo Land Fraud took place. When the federal government stepped in and had Georgia give up all land west of the Chattahoochee River, it also promised to move the Indi-

Bitterly angry over the amount of land being taken from the Indians, including his father's home in Savannah, Alexander McGillivray sent warriors against pioneer settlements.

ans out of the state. The federal government did little to carry out this promise. Then, in 1812, the United States was again at war.

Four hundred people died when the Red Stick Creek attacked Ft. Mims in Alabama.

WAR WAGED AGAINST THE CREEK

About this time, some Indian leaders from other parts of the country tried to get all Indians to fight for their right to the land. After the leaders talked with tribes in the southeast, the Indians became divided into two groups. Those who wanted war were called **Red Sticks**, and those who wanted peace were known as **White Sticks**.

During the War of 1812, many of the Red Stick Creek fought alongside the British. As you read earlier, the war ended with no real winner. However, something happened in 1813 that changed the future of the Creek Nation.

On August 30, one thousand Red Sticks attacked Fort Mims in present-day Alabama. During the battle, which lasted for hours, settlers, including women and children, White Stick Creek, and United

A few days after the Battle of Horseshoe Bend, Chief William Weatherford, also known as Red Eagle, rode into General Jackson's camp and surrendered.

States Army officers were killed. About four hundred people died at the hands of the Red Sticks, and the nation was alarmed. Cries of "Remember Fort Mims" were heard all over the country. Troops from Georgia, Tennessee, and the new Mississippi Territory began attacks in Creek territory.

Many battles were fought during the next year, but the Creek were no match for the United States Army. The last battle of the Creek Indian War began on March 27, 1814, at Horseshoe Bend in Alabama. As you learned in the previous chapter, over one thousand Red Sticks met two thousand members of the infantry, led by General Andrew Jackson. With the help of two cannon, seven hundred cavalrymen, and six hundred White Stick Cherokee, the Creek Indians were defeated.

In the following months, the Creek surrendered to Jackson and gave most of their lands to the United States government. Georgians were pleased with this outcome, because it meant that the Indians owned no more land in southern Georgia.

THE MONROE DOCTRINE

Between 1808 and 1822, various colonies in Latin America, including Chile, Peru, Columbia, and Mexico, declared their independence from Spain. Many people in the United States wanted to recognize the independence of these former colonies, because they believed that Latin American patriots were carrying on the revolutionary traditions begun by the founding of the United States in 1776.

President James Monroe and Secretary of State John Quincy Adams were sympathetic but moved slowly. They distrusted Spanish, French, British, and Russian intentions in the New World. In 1822, the United States recognized the newly independent Latin American nations. To block European ambitions in the New World, Adams crafted the so-called Monroe Doctrine.

President Monroe presented the doctrine named after himself to Congress on December 2, 1823. The doctrine had three principles. First, no European nation could establish colonies in the Western Hemisphere. The principle blocked Spain in Latin America and Russia on the West Coast. Second, no European nation could intervene in the affairs of independent nations of the New World. Third, Monroe promised that the United States would not interfere in European affairs, including any colonies Europe still owned in the New World.

The Monroe Doctrine became the foundation of American foreign policy in the Western Hemisphere. Americans viewed it as an assertion of their nationalism. In reality, it matched Great Britain's policies. The Royal Navy, not Monroe's words, gave force to the policy.

In a warning to European nations, President Monroe stated that the American continents were closed to "future colonization by any European powers."

As more and more of their land was ceded to the government, Creek tribes became separated from each other. There was little chance for them to talk together or to trade with each other. The strong Creek confederacy, which had united the tribes before the arrival of the settlers, was no more. Groups of Creek would sometimes sign treaties without asking the tribes to agree. This practice led to the death of one well-known Creek leader.

The Creek General Chief of the Cowetas, William McIntosh, was called Tustunugee Hutkee by fellow tribesmen, meaning "White Warrior." His signing of the Indian Springs Treaty giving up the last Creek Indian lands in Georgia was seen as a betrayal that led to his murder by fellow tribesmen.

Murder of Chief William McIntosh

By February 12, 1825, Creek Chief William McIntosh and his first cousin, Georgia Governor George Troup, had worked out the terms of the **Treaty of Indian Springs** in Butts County. The United States paid McIntosh and a large group of Lower Creek chiefs $200,000 to cede the last of Creek lands in Georgia to the federal government. The government, in turn, gave the use of that land to Georgia.

Groups of Creek who disagreed with the treaty met secretly to decide how to punish McIntosh. They agreed that, in accordance with Creek law, he should die. According to reports, somewhere between 170 and 400 Indians marched single file to McIntosh's home in Carroll County, Georgia. After two days, they were a mile from McIntosh's house. Many reports say the Indians got close enough to hear McIntosh and his son-in-law, Samuel Hawkins, talking, but McIntosh did not know theIndians were there.

At daybreak, the Creek set fire to the McIntosh home. The Indians allowed the women and children to leave before they exchanged gunfire with the chief they had come to kill. Smoke and his wounds stopped McIntosh from fighting. Indians dragged him from the house and stabbed him in the chest. McIntosh's scalp was taken as a warning to others who might want to give Creek land to white men.

Do You Remember?

1. What was the Yamasee War?
2. What event led to the Creek and Cherokee becoming enemies?
3. When did the Congress of Augusta take place?
4. Who was Alexander McGillivray?
5. Who were the Red Sticks?

JAMES FENIMORE COOPER

One of the first American writers to describe the adventures of our nation's pioneers as they blazed trails westward and to detail the problems between them and Indians was James Fenimore Cooper. Cooper, however, never actually lived in the unsettled West. He was born in Burlington, New Jersey, on September 15, 1789. The following year, his father established the settlement of Cooperstown, New York, a frontier village on the Susquehanna River.

After graduating from a preparatory school in 1803, Cooper entered Yale. He was expelled in his junior year and joined the navy. He soon discovered that he was no better suited to the rigors of the navy than he was to those of Yale, so he took a leave of absence and never returned to duty.

Cooper married in 1811, and for almost ten years thereafter, lived the life of a country gentleman, a far cry from the frontiersmen for which he was to become so well known. This life came to an end, however, when the need

arose for money to help pay for the care of his brothers' widows. To help defray these expenses, he turned to writing.

Cooper's first novel was not particularly successful, but his second, *The Spy*, was. His next book, *The Pioneers*, was the first of five in a series that became known as *The Leatherstocking Tales*. A major figure in these novels, which also included *The Last of the Mohicans*, was the frontiersman Natty Bumpo. Cooper's tales of life on the frontier were enormously popular, both in this country and abroad.

Cooper lived in Europe with his wife and family for a number of years and finally returned to Cooperstown, where he died on September 14, 1851.

James Fenimore Cooper's tales of the frontier made him America's favorite writer, in spite of the fact that he didn't start writing until he was in his thirties and had no experience on the frontier.

THE INDIAN REMOVAL

In 1828, Andrew Jackson was elected president of the United States. Jackson had been friendly to the Indians, especially the Cherokee when he needed their help to fight the Red Sticks. However, he was wise enough politically to know that white voters wanted the Indians removed from the southern states.

In 1830, Congress passed a bill, the Indian Removal Act, which called for the Indians to be moved to the western territories. There were strong feelings on both sides, and the bill passed by only fourteen votes. After Jackson signed the bill into law, however, there was no question about what would happen to Indians in the Southeast.

REMOVAL OF THE CREEK

The Choctaw, who lived in the newly created states of Alabama and Mississippi, were the first Indians to be moved. Hearing that hundreds of Choctaw died during the march to the west, the Creek refused to leave the lands of their fathers. When they did this, Alabama took away all Indian legal rights. The Creek could not defend themselves against whites who moved in and took their lands.

As a Major General in the United States Army, Andrew Jackson frequently used Indians in battles against the French, British, or Spanish forces or in fights supporting United States troops against other Indian tribes. However, when he was elected President in 1828, his debt to the various tribes was quickly forgotten.

Creek in Georgia, who no longer had hunting lands, were hungry. Some reports say they stood in the streets of Columbus and begged for food. To add to their hardships, smallpox broke out among the tribes in 1831, and many Indians died. Not long after that, the Treaty of Washington was signed. With this treaty, the Creek ceded the 5 million acres of land they still owned to the United States. In return, the government agreed to set aside 2 million acres on which the Creek would live and farm. Some terms in the treaty were favorable for both the Creek and the United States government. The government would protect Creek life and property from whites. Creek could own land, but only after living on it for five years. Then they could choose to sell the land and move west. The decision to stay on reserved land or to move to the western territory was up to each individual.

Once signed, the treaty was broken almost at once. Creek homes were burned, items were stolen from their farms, and Indians were killed. By 1835, some Creek gave up and began the trip west. However, in 1836, bands of Lower Creek attacked whites between Tuskegee, Alabama, and Columbus, Georgia. Afraid of another Indian war, the U.S. Army captured over one thousand Creek and took them to Indian Territory (present-day Oklahoma). During the next two years, a few Creek escaped and a few were made slaves, but the federal government forced thousands of them to move west.

Toward the end of the Creek removal in Georgia and Alabama, the United States became involved in another Indian war in Florida. They asked seven hundred Creek to help them fight the Seminole. After winning the war, the Creek returned to their families, who had been gathered in camps. Then the whole group, including those who had just fought with the army, was moved west.

REMOVAL OF THE CHEROKEE

At the same time that the Creek were being moved, Georgia was also making plans to remove the Cherokee. Georgians wanted to homestead the Cherokee land and mine the gold that had been found there.

Gold in Dahlonega

Gold was discovered in Dahlonega in the summer of 1829. In a matter of months, gold fever swept through the north Georgia mountain region. Although the Cherokee knew there was gold in the hills, the person given credit for the discovery was a farmer named Benjamin Parks. Parks found the valuable yellow metal while deer hunting in what was then Habersham (now White) County. Auraria, in nearby Lumpkin County, became the first gold mining center in the United States. Over ten thousand miners with gold pans, picks, and shovels moved onto Cherokee land.

The Georgia legislature passed a law that placed part of Cherokee land under state control. It said Cherokee laws were null and void, and the legislature would not let Indians speak against white men in a court of law. This meant any white person could hurt or even kill a Cherokee without much fear of punishment. A second law, passed on December 19, 1829, refused Indians any right to gold mined in the Dahlonega area. While the miners searched the mountains and streams for "a spot that showed good color," the Cherokee were losing their homes, lands, and legal rights.

The Indians' Last Hope

Most Georgians did not care what happened to the Indians, but a group of white missionaries living in Indian territory did. To remove the missionaries, the Georgia legislature passed a law on December 22, 1830, that said a white person could

The discovery of gold in Dahlonega ended any hope of the Cherokee retaining their lands. Once news spread that gold had been discovered, thousands swarmed into the small town.

Chief John Ross tried to obtain help for the Cherokee from the U.S. Congress.

not live on Indian land without taking an oath of allegiance. Eleven people, including the Reverend Samuel Worchester, postmaster at New Echota, refused to sign the oath and were put in jail in March 1831. They were set free, then arrested again in July of that year. This time they were chained and made to walk from the North Georgia mountains to Lawrenceville. At their trial in September, the jury took only fifteen minutes to return a verdict of guilty. Judge Augustin Clayton sentenced the group to four years at the state penitentiary in Milledgeville. Governor George Gilmer agreed to pardon anyone who would take an oath of loyalty to the state, and all but two agreed. Missionaries Worchester and Elizur Butler took their cases to the United States Supreme Court. Chief Justice John Marshall ruled that the decision of the Lawrenceville court could not stand because Cherokee territory was not under state law.

The Cherokee thought the ruling meant they might be able to keep their land and government. Chief Justice Marshall ordered Butler and Worchester set free, but the Gwinnett County Judge Clayton refused. Georgia's newly elected governor, Wilson Lumpkin, would not take a stand against Judge Clayton. Even President Andrew Jackson did not honor the Supreme Court order. Jackson thought that state governments should be in charge of Indian territories. He reportedly said, "John Marshall has rendered his 'decision'; now let him enforce it."

Cherokee lands were divided into lots of 40 and 160 acres. In 1832, the government held a state lottery to give Indian lands to white men. Even then, the Cherokee refused to leave their home.

On January 9, 1833, Butler and Worchester gave up and told Governor Lumpkin that they would "abandon litigation." **Litigation** means to sue in court. They agreed to leave the question of their prison sentence to the "**magnanimity** (generosity) of the State." The governor pardoned them, then said the two missionaries must leave the state and never return.

Cherokee Chief John Ross made several trips to Washington to ask Congress for help. He wanted the Indians protected and the terms of past treaties honored. No help was given. More and more, the Indians were run off their lands, whipped, and even killed. Time was running out for the Cherokee Nation.

In December 1835, the Cherokee were told to come to their capital, New Echota. There they were to sign a treaty giving up all the Cherokee land that remained in the Southeast. Any member of the tribe who did not come was considered to have been in agreement with the treaty. Three to five hundred Cherokee out of about seventeen thousand were at the meeting.

Cherokee trader Major Ridge, his son David, and a small number of Indians agreed to sign the government's treaty. The treaty said the Indians would move west, and Georgia would give them a little money and food for the trip.

By May of 1838, about two thousand Cherokee had gone. They left behind about fifteen thousand others who refused to leave their homes.

After moving to Oklahoma on the Trail of Tears, Major Ridge and his son David (above) were killed in 1839 for their role in bringing about the Cherokee removal from Georgia.

THE TRAIL OF TEARS

After the treaty was signed, some national leaders like Henry Clay, Daniel Webster, and Davy Crockett tried to get the United States government to give the Cherokee the rights due them. No one listened, and General Winfield Scott was ordered to remove the fifteen thousand or more Cherokee who were still in Georgia.

In May 1838, Scott and nearly seven thousand troops arrived in New Echota. The troops first built stockades to house the Cherokee. Then they went into homes and community buildings, forcibly moving the Cherokee to the stockades. Hundreds of men, women, and children died of cholera, dysentery, and fever while in the stockades. During the summer of 1838, the army loaded several thousand Cherokee onto crowded boats and sent them on the Tennessee, Mississippi, and Arkansas rivers to their new homes. The boats were dirty,

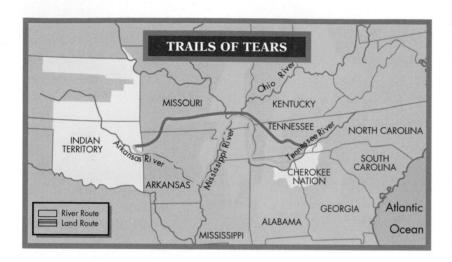

TRAILS OF TEARS

OHIO River

MISSOURI

KENTUCKY

TENNESSEE

Tennessee River

NORTH CAROLINA

INDIAN TERRITORY

Arkansas River

Mississippi River

ARKANSAS

CHEROKEE NATION

SOUTH CAROLINA

GEORGIA

Atlantic Ocean

ALABAMA

MISSISSIPPI

River Route
Land Route

This map shows the westward routes of the Cherokee by water and by land on the Trail of Tears.

and the food the government gave them was often not fit to eat. By the time these Indians arrived in the Oklahoma Territory, nearly one-third of the group had died.

A few Cherokee escaped and hid in the North Carolina mountains. The rest began a 700- to 800-mile walk to Indian Territory. It took some people six months to make the trip. Others were there in less time. However, winter winds, snow, and too little food led to the deaths of thousands of Cherokee. The exact number of Indians who were moved is not known, but about four thousand of this group died while they were in prison before they left or during the march west.

The Indians were not the only casualties of the treaty that removed the Cherokee from their land. Major Ridge, his son, and the editor of *Cherokee Phoenix*, Elias Boudinot, were killed by other Indians for breaking a tribal law forbidding individual Cherokee from signing away land rights without the permission of the entire tribe.

President Martin Van Buren, in his December 1838 address to Congress, said, "the measures of the Removal have had the happiest effect . . . the Cherokee have **emigrated** (moved out) without apparent reluctance." Today, we can only imagine the fear, despair, and hurt felt by those who had to leave the land of the "principal people." The Cherokee called the move to Indian Territory "ANuna-da-ut-sun'y," which means "the trail where they cried." To this day, the move is sadly remembered as the **Trail of Tears**.

Today we can only imagine the heartsick feelings of thousands of Cherokee as they were forced to leave their home, possessions, and lands behind and walk from Georgia to Oklahoma. This mural in the Oklahoma State Museum of History focuses on the family and servant of Chief John Ross.

Do You Remember?

1. What were Andrew Jackson's feelings about Indians?
2. What happened in Dahlonega in 1829?
3. Who was Samuel Worchester?
4. What Cherokee trader signed the treaty at New Echota?

SUMMARY

- Although most Indians still followed traditional ways, some had made great advances.
- The Cherokee were especially quick to adopt new methods.
- Sequoyah invented a syllabary that enabled Indians to communicate in writing.
- The Cherokee established a capital at New Echota.
- At first, Indians and white settlers were friendly, but bad feelings and mistrust soon developed.
- Indians sided with the French in the French and Indian War; then they sided with the British during the Revolutionary War and the War of 1812.
- U.S. treaties with the Indians were broken almost as soon as they were made.
- The Creek were forced west, and the Cherokee were gathered together and sent on their Trail of Tears.

CHAPTER REVIEW

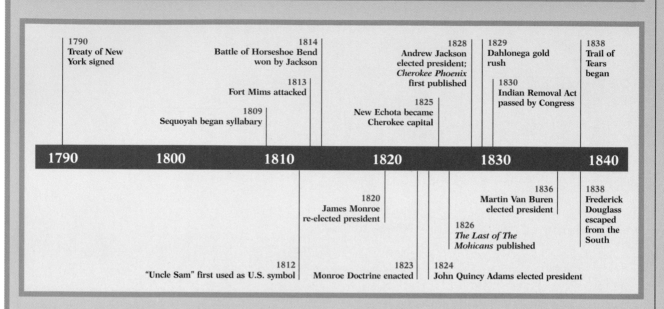

1790	1800	1810	1820	1830	1840

1790 Treaty of New York signed

1814 Battle of Horseshoe Bend won by Jackson

1813 Fort Mims attacked

1809 Sequoyah began syllabary

1828 Andrew Jackson elected president; *Cherokee Phoenix* first published

1825 New Echota became Cherokee capital

1829 Dahlonega gold rush

1830 Indian Removal Act passed by Congress

1838 Trail of Tears began

1820 James Monroe re-elected president

1836 Martin Van Buren elected president

1826 *The Last of The Mohicans* published

1838 Frederick Douglass escaped from the South

1812 "Uncle Sam" first used as U.S. symbol

1823 Monroe Doctrine enacted

1824 John Quincy Adams elected president

Reviewing People, Places, and Terms

Explain why each of the following appear in a chapter on The Indian Removal.

syllabary
Treaty of Paris (1763)
Proclamation of 1763
Cherokee Phoenix
Treaty of Indian Springs
Trail of Tears

Understanding the Facts

1. What was George Gist's Indian name?
2. How is a syllabary different from the alphabet?
3. In what month did the Cherokee leaders meet in New Echota to deal with tribal matters?
4. To which Indian group did the Yamasee tribe belong?
5. What did Europeans call the French and Indian War?
6. Who did Governor Dinwiddie of Virginia send to give an ultimatum to the French?
7. Which Creek chief signed the Treaty of New York?

8. How was the Creek chief who worked out the terms of the Treaty of Indian Springs punished?
9. Who was president when Congress passed the bill calling for the removal of the Indians to the western territories?
10. Which Indians were the first to be moved?

Developing Critical Thinking

1. Could the settlers and the Indians have lived together peacefully? Why or why not?
2. In your opinion, was the removal of the Indians right or wrong? Briefly explain your answer.
3. Why is the Trail of Tears often referred to as one of the darkest periods in the history of Georgia? Can you recall a similar "removal" anywhere in the world in more recent history?
4. Had you been a Cherokee during this period, would you have hidden in the mountains or would you have traveled to Indian territory on the Trail of Tears? Suppose you were married and had three small children who depended on you, what would you have done?

Applying Your Skills

1. Using a map of Georgia, locate ten communities, counties, or rivers that have Indian names.
2. Following the map on page 200 of your textbook that traces the Trail of Tears, list the states in order through which the Cherokee had to travel to reach Indian Territory.
3. Using whatever reference sources are available to you (including the Internet), research the history and use of the term "Uncle Sam." Compare an 1812 drawing of Uncle Sam with one made within the past ten years.

Making Connections

1. Natty Bumpo, the main character in *The Leatherstocking Tales*, was a fictional frontiersman. What real frontiersmen can you name that have been celebrated in books or songs?
2. Besides being known for its association with James Fenimore Cooper and his family, Cooperstown, New York, is also the site of an annual sports event. What is this event? With which sport is it connected?
3. Is the Monroe Doctrine still enforced by the United States today? What evidence is there to support your answer?

Did You Know?

• In the 1820s, nearly one-third of what is now Georgia still belonged to the Creek and Cherokee.
• By 1851, only 321 Cherokee were found still living in Georgia.
• The Indians referred to Georgia as "E-Cun-Nau-Nux-Udgee," which meant "people greedily grasping after the lands of red men."
• The giant redwood trees found in California are named in honor of Sequoyah.
• Twenty-eight of the fifty states in the United States have names with Indian origins.
• The largest groups of Indians in the mid-1990s are Cherokee.
• The sport of lacrosse originated with the North American Indians.

BUILDING SKILLS: FINDING INFORMATION

As you continue your studies of the history of Georgia, your teacher may assign topics for you to research. In addition to looking in the card catalog in your school media center, there are numerous reference books available, many of which are also published in electronic forms. Here are some of these references and the type of facts you are likely to find in them:

• **Almanac**: Facts about a variety of events and dates, often arranged by order of date.
• **Atlas**: Maps and place information.
• **Dictionary**: Meaning, spellings, and pronunciation of words; origin of words.
• **Encyclopedia:** Important details about people, places, and things, usually arranged alphabetically by subject or topic.

Read the descriptions of information needed and determine which reference source would be most appropriate to use. On a separate sheet of paper, write the number of the description and the abbreviation *AL*, if you would use an almanac; *AT*, if you would use an atlas; *DI*, if you would use a dictionary; and *EN*, if you would use an encyclopedia.

1. The distance between Atlanta and Darien
2. The date Georgia became a state
3. The yearly average rainfall in Georgia
4. The capital of Georgia
5. The definition of "goober peas"
6. An explanation of the War of 1812
7. The correct pronunciation of the word *poultry*
8. Another word for *Cherokee*
9. A map of Georgia's counties
10. Major crops grown in Georgia

THE INDIAN REMOVAL   **203**

UNIT IV

A NATION DIVIDED

*A house divided against itself cannot stand. I believe this government
cannot endure, permanently, half slave and half free. I do not expect
the Union to be dissolved; I do not expect the house to fall; but I do
expect it will cease to be divided. It will become all one thing, or all the
other. Either the opponents of slavery will arrest the further spread of
it and place it where the public mind shall rest in the belief that it is in
the course of ultimate extinction, or its advocates will push it forward
till it shall become alike lawful in all the states, old as well as new.
North as well as South.*

—Abraham Lincoln

THE UNITED STATES had been one nation since 1789.
However, society, politics, economics, and culture were
different in each major section of the country. The differences, perhaps, were sharpest between the northern and
the southern states. From the early 1800s until the middle 1800s,
people talked about these differences at socials and church meetings. Newspaper men wrote about them, and politicians made them
the subject of speeches. The differences eventually led to conflict. That
conflict led to secession, war, and reconstruction, and marks one of
the most difficult periods in Georgia's history.

*Today, Chickamauga National Military Park in Catoosa and Walker
counties serves as a reminder of the most divisive period in the
history of the United States, when disagreement over the issue of
slavery led Americans to take up arms against each other.*

CHAPTER SEVEN

ANTEBELLUM DAYS

We are a peculiar people, sir! You don't understand us . . . because we are known to you only by northern writers and northern papers . . . . We are an agricultural people; we are a primitive but a civilized people. We have no cities we don't want them. . . . We have no commercial navy no navy we don't want them. . . . We want no manufactures; we desire no trading, no mechanical or manufacturing classes. As long as we have our rice, our sugar, our tobacco, and our cotton, we can command wealth to produce all we want from those nations with which we are in amity, and to lay up money besides.
—Senator Lewis T. Wigfall of South Carolina

THE PERIOD BEFORE THE CIVIL WAR is called **antebellum,** which means before war. In 1850, when the last decade of the antebellum period began, the population of the United States was 23,191,876. California became the thirty-first state, and, following the death of President Zachary Taylor, Vice President Millard Fillmore became the thirteenth president. Americans were reading Nathaniel Hawthorne's novel, *The Scarlet Letter,* and Levi Strauss began making canvas pants called "Levis" for gold miners. Industry was growing in the North, and agriculture was profitable in the South.

Nevertheless, bad feelings between the North and South were spreading. Many issues such as sectionalism, economic considerations, and cultural differences divided the citizens of the United States. No issue, however, aroused the passions of most Americans as much as the issue of slavery.

The stately home of United States Senator Robert Toombs in Washington, Georgia, represented much of what the South wanted to save or perpetuate. The plantation classes lived a life of comfort and ease at the hands of others.

THE INSTITUTION OF SLAVERY

Although slavery was not the only cause of the Civil War, it did have a significant impact. The differences in sentiments between those states that permitted the owning of slaves and those that did not were sharp and reached out to affect many other aspects of life. Georgians were no different from the people in the other states where slavery was allowed.

The original 1732 charter of the trustees of Georgia had not permitted slavery. However, as land holdings grew in size, landowners needed help to work their fields. They asked the trustees appointed to manage the colony's affairs to allow them to import slaves. At first the trustees refused, influenced to a large degree by the Salzburger colonists, as well as by the Scottish Highlanders who had settled near Darien. However, in 1750, two years before Georgia became a royal colony, the trustees reconsidered and the institution of slavery began in Georgia.

By 1860, on the eve of the Civil War, there were over 4,000,000 slaves in the United States. Of that number, 465,000, or 11.6 percent, lived in Georgia. Most, but not all, of the other slaves were in the remaining southern states.

THE BEGINNINGS OF SLAVERY

The institution of slavery in North America began in 1619 when a Dutch trader brought sixty blacks to Virginia to work in the tobacco fields. At first, blacks and some whites were indentured servants. They agreed to work for a specified period of time, usually five to six years, after which they could do as they wished. In principle, they worked to repay the cost of their passage to the new land. However, by the mid-1600s, there were laws that made black indentured servants slaves for life.

SLAVE TRADING

People who traded slaves learned they could make a lot of money in this business. They began by going to Africa to get blacks to sell in the colonies. Traders tried to capture the strongest men and women in a village. In some cases, members of one African tribe would catch members of other tribes and sell them to slave traders for trinkets, blankets, or rum. There were also cases where a person who had broken a tribal law was sold as punishment. Sometimes, traders chained hundreds of Africans together and placed them in crowded ships going to the colonies. At least one chained tribe reportedly chose to walk into the sea and drown rather than get on board a slave ship waiting to take them overseas.

After Eli Whitney invented the cotton gin in 1793, farmers began to grow more cotton. They needed workers to plant, cultivate, and harvest this crop, so slave trading grew. Slave trading resulted in thousands of families being split up. Sometimes, even tribal kings whose families had ruled for hundreds of years were put in fields to hoe cotton because they had been enslaved.

Slave trading ships docked in places like New Orleans, Charleston, and Savannah. Traders led Africans to auction blocks and sold them to the highest bidder. During the slave trading years, prices ranged from a few hundred dollars to almost two thousand.

Once owners bought slaves, they moved them to their farms or plantations. Most of the slaves could not speak or understand English. Members of families and tribes were often sold to different owners. Since there were so many African tribal languages, new slaves might not be able to talk in their own language to any other slave who worked with them. Slave owners believed that the inability to communicate freely would prevent slave uprisings.

Slave market auctions were a time of fearful uncertainty and indignity for the slaves.

DAILY LIFE FOR SLAVES

Life was not easy for slaves, no matter where they worked. They usually ate fatback, molasses, and corn bread. On some plantations, slaves could grow a vegetable garden and fish in streams and ponds. Sometimes, plantation owners gave the slaves rabbits, opossums, squirrels, or other small game they had killed.

Slaves wore clothing made from materials that would last a long time. On big plantations, owners bought large amounts of wide-brimmed hats, heavy-duty shoes, socks or stockings, and underwear. The clothes did not always fit, and slaves sometimes worked barefoot in the fields. House slaves were generally treated better than field workers. House slaves were often given clothes that members of the plantation families no longer wore. These garments were usually much better than those given to field workers.

Most slaves lived in one-room huts with fireplaces for heating and cooking. They had little furniture—perhaps a table, some chairs, and pallets to sleep on. Slave housing was poorly built with inferior materials or with timber and stone found nearby. The house usually had stick-and-dirt chimneys, one door, and one window without glass. These slave huts were often small, crowded, and smoky. Some slaveholders did provide sturdier housing for their workers, but this was more the exception than the rule.

Opposite page: This rare portrait of a house servant was probably painted by a member of the family for whom she worked. House servants worked from sun-up to long past sun-down but they were usually spared the physical hardships of the field hands. Below: Slave quarters offered only the most basic shelter and furnishings.

WORK ROUTINES

The jobs done by slaves varied according to the crops grown in different parts of the state. Those who worked for rice planters were described as having the "hardest work" that slaves could have. The slaves worked long hours in flooded, swampy fields and were bent over most of the time. Each was expected to produce four or five barrels of rice a season. (A barrel weighed about 500 pounds.) It took two acres of land to produce the four or five barrels.

Cotton and tobacco were equally demanding crops. Slaves spent many hours in the hot summer sun "chopping cotton" to remove the never-ending weeds. From August to November, slaves had to pick the cotton by hand, stooping over each plant. Sometimes there were as many as six pickings during the season, because the cotton

Tobacco, the second major crop of the South, was as demanding to grow as cotton. Field hands worked six days a week, from before sunrise to sundown.

ripened gradually instead of all at once.

Field hands worked in the cotton, tobacco, or rice fields six days a week. They started before the sun came up and stayed until sundown. When crops were gathered, both adults and children had a set amount to bring in each day. If a slave did not harvest enough, the owner or overseer might whip or punish him or her in some other way. Owners and overseers always watched slaves to make sure they stayed busy.

Planters kept slaves busy at all times. Besides working in the cotton, tobacco, or rice fields, the slaves also cut down and sawed trees, rolled logs, and cleared vines and underbrush. They also loaded crops on vessels, repaired ditches, and built dikes.

Slave women worked just as hard as slave men. When not working in the fields, they spent much time spinning, sewing, weaving, preparing food, and minding children. Even the children worked, sometimes starting as early as five years old. They shooed chickens out of the garden and flies off the table. The children carried water to the workers in the field, gathered nuts and berries, and collected kindling for fires. They continued working until they were either too old or too sick to be of any use in the fields or the "big house."

THE OVERSEER

To manage the slaves on a day-to-day basis, a slaveholder hired an **overseer.** Overseers on large farms or plantations were paid from $200 to $1,000 a year. Income was based on the size of the farm and the number of slaves. An owner usually gave his overseer the use of a house and a small piece of land.

Many overseers carried whips or other means of punishment to remind slaves to work. The usual punishment for not working was thirty-nine lashes with a cowskin whip. However, the overseer had to know just how often and how such punishment could be administered. A "prime" field hand was worth as much as $1,800, which was a considerable sum of money in those days. Because a severely injured worker was of little use, an owner would dismiss an overseer who was so cruel to slaves as to make them unfit for work. To help them get the various tasks done, overseers used **drivers.** A driver was often an older slave who was loyal to the owner and who could manage the other slaves.

SLAVE FAMILIES

Given the harshness of their lives, the black family proved remarkably strong. The slave community extended far beyond a particular plantation. Slaves who could not find marriage partners on their own plantations often found them on other plantations. Masters encouraged slave women to marry men on adjoining farms or plantations because any children that came from such a union became the property of the woman's master.

Unfortunately, the law did not recognize slave marriages. Even though many masters tried not to separate black families, that tragedy often happened. Changes in a master's life made slaves especially vulnerable. Marriage, death, or relocation in the slaveholder's family were the greatest threats to a slave family's stability. Planters often made presents of slaves to newly married children. In their wills, planters divided slaves among white family members. Slaves were also sold to pay off debts or to remove black troublemakers. When a master warned, "I'm going to put you in my pocket," the master usually was threatening to sell the slave.

Slave children had an all too brief childhood, for by age six they generally joined their parents in the field.

Do You Remember?
1. What did Georgia's original charter say about slavery?
2. What were indentured servants?
3. What port in Georgia was used by slave-trading ships?
4. What was a driver?

RELIGION AND EDUCATION

Blacks took comfort in religion. During the Great Revival that occurred in the early 1800s, most blacks converted to Christianity.

Most large plantations had a church where both slaves and the plantation family attended services on Sunday mornings. The white ministers of these churches gave sermons on the theme "Servants obey your masters." In the slave quarters, black preachers delivered a far different message. Here and wherever slaves were allowed to have church meetings of their own, the black preachers voiced a strong desire for freedom and justice.

Spiritual songs were an important part of slave life. Slaves sang them at church, home, and work. The words gave them comfort and spoke of faith in God and belief in freedom. One of the most plaintive spiritual songs, "Go Down, Moses," is still sung today.

During the Great Revival, black preachers sometimes delivered sermons to mixed audiences. In the same period, black churches began to appear.

Education was almost nonexistent for most slaves. It was against the law for a slave owner to teach any slave to read or write. Some owners, however, recognized that it was useful to have slaves who could read well enough to distinguish labels on barrels of foodstuffs or to be able to write simple messages. In these instances, the slave owner or his wife used the Bible to teach their slaves the basics of reading and writing. However, the slaveholders also feared that slaves who could read and write might also use their talents to stir up discontent among other slaves.

SLAVES OFF THE PLANTATION

Not all slaves worked on a plantation. Close to 500,000 slaves could be found in cities and towns working as skilled artisans. These artisans included potters, weavers, shoemakers, engravers, dressmakers, printers, and woodworkers.

There were also another 500,000 blacks, fairly evenly divided between the North and the South, who were not slaves and were considered free. Free blacks generally were free in name only. Many free blacks suffered under discrimination. (**Discrimination** occurs when people are denied their rights because of prejudice.) They also faced restrictions in voting, owning property, and traveling from one place to another. Free blacks in the South generally could not enter-

SLAVE MUSIC

Music was an integral part of ceremonies and festivals in West African society. The music brought cheer to celebrations and to everyday life. Through slavery, African musical traditions reached the New World.

"Musicianers" played a key role in the slave community as teachers, entertainers, and preservers of African folk culture. Slave musicians played every instrument, and string instruments were prized the most. In the slave community, the fiddle was even more popular than the banjo, which was an African instrument. To be nicknamed "fiddler" was a high honor.

Slaveholders feared African drums and prohibited their use. They believed that drums might be used to signal a slave revolt, as, in fact, they were during the 1739 Stono Rebellion in South Carolina. To preserve the complex rhythms of West Africa, slaves resorted to "Jubba patting," which was hand clapping, body slapping, and foot tapping.

Slaves had many restraints on their freedom of expression and few outlets for their creativity or feelings. Slave songs provided both. The songs were also an "allowed" form of protest. "The songs of the slave," Frederick Douglass wrote, "represent the sorrows of his heart." Often, the songs conveyed images of broken families, the burden of work, and cruel treatment. But just as often they were filled with joy, deliverance, and the hope for a brighter future—even if that future lay in the next world.

African musical traditions were kept alive in the slave community. The fiddler was held in high esteem, and many times his music was accompanied by the hand clapping, body slapping, and foot tapping known as "Jubba patting."

tain slaves in their houses on Sundays or at night, nor could they trade with slaves. Nevertheless, some free blacks who had their own farms or plantations also owned slaves. In some instances, they owned their spouses and children. Black slave owners, needless to say, were few and far between.

The bloodiest slave revolt in American history occurred in 1831, in Virginia. Between fifty-seven and sixty-five white men, women, and children were killed. Nat Turner, a slave preacher, led the uprising, before being captured, put on trial, and hanged.

SLAVE UPRISINGS

As tobacco, cotton, rice, and sugar plantations continued to grow, there soon were many more blacks than whites on large farms and plantations. As a result, the thought of slave unrest frightened slaveholders, who took care to see that slaves anywhere had no chance to rise up against their masters.

It was hard for a group of slaves on one farm to get messages to groups in other places. When slaves left their plantation, they either went with the owner or overseer or had to have a pass. Because passes stated where slaves could go and when they must be back, secret meetings were almost impossible. Moreover, the fugitive slave laws, already implicit in the U. S. Constitution and which would be strengthened later on, required that runaway slaves be returned to their masters.

Other laws, called **slave codes,** took away nearly all the rights of slaves. It was against the law for them to testify against whites, show disrespect to white persons, make any type of physical contact, hit a white, or carry a weapon. On some plantations, overseers counted hoes, pitchforks, and shovels at the end of the day so they could not be kept for use as weapons. Slaves had little time to talk together. They were watched every day except Sundays, and on holidays like Christmas, New Year's Day, and the Fourth of July. Even some free blacks who owned slaves kept a careful eye on them. However, all the attention given by owners was not enough to stop some uprisings.

In 1800, Gabriel Prosser organized a band of several thousand slaves who were unhappy with their conditions. Prosser planned to attack Richmond, Virginia, at midnight on August 30. A few hours before the attack was to begin, two slaves told their owners about the planned uprising. The owners reported it to the authorities. Prosser did not know that he had been betrayed, but as it turned out, he was prevented from invading Richmond by an intense thunderstorm. Nevertheless, Prosser was arrested and executed along with thirty-four others. In 1822, Denmark Vesey, who had bought his freedom, reportedly led a force of 9,000 slaves who were prepared to take Charleston, South Carolina. He too was betrayed, and his plan failed.

In 1831, Nat Turner, who was born in the same year as Prosser's attempted uprising, led the bloodiest slave revolt in American history. Turner was a slave preacher in a Virginia town along the North Carolina border. During attacks he and his followers made in Virginia, between fifty-seven and sixty-five white men, women, and children were killed. Turner and twenty others were killed, but fear of uprisings spread.

ABOLITIONISTS

Many northern whites, some southern whites, and free blacks worked to get rid of slavery. These **abolitionists** made speeches, wrote books and articles, and offered their homes as safe houses for runaway slaves. White abolitionist William Lloyd Garrison published a newspaper called *The Liberator,* which, as its name suggests, urged freedom for all people. In *Uncle Tom's Cabin,* Harriet Beecher Stowe wrote about slaves as individuals rather than as a group. Although Stowe, who grew up in Connecticut, had seen slaves only once when visiting in Kentucky, her book described some of the worst things about slavery and the fugitive slave laws. The book was a huge success, and the information in it caused northerners to like slavery less and abolition more.

The best-known black abolitionist was a former slave, Frederick Douglass, who published a newspaper called the *North Star.* Douglass was also a spirited orator who traveled around the country describing the evils of slavery.

Sojourner Truth, another freed slave, was famous for her speeches, which asked for freedom for all blacks. Other blacks, like Harriet Tubman, helped slaves escape from the South to free states in the North and to Canada. Tubman was a leader in the **underground railroad,** a chain of homes, farms, and churches where runaway slaves could rest and hide from slave catchers. These slaves, either alone or in small groups, moved from place to place at night until they reached a free state or crossed the border into Canada. Tubman, and others like her, helped up to 50,000 slaves escape through the underground railroad between 1830 and 1860. Tubman personally led over 300 slaves to freedom.

GEORGIANS' FEELINGS TOWARD SLAVERY

Less than 40 percent of white Georgians owned any slaves during antebellum days, but the worth of Georgia's slaves ran into millions of dollars. Some whites in Georgia spoke out against slavery.

For forty years Sojourner Truth spoke out against slavery and for women's rights.

However, most of them simply accepted it as a way of life. Some thought that through slavery they were helping to care for blacks. Others said slavery allowed whites to teach blacks about Christianity.

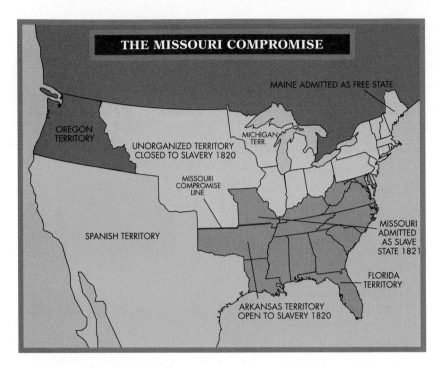

THE MISSOURI COMPROMISE

MAINE ADMITTED AS FREE STATE

OREGON TERRITORY

UNORGANIZED TERRITORY CLOSED TO SLAVERY 1820

MICHIGAN TERR.

MISSOURI COMPROMISE LINE

SPANISH TERRITORY

MISSOURI ADMITTED AS SLAVE STATE 1821

FLORIDA TERRITORY

ARKANSAS TERRITORY OPEN TO SLAVERY 1820

The Missouri Compromise of 1820 cooled the heated rhetoric over slavery for a short time, but the issue arose again in the 1820s and the 1830s.

THE MISSOURI COMPROMISE

The first serious disagreement between proslavery and antislavery forces was related to the distribution of power in Congress. By the end of 1819, there were eleven slave states and eleven free states. The number of members a state had in the United States House of Representatives depended on its population. Because population in the North was growing at a faster pace than in the South, southerners were afraid that northern states would soon have more influence in Congress.

In 1820, as Maine and Missouri prepared to enter the Union, Congress had to decide whether the future states would be admitted as **slave states** (states that permitted slavery) or **free states** (states that did not permit slavery).

When the Territory of Missouri applied for admission to the Union, it had about 2,000 slaves. While the House of Representatives considered the bill to admit Missouri, a New York representative, James Tallmadge, added an amendment requiring that Missouri abolish slavery. The House approved the bill with Tallmadge's amendment. The vote showed the free states voting for the amendment and the slave states voting against it. The Senate, where the votes of the free states and the slave states were equal, rejected the bill.

The disagreement over slavery became heated and pitted free states against slave states. After much discussion, northern and southern congressional leaders reached a compromise. Under the Compromise of 1820, which became known as the **Missouri Compromise,** Maine came into the Union as a free state and Missouri was admitted as a slave state. The Compromise stated there would be no slavery north of 36° 20' latitude, an area that included any lands west of the southern boundary of Missouri. For the time being, the question of slavery was at rest, but it was only a temporary solution to the questions of slavery and territorial rights.

THE ANTISLAVERY AND WOMEN'S RIGHTS MOVEMENTS

The religious revivals of the early 1800s led to a spirit of reform in the United States. Men and women increasingly began to address what they saw as the ills of society. In the 1830s, women became more involved with the antislavery movement. As they did, women realized the similarities between the oppression of slaves and the oppression of women.

Most men, however, would not accept women as equals in the movement, and women faced growing hostility for stepping out of their "place" in society. At the World Anti-Slavery Convention held in London in 1840, two American women delegates, Elizabeth Cady Stanton and Lucretia Mott, were refused permission to participate. Infuriated, they vowed to "form a society to advocate the rights of women" when they returned home.

Their vow resulted in the Seneca Falls Women's Rights Convention held in July 1848. A three-sentence announcement of the meeting to discuss "the social, civil, and religious rights of women" drew over three hundred people. Those attending adopted a 12-point Declaration of Sentiments, modeled after the Declaration of Independence. It detailed the injustices women had suffered; demanded the end of women's exclusion from trades, professions, and commerce; and denounced educational discrimination and unequal legal rights, including the right to vote. From this beginning, the women's rights movement spread across the country. However, after 1850, the country become more and more focused on the issue of slavery, and it was not until 1920 that women won the right to vote.

Elizabeth Cady Stanton (seated above), seen here with another pioneer of the women's rights movement, Susan B. Anthony, was refused permission to participate at an antislavery convention in London in 1840.

Do You Remember?

1. What were free blacks?
2. Who wrote *Uncle Tom's Cabin*?
3. Who was Harriet Tubman?
4. What percentage of Georgians owned slaves during the antebellum period?

A second cause of strife between the different parts of the nation was sectionalism. **Sectionalism** refers to a concept in which people in any given area think their ideas and interests are correct and more important than those of people in any other region. For example, in the 1850s, most northerners thought the federal government could pass laws for all the nation's citizens. They felt, if a law was bad, only the United States Supreme Court could have it removed. On the other hand, most southerners believed in states' rights, an idea that assumes that powers not given to the federal government in the Constitution belong to each state. To them, the principle of states' rights meant states could ignore federal laws that took away their rights.

Although people in the North and South as a whole disagreed on the institution of slavery, there was some degree of acceptance of each point of view. However, when westward expansion led to new territories requesting admission to the Union as either free or slave states, the issue of slavery could no longer avoid some kind of resolution.

THE COMPROMISE OF 1850

In 1848, gold was discovered at Sutter's Mill in California. People from all over the nation moved west to find gold. By late 1849, the population of California was over 100,000, enough to ask for statehood. In 1850, there were fifteen slave states and fifteen free states. California's constitution did not allow slavery. If California became a state, the balance in the Senate between slave states and free states would change. For eight months, what later came to be called "The Great Debate" raged as Congress tried to agree on what to do about California.

Seeing that these hotly debated issues might disrupt the Union, Senator Henry Clay of Kentucky proposed a compromise bill in early 1850. Strong leaders on both sides opposed certain parts of this bill. Senator John C. Calhoun of South Carolina would not accept any limits on slavery. President Zachary Taylor would not sign any bill that tied California statehood to other issues. It looked as though compromise was dead and the Union in danger. Instead, death took both men, Calhoun in March and Taylor in July. The new president, Millard Fillmore, favored the compromise.

Clay's **Compromise of 1850** was thus passed by Congress. The compromise offered something to please both North and South. For the North, there were three positive points. California came into the Union as a free state. Slave trading was ended in the District of Columbia. And Texas gave up its idea of annexing New Mexico, thus making the territory a part of a slave state.

Senator John C. Calhoun of South Carolina was opposed to Senator Clay's Compromise of 1850. He wanted slavery protected in the territories. His death in 1850 helped make compromise possible.

The South also gained three benefits. The territories of New Mexico and Utah would determine whether they wanted to be slave or free. The residents of the District of Columbia could keep the slaves they already had. Finally, Congress would pass a law stating that slaves who ran away to free states would be returned to their owners.

Senator Henry Clay of Kentucky was a Senate leader in 1850. Here, he urges the Senate to pass compromise legislation in order to preserve the Union.

KANSAS-NEBRASKA ACT

The slavery issue, however, would not die. People moved into the grassy plains west of Missouri and Iowa and needed territorial government. In 1854, Stephen Douglas of Illinois brought about passage of the **Kansas-Nebraska Act,** which created the territories of Kansas and Nebraska and which contained a clause on popular sovereignty. **Popular sovereignty** meant that when a territory asked for statehood, the people of that territory could vote to decide if they wanted to be a free or slave state. Northerners were angry because this law changed the Compromise of 1820, which did not permit slavery north of Missouri's southern boundary.

Most people in the new territories belonged to one of two groups: proslavery and free soil. **Free soilers** were against slavery and also wanted land to be given to western settlers for farming. After Congress passed the Kansas-Nebraska Act, fights broke out between proslavery and free soil groups. Abolitionists in other states promised to send antislavery settlers with guns into Kansas so they could oppose slavery. Missouri proslavery people promised to send men across the border to fight for slavery.

The result was such violence between the two sides that the territory was called "Bleeding Kansas." When Congress rejected Kansas's bid for statehood, southerners again realized that northern votes alone could keep slave states from the Union.

DRED SCOTT DECISION

In 1834, Dred Scott, a slave, was taken by his owner from the slave state of Missouri to the free state of Illinois. Later they went to Wisconsin, another free state. When Scott and his master returned to Missouri, Scott filed a lawsuit claiming he was free since he had lived in a free state. Abolitionists from the North raised enough money to take the case to the United States Supreme Court. In March 1857, the Supreme Court ruled on the case. The justices said Scott could not sue because he was a slave, and slaves were not citizens. The Court also said Congress had no right to stop slavery in territories. The Dred Scott decision further divided the North and South, and pushed them closer to war.

JOHN BROWN'S RAID

White abolitionist John Brown hated slavery. In 1859, he decided to try to help slaves in the South become free of their owners. To do this, Brown needed guns and ammunition.

Brown led a party of twenty-one men, blacks as well as whites, in a raid on the federal **arsenal** (arms storehouse) at Harpers Ferry, Virginia (now in West Virginia). They killed the mayor and made prisoners of forty citizens. Then Brown and his men took over a building at the railroad station. Within twenty-four hours, troops led by Colonel Robert E. Lee captured Brown. Two months later, the state of Virginia tried Brown for treason and sentenced him to be hanged. Not long before he died, Brown wrote to his family and said he was as content ". . . to die for God's eternal truth on the scaffold as in any other way."

Southerners thought John Brown was a murderer, and they were afraid others would try to lead slaves to rise up against owners. Many northerners were against the killings committed by Brown and his fellow raiders, but they saw Brown as a hero. Henry Wadsworth

Although he could neither read nor write, Dred Scott persevered in presenting his case all the way to the United States Supreme Court where the Dred Scott decision became a vital part of our nation's history.

Longfellow wrote, "This will be a great day in our history, the date of a new revolution. . . . As I write, they are leading old John Brown to execution. . . . This is sowing the wind to reap the whirlwind which will come soon."

Do You Remember?
1. What is sectionalism?
2. What is the definition of states' rights?
3. What senator led the fight against the Compromise of 1850?
4. Why was the Dred Scott decision important?

John Brown, a fanatical abolitionist, led an attack on the U.S. arsenal at Harper's Ferry. He intended to arm nearby slaves so they could fight for their freedom.

ECONOMIC CONSIDERATIONS

In addition to slavery and sectional differences, there were striking economic contrasts between the North and the South, including the major sources of their wealth. Because of these vastly different sources, the North and the South also disagreed on trade policies and restraints.

AGRICULTURE VERSUS INDUSTRY

The economy of the North was based on industry. A cold climate and short growing season in the New England states meant there was little profit in farming. Northerners worked in factories, mines, banks, stores, and on railroads to take care of their families. The railroad system carried industrial products to other parts of the country.

The South, on the other hand, depended on agriculture. Cotton and tobacco were the two main crops, but there were also rice plantations on the Georgia and South Carolina coasts. Even though cotton was King in the South, southerners shipped most of it to northern states where mills made thread and cloth. In 1850, there were 564 mills in New England. These mills employed 61,893 workers and

Although cotton was the most profitable crop in antebellum Georgia, the cultivation of rice was important along the coastal area. Here you see a picture of a rice plantation on the Altamaha River near Darien, owned by the Butler family. How do you think life on a cotton plantation might have differed from life on a rice plantation?

had a value of over $58 million. In the South, there were only 166 mills, with 10,043 workers and a value of $7.25 million. In fact, the antebellum South manufactured only 10 percent of the nation's goods. Few farmers and planters were interested in factories.

TARIFFS

Tariffs, or taxes on goods, were another source of conflict between the North and the South. Northern states wanted foreign countries that shipped goods to the United States to pay high tariffs. With high tariffs, items made in the North would cost less than imported ones. For example, a suit made and sold in Boston might cost $50. With an import tax of $20, an identical suit made in England and sold in Boston might cost $70.

Southern states had fewer factories and, therefore, bought many manufactured goods from foreign countries. Southerners did not want the prices they paid made higher by tariffs on imported goods.

In 1832, South Carolina threatened to secede from the Union because a new tariff was too high. South Carolinians began to arm themselves and hold practice drills. President Andrew Jackson asked Congress to allow him to take an army into South Carolina and force acceptance of the tariff. Instead, Congress passed a compromise tariff law, written by Henry Clay, which reduced the tariff over a ten-year period. The compromise pleased South Carolina, and their protests ended.

The differences over tariffs became worse when a depression, known as the Panic of 1857, hit the country. Before that time, many northern industrialists built their factories with borrowed money. Nearly five thousand of them went bankrupt during the depression. The factory owners asked Congress to pass higher tariffs to stop the British from shipping goods to the United States. Because there were so few factories in the South, the depression did not hurt southerners as badly. Their representatives, therefore, refused to support higher tariffs. The debates that followed further damaged feelings between the North and South.

In 1850, there were 564 mills in New England, employing 61,893 workers. In the South, there were only 166 mills, with 10,043 workers. The South manufactured only 10 percent of the nation's goods.

Do You Remember?
1. On what was the economy of the North based?
2. What percent of the nation's industrial goods were manufactured in the South?
3. Why did southerners not want higher tariffs?

Wearing the latest in fashion was only a part of the Northern lifestyle in the 1860s. Culture, education, and entertainment were also important parts of the lifestyle, and they all differed from the customs of the South.

The contrasts in the way people lived in the two sections of the country also added to the mistrust and misunderstanding that increased between North and South. The differences were most striking in the lifestyles and social structures of each section.

LIFESTYLES

Part of the reason for the differences in their lifestyles stems from the way in which each section developed. The North had several large cities, including New York, Philadelphia, Washington, Boston, and Chicago. People who lived there could visit museums or attend operas, lectures, or the theater. They might spend evenings at large dinner parties, receptions, and dances. Horse racing, already known in the South, and baseball became popular sports.

In the South, the rural lifestyle affected most things done for pleasure. There were few chances to attend lectures, concerts, or the theater except in towns such as Charleston, Richmond, Savannah, and Augusta. The actual day-to-day lives of planters were rarely like those depicted in movies such as *Gone with the Wind*. The planters had little time for parties and dances except on holidays when both whites and blacks had fewer duties. Most other times, they spent what little time they had away from work attending revivals, quilting bees, and hunting and horse racing parties. This quiet and predictable lifestyle stayed much the same from month to month. Whenever the sameness of the routine was broken up by, for example, the arrival in the area of a group of traveling performers, it was an exciting moment for everyone.

Although many house parties were given by the plantation owners, less is known about those held in the towns and cities. One party that has been recorded took place in 1850 at the Atlanta home of a Mrs. Mulligan. The party was to celebrate the laying of a wooden floor on top of the dirt floor in her cabin. According to reports, ale flowed freely; greased pig chases provided fun for both youngsters and adults; and hay rides were enjoyed by the young people. Guests danced until dawn, and a good time was had by all who attended. It was such a good time that soon all of the other women began to demand wooden floors in their houses. They, too, honored the occasion by holding even bigger celebration parties than Mrs. Mulligan's.

CLASS STRUCTURE

When used in reference to groups of people, **class structure** means the position one group has in relation to others. In the antebellum South, social classes were important. Most of the social structure of the South was based on land and slaves, and it was hard to move from one social class to another. A small but influential group of planters were at the top of the social ladder. Following them was the largest antebellum social group, the middle class. This included **yeoman farmers,** small farmers who owned less than five hundred acres of land; doctors; ministers; lawyers; and artisans. Next came poor whites who either owned very small farms, were seasonal laborers for planters or other farmers, or worked at low-paying jobs. Blacks and whites alike called a subclass of this group "poor white trash." These were drifters who could not read and write and who often lived on what other people gave them. Blacks were at the bottom of the South's class system, and there were social differences among them too. In the slave population, there was a difference between blacks who were house servants and those who worked in the fields. Slaves admired free blacks and wanted to be like them. Some free blacks owned farms and slaves, but most lived and worked in larger cities.

In the North, class structure was more often tied to wealth than to anything else. As a result, it was easier for people to move from one class to another. Many of the people worked in industry. Each of them had about the same chance to go to school, travel, and take part in cultural activities. Where there were separate classes, these classes seemed to be based on money more than on the group into which a person was born. By 1860, most people in the North did not understand or like the southern social system. Southerners, however, were not ready to change their lifestyle, especially for one they considered inferior to their own.

During the days before the Civil War, social life in the South was at a much slower pace than that of the North. Many social activities centered around farm life. Southerners used events like corn shucking to catch up on news and socialize while helping neighbors with the harvest.

Do You Remember?

1. Where were the cultural differences between the North and the South the most striking?
2. On what was the social structure of the South based?
3. What was the largest social group in the antebellum South?

As you learned in the last chapter, during the early part of the ante-bellum period, Georgians worked hard to get Indians removed from the state in order to obtain their land. After that was accomplished, the citizens of the state turned their full attention to other interests.

GEORGIA'S ECONOMY

The backbone of Georgia's economy was agriculture. By 1860, there were 68,000 farms in the state, and cotton was the main crop. The farms produced 700,000 bales of cotton in 1860. This was an increase from 326,000 bales in 1839. Most of Georgia's 31,000 farmers had less than one hundred acres of land. Only 3,500 farms had five hundred acres or more and could be called plantations. Because the land itself did not cost much, a plantation owner's worth was largely measured by the number of slaves he owned. Only 236 Georgians owned more than 100 slaves, and 60 percent had no slaves at all.

Just before the Civil War, half of Georgia's total wealth, or $400 million, was in slaves. In 1845, a prime field hand cost $600 but, by 1860, the price had risen to $1,800. In major slave markets, such as those in Savannah, Augusta, Macon, or Louisville, the monetary worth of a slave was determined by the cost of a pound of cotton. A planter had to sell 16,500 pounds of processed cotton to buy such a slave, and he bought the slave to increase his cotton production.

Most manufacturing in Georgia grew out of agriculture. The state had about forty cotton mills in the area where cotton was grown. There were also a few tanneries, shoe factories, iron foundries, grist mills, and brick and pottery factories. All told, Georgia had 1,890 factories by 1860 with a value of about $11 million. Even then, Georgia's in-dustrial base was far smaller than that of a comparable northern state.

TRANSPORTATION

For most of the early 1800s, little had changed in the way that people and cargo were transported both in Georgia and the rest of the South. Travel was still a time-consuming affair. Georgians trav-eled on horseback or in horse-drawn vehicles on the dirt roads and turnpikes that connected many of the communities in the state. Merchants and farmers also used these overland transportation methods to ship merchandise and agricultural products.

It took sixteen mules hitched to a wagon to pull the first locomotive, the Florida, *and two coach cars through miles of woods and over rough trails to the tiny town of Terminus, the terminal point of the Georgia railroad. Terminus later changed its name to Atlanta.*

Opposite page: Westville, near Lumpkin, recreates a Georgia town of 1850. **Top:** A demonstration of bootmaking. **Right:** A prosperous merchant's home. **Above:** A doctor's office.

The Stewart County Academy, built in 1832, is typical of county schools of the period. It has been reconstructed at Westville, near Lumpkin.

Travelers also could make use of the state's extensive river system and, by the late 1820s, the improved steamboats that had just come into fashion. The steamboats also carried cargo as did the slow-moving, flat-bottom barges and other river vessels.

Although river travel was certainly faster than overland travel, it did have a major drawback. River transportation was suitable only for transporting people or goods either north or south within the state. Most major rivers in Georgia, you may recall, flow from the north to the south. Transportation east or west still involved the snail's pace of the existing overland methods.

In 1825, the first railroad engine was built in England. Here at last was a promise of rapid overland travel. By the 1830s, the call for trains was heard everywhere in America, and Georgia was no exception. By 1833, a railroad line ran from Charleston, South Carolina, to Augusta. A second line, completed in 1843, went from Savannah to Macon. A few years later, the Western and Atlantic connected the Chattahoochee River at what is now Atlanta to Chattanooga, Tennessee.

By 1860, there were 1,226 miles of railroad tracks in the state. Railroads were often poorly built and frequently needed repairs. Still, they were necessary to the state's economy because growers were able to ship cotton by train to seaports or mills in the North.

EDUCATION

Education was not an important element in the lives of most antebellum Georgians. Some sons of wealthy planters had teachers in their homes or went to private academies. However, most Georgians had little education.

"Old field schools," built on fields that were no longer used, dotted the state. Members of a community built a school, hired the teacher, and bought a few books and supplies. Most students in old field schools attended only two or three years and learned basic reading, writing, and arithmetic.

In 1850, about 20 percent of Georgia's whites could not read or write. About half of Georgia's children were black and did not go to school at all. In 1858, the state legislature, using income from the state-owned Western and Atlantic Railroad, set aside $100,000 to

begin free schools. Before plans were finished, the war started and education was laid aside.

There were other developments in the field of education during the 1850s. In 1851, Georgia Military Institute was founded in Marietta. In the same year, the Georgia Academy for the Blind was begun in Macon. Later, in 1859, Joseph Lumpkin and Thomas Cobb founded Georgia's first law school in Athens.

Schoolrooms in the antebellum period, like the Stewart County Academy at Westville, were a far cry from today. Students of all ages were taught together in one room with limited materials.

RELIGION

Like many others in the South, Georgians were caught up in the Great Revival movement of the early 1800s. During the 1850s, church membership grew in Georgia; by 1860, there were 2,393 churches in the state. In the South, Georgia was second only to Virginia in the number of churches. Methodists and Baptists continued to have more members than any other group. The Episcopal, Catholic, and Presbyterian churches also grew. Jews, one of Georgia's earliest religious groups during settlement days, were small in number, but they added to the state's religious diversity. There were a few segregated churches, but slaves usually attended the same churches as their masters.

Climax Church, originally in Lumpkin, was built in 1850. Churches like this were the center of religious, civic, and social activity in the antebellum South. The church has been reconstructed at Westville.

Slavery caused great divisiveness among some denominations. Methodists in the South pulled out of their national organization and formed the Methodist Episcopal Church. In 1845, southern Baptists met in Augusta to begin the Southern Baptist Convention. Baptists in the South left the American Baptist Union when its foreign mission board would not accept slave owners as missionaries.

Religious revivals, often in the form of camp meetings, were popular, especially among Methodists. Sometimes people came from miles away and camped while attending a two- or three-day meeting. Often, the camp meetings lasted for a week or longer.

GEORGIA POLITICS

It was hard to keep up with political changes in Georgia during the twenty years before the state left the Union. In the 1840s, the two major political parties were Democrats and Whigs.

Democrats were for states' rights and took a strong stand for slavery. Their leaders were Herschel V. Johnson, Joseph E. Brown, and U.S. Congressman Howell Cobb.

Whigs were mostly members of the upper social classes. They favored a moderate protective tariff and federal help for the South. Robert Toombs and Alexander H. Stephens, both congressmen from Georgia, led the Whigs.

Although there was little real difference in what the two parties believed, each wanted to govern the state. During the 1840s, most governors were Democrats, while most members of the legislature were Whigs. In larger Georgia towns, there were two newspapers: one for Democrats and one for Whigs.

The 1850s brought about a change for both parties. Many Georgians did not like the Compromise of 1850. However, Democrat Cobb and Whigs Stephens and Toombs asked the citizens of Georgia to accept it. All three had been strong backers of the measure in the U.S. Congress. Cobb, in fact, was the speaker of the U.S. House of Representatives in 1849 and 1850. In part because of the persuasiveness of these congressmen, the "Georgia Platform" supporting the compromise was adopted at a convention held in the state capital of Milledgeville. It was clear even to Georgians who did not approve of it that the compromise was necessary if the state were to stay in the Union.

Not long after the platform was adopted, some Georgians formed the Constitutional Union party. Howell Cobb, an Athens lawyer who had been a Democrat, joined the new party along with former Whigs Stephens and Toombs. Cobb was elected governor in 1851. While he was in office, Cobb encouraged the growth of Georgia's railroad system and state support for schools.

At this same time, Joseph E. Brown, Herschel V. Johnson, and C. B. Strong gathered together some Georgians who did not agree with the Compromise of 1850. This group formed the States' Rights party. The party did not want to leave the Union, but its members felt southern states should not accept the Compromise until Congress agreed to protect slavery and states' rights.

Left: As governor of Georgia from 1851-1853, Howell Cobb approved the leasing of the state-owned Western and Atlantic Railroad and worked for increased state funding for education. In 1857, he became secretary of the treasury under President Buchanan but he resigned in 1860. Shortly thereafter, he became president of the Provisional Congress of the Confederacy. *Above:* As the only Georgia governor to serve four successive terms, Joseph E. Brown was a strong pro-slavery and states' rights proponent. Like many other Georgia politicians of the period, Brown favored secession and used his terms as governor to prepare the state for war.

*Above: The state capitol at Milledgeville. Milledgeville was Georgia's state capital from 1807 to 1867. The town was laid out in 1803 to serve as the seat of the state's government. It was named after John Milledge, Georgia's governor at that time and a former Revolutionary War hero. During its peak, Milledgeville was a cultural center of the state. **Opposite page:** This reconstruction of the old state capitol now houses a military academy.*

The Constitutional Union party broke up in August 1852. It had done what it set out to do: get Georgians to accept the Compromise of 1850. Toombs and Stephens joined the Democrats, while other Whigs joined the Know-Nothing party. The **Know-Nothing party** did not want immigrants to become citizens or anyone not born in the United States to hold political office. It was a secret group whose members answered questions with "I don't know," thus the name Know-Nothing.

After all the changes, the Democrats became the leading party. In 1856, James Buchanan, the Democratic presidential candidate, carried Georgia with no trouble. The next year, Democrat Joseph E. Brown became governor. Brown believed in states' rights and was also a good manager. He brought about railroad reforms and used money from state-owned railroads to begin a Common School Fund for public education. Brown was re-elected in 1859, and he served two more terms during the Civil War.

Do You Remember?

1. What was the name of the railroad that first connected Chattanooga to Atlanta?
2. Where was Georgia's first law school opened?
3. What were the two main church denominations in Georgia during this period?
4. What high position did Howell Cobb hold in the U.S. House of Representatives?

MORE NORTH-SOUTH DIVISION

By 1860, the division between the North and the South had become sharper and more vocal on a number of major issues, and the prospect for reconciling these differences was getting dimmer and dimmer. In addition to the various sectional problems that separated the North and South, new events on the national scene increased the tensions between the two sections. Chief among these were the rise of a new national party and the election in 1860 of its standard bearer.

THE RISE OF THE REPUBLICAN PARTY

Measures such as the Missouri Compromise and the Kansas-Nebraska Act had a significant effect on political parties. Up to this time, the major parties had been national ones. But this was soon to change. Just as it had in Georgia, the Whig party began to break up after the election of 1852. The northern wing of the party had become more antislavery and was less willing to compromise with the southern wing to keep internal peace.

The result was the creation in 1854 of a new political party—one that only existed in free states. This new party was called the **Republican party.** It grew quickly, attracting antislavery Whigs and Democrats. In 1856, the Republicans nominated John C. Fremont for president on a platform that opposed the spread of slavery. Democrat James Buchanan won, but Fremont managed to get 1.3 million votes.

THE ELECTION OF 1860

When the Democrats met in Charleston, South Carolina, for the national convention in 1860, a fight over the party platform brought matters to a head. (A **platform** is a statement of the principles and policies the party supports.) The supporters of Stephen A. Douglas of Illinois controlled the platform committee. They wanted to campaign on the issue of popular sovereignty. Southern Democrats did not agree and felt slaves should be allowed in all the territories. The two groups split over the issue. Northern Democrats nominated Stephen Douglas for president. Southern Democrats met separately in Baltimore and nominated Vice President John Breckinridge of Kentucky. Whigs from the border states also met in Baltimore to form the Constitutional Union party. They supported the Union and named John Bell of Tennessee as their candidate.

At the same time, the Republicans met in Chicago, where they nominated Abraham Lincoln, Illinois' "favorite son." The Republican platform was not just antislavery, although the party said it would not try to end slavery in the slave states. The platform supported a protective tariff, proposed a plan to give free western land to settlers, and

After the Democratic Party split during the National Convention in 1860, northern Democrats nominated Stephen A. Douglas (top) for president, while southern Democrats nominated John C. Breckinridge (above) of Kentucky.

GRACE BEDELL

As the story goes, in 1860, eleven-year-old Grace Bedell from Westfield, New York, saw a campaign poster of a beardless Abraham Lincoln. Grace thought Lincoln looked far too "homely" to win the election. She sat down and wrote him the following letter:

I hope you won't think me bold to write to such a great man as you are, but want you should be President of the United States very much. . . . I have got 4 brothers and part of them will vote for you any way, and if you will let your whiskers grow I will try to get the rest of them to vote for you [sic]. You would look a great deal better for your face is so thin. All the ladies like whiskers and they would tease their husbands to vote for you and then you would be President.

It thrilled Grace when she received a handwritten note from Lincoln. He replied, "As to the whiskers, having never worn any, do you not think people would call it a silly piece of affec[ta]tion if I were to begin it now?" Shortly after Lincoln won the election, he began to grow a beard.

As Lincoln traveled from Illinois to Washington for his inauguration, he stopped the train in Grace's hometown, where he received a warm welcome. It pleased the townspeople when Lincoln mentioned the letter Grace had written him and asked to meet her. A young man in the crowd pointed to an embarrassed Grace Bedell. Lincoln walked over and gave the child "several hearty kisses."

The next time you see a picture of bearded Abraham Lincoln, remember that an eleven-year-old girl influenced history.

Lincoln's gaunt features caused many jokes and cartoons before he grew a beard.

called for the construction of a transcontinental railroad with one end in the North. None of these measures would benefit the South. The Republican party and its presidential candidate, Abraham Lincoln, appeared to be against everything southerners wanted.

The election amounted to a revolution in politics. For the first time, a party getting votes from only one section of the nation won the election. Abraham Lincoln received 1.9 million votes (a minority of the votes cast) and was elected president. Douglas had 1.4 million votes,

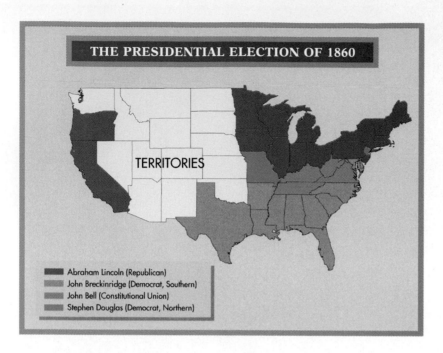

THE PRESIDENTIAL ELECTION OF 1860

TERRITORIES

- Abraham Lincoln (Republican)
- John Breckinridge (Democrat, Southern)
- John Bell (Constitutional Union)
- Stephen Douglas (Democrat, Northern)

The presidential election of 1860 split the country along sectional lines. Compare this map with the map of the original seven Confederate states on the facing page.

while Breckinridge had 850,000 and Bell 590,000. Almost all of Lincoln's electoral votes were from the free states. He won without receiving a single electoral vote from the states in the South.

GEORGIA REACTS TO LINCOLN'S ELECTION

After Lincoln's election to the presidency in November 1860, talk of secession and war swirled around every barbecue, quilting bee, and picnic. Wherever Georgians gathered, passionate debates took place. For eighty-four years, the nation had lived with the concept of a union of all states. Now southerners had to deal with questions over the conflict between states' rights and Union rights. Could they believe in the concept of the Union while maintaining a state's right to pass laws for the good of that state rather than to accept laws forced on a state by the federal government? There was no easy answer to the question. Georgians were, for the most part, for the Union; however, they were even more strongly for states' rights. Now they were suddenly forced to make a choice, and many households in Georgia found themselves in the midst of a bitter split.

THE CALL TO THE LEGISLATORS

Immediately after Lincoln's election, Georgia's Democratic governor, Joseph E. Brown, called for a legislative session to determine whether a special convention should be held to decide the question of **secession** (the act of pulling out of the Union). The special session could also suggest that Georgia bide its time and see what South Carolina would do. The legislative chamber was buzzing with activity as arguments resounded off the walls and memos and notes were passed back and forth. Speakers rose in quick succession to argue their views. Alexander Stephens of Crawfordville was especially stirring with his arguments against seceding.

...The first question that presents itself is, shall the people of Georgia secede from the Union in consequence of the election of Mr. Lincoln to the Presidency of the United States. My countrymen, I tell you

frankly, candidly, and earnestly, that I do not think they ought. In my judgment, the election of no man, constitutionally chosen to that high office, is sufficient cause to justify any State to separate from the Union. It ought to stand by and aid still in maintaining the Constitution of the country. . . .

Whatever fate is to befall this country, let it never be laid to the charge of the people of the South, and especially the people of Georgia, that we were untrue to our national engagements. Let the fault and the wrong rest upon others. If all our hopes are to be blasted, if the Republic is to go down, let us be found to the last moment standing on the deck with the Constitution of the United States waving over heads. . . .

THE ORIGINAL CONFEDERATE STATES

The original seven states that made up the Confederate States of America (C.S.A.) were South Carolina, Georgia, Alabama, Mississippi, Florida, Louisiana, and Texas. Eventually the C.S.A. would consist of eleven states.

Although Stephens' speech was interrupted many times by Robert Toombs, who along with Thomas Cobb strongly supported immediate secession, other conservative legislators loudly applauded Stephens' pleas for caution. But his eloquence was no match for the fiery leadership of Toombs, Cobb, and Governor Brown. On November 21, 1860, Governor Brown called for a Secession Convention.

SOUTH CAROLINA SECEDES

Other southerners, convinced that with the election of Lincoln Congress would not allow slavery in the territories, also were calling for definitive action. South Carolinians had been quite vocal about their feelings before the November election. They had repeatedly said that they would secede if Lincoln won the presidency. In December 1860, South Carolina held a state convention to talk about seceding from the Union and forming a separate government. On December 20, 1860, a little more than a month after Lincoln's election, South Carolina left the Union. Soon after, extremists in every other southern state were loudly yelling to follow South Carolina's lead.

Most Georgians supported South Carolina's action. On January 16, 1861, the special convention requested by Governor Brown was held in Milledgeville. When Eugenius Nisbet proposed a secession

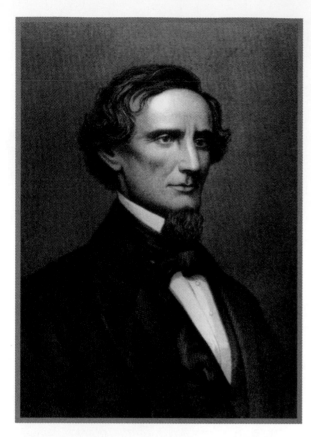

ordinance (bill) to the 297 delegates, 208 voted in favor. On January 19, 1861, Georgia was declared an independent republic with the following words: "The people of Georgia, having dissolved their political connection with the Government of the United States of America, present to their confederates and the world, the causes which have led to the separation."

By February 1, 1861, Florida, Alabama, Mississippi, Louisiana, and Texas had also voted to secede from the Union. On February 4, 1861, delegates from each of these states met in Montgomery, Alabama, and formed themselves into a new nation called the **Confederate States of America.** Jefferson Davis of Mississippi was elected president, and Robert Toombs of Georgia secretary of state. Georgian Alexander Stephens, who had argued so passionately against secession, was named vice president.

War was only two months away.

Above: At the age of fifty-two, Jefferson Davis was elected president of the Confederate States of America on February 9, 1861. **Opposite page:** *Born in Wilkes County in 1812, Alexander Stephens served as both a state senator and representative. In addition, he represented Georgia in the U. S. Congress. Many southerners opposed Alexander Stephens' selection as the Confederate vice president for he had openly spoken against secession from the Union in the days prior to the outbreak of the Civil War.*

Do You Remember?

1. Why were southerners against Lincoln's election to the presidency?
2. When was Abraham Lincoln elected president?
3. Which state seceded from the Union first?
4. What was the name the seceding states gave their new nation?

SUMMARY

- As the antebellum period drew to a close, differences between the North and South intensified.
- The issue that aroused the strongest passions was slavery.
- Slave traders bought or captured blacks in Africa and sold them as slaves in North America.
- The daily life of slaves was one of hard work and harsh treatment.
- Several slave revolts were attempted, but none were successful.
- The first serious disagreement between proslavery and antislavery forces was temporarily resolved by the Missouri Compromise of 1820; however, there would be others of increasing intensity and bad feelings.
- Other issues that divided North and South were sectionalism, economic considerations, cultural differences, and states' rights.
- Finally, national events, especially the election of Abraham Lincoln, caused southern states, including Georgia, to secede from the Union and form the Confederate States of America.

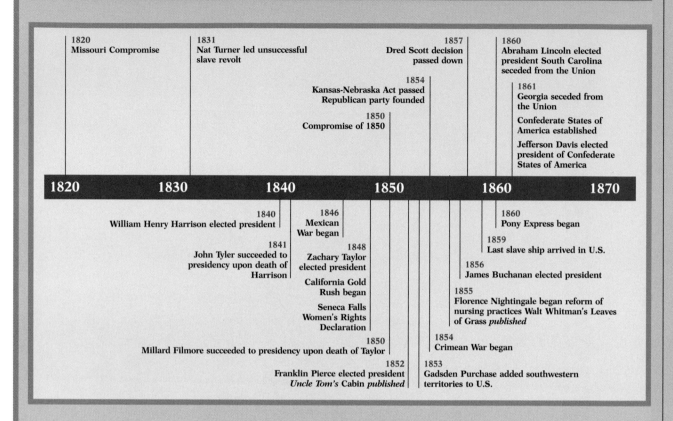

Timeline:

1820 Missouri Compromise

1831 Nat Turner led unsuccessful slave revolt

1857 Dred Scott decision passed down

1860 Abraham Lincoln elected president South Carolina seceded from the Union

1854 Kansas-Nebraska Act passed Republican party founded

1850 Compromise of 1850

1861 Georgia seceded from the Union

Confederate States of America established

Jefferson Davis elected president of Confederate States of America

| 1820 | 1830 | 1840 | 1850 | 1860 | 1870 |

1840 William Henry Harrison elected president

1846 Mexican War began

1860 Pony Express began

1841 John Tyler succeeded to presidency upon death of Harrison

1848 Zachary Taylor elected president

California Gold Rush began

Seneca Falls Women's Rights Declaration

1859 Last slave ship arrived in U.S.

1856 James Buchanan elected president

1855 Florence Nightingale began reform of nursing practices Walt Whitman's Leaves of Grass *published*

1850 Millard Filmore succeeded to presidency upon death of Taylor

1854 Crimean War began

1852 Franklin Pierce elected president *Uncle Tom's* Cabin *published*

1853 Gadsden Purchase added southwestern territories to U.S.

Reviewing People, Places, and Terms

Match each word or phrase with the correct definition below.

> antebellum
> class structure
> discrimination
> driver
> overseer
> platform
> slave code

1. A person responsible for seeing that slaves performed their assigned tasks
2. A set of laws that defined what slaves could or could not do
3. The period before the Civil War
4. A slave placed in charge of a group of slaves
5. Actions that deny people their rights because of prejudice
6. The position one group has in relation to other groups
7. A statement of the principles and policies that a political party supports

Understanding the Facts

1. When did the institution of slavery begin in North America?
2. What types of blacks did slave traders try to capture?
3. On what was the income of an overseer based?
4. Why did slave owners encourage slave women to marry slave men on adjoining plantations?
5. Approximately how many free blacks were there during the antebellum period?
6. Who was Gabriel Prosser?
7. What abolitionist published the newspaper

called *The Liberator*?

8. How many free states were there in 1850?

9. What was meant by *popular sovereignty*?

10. In what year was the Republican party created?

Developing Critical Thinking

1. Why do you think the slave codes were so effective in keeping blacks enslaved?

2. If rice, cotton, and tobacco were so difficult for slaves to produce, why do you think slave owners wanted to grow these crops?

3. Why do you think the white population in the antebellum period was so fearful of allowing slaves to read and write?

4. In what ways might slaves have learned to read in spite of the conditions that existed at the time?

Applying Your Skills

1. Prepare a report on the history and operation of the underground railroad, which helped slaves escape to free states and Canada.

2. Prepare a circle graph that shows the results of the 1860 presidential election. Use the figures given on pages 239-240.

3. Examine the map of the Missouri Compromise of 1820 shown on page 218. How did the map change as a result of the Compromise of 1850?

BUILDING SKILLS: UNDERSTANDING CAUSE AND EFFECT

An important part of the study of history is understanding the relationship between events. One relationship is *cause and effect*. Everything that happens does so because something makes it happen. The person, condition, or event that makes a thing happen is the *cause*, or reason. The thing that happens is the *effect*, or result. This relationship between what happens and what makes it happen is known as a cause-and-effect relationship.

Not all cause-and-effect relationships are clearcut. Indeed, to determine a true cause-and-effect relationship is usually very difficult. Sometimes an event may have more than one cause. At other times, the effects may not appear for a long time. The following guidelines will help you identify cause-and-effect relationships in written material.

1. Often statements contain "clue words" that will alert you to a cause-and-effect relationship. Be aware of and look for such words or phrases as *because, led to, brought about, produced, as a result of, so that, thus, since, outcome, as a consequence, resulted in, gave rise to,* and *therefore.*

2. There may not be clue words. In their place, you may find the word *and* or a comma.

3. Usually it takes more than one sentence or paragraph to describe a cause-and-effect relationship. If you are not sure whether a description illustrates a cause-and-effect relationship, ask yourself if economics, geography, religion, or technology is involved in the event or condition being studied. These are major forces in history that usually cause things to happen.

Complex historical events, such as the Civil War, have multiple causes; and a cause-and-effect relationship can be hard to identify even when it is obvious to you that one must be there. Try listing some causes of the Civil War; some causes of the underground railroad; some causes of Lincoln's election; and, some causes of the Compromise of 1850. Do you see that many of the causes you have identified are, in themselves, effects of other causes? Now you see why it is difficult to describe a simple cause-and-effect relationship.

Clue words are a writer's way of helping you keep cause and effect reactions in mind. Look back through the chapter and locate some clue words indicating a cause-effect relationship.

CHAPTER EIGHT

THE CIVIL WAR

I have no purpose . . . to interfere with the institution of slavery in the States where it exists. I believe I have no lawful right to do so, and I have no inclination to do so. This country, with its institutions, belongs to the people who inhabit it. Whenever they shall have grown weary of the existing government, they can exercise their constitutional right of amending it, or their revolutionary right to dismember or overthrow it. . . . We are not enemies but friends. We must not be enemies. . . . Though passion may have strained, it must not break our bonds of affection. . . . The mystic cords of memory . . . will yet swell the chorus of the Union, when again touched, as they surely will be, by the better angels of our nature.

—Abraham Lincoln

SEVEN DAYS AFTER ABRAHAM LINCOLN spoke the above words, the Congress of the Confederate States of America met in Montgomery, Alabama. Before the day was over, representatives from the seven member states adopted a constitution written in part by Thomas R. Cobb of Georgia. Among other items, the document declared the sovereignty of the states and forbade passage of any laws that would do away with slavery. The stage was set for war.

THE BEGINNING OF THE CIVIL WAR

On April 10, 1861, the Confederate government directed Brigadier General Pierre G. T. Beauregard to demand the surrender of Fort Sumter, South Carolina, by the United States Army **garrison** (military force) stationed there. The fort, located in Charleston harbor, was low on supplies, and a call had gone out for help. The leader of the garrison, Major Robert Anderson, believed that assistance in the form of both supplies and troops was on its way. Because he felt it was his duty to defend the fort until the relief troops came, Anderson refused to obey Beauregard's demand.

This Confederate memorial in front of the Bartow County Courthouse was also dedicated to Brigadier General Francis Bartow of Chatham County, the first Confederate general to die in battle in the Civil War.

SHOTS FIRED

At 4:30 a.m. on April 12, Confederate troops opened fire on Fort Sumter. During the bombardment, men and women of wealth and position stood on the Battery, an embankment across the harbor from the fort, and watched the exchange of fire without realizing what was to come. No help arrived for the Union troops, and thirty-six hours later a white flag waved over the fort. Major Anderson surrendered the fort on April 13, and he left it the following day.

OTHER ACTS OF WAR

Before the fall of Fort Sumter, Confederate forces had captured other federal garrisons in the South, including Fort Pulaski at Savannah, which fell to Confederate troops on January 3, 1861. However, there were two differences between Fort Sumter and the other captured garrisons: South Carolina had already seceded from the Union, and troops of the North and South exchanged gunfire at Fort Sumter.

The war that would be fought in ten thousand places on U.S. soil, the war in which seven future United States presidents fought, the war that would end slavery and cause the death of over 618,000 persons had begun.

PREPARATIONS FOR WAR

After the firing on Fort Sumter, both North and South stepped up preparations for war. They began training troops and gathering clothing, equipment, and supplies their soldiers would need. Arkansas, Tennessee, North Carolina, and Virginia joined the Confederacy, bringing the number of seceded states to eleven, and the capital was moved from Montgomery, Alabama, to Richmond, Virginia.

THE CONFEDERATE STATES OF AMERICA

■ Confederate States of America
□ Union States and Territories

Conditions in the North and the South were very different. There were about 9 million people in the South. This number included 3½ million slaves, who did not serve as soldiers. The South did not have a strong navy, a trained army, or even enough factories to make guns and ammunition. Railroads had been built to move farm products and cotton, the basis of the South's economy; the rails were too light to carry troop trains and heavy equipment effectively.

The North had about 22 million people. It had a strong, well-trained army and navy, both of which had protected the country for many years. The northern economy was based on industry, so the North could readily make the needed weapons, ammunition, and supplies that its forces would require. Northern railroads had been built to carry heavy industrial machinery, so movement of troops and equipment would not be much of a problem. Benefitting by the availability of troops from twenty-three northern and western states, it was relatively easy for the Union to gear up for war. The North also had a functioning government, one that was able to put the nation on a war footing quickly

The Confederacy, on the other hand, had to fight the war while putting together its national government. The Confederacy did, however, have some advantages. For the most part, the war was fought in the South. People fight harder when they are defending their homes. Also, the soldiers of the South were fighting on "familiar" territory.

Nevertheless, many citizens on both sides were of one mind. Both sides thought the war would be short, and both thought their side would win. But it was not only everyday citizens who had rosy expectations: President Lincoln's first call for volunteers for the Union's defense was for only a ninety-day period.

One of the North's biggest advantages over the South was a much larger population. Pro-Union meetings like the one shown here in New York City were commonplace before and after the war began as people demonstrated their support for the Union.

Do You Remember?

1. How many people were there in the South as the two sides prepared for war? How many in the North?
2. What was the economic base of the South as the war began? Of the North?

THE CIVIL WAR SOLDIER

Troops had only a few weeks or months to prepare for battle. Farmers, doctors, teachers, and merchants found themselves drilling with weapons they were unaccustomed to using.

Historians often write about the big battles and the great generals. The lives of common soldiers, however, give a truer picture of the war. Although they sometimes spoke with different accents and for different governments, the soldiers—nicknamed "Johnny Reb" and "Billy Yank"—were a lot alike. Most of the soldiers on both sides were under the age of 21. Over 250,000 were 16 years old or younger, and some were as young as 13. The majority of the soldiers came from the lower economic groups and knew nothing about war until the fighting actually started. In many cases, youths simply wanted to escape the boredom of farm life and seek adventure away from home. Soon, a very different reality was to emerge for these young soldiers.

DAILY FOOD RATION

Even from the very beginning of the war the northern troops generally ate better than their southern counterparts. Union records from 1864 give the basic daily **rations**, or portions of food, in ounces for Union soldiers. They received "20-beef; 18-flour; 2.56 dried beans; 1.6 green coffee; 2.4 sugar; .64 salt" and smaller amounts of pepper, yeast powder, soap, candles, and vinegar.

The same kind of records from the Army of Northern Virginia in 1863 lists rations for 100 Confederate soldiers over a 30-day period. Each day, they had to share "1/4 pound of bacon, 18 oz. of flour, 10 lbs. of rice, and a small amount of peas and dried fruits when they could be obtained."

Soldiers from both the North and the South had to depend on food found in the woods or taken from farms, or, as the soldiers explained it, "liberating chickens, hogs, pies, and eggs."

For soldiers with money, hunger pangs could be soothed by a visit to the sutler wagon. Though not part of the military, **sutler wagons** followed behind the troops and were packed with food, razors, writing papers, pens, sewing needles, and other goods. Prices, especially those for food, were frequently double or triple the item's normal cost. A dozen eggs, for example, could cost $6, which is expensive even by today's standards but was a small fortune in Civil War days.

CLOTHING

During the early battles of the war, it was often impossible to tell which side a typical soldier represented because uniforms were so seldom alike. The battlefields were a mass of colorful, often homespun, shirts, jackets, and trousers. One regiment even marched off to battle in kilts. In at least one instance, Union soldiers let a group of men in blue jackets into the line of fire thinking they were friendly forces. By the time the mistake was discovered, the Confederate unit had overrun the Union troops.

After a few months, Confederate soldiers dressed in double-breasted hip length coats and gray pants. These coats were later replaced by short-waisted, single-breasted jackets. Each branch of the army had a different trim on its uniforms. The artillery had red trim; the infantry, blue; and the **cavalry** (troops mounted on horseback), yellow. Officers' uniforms had buttons that indicated their branch of service. The uniforms of Union soldiers were blue, but the trim was much the same as the Confederate's. These troops also wore caps and hats with branch insignia in appropriate colors.

As the war dragged on, Confederate soldiers wore clothing made at home and sent by friends and relatives. Replacement uniforms soon became a luxury the Confederacy could ill afford.

Soldiers had knapsacks in which to carry writing paper, pictures, books, and toilet articles. However, soldiers found the knapsacks hard to keep up with and soon lost them. They wrapped personal items in a blanket and carried them in a tent canvas. Soldiers also carried a musket and a leather box for ammunition.

Under the leadership of twenty-nine-year-old John B. Gordon, a group of mountaineer miners suddenly found themselves Confederate soldiers. The troops were called the "Racoon Roughs" because the only thing they shared in common as a uniform was their coonskin caps.

These Civil War enthusiasts are re-enacting what life was like in a Civil War army camp. Experienced soldiers of the period learned to carry as little equipment as possible.

On their belts, they fastened a cap box, a bayonet in its sheath, a sewing kit, and mess equipment. The latter were eating tools and usually consisted of a knife, fork, spoon, cup, and, sometimes, a light cooking skillet. Together all of these items weighed about forty or fifty pounds. The longer a soldier stayed in the army, the more likely he was to leave things he could do without in camp or along the roadside.

HEALTH CARE

Although the first medical and nursing corps were established during the Civil War, the emergency medical care given to the soldiers on both sides of the conflict was far from adequate. Some soldiers preferred death in battle to a critical injury. Frequently, legs and arms were amputated without anesthesia. Infections in camp or battlefield hospitals were common and often resulted in death.

Do You Remember?
1. What were the nicknames for the Confederate and the Union soldiers?
2. What were the sutler wagons that followed the armies?
3. What was the color of the Confederate uniforms?

WAR STRATEGIES

After Fort Sumter, both Union and Confederate political and military leaders developed **strategies**, or plans, for winning the war. Over the course of the war, these strategies changed as new advances or setbacks called for different ways of proceeding with the conduct of the war. Sometimes the plans worked; sometimes, they did not. And sometimes one or another of the two sides became either victims or beneficiaries of everyday plain luck, luck that could not be foreseen by even the most able planner.

UNION STRATEGIES

Initially the Union strategy was to **blockade** (obstruct) all Confederate ports and seize the Mississippi River. The blockade was to prevent the South from selling cotton abroad and from getting war equipment and supplies from other nations. It was also politically important to the North to prevent other nations from recognizing the Confederacy so that the armies and navies of these countries would not become involved in the war. The capture of the Mississippi River was designed to split the Confederacy in half, leaving Texas, Arkansas, and Louisiana stranded. This strategy was known as the "Anaconda Plan" because, if successful, it would squeeze the Confederacy to death just like the giant anaconda snake squeezes its prey to death.

Much of the Confederacy's strategy had to do with breaking the Union blockade. In coastal waters, the Confederate Navy used ironclads (armored vessels) like the Atlanta *(below) to sink the Union's wooden ships and open southern ports for trade with other nations.*

As the war progressed, Union generals decided that the capture of the Confederate capital of Richmond could end the war. This strategy failed, however, because General Robert E. Lee was able to hold off Union armies from the doors of Richmond for several years.

In 1864 and 1865, Union Generals Ulysses S. Grant and William T. Sherman developed a strategy that finally brought victory to the North. Their plan was to destroy Confederate armies and lay waste to the land so that southern civilians would stop supporting the war.

CONFEDERATE STRATEGIES

The Confederate leaders also had strategies for winning the Civil War. On land, they planned to wear down the invading Union armies. They believed that rising casualties would cause northerners to tire of the war and, as a result, support for the war effort would weaken. At sea, the Confederates wanted to make sure that the Union blockade did not work. The Confederate Navy used swift *raiders* (fast and lightly armed ships) to capture Union merchant ships and

Ulysses S. Grant, who changed his name from Herman Ulysses Grant to avoid the initials HUG, was a brilliant military tactician. He served as commander of Union forces and later two terms as President of the United States.

draw the Union Navy away from the blockade. In coastal waters, the Confederates used *ironclads* (armored vessels) and even a submarine to sink the Union's wooden ships and open southern ports for trade with other nations.

The Confederacy's political strategy was called **King Cotton Diplomacy**. The South believed that the British and French textile mills needed the South's cotton to keep running. If the Confederacy stopped selling cotton abroad for a time, it believed that the French and British would be forced to help the South break the blockades and, in so doing, win the war. Unfortunately, the South's strategies were not successful.

BLOCKADES

Even before Virginia and North Carolina seceded from the Union, southern ports were blockaded. Early in the war, twenty-six Union ships steamed up and down the coast to keep boats from going into or out of the ports. Subsequently, the North spent millions of dollars to build additional vessels, seventy-four of which were ironclads. However, these vessels were no match for the Confederate navy or for the private ships, **blockade runners**, that tried to steal past the port blockades. There were over 650 private blockade runners during 1861, and nine out of every ten were able to run past the federal ships and sail into open waters.

Blockade running was a very profitable business. Captains were paid $5,000 for each trip, and pilots earned $3,500. Many ship owners and speculators made millions of dollars during the war. For example, the price of cotton was only 3 cents a pound in the South, but anywhere from 10 cents to $1 per pound in Great Britain. The profit on 1,000 bales of cotton sold in Britain was about $250,000. Blockade runners could also purchase military supplies, food items, and medical supplies in Great Britain and return to the South to sell these essentials to the Confederacy and earn yet another large profit.

As the war progressed, it became more and more difficult for blockade runners to get past federal ships. By 1863, one out of every four runners was captured before reaching the open sea. By 1865, only half of the blockade runners were able to outrun federal ships.

Abraham Lincoln's first choice for commander of the Union Army was Robert E. Lee. However, Lee decided to return to Virginia to command the Confederate troops instead.

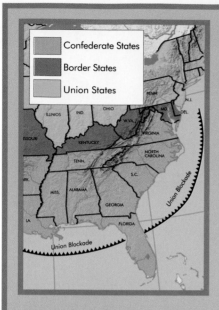

Confederate States
Border States
Union States

THE AMERICAN CIVIL WAR AND GREAT BRITAIN

During the Civil War, the fate of the Union rested partly in the hands of Great Britain. The British used millions of bales of cotton, most of it imported from the South. If the British recognized the Confederacy as an independent nation, they could claim the right to trade with her. British ships would sweep aside the North's blockading ships to get the cotton. President Lincoln sent Charles Francis Adams to London. Adams worked hard to prevent Great Britain from recognizing Confederate independence.

Two events threatened good relations between the United States and Great Britain. In November 1861, the U.S. Navy stopped the British steamer *Trent* and forcibly removed two Confederate diplomats. The British condemned the act and prepared for war. To end that crisis, President Lincoln released the diplomats.

The second event involved naval rams, which are armored steamships with 7-foot spikes jutting from the prow below the water line. Rams sink ships by punching holes in them below the water line. A British firm secretly began building rams for the Confederacy. Adams strongly protested, and the British government instead bought them.

In addition, poor wheat harvests in Europe meant the British needed northern wheat more than southern cotton. Great Britain was also strongly antislavery, having abolished slavery in 1833.

All of these factors prevented the British from becoming directly involved and thus contributed to Union victory.

Northern diplomacy kept the British and French from entering the war and breaking the blockades, and the South was increasingly unable to obtain war materials or money from abroad. Before, the South could export what it grew and import items it needed. Now the South was unable to get enough clothes, medicine, guns, and ammunition. The Union strategy of cutting off southern access to military and civilian supplies was an important step in the North's final victory.

Do You Remember?
1. Why was the northern strategy called the "Anaconda Plan"?
2. What was the southern political strategy called?
3. What did the South believe would happen if they stopped selling cotton abroad?

BATTLES OF THE WAR

The Civil War, which many had first thought would neither last long nor disrupt many lives, proved to be exceptionally costly, both in economic and human terms. During its course, some of the bloodiest battles in U.S. history were waged, battles that often pitted brother against brother and neighbor against neighbor.

BATTLES DURING 1861

During the first three months of the war, there were only minor skirmishes that led both the North and the South to think the war would be little more than a "cakewalk." However, on July 21, 1861, three months after the fall of Fort Sumter, the Battle of Bull Run took place.

The Battle of Bull Run

The Battle of Bull Run at Manassas, Virginia, was the first major battle of the Civil War. The Confederate forces won, but no one knows whether they won because they fought well or because there was a lot of confusion. Battle flags and uniforms for both sides were varied. During the battle, soldiers, many of whom had less than a month

The first Battle of Bull Run took place next to a creek with the same name. Close to Washington, D.C., the battle drew spectators with picnic baskets who gathered where they could cheer for the Union forces. They were disappointed when the Confederate troops won the first major battle of the war. Notice the variety of uniforms in the picture.

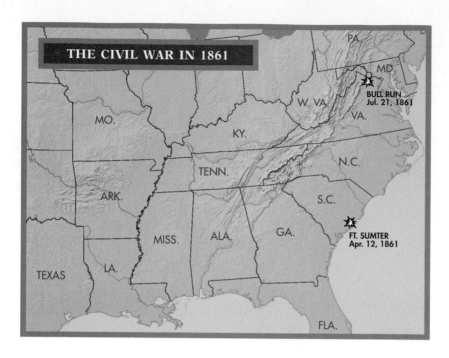

THE CIVIL WAR IN 1861

of training, often could not tell the difference between friends and enemies.

Confederate Generals P. G. T. Beauregard and Thomas "Stonewall" Jackson had not led large numbers of men into battle before. Neither had Union General Irwin McDowell, so mistakes were common. However, each side learned something important. Confederate leaders learned that their poorly trained army could fight. Union leaders began to understand that the war would last longer and be harder to win than they had first thought.

When the Battle of Bull Run ended, 4,500 soldiers were dead, wounded, or missing. Because Manassas is near Washington, D.C., historians will probably always wonder why, after their victory, the Confederate army did not try to capture the Union capital. One possible explanation is that, although the South's military leaders were fresh from the Mexican War, the Confederate troops did not have enough experience to take advantage of the situation.

Georgians Feel the First Pangs of War

At the first Battle of Bull Run, Georgia's 21st Regiment lost 184 of its 242 men—almost 76 percent of its troops. This hurt and alarmed those who thought the Yanks would be whipped with ease. Many young Georgians volunteered to fight, though, and soon there were more soldiers than guns. Some troops who went to fight in Virginia were not allowed to take guns out of Georgia because it was thought the guns would be needed to defend the state.

BATTLES DURING 1862

During 1862, the war escalated quickly. Thirty-seven battles were fought in the second year of the war. They had names like Pea Ridge in Arkansas, Shiloh in Tennessee, and the second Battle of Bull Run in Virginia. These and other battles, including Antietam in Maryland and Fredericksburg in Virginia, led to heavy losses on both sides. Many of the war records kept by the Confederacy were lost or destroyed, so historians have had to guess the number of Confederate casualties. Estimates of the dead, wounded, and missing soldiers during these battles number well over 137,000 for Union forces and over 164,000 for the Confederates.

Over 100,000 men took part in the Battle of Shiloh on April 6 and 7, 1862. Fresh Union troops arrived on the second day of the battle, enabling the Union Army to claim victory. However, the number of men hurt or killed made it clear to both sides during the second year of the war that the conflict would be costly.

The bloodiest one-day battle of the war was fought on September 17, 1862, at Antietam Creek near Sharpsburg, Maryland.

General Robert E. Lee, a West Point graduate and former federal army officer, had become the commander of the Confederate troops in Virginia in June of that year. At the Battle of Antietam, the Confederacy lost over 2,000 men, and more than 9,000 were wounded. Union forces under General McClellan also suffered large losses. When the South retreated, McClellan did not follow Lee's army and capture the remaining troops. If he had, many historians think the war might have ended then. Because General McClellan's army did not take advantage of Lee's retreat, President Lincoln removed him from command.

First Attacks in Georgia

On April 6 and 7, 1862, while Confederate forces were concentrated in Virginia, Union General Grant was winning a bloody and costly victory at Shiloh, Tennessee. At the same time, two areas of the Georgia coast were suffering their first major attacks. They were Tybee Island and Fort Pulaski, located about fifteen miles east of Savannah.

Fort Pulaski was a prime federal coastal defense site that U.S. troops first used in 1847. Named for Revolutionary War hero Count Casimir Pulaski, the fort was made of brick and considered strong enough to withstand any attack. However, on January 3, 1861, Confederate troops captured it. Inside the fort, the Confederates dug trenches and put down heavy pieces of wood to support their cannons. General Robert E. Lee visited the fort and thought it safe from Union fire.

In early April 1862, Union forces took Tybee Island, which was located only a mile across the Savannah River from the fort. They asked Fort Pulaski's 25-year-old commander and his 385 men to surrender

Known as the bloodiest one-day battle of the war, Antietam, near Sharpsburg, Maryland, may have been the result of a careless mistake. It is reported that a Confederate officer wrote down information about the impending battle and wrapped the paper around three cigars. The paper, which he then discarded, was later picked up by a federal soldier and the information on it led General McClellan to attack Lee's divided army. Although historians are unsure which stories about Antietam are true, they do illustrate the tremendous confusion during the ill-planned conflict.

THE GREAT LOCOMOTIVE CHASE

In the spring of 1862, Marietta played host to many strangers, so a few more spending time at the Fletcher House (now Kennesaw House) made little difference. One of the men was James Andrews (below), a Kentuckian who had been around for several weeks. In fact, he had even made a few friends, gaining the trust of Confederates by smuggling much needed quinine, a malaria medicine, across battle lines.

Andrews, however, was anything but a Confederate sympathizer. During the predawn hours on the morning of April 12, 1862, he nonchalantly boarded a train named *The General*, which was a special train of the Confederacy that carried not only regular passengers but also war

supplies from Atlanta to troops in Tennessee. Also boarding the train were twenty-one other men who, though dressed in civilian clothes, were really Union soldiers. They had trudged through heavy rain and muddy roads to reach the train.

The train stopped for a short while at Big Shanty station. During the stop, the conductor, Confederate Captain William Fuller, and his crew were eating inside the station when they heard a familiar sound—the noise of *The General* and its three freight cars pulling out of the station. Stunned, Captain Fuller and his crew raced out the door and began running after the train.

James Andrews and the twenty-one men with him on the train were Union spies who had carefully planned their raid. They chose Big Shanty station because it had no telegraph. Their intent was to head north to Huntsville to meet a Union commander, General Mitchell, and then move on to Chattanooga. Along the way, they planned to cut telegraph lines, burn bridges, and upend railroad ties. What they had not counted on was the spirit and determination of Fuller and his crew, who took the theft as a personal affront to their honor.

After running on the tracks for two miles, Fuller and his men found a platform handcar and pushed themselves along the tracks picking up two other men as they went along. They came upon a switch engine only to abandon it on tracks broken up by the Union raiders. Finally, after still another foot pursuit, the weary but angry band of men discovered an engine named *Texas* on the southbound tracks at Adairsville.

The General, which had been sidelined awaiting passage of other southbound train traffic, was north of Calhoun when the Union raiders saw an incredible sight. The mighty *Texas*, without any cars, was barreling down the railroad tracks in reverse.

Because the telegraph wires had been cut, people watching along the tracks had no idea what was happening. Fuller was able to get a message to Confederate General Ledbetter in Chattanooga informing him of the theft and chase.

Andrews' raiders were now filled with fear. The law was clear about the sentencing of spies, so the raiders first tossed crossties on the tracks to stop their pursuers. Then they released the freight boxcars, but the *Texas* pushed aside the cars and neared *The General*.

As they approached Chickamauga Creek, Andrews set fire to the last car *(left)* hoping that it would burn the bridge and stop the *Texas*. However, the bridge was soaked from rains the previous day and refused to burn. Again, the *Texas* pushed aside the burning boxcar and continued its race.

The race finally ended near Ringold Gap, eighteen miles south of Chattanooga, when *The General* ran out of fuel. The raiders fled *(below)* but were rounded up within two weeks. Two months later, James Andrews and seven of his men were court-martialed in Atlanta and hanged. The remaining fourteen were sent to Confederate prisons.

After the war, some of Andrews' raiding party received the Congressional Medal of Honor. However, because Andrews himself was not in the military, his family did not receive that final honor for him.

the fort back to Union control. Colonel Charles Olmstead refused; Union troops started firing on the fort at 8:00 a.m. on the morning of April 10. A day and a half later, the Union bombardment began breaking down the fort's brick walls, and Olmstead surrendered.

In a letter to his wife, Olmstead wrote, "I feel that I have done my duty, my whole duty, that I have been forced to yield only to [the] superior might of metal. Guns such as have never before been brought to bear against any fortification have overpowered me, but I trust to history to keep my name untarnished." The guns to which Olmstead was referring were the rifled cannons that were first used in modern warfare at Fort Pulaski. After the capture of Fort Pulaski, no more forts were built of brick.

The Emancipation Proclamation

On September 22, 1862, five days after the Battle of Antietam, President Lincoln issued the **Emancipation Proclamation**, a document that would ultimately affect 4 million slaves in the United States. The president wanted the Confederate states to end the war and return to the Union. In this now-famous document, Lincoln stated that unless the South surrendered by January 1, 1863, "all slaves in states or districts in rebellion against the United States on January 1, 1863, will be thenceforth and forever free." For the three months and nine days after the Emancipation Proclamation was issued, the Confederacy had a choice. If it surrendered, slavery would continue in the South. If it did not, the institution of slavery would end. The Confederate leaders elected to continue to fight for secession.

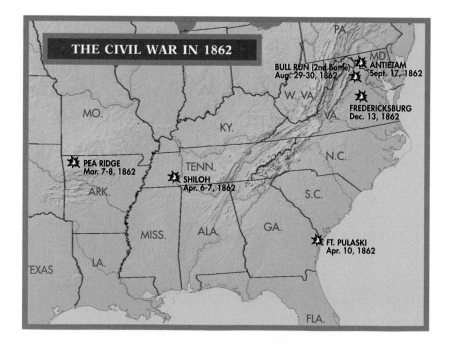

THE CIVIL WAR IN 1862

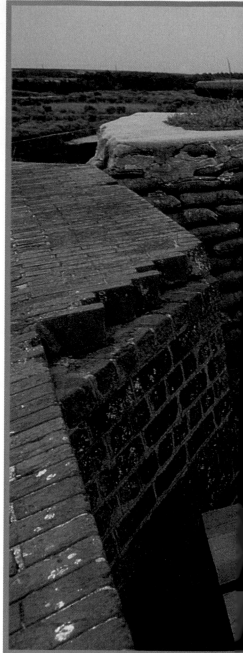

After the surrender of Fort Pulaski (above), Union General Hunter stated that "the result of this bombardment must cause. . .a change in the construction of fortifications. No works of stone or brick can resist the impact of rifled artillery of heavy caliber. . ."

Do You Remember?

1. At which battle did Georgia's 21st Regiment lose almost 76 percent of its troops?
2. What was the bloodiest one-day battle of the Civil War?
3. Who was Colonel Charles Olmstead?
4. In the Emancipation Proclamation, what did President Lincoln say would happen if the Confederates did not surrender by January 1, 1863?

BATTLES DURING 1863

The halfway point of the Civil War came in 1863. During that year, there were 627 battles, over half of which were in Virginia, Tennessee, and Mississippi. Most of the major battles of the third year of the war occurred in the spring and summer. Confederate forces were victorious in several, including the Battle of Chancellorsville in May and the Battle of Chickamauga in September. However, Union troops won most of the battles.

The Battle of Gettysburg

One of the most memorable battles of the Civil War happened during early July 1863, and it took place in the North. The Battle of Gettysburg was fought in a small Pennsylvania town of only 2,000 people, but it was considered to be the turning point in the Civil War. It began on July 1, and for the next three days 150,000 Confederate and Union soldiers met in meadows, woods, peach orchards, and foothills as General Lee attempted to smash through Union lines and take Washington, D.C.

The newly appointed commander of the Union troops, George Meade, had been sent to protect Washington and Baltimore. He ran into Lee's troops almost by accident. From the beginning, this his-

On July 1, 1863, Union General George Meade met a small force of Confederate troops at Gettysburg, Pennsylvania. For two days artillery blazed until Confederate General George Pickett led 15,000 men against Union forces in what has come to be known as "Pickett's Charge." The attack failed and Confederate forces were forced to retreat.

toric battle was a series of mistakes, arguments, and accidents. First, the fighting started before either army had all of its soldiers in Gettysburg. Second, Confederate General J.E.B. Stuart and his cavalry had gone off in another direction and could not be contacted. Third, Georgia-born General James Longstreet disagreed with Lee's tactics and wanted to withdraw from Gettysburg altogether. Historians offer different opinions as to what happened next. As Lee led his troops for a frontal attack, Longstreet and his men failed to join the rest of the force.

The bloody battle raged on and on. Firing on both sides was so inaccurate that it took almost a man's weight in lead to kill him. But there was plenty of gunpowder and lead, and by July 5, the North had lost 23,000 men while the South had lost approximately 28,000. After his defeat, a depressed and exhausted General Lee turned South, and fighting on northern soil was over. Thereafter, just the very mention of James Longstreet would be sure to cause an argument among many southerners.

To commemorate the victory, President Lincoln and others went to Gettysburg for a "few appropriate words." Lincoln, exhausted from presidential duties and worried about his wife Mary who had suffered head injuries in a fall from a carriage, began preparing for a cemetery dedication service. The day arrived and the main speaker, Edward Everett, spoke for two hours in front of a spellbound crowd from whom he received thunderous applause. Then Lincoln rose and spoke for less than two minutes. His speech was so short and over so quickly that the photographer had no time to take a picture. The remarks of Lincoln earned only a smattering of applause, and the speech was called "silly," "dull," and "commonplace" by the critics at the time. Today, almost 140 years later, the three-paragraph **Gettysburg Address** is heralded as one of the finest speeches of all time.

After the Battle of Gettysburg, the remaining battles of the Civil War were fought on southern soil. The Battle of Vicksburg in Mississippi resulted in another Union victory, one in which 31,277 southern soldiers were listed as dead, wounded, or missing. This battle gave the Union troops control of the Mississippi River, cutting the Confederacy in half and ending any hopes of a Confederate victory in the war.

THE CIVIL WAR IN 1863

GETTYSBURG
July 1-3, 1863

CHANCELLORSVILLE
May 1-4, 1863

CHATTANOOGA
Nov. 23-25, 1863

CHICKAMAUGA
Sept. 19-20, 1863

VICKSBURG
July 4, 1963

BLACKS IN THE ARMED FORCES

Black troops in the Union Army distinguished themselves at a number of major engagements such as the assault on Fort Wagner, near Charleston, South Carolina.

Some 178,985 enlisted men and 7,122 officers served in black regiments during the Civil War. These soldiers, about 3,500 of whom were from Georgia, took part in approximately 450 battles and skirmishes. The large-scale use of black troops was a central issue throughout the war years.

Blacks in the Union Forces

When the war began, the Union refused to allow blacks to serve in the army. Because blacks had fought in both the Revolutionary War and the War of 1812, black leaders like Frederick Douglass thought they should be allowed to fight again.

General David Hunter first organized black troops in 1862. When the war department would not support him, Hunter disbanded all but one company. General James Lane from Kansas organized black troops who took part in several western battles. Slowly, public opinion changed, and by 1863 the War Department allowed governors of several states to seek black soldiers. By October of that year, there were fifty-eight black regiments in the Union Army.

At first, many black troops built defenses, manned garrisons, and kept up the camps. Others acted as nurses, scouts, cooks, and spies. In some regiments, most of the infantrymen were black. During a federal attack on Port Hudson, near Baton Rouge on May 27, 1863, two of these regiments were praised for "meritorious performance." Other major engagements included Milliken's Bend near Vicksburg in June 1863 and an assault on Fort Wagner near Charleston, South Carolina. By the end of the war, nearly 10 percent of the Union Army was made up of free blacks and former slaves. About 37,300 lost their lives while serving. Seventeen black soldiers and four black sailors were awarded the Congressional Medal of Honor.

After General David Hunter organized the first black troops in 1862, it was over a year before a black regiment saw active military duty. This picture shows black Union troops fighting in Georgia.

Blacks in the Confederate Army

Taking note of the Union example, Confederate leaders began to discuss the use of blacks in their army. There was considerable opposition, because the Confederacy had gone to war to defend the social and political system of slavery. Georgia's General Howell Cobb summarized the thinking of those opposed to using blacks in the Confederate Army when he wrote, "You cannot make soldiers of slaves nor slaves of soldiers. . . . The day you make soldiers of them is the beginning of the end of our revolution. If slaves will make good soldiers, our whole theory of slavery is wrong." Governor Brown agreed stating, "If the negro is fit to be a soldier, he is not fit to be a slave."

General Robert E. Lee argued, "We must decide whether slavery shall be extinguished by our enemies and the slave used against us, or use them ourselves at the risk of the effects which may be produced upon our social institutions. . . . We should employ them without delay." Lee needed troops. On March 13, 1865, President Jefferson Davis took Lee's advice and signed the Negro Soldier Law, which allowed slaves to enlist in the Confederate Army. A few blacks enlisted in Richmond, but before a black regiment could be organized, Richmond had fallen to Union forces and the Civil War was drawing to an end.

In addition to the lives lost at the Battle of Chickamauga, the Confederacy failed to follow up on a strategic victory.

Battles Get Closer to Home in Georgia

During the third year of the war, Union General William Rosecrans and his army moved against Chattanooga, Tennessee. Chattanooga was a major railroad center from which supplies and munitions were sent to southern troops.

On September 19 and 20, Rosecrans' troops met those led by Confederate General Braxton Bragg seven miles south of Chattanooga at Chickamauga Creek, an Indian name meaning "River of Death." During the Chickamauga battle, 15,851 Union troops and 17,804 Confederate troops were killed, wounded, or missing. The Union general made several mistakes, allowing Bragg and his forces to win the battle and force the Union army back into Chattanooga.

However, Bragg did not follow the Union troops northward into Tennessee, and by November, General U. S. Grant arrived to reinforce the Union forces with more soldiers. The Battle of Chattanooga, on November 23, 24, and 25, placed the area in the hands of the Union. Bragg retreated to Dalton.

BATTLES DURING 1864

The height of the Civil War came in 1864. There were 779 battles, most of which were in Virginia, Tennessee, Arkansas, and Georgia. By this time, many Confederates had become disillusioned with the war. At one point, Confederate President Jefferson Davis guessed that approximately two-thirds of the army was absent from duty, many without permission.

Lee's Last Major Victory

Confederate General Robert E. Lee won his last major victory at Cold Harbor, Virginia, on June 3, 1864. Lee's 59,000 troops fought against 108,000 Union soldiers. Confederate forces had already lost many men in battles or to diseases, and between May 7 and June 3, they lost 32,000 more. During this same period, Union losses were about 50,000; however, while the North could replace lost soldiers, the South could not.

Ulysses S. Grant became the commander of the Union Army. During the next nine months, Lee and Grant met in battle again and again, with the Union winning almost every encounter.

At the Battle of Cold Harbor on June 3, 1864, Confederate forces under Robert E. Lee defeated a Union army almost twice as large. It was, however, Lee's last major victory.

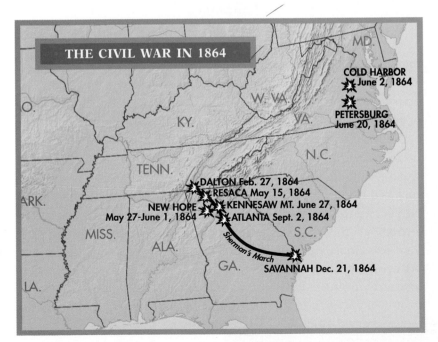

THE CIVIL WAR IN 1864

COLD HARBOR
June 2, 1864

PETERSBURG
June 20, 1864

DALTON Feb. 27, 1864
RESACA May 15, 1864
NEW HOPE
May 27-June 1, 1864
KENNESAW MT. June 27, 1864
ATLANTA Sept. 2, 1864

Sherman's March

SAVANNAH Dec. 21, 1864

MD.
W. VA.
KY.
VA.
N.C.
TENN.
ARK.
MISS.
ALA.
S.C.
GA.
LA.
O.

Beginning on June 27, 1864, the Battle of Kennesaw Mountain was a decisive military victory for Confederate General Johnston's troops against Sherman's troops. Although General Sherman (opposite page) lost nearly 3,000 men, it did not stop his march toward Atlanta. In addition, Jefferson Davis, dissatisfied with Johnston's constant retreating tactics, replaced the brilliant warrior with General John B. Hood on July 18, to the dismay of the weary Confederate troops.

Sherman's March Through Georgia

Of the 108 Civil War battles in Georgia, 92 of them took place in 1864. Most of Georgia's battles were a result of the Battle of Chickamauga when General Bragg allowed Union General Grant to capture Chattanooga. When Grant moved his army east to meet his Confederate counterpart, Robert E. Lee, he placed 112,000 men in Chattanooga under the command of General William Tecumseh Sherman.

Sherman's immediate goal was to capture Atlanta, the final transportation center of the South. Sherman led his troops southward toward Atlanta. Confederate General Joseph E. Johnston, who had replaced Bragg because of the military mistakes at Chickamauga, had only 60,000 troops to hold back Sherman's army. During the late spring and early summer of 1864, the two armies fought at Dalton, Resaca, and New Hope. Johnston had to retreat at each of these battles, but he burned bridges and blocked roads as he went. This slowed Sherman's forward movement to about two miles a day. The movement of troops from Chattanooga to Atlanta—a distance that now takes about 1½ hours to drive—took General Sherman four months to cover.

Above: From July 28 to August 31, Atlanta was attacked by Union troops on the north and east. The lack of a clear victory forced General Sherman to move his troops south to Jonesboro. The fighting was fierce for the next two days but Hood's outnumbered army was unable to hold out and evacuated Atlanta on September 1.

***Opposite page, below:** This map shows the $100 million path of destruction wrought by Sherman's "march to the sea."*

In June, Sherman attacked Confederate forces at Kennesaw Mountain, but Johnston's army won. Jefferson Davis, President of the Confederacy, wanted Sherman's army attacked head on, so he replaced General Johnston with John Bell Hood, who was called "Old Woodenhead" by his men. In July, Hood led his men against the Union forces and lost over 11,000 troops in two days. The two armies fought throughout July and August until Sherman's forces encircled Atlanta. Hood left the city on September 1 following the evacuation of Atlanta's citizens. The next day, the Union Army moved into Atlanta and took over Georgia's major railroads and factories. Sherman telegraphed the president with the message, "Atlanta is ours and fairly won." His troops remained there until November 15, when they set fire to the city destroying businesses, transportation facilities, homes, gardens, and even the pens for livestock.

Sherman's strategy of laying waste to the land to end civilian support for the war effort was in full force by November. On November

16, Sherman's army began its famous "march to the sea." His army moved quickly through the state. Sixty-two thousand soldiers cut a path sixty miles wide on the three-hundred-mile trip from Atlanta to Savannah. Mostly, the soldiers lived by killing livestock and taking food from farms, stores, and homes they burned along the way.

On December 24, 1864, General Sherman sent a message to Abraham Lincoln, who earlier had been re-elected to the presidency: "I beg to present you as a Christmas gift the City of Savannah, with one hundred fifty heavy guns, and plenty of ammunition, also about twenty-five thousand bales of cotton." On Christmas Day, Union troops overran Savannah.

General Sherman had completed his plan. The lower South was now cut off from the rest of the Confederacy, and a pathway of fire and destruction lay across the state from the capital to the coast. Estimates of damages from Sherman's march to the sea were as high as $100 million.

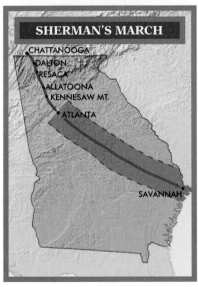

SHERMAN'S MARCH

CHATTANOOGA
DALTON
RESACA
ALLATOONA
KENNESAW MT.
ATLANTA
SAVANNAH

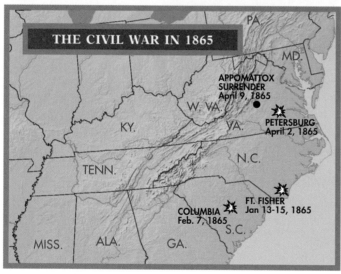

THE CIVIL WAR IN 1865

APPOMATTOX
SURRENDER
April 9, 1865

PETERSBURG
April 2, 1865

FT. FISHER
Jan 13-15, 1865

COLUMBIA
Feb. 7, 1865

PA.

MD.

W. VA.

KY.

VA.

TENN.

N.C.

MISS.

ALA.

GA.

S.C.

Top: *From September 2 until November 15, federal troops systematically destroyed Atlanta. The city was set afire as Sherman left Atlanta on his march to Savannah. The skyline of the blazing city could be seen for miles.*

THE FINAL BATTLES OF THE WAR

On January 13, 1865, the last Confederate blockade-running port was closed when Fort Fisher in North Carolina was captured by the North. In Virginia, Lee's troops continued to fight Grant's army, which was over twice the size of the remaining Confederate force. On March 2, Lee asked for a meeting with Grant to talk about ending the war, but President Lincoln refused to allow the meeting unless the South surrendered.

Lee tried one final time to push Union troops back from Petersburg, Virginia. He failed, and before he could reach the remaining Confederate forces in North Carolina, Union troops cut off his retreat. President Jefferson Davis knew the war was near its end, so he left Richmond and went to Danville, Virginia, to avoid capture.

On April 9, 1865, General Lee surrendered to Grant at Appomattox Courthouse in Virginia. While there were still a few small skirmishes in North Carolina, the Civil War was officially over.

Although the official surrender was in April, the war had really ended much sooner in Georgia. The main concern of most Georgians during the final year of the war was to find food and shelter. Factories, rail lines, mills, plantations, towns, farms, and fields lay in ruins as the war drew to an end.

After the final gunshots were heard and the drums and bugles were silent, hundreds of thousands began the long trek home. In the South, dirt roads were filled with groups of men in tattered uniforms trudging along. All were burdened with a tiredness that comes only with defeat, but many still swore that if things had worked out a little bit better, maybe they could have whipped "those Yanks."

In Washington, D.C., 200,000 smartly dressed Union soldiers marched up Pennsylvania Avenue past the president, cabinet members, and throngs of cheering civilians feeling the elation of victory. Both the Union and the Confederate soldiers, however, came home to the love of family and friends, and both groups had to begin the process of healing.

Do You Remember?
1. What occasion in Gettysburg led to President Lincoln's most famous speech?
2. Why did Union troops want to take Chattanooga?
3. What did General Sherman do to Atlanta?
4. What were the results of Sherman's "march to the sea"?

On Sunday, April 9, 1865, the Civil War was over. Georgia's Major General John B. Gordon (above) was chosen by General Robert E. Lee to lead his men down the street to the house of Wilmer McLean at Appomattox Court House in Virginia. In McLean's home, Lee and Union General Ulysses Grant met (below). General Grant then wrote out the terms of the Confederate surrender.

PHOTOGRAPHY IN THE CIVIL WAR

The Civil War was the first major national event to be photographed. In 1839, a Frenchman named Daguerre developed a process to take a picture using a copper plate coated with silver. Samuel F. B. Morse (inventor of the telegraph) happened to be in Paris then and learned the process. Back in New York, Morse opened a studio, and the photography craze soon swept America.

When the Civil War began, some 3,154 Americans listed their occupation as photographers. At least 1,500 of them took war photographs, and practically all of these worked with Union forces. The

Union blockade made it difficult for southern photographers to get the chemicals needed to coat plates and develop them.

Photographers mainly reached the battlefields after the battles were over. And because exposure times were long, photographers took pictures of still scenes: dead people and animals, splintered trees, destroyed buildings, and the debris of war. The most popular pictures were those of individual soldiers. Illustrated newspapers bought photographs from which they made wood engravings. Important photographers included Matthew Brady, Edward and Henry Anthony, Alexander Gardner, George Bernard, Timothy O'Sullivan, and Henry P. Moore.

Artists argued about whether photographs were art. Some people regarded them as depictions of reality. Others argued that the photographer posed his subjects, determined the light, and thus took pictures that had the elements of art. Art or not, the nation is fortunate to have an extensive pictorial record of the Civil War.

Mathew Brady (opposite page, above) took this photograph (opposite page, below) at the Battle of Chancellorsville on May 3, 1863. The photograph above shows the destruction of Confederate railroad tracks in Georgia during Sherman's "march to the sea" in 1864.

In 1863, the decision was made to build a prison in the deep South. Andersonville, a railroad station twelve miles from Americus, Georgia, was chosen as the site. The stockade was built to hold 8,000 to 10,000 men. By May 1864, over 22,000 men were so piled in that each man had a space of 33 square feet. A severe lack of medical supplies and food caused the deaths of more than 13,000 Union soldiers, many of whom are buried in Andersonville.

CIVIL WAR PRISONS

A particularly dark side of the Civil War was seen in the way prisoners of both sides were treated by their captors. At first, each side routinely exchanged prisoners. However, in 1864, after an incident in which northern black military prisoners were reported to have been killed by their Confederate captors, General Grant stopped exchanging prisoners with the South. This kept the Confederacy from getting back men needed for the army. It also made military prisons overflow.

One of the Confederate prisons for Union soldiers was in Andersonville, Georgia. The prison was dirty; the only shelter was whatever the prisoners could put together; and there was not enough food, water, or medical supplies. Much of the water that was available was contaminated. Between 1864 and 1865, close to 30 percent of the 40,000 Union prisoners at Andersonville died. Although all of these men were not at Andersonville at the same time, the prison was always crowded beyond reason.

Stories of the conditions from Andersonville were so bad that the Confederate War Department had a medical team look at the prison. The team recommended moving the soldiers to better places. Andersonville's commander, Captain Henry Wirz, was executed in

1865 for "excessive cruelty," although records indicate he did try to improve conditions at the prison. Today, Andersonville is a national cemetery where 13,700 Union dead are buried.

Although conditions at Andersonville Prison were horrible, the problems in prison camps were not limited to the South. Over 26,000 southerners died in northern camps such as Point Lookout, Maryland, and Camp Douglas, Illinois.

One Union prison was located at Elmira, New York. Before the war's end, one-fourth of the 12,123 Confederate prisoners at Elmira died. Malnutrition, exposure to the cold, and poor medical conditions were constant. A man gnawing on a meat bone was envied by those about him. Broken arms and legs frequently were not mended. Prisoners, unaccustomed to the severe cold of New York winters, were often made to stand at attention barefooted on the snowy, ice-cold grounds. During summer months, prisoners were often made to stand for days in a sweat box seven feet high, twenty inches wide, and twelve inches deep without food, water, or ventilation.

Neither the North nor the South had foreseen the problems that would be caused by large numbers of prisoners over a prolonged war period. They had not planned how to house and feed and care for thousands of military prisoners, and they were unable to do so.

While the leaders of both sides planned strategies and waged battles, others in the both the North and the South made their contributions to the war effort. Women played major parts during the war, some in military roles and others on the home front. People underwent tremendous hardships, including the loss of loved ones.

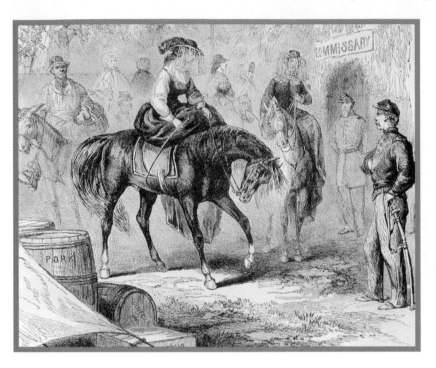

In towns under occupation by the Union Army, southern women were sometimes reduced to asking the Union soldiers for food.

LIFE ON THE HOME FRONT

Both northern and southern communities endured hardships during the Civil War, and the civilians at home suffered no matter which side of the conflict they were on. Even though the North and South were very different in their social activities, politics, economies, and industries, life grew much more difficult on both Union and Confederate home fronts.

In 1863, the South had to import everything from a hair pin to a toothpick, from a cradle to a coffin. Southerners found it difficult to get farm supplies, including seed, horse harnesses, ropes, and water tubs. The cost of feed for the animals and salt to cure, or preserve, meat was high. It was almost impossible to get items such as coffee or sugar. Household items, such as soap, candles, and matches were hard to come by. People often went without oil or gas for lighting and wood or coal for heating. There were not enough medical supplies for the civilians or the army. Many of the rail lines were inoperable for there were no tracks to replace war damaged lines. Although manufactured goods were in desperate need, there was a severe lack of machine parts when replacements were needed. The few manufacturing facilities in the South were not functional as the war wore on. Life in Georgia, as in all southern states, became very difficult.

Bread riots broke out in Richmond, Virginia. Many southerners used food items they had never tried before. Some ate mule meat and rats. Molasses was used as a sweetener instead of sugar. When they had no more coffee, people made drinks from chicory, peanuts, okra seed, and sweet potatoes.

Women used curtains or carpets to make clothes. Shoes were made from horsehide, deer, or pigskin and, sometimes, book covers. When they could not find the right kind of paper, some publishers used multicolored or patterned wallpaper for newsprint.

Prices in the South shot up, and money became worth less and less. Salt, which had cost a penny a pound before the war, rose to 50 cents a pound. Flour jumped to $200 a barrel. Dress shoes cost as much as $100. People began to barter, or trade items. According to one news report, a woman traded a $600 hat for five turkeys. Newspaper ads with barter requests were common.

There were not enough teachers or books to keep most schools open. Soldiers needed ammunition and horses, so there were few hunts or races. Some communities tried to raise money for the war with talent shows, musicals, or, occasionally, road shows. The admission price of one such show in Uniontown, Alabama, was $2 or "one pair of socks."

Neighbors and friends still visited each other, but these gatherings were no longer carefree parties. Southern women, trying to keep up family farms, did not always look forward to getting mail. They knew any letter might bring news of an injured or dead husband, son, or brother.

By the war's end Confederate money was worthless, making the rebuilding of Georgia even more difficult.

THE ROLE OF WOMEN IN THE CIVIL WAR

Women played a variety of roles in the war. In addition to running farms or working in factories, jobs traditionally held before the war by men, women served in other ways. Approximately four hundred women, according to some reports, actually disguised themselves as men and fought as soldiers. On more than one occasion, women acted as spies and Army scouts for both Union and Confederate troops while others served in the official army as stewardesses, laundresses, and nurses. When the Confederate Army in Tennessee was desperate for ammunition, women in Augusta at the Powder Works Gunpowder Plant were called in to help produce 75,000 cartridges a day. Thousands of women worked as paid or unpaid volunteers, and some were placed in positions of major importance.

Thirty-nine-year-old Phoebe Pember of Savannah was in charge of housekeeping and patient diet at one of the divisions of Richmond's Chimborazo Hospital. During the war, 15,000 patients were under her direct care. Dorothea Dix, who was known for her tireless campaign on behalf of the mentally ill, was head of the Union's Nursing Corps. Sally Tompkins, who ran a southern military hospital, was made a captain by Jefferson Davis and was the only woman to receive an officer's rank in the Confederate Army. Another well-known woman was Clara Barton, a Union Army nurse supervisor. After the war, she used her field-hospital experiences to found the American Red Cross in 1881.

Other women, such as Mary Boykin Chesnut of South Carolina, used their literary talents to record the drama of the Civil War. Chesnut's *A Diary from Dixie* was a shortened version of a 400,000-page manuscript about life during the period. Abolitionists, such as Elizabeth Cady Stanton and Susan B. Anthony, not only promoted the abolition of slavery but worked to obtain equal rights and suffrage for women.

Dorothea Dix, a famous mental health reformer, was head of the Union's Nursing Corps.

Women helped in the war effort in a very important way by simply keeping in touch with husbands, sons, brothers, and friends. By some accounts, close to 150,000 letters were sent out from Union post offices each day. Although southern mail took far longer, the same support was given to Confederate troops.

Occasionally, women supported the war effort in a less-than-dignified fashion. When New Orleans was occupied by Union soldiers, women would cast hateful glances at the soldiers as they passed by. They would sing Confederate songs in loud voices and would even spit on Union troops. Things got so out of hand, one woman emptied a bed chamber pot out a window on the head of Captain David Farragut. Shortly thereafter, Union officials passed the "Woman's Order," which made it a crime to treat soldiers in an undignified manner.

Most women, however, were content to assist in the war effort by keeping home and hearth going, by making clothes and bandages for soldiers, or filling the more traditional role of nursing the wounded.

A FINAL NOTE— THE COST OF THE CIVIL WAR

The Civil War cost our nation much more than the devastation and destruction of the towns and lands upon which battles were fought. It cost much more than the emotional heartache of a war that split our nation in two for five bloody years.

The war cost the United States government $2 million a day, or over $6 billion total. By 1910, after benefits were paid to veterans and their widows, that cost soared to $11.5 billion. Although the Confederate records were mostly destroyed, estimates show that the South spent about $4 billion. The expenditures of war were a severe financial drain on a young nation.

More importantly, however, over 620,000 soldiers died in the Civil War. About one-third of those men died on the battlefield, but most died from diseases, wounds, or the hardships of military prisons. On both sides of the tragic conflict, some of the men fought out of a sense of loyalty and duty, and others fought from a sense of adventure. Neither the North nor the South was ever the same again. The healing of emotional wounds would take far longer than the war itself. In the end, all that remained was the challenge of rebuilding a nation that was almost destroyed by the war.

Do You Remember?
1. Who was executed for "excessive cruelty" towards the Union prisoners at Andersonville?
2. Who was the only woman officer in the Confederacy?
3. What was the "Woman's Order"?
4. How many soldiers died in the Civil War?

SUMMARY

Nurse supervisor Clara Barton used her experience in Civil War field hospitals to found the American Red Cross.

- Confederate troops opened fire on Fort Sumter on April 12, 1861.
- Both sides began to prepare for war.
- The North had a standing army, more citizens to call to arms, and a stronger economy.
- Each side developed military and diplomatic strategies for winning the war.
- The first major battle, the Battle of Bull Run, was won by the Confederates.
- The bloodiest battle of the war was fought at Antietam Creek.
- Shortly after Antietam, on September 22, 1862, President Lincoln issued the Emancipation Proclamation.
- Although at first they were not allowed to serve, blacks ultimately fought for the Union forces.
- After Chattanooga fell in 1864, General Sherman's troops began their invasion of Georgia.
- With the fall of Savannah, the lower South was cut off from the rest of the Confederacy.
- General Robert E. Lee surrendered to General Ulysses S. Grant at Appomattox Courthouse on April 9, 1865.
- Women played important roles in the Civil War, in the battlefield as spies, soldiers, and nurses as well as on the home front.
- The North's blockades of southern ports hastened the end of the war.
- The final cost of the war was enormous, especially in terms of the loss of life and the long-term bitterness that remained between the two opponents

CHAPTER REVIEW

1861	1862	1863	1864	1865
Fort Pulaski taken by Confederate troops Battle of Bull Run	Battle of Antietam	Emancipation Proclamation put into effect Battle of Gettysburg Battle of Chickamauga	Atlanta occupied by Union troops Sherman's "march to the sea" Lincoln re-elected Savannah occupied by Union troops	Lee surrenders at Appomattox Courthouse

1861   1862   1863   1864   1865

1861	1862	1863	1864	1865
First transcontinental telegraph message sent Yale awards first Ph.D. degrees in the nation	Homestead Act signed Battle of the *Monitor* and the *Merrimack* "Battle Hymn of the Republic" published First federal income tax goes into effect	Thanksgiving declared a national holiday First Medal of Honor awarded Ebenezer Butterick invented the paper dress pattern	Motto "In God We Trust" introduced George Pullman began construction of railroad sleeping cars Arlington National Cemetery established	Stetson hat introduced Ku Klux Klan founded

Reviewing People, Places, and Terms

Define, identify, or explain the importance of each of the following.

1. blockade runner
2. garrison
3. rations
4. strategies
5. sutler wagons

Understanding the Facts

1. Where were the first shots of the Civil War fired?
2. What four states joined the Confederacy after the start of the war?
3. What was the northern strategy called that involved splitting the Confederacy in half by capturing the Mississippi River?
4. Which side was victorious at Manassas?
5. What did General Longstreet's forces do at the Battle of Gettysburg?
6. Who were the two opposing generals in the battle at Chickamauga Creek?

7. What was Sherman's strategy to end the support of southern civilians for the war?

Developing Critical Thinking

1. What do you think was the greatest factor in the Confederacy's defeat?
2. One southern newspaper owner called the Civil War, "a rich man's war and a poor man's fight." What do you think he meant by that?
3. How could the South's "King Cotton Diplomacy" political strategy for winning the war have been defended? Can you think of a strategy that might have been more defensible?
4. Why are historians unsure of the exact numbers of Confederate casualties?
5. Why do you think so many southerners thought the Confederacy could win the war in such short order?

Applying Your Skills

1. On a map of the United States, highlight using different colors (a) the Union states, (b) the

Confederate states, and (c) the border states that did not secede.

2. Choose one of the years 1861 to 1865 and prepare an expanded timeline that includes all events that occurred in the year that are mentioned in this chapter.

3. Using a Georgia road map and colored pencils or ink, identify in a distinctive color the counties and communities that lay in the route of destruction from Sherman's "march to the sea."

4. Imagine that you are a reporter covering the Gettysburg Cemetery dedication ceremonies. Write a brief news story about President Abraham Lincoln's appearance and remarks at the dedication.

Making Connections

1. From the library or other reference source, find a photograph taken during the Civil War that you find particularly moving. Why do you think it affected you so?

2. Have photographic images affected people's impressions of or reactions to wars or fighting in recent times? Give examples.

3. In what ways do you think Matthew Brady's coverage of events during the Civil War differs from today's typical television coverage of, say, the conflict in Kosovo?

4. What factors led Great Britain to support the Union against the Confederacy in the Civil War?

Did You Know?

- Four of Abraham Lincoln's brothers were Confederates.
- In 1864, the monthly pay of a private in the Confederate forces was $18.
- One of every sixty-five men in the Union Army was killed in action; one of every fifty-six died of wounds; one of every thirteen died from diseases; one of every ten was wounded; and one of every fifteen was captured.
- The Civil War was the first war in which servicemen in the field voted during a national election.
- Andersonville Prison, located about fifty miles south of Macon, is open today as a major tourist attraction.
- Fort Benning, near Columbus, is named after Henry Benning, a Confederate general.

BUILDING SKILLS: EXAMINING ALL SIDES OF AN ISSUE

People rarely, if ever, agree on an issue. And they frequently have a wide variety of reasons for feeling the way they do about an issue or for making the choices they do. Often, when making decisions, it is important to examine *all* reasons or alternatives in order to make the best decision possible. Reread the following paragraph from this chapter:

The Confederacy's political strategy was called King Cotton Diplomacy. The South believed that the British and French textile mills needed the South's cotton to keep running. If the Confederacy stopped selling cotton abroad for a time, it believed that the French and British would be forced *to help the South break the blockades and, in so doing, win the war.*

Put yourself in the place of French and British leaders considering the choices open to them. Analyze the reasons for (1) helping the South break the blockades, (2) providing assistance to the North, or (3) remaining neutral during the conflict.

On a sheet of paper, make three columns with these headings: Help the South, Help the North, Remain Neutral. Under each heading, make a "for" and an "against" list. In other words, list the reasons why the choice should be supported and the reasons why it would be a mistake to make that choice.

CHAPTER NINE

THE REBUILDING YEARS

With malice toward none, with charity for all . . . let us strive to finish the work we are in, to bind up the nation's wounds . . . .
—Abraham Lincoln

THE CIVIL WAR WAS OVER, and the enormous task of rebuilding the nation was about to begin. First, however, a number of questions had to be answered. What could be done to prevent another civil war? What might the conquering forces of the North do to the states of the Confederacy? How could the bonds of affection that had tied the southern states to the Union be restored? What should be done with four million freed slaves? What should be done about the sectional political parties that had helped cause the war? What could be done to restore economic and social well-being to those regions, especially in the South, that had borne the greatest part of the war's destruction?

THE AFTERMATH OF THE WAR

When the Civil War ended in 1865, Georgia, along with the rest of the South, faced great challenges. The Georgia to which the war-weary Confederate soldiers returned home was not as they had left it. Fields lay in ruins. Most houses were badly run down or had been destroyed. Owners of many factories, railroads, and stores had stopped doing business. Some quit because of wartime danger.

In addition to rebuilding as a direct result of Sherman's devastation, Georgia also had to replace railroad tracks and factories, like this rolling mill outside Atlanta, that the Confederate troops had destroyed in order to keep Sherman's men from using them.

Congress created the Freedmen's Bureau to help feed, clothe, and educate destitute freedmen. They lined up at Bureau offices all over the state to get help.

Others did not have enough money to stay open. There was not enough food, and many people were starving. Confederate paper money was worthless, and numbers of banks had closed their doors. Georgia faced a war debt of $20 million.

Many of Georgia's adult white male population died during the war or returned home unable to work because of their injuries. Some who had owned land sold it, or at least sold enough of it to raise cash badly needed for rebuilding. Many others returned to farms, homes, and businesses that had been destroyed or badly damaged.

At first, life for both blacks and whites was hard. During Sherman's march to the sea, his soldiers burned whole communities—houses as well as farms and businesses. Many people had to live in makeshift housing or tents. For most Georgians, there were new struggles each day. These struggles grew worse over the next several years.

FREEDMEN

The several hundred thousand **freedmen** (former slaves) faced even greater hardships. Homeless, uneducated, and free for the first time in their lives, the freedmen had little more than the clothes on their backs. Many went from place to place looking for food, shelter, and work. Some traveled just to demonstrate their new-found freedom. Others searched for spouses, children, other family members, or friends who had been sold away from them during slavery.

When the Civil War broke the chains of slavery, it also destroyed the old social order of master and slave. A new relationship had to be developed between black and white Georgians. But the attitudes of whites and blacks made that hard to do. Blacks feared that their old masters would try to re-enslave them. Whites found it difficult to accept blacks as free persons and did not accept them as equals.

THE FREEDMEN'S BUREAU

In response to the needs of the struggling whites and freedmen, the United States government established the Bureau of Refugees, Freedmen, and Abandoned Lands in March 1865. Its first commissioner was Union General Oliver O. Howard, who later founded Howard University in Washington, D.C. The original purpose of the agency, which soon became known as the **Freedmen's Bureau**, was to help both blacks and whites cope with their everyday problems by offering them clothing, food, and other necessities. However, after a while, the bureau's focus changed so that it became concerned primarily with helping freedmen adjust to their new circumstances. Freedmen, for their part, now regarded the ballot, land, and education as the primary means to independence.

Scores of Northern teachers came to the South after the Civil War to teach freedmen.

POLITICAL RECONSTRUCTION

The people of the now conquered South were fearful of what the victorious North might do to them. Would they be punished for their war against the Union? Would their property be taken away from them? Would they forever lose their rights as citizens? At first, the fears of most southerners were put to rest when they learned of the plans of President Lincoln and his successor for bringing them back into the Union. Subsequent events, however, would once again cause them to feel uneasy.

LINCOLN'S PLAN FOR RECONSTRUCTION

During the closing days of the war, President Lincoln developed a plan to rebuild the South and restore the southern states to the Union as quickly and easily as possible. The process was known as **Reconstruction**. Lincoln's plan had two simple steps: (1) All southerners, except for high-ranking Confederate civil and military leaders, would be pardoned after taking an oath of allegiance to the United States; and (2) when 10 percent of the voters in each state had taken the oath of loyalty, the state would be permitted to form a legal government and rejoin the Union.

John Wilkes Booth's decision to shoot Abraham Lincoln had a dramatic impact on Reconstruction and, perhaps, on the future history of our nation.

The Assassination of President Lincoln

On Good Friday, April 14, 1865, only five days after Lee's surrender, Abraham Lincoln turned to his wife, Mary Todd Lincoln, and said, "I never felt so happy in my life." That evening the couple and some friends went to Ford's Theatre to see an English play, *Our American Cousin.*

The play was nearly over when John Wilkes Booth, an actor who had been loyal to the Confederacy, entered Lincoln's theater box. At 10:15 p.m., timing his action with the play's biggest laugh, Booth shot the president in the back of the head. Lincoln was carried to a boarding house near the theater. He died there at 7:22 the following morning.

Booth Flees and Is Captured

After shooting the president, Booth then leaped from the box, shouting the state motto of Virginia, *Sic Semper Tyrannis* (Thus ever be to tyrants). During his jump, Booth caught his right spur on the treasury regiment flag displayed in the president's box. He fell, breaking his foot, and escaped the theater. He slipped out of Washington without getting caught.

Booth was able to elude his pursuers for several days. On April 26, 1865, federal troops and secret service agents found him hiding in a barn in Virginia and moved in to capture him. Acting against orders, Sergeant Boston Corbett fired into the barn and hit Booth in the neck. Booth died the next day.

JOHNSON'S RECONSTRUCTION PLAN

Lincoln's assassination took place before his plan for Reconstruction went into effect. Upon Lincoln's death, Vice President Andrew Johnson became the nation's seventeenth president. Soon after taking office, he took on the responsibility for returning the former Confederate states to the Union.

President Johnson's Reconstruction plan was much like Lincoln's, except that Johnson expanded the group of southerners who were not covered by the general pardon. Men who held high-ranking positions in the Confederate government and military and those who owned property worth more than $20,000 had to apply directly to the president for a pardon. Johnson, who was born in North Carolina and later moved to Tennessee, also required the southern states to write new constitutions that abolished slavery.

Johnson's plan, like Lincoln's, disappointed a group of radical Republicans who had gained control of Congress. One of the concerns of this group of Republicans was that blacks would be **disfranchised** (have voting rights taken away). They also felt that both Lincoln's and Johnson's plans did not punish the South

Vice President Andrew Johnson, the former governor of Tennessee, was as stunned as the rest of the nation over the assassination of President Lincoln. He quickly decided to carry out Lincoln's moderate plan of Reconstruction, but the radical Republicans had other ideas.

enough and called for stronger requirements for readmission. Under pressure from the public and Congress, Johnson added three more requirements to his plan. Southern states had to (1) repeal their secession ordinances; (2) *repudiate* (void) their war debt; and (3) ratify the **Thirteenth Amendment**, which ended slavery. When that was done, the states could return representatives to the United States Congress, and the government would forgive each state's war debt.

Do You Remember?

1. What was Georgia's war debt after the Civil War?
2. Who was the first commissioner of the Freedmen's Bureau?
3. What were the two conditions in Lincoln's plan for Reconstruction?
4. Which Congressional group wanted stronger punishment for the South?
5. What was the Thirteenth Amendment?

POLITICAL RECONSTRUCTION IN GEORGIA

During the mid- to late-1860s, it was often hard to tell who was in charge of Georgia politics. In order to be readmitted into the Union, the state worked through three separate phases of political reconstruction: President Johnson's Reconstruction plan, Congressional Reconstruction plans, and—for a short period of time—military occupation.

Appointed by President Andrew Johnson, former Congressman James Johnson served as Georgia's provisional governor from June to December 1865.

PHASE I:
PRESIDENTIAL RECONSTRUCTION

In June 1865, President Johnson appointed James Johnson as **provisional** (temporary) governor of Georgia. Johnson earlier had been one of the state's congressmen opposed to secession. The president directed Governor Johnson to hold a constitutional convention in Milledgeville in October, six months after Lee surrendered at Appomattox.

The Constitutional Convention of 1865

The convention repealed the Ordinance of Secession and voted to do away with slavery. It wrote a new constitution that, although quite similar to the Constitution of 1861, was acceptable to the president.

In November, the state elected Charles Jenkins as governor (he was the only candidate) and representatives to the United States Congress. In the following month, the legislature met and formally ratified the Thirteenth Amendment to the U.S. Constitution. Also in December 1865, after President Johnson removed the provisional governor, the state inaugurated Jenkins as its governor.

The Georgia General Assembly met again in January 1866 and elected two United States senators: Alexander Stephens, former vice president of the Confederacy, and Herschel Johnson. The General Assembly also voted to give civil rights to freed blacks. However, like other southern states, Georgia limited those rights.

Black Codes

The Thirteenth Amendment, passed in 1865, abolished slavery. However, it did not abolish discrimination.

By 1865, most of the southern states, including Georgia, had passed a number of laws known as **Black Codes** that were designed to restrict the rights of freedmen. The codes included regulations that controlled the types of employment freedmen could have; permitted whipping as punishment; and established labor periods from sunrise to sunset, six days a week. Because these codes permitted the imprisonment of jobless blacks, freedmen were forced to take whatever jobs they could find regardless of low wages or other conditions. Although the Freedmen's Bureau recommended wages of $144 a year plus food and shelter, most workers were paid between $50 and $100 a year. Any days not worked were charged against the worker, with penalties ranging from $1 for an illness to $5 for political activity.

Other sections of the Black Codes restricted freedmen from serving on juries or testifying in court against whites. The codes declared intermarriage between the races illegal, and they denied voting rights to the freedmen.

Even with the codes, Georgia had done what President Johnson's plan required, and it was ready to re-enter the Union. But President Johnson, who barely survived a vote calling for his **impeachment** (charges brought to seek removal from office), no longer had the influence he once had. Instead, the balance of power now was in the hands of the more radical groups in Congress.

PHASE II:
CONGRESSIONAL RECONSTRUCTION

Reaction in the North to the Black Codes was fairly swift. In 1866, the **Fourteenth Amendment** to the U.S. Constitution was passed forbidding any state from making laws that would limit the rights and privileges of any citizen. The amendment also included clauses pertaining to the due process of law and to equal protection under it.

As a leader in the state convention while James Johnson was governor, Herschel Vespasian Johnson was elected as one of Georgia's two U.S. Senators in January 1866.

The radical Republicans, who took control of the U.S. Congress in 1866, also felt that the southern states were not "adequately reconstructed." They called for additional requirements for re-entry into the Union. They said the southern states must ratify the Fourteenth Amendment, the amendment that gave blacks full citizenship and equal protection under the law. In November 1866, Georgia joined all other southern states except Tennessee in refusing to ratify that amendment.

Five months later, in April 1867, the U.S. Congress acted. The states, including Georgia, that refused to ratify the Fourteenth Amendment were again placed under military rule. Congress divided these states into five military districts and appointed an army general to govern each of them, along with federal troops to keep order. Georgia, Alabama, and Florida were in the third military district governed by General John Pope.

PUNISHMENT OF EX-CONFEDERATES

After the war, those who took up arms against the United States could have been charged with treason and, if found guilty, executed. Presidents Abraham Lincoln and Andrew Johnson, however, favored lenient treatment. They believed leniency would make it easier to restore the Union in spirit.

In 1865, President Johnson issued a proclamation that pardoned all Confederates who had supported the war except those in fourteen classifications. The classes generally included Confederate leaders and wealthy southerners. These people could personally apply to the president for pardons, and thousands did. Johnson pardoned some 13,500 people.

Still, scores of Confederate leaders were imprisoned until Johnson could decide what to do with them. Chief among them was Jefferson Davis, who was imprisoned for two years at Fortress Monroe. He was charged with treason, but in 1867 the federal government decided not to prosecute him. He was freed but never pardoned.

The ratification of the Fourteenth Amendment in 1868 created new problems for ex-Confederates. It prohibited them from holding office until pardoned by a two-thirds vote of Congress. Those who were elected to office in 1868 as Republicans were easily pardoned. By 1877, Congress had pardoned all but about 500 ex-Confederate leaders. In 1898, Congress finally passed an act of general amnesty.

Overall, the United States government was most lenient and forgiving of ex-Confederate leaders. It thus secured their loyalty and the loyalty of the South.

One of General Pope's first tasks was to register all eligible voters, a category that included all adult males, black as well as white, who swore allegiance to the United States. Only certain former high-ranking Confederate military and political leaders were excluded.

The Constitutional Convention of 1867

During the fall of 1867, an election was held to decide if there should be a constitutional convention and to elect delegates to it. This election marked the first time blacks could run for and hold public office in Georgia. The voters did decide to hold a constitutional convention, which began in Atlanta on December 9, 1867. The convention worked for three months to draw up a new constitution. Most of the 169 delegates were **scalawags**, a term used to describe southerners who supported the radical Republicans. There were also twelve conservative whites and nine northerners who had moved into the state to help carry out Congress's Reconstruction plan. These northerners were called **carpetbaggers** because they supposedly arrived in the South with all their belongings packed in cheap luggage made from carpets. Thirty-seven delegates were black.

The delegates had varied backgrounds. Some had moved to the South after the war. Some could neither read nor write and had no experience in government. Others were educated professionals, such as ministers, lawyers, teachers, and government employees.

Three of the better known black delegates were Tunis G. Campbell, Henry McNeal Turner, and Aaron A. Bradley. Campbell was a native of New Jersey and a Freedmen's Bureau agent. He is

BUFFALO SOLDIERS

During Reconstruction, many families headed to the West, lured by the promises of open land, opportunities for free or inexpensive homesteads, claims of gold, and assurances of excitement and adventure. Among those who rushed there were blacks. Some blacks went there as soldiers, others went to become cowboys.

The geography of these territories presented challenges for the new settlers as they tried to establish and protect their homesteads. The areas were much more vast and remote than those left behind in the East. In many places, rivers and streams were less plentiful, so arguments arose over water and grazing rights. Usually, great distances separated one settlement from another, and communications between them were often primitive. Frequently, this remoteness and isolation made the settler more vulnerable to attacks by roving bands of unfriendly Indians or lawless whites.

In 1866, Congress passed a bill establishing a post-war military force to help protect citizens in the western territories. A distinctive part of this force were units of the U.S. cavalry called the "Buffalo Soldiers" by Indians because of the buffalo-hide coats the troops wore in the winter. Included among the Buffalo Soldiers were six black regiments, which were later reorganized into four regiments.

The duties of the western troops were varied depending on a unit's location. Some units escorted wagon trains and stagecoaches, helping build forts and roads as they mapped uncharted areas. Some of the maps proved invaluable to settlement of the area. Other units protected settlers in the western lands from Indian attacks, cattle rustlers, or Mexican revolutionaries. The black regiments distinguished themselves for many years, participating in several major campaigns against the Indians and later serving as lead troops in the Spanish-American War.

Clad in full-dress uniforms, soldiers of Company B, 25th U.S. Infantry, stand at attention outside their barracks at Fort Randall in Dakota Territory. Before coming to the northern plains in 1880, these soldiers had fought Apaches along the Texas-Mexico border.

remembered for introducing **legislation** (laws) that kept people who could not pay their debts from going to prison. Henry Turner was born free in South Carolina and worked with the Freedmen's Bureau immediately after the war. Turner was an advocate of civil rights and public education and was the first black chaplain in the United States Army. He later served as a minister in Macon, Georgia.

Aaron Bradley had been a slave in Georgia until he escaped to New York twenty-six years before the Civil War. After the war, he settled in Savannah. Bradley was outspoken and had an angry, quick temper. After several outbursts, the convention *expelled* (removed) him by a unanimous vote. Bradley, however, was popular with blacks and was elected to the Georgia Senate in 1868.

Ku Klux Klan

Another group, the **Ku Klux Klan**, became powerful during early Reconstruction. The Klan was one of several secret organizations that tried to keep blacks from using their newly granted civil rights.

The Ku Klux Klan began in Pulaski, Tennessee, in 1865 as a social club for returned soldiers. However, it very quickly changed into a force of terror. Members dressed in white robes and hoods so no one would

Above: For freedmen, the rise of the Ku Klux Klan was another terrifying experience as the Klan worked to prevent former slaves from using their newly won freedom and rights. Right: Begging for one's life had little effect on the hardened Klansmen embittered over the South's defeat in the war and the economic hardships of Reconstruction.

know them. They moved at night and frightened black leaders with whippings and murders.

By 1868, the Ku Klux Klan was active in Georgia. It tried to keep black citizens from voting or taking any part in government. The Klan became so powerful in the South that Congress later passed laws, including the **Force Act of 1870**, to end its activities. The military enforced the laws and, by 1871, most of the terrorism of the Klan seemed over.

Georgians Approve New Constitution

Even though they had heated debates during the convention, the delegates were pleased with the results of their attempts at rewriting the state's constitution. The new constitution gave civil rights to all the state's citizens. It approved free public education for all children and made Georgia the first state to allow married women to control their own property.

In April 1868, Georgia voters approved the new constitution. They also elected Republican Rufus Bullock as governor by a 7,000-vote majority. Bullock, a native of New York, had been in Georgia for only nine years. He defeated John B. Gordon, a well-known Confederate commander who was said to be a leader in the Ku Klux Klan. In July, the General Assembly ratified the Fourteenth Amendment to the United States Constitution, and Bullock was inaugurated. Georgia had, for a second time, met the requirements to be readmitted to the Union.

The convention had one other, long-lasting effect on politics in Georgia. Delegates to the constitutional convention enjoyed their stay in Atlanta. Milledgeville hotels would not house black legislators, but those in Atlanta would. Perhaps this may have been a major influence on the legislature's decision later in 1868 to move the state capital to Atlanta.

Once the state ratified its new constitution, federal troops left the state. They were, however, to return shortly.

A New Yorker, Rufus Bullock had served in the Confederacy during the war. Although elected governor of Georgia in 1868 by popular vote, his administration was marked with scandals of embezzlement and corruption. After resigning as governor and fleeing the state, he was arrested but later acquitted of illegally using public funds.

PHASE III:
RETURN TO MILITARY RULE

Once again, Congress would not let Georgia re-enter the Union. When the legislature met in September, the conservatives who had opposed Bullock were in control. Over Governor Bullock's strong objections, they expelled twenty-eight of the thirty-two black legislators. The conservatives said the right to vote did not carry with it the right to hold public office.

The Georgia Act

Because of evidence that increased Ku Klux Klan activity kept blacks from voting in the 1868 presidential election, Governor Bullock appealed to the federal government for help. Congress responded by passing the **Georgia Act** in December 1869. The Georgia Act placed Georgia under military rule for the third time. General Alfred Terry became Georgia's new military commander, and Bullock became provisional governor.

Benjamin Conley became governor when Rufus Bullock suddenly resigned. He is most well known for being the state's last Republican governor.

The Georgia Act also declared that Georgia would have to ratify the **Fifteenth Amendment** to the United States Constitution before the state could be readmitted to the Union. The Fifteenth Amendment states that the "right of citizens of the United States to vote shall not be denied . . . on account of race, color, or previous condition of servitude."

End of Reconstruction

The Georgia Supreme Court ruled that blacks were eligible to hold office. When the General Assembly met in January 1870, it reseated the expelled representatives. The legislature again approved the Fourteenth Amendment and ratified the Fifteenth Amendment. Georgia was readmitted to the Union in July 1870. Senators Joshua Hill and H. V. M. Miller, elected in 1868, were seated in Congress. For Georgia, Reconstruction was officially over.

Democrats Regain Control of State Politics

There was one final political note to the end of Reconstruction. The Democrats regained control of both houses of the Georgia General Assembly in the December 1870 election. Governor Bullock, a Republican, knew the General Assembly would impeach him when they met in November 1871. Rather than face impeachment, Bullock resigned. He secretly swore in as governor a friend, Benjamin Conley, who had been president of the senate during the last legislative session. Conley served as governor only two months before the General Assembly ordered a special election. In December, Democrat James M. Smith, former speaker of the house of representatives and a lawyer from Columbus, ran unopposed for the office of governor.

Smith was inaugurated on January 12, 1872. From his election in December 1871 through 1999, Georgia's governors have been members of the Democratic party.

James M. Smith, a Democrat from Twiggs County and former speaker of the house of representatives, followed Benjamin Conley as governor and served from 1872 to 1877.

Do You Remember?

1. What were the Black Codes designed to do?
2. What did the Fourteenth Amendment give to blacks?
3. What were carpetbaggers?
4. Who was the last Republican governor of the state?

ECONOMIC RECONSTRUCTION

It was necessary for Georgia to rebuild economically as well as politically. Banks had failed all over the South. Confederate money was worthless, and at least two-thirds of the railroads could not be used. Southern states owed millions of dollars in war debts. Former slaves, who had lived and worked on large farms and plantations, now had no jobs. Most whites who owned farms needed laborers but could not pay them. Those in charge of Reconstruction had promised freed blacks "forty acres and a mule," but that promise was never kept. As a result, land owners and workers agreed on two new ways to farm.

SHARECROPPING AND TENANT FARMING

Workers who had nothing but their labor to offer often resorted to **sharecropping**. Under this system, the landowner provided land, a house, farming tools and animals, seed, and fertilizer. The workers agreed to give the owner a share of the harvest. Until the workers sold their crops, the owners often let them have food, medicine, clothing, and other supplies at high prices on credit.

For many, this credit was their undoing. For example, cotton was a major crop in Georgia. If a sharecropper harvested 500 bales of cotton and had agreed to give the landowner half, each would get 250 bales. After selling the harvested cotton and paying the bills, the typical sharecropper had little, if any, cash left. Moreover, because few sharecroppers could read or count, the planter or the store owner could easily cheat them, and many did. Year after year, sharecroppers were in debt. There was little hope they could ever save enough to buy their own land and equipment.

Tenant farming was similar to sharecropping. The main difference was that tenants usually owned agricultural equipment and farm animals, such as mules. They also bought their

Right: For many freed slaves, work as a sharecropper during Reconstruction was much as it had been before the war.
Above: A living history demonstration at Tifton's Agrirama recreates the life of a late nineteenth-century tenant farmer.

own seed and fertilizer. Tenants worked the owner's land using their own equipment and supplies. At the end of the year, they either paid the landowner a set amount of cash or gave the agreed-on share of the crop. Tenant farmers owned more than sharecroppers, and they usually made a small profit for working the land. However, the lives of both groups were very hard. The tenant farming and sharecropper systems allowed landowners to keep their farms in operation without having to spend money for labor.

On the surface, it seemed that landowners who used tenants and sharecroppers to work their land made a profit while taking few risks. However, many owners who did not have enough money to buy the seed, fertilizer, and tools needed by sharecroppers would mortgage crops before they were planted. Interest on such loans was often more than the crops were worth. Because bankers expected farmers to grow cotton or tobacco in the same place year after year, much of the soil was ruined. In time, many landowners in the South, like the sharecroppers and tenants who worked their land, became poorer each year.

At the end of Reconstruction, cotton was again the most important crop in many parts of Georgia. In 1870, the state produced 726,406 bales of cotton, more, in fact, than the number of bales grown in the year before the Civil War. Not all parts of the state fared equally well. The coastal region, for example, never regained its prewar position in either cotton or rice production.

INDUSTRY, RAILROADS, BUSINESS, AND SHIPPING

Increasing cotton production brought industry to some parts of Georgia. Northern investors put money into building textile mills. Slowly, banks began to reopen and were able to loan money to merchants and businessmen.

By the late 1860s, dry goods stores, shops, and hotels were again in business. Atlanta, almost completely destroyed during the war, was rebuilt and grew rapidly after it became the state capital.

Railroads, which were necessary to the success of Georgia's economy, expanded during this time. At the end of the Civil War, only the state-owned Western and Atlantic Railroad was still in operation. Union soldiers had kept it up to transport troops and equipment. In the eight years immediately following the war, rail companies laid 840 miles of track in Georgia. Rail lines began to compete with each other.

Shipping companies also took on new life. Savannah again became the major port for exporting cotton, and Brunswick was a close second. Even with the growth of banks, rail lines, and shipping companies, economic reconstruction was slow. However, as Georgians worked together, they made steady progress.

Only one railway company was still in operation at the end of the Civil War. In the eight years following, rail companies laid 840 miles of track in Georgia.

A CITY RISES FROM ITS ASHES

At the beginning of Reconstruction, Atlanta literally had to rebuild itself from the ashes of what once had been Georgia's transportation and communications center. When Sherman's troops moved out of Atlanta on their infamous march to the sea, they left the city in flames. Stores had been gutted, homes had been burned, warehouses had been destroyed, telegraphs lines had been cut, and even the iron rails of the railroad tracks had been wrapped around trees to prevent their being reused.

Atlanta had begun in 1837 when a railroad engineer, Stephen Long, surveyed the best route for the Georgia State Railroad. He wrote that a collection of shacks known as the *Terminus* (end) might be "a good location for one tavern, a blacksmith shop, a grocery store, and

Above: In 1843, Terminus was renamed Marthasville, and the small settlement began to grow. **Right:** *In 1845, Marthasville was renamed Atlanta, for the Western and Atlantic Railroads. The paintings on these and the next two pages are by Georgia artist Wilbur G. Kurtz, who did many paintings depicting the early history of Atlanta.*

Above: By 1860, Atlanta had a population of 9,500 and was Georgia's fourth largest city, after Savannah, Augusta, and Columbus. **Opposite page:** *This painting shows Atlanta in 1864, before Sherman's occupation. After Sherman left on his march to the sea, the city lay in wood cinders and chunks of brick. However, the spirit of Atlanta had not burned, and rebuilding began at once. In 1866, the population was 20,000, and there were 250 stores in a 3-mile downtown area. Street lamps and gas lights were back in place.*

nothing else." By 1842, railroad lines into Terminus had grown, and it was home to almost thirty people. In that year, the community was renamed Marthasville, in honor of Governor Lumpkin's daughter.

During the next few years, the growing community added a sawmill, a general store, a bonnet and hat shop, and several small grocery stores. The town also had a real estate office and a small hotel. Because freight shipped to the city was marked "Atlanta," a feminine form of the word *Atlantic* in Atlantic and Pacific Railroad, the town was called Atlanta by railroad officials and crews. Soon the name Marthasville was discarded, and the state issued a municipal charter for the city to be named Atlanta.

By 1847, the population of Atlanta had grown to 2,500. The city now had its first bookstore, thirty or so other stores, a second hotel, two newspapers, and two schools. A visitor reported that 187 buildings were constructed during an eight-month period.

At the beginning of the Civil War, Atlanta was Georgia's fourth largest city, with a population of over 9,500. Only Savannah, Augusta, and Columbus were larger. During the war, Atlanta grew even more in population and importance as the South's center for communications and supplies.

An aerial view of Atlanta in 1871. Downtown Atlanta began a slow but steady rebuilding process following the destruction caused by Sherman's burning of the city as he began his infamous "March to the Sea."

After Sherman's troops left, the city lay smouldering and in ruins, with black smoke rising in the air. But the city had a proud past and the heart to rebuild for a proud future.

About fifty families had remained in the city despite evacuation orders. Those who remained were determined to rebuild. Joined by others, they worked throughout the Reconstruction period to build a city that was to rise out of the ashes like a *phoenix*, a mythical Egyptian symbol of resurrected life that supposedly reappeared periodically after self-destruction ended each life span.

The city grew rapidly during the period, both commercially and politically. Finally, in 1868, Atlanta become the capital city of Georgia.

Do You Remember?

1. What was the difference between a sharecropper and a tenant farmer?
2. How much cotton did Georgia produce in 1870? How did that compare to pre-war production?
3. What were Georgia's two major seaports after the war?
4. What was Atlanta called before a state municipal charter changed its name?

"DOC" HOLLIDAY

Every state has one or more notorious citizens, and Georgia is no exception. One of Georgia's more infamous citizens was John Henry Holliday, better known as "Doc" Holliday. Born in Griffin, John Henry grew up in Valdosta as the only child of a Confederate major who was also the mayor of Valdosta.

In 1870, at the age of 19, Holliday headed north to attend dental school. He returned to Georgia and opened a dental practice in Atlanta. Not everyone agrees on the exact sequence of events in Holliday's life over the next few years, but this much we do know. Doc Holliday contracted tuberculosis and was told that he had only six or seven months left to live. He moved west to a drier climate because of his illness. As his coughing became more "bone-wracking" and constant, he could no longer practice dentistry so he turned a favored pastime, gambling, into a full-time profession.

Doc lived in Dallas for a while until he killed a man in a gunfight. For a few years, he wandered between Colorado and Texas, usually moving two steps ahead of the law. On one of his jaunts, he met and became fast friends with the famous western lawman Wyatt Earp and Earp's two brothers. Holliday even saved Earp's life.

Eventually Holliday joined the trio in Tombstone, Arizona. Members of a gang called the "Cowboys" were looking for trouble and sent word that they would arrive in Tombstone with guns, something that was forbidden by the town's laws. Things heated up quickly after their arrival, and around 2:30 p.m. on October 26, 1881, the legendary shootout at the O.K. Corral occurred. The gunfight was not actually in the corral but in an alley next to it. After a brief blaze of bullets, three men were dead and everyone but Wyatt Earp was injured. Soon afterward, both Wyatt and Doc headed for Denver where Doc was promptly arrested. However, Bat Masterson, another legendary lawman, persuaded the governor of Colorado to release the dentist turned gambler and gunfighter.

In May 1887, Doc went to Glenwood Springs in Colorado to try the sulfur vapors believed to be helpful in treating tuberculosis. But the disease had ravaged his body. On November 8, he awoke from a partial coma and said, "This is funny." Then Doc Holliday died, marking the end of a man's life and the beginning of the legend of a famous western gunfighter.

Former dentist, professional gambler, and gunfighter, John Henry "Doc" Holliday is one of the most colorful characters to have come from Georgia.

Above: The Hebrew Benevolent Society provided a permanent home for Atlanta's Jewish population in 1875 when the first synagogue was built in the city. Opposite page: After serving one term in the Georgia legislature from 1868 to 1870, Henry McNeal Turner became actively involved in the A.M.E. Church. A fiery orator and writer, Turner later actually favored African colonization. Why do you think Henry Turner advocated black migration to Africa?

SOCIAL AND CULTURAL PROGRESS

The Civil War also tore apart the social and cultural institutions of southerners, and these, too, had to be put back together during the years immediately following the South's defeat. Fairly quickly, however, new places of worship and education were established. At the same time, various outlets for creative expression emerged.

RELIGION

Churches suffered in several ways during the Civil War. Many church buildings had been burned and had to be rebuilt. Issues such as slavery and secession had led to divisions in many of the major Christian denominations. As a result of these divisions and the war casualties, there was also a shortage of ministers.

During the Reconstruction period, however, church membership grew rapidly, and people began to replace their houses of worship. Some of the once-divided denominations, like the Episcopalians, chose to reunite their churches with those in the North. Others, like the Baptists, did not, and they remain part of a southern religious organization to this day.

Jews, who had been among the first colonists in Georgia, were also active in restoring old houses of worship or establishing new ones. In 1875, the Hebrew Benevolent Congregation built its first synagogue in Atlanta.

Black churches grew in number and influence. A few blacks continued to attend white churches, but most went to churches begun by blacks. Soon these churches became centers of social and religious life; black ministers quickly became leaders in religious, community, and civil rights matters. Also during this period, Henry Turner, a representative to the Georgia General Assembly, established the African Methodist Episcopal Church (AME).

EDUCATION

The 1868 Georgia constitution provided for schools "free to all children of the state" but did not fund them. Following the provisions of the state constitution, the General Assembly in 1870 passed an act to "establish a system of public education." The legislation divided the state into local school districts. It also provided for a state school commissioner and a state board of education. The Georgia Education Association was formed in 1869, with Gustavus J. Orr as its first chairman. Most educational gains during Reconstruction came about mainly as a result of Orr's work.

The 1870 school law provided for separate but "equal" schools for black and white children, but two years later, a new law read,

As a journalist for the Atlanta Constitution, *attorney Charles Henry Smith used Bill Arp as a pseudonym, or pen name.*

"equal as far as practicable." In many towns, the school "year" was actually only four months. The four-month school "year" was largely due to the need for farmers' children to help in the fields during the time of planting and harvesting. General J. R. Lewis was the first state school commissioner. In 1872, he was replaced by Orr, who is called the father of public education in Georgia. Public schools, nevertheless, did not receive any state support until 1873. Cities such as Savannah, Atlanta, and Columbus did not wait for the state and began their own school systems. However, the public school system that we know today did not make much progress until the early 1900s.

Other educational groups and institutions also made an impact on the state during the Reconstruction period. The Freedmen's Bureau started over 4,000 primary schools, 64 industrial schools, and 74 teacher-training institutions for young black people in the South. Northern individuals and missionary societies helped by sending both money and teachers. In 1867, the American Missionary Association sponsored the chartering of Georgia's Atlanta University. That same year, the American Baptist Home Mission Society organized Morehouse College in Augusta. The Augusta school, which moved to Atlanta in 1870, is still in operation. A third Georgia Reconstruction school was Clark College in Atlanta. It first opened as a school for children, and, by 1877, it had become a college.

LITERATURE

There were several popular works of American literature published during the post-war period. These included *Hans Brinker or The Silver Skates* by Mary Mapes Dodge, *The Story of a Bad Boy* by Thomas Aldrich, and Mark Twain's *Innocents Abroad*. No story was more popular with girls than *Little Women*, by Louisa Mae Alcott. This story of the trials of a New England family during the Civil War continues to this day to be a lasting and loved work of American literature.

A well-known Georgia author of the period was Charles H. Smith, who used the pen name Bill Arp. His books included *Bill Arp, So-Called, A Side Show of the Southern Side of the War*, published in 1866, and *Bill Arp's Letters*, published in 1868. Both books used humor to describe the woes of the defeated South.

Southern Cultivator, the only Georgia magazine that did not stop publication during the war, continued to give farming information. Magazines such as *The Atlantic Monthly* and *The Saturday Press* had readers all over the country. The latter magazine, published in New York, played a major part in bringing fame to Samuel Langhorne

Clemens. Clemens, better known as Mark Twain, wrote a tall tale called "Jim Smiley and His Jumping Frog," which *The Saturday Press* printed in 1865. Major newspapers in the country reprinted the story, known today as "The Celebrated Jumping Frog of Calaveras County."

After the wartime paper shortage was over, newspapers grew both in circulation and in number of pages. Unlike the two or four sheets that some of them were reduced to in wartime, they now began to look more like the ones we see today, reporting state and local events. The *Atlanta Constitution*, started in 1868, soon became the "Voice of the South."

Do You Remember?

1. Who founded the African Methodist Episcopal Church?
2. Who was Gustavus Orr?
3. What was the major reason for the four-month school year?
4. In what city was Morehouse College first located?
5. Who was Charles H. Smith?

Carey W. Styles, who served as a colonel in the Civil War, founded the Atlanta Constitution *on June 16, 1868.*

SUMMARY

- Following the war, much of the South lay in ruin.
- Lincoln drafted a Reconstruction plan but was assassinated before he could put it to work.
- Lincoln and his successor, Andrew Johnson, wanted the South readmitted to the Union as quickly and painlessly as possible.
- To gain readmission, Confederate states had to swear allegiance, abolish slavery, and repeal the Ordinance of Secession.
- A group of radical Republicans, who gained control of Congress, passed a series of acts that made re-entry into the Union much more difficult. States wanting readmission had to adopt the Thirteenth, Fourteenth, and Fifteenth amendments to the U.S. Constitution.
- Georgia went through three phases of political reconstruction before being readmitted to the Union—presidential Reconstruction, congressional Reconstruction, and military occupation.
- After blacks who had been elected to the General Assembly were expelled, Congress passed the Georgia Act, and the state returned to military rule.
- During Reconstruction, Georgia's farmers operated with little money for labor by using the systems of sharecropping and tenant farming.
- After the war, churches and schools had to be re-established, and cultural life had to be renewed.
- Georgia was finally readmitted to the Union in July 1870.

CHAPTER REVIEW

1865	1866	1867	1868	1869	1870	1872
Lincoln assassinated; Johnson becomes president	Georgia refused to ratify the Fourteenth Amendment	Georgia returned to military rule	Fourteenth Amendment ratified	Georgia Act passed	Fifteenth Amendment ratified	Freedmen's Bureau abolished
Thirteenth Amendment ratified			New state constitution adopted		Georgia readmitted into the Union	
			Atlanta Constitution founded			

1865   1866   1867   1868   1869   1870   1871   1872

1865	1866	1867	1868	1869	1870
Lister discovered use of antiseptic	Nobel invented dynamite	U.S. bought Alaska from Russia	Westinghouse invented air brake for trains	Transcontinental railroad completed	Hiram R. Revels of Mississippi became first black U.S. Senator
Lewis Carroll published *Alice's Adventures in Wonderland*		Sholes invented first practical typewriter		Wyoming passed law granting women the right to vote	

Reviewing People, Places, and Terms

Use the following terms in a paragraph describing Georgia after the Civil War.

Black Codes
carpetbaggers
freedmen
Reconstruction
scalawags

Understanding the Facts

1. What did freed blacks fear their former owners would try to do?
2. What was the original purpose of the Freedmen's Bureau?
3. What play was Lincoln watching when shot?
4. What was the major difference between Johnson's original Reconstruction plan and Lincoln's?
5. What were the three phases of political Reconstruction in Georgia?
6. What act did Congress pass in an attempt to end the activities of the Ku Klux Klan?
7. What did the Fifteenth Amendment state?
8. How did Atlanta get its name?
9. What group sponsored the chartering of Atlanta University?

Developing Critical Thinking

1. If Lincoln had lived, do you think Reconstruction in the South would have been different? Explain your answer.
2. Compare and contrast scalawags and carpetbaggers.
3. Some historians have said that one of the biggest mistakes of Reconstruction was the decision by the federal government not to give land grants to blacks. In a short paragraph, argue either for or against such land grants.

Applying Your Skills

1. Pretend you are a Confederate soldier returning home in 1865 from the war after four years of being away. Write a letter to a friend in another state describing how things have changed in Georgia since you were last home.
2. Choose one of the following people, and write a short report on that person's life: (a) Andrew Johnson, (b) John Wilkes Booth, (c) Louisa May Alcott, (d) Henry Turner, or (e) Jefferson Davis.
3. Research and write a one-page report on either sharecropping or tenant farming that contains information not already covered in this textbook.

Making Connections

1. Read the novel *Lonesome Dove* or look at a video of the television series adapted from it. Can you find any parallels between the cowboy life as depicted in the book or television series and that described in this chapter? What are they?

2. Another recent television film, *Buffalo Soldiers*, traces the lives of members of the post-Civil War western troops. How closely do the events in that film correspond with the descriptions in your textbook? How do they differ?

3. Jefferson Davis was never pardoned for his participation in the Confederacy. Prepare a short report on why this was so.

4. The victorious side in a war often charges those on the losing side with "war crimes." What are "war crimes"? Give examples of this practice in the twentieth century.

BUILDING SKILLS
STUDYING HISTORIC DOCUMENTS

The night President Abraham Lincoln was assassinated by John Wilkes Booth, he was attending a performance of *Our American Cousin* at Ford's Theatre in Washington, D.C. Pictured here is Lincoln's original program. Notice the bloodstains on the program.

Read the program, then see if you can answer the following questions:

1. What was the date of Lincoln's assassination? What day of the week was it?

2. What was the name of the patriotic song and chorus?

3. Who was the featured actress for the performance of "Our American Cousin"?

4. When you attend a movie today, you are shown "coming attractions." What was the "coming attraction" at Ford's Theatre?

5. Who was the star of the "coming attraction"?

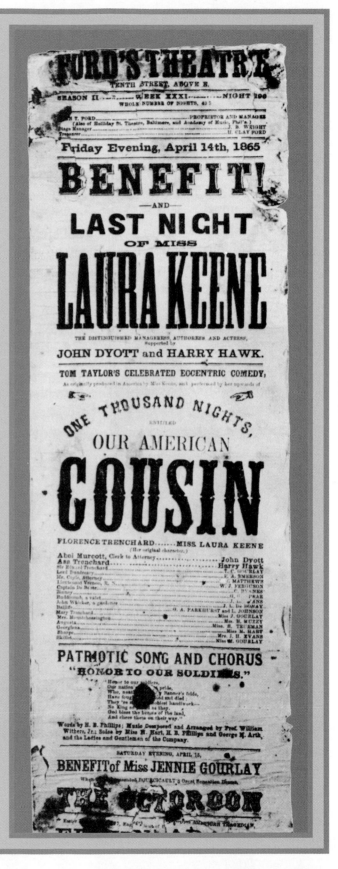

UNIT V

A NEW SPIRIT

It is among the factory workers and the small farmers of Georgia that one finds the chief prosperity of the State. Here there is little or no debt; money circulates rapidly; improvements are seen; and there are patient, hopeful labor, thrift and enterprise, which affect, as it seems to me, the whole population. . . .

—Charles Nordhoff

IN THE YEARS BETWEEN the end of Reconstruction and the end of World War I, the United States and Georgia underwent important and far-reaching changes. The nation now was both politically and geographically united. It stretched westward from the Atlantic to the Pacific and southward from the Great Lakes to the Gulf of Mexico. Within these broad boundaries, millions of Americans, including many hundreds of thousands of newly arrived immigrants, were engaged in an effort to develop a rapidly expanding industrial base. In so doing, they created a great world power, one that in the new century would become increasingly involved in world affairs.

During this period, huge advances were made in technology and science. However, while Georgia and the rest of the nation were busy working to keep pace with this progress, both had to deal with a series of other problems. Political scandals tested the patience of the American public. And racial and civil unrest during the late 1800s and early 1900s drew attention to the need to make the rights of all citizens equal. Nevertheless, even with the problems they faced, Georgians—like most Americans during this period—were filled with pride in their nation's accomplishments and hope for a better future.

In Georgia, these nearly fifty years can be divided into two major time periods: the "New South Era," covered in Chapters 10 and 11, and the "Progressive Period," treated in Chapters 12 and 13.

This memorial statue to Henry W. Grady in downtown Atlanta is surrounded by the city he helped rebuild after the Civil War.

Opposite: Henry W. Grady was a spokesman for the New South.

CHAPTER TEN

THE NEW SOUTH ERA: POLITICAL REDEMPTION

The New South is enamored of her work. Her soul is stirred with the breath of a new life. . . . She is thrilling with the consciousness of growing power and prosperity.

—Henry W. Grady

WHEN THE CIVIL WAR ENDED, many people wondered about the "New South" that would arise from the ashes of war. Would the New South remain a land devoted to agriculture? Would it try to be more like the industrial North and build factories and businesses?

THE NEW SOUTH

Athens-born Henry W. Grady was a journalist and speaker. He also was the first to use the phrase **New South** to describe southern progress in the late 1800s, reportedly in an 1874 *Atlanta Daily Herald* editorial. In the article, Grady described the need for Georgia and the rest of the South to become more like the industrialized North.

In 1880, Grady became managing editor of another Atlanta newspaper, the *Atlanta Constitution*. During his brief but brilliant career, Grady made many speeches in Georgia and across the country. He also published many articles describing a South that could compete economically with its northern neighbors. Grady died of pneumonia on December 23, 1889, but ten days before his death, he spoke in Boston of the need for industry in Georgia:

I attended a funeral in a Georgia county. It was a poor one-gallused fellow. They buried him in the midst of a marble quarry; they cut

through solid marble to make his grave; yet the little tombstone they put above him was from Vermont. They buried him in the midst of a pine forest, but his pine coffin was imported from Cincinnati. They buried him within touch of an iron mine, but the nails in his coffin and the iron in the shovel that dug his grave were from Pittsburgh. They buried him near the best sheep-grazing country in the world, yet the wool in the coffin bands was brought from the North. They buried him in a New York coat, a Boston pair of shoes, a pair of breeches from Chicago, and a shirt from Cincinnati. Georgia furnished only the corpse and a hole in the ground.

THE BOURBON TRIUMVIRATE

Before there was a "New South," however, there was a period right after Reconstruction known as the **Redemption Era**. The purpose of the time was to "redeem" the state from the hardships that followed the Civil War years and especially from the leadership of the Republican party that had ruled during Reconstruction. The job of redemption fell mainly to three Democrats: Joseph E. Brown, Alfred H. Colquitt, and John B. Gordon. Like Grady, these men wanted stronger economic bonds with the industrial North. Unlike Grady, they wanted to keep many old southern traditions, particularly white supremacy. Brown, Colquitt, and Gordon were active in Georgia politics from 1872 to 1890, but their influence carried over into the twentieth century.

The three Georgia leaders were called the **Bourbon Triumvirate**. *Bourbon* was the name of a castle and state in France, as well as a line of French kings who ruled for 231 years. *Triumvirate* refers to a ruling body of three. Although the background of each man was different, politics and power drew them together.

JOSEPH E. BROWN

Joseph E. Brown, the oldest member of the triumvirate, was born on April 15, 1821, near Pickens, South Carolina. During his youth, his family moved to Union County in the North Georgia mountains. There he worked as a day laborer to repay money borrowed for a year of tuition at a school in South Carolina. Brown, who was a bright student, attended a rural school in Georgia and became a teacher. At night, he studied law, preparing to attend Yale Law School. After graduating from Yale in 1846, Brown opened a law office in Canton, Georgia. He was elected to the state senate in 1849 and served there until 1855. Brown then became a judge for the Blue Ridge Judicial Circuit. During the time he served as a judge, he was also a farmer, raising wheat on his North Georgia farm.

Opposite page: After serving as one of Georgia's U.S. Senators, Joseph E. Brown retired from active politics in 1891 and turned his attention to educational interests. **Above:** *Benjamin Hill, a sparkling orator, was shocked at his defeat for governor by Joseph E. Brown.*

Opposite page: As the second member of the Bourbon Triumvirate, Alfred Holt Colquitt served as Georgia's governor from 1877-1882. As governor, Colquitt provided leadership for a new state constitution.
Above: Virginia-born Walter Colquitt was the father of Governor Alfred H. Colquitt. A Methodist minister, Walter Colquitt served Georgia as an attorney, judge, and United States Senator. Colquitt County is named for him.

In 1857, the state Democratic Convention had trouble selecting a candidate for governor. After twenty ballots, and without his consent, Brown was suggested as a compromise candidate. The shy, serious judge and farmer shocked the rival American party by narrowly defeating well-known politician Benjamin Hill. Brown became a popular "states' rights" governor and was re-elected to a second term. He knew the Civil War was coming, so he **appropriated** (budgeted) a million dollars to equip the Georgia State Militia. He was re-elected for an unprecedented third term even though he did not seek the post.

Governor Brown guided the state through the difficult war years and was re-elected to a fourth term. When Reconstruction began, Brown lost much of his popularity by asking Georgians to go along with radical reconstruction policies. He believed this would shorten Reconstruction. Brown remained in office until June 1865, when federal officials took over Reconstruction. Governor Rufus Bullock appointed Brown chief justice of the Georgia Supreme Court. He served there two years before resigning to head a company that leased the Western and Atlantic Railroad.

Brown was a talented businessman, and he made a large fortune. In 1880, he entered politics again. When John Gordon resigned from the United States Senate, Governor Colquitt appointed Brown to Gordon's Senate seat. Brown stayed in the Senate until 1891.

During his retirement years, Brown continued his public service in education. He was a trustee of the University of Georgia for thirty-two years and president of the Atlanta Board of Education.

Brown, born into poverty, died a millionaire on November 30, 1894. Fifteen years later, his son, "Little Joe," became governor of Georgia. Brown's tombstone in Atlanta's Oakland Cemetery reads: "His history is written in the **annals** (records) of Georgia."

ALFRED H. COLQUITT

Alfred H. Colquitt was born April 20, 1824, in Walton County. He was the son of United States Senator Walter Colquitt, for whom Colquitt County is named. He graduated from Princeton University with a law degree, then fought in the Mexican War from 1846 to 1848. He was twenty-five when he entered Georgia politics, joining Joseph E. Brown in the state senate in 1849. The two developed a political bond that lasted for the next forty-four years. Before the Civil War, Colquitt also served in Congress and at Georgia's Secession Convention. During the war years, he was an able military leader and rose to the rank of major general.

Colquitt became a wealthy farmer and businessman during Reconstruction. He re-entered politics and was elected governor in 1876.

Around that time, several thousand friends asked for about thirty open government jobs. Those who did not get one of the jobs tried to turn voters against Colquitt. There also were rumors that Colquitt had been involved in illegal dealings with the Northeastern Railroad. Colquitt himself called for an investigation, hoping to end the scandal.

A legislative committee found Colquitt innocent of the charges. However, other members of the executive branch of Georgia's government were found guilty. Colquitt was re-elected and served until 1882. During his administration, the state's debt was reduced and, in 1877, a new state constitution was approved. This constitution was not rewritten until 1945.

Colquitt was elected to the United States Senate in 1883 and 1888. He died in March 1894, three months after the death of his political **ally** (one who shares a common cause), Joseph E. Brown.

JOHN B. GORDON

John B. Gordon, the third member of the Bourbon Triumvirate, was the son of a minister. He was born in 1832 in Upson County and attended the University of Georgia. Gordon left the university to study law with Logan Bleckley, an attorney who became a Georgia chief justice.

Gordon decided against being a lawyer. He worked for a while as a newspaper correspondent, then as manager of a coal mine in Dade County. When the Civil War broke out in 1861, Gordon was twenty-nine years old. He had no military experience or definite career plans.

During the war, Gordon proved an able leader. He fought in many major battles and became one of three Georgia officers who reached the rank of lieutenant general. Gordon's wife often traveled with him and occasionally followed him into battle. After the war, Gordon wrote a book, titled *Reminiscences*, and became a popular speaker across the nation. It has been said, but never proved, that he was head of Georgia's Ku Klux Klan during Reconstruction.

In 1872, Gordon defeated Alexander Stephens to become a United States Senator. In 1880, he resigned from the Senate and accepted a position with one of the railroads.

In 1886, John Gordon began one of two terms as governor of Georgia in the new state capitol building. While governor, Gordon reduced the state's debt and brought new industry into the area.

Above: Former Governor John B. Gordon is the only statue figure on horseback on the grounds of the state capitol.
Opposite page: As the third member of the Bourbon Triumvirate, Gordon was a United States Senator from 1873-1880 and governor from 1886-1890. It is interesting to note that none of the three members of the Bourbon Triumvirate had a Georgia county named for him.

ALEXANDER H. STEPHENS

Gordon returned to the United States Senate in 1891, and he served until 1897. He died on January 4, 1904, while visiting the family farm in Miami, Florida. On the day his body was returned to Atlanta for a hero's burial, one newspaper headline read "Hat's Off! Gordon Comes Home Today."

Gordon College in Barnesville is named for him. His is the only statue of a man on horseback on the state capitol grounds.

*Below: The former vice president of the Confederacy, Alexander H. Stephens' last period of public service came in November 1882, when he was elected as governor. Ill health prevented him from serving more than four months, and he died on March 4, 1883. **Left:** Liberty Hall, the home of Alexander Stephens, is located in Crawfordville and is now a state park. Stephens, despite poor health much of his life, served Georgia in the state assembly, as governor, and in the U.S. Senate.*

Do You Remember?

1. To what does *New South* refer? Where and when was the phrase first used?
2. Henry W. Grady was the managing editor of what newspaper?
3. What was the topic of Henry Grady's Boston speech?
4. What old southern tradition did the Bourbon Triumvirate especially want to keep?

THE DECLINE OF THE BOURBON TRIUMVIRATE

Brown, Colquitt, and Gordon helped carry Georgia through economic reconstruction. Under their leadership, taxes in the state were lowered, the state's war debts were reduced, and business and industry expanded. Those who did not like the triumvirate, however, had an even larger list of things the triumvirate failed to do. They said the triumvirate did little to improve the lives of the poor, especially tenant farmers. In addition, education suffered when funds were cut. There was little support for reforms in prisons and mental hospitals, and working conditions in factories were not improved.

After Reconstruction, the Republican party was just about wiped out in Georgia. They did not select a candidate for governor in 1872. However, not all Georgians agreed with the beliefs or practices of the Democrats who controlled state politics.

THE FELTONS CHALLENGE THE BOURBONS

In 1874, the triumvirate and other Bourbons like Robert Toombs faced a new type of Democrat: the Independent Democrat. The change began in North Georgia in the Seventh Congressional District. A group of independents, led by William H. Felton of Cartersville, began to seek offices in local elections. Dr. Felton was both the leading spokesman for this group and its candidate for Congress.

William Felton was a doctor, farmer, Methodist preacher, and convincing public speaker. He and his wife, Rebecca Latimer Felton, traveled around the Seventh District, speaking against the Bourbons. The Feltons argued that the regular Democratic party was not concerned with the poor and the lower middle-income farmers. Instead, the party supported a "planter aristocracy" and new businesses. Rebecca Felton continued the attack in the family-owned newspaper, *The Cartersville Courant.* She wrote often about the evils of the Bourbons. One of her special concerns was the Georgia convict lease system, which Brown and Gordon used.

As the New South era emerged, the influence of Bourbons like Robert Toombs (top) was diminishing. Following the war, Toombs refused to sign the Oath of Allegiance to the Union and never regained his U.S. citizenship. Rebecca Latimer Felton (above) and her husband William H. Felton were reformers who helped end the influence of the Bourbon Triumvirate.

The Convict Lease System

One of the most serious problems facing Georgia during the New South era was the treatment of prisoners. Many prisons were destroyed during the Civil War. After the war, the lack of jobs led to an increase in the number of people who committed crimes, particularly those who stole to feed their families. The state had to decide what to do with the added prison population, of which nearly 90 percent were blacks. One solution was the **convict lease system**. Under this plan, prisoners were leased to people who provided them with housing and food in exchange for labor.

When the convict lease system began in 1866, the prisoners were used to complete public works projects, such as rebuilding roads destroyed during the war. However, by 1879, most of the prisoners were leased to one of three large companies. Each of the companies **contracted** (agreed) to pay the state $25,000 a year, no matter how many convicts they used. Two of these companies were owned by Bourbons Joseph E. Brown and John B. Gordon. The third was a railroad construction company. Leases were increased from the original five-year period to twenty years. Work ranged from clearing land and farming to mining coal and building railroads.

Companies who leased convicts agreed to provide medical care, allow prisoners to rest on Sundays, and see that housing and clothing were adequate. However, these rules were widely ignored. All too often the prisoners received no clothes, no medical care, and little food. Some contractors literally worked the prisoners to death and then simply leased more.

Prisoners were not the only ones to suffer from the lease system. Paid laborers were not given jobs convicts could do. Instead, they had to compete for limited numbers of available jobs, most of which paid very low wages. This increased the large number of poor and unemployed. In 1880, a special legislative committee was formed to look into the handling of leased prisoners, but few changes were made. Although William and Rebecca Felton continued to demand reforms, it was not until 1897 that the convict lease law was changed.

Leased convict labor provided Georgia companies, especially railroads, with workers who had no choice other than to work long hours of back-breaking labor and to face imprisonment at the end of the workday. The state gained little economic profits from leasing the convict labor, and the workers gained none. Only the companies who received the cheap labor profited from the system.

Much later, a commission appointed to study the convict lease system created state-run prison farms where, at least, youthful male offenders and old or sick inmates could be separated from other prisoners. The commission also established a separate prison farm for females.

Dr. Felton Elected to Congress

In 1874, Dr. Felton was elected to Congress and served there for three terms, from 1874 to 1880. In 1880, he became a member of the Georgia General Assembly. While in the legislature, Felton pushed for improvements in education and prison reform and limits on alcohol traffic in the state. Because of the work of the Feltons, the roots of the Populist Movement were planted in the state.

Rebecca Latimer Felton

Just like her husband, Rebecca Latimer Felton was a tireless worker for fairness and justice and was deeply involved with many causes. She was a leader in the **suffrage** (votes, particularly for women) and **temperance** (anti-alcohol) movements. Long before the early 1900s, when women began to push for equal rights, she was already publicly active. Moreover, she had a platform from which to publish her views. In 1889, Hoke Smith, publisher of the *Atlanta Journal*, asked her to be a columnist. She was a popular writer, and she continued to work for the newspaper until her death in 1930.

At age 87, Rebecca Felton became the first female to serve in the United States Senate. Although her appointment was an honorary one and she served only ten days until the election of Walter F. George, it was a tribute to her diligence and her efforts supporting causes like prison reform, women's rights, and education.

Rebecca Felton pushed for a variety of social changes. She wanted the state to fund public education adequately. She supported vocational training for poor white girls, and in 1915, together with Margaret Olivia Slocum Sage of New York, she began the Georgia Training School for Girls in Atlanta. Rebecca Felton worked to get the University of Georgia, where her husband graduated, to accept women students.

On October 4, 1922, Governor Thomas Hardwick named Rebecca Felton as the junior U.S. senator from Georgia until an election to fill the seat of Senator Tom Watson who had just died. In a black dress and bonnet, the 87-year-old woman was sworn in as the first female U. S. senator in the nation's history. Ten days later, the Georgia legislature elected Walter F. George as the new senator. Rebecca Felton died in 1930, still active in trying to right social injustices.

Rebecca Ann Latimer Felton died on January 24, 1930, in Atlanta at age 94. Some say had she lived in a more enlightened time, her contributions to society would have been far greater. After reading about Mrs. Felton, which reform causes do you think she would support today?

Do You Remember?

1. According to William H. Felton, what two groups did the regular Democratic party show no concern for?
2. To how many companies were the prisoners in Georgia contracted under the convict lease plan?
3. How long did Rebecca Felton serve as a United States senator? Who succeeded her?

Terror filled the city of Chicago from October 8 to 11 in 1871 when fire raged through three and one-half square miles of the city. Some 17,500 buildings were destroyed, and 250 people died.

In 1871, a major topic of conversation all over the nation was the great fire in Chicago. The fire, which started in the barn of a horse-cart driver named Daniel Sullivan, raged through the city for four days. When it was over, 17,500 buildings had been destroyed, about 250 people killed, and 98,500 others left homeless. Over $200 million worth of damage was done to the city and its citizens.

Soon, however, Chicago rebuilt and became the nation's second largest city. But Chicago was not the only city that was to take advantage of the great events that were occurring throughout the nation.

THE RISE OF CITIES

Elsewhere, cities were sprouting up all over as the nation became increasingly more and more **urban** (city-like) and less and less rural. People were moving into the cities from the country to take part in the great industrial revolution that was occurring in the United States. Immigrants, especially from southern and eastern Europe, swarmed to the United States in search of work and better lives. Workers were needed for the machines that were now making a greater variety of goods than the world had ever seen before. New inventions were appearing almost every day—more new things than could have even been imagined before. And people were demanding huge numbers of these marvels designed to make life at home and at work easier.

To meet the demand, the nation's factories and blast furnaces sometimes were kept busy day and night. Working conditions, however, often were difficult and dangerous. Labor unions were organized to bring about improvements in the worker's lot. And various religious and **philanthropic** (charitable) groups sprang up to aid the workers, especially the child laborers whose lives were particularly hard. At the same time, farmers, who were beginning to see their power and influence decline in proportion to their decline in numbers, sought ways of regrouping into stronger voices.

IMMIGRATION

Immigration helped create modern America. In the nineteenth and twentieth centuries, immigrants arrived in two waves. The first wave began in the 1840s and reached a climax in the 1880s. These immigrants were mainly from western Europe. The second wave surged in the first decade of the twentieth century, from 1900 to 1910, and brought large numbers of people from southern and eastern Europe.

Between 1870 and 1920, 26 million European immigrants entered the United States. Most settled in cities. Soon southern blacks joined the mass movement to the cities, especially after 1915. As the nation became more urbanized, modern American culture flourished. That culture came to include African-American jazz, Jewish theater and music, Irish comedy, Italian food, and American folk music and literature. Newcomers changed society as much as it changed them.

Even so, Americans whose families had arrived before the Revolution feared the arrival of so many foreigners with their "different" religions and cultures. During the 1920s, Congress passed acts to restrict immigration. The National Origins Act of 1924 set quotas for each nationality, favoring immigrants from northern and western Europe and limiting those from southern and eastern Europe. The laws virtually excluded people of Asian ancestry. The laws did not restrict immigrants from the Western Hemisphere. As a result, Mexicans and Puerto Ricans soon became the largest groups of newcomers.

After the Civil War, millions of immigrants poured into the United States. Most settled in the Northeast and Midwest.

POLITICAL SCANDALS

President Ulysses S. Grant's first administration had been filled with scandal, yet he was re-elected in 1872. Although Grant was an honest man, many of his advisers were not. One of these scandals, the **Crédit Mobilier scandal**, centered on the construction of the **transcontinental** (across the continent) railroad and became one of the greatest political and financial sensations of the century.

Rutherford B. Hayes, a Republican, became President in 1877, despite losing the popular vote to Democrat Samuel J. Tilden.

Congress had given a great deal of money to the Union Pacific and Central Pacific railroads during the Civil War to build a transcontinental railroad. The Union Pacific formed a new company, Crédit Mobilier, to do the actual work of building it. Crédit Mobilier charged more than the work cost, kept the extra money, and saw the price of its stock soar. When people started to suspect a connection between Union Pacific and Crédit Mobilier, shares of stock in the company were given to members of Congress in the hope that a Congressional investigation would be avoided if enough shares were distributed. When the scandal was discovered, many congressmen were forced to resign. Among those involved was Vice President Schuyler Colfax, who quickly retired from office.

An even bigger national scandal involved William M. Tweed, who headed the New York Democratic organization called Tammany Hall. "Boss" Tweed, as he was often called, was found guilty of robbing the city of over $100 million. These scandals and the economic panic of 1869, which wiped out hundreds of businesses, all reflected on President Grant's leadership. In 1873, another more widespread panic led to long-term economic disruptions.

HAYES WINS DISPUTED ELECTION FOR PRESIDENT

In 1877, one of the most disputed national elections of all time was settled between Republican Rutherford B. Hayes and Democrat Samuel Tilden. In the 1876 election, Tilden won the popular vote. However, the Republicans would not concede the election because of disputed returns from Florida, Louisiana, South Carolina, and Oregon. The disputed vote from Oregon was settled in favor of Hayes. The other three states had both Democratic and Republican election boards, each of which declared its party's candidate the winner of its state's electoral votes.

To resolve the dispute, Congress appointed a special commission to decide who would become president. The commission consisted of fifteen members, five each from the Senate, the House of Representatives, and the Supreme Court. There were eight Republicans and seven Democrats. Tilden had 184 electoral votes and needed only one more to become president. The commission voted along party lines, and the disputed votes went to Hayes. This gave Hayes 185 electoral votes and the presidency.

After his election, in an effort to bring the states together, Hayes ended carpetbag rule and removed all federal troops from Louisiana and South Carolina. Some say that, in making these friendly overtures toward the South, he was only paying off on promises he made during the commission's consideration of his disputed election.

ANOTHER PRESIDENTIAL ASSASSINATION

A scant sixteen years after the nation was stunned by the death of Abraham Lincoln, another U.S. president was downed by an assassin's bullet. The president was James Abram Garfield, who like Lincoln had been born in a log cabin and worked his way up to the nation's highest office. At one time, Garfield had been a mule driver in his native Ohio. He served in Congress before his election as a Republican president and had been one of the Congressmen involved in the Crédit Mobilier scandal.

On July 2, 1881, Garfield was in a Washington railroad station preparing to travel to Williamstown, Massachusetts, where he was to give a commencement address at his former school, Williams College. Suddenly, shots rang out and the president was struck by a bullet in his back. Garfield lived for eighty days in extreme pain and died on September 19, 1881.

His assassin was Charles J. Guiteau, an unhappy Republican federal job seeker who had been overlooked for a job with the secretary of state. People were deeply disturbed by Guiteau's motives for killing the president. For years, many government employees had gotten their jobs simply because they were friends of the president or a member of his political party. **Patronage**, appointing people to government jobs in return for political support, was a widely accepted practice. At the time, many workers at different levels of government held their jobs in reward for support on various pieces of legislation.

After Garfield's assassination, however, civil service reforms were implemented to reduce patronage. Garfield's death led to the passage of the **Pendleton Civil Service Act of 1883**, which established a series of competitive civil service examinations for job vacancies. These reforms help ensure that the person best suited for a job would be chosen for it, regardless of political party. Such a merit system remains today at both the federal and state levels.

Sixteen years after the death of Lincoln, James A. Garfield became the second American president to die by an assassin's bullet, killed by Charles J. Guiteau, a frustrated job-seeker.

Do You Remember?
1. Where did the Chicago fire of 1871 start?
2. What was the Crédit Mobilier scandal?
3. Who was elected president in 1876? Did he receive the majority of the popular vote?
4. What did the Pendleton Civil Service Act of 1883 do?

"A SPLENDID LITTLE WAR"

On February 15, 1898, one of America's newest battleships, the Maine, blew up in Havana harbor. Two hundred sixty men died in the explosion. No one ever knew who sank the Maine, but American newspapers reported that it was the work of a Spanish submarine, and Americans demanded retaliation.

By the end of the nineteenth century, railroads and the closing of the frontier had brought an end to continental expansion within the United States. Now, some in the country sought an American empire on which the sun never set. America had built up its sea power, and calls for using it were sounded in newspaper articles and editorials throughout the country. Cuba, the large, rich island that lay ninety miles south of Florida, was of particular interest to the United States. For years, Americans had dreamed of annexing it. However, it was owned by Spain.

Many Cubans wanted to be free from Spain, and some groups came to the United States seeking money and arms for a revolution. Backed by American aid, Cubans unsuccessfully rose up against the Spanish in rebellions from 1868 to 1878, and again in 1895.

In late 1897, the U.S. battleship *Maine* was ordered to sail into the harbor at Havana, supposedly just to pay a courtesy call. In the evening of February 15, 1898, the *Maine* exploded, killing or wounding hundreds of American sailors. The sinking of the *Maine* was condemned throughout the country. Hunger for revenge was fed by headlines in the sensationalist newspapers of the day—particularly those of William Randolph Hearst. Soon the slogan "Remember the *Maine*" became a rallying cry for those Americans seeking war.

On April 11, 1898, President McKinley sent a message to Congress asking for "forcible intervention" to establish peace in Cuba. Congress responded with a resolution stating that because Cuba was independent, the president could use force to make Spain leave the island. The stage was set for the Spanish-American War, called by diplomat John Hay "a splendid little war."

The first part of the war began thousands of miles away from Cuba in Manila in the Philippine Islands, another Spanish possession. Commodore George Dewey was sent to wreck the Spanish fleet harbored there. The Spanish were not prepared, and their fleet was destroyed with heavy casualties. The six-ship American fleet was hardly touched.

On June 14, 17,000 American soldiers and marines left Tampa, Florida, on route to Cuba. Among the most famous of the troops were the Rough Riders, led by Theodore Roosevelt, soon to be president of the United States. Accounts at the time had Roosevelt leading his band of soldiers in a charge on San Juan Hill. The real facts of this event, however, have been disputed. In any event, American troops quickly defeated the Spanish army.

In December 1898, representatives of both governments met in Paris to sign a formal treaty ending the Spanish-American War. America came out extremely well from these peace negotiations. Spain gave up control of Cuba. Equally important, Spain ceded the Philippines, Puerto Rico, and Guam to the United States for $20 million.

Future president Theodore Roosevelt (second row, second from the left) led the Rough Riders' (above) famous charge up San Juan Hill in Cuba during the Spanish-American War. The charge was made mostly on foot, as their horses hadn't arrived yet.

AGRICULTURE AND THE RISE
OF POPULIST MOVEMENTS

When the United States was formed, farm families made up most of the population. As the country grew, so did the need for farm products. To produce needed crops, farmers had to be willing to work hard and take risks. Weather, insects, plant diseases, bank loan interest, shipping costs, and market prices were all beyond the farmers' control.

THE GRANGE IS FORMED

In 1866, a clerk in the Bureau of Agriculture toured the South and found farmers discouraged, tired, and often without enough money. The next year he formed the "Patrons of Husbandry," which

Above: Market day in Newnan. Market day offered farmers the chance to sell their cotton, exchange news, and socialize.
Right: *The Grange had become a major political force by 1875.*

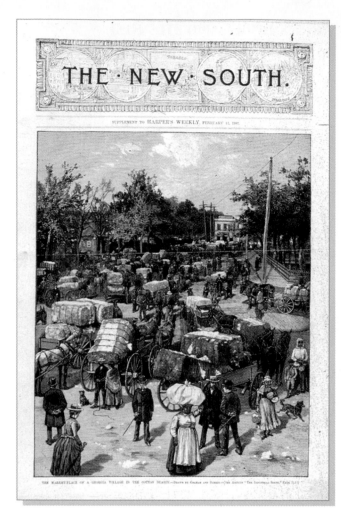

THE · NEW · SOUTH.

SUPPLEMENT TO HARPER'S WEEKLY, FEBRUARY 11, 1887.

THE MARKET-PLACE OF A GEORGIA VILLAGE IN THE COTTON SEASON.—DRAWN BY GRAHAM AND DURKIN.—[SEE ARTICLE "THE INDUSTRIAL SOUTH," PAGE 312.]

During the New South Era as industry became the focus of future development, farming remained the fundamental economic model of the present, as indicated on the cover of the special edition of Harper's Weekly *shown here.*

soon became known as the **Grange**. *Grange* is a word that means a farm and its buildings.

At first, Grange meetings were mostly social. Farmers gathered and talked about common problems. Sometimes there were dances or other social activities or speakers who talked about farming improvements.

After the early 1870s, farm prices began to drop. A bushel of wheat, which sold for $1.21 in 1873, dropped to $0.49 by 1885. In 1873, a pound of cotton sold for $0.21, but by 1893 the price was only $0.05. During this same time, banks were not lending farmers as much money as before. Many farmers were forced into bankruptcy. In the 1880s, after paying the landowner, a small Georgia sharecropper might not make more than $130 for his cotton crop.

THE GRANGE BECOMES A POLITICAL FORCE

Because of such economic conditions, the Grange became more political. In 1872, Granges began organizing and meeting in Georgia. By 1875, there were 18,000 members of Georgia's Grange chapter, and about 750,000 members in the nation. Georgia's Grange put enough pressure on the state legislature to force the formation of a state department of agriculture in 1874, making Georgia the first state in the nation to have a government agency concerned entirely with farming. Some midwestern groups elected legislators who favored farm supports. They were also able to get laws passed to regulate railroad freight rates. However, in the rest of the country, the Grange was not a major political power.

FORMATION OF THE FARMERS' ALLIANCE

During the late 1870s and early 1880s, the **Farmers' Alliance** was formed. There was one large group in the Northwest and another in the South. Like the Grange, the alliances began as social organizations. However, many of the local alliances formed cooperative buying stores, or **co-ops.** The co-ops purchased goods and equipment directly from producers. This allowed farmers to buy seed, fertilizer, and farm tools at wholesale prices.

Farmers' Alliance leaders worked against high railroad freight rates and high interest rates charged by banks for farm loans. The Alliance wanted to change the federal government's money policy. The government had followed a "tight" money policy since the Civil War. That is, it limited the amount of money in circulation and measured the money against the value of gold. The Alliance believed this policy caused prices for crops and other goods to fall. The policy also limited the amount of credit available to farmers. The Alliance wanted the federal government to issue more paper money and to circulate silver coins.

THE POPULIST PARTY

The Alliance's political influence grew along with its membership and, in 1890, forty-five "Alliancemen" were elected to Congress. Alliance-backed men became governors in several southern states. Encouraged, the Alliance began talking about selecting the president of the United States in the 1892 election.

Members of labor organizations joined with the Alliance to form a new political party in 1891. They named it the People's party, but it was usually called the **Populist party**. The first business of the Populist party was protest. Surpluses of cereal crops, cotton, and silver had lowered market prices, forced both farmers and miners into poverty, and caused "suffering amidst plenty." The first Populist party nominating convention met in Omaha, Nebraska, in July 1892. The platform contained many "futuristic" reforms. Among them were the following:

- an eight-hour workday
- government ownership of railroads and telephone and telegraph services
- a graduated federal income tax
- "free" or unlimited coinage of silver into dollars
- the direct election of U.S. senators
- restrictions on immigration
- use of the **Australian ballot** (a ballot printed by the government rather than by a political party, distributed at voting places, and collected there in sealed boxes so the votes would be kept secret)
- a program of government loans to farmers who would store crops in government warehouses as security for the loans

The Populist candidate for president in the 1892 election was James B. Weaver. Democrat Grover Cleveland won the election, but Weaver received over a million popular votes and twenty-two electoral votes—a large number for a third-party candidate. By openly asking for black votes, the Populist party lost much of its popularity and support in the South. Nevertheless, its platform of reform paved the way for future changes.

Grover Cleveland, the nation's 22nd and 24th president, served from 1885 to 1889 and 1893 to 1897. Georgia's Hoke Smith served as Cleveland's Secretary of the Interior from 1893 to 1896.

GEORGIA'S BEST-KNOWN POPULIST

A colorful national leader of the Populist party was Georgian Tom Watson. Born near Thomson in 1856, Thomas Edward Watson became one of the state's most controversial politicians.

As a youth, the slim, red-haired Watson was an excellent student. By the age of fourteen, he had written a series of essays, poems, and speeches. He had to drop out of Mercer University when his father went bankrupt during the economic panic of 1873. Nevertheless, Watson taught school and studied law until he passed the state bar exam in 1877, at the age of twenty-one. In 1882, he was elected to the General Assembly.

Watson was a criminal lawyer known for his "down-to-earth" style of defense. Even though he became wealthy, Watson was concerned because poor and struggling farmers in Georgia needed help. He accepted the goals of the Farmers' Alliance and, with their backing, was elected to Congress in 1890. Watson, a Democrat, represented the Tenth Congressional District, which stretched from Augusta west across the state.

A year later, Watson switched political sides and spoke for the causes of the Populist party. In one of his many Congressional speeches for farmers, the firebrand Watson declared, "Before I give up this fight, I will stay here 'til the ants tote me out of the keyhole."

Above: Born in 1856 near Thomson, Georgia, the young Tom Watson was viewed as a hero to the struggling Georgia farmers whom he wanted to represent. Opposite page: Elected to Congress in 1890, Thomas Watson's greatest accomplishment was getting the Rural Free Delivery bill passed in Congress. The RFD bill enabled people living in rural areas to receive free mail delivery at their homes.

Watson Introduces Rural Free Delivery Bill

Watson represented Georgia in the U.S. House of Representatives only two years. However, he gained a place in Congressional history by introducing the **Rural Free Delivery (RFD) bill.** The RFD bill required the United States postmaster general to spend $10,000 to find a way to deliver mail to rural homes free of charge. It took several years to put the system into action in rural areas. However, Watson's bill resulted in farm families no longer having to go to the nearest post office for their mail. The first official Rural Free Delivery route in Georgia was in Warren County.

Watson was known all over the country because of the RFD bill and his support of farmers. In 1892, the Democrat-turned-Populist became a candidate for re-election from the Tenth District. However, the state's Democratic party wanted Watson out of Georgia politics. Because he had no organized support, Watson tried to get black farmers to join white farmers and return him to Congress. By election day, there were reports of vote-buying, physical attacks, and attempts to frighten people. Watson supporters claimed that the Tenth District's black voters were denied credit at stores if they supported Watson. They said murders had been committed to keep black farmers from backing Watson. When the **polls** (voting places) closed and the votes were counted,

RURAL FREE DELIVERY

In the later years of the nineteenth century, farmers and others living in rural areas of the United States still did not have mail delivery service. In order to send or receive mail, rural people—as they had always done in the past—had to travel to the nearest community that had mail services. People in larger communities, however, had long enjoyed home delivery.

In October 1890, Congress appropriated $10,000 for Postmaster General John Wanamaker to test the free delivery system in small towns and villages. He experimented with delivery in 46 communities having populations under 4,000. By all accounts, the experiment was a great success.

Nevertheless, in 1892 the House Committee on the Post Office and Post Roads, rejected a bill that called for the permanent establishment of rural free delivery, as well as an amendment providing $100,000 for the service.

In 1893, Georgia Congressman Tom Watson proposed legislation for another experiment. His bill called for mail delivery not just to small towns and villages, but also directly to farmers. A new postmaster general, William S. Bissell, rejected the idea, saying that it would bankrupt the nation.

Despite many letters to Congress supporting rural free delivery, Bissell continued to refuse to spend the money that Congress appropriated. Finally, in 1895, Congress directed Bissell to spend $20,000 on Watson's experiment and to report back on its results. Bissell was still opposed to the plan, and he resigned rather than put it into action.

Bissell's successor, William L. Wilson, agreed to implement the experiment, choosing three villages in West Virginia as test sites. On October 1, 1896, the trial began with 5 routes. Within nine months, 82 routes were operating from 43 post offices in 29 states. Today, a century later, rural carriers deliver the mail daily on over 50,000 rural routes to almost 25 million delivery points.

Watson had lost his bid for re-election. He ran for Congress again in 1894 and was again defeated. Watson returned to his home, Hickory Hill near Thomson, to influence politics through the press. He began two magazines: *The Weekly Jeffersonian* and the monthly *Watson's Jeffersonian*. He also wrote a ten-volume *Story of France* and biographies of Andrew Jackson and Thomas Jefferson.

Watson Is Nominee for Vice President

In 1896, Watson was the Populist party's nominee for vice president of the United States. He ran with Democrat and "free-silver advocate" William Jennings Bryan. The election ended in another defeat, and Watson returned to writing.

In 1904, the dying Populist party nominated Watson for president and, once again, he lost. The next year, Watson returned to the Democratic party and successfully backed Hoke Smith for governor of Georgia. However, his stand on civil rights had changed. Fifteen years earlier, Watson had asked for black votes. Now, his opposition to minority rights included those for blacks, Catholics, and Jews. In 1920, Watson ran against Hoke Smith and won the United States Senate race. Two years later, he died in Washington, D.C.

A statue of Tom Watson stands by the main entrance to the state capitol. On it are the following words:

Democratic institutions exist by reason of their virtue. If ever they perish it will be when you have forgotten the past, become indifferent to the present, and utterly reckless as to the future.

Do You Remember?

1. Why was the Farmers' Alliance formed?
2. By what other name was the People's party known?
3. What major bill did Tom Watson get passed during his only term in the U.S. House of Representatives?

SUMMARY

- The period after Reconstruction is known as the New South era, a phrase coined by Henry W. Grady.
- Georgia was controlled by a group of three powerful politicians known as the Bourbon Triumvirate.
- The decline of the Bourbon Triumvirate came about because social reforms and educational progress were limited during their rule.
- The groundwork for social reform was laid by William H. Felton and his wife, Rebecca Latimer Felton.
- The late 1800s saw the rise of big cities.
- The 1870s were marked by a series of scandals.
- Two national political movements, the Grange and the Farmers' Alliance, arose to give farmers a stronger voice.
- The Farmers' Alliance joined forces with members of labor unions to form a new party, the Populist party.

Today a statue of Thomas Watson stands at the main entrance to the state capitol building in Atlanta.

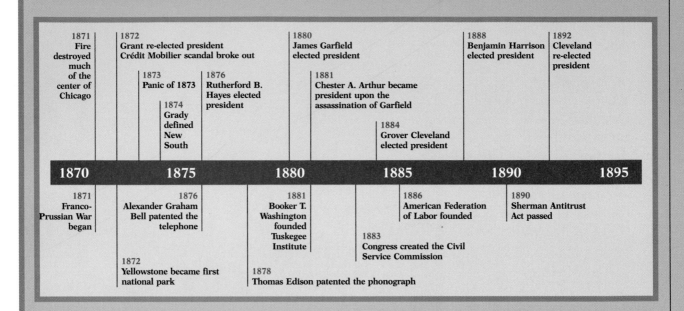

1871
Fire destroyed much of the center of Chicago

1872
Grant re-elected president
Crédit Mobilier scandal broke out

1873
Panic of 1873

1874
Grady defined New South

1876
Rutherford B. Hayes elected president

1880
James Garfield elected president

1881
Chester A. Arthur became president upon the assassination of Garfield

1884
Grover Cleveland elected president

1888
Benjamin Harrison elected president

1892
Cleveland re-elected president

| 1870 | 1875 | 1880 | 1885 | 1890 | 1895 |

1871
Franco-Prussian War began

1876
Alexander Graham Bell patented the telephone

1881
Booker T. Washington founded Tuskegee Institute

1886
American Federation of Labor founded

1890
Sherman Antitrust Act passed

1883
Congress created the Civil Service Commission

1872
Yellowstone became first national park

1878
Thomas Edison patented the phonograph

Reviewing People, Places, and Terms

Define, identify, or explain the importance of the following.

1. Australian ballot
2. Bourbon Triumvirate
3. convict lease system
4. Crédit Mobilier scandal
5. Farmers' Alliance
6. Populist party

Understanding the Facts

1. What was the purpose of the Redemption Era?
2. Which member of the Bourbon Triumvirate reached the rank of major general in the Civil War?
3. List three things that their opponents felt the triumvirate failed to do.
4. Besides the prisoners, what other group of people were badly affected by the convict lease system?
5. Who was the publisher of the *Atlanta Journal* who provided Rebecca Felton with a platform from which to publish her views?

6. To which two railroads did Congress give huge sums of money to build a transcontinental railroad?
7. What were the four states whose returns in the 1876 election were disputed by the Republican party?
8. By what name do we know the group called the "Patrons of Husbandry"?
9. What was the "tight" money policy that the federal government had followed since the Civil War?
10. Who is considered Georgia's best-known Populist?

Developing Critical Thinking

1. Compare and contrast the beliefs of the Bourbon Triumvirate with those of William and Rebecca Felton.
2. When the Populist party's nominating convention met in Omaha in 1892, it urged the passage of many reforms. Which reforms called for at that time are in effect today?
3. What do you suppose have been the long-term

effects of the Democratic party's control of the governorship of Georgia?

Applying Your Skills

1. The Grange and the Farmers' Alliance were two national groups organized to help farmers in the late 1800s. Today, many young people belong to a 4-H Club or the Future Farmers of America. Prepare a report on the activities of one of these two groups.
2. Prepare a short report on the existence of third parties in our nation's history. What issues might be the basis for a third party today?

Making Connections

1. Today, you can order merchandise through on-line services, television shopping, and the telephone. Find out from friends, neighbors, or relatives how often they use these services and what they typically order from them.
2. Imagine ordering a house and all its furnishing, including pots and pans, through a mail-order house. At the turn of the century, many people did exactly that through companies such as Sears, Roebuck. Find out if any of these houses are still standing in your community.

Did You Know?

• During the Great Chicago Fire of 1871, the original draft of Lincoln's Emancipation Proclamation was destroyed.
• In 1875, the Atlanta City Council passed a cow ordinance. Any cow found roaming the streets of the city at night cost its owner a $2 fine.

BUILDING SKILLS: RECOGNIZING PROPAGANDA

After reading about scandals of the Grant administration and the political campaigns of the 1880s and 1890s, you probably thought nothing has changed in the past century. The use of propaganda to persuade people to make certain decisions has been a part of political life since political parties were organized. What we sometimes forget is that some of these same techniques are used today in advertising.

Bandwagon approach. You've probably used this technique on your parents to try to convince them to let you do something or go somewhere because "everybody else is." You hope your parents will think it's all right since other parents are allowing their sons and daughters to go.

Testimonial. With this technique, a well-known person—an athlete or a movie star, for example—describes how great a particular product or brand (of motor oil, athletic shoes, sport drink, and so on) is. This technique is also used when movie stars campaign for political candidates. When an influential person is shown with another person or thing, it is an attempt to transfer honor and respect from one individual to another. Think of all the television commercials that try to transfer the good feeling about an athlete to a particular product. Has this technique ever influenced your decision about buying a product?

Repetition. Watch television one evening and you'll see that many short commercials are repeated several times during a particular show. Advertisers use repetition to drive home a particular message. They're hoping that if you see the message often enough, you'll remember it.

Cause-and-effect relationship. A misleading cause-and-effect relationship is often used to persuade. "Twenty students in the class who used computer X to write their history reports got an A." The implication here is that those twenty students only got an A because they used computer X. Would this persuade you to go buy computer X if you got a poor grade? Why or why not?

Write an ad for a newspaper or television station for a product or a political candidate using one or more of the above techniques. Make a video tape of your ad if you have a video camera available.

CHAPTER ELEVEN

TECHNOLOGY, SOCIETY, AND CULTURE IN THE NEW SOUTH

The first duty of government is to see that people have food, fuel, and clothes. The second, that they have means of moral and intellectual education.

—John Ruskin

THE PERIOD LEADING UP TO the turn of the century was one of great change, with breakthroughs and innovations in many fields. Important advancements were made in science and technology. New businesses were developed and grew rapidly. Not only work, but also education and leisure were different from what they had been previously. And new voices were heard to comment in songs, paintings, and writings on the changes taking place.

ADVANCES IN SCIENCE AND TECHNOLOGY

By the late 1800s, industrial expansion was in full force in the United States. The opening of the West provided access to vast sources of natural resources that could be developed by what seemed to be a never-ending supply of cheap immigrant labor.

To convert these resources into the relatively inexpensive products that America and the rest of the world so badly wanted, new inventions and techniques were required. And the United States had the people with the imagination and the money to develop and finance these innovations. The U.S. Patent Office, which has the responsibility for registering and protecting new inventions, was flooded with new ideas, processes, and ways of getting things done in all fields.

One of the best known writers of the New South era, Joel Chandler Harris did much of his writing at his Atlanta home, "Wren's Nest."

COMMUNICATIONS

The rapid development and use of electricity gave rise to a variety of improvements in the way people communicated with each other. In 1876, Alexander Graham Bell received the first patent issued in the United States for the telephone. On March 10 of that year, Bell was working on his invention when he spilled acid on his clothes. He shouted to his assistant, "Mr. Watson, come here. I want you." Watson, working in the next room, heard Bell's voice over the telephone.

Although in the beginning telephone service was limited largely to calls within a local area, telephone use grew rapidly. The first telephone conversation in Atlanta took place on September 21, 1881. Around noon, workers finished connecting a telephone line from the Western and Atlantic freight station to the dispatcher's office in Union Station. The first telephone call in the city was between two railroad workers. It was short and practical:

B. W. Wrenn: *"Who's there?"*
Anton Kontz: *"Anton Kontz. That's Wrenn, ain't it?"*
B. W. Wrenn: *"Yes. I'm hungry. Send word to Henry Durnad to get me a good dinner."*

By 1883, telephone service was established between New York and Chicago. In 1900, 1,335,991 telephones were in use across America.

In 1876, Thomas A. Edison invented the mimeograph. In 1884, Lewis Waterman patented the fountain pen, which replaced the pens dipped in ink that had been used. Because of the **linotype machine** (a mechanical typesetting device) invented in 1885 by Ottmar Mergenthaler, newspapers were able to print late-breaking news faster. In 1886, *The New York Tribune* put the linotype machine into use.

TRANSPORTATION

The later part of the nineteenth century also ushered in a new era in the way people traveled from one place to another. With the development of electricity and various means of harnessing its power, innovations such as the electric railway sprang up throughout the nation. In 1888, Frank Sprague introduced the modern **electric street trolley** (streetcar) in Richmond, Virginia. Soon this method of transportation was adopted by other cities, including communities in Georgia. Often, businessmen and other civic promoters built attractions such as amusement parks at the end of the trolley line to lure riders. However, the availability of inexpensive rapid transit soon extended the boundaries of the nation's cities and led to the development of **suburbs** (communities on the outskirts of cities). In 1889, Inman Park, reached by an electric streetcar, became Atlanta's first suburb.

*Opposite page: Of Thomas Edison's many inventions, none had a greater impact than the electric lightbulb. Here, he is at work in his Menlo Park, New Jersey, laboratory. **Above:** In 1892, the American brothers Charles and Frank Duryea built the first practical gasoline automobile in the United States.*

Shortly after this time, another even more startling form of "horseless" carriage appeared. Earlier in the 1880s, two Germans—Karl Benz and Gottlieb Daimler—had demonstrated automobiles with gasoline-powered engines. In 1892, the American brothers Charles and Frank Duryea perfected their own version of an automobile and drove it through the roads of New England.

In Detroit, another American, Henry Ford, was also hard at work developing a practical car. At two o'clock on the morning of June 4, 1896, the first Ford automobile was completed. The car had been built in a brick shed, but no one noticed that it was wider than the shed door. Before the car could be taken outside to drive, workers had to use an ax to knock out the bricks that framed the door. Thus, in a sense, the American automobile industry was "hatched."

Within a few years, automobiles were almost everywhere in the nation's cities and towns. However, because most of the roads in the country were little more than dirt paths with ruts, rocks, and protruding tree trunks, travel elsewhere was extremely difficult. And of course, when heavy rains or melting snow turned the good Georgia soil into seas of mud, those roads were practically impassable.

Early automobiles quickly became popular in cities and towns, but travel elsewhere was extremely difficult due to the poor condition of rural roads.

INDUSTRY

Every year brought new inventions and improved methods to industry. Although it had been invented during the Civil War, **celluloid**, a hard plastic-like material, was produced commercially for the first time in 1872. In 1873, nitroglycerin was used to blast a railroad tunnel in Massachusetts. In 1883, black inventor Jan Matzeliger revolutionized the shoe industry with a machine that attached soles to shoes by sewing the leather together. Before Matzeliger's invention, a cobbler could make only six to eight pairs of shoes a day. With the new machine, about a thousand pairs could be made in a day. In 1886, Charles Hall and a Frenchman, Paul Héroult, independently and simultaneously discovered an economical way to take aluminum from ore. The Hall-Héroult process was so successful that the price of aluminum dropped from $5 a pound in 1888 to 18 cents a pound in 1914.

AGRICULTURE

Electricity and gas-powered engines also transformed life on Georgia's farms. Electricity was used to generate power for a variety of agricultural applications, although electrical power would not be available for everyone until much later. Gas-driven machines, however, could be used almost everywhere. Soon, gas-driven tractors replaced horses, speeding up a farmer's work by several fold.

Farm productivity was also increased with the introduction of new ways of **tilling** (plowing) soil and improved seeds. In 1872, Luther Burbank developed a strain of potato plants that produced seed balls. From the seeds, Burbank produced hearty plants that were later called the "Burbank potato." During the next few years, Burbank's research produced many new types of fruits, vegetables, and grains.

In 1873, Illinois-born Joseph Glidden invented barbed wire. Ranchers used it to fence land on which they raised cattle. The use of fences made it possible for ranchers and farmers to live in peace and helped end the battles over land use that had been waged between the two groups. Fences also meant that fewer cowboys were needed to keep the cattle where they belonged.

Daniel Halladay invented the Halladay windmill in 1854. The use of windmills spread in the 1870s and 1880s as they were used to pump enough well water to supply the needs of farms and ranches.

In Georgia, agriculture and technology joined hands when a peach planter near Montezuma invented a wooden packing crate that could be stored in a refrigerated carrier. This invention of Samuel Rumph led to the growth of Georgia's peach industry because peaches could now be shipped throughout the nation. Today, the state ranks third in the nation in the production of peaches.

Rumph's interest in perfecting peaches also made his wife quite famous. He named a type of peach, the Elberta, after her. When this peach proved to be very popular in northern states, the market for Georgia's peaches was once again expanded.

MEDICINE

The late nineteenth century also saw many new advancements in the field of medicine. In 1880, French biologist Louis Pasteur discovered a vaccine for chicken cholera. He also developed a successful vaccine against rabies in 1885. Within a few years, rabies, one of the most dreaded diseases of the times, was controllable.

Pasteur was also responsible for another discovery from which we still benefit. Fresh cow's milk sours after several days because of the bacteria in it. Pasteur invented a process that would keep milk fresh longer. He heated the milk to a high temperature, thus killing

Known as the "plant wizard," Massachusetts-born Luther Burbank was famous throughout the world for his improvement of plants through crossbreeding. From 1875 when he opened a nursery in Santa Rosa, California, until his death in 1926, he developed numerous varieties of plums, berries, roses, and daisies. Research the work of Luther Burbank and determine which foods you eat are a result of his efforts.

PUBLIC HEALTH

The movement for public health grew out of the Civil War experience. Before the war, most Americans lived in dirt and grime. In caring for the sick and wounded during the war, reformers realized that there was a connection between cleanliness and good health.

In the decades after the war, urban areas became the centers of the public health movement. Because urban areas were crowded, smelly, dirty, and noisy, disease spread quickly. The most feared diseases were cholera, typhoid, and yellow fever. Cholera outbreaks in the United States occurred in 1832, 1849, and 1866. Yellow fever visited nearly every year. The 1878 epidemic killed 8,100 people in New Orleans and 5,100 in Memphis.

To halt these epidemics, health boards were created and took steps to cleanse cities, quarantine (isolate) the sick, protect water supplies, and remove garbage and waste. Physicians made house-to-house visits. Volunteers distributed circulars giving advice on personal hygiene. Diseased areas received large doses of disinfectant.

By 1900, nearly every major city and state had a health department. Cities began to install running water and sewers. Ordinances prevented businesses and private citizens from simply dumping waste and debris in the streets. Where public health was concerned, Americans learned that they had to be their "brothers' keepers."

the bacteria, and then transferred the milk into a sterilized bottle and sealed the top. His process, called **pasteurization**, is used today, not only for milk but also for products such as cider, to prevent spoilage and possible disease.

In 1895, German Wilhelm Roentgen discovered rays that could pass through solids. Because he did not completely understand them, Roentgen called them "x rays." Today, doctors and dentists use them to take pictures of broken bones, determine the healthiness of lungs, or check for cavities in the teeth.

For some time, one of the deadliest diseases in parts of the South and in tropical countries was yellow fever. Each year, it caused the death of scores of people and made certain areas unlivable in hot weather. In 1898, during the Spanish-American War, Dr. Walter Reed learned that mosquitoes carried yellow fever. Later, when the Panama Canal was built, his discovery saved hundreds of lives. Doctors were able to end the spread of malaria and yellow fever by killing the mosquito population. Areas that had once been avoided during the summer months now could be sprayed and made habitable.

HOME

A variety of inventions affected the way people lived and worked at home. In 1877, Thomas Edison introduced the phonograph, the first device to bring into the home real people performing works of entertainment. The first words recorded on it were "Mary had a little lamb." Two years later, Edison developed the **incandescent** (glowing) lamp using a carbon filament made of cotton that would last forty hours. Soon his electric lights began to replace oil and kerosene lamps. Edison also supervised the building of the first central electrical power plant in the world. By 1881, the New York plant was in operation, providing power to local homes, businesses, and industries.

Photography became popular when George Eastman introduced the hand-held camera. Earlier, bulky cameras that captured images on hard-to-handle glass or copper plates were used to take photographs. Eastman's camera was a square box that used a film roll. At first, the camera—with the used roll of film still in it—was sent to the factory. The film was developed, the camera was reloaded with new film, and both were returned to the owner.

Sewing clothes and linens, whether for home use or for manufacture, had always been done by hand, a time-consuming affair. Although sewing machines had been around since the mid-1800s, they did not become a common household item until the late 1800s when Singer Manufacturing Company perfected and marketed them. Their machines greatly reduced the time and cost of making garments and other items and were welcomed by homemakers and the sewing industry.

In 1891, Thomas Edison received a patent for the first motion picture camera. Silent films did not become common until the early 1900s; however, Edison's invention was the beginning of the movie industry.

Sewing machines became a common household item in the late nineteenth century.

Do You Remember?
1. When was the telephone invented? By whom?
2. What did Luther Burbank accomplish?
3. Why was the invention of barbed wire important?
4. Who discovered x rays?
5. What invention popularized photography?
6. Who received a patent for the first motion picture camera?

THE DEVELOPMENT OF INDUSTRIES IN GEORGIA

Toward the end of the nineteenth century, much of Georgia was still primarily agricultural. However, Henry Grady's dream of a New South based on business and industry was, in part, coming to pass. The expansion of railroads played an important part in the development and growth of industries that were able to take advantage of the network of railroad lines to transport their products. Among these emerging new industries were textiles, forest products, and mining.

TEXTILES

One of the state's first industries was **textiles** (woven materials). Textile mills used raw materials, including cotton and wool, to produce textiles for clothing, bed sheets, blankets, and carpets. Before the Civil War, the center of the textile industry was in New England.

Mills Come to Georgia

In the late 1800s, mills began to spring up in Georgia. Today, over 176,000 Georgians are employed in the textile industry.

Once begun, Georgia's textile industry experienced steady growth. The main manufacturing centers were located along the fall line in Augusta, Columbus, and Macon. There, major rivers provided water power. There were also mills in smaller towns. By 1890, Georgia's textile industry produced over $12.5 million worth of goods.

Life in a Mill Village

In order to house textile workers, mill owners built villages. The small houses were usually all alike. Mill houses were often not in good repair and lacked indoor bathrooms or running water. Sometimes, families with five or six children lived in houses with two rooms, plus a kitchen and front and back porches. A fireplace provided the only heat, and a wood stove in the kitchen was used to prepare the few scant meals the workers could afford. Christmas in these homes was a sparse celebration. Children usually received one or two toys, either handmade or purchased at a five-and-ten-cent store. Oranges were a special Christmas treat, as were peppermint sticks.

Mill pay was small, often only a few cents an hour. Parents and children sometimes worked up to seventy hours a week. Mill workers usually bought food, clothes, and supplies from company-owned stores. Most families had to charge purchases, and many owed the company stores more than they could make in a year. Workers, therefore, were locked into jobs with the company.

In many mill villages, even the churches were owned by the mills. Sermons were about the values of hard work, loyalty to employers,

Workers in early Georgia cotton mills like this one endured long hours and sometimes dangerous conditions for very low wages. Much of the work was done by women and children.

Top: The Scottsdale Cotton Mill in Decatur, built in 1900, was surrounded by tiny one- and two-room houses for the mill workers. **Above right:** *Mill village houses like the ones shown here, built in Roswell in 1839, were barely adequate and frequently unsanitary.* **Above left:** *The Eagle and Phenix Mill in Columbus was one of the state's first textile mills. Destroyed during the Civil War, the mill was quickly rebuilt.*

and the evils of unions. There was enough medical care to keep the work force healthy so women and children, especially, would not miss work. Often, workers suffered with lung illnesses from breathing cotton lint. However, even with the hardships, many second- and third-generation families kept working in the mills.

FOREST PRODUCTS

Georgia's rich timberlands provided another major source of income. Trees from the forests were turned into lumber that was used in the construction of buildings both to replace those destroyed in the Civil War as well as those needed to house growing industries and the people who worked in them. The forest furnished the raw materials that would wind up in a variety of products, from furniture to the **naval stores** (turpentine, rosin, tar, and pitch) used in shipbuilding.

Not only did Georgia's forests provide raw materials, they also created work. Sawmills, often the center of new communities, were needed to convert the raw lumber into boards. Railroads were improved or extended to transport the materials to customers both within the state and elsewhere. Factories were built to manufacture furniture and other household items.

Naval stores, like those seen here on one of the Savannah docks, represented one of Georgia's leading industries during the New South era.

MINING

Other of the state's natural resources also spurred new or expanded industries. Georgia's rich stores of **kaolin** (a white clay used in the manufacture of paper and other products), gold, coal, and iron led to a growth in the mining industry. Mining for **bauxite**, a mineral used in the manufacture of aluminum, increased after the development of an inexpensive method of converting bauxite into the metal.

Do You Remember?
1. What type of transportation played a major role in Georgia's industrial expansion?
2. Where did mill workers usually buy their food and clothing?
3. What are two industries besides textiles that grew in Georgia during this period?

Above: Three expositions were held in Atlanta between 1881 and 1895. The Piedmont Exposition was held in 1887.
Opposite: This special newspaper supplement celebrates President Cleveland's visit to the Piedmont Exposition.

ATLANTA HOSTS THREE NATIONAL EXHIBITIONS

Three **exhibitions** (shows) in Atlanta during the 1880s and 1890s drew the nation's attention to Georgia. They had been the dream of Henry Grady, who wanted the nation to know about progress in the South. In 1881, the International Cotton Exposition had over a thousand displays from many states and several foreign countries. In 1887, the Piedmont Exposition brought over 200,000 visitors, including President Cleveland, to Georgia. The largest and most publicized exhibition was in 1895, when 800,000 visitors came to Atlanta during the three-month-long Cotton States and International Exposition. There, they saw new machinery and learned how cotton was made into marketable products.

Visitors also enjoyed Buffalo Bill's Wild West Show and tapped their feet to the lively patriotic music of John Philip Sousa. Booker T. Washington became nationally known when he dedicated an exhibit building that highlighted black contributions to the southern economy.

WELCOME
· TO ·
· ATLANTA ·

1. ILLUMINATION OF KENNESAW MOUNTAIN, NEAR MARIETTA.   2. THE UNION RAILWAY STATION—AWAITING THE ARRIVAL OF THE PRESIDENT.   3. A PARADE OF THE YOUNG MEN'S DEMOCRATIC CLUB ON MARIETTA STREET, ATLANTA.
THE WELCOME OF THE NEW SOUTH TO PRESIDENT CLEVELAND.—SCENES IN ATLANTA.—THE ILLUMINATION OF KENNESAW MOUNTAIN, SCENE OF ONE OF
THE HISTORIC BATTLES OF THE CIVIL WAR.

BUSINESS IN THE NEW SOUTH

The period between the end of the Civil War and the early 1900s also saw the rise of many new businesses and a new breed of business people to run them. Among these were two Atlanta institutions—Rich's Department Store and Coca-Cola—that were to leave a lasting impression on Georgia and the world of marketing.

RICH'S DEPARTMENT STORE

Morris Reichs was born in Hungary in 1847 but moved with his family to America and settled in Cleveland, Ohio. The young immigrant, now called Morris Rich, set out with his brothers to make a living. He moved to Georgia and traveled the state as a peddler, selling items such as needles, thread, cooking pots, and other household goods. In 1867, after managing stores in Albany and Chattanooga, Rich decided to settle in Atlanta.

Above: Hungarian immigrant Morris Rich was typical of the entrepreneurs who, through diligent and hard work, built prosperous businesses in Atlanta. *Right:* The small Rich's store of 1867 rapidly grew into one of Atlanta's shopping institutions. During the early to mid-1900s, it was a social highlight for Atlantans to don hats and gloves, shop for a while, and eat lunch in the store tearoom.

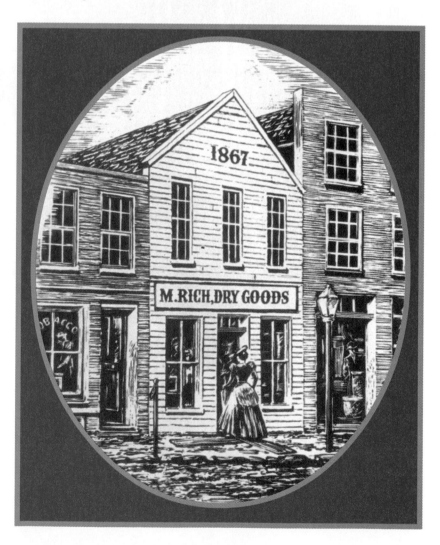

Rich's Builds and Grows

Rich borrowed $500 from his older brother, William, who was an Atlanta merchant. With it, he bought a small wooden building near the railroad tracks. In those days, many of the streets in Atlanta were dirt. Walking in these streets after a rainstorm could be rather messy, particularly to the hems of women's dresses. One of Rich's first services to customers was to cover a mud hole in front of the store with planks.

Rich stocked many items, but the best selling goods were corsets and calfskin boots. When customers did not have cash to pay for their purchases, Rich was willing to exchange goods for chickens, eggs, or vegetables.

In 1881, Morris Rich and two of his brothers bought a new and larger store on Whitehall Street. The inside of the building was decorated in black and gold, and it had Atlanta's first plate glass store windows. In 1924, his store moved to the corner of Broad and Alabama streets in the heart of downtown Atlanta.

Rich's Generosity

For sixty-one years, until his death in 1928, Morris Rich was an example of the best of the rising merchant class. Most Georgians know Rich's because of the annual "Lighting of the Great Tree" each Thanksgiving night to begin the Christmas and Hanukkah holidays. Atlanta teachers remember another gift of the Rich family. During the 1930 depression, Atlanta had no money for teachers' salaries, so it paid them in **scrip** (paper money that is not legal currency). Rich's accepted the scrip at face value in payment for goods bought in their stores. It is not known if the business later got full value for the scrip after the depression. However, the help given to teachers was long remembered.

Teachers were not the only group to benefit from Rich's generosity. In 1931, Rich's accepted up to 5,000 bales of cotton from Georgia farmers in exchange for merchandise.

For many years, many Georgians made yearly trips to Atlanta to shop at Rich's. In the early 1960s, shopping malls became popular and large department stores opened mall branches. The advertising department at Rich's ran newspaper ads to let shoppers know the downtown Atlanta store would stay as it was. However, the ads also said, "You don't have to wear a hat and gloves to shop at Rich's! You can always shop at the new suburban mall Rich's at Lenox Square." Although the downtown store closed in the summer of 1991, Rich's still can be found in other areas of Atlanta and across the Southeast.

From 1948 until the closing of the downtown Rich's store in 1991, the lighting of the "great tree" on Thanksgiving night meant the beginning of the holiday season for Georgians.

COCA-COLA—THE HEADACHE THAT CREATED A FORTUNE

Coca-Cola began in the backyard of Atlanta druggist John Styth Pemberton. Pemberton was a successful wholesale pharmacist in Columbus before the Civil War. He served in the Confederate cavalry and then moved to Atlanta. There, he mixed and sold medicines such as Globe of Flower Cough Syrup and Triplex Liver Pills. The most popular of "Doc" Pemberton's mixtures was a tonic called "French Wine Coca," a syrup that included alcohol and coca. The coca came from the South American coca plant, the same plant that produces cocaine. There is no record of the amount of coca in the tonic, but there was a good bit of alcohol. To keep up with the demand for his "Delightful Nerve Tonic and Stimulant That Never Intoxicates," Pemberton built a small chemical plant for $160.

The Temperance Movement Changes the Formula

In 1885, the temperance movement that swept most of the country led citizens of Fulton County to vote their county "dry" (free of alcoholic beverages), effective July 1, 1886. Pemberton began looking for a way to remove the alcohol from his tonic and still have its good taste. He put a three-legged, thirty-gallon brass stirring kettle over a fire and started work on a new recipe. Instead of alcohol, Pemberton used an extract of the African kola nut, a stimulant brought to the South during antebellum days. After months of measuring and mixing, Pemberton came up with a new syrup that was both stimulating and pleasant tasting. This new "Brain Tonic" was named Coca-Cola after its two main ingredients, the coca plant and the kola nut. It was put into pint beer bottles, labeled the "Intellec-

Above: After the Civil War, pharmacist John S. Pemberton, better known as "Doc," settled in Atlanta and began distributing his popular nerve tonic, "French Wine Coca." Right: In the backyard of "Doc" Pemberton's home was a three-legged iron pot used to mix his newest concoction, Coca-Cola.

tual Beverage and Temperance Drink," and sold for twenty-five cents in several Atlanta drug stores. The exact formula is still a closely guarded secret, one that is known to very few.

According to Coca-Cola Company historians, a chance event changed the course of the beverage industry. Willis Venable was the soda fountain man at Jacob's Drug Store. One day a customer came in with a severe headache. He bought Coca-Cola syrup and asked Venable to mix some with water so he could take it immediately. The tap water faucet was at the other end of the counter, so Venable suggested soda water instead of plain water. The customer agreed and, when he drank the mixture, said it was much better than with plain water. Within weeks, several other drug stores began mixing the medicine with soda rather than with tap water. By the time the "dry" law went into effect, syrup sales had jumped. Within a year, they grew from 25 to 1,049 gallons.

*Above left: A 1910 Coca-Cola fountain tray. Today, Coke memorabilia is almost an industry within itself. **Above right:** Asa G. Candler traveled to Atlanta from Villa Rica with a dollar and some change in his pocket. After selling patent medicines for a few years, the wholesale druggist managed to purchase Pemberton's business and the Coca-Cola secret mixture for $2,300.*

Coca-Cola Changes Hands

In July 1887, Pemberton's health began to fail. He needed money, so he sold Venable a two-thirds interest in his company. Equipment, supplies, and advertising items were moved from Pemberton's home to the basement of Jacob's Pharmacy. Among the items were the brass stirring kettle, five hundred street car signs, four Coca-Cola cards, and oils of nutmeg, spice, lemon, lime, and vanilla. Other ingredients in the mixture included extract of coca leaves, citric acid, orange elixir, oil of neroli, and caffeine. Later, in 1903, the coca leaves were eliminated from the drink. The total value of the items removed was $283.24.

Pemberton died penniless in August 1888. But before his death, a Villa Rica native and druggist named Asa Candler bought all the Coca-Cola stock. The amount paid by Candler was $2,300.

By 1892, the drink had become so popular that Candler sold his drug store and formed the Coca-Cola Company. Candler grew wealthy and gave money to establish Emory University and Hospital. He also served without pay for several years as mayor of Atlanta.

In February 1919, Candler's wife Lizzie died, and he went into a deep depression. The following September, Candler's son quietly sold

Above: *The early straight-sided bottle on the left was replaced by the familiar curved bottle on the right in 1916.* **Right:** *During World War II, the Coca-Cola Company provided American soldiers with a taste of home.*

the company to Atlanta businessman Ernest Woodruff for $25,000,000. At that time, it was the largest business deal ever made in the South.

Under the new ownership, Coca-Cola continued to grow. However, by 1920, the company was in financial trouble. In 1923, Ernest Woodruff's son Robert became president. Robert Woodruff was only three years old when Pemberton mixed the formula for Coca-Cola. As an adult, he led the company into a multibillion dollar, international business.

Woodruff continued the clever marketing policies that had been begun earlier. The beverage's uniquely shaped green bottle and its wholesome advertisements were everywhere, both in this country and abroad. He built bottling plants in Europe during World War II. This gave American soldiers a little touch of home, and Europeans began to enjoy the American "pause that refreshes."

Like Asa Candler, Robert Woodruff gave money to worthy causes. His gifts included $105,000,000 worth of Coca-Cola stock to Emory University. For many years, this remained one of the largest single gifts in American history.

Today Coca-Cola products are enjoyed around the world by over 470 million people each day. What was begun by "Doc" Pemberton, soda fountain man Willis Venable, and the customer with a headache has mushroomed into a giant international company with annual sales in the billions of dollars.

After World War I, millionaire Asa Candler sold Coca-Cola to a group of investors headed by banker Ernest Woodruff. His son, Robert Woodruff (above), took over the company shortly thereafter and ran the global enterprise for almost 50 years.

Do You Remember?

1. How old was Morris Rich when he opened his store on Whitehall Street?
2. What did Rich sometimes accept as payment for goods instead of money?
3. Why did Pemberton change his original tonic formula?
4. Who purchased Coca-Cola from Asa Candler?

EDUCATION IN THE NEW SOUTH

As you learned in Chapter 9, when Georgia lawmakers rewrote the state constitution in 1868, the new constitution approved "free public education for all children of the state." Later, in 1870, the General Assembly passed an act to establish a system of public instruction. The legislation also established a state board chief executive officer to supervise public schools.

Although the basic elements of a public school system were finally in place, education in Georgia in the late 1800s and early 1900s was quite different from education in the state today. There was little support for education, both from a large portion of the public and from their elected officials. Teachers were badly paid and usually not formally trained, school terms were much shorter, and classroom discipline was much stricter.

PUBLIC SUPPORT FOR SCHOOLS

Not all Georgians favored public education, especially at the high school level. Parents depended on their teenaged children to either help with work on family farms or bring in income from their labor in the textile mills and other factories that were sprouting up all over the state. In some communities, local schools were paid for by property taxes. Because there still were relatively few property owners, this source was not enough to meet the needs. Moreover, many property owners were reluctant to pay for the education of all children—especially if they were black.

STATE SUPPORT FOR SCHOOLS

In 1871, the first year Georgia had state-funded schools, 49,570 students enrolled. Only 13 percent of the pupils were black. The state agreed to spend $175,000 for a school term. Because that was not enough money to fund the schools, many teachers were not paid during the first year.

Dr. Gustavus James Orr, who began the Georgia Teachers' Association, was appointed state school commissioner in 1872. Two of his goals were to improve funding and to provide equal treatment for black students. Orr said, "I am in favor of affording them [black students] a fair field for self-development, that they may have the opportunity of exhibiting to the world . . . what they can accomplish." Orr worked with Atlanta University to train black teachers. In 1874, the Georgia General Assembly agreed to give the university $8,000 a year. In return, Atlanta University would admit, free of tuition, as many black students as there were members in the Georgia House of Representatives.

Education during the New South Era was a serious undertaking. There was little time for play or "extra" activities. Students who did not behave appropriately were severely chastised.

Orr also believed in vocational education. He thought it would help students learn skills to fill the needs of a growing labor market. However, despite Orr's work, lack of money kept many communities from having these schools.

COMMUNITY SUPPORT FOR SCHOOLS

In 1887, Commissioner Orr died. He was replaced by Sandersville attorney James S. Hook. Like Orr, Hook worked to establish a state **normal school** (teacher training school). One was established in 1895. Monies raised from school taxation also increased, so that by 1893, $699,650 was spent on public schools. Still, teachers made little more than farm laborers. Most schools had about forty-five students and an average attendance of thirty. This meant that, on average, most teachers were paid about a dollar a month for each student.

By 1895, due largely to efforts of local newspapers such as the *Atlanta Constitution* and the *Augusta Chronicle*, $100,000 a year was raised for school buildings. Most of the money came from local communities. Landscaping of school grounds came about because of an 1890 law that required students to observe Arbor Day on the first Friday in December.

THE THREE-MONTH SCHOOL YEAR

The **three-month school year** (a school term of three months) met two important needs. It enabled children to both get a public school education and work either in the factories or mills. It also offset the difference between the need for teachers and the availability of them.

The three-month-school year was held at different times in different counties. Because of this, it was possible for teachers to teach in more than one county. In addition, this flexibility took into consideration the different work needs of the students.

Each local district decided where school would be held. In one rural county, the citizens used a building "good enough to winter a cow." In another, forty or fifty children crowded into a poor building with sawmill slabs for seats. Restrooms were outdoors, and drinking water was in buckets. Some schools had a hand bell. In others, teachers hit the door with a stick to call children to class.

TEACHER TRAINING

In 1870, local school commissioners made up tests for people who wanted to teach. In most cases, a passing grade was 70. The tests covered such subjects as *orthography* (spelling), reading, writing, English grammar, and geography. Sometimes, when a county needed teachers, the tests were no more than a spur-of-the-moment question-and-answer session between the school officials and the potential teachers.

Gustavus James Orr, known as the "Father of the Common School System" in Georgia, when he was named state school commissioner in 1872. He worked to improve education until his death in 1887.

It was as important for a teacher to show good moral character as to be able to teach. Very few teachers had been to college. Most finished common school, then took the teacher's test. An 1872 job description for teachers included the following:

1. Teachers each day will fill lamps, clean chimneys;
2. Each teacher will bring a bucket of water and a scuttle of coal for the day's session;
3. Make your pens carefully. You may whittle nubs to the individual taste of the pupils;
4. Men teachers may take one evening each week for courting purposes, or two evenings a week if they go to church regularly;
5. After ten hours in school, the teachers may spend the remaining time reading the Bible or other good books;
6. Women teachers who marry or engage in unseemly conduct will be dismissed;
7. Every teacher should lay aside from each day's pay a goodly sum of his earnings for his benefit during his declining years so that he will not become a burden on society;
8. Any teacher who smokes, uses liquor in any form, frequents pool or public halls, or gets shaved in a barber shop will give good

In 1871, Girl's High in Atlanta was established and opened with 153 female students. List some differences you can observe between the class of 1875 shown here and the graduating classes of today.

reason to suspect his worth, intention, integrity and honesty; and,

9. The teacher who performs his labor faithfully and without fault for five years will be given an increase of twenty-five cents per week in his pay providing the Board of Education approves.

In December 1894, Gustavus Glenn, a former physics professor at Macon's Wesleyan College, became the new education commissioner. During his term, grades required on teacher exams were increased to 100 for a three-year license and 70 for a one-year license. Teachers who had taught many years and who managed their classrooms well were given permanent licenses. Glenn said, "We adopt books for five years; why not adopt teachers for five years?"

Teacher-Training Schools

In 1870, Georgia tried to start a normal school. The legislature agreed to pay $6,000 a year if Peabody Normal School would move from Nashville to Georgia. The proposal was rejected by Peabody, and there was no formal teacher education in the state until 1882.

In 1882, the legislature set aside funds to send 252 teachers (154 white and 98 black) to a one-month training institute in either Americus, Milledgeville, or Toccoa. There were 6,128 teachers instructing 243,000 Georgia school children at that time. These institutes were the state's first efforts to improve the skills of teachers.

Teacher Salaries

Each county set salaries for those who taught in its schools. In 1900, the average salary of a black male teacher was $25 a month. A white male might be paid as much as $65 a month. Sixteen counties paid teachers the same amount, no matter what their race or sex. One county, Oconee, paid black teachers more than white ones because black teachers were harder to find.

DISCIPLINE IN THE SCHOOLS

Not only were teachers expected to teach basic subjects, they were also expected to see that students behaved. Student behavior had to measure up to strict standards. An 1871 set of rules describing what was required of them had to be learned in rhyme:

For study each pupil is furnished a seat; he must keep it in order and perfectly neat; his books and his desk, with what appertains, he must notice and care for, with similar pains; and the floor close about him must also be kept. . .as free from all litter as when it was swept.

Suspension or even expulsion from school. . .may follow persistent breaches of rule. . .disobedience stubborn, repeatedly shown. . .

Gustavus Glenn, a former professor at Wesleyan College, became Georgia's school commissioner in 1894. He made the improvement of teacher licensing one of his priorities.

disorderly conduct or quarrel alone. . .or truancy, too, or indolent waste. . .profanity's words or language unchaste. . . .

Students who did not behave were usually whipped by the teacher. There were two popular ways to do this. The first was called "the horse and rider." The child to be punished was placed on the back of another student so that the hickory rod was closer to the target. The second was called the "circus wag." A group of students who had misbehaved or who had done their lessons poorly were marched clockwise in a circle and hit with a hickory stick as they passed by.

EDUCATION TAKES A GIANT STEP BACKWARD

In the 1877 Georgia constitution, public education was still limited to elementary school. Again, most Georgians believed that education beyond eighth grade was not particularly useful, especially when an adolescent's time could be better spent at work. They also felt that too much schooling might cause teenagers to be dissatisfied with their lot in life and, worst of all, to long for a much better one.

The constitution of 1877 also called for segregation of schools. From then until the 1950s, black students would be left to be schooled, for the most part, in second-rate school buildings; to be given outdated materials and equipment; and to be taught by teachers who were often underpaid.

GEORGIA TECH OPENS

A further sign that the state wanted Georgia's role in the nation's industrial economy to grow was provided in 1888 with opening of the Georgia School of Technology. The school, better known as Georgia Tech, is located in Atlanta. It continues to attract students who are interested in using technology to improve industry.

At the suggestion of Macon industrialist John Hanson, State Representative Nathaniel Harris proposed a bill in the General Assembly to establish a state technical school. The result of that bill was that the Georgia School of Technology (Georgia Tech) opened its doors in 1888 with two buildings. Today it is known throughout the country as one of the nation's leading colleges of engineering.

Do You Remember?
1. When did Georgia first have state-funded schools?
2. What is a normal school?
3. In what year did Georgia first begin formal teacher education?
4. When did the state constitution call for segregated schools?

THE ARTS DURING THE NEW SOUTH ERA

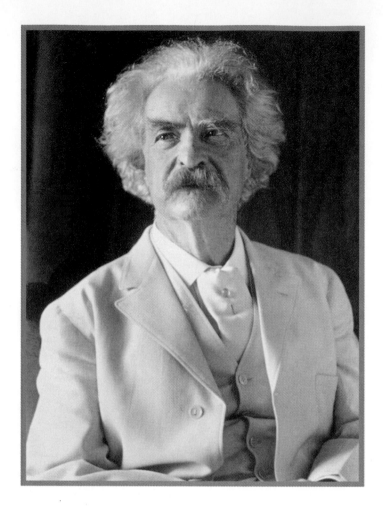

Samuel Langhorne Clemens, better known by his pen name Mark Twain, was one of the most popular American writers of the latter part of the century.

During the late nineteenth and early twentieth centuries, artists, musicians, and writers reflected the events and culture of the period. Winslow Homer painted anything that interested him, but he was best known for his pictures of the sea and of ordinary people. Frederick Remington worked as a cowboy and panned for gold to get ideas for his paintings of the American West. John Singer Sargent was famous for his portraits.

Blues and ragtime were popular in the New South. Musicians like Scott Joplin, W. C. Handy, and "Jelly Roll" Morton wrote songs still heard today. The marches of John Philip Sousa and "America the Beautiful" by Katherine Lee Bates stirred patriotic feelings.

Architect Louis Sullivan was known around the world for the new look of his buildings which were based on the use of steel frames. John Roebling and his son Washington Roebling oversaw the construction of a bridge that connected Manhattan to Brooklyn and which was held up by woven steel cables. And a Frenchman, Frédéric Bartholdi, created the Statue of Liberty, which towers over the entrance to the New York harbor.

Writers like Mark Twain, Stephen Crane, Sarah Orne Jewett, Zane Grey, Ida Tarbell, Upton Sinclair, Booth Tarkington, and Sinclair Lewis told about both the good and the bad in America during the late 1800s and early 1900s. Adventure stories, mysteries, and tales for children became more popular. The poems of Henry Wadsworth Longfellow, Emily Dickinson, Edwin Arlington Robinson, Amy Lowell, and Carl Sandburg were read all over the world. The black poet Paul Laurence Dunbar, who wrote his first poem at the age of six, published his first book of poems, *Oak and Ivy*. These works spoke of the past glories and future hopes of the nation.

TWO GEORGIAN WRITERS

Georgia was the birthplace of two widely read authors of the period: Sidney Lanier and Joel Chandler Harris. Although they were both Georgians, the two men had little in common.

Sidney Lanier

Sidney Lanier was born in Macon in 1842. His family was musical and, even as a young child Lanier could play the flute, violin, organ, piano, and guitar. Lanier entered Oglethorpe University in Midway at the age of fourteen, graduated in 1860, and became a tutor. In 1861, Lanier and his brother, Cliff, enlisted as privates in the Confederate Army. The brothers turned down promotions so they could stay together. They became army scouts and later joined the Signal Service.

Union troops captured Sidney Lanier while he was running a blockade off the coast of Wilmington, North Carolina. He was in prison for five months at Point Lookout, Maryland. During that time, he became ill with tuberculosis.

Upon his release from prison, Lanier and a friend walked most of the way back to Macon. He reached home on November 15, 1865, and spent the next few months trying to get back his strength.

Lanier wrote his first novel, *Tiger Lilies*, while working in a store in Montgomery, Alabama. The book did not sell, and Lanier lost confidence in his writing. In 1867 he opened a school in Prattville, Alabama, and married Mary Day from Macon.

Pictured here at age 37, Sidney Lanier died in Lynn, North Carolina, two years later in 1881. His last verse started, "I was the earliest bird awake, It was a while before dawn, I believe, But somehow I saw around the world, And the eastern mountaintop did not hinder me. I knew the dawn by my heart, not by mine eyes."

Because of his poor health, Lanier and his wife returned to Macon. There he worked as an assistant in his father's law office. In December 1872, he moved to Texas, but the dry heat was not good for him. While in Texas, Lanier felt he had little time to live. He wanted to spend that time with the books and music he loved. In 1873 the family moved to Baltimore where he played first flute in the Peabody Symphony.

It was in Baltimore that Lanier had his first success as a writer. His first poems, published in 1875, were well received. Lanier was asked to write words for a *cantata* (an orchestral piece with words) to celebrate America's 100th birthday. The music was sung at the Centennial Exposition in Philadelphia. One of his better known works, "Evening Song," was written during 1876.

Lanier went to other states looking for a climate in which he could feel well. However, he returned to Baltimore to play with the

Sidney Lanier was born on February 3, 1842, in this house in Macon. He graduated from Oglethorpe University, a Presbyterian school at Midway near Milledgeville, in 1860 and became a tutor.

symphony and give private lectures on Elizabethan verse. On his birthday in 1879, he was asked to teach at Johns Hopkins University. This job provided his first steady income since his marriage.

Lanier published "The Song of the Chattahoochee" and "The Marshes of Glynn." He also began a group of poems, "Hymns of the Marshes," which was never finished. One of those poems, "Sunrise," is perhaps his most famous.

Lanier's health grew worse and, on the advice of his doctors, the family moved to the crisp, clean air near Asheville, North Carolina, to live in a tent. His final move was to Lynn, North Carolina, where he died in 1881.

Joel Chandler Harris

Joel Chandler Harris was born in Eatonton in 1848. Because his father left the family before Joel's birth, Mary Harris had to raise her son alone. Although Harris joked with friends, he was shy when among strangers. He went to school in Eatonton until he was twelve. At that time, Joseph Addison Turner of Turnwold Plantation, nine miles from Eatonton, asked Harris to live with him. Turner owned the only newspaper ever published on a plantation, and Harris became an apprentice for that paper, *The Countryman*. Some days, after he finished his work, the thirteen-year-old read books borrowed from Turner's library. On other days, he walked around the plantation and listened to tales told by the workers. Harris learned to speak the workers' dialect very well. With Turner's approval, Harris began writing both serious and funny stories for the paper.

Shortly before Sherman's march through Georgia, Harris became a printer for the *Macon Telegraph*. He stuttered and, when invited to lecture at Vanderbilt University, said, "I could not deliver a lecture in public for a million dollars."

After a short time Harris moved to New Orleans and worked six months as secretary to a newspaper publisher. His next move was to Forsyth, Georgia, where he wrote humorous articles for the *Monroe Advertiser*. The *Savannah Morning News* named him as an associate editor and, while living there, Harris married Esther LaRose.

In 1876, yellow fever swept through Savannah. The 28-year-old Harris, his wife, two children, and their nurse, fled to Atlanta. In that city, he met *Atlanta Constitution* editor Henry Grady and accepted a position with the newspaper. Harris helped Grady make the *Atlanta Constitution* a New South paper.

Harris's most popular and lasting contributions to southern literature were the legends and folk tales that were told to him by former slaves. *Uncle Remus, His Songs and His Sayings*, written in 1880

Wren's Nest was such a safe haven for the shy writer Joel Chandler Harris that he rarely left home even to go to the Atlanta Constitution *offices to write his editorials. When President Cleveland visited Atlanta and wanted to meet Harris, editor Henry Grady had to send another reporter to be sure the writer would leave his home for the meeting.*

The shy and retiring Joel Chandler Harris (on the right) had among his many friends, industrialist Andrew Carnegie. Atlantans owe Carnegie a special thanks. In 1889 the wealthy Carnegie gave $100,000—an enormous amount of money at that time—to Atlanta to build a library.

when Harris was thirty-two, began as a column in the *Atlanta Constitution*. During the next twenty-six years, he wrote *Uncle Remus and His Friends, Told by Uncle Remus* and *Uncle Remus and Br'er Rabbit*.

Harris did much of his writing at his Atlanta home, "Wren's Nest." It is said that Harris gave his home its name after a family of wrens built a nest on the mailbox. Today, Wren's Nest, located in Atlanta's West End, is a museum.

Joel Chandler Harris never outgrew his childhood shyness. In 1905 President Teddy Roosevelt visited Atlanta and wanted to meet the popular writer. The *Atlanta Constitution*'s publisher is said to have had three reporters take Harris to the president's train to "see that he's there if you have to hogtie him."

Harris died on July 3, 1908, at the age of fifty-nine. He wrote the words carved in stone over his grave in Atlanta's Westview Cemetery:

I seem to see before me the smiling faces of thousands of children—some young and fresh—and some wearing the friendly marks of age, but all children at heart, and not an unfriendly face among them. And while I am trying hard to speak the right word, I seem to hear a voice lifted above the rest, saying, 'You have made some of us happy,' and so I feel my heart fluttering and my lips trembling and I have to bow silently and turn away and hurry into the obscurity that fits me best.

Do You Remember?

1. For what type of art was American painter Fredrick Remington known?
2. Who created the Statue of Liberty?
3. What was the title of Paul Dunbar's book of poems?
4. What was the name of Sidney Lanier's first novel?
5. Why did Joel Chandler Harris and his family flee Savannah?
6. What is the name of Joel Chandler Harris's home? Where is it located?

LEISURE AND RECREATION

During the years after the Civil War, leisure and recreational activities differed according to economic status. In 1876, the average factory worker in the nation earned $500 a year, and those in the South earned far less. The average farm worker brought home less than $15 a month. Twenty percent of American's young men and 10 percent of its young women worked either in factories or on farms.

Most leisure time was spent in church-related activities or in home parties that featured inexpensive events such as candy pulls or corn popping. On southern farms, families and friends generally lived far from each other, so house parties were popular. Such gatherings occasionally included a barbecue and often singalongs. Cycling continued to be a popular pastime as well as a means of transportation. In many communities, dancing and card playing offered a break from the monotony of work. However, in other communities these forms of entertainment were frowned on by church officials.

Leisure time activities for the wealthy were quite different from those of factory workers, farmers, and small shop owners. Those who

Toward the end of the century, the beach became a popular destination for wealthier southerners. Notice the modes of transportation and fashions in this turn-of-the-century photograph of Daytona Beach.

THE BIRTH OF MASS CULTURE

Bicycling was a favorite pastime at the turn of the century for men and women. Informal bicycling clothing eventually gave women the freedom to wear more casual attire.

Until the late 1800s, Americans had little leisure time. But as the workweek and the workday shortened, people turned to leisurely pursuits.

Baseball, primarily an urban game, was the first and most popular sport. The Cincinnati Red Stockings became the first professional club in 1869. With the formation of the National League in 1876, baseball became a big business.

In the 1890s, bicycling was almost as popular. Both men and women rode bicycles. In order to ride, women had to give up the formal Victorian fashions of the period. Informal bicycling clothing eventually gave women the freedom to wear more casual attire.

American show business appealed to all classes of people. Musical comedies featured song, humor, and dance. George M. Cohan set the standard with such popular songs as "Yankee Doodle Dandy." Vaudeville was probably the most popular form of entertainment at the beginning of the twentieth century. Shows included song, dance, magic, ethnic humor, and animal acts.

Thomas Edison's invention of moving pictures in the late 1880s grew into the most popular art form of the twentieth century. The most famous movie of the period was D. W. Griffith's *The Birth of a Nation*, although flawed by its racism and glorified treatment of the Ku Klux Klan. Technology—photography, phonographs, and movies—put mass entertainment within the reach of all Americans.

were well-off had elegant carriages with drivers who would transport them to teas, garden parties, shopping trips, or private clubs. In many cities, young people gathered at soda shops to exchange gossip and to see and be seen by other young people. Formal balls remained popular, and a recent invention, the phonograph—even in its earliest forms—provided an new type of entertainment. Some of the phonographs had six or eight earphones, thus allowing friends to gather around and enjoy music without disturbing others in the household.

In the early 1890s, football joined baseball as a popular sport for men and young boys. One baseball game of the period was played between the Atlanta Baseball Club and the Gate City Nine, another Atlanta team. Playing without baseball mitts, the Gate City Nine won 127 to 9. In 1892, intercollegiate football began in Georgia with a game played in Atlanta's Piedmont Park between the University of Georgia and Auburn University. Instead of today's bulldog, the mascot of the University of Georgia at that time was a billy goat. Other teams, including Georgia Tech, also joined in intercollegiate sports.

Do You Remember?

1. How much did the average farm worker bring home each month?
2. What type of parties were particularly popular on southern farms?
3. What recent invention provided a new type of entertainment in the late 1800s?
4. Who won the baseball game between the Atlanta Baseball Club and the Gate City Nine?

SUMMARY

- The later part of the nineteenth century was an era of great change in many fields.
- Advances in science and technology included the telephone, the phonograph, the electric street trolley, and the automobile.
- Edison perfected the incandescent lamp, and Eastman revolutionized photography.
- Medical advances included Pasteur's discoveries of a rabies vaccine and a method to prolong the life of milk, Roentgen's discovery of the x ray, and Reed's linkage of a mosquito to the disease of yellow fever.
- Business and industry in Georgia prospered with growing industries in textiles and mining.
- Two Atlanta business institutions—Rich's and Coca-Cola— left an indelible mark.
- A state public school system was begun, although funds were limited.
- Teaching conditions were difficult and salaries were low; however, some progress was made in the training and licensing of teachers.
- Educational progress took a step backward when the 1877 state constitution called for segregation of schools.
- The arts flourished in Georgia and the rest of the nation.
- New forms of leisure were introduced.

Ty Cobb, the "Georgia Peach," was born in 1886 when baseball was the most popular sport of the New South era. Famous as a hitter and base-stealer, he was the first player elected to the Baseball Hall of Fame.

CHAPTER REVIEW

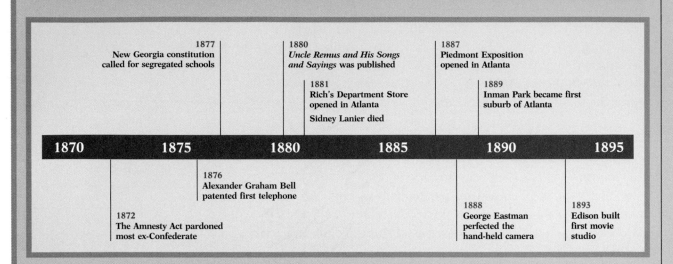

1877
New Georgia constitution
called for segregated schools

1880
*Uncle Remus and His Songs
and Sayings* was published

1887
Piedmont Exposition
opened in Atlanta

1881
Rich's Department Store
opened in Atlanta

Sidney Lanier died

1889
Inman Park became first
suburb of Atlanta

1870	1875	1880	1885	1890	1895

1876
Alexander Graham Bell
patented first telephone

1888
George Eastman
perfected the
hand-held camera

1893
Edison built
first movie
studio

1872
The Amnesty Act pardoned
most ex-Confederate

Reviewing People, Places, and Terms

Define, identify, or explain the importance of the following.

1. bauxite
2. electric street trolley
3. kaolin
4. normal school
5. pasteurization
6. scrip
7. suburbs
8. textiles
9. three-month school year

Understanding the Facts

1. What was Atlanta's first suburb?
2. What important discovery was made by Walter Reed?
3. What inventor introduced the phonograph?
4. What three cities in Georgia were most important to textile manufacturing?
5. What mineral is used in the manufacture of aluminum?
6. Who began the Georgia Teachers' Association?
7. Name three other writers of this period besides Sidney Lanier and Joel Chandler Harris.
8. Where was Lanier's cantata celebrating America's 100th birthday sung?
9. Where did young people gather in many cities during this period?

Developing Critical Thinking

1. Why do you think many Georgians did not support taxes for the state's school system?
2. How do you think the opening of Georgia Tech was "A further sign that the state wanted Georgia's role in the national economy to grow"?
3. What effect did the use of steel frames have on the size and appearance of buildings?

Applying Your Skills

1. Using whatever library or Internet resources are available to you, research and prepare a short report on at least three other inventions of the late 1800s that made work easier for the homemaker.
2. Collectors of Americana prize many of the posters, serving trays, and other soda fountain accessories that bear the Coca-Cola name. Using whatever research sources are available to you, try to determine the most current prices paid for some of these items.

3. Prepare a short report of one or two pages on any of the colleges or universities mentioned in this chapter.

Making Connections
1. Prepare a table that lists the deadly diseases smallpox, cholera, typhoid, yellow fever, influenza, tuberculosis, and polio. For each disease, indicate (a) the average number of deaths per year in the United States, (b) the highest number of deaths in a one-year period, (c) the year in which this happened, and (d) the current status (eradication, under control, and so on).
2. Prepare a report on what your local board of health does to protect the public health. Are there any other organizations in your area that work to protect the public health? If so, list two or three of them.
3. List five inventions that you believe have been the most instrumental in giving Americans more leisure time.
4. Today there are arguments over whether entertainment reflects our culture or whether culture reflects our entertainment. What do you think about this issue?

Did You Know?
• The Atlanta Cyclorama, which depicts the Battle of Atlanta, was painted in 1886 by a group of German, Austrian, and Polish artists.
• In 1867, philanthropist George Peabody established a million-dollar fund to help schools in the South.

BUILDING SKILLS: NOTETAKING

In your school career, you have no doubt found that it is impossible to remember all of the information you need for assignments or when studying for tests. One of the best ways to remember something is to write it down. *Notetaking*—writing down information in a brief and orderly manner—will not only help you remember information but also make studying easier.

Notetaking only works if you use it and can understand the notes you have taken. Your system for notetaking may be different from the student next to you, but there are some general guidelines that everyone should find helpful.

Take a sheet of plain or lined notebook paper and draw a vertical line down the page about six inches from the left edge. Draw a horizontal line across the page about two inches up from the bottom of the page.

Identify the subject by writing it at the top of the sheet. You might, for example, write "Advances in Science and Technology" at the top of the page for the notes you take on this chapter.

Write your notes in the wide, left-hand column.

Periodically, write down key words or key ideas in the narrow, right-hand column.

Don't try to write down everything. Listen carefully to what your teacher says. If your teacher stresses or repeats something or spends a good deal of time on a topic, that is a clue to its importance. If you are doing research, you might want to write down topic sentences or key words or phrases.

Learn to *paraphrase,* or write down the information in your own words. This will help you think about what was said or written.

Make sure your notes are legible and neat so that you can understand them when you read them again.

At the bottom of each sheet of notes, write out several questions that could be answered by the notes on the page. You might want to work with a classmate and practice answering the questions.

Try This! Practice your notetaking skills by completing Activity 1 under the Applying Your Skills head. Use the notes you take to help you prepare the report.

THE PROGRESSIVE ERA: A TIME OF REFORM

Generally, graduation is a time for joy and excitement, but for many in the Georgia Tech class of 1917 it was a day filled with apprehension. Why?

We see in many things that life is very great . . . but the evil has come with the good. . . . Our duty is to cleanse, to reconsider, to restore, to correct the evil without impairing the good.

—Woodrow Wilson

FOR THE MOST PART, the first twenty years of the twentieth century were a period of peace, prosperity, and general good feelings in Georgia and the rest of the nation. The rapid growth of industry and cities throughout the country created great wealth. Major advancements continued to be made in science and technology that would help improve the lifestyles of many people. But not all people shared in this wealth or could take advantage of these advancements, and the gap between the "haves" and the "have-nots" was sharper than ever before. Cities were filled with newcomers from rural America and overseas who sought work in factories and offices. Living in crowded, often unsanitary buildings and working long hours in drab, poorly lit or heated plants and mills, these workers were fast becoming a new breed of "forgotten people."

At the end of this period, many conditions had changed considerably. A new movement of reform swept the country. And a world war would forever alter life and lifestyles in this country and elsewhere.

THE PROGRESSIVE MOVEMENT

During the late 1800s and early 1900s, the **progressive movement** swept the country. Progressives believed that government—local, state, and national—was best equipped to correct the ills of society. They had faith in the idea of progress, the belief that humans could keep improving society to make it better and better.

The progressive movement, which was actually a series of movements, worked to reform society in three main ways. First, progressives wanted government to fight poverty and improve the living conditions of its citizens. Progressives worked hard to reform prisons, improve working conditions, outlaw alcohol, and extend voting rights to women. Second, they wanted to break up large corporations and regulate business. They hoped to decrease corporations' voice in government. Third, they wanted voters to have more influence in government. Progressives had great faith in the people's ability to improve society. They believed people could do this if they only had a greater voice. Strangely, however, progressives also justified the disfranchisement of African Americans on the ground that the black vote could be bought.

The reform movements were largely due to changes in industry and agriculture. Many people left farms to work in city manufacturing plants. Such moves did not always improve financial or housing conditions. Newspapers, magazines, and books printed stories about dishonesty in business, corruption in government and politics, and the horrors of being poor. Theodore Roosevelt said these writers "raked filth for their reports." From then on, writers who wrote about the problems of American life in the early twentieth century were called *muckrakers.*

One of the most famous muckrakers was Upton Sinclair. His book *The Jungle* was published in 1906. The novel described the horrible working conditions in Chicago's meat-packing plants and told how meat was produced in dirty conditions. As a result of this book, President Roosevelt pushed for a congressional bill that same year. The Meat Inspection Bill required sanitary conditions in packing plants. It also allowed federal inspection of plants that shipped meats to other states.

Other famous muckrakers include Ida Tarbell, Lincoln Steffens, and Jacob Riis. Tarbell exposed the greed and power plays of the Standard Oil Company. In his book *The Shame of the Cities* Steffens described the corruption of many city governments. Riis, an immigrant from Denmark, graphically portrayed life in the slums of New York in *How the Other Half Lives*.

Another cause of the reform movements in the Progressive Era was the influence of the Populist party. Populists made voters more aware of problems facing the nation in the 1890s. By 1900, the party had little political power, but its earlier work caused Americans to understand the need for governmental and social reform.

Inventions of the late 1800s and early 1900s made it easier for reformers to spread the word about conditions they felt needed correction. Reformers now had at their disposal typewriters, telephones, and wireless telegraph. All of these were put to use to deliver the calls for reform quickly across the country.

PRISON REFORM

In Georgia, as in some of the other southern states, a convict lease system was still in effect. Although a special legislative committee was formed in 1880 to look into the handling of leased prisoners, few changes were made. It was not until 1897 that major changes in the lease system were made. A commission was appointed to buy a prison farm so youthful offenders and old or sick inmates could be separated from other prisoners. The farm, located near Milledgeville, was built in 1900. On the farm, prisoners grew their own food and built and kept up their living quarters. Another prison was set aside for females, and in the following year, a large federal penitentiary was built in nearby Atlanta.

Chain Gangs Replace Convict Lease System

In 1908, the convict lease system was eliminated completely. It was replaced with another method of handling prisoners: county work camps, or **chain gangs**. Prisoners in work camps wore distinctive black-and-white-striped uniforms and were chained by their wrists and ankles so they could not escape. The work they did was hard, and

During the first part of the twentieth century, attempts to design programs to rehabilitate prisoners were unheard of. The chain gang shown here, building roads near Atlanta, was considered just punishment for criminals. Do you think the threat of being placed on a chain gang would be a deterrent to crime today? Why or why not?

A cigarmaker by trade, English-born immigrant Samuel Gompers worked tirelessly for labor reforms that would provide men and women with a life without poverty and despair. He helped found the Federation of Organized Trade and Labor Union in 1881. When the union reorganized in 1886 into the American Federation of Labor, Gompers became its president.

whippings were common. There was no training or any other effort to prepare them for life after they had served their prison sentences. Housing, sanitary conditions, and the quality of food were often poor.

Juvenile Court System Created

Georgia's ways of dealing with criminals did not improve greatly until the early 1940s. Then, modern equipment replaced chain-gang workers. However, one positive change was made during the Progressive Era. In 1915, at the urging of social reformers, the Georgia General Assembly created the juvenile court system. For the first time, young offenders were tried and punished differently from adults.

LABOR REFORMS

In 1900, unskilled employees were earning 10 cents an hour working twelve-hour days in factories and manufacturing plants. Many of these workers were children. Across the nation, weekly pay was less than $10. A man's shirt cost 50 cents, and meat was 10 cents a pound. Workers could barely provide for their families and had little hope of things getting better.

The American Federation of Labor is Formed

Factories were often unsafe, and job-related accidents and deaths were common in both factories and mines. People who tried to form labor unions were often punished or fired. However, one organization, the **American Federation of Labor** (AFL), was successful. It was begun in 1886 with Samuel Gompers as president. AFL members worked to bring about collective bargaining, higher wages, shorter working hours, and better working conditions.

During the Progressive Era, Georgians, like most other southerners, did not support the growth of unions. In many cases, industries were locally owned, and workers lived in the community. They attended church, social activities, and ball games with the factory, mill, or mine owners. In Georgia's mill towns, the homes of many workers and many of the town stores belonged to mill owners. Most workers thought that if they caused trouble or took part in unions, they would lose their jobs and the houses in which they lived.

A Strike Fails at the Columbus Textile Mill

In 1898, Prince W. Greene organized workers at the Columbus Textile Mill and led them in a strike against the company. This strike and efforts by workers in Atlanta and Augusta to promote membership in the National Union of Textile Workers, part of the AFL, were not successful. By the early 1900s, while unions were gaining influence in other parts of the country, attempts to form unions ended in Georgia.

The Triangle Shirtwaist Fire

One event in the early 1900s drew national attention to the need for improved working conditions. The Triangle Shirtwaist Company in New York made women's blouses. On Saturday, March 25, 1911, just before closing time, a fire broke out. Eight hundred fifty employees, most of them young women, were in the building, which was thought to be fireproof. Burning fabric spread fire through the building. The one fire escape was blocked, and screaming employees jumped out windows. One hundred forty-six workers were killed in the thirty-minute fire. As a result, local building codes and labor laws were changed to make workplaces safer. There was also an increase in the membership of the **International Ladies Garment Workers Union** (ILGU), which had been formed in 1900.

Child Labor Laws Passed

Child labor reform was slow. In 1900, over 1,000,000 children under the age of sixteen worked thirteen or more hours a day in northern **sweatshops** (factories with especially harsh working conditions) or in southern cotton fields and textile plants. Most made only a few cents

Photographer Lewis Hine, famous for his pictures showing the hardships of the downtrodden, captured this young girl working at a textile mill in Macon before child labor laws were passed. In his notes about her, he wrote, "She was so small, she had to climb up on the spinning frame to mend the broken thread." How do you think photographs like this one helped ensure the passage of child labor reforms in Congress?

an hour. Slowly, state legislatures, including Georgia's, set minimum wages for children. School attendance was required, and children could no longer work in dangerous places, such as around fast-moving machines or in some types of mining. However, it was the 1930s before there was adequate legal protection for child workers.

THE TEMPERANCE MOVEMENT

One of the most successful organized attempts at reform during the Progressive Era was the temperance movement. Since colonial days, groups had tried to end the production and use of alcoholic beverages. In 1873, after some women in Hillsboro, Ohio, heard a lecture by a health authority, they began a crusade to close the town saloons. The campaign spread to other communities, and within two months twenty states had become "dry" without any laws being passed.

The Women's Christian Temperance Union

In November 1874, women from seventeen states gathered in Cleveland, Ohio, to form a permanent organization. It was called the **Women's Christian Temperance Union** (WCTU). Led by Frances Willard, the WCTU grew rapidly. In 1893, a second group, the Anti-Saloon League, was formed to force saloons to close.

The early Temperance movement wanted only to moderate the use of alcohol, but by 1874, the year this Currier and Ives lithograph entitled "Women's Holy War" was published, the goal was to prohibit alcohol.

Carrie Nation

One of the most colorful persons of the period was Carrie Nation. The six-foot-tall, 175-pound woman entered Dobson's Saloon in Kiowa, Kansas, on June 7, 1900. Armed with rocks, she took careful aim at the bottles behind the bar.

Within minutes, the floor was covered with broken glass. Looking at the speechless bar owner, Nation is reported to have said, "Now, Mr. Dobson, I have finished! God be with you." She walked out of the bar and, taking a buggy load of rocks, went down the street and wrecked two other bars. Nation demanded that the sheriff arrest her, but the shocked lawman just asked her to leave town quickly.

As president of the local WCTU, Nation then started a series of raids on saloons in Topeka and Wichita. For those, she carried a hatchet in one hand and a Bible in the other. Her "hatchetations" continued in other parts of Kansas and in such cities as New York, Washington, and San Francisco. Conservative prohibitionists disagreed with Nation's tactics, but other women followed her example. Nation was arrested more than thirty times. She raised money to pay her fines by making speeches and selling tiny silver hatchets as souvenirs.

Georgia Women Speak Out Against "Demon Rum"

About the same time, Georgia reformer Mary Harris Armor was also speaking against "demon rum." She was a skillful speaker and raised money for the temperance movement. Armor spoke to conventions in Boston, London, Glasgow, and Toronto. During World War I, President Woodrow Wilson asked her to be the official United States representative to the World Congress on Alcoholism in Milan, Italy.

Rebecca Latimer Felton also joined hundreds of Georgia women in the WCTU. These women did not have the right to vote but had a great deal of political influence. As the movement grew stronger, temperance leaders persuaded the Georgia General Assembly to outlaw the sale of liquor in areas near schools and churches. This was followed with laws that called for each county to decide if it wanted to be "wet" (allow alcohol) or "dry" (ban alcohol).

Georgia Acts to Ban the Use of Alcohol

By 1881, forty-eight Georgia counties had banned the sale of alcohol. A state temperance conference was held in Atlanta in July 1881 during which the attendees committed themselves to making the

Above right: The six-foot-tall Carrie Nation was an impressive and intimidating sight. Armed with her Bible and hatchet, she took messages of temperance to anyone who would listen and many who would not. Above left: This 1908 cartoon shows "Carrie Nation cadets" marching through Georgia. Had you lived during the days of the temperance movement, would you have supported "hatchetations"? Why or why not?

entire state dry. By 1884, **prohibition** (the banning of alcohol) was one of the main topics of conversation in churches, political meetings, and at many dinner tables. Ninety counties had voted to go dry. Atlanta and Fulton County joined them in 1885.

In 1887, however, the tide started to turn against prohibition. Businesses that depended on the sale of alcohol formed an anti-prohibition group, and temperance forces in Fulton County lost. By the end of 1888, twenty-six other counties were again wet.

Prohibition activists (people who work for or against issues) tried to get rid of distilleries (places where alcohol is made); in 1900, there were 135 of them in the state. But making liquor raised tax money for counties where the distilleries were located and provided $150,000 for education in the state. In 1907, with the support of Governor Hoke Smith, the legislature passed a law prohibiting alcohol. The law was hard to enforce, however, and saloons selling "near-beer'" began to open. Soon, they were selling liquor and officers of the law paid little attention. Individuals could buy liquor outside the state and bring it into Georgia. It was not long until the loading platforms at railroad stations were filled with small boxes of liquor. In 1909, Joseph M. Brown, the son of a former Bourbon Triumvirate leader, became governor. He thought the state should go back to earlier laws that allowed counties to decide if prohibition was best for them.

In 1913, the U.S. Congress passed the Webb-Kenyon Bill, making it illegal for railroads to carry alcohol into dry states. Nevertheless, the near-beer saloons and clubs that kept liquor on hand for members grew in number. In 1914, Georgians elected Nathaniel E. Harris as governor. Harris called a special legislative session and pushed through a bill to close the near-beer saloons and private clubs. By 1919, it was illegal for a Georgian to have any alcoholic beverage at all.

Also in 1919, the last of the nation's then forty-eight states voted to ratify the **Eighteenth Amendment** to the Constitution. This amendment prohibited the manufacture, sale, and transportation of "intoxicating beverages." For the next fourteen years, the nation was legally dry. Carrie Nation could put away her hatchet.

WOMEN'S SUFFRAGE

The fight for women's suffrage began long before the Progressive era. In the late 1700s and early 1800s, there was little difference between the roles of men and women. Women who moved west with their families were equal pioneers with their husbands. In the industrialized North, factory jobs and teaching positions were filled by both men and women. However, by 1830, "a woman's place was in the home." Married women had few chances to earn money, and what they had was controlled by their husbands.

Attorney Nat Harris, Georgia's governor from 1915 to 1917, was the last Confederate veteran to serve as the head of state. His effectiveness as governor was sorely tested by the state's division over the issue of alcohol sales. Read about his actions and discuss what you would have done in his place.

Women Organize for the Right to Vote

There was little hope that a woman could be a political or business leader. Those who wanted freedom for slaves began to speak out for the rights of women also. In July 1848, Lucretia Mott, Elizabeth Cady Stanton, and three other women met at the Stanton home in Seneca Falls, New York. They decided to get others involved in the cause of women's rights. On July 19, more than three hundred people, including black publisher Frederick Douglass, gathered in the Seneca Falls Methodist Church. The group talked about a variety of subjects including property rights, divorce laws, and voting rights.

As word of the convention spread, thousands of women joined to demand the right of women and blacks to vote. A few years later, Susan B. Anthony and Elizabeth Stanton met, became friends, and went all over the country to share their beliefs.

The Fifteenth Amendment, passed in 1870, gave black men the right to vote, but it did nothing for women. The **suffragettes**, as those fighting for women's rights were called, felt they were getting somewhere when, in 1869, the territory of Wyoming gave women the right to vote.

Georgia suffragettes cared little that they were the recipients of catcalls and jokes as they paraded in downtown Atlanta. In most parades, they were put at the end of the procession behind the cleanup carts.

When the territory applied for statehood, some Congressmen asked them to change the suffrage law. Wyoming leaders wired their answer: "We will remain out of the Union 100 years rather than come in without the women." In 1890, they became the first "women's suffrage state." By 1900, women could also vote in Utah, Colorado, and Idaho.

Rebecca Felton supported many progressive causes and reforms, including temperance and women's suffrage. She assisted her husband, Reverend William Felton, in his successful political campaigns. Their campaigns led to this popular jingle: "Some parsons hide behind their coat, To save their precious life; But Parson Felton beats them all, He hides behind his wife."

Georgia Women Work for Suffrage

Women in Georgia were also busy working for women's rights. Augusta Howard organized Georgia women to work for suffrage, and their first meeting was in Columbus in July 1890. Several years later, the National Woman Suffrage Association Convention met in Atlanta.

In 1914, the Equal Suffrage party was formed by Georgia women, including W. G. Raoul, Mary Raoul, and Emily MacDougald. They wanted to get support for passage of the **Nineteenth Amendment**, which would give women the right to vote. Within a year, the party had 2,000 members. In November 1915, some of them marched in Atlanta's annual Harvest Festival Parade. The place assigned to them was at the end of the parade, behind the city trash carts.

Thirty-five states had ratified the Nineteenth Amendment by the summer of 1920. One more was needed to make it law. On Wednesday, August 18, 1920, the Tennessee legislature met to consider the amendment. Legislators in favor of it wore yellow roses in their lapels. Those against it wore red roses. Harry Burn, a young legislator who had promised his support, had on a red rose. People in the visitors' gallery watched as the first vote ended in a tie. On the second vote, Burn changed his "no" to "aye," and the Nineteenth Amendment became the law of the land.

Georgia was one of five states that did not ratify the Nineteenth Amendment. Suffragette Rebecca Felton said, "It is embarrassing to apologize for the ignorance and stupidity of the state legislature."

Do You Remember?

1. What prison method replaced the convict lease system?
2. What event led to changes in building codes and labor laws to make workplaces safer?
3. What did the Eighteenth Amendment to the Constitution prohibit?
4. Which amendment gave women the right to vote?

LIFE IN THE PROGRESSIVE ERA

Many Americans in the late 1890s and early 1900s now had more leisure than ever before, and some had the money to enjoy it fully. As always, though, there were sharp distinctions between the lives of the rich and the poor. But even those at the middle and the lower ends of the economic scale now had some everyday comforts once known only to the very wealthy. America was beginning to move into a consumer economy as a broad variety of relatively inexpensive items appeared on store shelves throughout the nation.

THE GILDED AGE

During the early part of the Progressive Era, a new group of people emerged in the nation, whose population now numbered almost 76 million people. This group, called the nouveau riche (new rich), made a great deal of money buying and selling land and taking financial risks in business. They spent money so freely that the late 1880s through the early 1900s became known as the "Gilded Age."

Houses of the noveau riche were showy. They usually had expensive woven rugs, heavy furniture, carved staircases, and many original paintings. Bigger was better, and many people like Jay Cooke, William Vanderbilt, and Jay Gould built giant stone mansions with fifty to seventy rooms. Steel baron Andrew Carnegie had beautiful personal railroad cars with living and office space. In New York, he had a huge house complete with gold plumbing fixtures. On Nob Hill in San Francisco, mining tycoon James Flood built a 42-room house surrounded by a block-long bronze fence. It took a full-time employee just to keep the fence polished.

Georgia's Jekyll Island became a retreat for such wealthy families as the Astors, Vanderbilts, and Rockefellers. Their winter "cottages," were, in reality, large estates. Jekyll Island was a playground for the rich and famous from 1888 to the early 1940s.

Many wealthy people in the Gilded Age built their large houses outside the cities in areas where there was enough land for them. This was part of a cycle, with middle income families moving to the outer circles of the cities, and poorer families staying near the center.

A few Americans, like industrialist Andrew Carnegie, could afford a life of untold luxuries. However, the Scottish-born immigrant first worked as a bobbin boy in a cotton mill, a telegrapher, and a railroad superintendent before becoming a wealthy steel industrialist. He gave away enough money to open 2,800 public libraries across the country, including a number in Georgia.

LIFE FOR MOST AMERICANS

Life for the middle class and poor was quite different from that of the very rich. The length of the workweek began to decline at the turn of the century. The typical workweek of 59 hours had dropped to 48 to 50 hours by 1920. The extra time away from work was made even more pleasant as conveniences became more and more commonplace. Ready-made clothes did away with the need to create every garment by hand. Markets carried a variety of food products, thus eliminating the need of churning butter, feeding chickens, and tending vegetable gardens. Iceboxes, the predecessor of today's refrigerators and freezers, meant that women no longer had to shop every day. A block of ice, delivered by the iceman straight to the icebox, allowed vegetables, milk, and butter to stay fresh longer.

In 1900, a 1-pound bag of coffee cost 25 cents; a rocking chair might run several dollars; bed sheets could be had for 45 cents; and tickets to shows were 50 cents. However, many workers made as little as 22 cents an hour. Just as always, trying to make one's salary cover the needs of a family was quite a challenge.

Outdoor sports were a major means of recreation. Baseball became more popular, and people both played in their neighborhoods and attended professional games. Dr. James Naismith of the Young Men's Christian Association College in Springfield, Massachusetts, introduced basketball, the only major sport that originated in the United States. Within a few years, people of all ages were enjoying the new game. College football, an American form of the English game of rugby, caught on slowly. Often, the players were also the cheering section.

Bicycling was an important means of transportation. Some larger cities had streetcars. Automobiles were not widely used until after World War I. Other favorite pastimes included going to vaudeville (a type of variety show) and musical comedy shows. Growing in popularity was a new form of entertainment: movies. The first moving pictures in America were shown in 1905 at a Pittsburgh movie theater and quickly spread across the country. Because it usually cost a nickel to see a movie, people called the movie theaters "nickelodeons."

Popular books of the era included Rudyard Kipling's *Captains Courageous*; L. Frank Baum's *The Wonderful Wizard of Oz*; Alice Rice's *Mrs. Wiggs of the Cabbage Patch*; and the stories of Jack London, including *White Fang*, *The Call of the Wild*, and *The Sea Wolf*. Newspapers and magazines were widely read, and most Americans became better informed about events affecting their lives.

After the first game of basketball was played in 1891, the sport quickly grew in popularity. Here you see a game between Atlanta's Boys' High and Tech High in 1919.

Mail-order shopping grew into a major business during this period. Sears, Roebuck and Company competed with Montgomery Ward and several other retailers in selling items through catalogs. Catalogs offered almost any needed item at a price working people could afford. For example, in 1902, Sears, Roebuck and Company offered a baseball for 55 cents, a 100-piece set of china for under $6, and a top-of-the line wood and coal stove for less than $15. For cold winters, a person could buy a calfskin fur coat for $16 or an all-wool coat for $4. One could also get a new pair of boots for $11 and a hat for only 75 cents.

STILL ANOTHER PRESIDENT ASSASSINATED

William McKinley had high hopes for his re-election in 1900. Although the nation still mourned the deaths of 6,000 people killed by a hurricane in Galveston, Texas, the mood of the country was upbeat. Henry Ford's new mode of transportation, the Model T, was the talk of the country. Economically, the nation was growing and, little by little, life was getting easier for many people.

On September 6, 1901, President McKinley traveled to Buffalo, New York, to deliver a speech at the Pan American Exposition, an exhibition celebrating the country's progress. Crowds surrounded the president as he stood shaking hands and chatting with well-wishers. As a man in a black suit approached, McKinley reached out his hand to greet the next potential voter.

Top left: *The bicycle remained a favorite mode of transportation.* *Top right:* *This 1911 Georgia Tech football team was coached by John W. Heisman, for whom the Heisman Trophy is named.* *Above:* *President McKinley was assassinated in 1901.*

398 GEORGIA: THE HISTORY OF AN AMERICAN STATE

Suddenly, two shots rang out. The president clutched his chest and asked, "Am I shot?" Then he fell forward. The shooter, who had hidden a gun under his handkerchief, turned to run but was immediately stopped by onlookers who began to beat him. McKinley stopped their assaults by saying, "Let no one hurt him." Although in obvious pain, the president turned to his aide and whispered, "My wife—Be careful how you tell her—Oh, be careful."

McKinley was rushed to the hospital and treated, and his recovery seemed assured. However, eight days later, he took a turn for the worse. On September 14, the 58-year-old president became the third American chief executive to die by an assassin's hand. McKinley's vice president, Theodore Roosevelt, was then sworn in as president.

McKinley's killer, Leon Czolgosz, was an **anarchist**, an anti-government terrorist. Like other anarchists, Czolgosz was opposed to all forms of government. He had dreamed of killing a major world leader and chose the American president.

RELIGION DURING THE PROGRESSIVE ERA

During the Progressive Era, many social and political events centered around religion. Baptists and Methodists remained the major Protestant denominations in Georgia. Churches tried to help members in need. They also developed programs for young people.

Revivals and Evangelism

After the major work of planting was done but before time to harvest, most churches had summer revivals. People came from miles around to hear famous preachers who spoke each night for one or two weeks. Sin and the devil were the main targets of loud, foot-stomping sermons. Georgia enjoyed the preaching of Cartersville resident Samuel Porter Jones. Jones was a Methodist circuit rider who preached against drinking, gambling, card-playing, baseball, bicycling, novel reading, and dancing.

Billy Sunday Comes to Atlanta

In the early twentieth century, there was a spirit of religious revival all over the nation. Former professional baseball player and YMCA worker William Ashley "Billy" Sunday was one of the most popular preachers of the day. Sunday came to Atlanta in 1917. When he arrived, he said, "I expect Atlanta to come to the plate and line them out so fast that the Devil will have his tongue hanging out and . . . the score will be one of which Atlanta will be proud." During his seven-week revival, thousands came to a huge tent in the city to hear the fiery evangelist speak out on sin in general, and the evils of alcohol in particular.

Top: *Methodist evangelist Samuel Jones traveled throughout the state preaching against many of the "new-fangled" ideas and leisure time activities of the early 1900s.* ***Above:*** *Well-known preacher Billy Sunday came to Atlanta in 1917.*

THE BERRY SCHOOLS

Martha McChesney Berry was born into a wealthy family near Rome on October 7, 1866. She attended private school in Boston, then traveled in Europe. After returning to Oak Hill, the family plantation, Berry often rode with her father to deliver food and clothing to the poor.

Berry's study, where she liked to write, was a log cabin on the plantation. One Sunday afternoon, three boys in ragged overalls were playing outside the study. Martha asked them to come in, gave them apples, and told them Bible stories. The next Sunday, the boys brought their brothers and sisters. Soon, parents came for Berry's weekly "Sunday School." The group outgrew the cabin, so they moved to an old church building at Possum Trot. When there were too many people to get in that building, Berry began other Sunday Schools in nearby communities. The people of the area called Martha Berry the "Sunday Lady of Possum Trot." In addition to sharing Bible stories, Berry taught reading, singing, and good health practices.

In 1901, Berry used $1,000 of her own money and 83 acres of land to establish a school. With the help of her students, she built a small schoolhouse across the road from her home. The next year, Berry, her sister, and Elizabeth Brewster added a dormitory so students could

Right: When she was not horseback riding or strolling the 300-acre grounds of her comfortable home, Martha Berry could often be found working in her study. *Above:* Martha Berry's family plantation, Oak Hill, near Rome, Georgia.

live at the school. There was no tuition, but each student worked. Students grew vegetables, raised cattle, and helped build roads and other school structures as needed. Berry called the entrance to the school the "Gate of Opportunity." Here, poor young boys of the mountain area learned to read, write, and do arithmetic. They also got job training that would help them find work when school days were over.

Like the Sunday classes, the school quickly became overcrowded. Berry asked for and got help from two of America's wealthiest businessmen, Andrew Carnegie and Henry Ford. In 1909, she started a girl's division of the school and renamed it The Berry Schools.

After World War I, when more students were entering high school, Berry knew she needed additional teachers. In 1926, she opened Berry Junior College to train them and, by 1932, the small college had become a four-year institution. Martha Berry died in 1942. The school she started now covers 30,000 acres and has modern buildings and courses. Her goal was "to free the children of the mountain forests; to give them to America, strong of heart, mind, and soul."

Martha Berry's dream of helping others by providing educational opportunities is still carried on today at Berry College.

Above: A multi-talented woman, Juliette Gordon Low, who founded the Girl Scouts of America in Savannah, Georgia, was an artist, sculptor, world traveler, and wealthy socialite. Her talents also extended to writing the Girl Scout Handbook. ***Above right:*** *"Daisy" Low presents a scout with the Golden Eaglet, then the highest Girl Scouting award. Although Mrs. Low did not have any children of her own, she has influenced millions of young girls through the scouting program she began in 1912.*

GIRL SCOUTS ORGANIZED

Juliette Gordon Low was the daughter of a wealthy Confederate Army captain. Daisy, as she was called, met her husband "Willy" Low while traveling in England after the Civil War. Daisy knew people like King Edward VII, Winston Churchill, and Rudyard Kipling. She introduced her English friends to southern foods, such as grits, sweet potatoes, and cucumber pickles.

After her husband died, Low met Sir Robert Baden-Powell, the founder of the Boy Scouts. His sister had organized a group for girls called Girl Guides. The brother and sister got Daisy to start Girl Guides in Scotland. She then began two more groups in London. Low thought American girls would enjoy scouting activities. She returned to her native Savannah and, with the help of her family, started a Girl's Guide group with fifteen members. The girls wore uniforms of dark blue skirts, middy blouses, black cotton stockings, and black hair ribbons.

The group was immediately successful and, in 1915, a national headquarters was established in Washington, D.C., under the name of **Girl Scouts of America**. Until her death in 1927, Low worked to promote Girl Scouts. Today there are over 3 million Girls Scouts who enjoy the fun of scouting Low brought to the United States from England.

Do You Remember?
1. What name was given to the period in the late 1800s and early 1900s because of the way some of the wealthy lived?
2. What sport did Dr. James Naismith introduce?
3. Who was Billy Sunday?
4. Who encouraged Juliette Gordon Low to organize her first group of Girl Guides?

CHANGES IN THE WIND

For some Americans, 1906 was one of the most memorable years during the Progressive Era. On April 18, an earthquake rocked San Francisco, California. At 5:12 a.m., the earth began to shake. Although it seemed longer, the quake lasted only forty seconds. After several seconds of relief, another wave struck and lasted twenty-five seconds.

Finally, the earth rested and everyone gave sighs of relief. Their relief, however, was short-lived. Soon over fifty fires had broken out all over San Francisco causing far more damage than the initial quake. Because most of the city's water mains were broken by the earthquake, firemen had to stand by helplessly as buildings burned and crumbled into ashes. Fires burned around the city for three days. When the smoke cleared, 452 people were dead and 225,000 were homeless.

On a more positive side, 1906 was also the year that President Theodore Roosevelt became the first American to receive the Nobel Peace Prize. Novelist Zane Grey published the first of sixty books, many of which were westerns. And both the Meat Inspection Act and the Pure Food and Drug Act were made into law. Both of these measures were aimed at protecting the health of the American public.

In only sixty-five seconds, in 1906, an earthquake devastated San Francisco, causing fires and destruction that would kill 452 people and leave 225,000 homeless. This photograph shows the remains of the San Francisco City Hall.

GEORGIA POLITICS

The year 1906 was an election year in Georgia. Two newspaper men ran against each other for the office of governor. Clarke Howell, publisher of the *Atlanta Constitution*, ran for the state's highest office as a conservative Democrat. His opponent was attorney Hoke Smith, owner of the *Atlanta Evening Journal*, known today as the *Atlanta Journal*. Smith was a reform candidate. He promised that corporations and private railroad companies would no longer have any power in state government.

Hoke Smith Elected Governor

Populist Tom Watson agreed to support Smith's campaign if Smith would support a law to disfranchise blacks. Each of the candidates ran as a conservative **white supremacist**, someone who believes the white race is superior to the black race or to any other race. A statement in the black-owned *Savannah Tribune* read: "God help the civilization and future of the Democratic white man if Hoke Smith represents his ideas." Nevertheless, Smith won by a landslide. His election was seen as a victory for both the state's reformers and farmers. Smith gained farm support by promising to take political power away from the cities and return it to the rural areas. After Smith's election, rural Georgia remained the principal power base of state politics for the next fifty-six years.

Above: The publisher of the Atlanta Constitution, *Clarke Howell, was unsuccessful in his 1906 bid for governor against rival* Atlanta Evening Journal *owner, Hoke Smith.*

Opposite page: Attorney Hoke Smith, publisher of the Atlanta Evening Journal, *served as Georgia's governor from 1907-1909. In the 1908 campaign, Smith lost his bid for re-election. One of the main reasons was the influence of Thomas Watson who threw his support behind opponent Joseph Brown.*

Little Joe" Brown Elected Governor

Joseph M. Brown defeated Hoke Smith in the 1908 governor's election. Brown, the son of Civil War Governor Joseph E. Brown, was called "Little Joe" Brown. He used the problems caused by a 1907 economic depression to blame Smith for Georgia's difficulty. One of Brown's slogans was "Hoke and Hunger; Brown and Bread."

Another cause for Smith's defeat was that Tom Watson changed his support to Brown. Watson's friend Arthur Glover was convicted of murdering a woman in Augusta and sentenced to be hanged. Watson asked Governor Smith to change the sentence to life in prison. Smith refused, and Watson withdrew his support.

Smith Re-elected

Hoke Smith was re-elected in 1910. He still believed in white supremacy and supported anti-black laws. Under his leadership, the Georgia General Assembly passed a constitutional amendment that said a person had to own property and be able to read in order to

vote. As a result, most blacks and many poor whites were removed from the voter rolls.

At the same time, there were also positive changes during Smith's two terms in office. The Railroad Commission became responsible for the regulation of gas lines, electric power companies, and trolley cars. Public schools received better funding, and child labor laws changed. Smith worked with the legislature to regulate lobbying groups and to place limits on campaign contributions.

Above: Thomas Watson won his 1920 Senate race against incumbent Hoke Smith because he had the unlikely backing of reformer Rebecca Felton.

Opposite page: The county unit system gave rural areas, such as Baldwin County (county seat, Milledgeville, top), considerable political power when united with other rural areas. Smaller counties of the state received two unit votes. Larger counties, such as the 254-square-mile Bibb County (county seat, Macon, below), with a far larger population than small rural areas, received only six county unit votes. This system allowed rural Georgia to dominate state politics and decision making until 1962.

Smith Appointed to Senate

In 1911, the Georgia General Assembly named Hoke Smith to succeed Joseph M. Terrell in the United States Senate. While in the Senate, where he served until 1921, Smith was responsible for two major pieces of legislation: the **Smith-Lever Act** and the **Smith-Hughes Act**. The 1914 Smith-Lever Act created the **Agricultural Extension Service**. It gave matching federal funds to states that spent money to teach young people better farming methods. The Smith-Hughes Act helped establish vocational programs in public schools across the nation. The Act also set up a federal board for vocational education to help states plan and carry out vocational training goals. By the 1920s, young people were being trained in trades, agriculture, and home economics as a result of Smith's legislation.

The County Unit System

The 1917 **Neill Primary Act** established a **county unit system** for political primaries. At that time, the Democratic party was the only active political party in the state. This meant the outcomes of primary elections and general elections were usually the same. Because that was true, the county unit system, in fact, affected both elections. The Neill Primary Act provided:

1. All primary elections for major offices, such as governor, U.S. senators, justices of the supreme court, court of appeals judges, and statehouse offices would be held on the second Wednesday in September in the years of general elections;
2. Candidates who received the largest popular vote in a county would "carry that county" and receive all of the county's unit votes;

3. County unit votes would be determined by the number of lower house representatives in the General Assembly, with counties receiving two unit votes per representative;

4. In the event of a tie between two candidates in a county's primary election, the unit votes for that county would be split;

5. A majority of the county unit votes would be required to nominate a candidate for governor or for the United States Senate. If there was a tie, the candidate who received the most popular votes would be nominated;

6. For all other offices, a tie would result in a second primary election, allowing the top two county unit winners to run against each other again;

7. A **plurality** (the margin of victory for the winner over the nearest rival) of county unit votes was required to elect an individual in any race except those for governor and the United States Senate.

Rural Counties Control Politics Under County Unit System

Under the county unit system, the 8 most populated counties had 6 county unit votes each. The next 30 counties had 4, and the remaining 121 counties had 2. In small counties, a unit vote could represent 879 people. In larger counties, it might represent as many as 91,687 people. The 38 largest counties had two-thirds of Georgia's voters, but the other 121 counties together could decide a state election. Those against the county unit system pointed out that people were elected to office without a majority of the state's popular vote. Those for it said the system allowed small, less populated counties to have the same power and influence as larger ones. The county unit system remained in effect until 1962.

Do You Remember?

1. Who was elected governor in 1906?
2. What act created the Agricultural Extension Service?
3. What were the reasons people opposed the county unit system?
4. What were the reasons people supported the county unit system?

SCIENCE AND TECHNOLOGY

During the Progressive Era, major developments in science and technology took place. Communication between people in far-flung areas of the world was made possible. And the search for a practical means of air transportation was finally realized.

COMMUNICATIONS

Some of the major advances of the era were those made in the field of communications. Now, people could phone others not only in different parts of a city or state, but in different parts of the country and world as well. And a device was developed that would bring information and entertainment directly into one's home: the radio.

Transcontinental Phone Communication

On January 25, 1915, Alexander Graham Bell sat with Bell Telephone Company officials in New York. At 4:30 p.m., Bell lifted a telephone receiver and said, "Ahoy, Ahoy! Mr. Watson. Are you there? Do you hear me"? In San Francisco, 3,400 miles away, Bell's assistant responded, "Yes, Dr. Bell, I hear you perfectly." The first transcontinental telephone call had been completed. Messages that once took hours, days, even weeks, now were sent and received in just a matter of minutes. The communications gap had been closed.

Less than thirty years after Alexander Graham Bell (above) invented the telephone, the first transatlantic phone call was made, on January 25, 1915.

The Telegraph Leads to Radio

Italian Guglielmo Marconi received a British patent for his invention of the wireless telegraph in 1897. Using a code of dots and dashes, messages could be sent immediately for long distances—even overseas. Reginald Fessenden wondered if wireless messages could be sent in waves like sound vibrations. If they could, music and speech could be transmitted. Fessenden's experiments worked. At 8:00 p.m. on Christmas Eve, 1906, shipboard wireless operators off the New England coast heard human voices instead of the usual dots and dashes. A woman sang a Christmas carol; someone played the violin; another person read a passage from the Bible. At the end, Fessenden wished the operators "Merry Christmas." The first radio program had been broadcast. In the years that followed, Fessenden continued to improve radio transmission. The word *broadcast* took on a new meaning. In 1901, it was defined as "the act or process of scattering seeds." By 1927, it meant "to scatter or disseminate, specifically, radio messages, speeches. . . ." In 1922, Georgia joined the radio generation when WSB radio was established in Atlanta.

TRANSPORTATION

In 1901, France admitted the failure of a twenty-year effort to build a canal in Panama to connect the Atlantic and Pacific oceans. With President Theodore Roosevelt's encouragement, the United States took over the project in 1902. Colonel George Goethals was in charge of 30,000 to 40,000 workers. They removed 240 million cubic yards of earth to build over 50 miles of locks. When the canal opened in 1914, it had cost $380 million. But the eventual savings in the time and human life far outweighed that cost. Ships no longer had to make the long and dangerous voyage around Cape Horn at the southern tip of South America.

Henry Ford and Mass Production

After Henry Ford finished his first automobile, he built a factory for making cars. It was ready for operation in 1903. People no longer laughed at the "new-fangled contraption." Instead, they bought it in ever-increasing numbers. In 1900, 4,000 cars were made. In 1910, 187,000 Model T Fords rolled out of factories.

In 1913, Ford began building cars on an assembly line, a moving track or belt. Using this method, a car could be put together in 93 minutes instead of several hours. As a result, the number of cars produced rose from 570,000 in 1914 to 1,600,000 in 1919. The assembly line worked so well that by 1924, the price of a black Model T dropped to $290.

But Ford had created much more than just another way to build cars. With the assembly line, he created the concept of mass production. Mass production is the manufacture of great quantities of an item through the assembly of interchangeable parts. Mass production enabled Ford to make cars available to the average person. Unlike the earlier automobiles that were handmade and so expensive only the wealthy bought them, now almost everyone could afford a car. For example, at the time when an average three-bedroom house cost $2,650, a new Ford could be purchased for a little over $500. Moreover, the principles of the assembly line and mass production could

Shown here is the Ford Model T assembly line. With this innovation in manufacturing, cars could be made much more quickly and at far less expense. Once the assembly line went into operation, Ford could produce a car in 93 minutes compared with the several hours required to make a car before the line was completed.

BERNOULLI'S THEOREM

The Wright brothers made use of the theorem on the flow of fluids developed by Daniel Bernoulli (top) to design wings used in the first powered flights at Kitty Hawk on December 17, 1903 (above). The cross section diagram shows how a curved wing creates unequal air pressure above and below the wing, causing it to lift.

The Wright brothers used science to design their gliders and airplanes. One scientist whose work helped them was Daniel Bernoulli. Born in 1700 in Switzerland, Bernoulli was a mathematician, physicist, and philosopher. In 1738, Bernoulli published (in Latin) an important work called "Hydrodynamica" ("The Dynamics of Water"), which contained his theorem (or principle) on the flow of fluids. Bernoulli's theorem states that the pressure of a fluid decreases as the speed of the fluid increases.

If you think of air as a "fluid," the theorem can be applied to aircraft design. Look at this cross section of an aircraft wing. Because the air moving over the top of the wing moves faster than the air moving across the bottom, the air pressure on the top is less. Since the air pressure on the bottom is more, the air pushes *up* on the wing and lifts the whole airplane.

The Wright brothers built a small wind tunnel to test Bernoulli's principle on different wing shapes. They used the data they gathered to build new and larger wings. Finally, they were ready to add power to their glider. And the rest is history.

be applied to the manufacture of almost anything. Thus, a great variety of items could now be produced faster at a much lower cost.

The Wright Brothers' First Flight

Another major advance in transportation was made on December 17, 1903, by two brothers from Dayton, Ohio. On a cold and windy Thursday in Kitty Hawk, North Carolina, Wilbur and Orville Wright and five helpers dragged a 605-pound machine along the beach to the base of Kill Devil Hill. The machine, which looked like a giant box kite, was named "Flyer." Its 40-foot wings were covered with thin muslin cloth. Reportedly, one of the men helping the Wright brothers joked, "All that thing needs is a good coat of feathers to make it fly."

"Flyer" was pulled up the hill and placed on a 60-foot-long, greased launching track. At 10:30 a.m., the final adjustments were made, and the engine was started to turn the plane's propellers. Orville lay face down, strapped to the lower wing. Slowly, the throttle was pushed, and the 4-cylinder, 12-horsepower aircraft came to life. Five minutes later, Orville released the restraining wire and entered history.

The flight lasted only 12 seconds, during which time Flyer went up 10 feet and traveled 120 feet. The Wright brothers made three other flights that day. The longest was 852 feet and lasted 59 seconds. Air travel had begun.

Other Events in Transportation

In 1904, the first New York City subway opened. Soon it was to become part of the country's largest underground transportation system. Also in 1904, the diesel engine, named after its German inventor Rudolf Diesel, was shown at the St. Louis Exposition.

A far more tragic event in transportation occurred on April 14, 1912. The British liner *Titanic*, highly publicized as "unsinkable," struck an iceberg in the North Atlantic. Within 3 hours, the ship sank and over 1,500 of its 2,227 passengers and crew were carried to their deaths.

Those that survived did so in large part because of the use of the wireless telegraph, which was able to summon nearby vessels to their aid. Perhaps the tragedy could have been averted completely if the *Titanic's* officers had heeded warnings of icebergs that were transmitted to them by wire earlier in the day.

Do You Remember?
1. Who invented the wireless telegraph?
2. What concept of Henry Ford's revolutionized the way automobiles and a variety of other products were manufactured?
3. What happened at Kitty Hawk, North Carolina, to change modern-day transportation?

As early as the late 1400s when Italian Renaissance artist Leonardo da Vinci first tried to fly with wings attached to his back, man had long dreamed of flight. In 1903, two brothers, Orville (left) and Wilbur (right) Wright, came a step closer to realizing this dream at Kitty Hawk, North Carolina.

WORLD WAR I

War broke out in Europe in August 1914. President Woodrow Wilson, who had been elected in 1912, declared America a **neutral** nation. In other words, the United States would not take sides between the Central Powers led by Germany and Austria-Hungary and the Allied Powers led by France, Great Britain, and Russia.

Some Georgians, however, did take sides. They volunteered to fight for the French and British, serving as aviators, soldiers, ambulance drivers, and nurses. Some joined with other Americans and flew with the Lafayette Escadrille, a squadron of American aviators who fought for France.

The automatic machine gun was invented in 1882 by Hiram Maxim and was first used in battle during World War I. The weapon could fire over ten shots per second and resulted in the deaths of thousands of soldiers on both sides of the battle.

THE UNITED STATES ENTERS THE WAR

President Wilson wanted the United States to remain neutral and had based his campaign for re-election in 1916 on the slogan, "He kept us out of war." However, a series of hostile actions taken by Germany led him to ask Congress to declare war on Germany in April 1917. When President Wilson spoke to Congress, he asked Americans to fight a war "to make the world safe for democracy." This war has come to be known as **World War I.**

THE UNITED STATES AND WORLD WAR I

When World War I began in 1914, the United States remained neutral. By international law, the United States could trade with both warring sides. This was called "freedom of the seas." The British tried to stop neutrals' trade with Germany by mining the North Sea with explosives. Germany hoped to use its submarines to sink ships trading with the British.

In May 1915, a German submarine sank the British liner *Lusitania* off Ireland. Among the hundreds killed were 128 Americans. President Wilson warned Germany of dire results if it continued to violate international law requiring warships to provide for the safety of passengers and crews of trading ships they sank. Germany apologized and stopped the submarine warfare lest the United States enter the war.

Meanwhile the United States became more committed to the Allies, who depended on the United States for food and war supplies. The British bombarded America with anti-German propaganda. Americans believed the propaganda, especially after German spies tried to sabotage American industry. Congress began preparing for war.

In early 1917, Germany resumed submarine attacks, and in March 1917 its submarines sank several American ships. Meanwhile the British intercepted and decoded a secret radio message from Germany to Mexico. In this "Zimmerman Telegram," Germany urged Mexico to attack the United States in return for getting the southwestern United States. This was the final blow. President Wilson asked Congress to declare war.

German U-boat attacks on American shipping were one of the main reasons for the United States' entry into the war. Here we see a captured German U-boat crew being transported to the prisoner of war camp located at Fort McPherson in East Point, just outside Atlanta, to wait out the war's end.

GEORGIA AND WORLD WAR I

When the United States declared war, Georgia's citizens were ready to help. Between 85,000 and 100,000 of them joined the armed forces. Soldiers came from other states to be trained at military posts located throughout the state, including Camp Benning, Fort McPherson, and Camp Gordon. Camp Benning was opened in 1917 as a result of orders from General John Pershing, the leader of the American armed forces. Located near Columbus, Camp Benning trained infantry troops. Named in honor of Confederate General Henry Benning, it became Fort Benning in 1922. During the war, a German submarine crew was imprisoned at Fort McPherson, which was just outside of Atlanta. Camp Gordon (later called Fort Gordon), is located outside of Augusta. These and other military installations were to be a major factor in the state's economy.

Georgians contributed to the war effort in other ways. Textile mills made fabric for military uniforms. Railroads carried arms, ammunition, and soldiers to ports where ships waited to sail for Europe. Farmers grew more food crops, tobacco, and livestock. Many town residents planted victory gardens to release other food for the military. Women gave their time to work for the Red Cross, welcome soldiers, knit, and help sell bonds. However, Georgia's most important contribution was the 3,000 young people from all over the state who died in an effort to "make the world safe for democracy."

With the entry of the United States and the vast amounts of supplies and equipment it was able to contribute, the Central Powers were defeated. On November 11, 1918, the war officially ended when both sides signed an **armistice** (an agreement to stop fighting). For years afterward, Georgia and the rest of the nation rang church bells and held ceremonies at the 11th hour on the 11th day of the 11th month to commemorate victory and peace.

These 1917 postcards of Camp Gordon shows only one of five World War I Georgia training camps. Troops shown above are hearing a lecture on military tactics. Today the army post is located outside of Augusta and is known as Fort Gordon.

THE ATLANTA FIRE

On May 21, 1917, Atlanta's attention was drawn sharply back to a local event. Early that morning, many residents were told to collect water needed for the day because the city's supply would be off for a while. Fire broke out in the west end of town, and firemen had little water to put it out. During the next ten to twelve hours, more than eighty blocks were destroyed.

Dry weather and wooden houses built close together made it easy for the fire to spread. About 1,900 houses and 1,553 other buildings were destroyed. There were between 6,000 and 10,000 people left homeless.

Do You Remember?
1. Who were the Central Powers?
2. What slogan did Wilson use in his 1916 presidential campaign?
3. When did the United States enter the war?
4. When did the war end?

SUMMARY

- The Progressive Era was marked by major economic, social, and political changes.
- The textile industry grew rapidly, but working conditions were difficult and wages low.
- Among the social changes were prison reform, labor reform, and prohibition.
- Suffragettes' struggle to gain the right to vote resulted in the Nineteenth Amendment.
- Political changes included the establishment of a county unit system that gave rural politicians disproportionate influence.
- World War I broke out in Europe between the Allied Powers and the Central Powers.
- After several years of neutrality, America entered the war on the side of the Allied Powers.
- The war ended in victory for the Allied Powers.

Top: Atlanta's West End fire left 6,000 residents of the city homeless. *Above:* After the Atlanta fire in 1917, all that was left of 300 acres were chimneys, which were a tragic reminder of the city's loss.

1901 McKinley assassinated	1903 Wright brothers made first successful airplane flight			1914 World War I began	1917 United States entered World War I
	1906 Hoke Smith elected governor				1918 World War I ended
		1908 "Little Joe" Brown elected governor			

1900 **1905** **1910** **1915** **1920**

1901 Oil discovered at Spindletop, Texas	1903 First child labor law passed	1909 Admiral Perry and Matthew Henson reached the North Pole	1911 American Tobacco Company broken up / Triangle Shirtwaist Company fire occurred	
	1906 San Francisco rocked by earthquake / First school of forestry in the South formed at University of Georgia	1908 William Howard Taft elected president / Henry Ford introduced Model T	1918 Worldwide influenza epidemic broke out / First women admitted to University of Georgia	1919 Charter of the League of Nations is written

Reviewing People, Places, and Terms

Explain why each of the following terms appears in a chapter on the Progressive Era.
1. chain gang
2. county unit system
3. sweatshop
4. suffragettes
5. prohibition

Understanding the Facts

1. Who did the progressives feel was best equipped to correct the ills of society?
2. What piece of legislation led to improved sanitary conditions in meat-packing plants?
3. In what year did the American Federation of Labor begin?
4. What did Prince W. Greene do?
5. Which Georgia reformer spoke out against "demon rum"?
6. When did the Nineteenth Amendment become the law of the land?

7. What place in Georgia became a playground for the wealthy?
8. What did the Neill Primary Act establish?
9. Which three European countries formed the Allied Powers at the beginning of World War I?

Developing Critical Thinking

1. What impact do you think child labor had on the U.S. economy?
2. The practice of using prisoners to maintain roads or to do other maintenance work has recently been reinstated in some areas of the country. Do you think this is a good policy? Why or why not?
3. Which of the Central Powers and Allied Powers do you think was most responsible for the outbreak of World War I? Research the topic and give reasons to support your answer.
4. Do you think that the county unit system was in the best interest of the state of Georgia? Defend your answer.

5. Why do you think it took so many years before women were given the right to vote?

Applying Your Skills

1. Re-read the sections in this chapter that describe how much an average worker was paid in a year and how much a stove from Sears, Roebuck and Company cost. If an individual making an average salary wanted to buy that stove but could only save 75 cents a month, how many months would it take before the stove would be paid off?

2. At the beginning of the twentieth century, the number of corporations increased rapidly. Research how a corporation is formed. Try to find out whether any businesses in your community are organized as corporations.

3. Susan B. Anthony and Elizabeth Cady Stanton were leaders in the national women's suffrage movement. Prepare a report on one of them.

Making Connections

1. Find out if wind tunnels are used today. If so, how?

2. Cut a 2-inch square piece of heavy paper. Put a straight pin through the center of it. Place a thread spool over the pin and the paper. Hold the paper, pin, and spool in the palm of one hand. Blow through the top of the spool and see what happens. As you blow, take the supporting hand away. The paper should appear to stick to the spool the harder you blow. When you stop blowing, the paper and pin fall away. Why do you suppose this is so?

3. World War I was fought to make the world "safe for democracy." Do you think it did that? Why or why not?

4. Could a major metropolitan area be as devastated by a fire today as Atlanta was in 1906? Why or why not?

Did You Know?

- The *Titanic* was the equivalent of an eleven-story building in height.
- Although almost 250,000 people lost their homes in the San Francisco earthquakes and fires, less than 500 people were killed.
- When the zipper was introduced, it was primarily used by actors as a fastener for quick clothing changes between scenes.
- President Woodrow Wilson lived in Augusta as a youngster and later practiced law in Atlanta.

BUILDING SKILLS: ASKING EFFECTIVE QUESTIONS

Effective questions are questions that serve a specific purpose and provide desired information. Asking effective questions involves a three-step process. If you ask questions without having a carefully planned strategy for doing so, you can spend a great deal of time and end up with confusing data. Effective questions help you "get to the point" and allow you to better understand the given topic.

The three steps involved in developing effective questions are the following:

1. Determine what information you need to know.

2. Decide what materials or people you should consult.

3. Consider what questions you should ask.

By following these guidelines, the questions you ask will be effective ones. Now, imagine that your teacher has asked you and three of your classmates to do a group report on the causes of World War I. Use the three-step approach to develop effective questions about the series of events that brought about the war.

CHAPTER THIRTEEN

A NEW ERA IN CIVIL RIGHTS

I am as good as anybody else. God had no different dirt to make me out of than that used in making the first lady of the land.

—Lucy C. Laney

Opposite page: The ninth of ten children, Macon-born Lucy Craft Laney graduated from the original Atlanta University in 1873. She went on to become a leading Georgia educator. Above: The Atlanta of the 1870s and 1880s before Plessy v. Ferguson *was, to a limited degree, integrated. However, the social actuality was far different from the picture seen here. Notice the stereotyped depiction of blacks and whites. What messages does the picture give?*

ALTHOUGH BLACKS BECAME CITIZENS of the United States with the ratification of the Fourteenth Amendment in 1868, they did not enjoy the full rights of citizens. Not only did that amendment to the U.S. Constitution make blacks citizens of the United States, but it also placed restrictions on the states to make sure that they did not take away from blacks their rights as citizens. For example, a state could not have separate sets of laws for blacks and whites. A state could not take away a person's life, liberty, or property without proper legal steps. In 1870, the Fifteenth Amendment ensured that blacks had the right to vote.

THE FIGHT FOR CIVIL RIGHTS

The rights of citizens are called **civil rights**. There is no complete list of these rights, but most people include the following: free speech, freedom of religion, access to courts, trial by a jury of one's peers (equals), property ownership, voting (if qualified), access to jobs, privacy, and the ability to travel wherever one wishes inside the country.

Over the years, various laws relating to these civil rights have been passed. However, getting a law passed does not always mean it will be enforced. During the late 1800s and early 1900s, the concept of "white supremacy" was popular, not only in the South, but in other areas of the western world as well. During Reconstruction and the New South era, most whites and many blacks accepted racial **segregation** (separation of races) as a way of life.

For example, Congress enacted the **Civil Rights Act of 1875**, which provided for equal accommodations for blacks and whites and said that blacks must be allowed to serve on juries. However, in 1883, the U.S. Supreme Court ruled the act unconstitutional. Georgia's public schools, which in 1871 were open to all students, were totally

segregated by 1877. The Georgia constitution of 1877 allowed only blacks who had paid taxes to vote. Federal laws and the judges who reviewed them had little, if any, impact on customs and traditions. Sociologist William Sumner said, "Stateways cannot change folkways."

SEPARATE BUT EQUAL

A new direction in civil rights was caused by the U.S. Supreme Court decision entitled ***Plessy v. Ferguson***. The Supreme Court ruling in this case created the **separate-but-equal concept**, which allowed states to pass laws to segregate facilities for blacks and whites.

In 1881, Tennessee became the first southern state to pass a bill to segregate railroad cars. Every other southern state followed. These separate-but-equal laws in the South were unofficially called **Jim Crow laws**. (The name "Jim Crow," which came from a song-and-dance routine of the 1830s, was used as a derogatory synonym for blacks.) The Jim Crow laws resulted in separate restrooms, water fountains, railroad cars, waiting rooms, dining areas, and schools. Although the facilities for blacks were separate, they were rarely equal to those for whites. Blacks protested these laws in public meetings from Maine to Florida. Georgia's Henry McNeal Turner, an African Methodist Episcopal (AME) bishop, called the new civil rights laws, and the segregation that followed as a result of them, "barbarous."

The decision in *Plessy v. Ferguson* opened the door for more Jim Crow laws. Soon sports, hospitals, orphanages, funeral homes, and cemeteries were added to the list of "separate-but-equal" facilities. The Georgia General Assembly in 1889 segregated a number of public facilities including theaters, prison camps, water fountains, and restrooms. In actual practice, the decision in *Plessy v. Ferguson* made segregation the law of the land until 1954.

BLACKS IN GEORGIA

In the 1870s and early 1880s, black and white Georgians sat together on streetcars, shopped in integrated business districts, shared public parks and playgrounds and, sometimes, lived in the same neighborhoods. With the spread of the "separate-but-equal" concept, integration became part of the past.

By 1900, close to 12 percent of the blacks in the nation lived in Georgia. These 1 million black citizens were 49 percent of the state's population. Most of them lived in the farming centers of middle and southwest Georgia. However, a number of them moved to the cities and built social, business, religious, and educational centers. Nearly one-third of Georgia's cities had black majorities, and half of this population lived in Atlanta, Savannah, and Augusta. It was in these cities that people protested most against Jim Crow laws. However, protests were not the same as votes.

Although federal law ensured that blacks could vote in general elections, Georgia law allowed only white males to vote in primary elections. More and more, blacks felt pushed aside and without power. Black leaders began to speak against segregation. Black protests continued, but so did segregation.

CONNECTING HISTORY AND LAW

PLESSY v. FERGUSON

In 1892, Homer Plessy bought a train ticket from New Orleans to Covington, Louisiana. Because he was seven-eighths white and one-eighth black, he took a seat in the "whites only" car. When he refused to move, he was arrested under the "Jim Crow Car Act of 1890," which required separate-but-equal accommodations for whites and blacks on railroad cars.

Plessy staged the incident to test the constitutionality of the 1890 law. In 1896, the U.S. Supreme Court heard the case and, by a 7-1 vote, upheld the law. A southerner, Justice John Marshall Harlan, cast the single dissenting vote. Harlan argued: "Our Constitution is color-blind, and neither knows nor tolerates classes among citizens. In respect of civil rights, all citizens are equal before the law."

Plessy v. Ferguson gave states the right to control social discrimination and to promote segregation of the races. Throughout the South, numerous laws forced blacks to use separate facilities such as schools, parks, and public transportation. Those facilities were almost never equal to ones available to whites.

Not until *Brown v. Board of Education* (1954) did the Supreme Court reverse itself. In that landmark decision, the Court determined that separate educational facilities were "inherently unequal" and harmful to black students' self-esteem. The *Brown* case led to the end of legal segregation.

Do You Remember?

1. What concept was created by the Supreme Court ruling in *Plessy v. Ferguson*?
2. Which was the first southern state to pass a law segregating railways?
3. By 1900, approximately what percent of the nation's blacks lived in Georgia?

Opposite page: During the New South and Progressive eras, African Americans had few economic options and were often either teachers, ministers, laborers, sharecroppers, farm hands, or servants.

BOOKER T. WASHINGTON

One leader who stood out was Booker Taliaferro Washington. Booker Taliaferro, as he was first named, was born into a slave family in Virginia in 1856. After the Civil War, his family moved to Malden, West Virginia, and Booker was put to work in a salt furnace. Although it was quite difficult to work and get an education at the same time, young Booker was determined to do both. When the local black community finally got a schoolteacher, Booker first had to work during the day and be taught at night. Later, an arrangement was made under which he was allowed to work before and after day classes.

When asked for his name at school, he called himself "Washington" because, as he later explained, "it made me feel equal to the situation."

At sixteen, Booker Taliaferro Washington entered Hampton Institute, a vocational school for blacks in Virginia. He graduated in 1875 as a brick mason. Four years later, he became a night instructor at Hampton. From the very beginning, Washington spoke out on the issue of civil rights. In 1876, he addressed the National Education Association at their meeting in Wisconsin.

Opposite page: Booker T. Washington worked his entire adult life to build Tuskegee Institute in Alabama into an institution known throughout the world. Above: Students at Tuskegee studied and worked from the wake-up bell at 5:00 in the morning until retiring at 9:30 at night. Students learned practical skills like harness making (shown here), carpentry, cabinet making, printing, farming, shoemaking, and others.

Brains, property, and character for the Negro will settle the question of civil rights. The best course to pursue in regards to the civil rights bill in the South is to let it alone; let it alone and it will settle itself. Good schoolteachers and plenty of money to pay them will be more potent in settling the race question than many civil rights and investigating committees.

Tuskegee Institute

Booker T. Washington's belief in the power of education became well known. In 1881, two men from Tuskegee, Alabama, wrote to Samuel Armstrong, who had founded Hampton Institute. They were looking for an educator to establish an industrial and professional school for black students. Armstrong suggested Washington. Because Washington believed economic independence for blacks would lead to social and political equality, he agreed to take the job. The school began in a church and a run-down house. During

the next thirty-four years, Washington worked beside teachers and students as they built Tuskegee Institute's buildings.

Students received a "hands-on" approach to education as they shaped bricks, poured foundations for buildings, built walls, and made furniture. In addition to his work at Tuskegee, Washington traveled in the United States and Europe, speaking and asking for money to expand the new school.

Washington and the "Atlanta Compromise"

On September 18, 1895, in Atlanta, Washington made one of his most famous speeches. Visitors from all over the nation were there for the opening of the Cotton States Exposition. A racially integrated crowd heard the opening-day speeches in Exposition Hall.

After several remarks by industrialists and politicians, Booker T. Washington was introduced. What he said that day shaped race relations and strongly influenced black leadership for the next twenty years. Washington, a tall, muscular man with a strong, clear voice, began to speak:

During the 1895 Atlanta Cotton States Exposition, Booker T. Washington electrified the crowd with his "Cast down your bucket" speech. His influence was extended during the administrations of Presidents Theodore Roosevelt and William Howard Taft as both men consulted with the Tuskegee Institute founder.

A ship lost at sea for many days suddenly sighted a friendly vessel. From the mast of the unfortunate vessel was seen a signal, "Water, water; we die of thirst!" The answer from the friendly vessel at once came back, "Cast down your bucket where you are." A second time the signal "Water, water; send us water!" ran up from the distressed vessel, and was answered, "Cast down your bucket where you are!" A third and fourth signal for water was answered, "Cast down your bucket where you are."

The captain of the distressed vessel, at last heeding the injunction, cast down his bucket and it came up full of fresh, sparkling water from the mouth of the Amazon River. To those of my race who depend on bettering their condition in a foreign land or who underestimate the importance of cultivating friendly relations with the southern white man, who is their next door neighbor, I would say: "Cast down your bucket where you are. . . ."

To whites, Washington offered the same advice:

Cast down your bucket. . .among the eight millions of Negroes . . .who have, without strikes and labor wars, tilled your fields, cleared your forests, builded your railroads and cities. . .the most patient, faithful, law-abiding, and unresentful people that the world has seen.

Suddenly, Washington flung his hand up, the fingers held apart and said:

In all things that are purely social, we can be as separate as the fingers. . .

He balled up his fingers into a fist and continued:

. . .yet one as the hand in all things essential to mutual progress.

The crowd in Exposition Hall went wild. People cheered and waved handkerchiefs. Loud applause interrupted the speech. After the shouts finally died down, Washington addressed the problems of social equality:

The wisest among my race understand that the agitation of questions of social equality is the extremist folly, and that progress in the enjoyment of all the privileges that will come to us must be the result of severe and constant struggle rather than of artificial forcing. . . .

No race that has anything to contribute to the markets of the world is long in any degree ostracized. It is important and right that all privileges of the law be ours, but it is vastly more important that we be prepared for the exercise of those privileges. The opportunity to earn a dollar in a factory just now is worth infinitely more than the opportunity to spend a dollar in an opera house.

Booker T. Washington urged southern blacks to remain in the South and rebuild the region rather than migrating to northern cities to seek prosperity from factory jobs.

When Washington made his comments on social equality, he believed in them from a practical and realistic point of view that reflected the time. His speech became known as the **Atlanta Compromise speech**, because it proposed that blacks and whites should agree to benefit from each other.

Do You Remember?
1. Why did Booker Taliaferro call himself "Washington"?
2. What school did Booker T. Washington begin?
3. What did Washington propose in his Atlanta Compromise speech?

W. E. B. DUBOIS AND RACIAL UNREST

William Edward Burghardt DuBois (pronounced Du Boyce) did not agree with Booker T. Washington. DuBois was born in Great Barrington, Massachusetts, on February 12, 1868, the year Congress passed the Fourteenth Amendment. His ancestors were French, Dutch, and African.

Will, as he was called, was left penniless at sixteen when his mother died. He worked as a timekeeper in a textile mill and became the first black student to graduate from Barrington High School. DuBois received a scholarship to Fisk University in Nashville, Tennessee. After he graduated from Fisk, he earned a master's degree from Harvard University. DuBois then studied at the University of Berlin in Germany before returning to Harvard, where he became the first black to receive its doctor of philosophy degree. DuBois taught in colleges in Ohio and Pennsylvania before coming to Atlanta University in 1897.

In Atlanta, Dr. DuBois taught economics and political science.

The originator of the "Talented Tenth" philosophy, Dr. W. E. B. DuBois, had a far different view of black progress than did Booker T. Washington. After reading the opinions of both men, what is your view of their philosophies?

At first, he thought truth and knowledge would help blacks and whites understand and accept each other. DuBois wanted social and political integration, as well as higher education for 10 percent—what he called a "Talented Tenth"— of the black population. He believed this group could become leaders for all other blacks.

However, the late 1800s were a time of extreme racial unrest. Between 1884 and 1918, there were over 2,500 reported **lynchings** (illegal hangings, usually by mobs) of blacks in the United States. DuBois described each death by lynching as "a scar upon my soul." He decided that knowledge and truth alone were not enough. There must also be action if blacks and whites were to understand and accept each other.

After Booker T. Washington made his famous Atlanta Compromise speech at the Cotton Exposition, differences in their approaches to racial problems caused a split between Washington and DuBois. DuBois did not like what he called the "Tuskegee Machine." He thought Washington was making social, political, and economic decisions that affected all blacks. DuBois also disagreed with Washington's idea that blacks who became economically successful and waited long enough would see race relations improve. In his book, *The Souls of Black Folk*, DuBois wrote:

Manly self-respect is worth more than land and houses, and. . .a people who voluntarily surrender such respect, or cease striving for it, are not worth criticizing.

DuBois concluded:

So far as Mr. Washington preaches Thrift, Patience, and Industrial Training for the masses, we must hold up his hands and strive with him. . . . But, as far as Mr. Washington apologizes for injustices, North or South, does not rightly value the privilege and duty of voting, belittles the emasculating effects of caste distinctions, and opposes the higher training and ambition of our brighter minds,—as far as he, the South or the Nation, does this—we must unceasingly and firmly oppose them.

The Niagara Movement

In order to work for what he believed, DuBois, with the help of William Trotter, gathered together some black educators and professional men. They met secretly near Niagara Falls, New York, in 1905 and drew up a list of demands that included the abolition of discrimination based on race or color. The following year, the group held its first national convention at the site of John Brown's raid in Harpers Ferry, West Virginia. At this meeting, the **Niagara Movement**, as the group was called, published its purpose and goals:

Considering the uneasy racial times in the first decade of the 1900s, the formation of the Niagara Movement to protest racial injustices was a brave and daring step.

We will not be satisfied with less than our full manhood rights. We claim for ourselves every right that belongs to a free-born American—political, civil and social—and until we get these rights, we will never cease to protest and assail the ears of America with the story of its shameful deeds towards us. We want full manhood suffrage and we want it now, henceforth and forever.

Blacks in Georgia Also Protest

When blacks in Georgia learned about the Niagara Movement, a number of them came together to protest injustices. Augusta educator and political leader William White led several hundred teachers, farmers, ministers, and other professionals who met in Macon in February 1906. There were speeches against the convict lease system and the fact that blacks were not allowed to serve on juries. Some speakers also pointed out that white and black schools did not get the same amount of money. Others spoke against paying low wages to blacks for hard labor. William White told the audience that, to improve their condition, they must:

William Monroe Trotter was born in 1872 near Chillicothe, Ohio, and graduated from Harvard College. After several years in the real estate business, Trotter was frustrated by the Jim Crow system and began publishing a newspaper called the Guardian. *An overnight success, the* Guardian *publicly opposed the philosophy of Booker T. Washington and the "Tuskegee Machine" in support of the position of W. E. B. DuBois.*

. . . buy lands and homes. We must encourage Negro businessmen . . . we must agitate, complain, protest, and keep protesting against the invasion of our manhood rights. . . . And above all, organize these million brothers of ours into one great fist which shall never cease to pound at the gates of opportunity until they shall fly open.

Race Riot in Atlanta

The year 1906 was also a memorable year in Atlanta's history. While Georgia's politicians worked for political control, Atlanta experienced one of the worst race riots in the nation's history. Some thought the riot came about because men like Tom Watson were spreading racial fears. Others felt that Hoke Smith had used racial fears to gain votes during the gubernatorial campaign of that year. Still others blamed Atlanta newspapers, which printed story after story of black violence against whites.

On the afternoon of Saturday, September 22, local newspaper headlines carried false reports of black assaults. By 9 p.m., there was a crowd of over 5,000 whites and blacks on Decatur Street. Some accounts reported that thousands of whites brought guns and began to roam through the downtown area. Fears grew, and the attacks became real.

The riot lasted two days. **Martial law** (military rule) was declared before the city once again became calm. The cost in human life was high. At least eighteen blacks and three whites were killed, and hundreds of people were injured. The value of property destroyed was also high, but it could not be estimated accurately.

BLACKS ORGANIZE

In the early 1900s, there were periods of racial unrest in numbers of cities across the country besides the 1906 Atlanta riot. From August 14 to 19, 1908, black homes and businesses in Springfield, Illinois, were burned and some blacks were killed. Abraham Lincoln had lived in Springfield, and some historians think this is why riots there drew the attention of white liberals. The unrest helped move blacks to seek out new ways to achieve equality, including forming new organizations.

THE NAACP

Oswald Garrison Villard, grandson of the abolitionist William Lloyd Garrison, asked white liberals to join with the Niagara Movement and form a new organization. This group became known as the **National Association for the Advancement of Colored People** (NAACP), which was founded in 1909. Soon other groups would be organized to help blacks in their struggle for equality.

The goal of the National Association for the Advancement of Colored People was to work for the rights of black Americans. W. E. B. DuBois left Atlanta University to live in New York and edit *The Crisis*, a monthly NAACP publication. In his column, "As The Crow Flies," DuBois used humor and wit to support black protest. NAACP chapters were organized all over the country, and, during World War I, the organization became strong in Georgia.

THE BACK-TO-AFRICA MOVEMENT

Some Georgia blacks did not agree with either Booker T. Washington or W. E. B. DuBois. Instead they were influenced by Marcus Garvey and A.M.E. Bishop Henry Turner. These men favored the **Back-to-Africa movement**. Popular in the 1890s, the movement promised cheap transportation to Liberia for the purpose of establishing colonies. Small groups did go to Liberia, but tales of hardship, starvation, and death from fever discouraged future settlements. By 1900, the movement had ended.

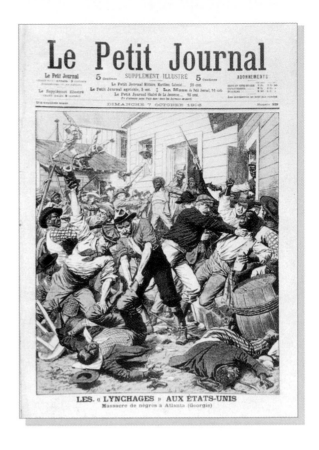

LES « LYNCHAGES » AUX ÉTATS-UNIS
Massacre de nègres à Atlanta (Georgie)

Atlanta gained international news coverage as a result of the 1906 race riot. During the ten-year period prior to the Atlanta riot, there had been instances of racial violence in Danville, Virginia; Carrollton, Mississippi; New Orleans, Louisiana; Wilmington, North Carolina; and Brownsville, Texas. In each instance there had been multiple injuries, deaths, or both. But news reports of these instances did little to prepare Atlantans, both black and white, for the two days and nights of rioting. It would take years to heal the emotional damage that resulted from the riot.

THE NATIONAL URBAN LEAGUE

A third organization, the **National Urban League**, was begun in 1910. It was an interracial group that worked to solve social problems facing blacks who lived in the cities. During this period, many blacks had moved from the rural South to cities in the North during what is called the **Great Migration**. They were looking for better jobs and less racial segregation. The National Urban League was able to help deal with the problems of living in the cities and to make the adjustment to city life easier for many.

MOST BLACK GEORGIANS DENIED VOTING RIGHTS

While Washington, DuBois, and others were working in their own ways for racial equality, blacks continued to have problems trying to exercise one of the most essential rights of any citizen—the right to vote. Throughout the South, law after law was passed with the sole aim to keep blacks from voting.

In 1908, Georgia followed other southern states and enacted a **grandfather clause**. The clause stated that only those men whose fathers or grandfathers had been eligible to vote in 1867 were eligible to vote. Because few blacks were able to vote in 1867, the grandfather clause kept most of Georgia's blacks from voting.

Even those blacks who could pass the standards of the grandfather clause faced problems at the voting booth. The state and local areas passed a series of additional qualifications for blacks. They had to own property, pay a **poll tax** (a tax to be able to vote), and pass literacy tests. Because the literacy tests were not standard, the questions could and did contain almost anything the voting clerk thought would stump the potential voter. One story—that may or may not be true—told of a black teacher with a degree from Harvard who tried to register to vote in a southern state after 1908. The voting clerk had the teacher read parts of the U.S. Constitution and pages from several books. He then had the teacher read in Latin, French, German, and Spanish—all of which he did successfully. Finally, the frustrated clerk held up a page of Chinese characters and asked, "What does this mean?" The teacher responded, "It means that you do not want me to vote."

A.M.E. Bishop Henry McNeal Turner favored the Back-to-Africa movement. Popular in the 1890s, the movement promised cheap transportation to Liberia for the purpose of establishing colonies. By 1900, the movement had ended.

Do You Remember?

1. Who wrote *The Souls of Black Folk?*
2. What group was formed when the Niagara Movement was joined with white liberals?
3. Which movement was led by Marcus Garvey?
4. What were two ways used in the South to keep blacks from voting?

THE GREAT MIGRATION

Between 1916 and 1930, one of the largest population movements inside our nation took place. Over 1 million African Americans moved from the South to the North and West. This movement came to be called the "Great Migration," and it continued well into the 1960s.

Overproduction in the 1920s created an agricultural depression, forcing tenants (many of them black) off farms. In the South, African Americans had few economic opportunities; most well-paying jobs went to whites. Better jobs and higher pay were available in the North. In fact, northern companies actively recruited African Americans for jobs.

There were other reasons for the migration. Few blacks could vote in the southern states, while the North offered the hope of full citizenship rights. Public schools for blacks were poor in the South but better in northern cities. Health care was better in the North. Segregation in the South kept blacks from hotels, restaurants, and recreation areas, but the North offered access to these facilities.

Because they usually did not have enough money to move everyone at once, black families first sent their young men to get jobs. Most were unskilled and found work in the meat-packing plants, shipyards, and steel mills. When the young men had saved enough money, they sent for the rest of their families.

Blacks generally improved their lives by moving north. But they were also crowded into segregated housing and faced prejudice.

Slowly, race relations began to improve in the South in the late 60s and early 70s. As a result, many African-American families returned to the South. Accustomed to large northern cities, many of the migrators moved to cities like Atlanta and Birmingham.

Many black families sent their young men to the North to get jobs to earn money for the rest of the family to migrate to the North. These young men found work in shipyards, meat-packing plants, and steel mills.

Many black Georgians worked hard during the Progressive Era to improve life for their race. Among them were educators, political leaders, business people, and religious leaders.

JOHN HOPE

John Hope was a Georgian who earned national respect for his work as an educator and civic leader. Hope was born in Augusta, Georgia, on June 2, 1868, to a white father and a black mother. During early childhood, he was treated as the son of a plantation owner. However, his father died when John was eight, and afterwards he had neither money nor social acceptance. Although he could have made things a bit easier by passing as a white person, he was proud of his black heritage.

Hope attended Augusta public schools and, in 1886, went to Worchester Academy in Massachusetts. He graduated from Brown University and taught at Roger Williams University in Nashville from 1894 to 1898. He then joined the faculty of Atlanta Baptist College, which became Morehouse in 1913. Hope became the school's first black president in 1906. In 1929, he was selected as president of the new Atlanta University.

Hope worked for social equality all his adult life. He heard Booker T. Washington's Atlanta Compromise speech in 1895 but did not share his views. Speaking to a debating society in 1896, Hope said:

If we are not striving for equality, in heaven's name, for what are we living? . . . Now catch your breath, for I am going to use an adjective. I am going to say we demand social equality!

Hope believed in a type of education different from Washington's vocational training.

The Negro must enter the higher fields of learning. He must be prepared for advanced and original investigation. . . . More honesty, more wealth will not give us rank among the other peoples of the civilized world; and, what is more, we ourselves will never be possessed of conscious self-respect until we can point to men in our own ranks who are easily the equal of any race.

While he was at Atlanta Baptist College, Hope became close friends with W. E. B. DuBois, who was then on the faculty at Atlanta University. Hope attended the Niagara Movement meeting with DuBois. He was the only college president at the 1909 protest meeting in New

As a teacher, college and university president, and political activist, John Hope made significant contributions in education and in raising the collective consciousness of both blacks and whites. Dr. Hope was buried in a grave below what had been his office on the Atlanta University campus.

York that resulted in the founding of the NAACP. During the Atlanta race riot, Hope was an active civic leader who worked to restore calm to the city.

John Hope was president of the National Association of Teachers of Colored Schools and a leader in the Association for the Study of Negro Life and History. He gained international recognition for his work with the YMCA. Under Hope's leadership, Morehouse, Spelman, Morris Brown, and Clark colleges, Gannon Theological Seminary, and Atlanta University formed the Atlanta University Center. These six schools, all located on adjoining campuses in Atlanta's West End, form the largest complex of predominantly black educational institutions in the world.

John Hope's wife, Lugenia, was also a well-known civic leader. She organized the Neighborhood Union, which offered vocational classes for children, a health center, and clubs for boys and girls. As a community action organization, the Neighborhood Union provided financial aid for needy families. It also put pressure on city leaders to improve roads, lighting, and sanitation in the black neighborhoods of Atlanta.

Improving life in the black community and increasing cultural understanding between blacks and whites was a family affair for John Hope and his wife Lugenia, and their sons, Edward and John, Jr. Lugenia, a former social worker, began volunteer work in 1898 which resulted in the founding of the Neighborhood Union in 1908.

Educator Lucy Craft Laney was an inspiration to all who knew and worked with her. One of her most notable students was John Hope.

LUCY C. LANEY

To many, Lucy C. Laney was as well known as John Hope. She was the ninth of ten children born to carpenter David Laney and his wife Louisa. Lucy could read by the time she was four. In 1873, she was a member of the first graduating class of Atlanta University. After graduation, Laney taught in Savannah for ten years and then moved to Augusta and opened a school in the basement of Christ Presbyterian Church. There were only five pupils the first year, but by the end of the second year, over two hundred students were enrolled.

In 1886, Francine Haines, a white Presbyterian churchwoman from the North, offered help and financial support. With her backing, Laney opened the Haines Normal and Industrial Institute in Augusta. For sixty years, the school was known for excellent instruction and teacher training. Mary McLeod Bethune, founder of Bethune-Cookman College in Florida, did her first teaching at Haines.

Laney also began Augusta's first black kindergarten and a nursing training program. When she died in 1933, the *Augusta Chronicle* wrote, "Lucy Laney was great because she loved people." Laney's portrait was hung in the Georgia Capitol in 1974.

SELENA SLOAN BUTLER

Another Georgian concerned about the welfare of children was Selena Sloan Butler, who was raised in Thomasville. After graduating from Spelman College at sixteen, Butler taught English in the Atlanta school system. While her husband, Henry Butler, attended medical school, she moved to Boston.

Upon returning to Atlanta, Selena Sloan Butler founded the first black PTA at Yonge Street School. Through her work, the **National Congress of Colored Parents and Teachers** (NCCPT) was organized in 1926. NCCPT was dedicated to protecting the rights of all children, regardless of their race. She also founded the Phyllis Wheatley YWCA in Atlanta, a longtime haven for young black women. Butler also organized the first night school for blacks in the city.

In 1929, President Herbert Hoover appointed Selena Sloan Butler to serve on the White House Conference on Child and Health Protection. Throughout her life, she dedicated herself to improving race relations and providing civil rights for all children.

WILLIAM FINCH

William Finch was known as the "Father of Black Public Schools" in Atlanta. In 1870, Finch, a successful tailor, was elected to Atlanta's city council. At that time, only two Atlanta public schools were open to black students. While on the city council and after returning to private life, Finch worked successfully for more schools for black youth.

RICHARD ROBERT WRIGHT, SR.

Richard Robert Wright, Sr., was born in 1855 in Dalton. He graduated from Atlanta University with Lucy Laney. Wright became principal of an elementary school in Cuthbert. While in Cuthbert, he organized farming cooperatives and conducted the state's first black agricultural county fair. Wright is credited with organizing the Georgia State Teachers' Association. In 1900, he started the state's first public high school for blacks in Augusta.

President McKinley appointed Wright, an active Republican, as army paymaster during the Spanish-American War. He was given the rank of major, the highest military rank held by a black man at that time. After the war, Wright became president of the State College of Industry for Colored, now known as Savannah State College.

After thirty years with the college, Wright joined his son and daughter in Philadelphia. There he founded the Citizens and Southern Bank and Trust Company, the first black-owned trust company in the United States. He was asked to be the United States ambassador to Liberia but did not accept because of his family and business.

A multi-talented man, Richard Wright, Sr., was an educator, politician, editor, and banker. Here, he is wearing the uniform of the army paymaster during the Spanish-American War.

IDA WELLS

In the late 1800s and early 1900s, many black writers used their skills to help bring about a spirit of equality. Some, like Paul Dunbar and James Weldon Johnson, used their creative talents to arouse emotions from their readers. Others simply reported news events as they occurred, letting the happenings speak for themselves. One such writer was the reporter and teacher Ida Wells.

As the nation moved into the twentieth century, job and social discrimination was widespread and riots were increasing. The most frightening occurrences, however, were the lynchings, many of which

were conducted in secret. Wells broke the cover of secrecy and, unlike many reporters, described these events in her newspaper articles.

Ida Wells did not start out to be a reporter. Instead, she began her professional life as a classroom teacher and activist in Memphis. In 1884, Wells was refused seating on a train because of her race. She sued the railroad and lost, and then she began writing part-time for a local newspaper reporting on various injustices. One series of articles dealt with the poor quality of the teaching materials and resources in the school system in which she taught. As a result of these articles, she lost her teaching position. Still determined to report what she saw, she became a full-time newswriter and, later, a part owner of the newspaper.

After losing a friend to a lynch mob, Ida Wells turned her investigative skills and reporting talents to exposing the ugliness and lawless horrors of lynching. She also reported on race riots, both local and national. Throughout her career, she crusaded for fairness and full rights for black people.

Alonzo Franklin Herndon was one of the most astute businessmen of his time. Through hard work, Herndon built a business empire worth millions of dollars. Visitors can walk through his palatial 1910 mansion in Atlanta. Read this section to find his secret to success. What does his statement mean?

ALONZO FRANKLIN HERNDON

Perhaps the best-known black business leader of the Progressive Era was Alonzo Franklin Herndon. Herndon was born a slave in 1858 on a Walton County plantation and grew up in Social Circle. After the Civil War, he worked for his former master for a short time at a salary of $25 a year.

Herndon learned to be a barber and moved to Jonesboro to open his own barber shop. He thought business would be better in Atlanta, so he moved there to work in a barber shop. Within six months, he owned a half interest in the business. By the early 1900s, he had opened three new shops for white customers. Herndon began buying property, and soon he owned a block of office buildings on Auburn Avenue and a hundred rental houses.

In 1905, Herndon purchased a small insurance company for $140. He knew little about insurance, so he hired black college graduates to run the Atlanta Mutual Insurance Company.

Along with W.E.B. DuBois and John Hope, Herndon was present at the first meeting of the Niagara Movement in New York. He gave freely of his wealth to civil rights causes. Herndon was still president of his insurance company when he died in 1927. That company is now the Atlanta Life Insurance Company. It is one of the largest black-owned businesses in the United States, and has a net worth of over $100 million. Perhaps the secret of Herndon's success was best explained when he said, "Some of us sit and wait for opportunity when it is always with us."

HENRY O. FLIPPER

Henry O. Flipper was born in Thomasville in 1856. His slave father was a skilled workman who bought his family's freedom. After the Civil War, Flipper attended Freedman's Bureau American Missionary Association schools. He next went to Atlanta University and, in 1873, was appointed to West Point Military Academy.

Second Lieutenant Flipper was the first black to graduate from West Point. He was assigned to the all-black Tenth Cavalry. During the next four years, he served on five army posts in Texas. At Fort Davis, Flipper's commanding officer accused him of "embezzling funds and conduct unbecoming an officer and gentleman." The officer said Flipper failed to turn in $4,000 of commissary funds. At a general court martial, Flipper was found innocent of taking the money but guilty of "bad conduct." On June 30, 1882, he was discharged from the Army.

Flipper remained in the West and became a successful engineer and special agent for the United States Department of Justice. When the Spanish-American War broke out, he offered his services to the army. Bills were introduced in both houses of Congress to have Flipper's army rank restored. Both bills were defeated.

Senator Albert Fall brought Flipper to Washington as a congressional subcommittee translator and interpreter. Flipper later went to Venezuela and worked for an oil company. In 1930, he returned to Atlanta and lived with his brother Joseph, an A.M.E. Church bishop. Until his death in 1940, Flipper maintained that he was innocent of the army's charges. He believed he had been accused because while at Fort Davis, he had gone horseback riding with one of the few white women in the territory. In 1973, Flipper was cleared of all charges.

The following year, a bust of Flipper was unveiled at West Point. At the ceremony, the superintendent of the Academy said Flipper had "become one of the most honored citizens of the nation, a credit to all of its people and its rich diversity."

"I hardly know how I endured it all so long." These were the sentiments of Henry O. Flipper describing his years as the first black graduate of West Point Military Academy. But endure he did and went on to attain success despite an unfair army discharge that was not rectified until 91 years later when his name and record were cleared.

Top: Henry Hugh Proctor distinguished himself as a minister, community activist, and race relations mediator.
Above: Carrie Steele could not bear to see children suffer from hunger and neglect. Her life's work was to provide a safe, caring environment for children in need.

HENRY HUGH PROCTOR

Henry Hugh Proctor, who was born in Tennessee in 1868, became pastor of the First Congregational Church in Atlanta in 1894. From the time he moved to Georgia, Proctor established missions among the city's poor and in Atlanta's jails. Proctor received national attention following the Atlanta riots in 1906, when he and a white attorney, Charles Hopkins, formed a committee of forty blacks and whites to work against racial tension in the city.

Under Dr. Proctor's leadership, his church built a gymnasium, opened a library and an employment bureau, and began a counseling program. The church also provided a home for working girls and a kindergarten. Many visitors came to Atlanta to see these community-action services including two U.S. presidents, Theodore Roosevelt and William Howard Taft.

During World War I, Dr. Proctor was appointed to a special position to encourage black troops. In 1919, he traveled in Europe, speaking to and helping over 100,000 black soldiers.

THE HEALY FAMILY

James Augustine Healy was born in 1830 near Macon. He left Georgia while a young man to attend Holy Cross College in Worcester, Massachusetts, where he was valedictorian of his class. Healy became a Catholic priest and, in 1875, became the first black Catholic bishop in the United States. Bishop Healy worked in Portland, Maine, until his death in 1900.

Father Healy's sister, Eliza, was Mother Superior in a Vermont convent school. His younger brother, Patrick, also a Catholic priest, became the first black president of Georgetown University in Washington, D.C. Another brother, Michael, was an officer in the United States Revenue Cutter Service, the forerunner of the modern United States Coast Guard.

ADAM DANIEL WILLIAMS

Adam Daniel Williams was born January 2, 1863, and grew up in Greene County. He entered the ministry and became pastor of Ebenezer Baptist Church in Atlanta in 1894. At that time, the church had thirteen members. Under Williams' leadership, church membership increased and became a focal point for community and civil rights causes. Williams organized boycotts and rallies to demand equal treatment for blacks. He supported W. E. B. DuBois and was a charter member of the Atlanta chapter of the NAACP.

When Williams died in 1937, his son-in-law, Martin Luther King, Sr., continued his work. Martin Luther King, Sr., in turn was followed by his son, civil rights leader Dr. Martin Luther King, Jr.

CARRIE STEELE

Carrie Steele worked as a maid at Atlanta's Union Railroad Station. At the station, she found children left by parents who could not care for them. Steele took the children to her home and fed, clothed, and cared for them. Soon, there were more children than her house could hold. She sold her house and, using money donated by people in the community, opened the Carrie Steele Orphanage in 1888. Carrie Steele died in 1900, but the orphanage—today called the Carrie Steele Pitts Home—has cared for over 20,000 children.

AMANDA DICKSON

Amanda Dickson was born in Hancock County in 1849, the daughter of David Dickson, a white planter, and a slave named Julia. When Dickson died, he left control of his **estate** (possessions) to Amanda. Dickson's white relatives filed suit, charging that a white man could not leave property to nonwhite children. Amanda Dickson fought the suit all the way to the Georgia Supreme Court. In 1887, the court ruled that a person with black and white ancestry could inherit from a white parent. The ruling awarded the estate, worth $300,000, to Amanda Dickson, who moved to Augusta and lived in comfort until her death in 1893.

SPOTLIGHT

THOMAS A. DORSEY

Historically, religion has played a vital role in the black community, and music has always been an important component of church services. During the 1930s, a new style of church music—gospel music—became popular in black churches throughout the country. In large part, the popularity of gospel music was due to the talents of Georgian Thomas A. Dorsey, generally regarded as the "Father of Gospel."

Dorsey was born in Villa Rica, but spent most of his youth in Atlanta. He was an excellent pianist and sang blues in private clubs all over Atlanta. In 1920, Dorsey revolutionized blues music when he copyrighted his song, "If You Don't Believe I'm Leaving, You Can Count the Days I'm Gone." Before his copyright of the song, most black artists felt that their music belonged to all in the black community. However, copyrighting a song assured that royalties would be paid to the composer.

In 1932, Dorsey, who was the son of a minister, turned his attention to gospel music working with gospel singers such as Mahalia Jackson and Sallie Martin. He was a prolific composer and wrote some five hundred gospel songs including "There Will Be Peace in the Valley," "Precious Lord, Take My Hand," "Move On Up a Little Higher," and "Surely, God is Able."

After World War II, black gospel music was to become popular with new generations of listeners. Other composers and performers, including Elvis Presley, were to be greatly influenced by gospel music and by the art of Thomas A. Dorsey.

Do You Remember?
1. Who was the only college president at the meeting in 1909 that resulted in the founding of the NAACP?
2. Who opened the Haines Normal and Industrial Institute?
3. What major civil rights leader was the grandson of Adam Daniel Williams?

Probably the most sensational trial in Georgia's history, the Leo Frank case in 1915, brought reporters from across the nation. Governor Slaton commuted Frank's sentence based on what he called "conflicting testimony." The governor received over 100,000 national appeals to grant clemency to Frank. Frank's hanging and the resulting demonstration showed the degree of racial and religious intolerance during the Progressive era.

A SETBACK FOR CIVIL RIGHTS

While there were gains made in civil rights for blacks during the Progressive Era, there was also a major setback. The setback centered on a court case that attracted national attention and that resulted in the rebirth of the Ku Klux Klan.

THE TRIAL OF LEO M. FRANK

On August 16, 1915, Georgia became the center of national attention when 29-year-old Leo M. Frank was lynched in Marietta.

Frank was superintendent of the National Pencil Company factory in Atlanta. On April 26, 1913, he was charged with the murder of Mary Phagan, a 14-year-old employee. The trial that followed was one of the most debated in Georgia's history. Although there was little evidence, Frank was convicted and sentenced to death, largely because of the testimony of Jim Conley, the factory's black janitor. Because Conley was also a suspect, his testimony normally would not have been heard. However, these were not normal times. Frank was Jewish, and during that time, many people disliked Jews.

Frank's lawyers appealed the case to the Supreme Court. Georgia Governor John Slaton was under pressure to pardon Frank. The day before his term of office ended in June 1915, Slaton changed Frank's sentence from death to life imprisonment. Tom Watson used his magazine, *The Weekly Jeffersonian*, to lead a public outcry against Slaton's action. In July, amid **anti-Semitic** (anti-Jewish) feelings and continuing racial discord, the Ku Klux Klan received a charter from the Fulton County Superior Court.

Anger directed toward Slaton because of his change of Frank's sentence caused him to leave the state. Two months after the sentence change, twenty-five armed men walked into the state penitentiary in Milledgeville and took Frank from his prison cell. They drove to Marietta, the home of Mary Phagan, and hanged Frank from a tree. The next day, about 15,000 people filed by Frank's open casket in an Atlanta mortuary. Pictures of Frank's hanging body were sold, and a song, "The Ballad of Mary Phagan," became popular.

Seventy-one years after Leo Frank was hanged, Governor Joe Frank Harris issued him a pardon. Frank's family asked for the pardon because the convicted murderer's appeals process had been stopped by the lynching.

THE KLAN IS REBORN

On Thanksgiving night, 1915, Atlanta preacher and salesman William Simmons and thirty-four others climbed to the top of Stone Mountain near Atlanta. There, the group lit torches as they circled a

burning cross. The Ku Klux Klan was reborn in Georgia and elsewhere in the country.

By 1924, the modern Ku Klux Klan was strong in all southern states as well as in California, Oregon, Indiana, and Ohio. At its peak, the Klan claimed over 4 million members. Today, Stone Mountain, the home of frequent Klan gatherings, has a black mayor. Ironically, the mayor also owns the home that formerly belonged to James Venerable, a major Klan leader.

The reorganization of the Ku Klux Klan, depicted here at Stone Mountain in 1921, revived feelings of fear and intolerance that had been buried since Reconstruction days. Between 1920 and 1923, Ku Klux Klan membership nationwide grew from 5,000 to several million members.

Do You Remember?
1. Who was Leo Frank accused of murdering?
2. Whose magazine led the public outcry against Governor Slaton?
3. How many members did the Ku Klux Klan claim at its peak?

SUMMARY

- After the U.S. Supreme Court struck down the Civil Rights Act of 1875 as unconstitutional and created the separate-but-equal concept in the 1896 *Plessy v. Ferguson* case, segregation became legal as states passed Jim Crow laws.
- In his Atlanta Compromise speech, Booker T. Washington urged blacks and whites to benefit from the strengths of each other.
- Other blacks, including W. E. B. DuBois, encouraged blacks to achieve social equality through economic power.
- Blacks organized into several national groups, including the NAACP and the National Urban League.
- Many blacks, such as John Hope and Alonzo Herndon in Georgia and others elsewhere, worked to bring about positive changes.

C H A P T E R R E V I E W

1883	1895		1905	1910
Supreme Court struck down Civil Rights Act of 1875	Booker T. Washington delivered Atlanta Compromise speech		Niagara Movement organized	National Urban League founded
			1903 W. E. B. DuBois published *Souls of Black Folk*	**1909** NAACP formed
	1889 Georgia General Assembly passed segregation laws	**1896** Supreme Court ruled on *Plessy v. Ferguson*		

1880	**1890**	**1900**	**1910**

1882 Ida Wells published exposé on lynching	**1896** First modern Olympic Games held in Athens, Greece	**1908** Jack Johnson became first black to hold the heavyweight boxing title

Reviewing People, Places, and Terms

Define, identify, or explain the importance of each of the following terms.

1. the Atlanta Compromise speech
2. Great Migration
3. Jim Crow laws
4. NAACP
5. *Plessy v. Ferguson*
6. poll tax
7. segregation

Understanding the Facts

1. What are the rights of citizens called?
2. What did the Civil Rights Act of 1875 provide?
3. How did W. E. B. DuBois describe each death by lynching?
4. At what historic site did the Niagara Movement hold its first national convention?
5. What interracial group was organized in 1910 to help rural people adjust to the problems of city life?
6. Which well-known civic leader organized Atlanta's Neighborhood Union?
7. Who was known as "Father of Black Public Schools" in Atlanta?
8. Who was the first black to graduate from West Point?
9. Who issued a pardon to Leo Frank?
10. At which of the state's natural attractions was the Ku Klux Klan reborn in Georgia?

Developing Critical Thinking

1. Why do you think most black Georgians were either denied the right to vote or frustrated in their attempts to vote?
2. How was the grandfather clause openly discriminatory? How did it contribute to the white supremacy movement?
3. Compare and contrast the philosophies of Booker T. Washington and W. E. B. DuBois.
4. What effect, if any, do you think the practice of white supremacy had on Georgia's economic growth?

Applying Your Skills

1. Research the Great Migration. Using a map of the United States, indicate those northern and western states in which a majority of blacks settled following World War I. In what way did this migration change the demo-

graphics of the nation?

2. Frank J. Ferrell, Lewis Howard Latimer, and Norbert Rillieux were among the black inventors of this period. Research their lives, and prepare a short report summarizing their inventions and the dates of these inventions.

Making Connections

1. Why was the separate-but-equal concept an impossibility from the start?
2. Research a Supreme Court decision other than *Plessy v. Ferguson* that has greatly affected Americans either politically, economically, or socially. Prepare a short report to share with your classmates.

3. Give three reasons that led to the Great Migration.
4. What effects do you feel the Great Migration had on Georgia?

Did You Know?

- The first recorded transportation boycott by blacks occurred in Louisville, Kentucky, in 1871, when blacks refused to use the city's trolley cars until they were allowed to ride with whites.
- Spelman College, the nation's oldest school for black women, was started by Sophia Packard and Harriet Giles in 1881 with just $100.

BUILDING SKILLS: RESEARCHING TOPICS

An historian must do research as part of his or her work. Historians are much like detectives looking for clues and possible solutions to questions or mysteries. The work is much easier when the historian feels that the place to find much needed information is a library. A library is often a researcher's best friend.

Library work gives the historian a good foundation for further research outside the library. Knowing where and how to find needed information makes research much easier and, like everything else, requires practice to become proficient.

During the year, you will be given assignments that make it necessary to use information in a library to find answers to questions. You may, at other times, simply want to know more about a certain topic you have been studying about in class. When you visit a library for research, there are specific places to look for information. Your key aids in the library are the card catalogue and the *Reader's Guide to Periodic Literature*.

Visit your school library or media center and find information on the following subjects: civil rights in Georgia, Ku Klux Klan activities in Georgia, black inventors of the early 1900s, and Jim Crow laws. All of these topics have to do with the early civil rights era. For each of these topics, find one reference in each of the following sources: encyclopedia, periodical, biographic or historical dictionary, and general history book. Once you find a book, use its index to locate the pages on which your topic is discussed.

Once you locate your sources, list the name of the book or periodical, making sure to include all the information you need for a bibliography. You do not need to write a report. The information should include the title of each book or article, the date of publication, the publisher, and the author. It is very important to keep a list of the sources you find during your research, because you must be able to find the information again if necessary. Your sources are your evidence to back up the accuracy of your work.

After completing this task, think about these questions. Are there sources in your library that emphasize Georgia history or give information on the state? Do general references books on United States history contain all the information you may need on the four topics? Does your library have a "Georgia Collection"? In which of the four topics listed above was it most difficult to locate the information you needed? Why do you think this was so?

CHAPTER FOURTEEN

GEORGIA IN THE DEPRESSION AND WAR

*I hope for a world founded upon four essential freedoms—
freedom of speech, freedom of religion, freedom from want,
and freedom from fear.*

—Franklin Delano Roosevelt

AFTER WORLD WAR I, most Americans enjoyed a time of prosperity that had begun with the production of war goods. By the late 1920s, no one expected the prosperity to end. With the exception of rural areas, most homes had electricity and modern appliances. Wages were the highest in the nation's history. People spent freely for goods and services.

However, all this would shortly come to a halt. In the period from the end of the 1920s to 1945, Georgia and the rest of the world would experience great suffering and change. The stock market crash of 1929 brought the worst economic depression the nation had ever known. Agriculture and industry declined while unemployment was widespread. Moreover, Georgia's cotton industry was threatened by a crop-destroying beetle.

All levels of government tried to ease the suffering and bring about an economic recovery. The nation had little success against the depression until Congress passed Franklin D. Roosevelt's New Deal proposals. Although the New Deal gave people hope, it did not end the depression. What ended it was America's entry into World War II.

*Georgia governors from 1911 to 1941 represented a period of change
in the state's history. Posing together in 1939 are some of Georgia's
most powerful politicians. They had a direct impact on the state for
32 years (left to right, Ed Rivers, Eugene Talmadge, Richard B. Russell,
Jr., Clifford Walker, Thomas Hardwick, Hugh Dorsey, John Slaton).*

Beginning operations in 1922, WSB radio provided millions of hours of entertainment and information long before the advent of television.

For many, the 1920s was a time when they were able to break free of the restraints of earlier eras. During World War I, Americans who had never before been far from birthplaces and local customs were exposed to a variety of other cultures. Returning from overseas, some of these men and women were now willing to try new ways of doing things and of expressing themselves. Perhaps as a result of the swiftness of its victory in the war, the country was filled with a "can-do" attitude. American know-how could do anything, and the sky was the limit as far as the country's continued economic success was concerned.

After the restrictions of wartime, people went on a spending spree. No longer was it unusual for families in Georgia to have radios. In 1922, WSB in Atlanta began operation as "the voice of the South." By 1924, there were 580 radio stations complete with live bands. Automobiles were relatively inexpensive. Gasoline stations and garages sprang up to provide services for these automobiles. Motor hotels, called **motels**, were built for the convenience of the traveling public. More money was spent on education in the United States than in the rest of the nations of the world put together. With advanced medical knowledge, the fear of childhood diseases such as typhoid, measles, and diphtheria was ending. Catalog orders from businesses like Sears, Roebuck and Montgomery Ward were at an all-time high.

The twenties were also an age of abandon. Flappers—young women who boldly displayed their independent spirit both in conduct and dress—danced the "Charleston," and jazz music became popular. Prohibition became law on January 17, 1920, so drinkers went to "speakeasy" night clubs, where alcohol was served in teacups. Groups headed by such people as "Scarface" Al Capone, Jack "Legs" Diamond, and Frank "the Enforcer" Nitti became organized crime "families." They grew wealthy selling illegal liquor to thousands of private "clubs."

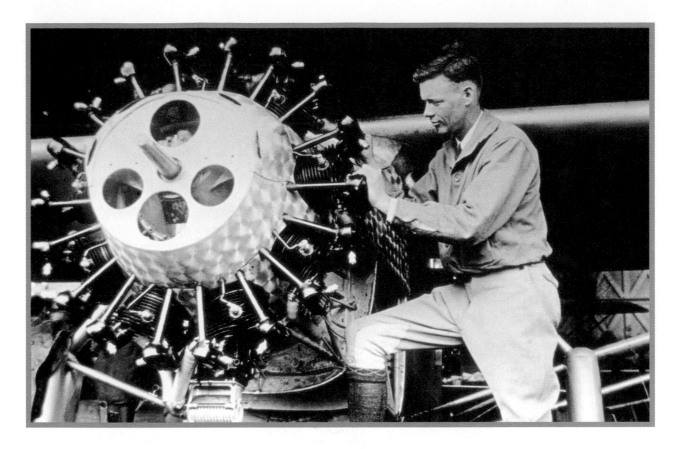

Charles Lindbergh, the "Lone Eagle," checks the engine of the Spirit of St. Louis, *prior to his record-breaking flight to France.*

THE "LONE EAGLE"

The twenties were an era of new heroes, as people like Gertrude Ederle swam the English Channel and Babe Ruth broke baseball records. But no hero was as celebrated as Charles A. Lindbergh. In 1927, Lindbergh took off from Roosevelt Field, New York, in his airplane, "The Spirit of St. Louis," on a flight across the Atlantic Ocean to Paris, France.

Lindbergh accomplished the first recorded nonstop transatlantic flight. He flew alone, without the help of navigational or weather instruments, using only landmarks to guide him. Upon his arrival in France, he became an overnight hero. Songs were written about him, including one called "Lucky Lindy." Wherever he went, crowds of people gathered to see him. In October 1927, six months after his historic flight, Lindbergh flew into Atlanta where he was welcomed by over 20,000 admirers. Soon afterward, a street in the city was named Lindbergh Drive in honor of the "Lone Eagle," Charles Lindbergh.

THE DESTRUCTION OF KING COTTON

For many Georgians, however, the twenties were not a time of abundance. A small, grayish, long-snouted beetle, the **boll weevil**, was destroying the primary source of income for many Georgia farmers:

STRATFORD CALCIUM ARSENATE
Death To The Boll Weevil

Top: By the time the boll weevil and the 1925 drought hit Georgia, there was little farmers could do to stop the devastation. Low cotton prices at the time were the final blow to Georgia's rural economy, so the farm depression arrived in Georgia long before the general depression hit the nation in the 1930s.
Above: Regardless of the advertisement's promise, there was little Georgia farmers could do to stop the ravages of the small but deadly boll weevil.

cotton. The boll weevil came from Mexico, moved through Texas, and then into the southern states in the 1890s. The beetles hatch in the yellow flower of the cotton plant. As the flower becomes a **boll** (the place where the fibers are formed), the larvae feeds on the growing white, fluffy cotton, making it useless.

The boll weevil appeared in southwest Georgia in 1918. It quickly spread across the state, destroying thousands of acres of Georgia's major agricultural crop. By 1923, cotton production had dropped from over two million bales in 1918 to slightly more than a half million bales. The postwar price was only fifteen to seventeen cents a pound.

In 1925, Georgia farmers were hit with another natural disaster a—major **drought,** an extended period of extreme dryness from the lack of rain. The sun-baked fields slowed down the destructive work of the boll weevil, but ruined most of Georgia's other crops while doing so. Over 375,000 farm workers left Georgia between 1920 and 1925. The number of working farms fell from 310,132 to 249,095. Black farmers, in particular, moved to northern industrial cities such as Chicago and Detroit, hoping to find work in factories and assembly plants.

When farms failed, banks that had loaned the farmers money took huge losses. Many farm-related businesses closed. Georgia was in a deep economic depression.

Do You Remember?
1. Which Atlanta radio station was known as "the voice of the South"?
2. What did Charles Lindbergh accomplish in 1927 that made him an overnight hero?
3. In which part of the cotton plant are the fibers formed?

THE GREAT DEPRESSION

In his March 1929 inaugural address, President Herbert Hoover confidently declared that the end of poverty was near. At the same time, the stock market was unstable, some banks had closed, and factories had to lay off workers. However, few people stopped spending long enough to notice.

Many banks were in trouble. Farmers were not able to pay off loans, and more and more Americans were borrowing money to buy houses, cars, and household goods. Factories produced too much, then had to cut back on the number of workers until the goods sold. This left workers without money to repay the bank loans that had been so easy to get.

Many Americans were now investing in the **stock market**, the place where shares of stock in corporations are bought and sold. To make things worse, many had invested with borrowed money, hoping the value of the stock would rise and they could sell the stock to earn more money. Some people became millionaires by buying stocks at low prices and selling them when the prices went up. The stock market was like a roller coaster. Prices shot up one day, then fell several weeks later. If a buyer waited too long to sell, the original investment was lost. If that investment was borrowed, the buyer could not repay the bank. As a result, banks failed, businesses closed, and many people were out of work.

A stunned crowd mills around on Wall Street in New York City on the day of the great stock market crash, October 29, 1929, "Black Tuesday."

THE STOCK MARKET CRASHES

On October 24, 1929, the bubble of prosperity burst when the value of stocks suddenly dropped. Investors tried to sell their stocks at any price. On that day alone, 13,000,000 shares of stock changed hands. Thousands of stockholders across the country lost a great deal of money.

The market continued to fall and, on October 29—now known as "Black Tuesday"—the stock market "crashed." Over 16,400,030 shares of stock were unloaded. With each day that passed, the nation went deeper into an economic downturn, which today we call the **Great Depression**. The values of stocks on the market fell by $40 billion before the end of 1929. A share of United States Steel that had sold for $262 dropped to $22. Montgomery Ward stock sank from $138 to $4 a share, and a share of General Motors plunged from $78 to $8.

BANKS CLOSE THEIR DOORS

In 1928 and 1929, hundreds of banks closed their doors because of unpaid loans. People who had money in the closed banks could not get it out. All over the country, lines formed at bank doors as people tried to take out their savings. Banks that could not meet the demands of their customers for cash failed. Over 650 banks closed during the first year of the depression. Thirteen hundred failed in 1930, and another thousand in 1931.

GEORGIANS HIT BY DEPRESSION

Georgia was already in an economic depression when the stock market crashed. Georgians did not immediately feel the impact of "Black Tuesday," as did those in other states. However, between 1929 and 1932, an average farmer's income dropped from $206 a year to $83, and cotton fell to $.05 a pound. By 1930, over 60 percent of Georgia's farms were worked by tenants.

During the depression, most Georgians were challenged simply by trying to meet their everyday needs. Many workers in the state lost their jobs, resulting in great suffering and despair. Children of the unemployed often did not go to school because they had no shoes or proper clothes. Families went hungry, with many living for weeks on a single food like cornmeal or rice.

Images of the Great Depression in Georgia: (top) a one-teacher black school in Veazy ; (above) a Greene County cotton farmer, forced to mortgage the farm he had inherited; (opposite) Collie Smith reading, Carroll County.

State services suffered. Many rural children did not get an education. Georgia's health care and highway construction were not funded. The economic advances of the previous several decades were stopped dead in their tracks.

EASING THE BURDEN

With earlier depressions, the American economy had always begun to recover after a year or two. This depression, however, went on year after year. As the years passed, the mood of the country became more and more discouraged.

President Herbert Hoover was the first president to use the power of the federal government to help the economy recover. In one program designed to help farmers, the government bought large amounts of cotton, wheat, and other commodities. This, it was believed, would cause farm prices to rise. The government would sell its commodities on the market later, after the prices had risen. The government bought too little of the commodities, however, and the plan did not work.

President Hoover approved a program that loaned federal money to needy businesses. He also supported public works projects, such as the building of post offices, parks, courthouses, and roads. These projects put many unemployed men back to work. With Hoover's urging, the government loaned money to the states for their own public works projects. He also used the government's stored wheat and cotton to provide flour and cloth for the needy. Hoover's programs helped, but they did not end the depression or provide adequate relief for the poor. Unfortunately, the man who had spearheaded mammoth worldwide relief efforts after World War I was unable to ease the problems of his own countrymen. Soon, the clusters of packing-crate shanties inhabited by the unemployed became known as "Hoovervilles."

Besides the federal and state governments, many local agencies also helped. The most effective were the Red Cross and the Salvation Army. Hospitals provided free lunches for the needy. Local governments paid men low wages to sweep streets, plant trees, drain swamps, cut firewood, and plant gardens. They also provided free lunches for needy children. Still, public and private efforts to provide **relief** (money and goods given to people in special need) were not enough. What was needed was a program that coordinated efforts at all levels.

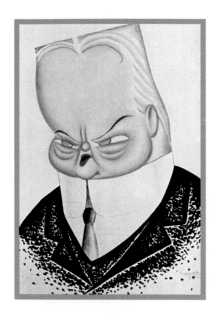

Unable to cope with the problems of the Great Depression, Herbert Hoover became the subject of cruel caricatures at the end of his term in 1932.

Do You Remember?
1. What happened on "Black Tuesday"?
2. What happened to banks that caused them to be unable to meet the demand of their customers for cash?
3. What were "Hoovervilles"?

UNEMPLOYMENT IN THE GREAT DEPRESSION

The worst aspect of an economic depression is the suffering it causes the unemployed. Today, an unemployment rate of 5-6 percent is considered acceptable. In 1933, the worst year of the depression, the unemployment rate was 25 percent. African Americans experienced the greatest loss of jobs. By 1933, half of black workers were unemployed. Many single women were fired so that their jobs could go to men or women with children to support.

People who lost their jobs for a long time suffered greatly. They lost their sense of personal worth, blamed themselves for their misfortune, and avoided friends. Many of those who accepted a handout felt ashamed and became indifferent. Families with children suffered more; many families went hungry and lacked adequate medical care. Children without clothes and shoes often did not want to attend school.

Before 1932, people believed that families, churches, and private agencies like the Red Cross should help the jobless. If more help were needed, the unemployed should turn to local governments. People did not believe that the state or federal government should be involved. But so many people were unemployed and hungry that this idea changed—and brought a fundamental change in government. State and federal relief agencies were established to spend money on public projects, mainly to give work to the unemployed. Other safety nets to help the unfortunate in society include programs like Social Security, the Job Corps, Medicaid, and food stamps.

The unemployed resorted to a variety of methods to get work during the Great Depression, like this man in Detroit.

THE NEW DEAL

In the fall of 1932, the depression was at its worst. One of the musical hits of the year was "Brother, Can You Spare A Dime?" It was also an election year. Herbert Hoover was running for a second term on the Republican ticket. His opponent was New York Governor Franklin Delano Roosevelt. At the Democratic Convention in Chicago, Roosevelt easily won his party's nomination on the first ballot.

Just before Roosevelt made his acceptance speech, his chief writer added this final sentence: "I pledge you, I pledge myself, to a new deal for the American People." Campaigning was difficult at times, because he was struck with polio in 1921 and wore steel leg braces. Sometimes, when he was out of sight of the public, he used a wheelchair. However, his spirits were high as he campaigned for the presidency, and he became very popular with the American people. Roosevelt won with an electoral majority of 472 votes to Hoover's 59. In his inaugural address, Roosevelt said:

We are stricken by no plague of locusts. Compared with the perils which our forefathers conquered because they believed and were not afraid, we have still much to be thankful for. Nature still offers her bounty and human efforts have multiplied it. Plenty is at our doorstep. . . . The only thing we have to fear is fear itself.

His speech and his natural optimism won the people's confidence. They believed Roosevelt would try new ways to end the depression, which was, by then, felt all over the world. Roosevelt spent many

Garnering support in Atlanta during his 1932 campaign, Franklin Delano Roosevelt always felt comfortable in his second home—Georgia.

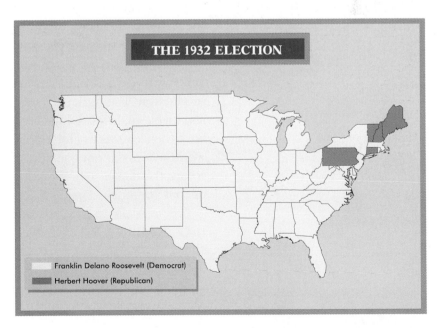

THE 1932 ELECTION

Franklin Delano Roosevelt (Democrat)
Herbert Hoover (Republican)

summers at what became known as the "Little White House" in Warm Springs, Georgia, where he could bathe his crippled legs in the healing water of the springs. Because of his frequent visits, Georgians in the area came to know FDR, as he was called, on a personal basis.

When Roosevelt took office on March 4, 1933, he took steps to fulfill his promise of "a new deal for the American people." Roosevelt had no clear idea of how to deal with the depression. He gathered together a group of advisers from all over the country who became known as the **brain trust**. With their help and at his urging, however, Congress passed a series of laws that came to be known as the **New Deal**. These laws were to bring about economic recovery, relieve the suffering of the unemployed, reform defects in the economy, and improve society.

This 1934 cartoon pokes fun at President Roosevelt and the proliferation of "alphabet" agencies under the New Deal.

ECONOMIC RECOVERY

The first objective of the New Deal was economic recovery—bringing the nation's economy back to the same level it had been in 1929. The first need was to make sure the banking system was sound. On the day after his inauguration, President Roosevelt ordered all banks closed until government inspectors could examine them. In a few days, the banks that seemed sound reopened. The government loaned money to banks that were weak in order to make them stronger and prevent their failure.

Congress then passed a number of laws designed to help farmers. To increase farm prices, the government asked farmers to cut production. The Agricultural Adjustment Act (AAA) provided **price supports** (guaranteed higher prices) to farmers who agreed to cut back their cotton and tobacco crops. Georgia's farmers agreed, but world prices did not go higher than about one-half what they were before the depression. When the Supreme Court declared the AAA unconstitutional, Congress passed other laws to help farmers.

Congress also passed the National Industrial Recovery Act (NIRA). In Georgia, the NIRA applied mainly to cotton textile manufacturers. To increase prices and profits, the law allowed the manufacturers to regulate themselves by cutting production. The textile manufacturers agreed to reduce their hours of operation. They also promised workers a 40-hour workweek and to pay them a minimum wage. A **mini-**

FDR'S FIRESIDE CHATS

Those who framed our government expected the House of Representatives to become the part of government closest to the people. After 1933, though, people expected the president to hear their pleas. This change occurred in part because President Franklin D. Roosevelt was an excellent communicator. In fact, he was so popular that the people elected him to four terms in office.

Roosevelt could attribute part of this popularity to his direct communication with the American people by radio. From 1933 to 1945, he spoke to the American people about thirty times. After the first program, a broadcaster called Roosevelt's talk a "fireside chat." The name stuck.

President Roosevelt's "fireside chats" did much to restore the morale of the American people.

Why did these fireside chats resonate in the hearts of Americans? One reason is that Roosevelt referred to his listeners as "my friends," and he spoke like one friend to another. He used the simplest language and concrete examples. Roosevelt was personable, optimistic, and even charming. He instilled hope in the people. After calling attention to the opponents of his programs, he made references to American traditions. And, after every radio address, the national anthem was played. These techniques helped Roosevelt establish good rapport with the people and gained their support for his programs.

mum wage is the least amount an employer can pay an employee for a certain number of hours worked. Congress hoped this would put more people to work at higher wages. The law also permitted workers to organize themselves into unions, which would bargain collectively for higher wages. Although they were common in the North, unions were a relatively new concept in the South. Nevertheless, between September 1933 and August 1934, membership in the United Textile Workers of America union jumped from 40,000 to over 270,000.

Textile workers across the South went on strike in August 1934 to protest the unfair treatment by the mill owners.

Textile mill owners reacted strongly to these changes in the way they had been accustomed to treating their mill workers. The owners wanted to destroy the unions. They fired activists and other union members. The mill owners also blacklisted many workers (put out the word that they should not be hired). The owners also resorted to the **stretch out**, a practice requiring workers to tend more machines. In this practice, workers had to do the same amount of work in an 8-hour shift that had been done in a 12-hour shift. It was a brutal, if not impossible, schedule and clearly against the intent of the law.

Textile workers all over the South joined in a strike called by the union in August 1934. Workers immediately left their jobs and went into the streets of cities such as Macon, where 3,500 mill workers protested their treatment. Throughout Georgia, the scene was repeated by 45,000 union workers, a large portion of the 60,000 mill hands in the state. Groups of striking workers, called "flying squadrons," traveled from mill to mill stirring up workers and closing down production. At one point, things were so bad that Governor Eugene Talmadge called out the National Guard and had thousands of workers arrested.

For many mill workers, family needs caused them to end their strike and return to work. On September 22, the union called off the strike. Although mill workers returned to their jobs, many things were never the same as before. Feuds between strikers and non-strikers mushroomed. Additional union activists were blacklisted and unable to find work. The workers were forced to leave their mill homes. Feelings of disillusionment and fear of authority became common among workers in the textile industry. The failed strike and the subsequent hardships were to make an impression on Georgia workers that would last for many years.

The Supreme Court later declared the NIRA unconstitutional. To replace it, Congress quickly passed several laws to protect workers. The Wagner Act of 1935 guaranteed workers the right of **collective bargaining**, discussions between a union and employer to determine such things as working conditions and employees' wages, hours, and benefits. It also outlawed many unfair labor practices (such as firing union members) and established a board to enforce the law. Thereafter, when workers asked for a union in a mill, the board oversaw the election. Congress hoped workers would organize for higher wages. With higher wages, workers could buy more consumer goods and help the economy recover.

Do You Remember?
1. What was the "New Deal"?
2. How did the federal government revive the banking system?
3. What did the Wagner Act do?

RELIEF

A number of New Deal measures were designed to help the unemployed. The Federal Emergency Relief Administration (FERA) gave money to the states to provide jobs, food, and clothes. The Public Works Administration (PWA) built useful public projects to help the economy recover. In 1935, Congress created the Works Progress Administration (WPA) to provide jobs for workers as quickly as possible. WPA projects included building schools, parks, roads, and airports. Nationwide, the WPA employed over 4,000,000 persons. The WPA also provided work for artists, musicians, and actors. They painted murals for government buildings, created statues in parks, and put on plays and musical performances.

In 1933, the Civilian Conservation Corps (CCC) was established. Operated by the army, this agency established close to 1,300 camps across the country for unemployed young men just out of high school. The men were paid $30 a month, $22 of which was sent home to their families. The CCC put some 2.5 million young men to work preserving the soil and purifying the water. They cleared brush, planted trees, built parks, and worked on roads. They drained swamps and built firebreaks in the nation's forests. The CCC lasted until 1945 and was one of the most popular New Deal programs. Another program, the National Youth Administration (NYA), paid college students to grade papers and do office chores.

These relief efforts could not reach those people who could not work—children, the blind, widows with small children, and the elderly. In addition, workers needed some protection against unemployment. In 1935, Congress passed the **Social Security Act**. The federal

More than three million young men were provided with jobs for a dollar a day from the Civilian Conservation Corps, the CCC.

Governor E. D. Rivers breaking ground for a new hospital, a Works Progress Administration (WPA) project in Milledgeville.

government would provide old-age insurance from taxes paid by both workers and their employers. The states, helped by the federal government, would meet the other needs.

ECONOMIC REFORMS

The New Deal also tried to correct weaknesses in the economy that may have added to the depression. One important reform was the creation of the Federal Deposit Insurance Corporation (FDIC). The FDIC insured depositors' accounts in banks. That is, if the banks failed, the FDIC would see that the depositors got their money back.

Congress also tried to reform the stock exchanges, where investigators found many abuses. One abuse was *insider trading*. People "inside" corporations or stock exchanges used information they knew about their companies to make fortunes or avoid losses. Another abuse was giving out false information about corporations in order to sell their stocks. Congress also discovered that investors bought too much stock with borrowed money. The Securities Exchange Act of 1934 was passed to eliminate these abuses.

Another reform involved the regulation of electrical utility holding companies. Thirteen companies controlled three-fourths of the power companies in the nation. Investors in these holding companies took the power companies' profits out of the business. This left little money for expansion and led to higher utility rates for customers. Congress passed a law abolishing all electrical holding companies. The law also permitted the government to organize power companies into regional systems to provide more power cheaply and efficiently.

SOCIAL IMPROVEMENT

The New Deal went beyond trying to solve the problems of the depression. It also tried to improve people's lives.

Congress started a huge social improvement project when it created the **Tennessee Valley Authority** (TVA) in 1933. The Tennessee River valley stretched through seven states. The TVA built a number of dams on the Tennessee River and its tributaries. The dams provided cheap electricity to states including Georgia, improved navi-

gation on the rivers, attracted industry, controlled flooding, improved farming, and created recreational areas.

The TVA was also involved in **conservation** (the management of a natural resource to prevent its destruction). The "dust bowl" in Oklahoma and other midwestern states showed what happened when drought and wind eroded the soil. People could no longer live on the land, and many had to relocate. The TVA built model farms to show farmers how to conserve the soil and restore its fertility.

Another New Deal program involved **rural electrification**. In the 1920s, power companies mainly ran lines to towns and cities. Because the rural population was spread out, power lines were expensive to build and maintain. The Rural Electrification Authority (REA) reportedly was a result of President Roosevelt's first night at Warm Springs. He was sitting on his porch, trying to catch a breeze on a hot, sultry, summer night. He noticed that no lights were showing from neighboring farms. When he received his electric bill at the end of the month, he saw that it was many times higher than what he paid at his mansion in Hyde Park, New York. Roosevelt never forgot that night, and on May 11, 1935, he signed into law the act creating the REA. The REA loaned over $300 million to farmers' cooperatives to help them extend their own power lines and buy power wholesale. This program was one on the most important and far-reaching of the New Deal programs. By 1940, a significant percentage of farmers in Georgia and other parts of the nation had electricity. Electric water pumps, lights, milking machines, and appliances made farm life much easier.

TVA dams built during the Great Depression, like Norris Dam on the Tennessee River in Alabama, still provide needed electricity to the region.

BLACK AMERICA DURING THE NEW DEAL

Although most African Americans supported President Roosevelt, the black community as a whole did not make great gains under New Deal reforms. For example, under the AAA, farm subsidies went to property owners rather than to the tenant farmers, who were predominantly black.

The Social Security Act was not designed to provide an income for farm and household workers. Therefore, those working at such jobs received no share of the pension and unemployment benefits. When the WPA and other federal relief programs were organized, President Roosevelt ordered state relief officers "not to discriminate . . . because of race or religion or politics." In spite of a lack of support from Governor Eugene Talmadge, those responsible for New Deal programs in Georgia made every effort to equally distribute WPA programs.

Right: Perhaps the most prominent black to serve in the government during the New Deal was Mary McLeod Bethune. In addition to founding Bethune-Cookman College, she became a high-ranking official under President Roosevelt. In 1936, Bethune was given charge of the Office of Minority Affairs in the National Youth Administration (NYA). Above: Robert Weaver, a native of Washington, D.C., served as Secretary of the new Department of Housing and Urban Development. He was the first African American to hold a cabinet position.

Several prominent blacks were instrumental in leading the New Deal programs, including Clark Foreman, a staff member at the office of the secretary of the interior. Foreman brought qualified blacks into government agencies and checked on complaints about racial discrimination. Another African American, Robert Weaver, started his government career during the New Deal. Later, in the 1960s, he became the first head of the Department of Housing and Urban Development. William Hastie, also a leading black figure in the New Deal, later became a federal judge.

Another Georgia organization was the Atlanta-based Commission on Interracial Cooperation. This group worked to ensure the equal administration of federal relief efforts. By 1944, the commission had become the Southern Regional Council (SRC), which played a major role in civil rights programs of the 1960s.

William Henry Hastie, an NAACP attorney during President Roosevelt's terms, was the first African American to be appointed a federal judge in the United States, and the first African-American territorial governor (of the Virgin Islands).

Do You Remember?
1. What were four government agencies established to put people to work during the Great Depression?
2. How did the government try to help those who could not work?
3. What good did the TVA do?

The depression years brought new leadership to Georgia. Like the people in the rest of the nation, Georgians based their hopes for a better future in this new leadership. Some of Georgia's governors were to prove themselves forward-looking, but at least one of them appeared at first to be an echo from the past.

As governor, Richard B. Russell, Jr., son of a Georgia Supreme Court Chief Justice, gained recognition by reorganizing Georgia's government. As a U.S. Senator, he spent more than half his life in the service of his state and nation. **Opposite page:** *Known for his red suspenders and "down home" ways, Eugene Talmadge was a powerful figure in Georgia politics.*

RICHARD RUSSELL, JR.

On June 27, 1931, Winder resident Richard Russell, Jr., succeeded Lamartine Hardman as governor. A former member and speaker of the Georgia house of representatives, Russell used this experience to make some needed changes. One of his first acts was to reduce the number of state boards from 102 to 18. In an equally daring political move, he combined the boards of trustees of state colleges and universities into one governing group called the University System of Georgia Board of Regents. During the creation of the new system, some colleges were closed while others were combined. Russell appointed Hughes Spalding, an Atlanta lawyer, as the first chairman of the board of regents.

Russell tried to run the state like a successful business. His approach eased some of the problems brought on by the depression. In 1932, Governor Russell was elected to the United States Senate, where he served for the next thirty-eight years. Russell favored national military preparedness and states' rights. He became a respected advisor to six United States presidents and, when he served as president pro tempore of the Senate, he was third in line for the presidency.

EUGENE TALMADGE

State government changed greatly when Eugene Talmadge became governor in 1933. The Forsyth farmer, lawyer, and sawmill owner had been elected commissioner of agriculture in 1926 and served three years in that position. Talmadge was a dramatic politician in the style of Tom Watson. He often compared himself with Watson, especially when trying to get the support of rural voters. He was a conservative white supremacist who did not like federal government intervention or government debts. Talmadge especially disliked relief efforts, public welfare, and federal assistance programs.

After becoming governor, Talmadge tried to rid the state of New Deal programs. He used federal funds to build highways more often than for needed relief of the unemployed. He also reduced property taxes, utility rates, and some license fees. Car tags, which had been $5 or $10, could be bought for $3.

Talmadge was elected to a second term in 1934 by a landslide margin. However, because he refused to follow federal New Deal regulations, the federal government took over New Deal programs in Georgia. Officials who disagreed with Talmadge were fired and replaced with his supporters. Once, Talmadge ordered the highway commissioner to reduce spending or resign. The commissioner refused to do as asked. Talmadge called in the National Guard, declared martial law, and had the commissioner physically removed from his office. A Talmadge supporter was named as the new commissioner.

In 1934, during the state's worst textile strike, the governor declared martial law again and used the National Guard to arrest strikers. However, Talmadge's political power plays did not change the fact that Georgia law would not allow him to serve more than two consecutive terms.

EURITH RIVERS

Because he could not run for governor, Talmadge ran for the United States Senate in 1936 against Richard Russell and was soundly defeated. His hand-picked successor for governor, Charles Redwine, was beaten by Lanier County resident Eurith "Ed" Rivers.

Governor Rivers served from 1937 to 1941. A former newspaperman and speaker of the Georgia house of representatives, Rivers supported President Roosevelt's New Deal programs. He also supported and gained passage of constitutional amendments granting health services for all Georgians, old age pensions, teacher pay raises, a seven-month school year, homestead exemptions for taxes, and expansion of the state's highway system.

Under Rivers' leadership, electrical services were expanded to rural areas of the state. Georgia moved from the lowest ranked state to the top of the list in the

E. D. "Ed" Rivers campaigned across the state in support of Roosevelt's New Deal policies during the 1936 governor's race against Charles Redwine.

number of rural electrification associations. While he was in office, the State Bureau of Unemployment Compensation was created, allowing Georgians to receive unemployment benefits.

After Rivers' re-election in 1938, he ran into problems financing many of his improvement programs. The budget was reduced by 25 percent. Even so, he was able to influence the legislature to create the Georgia Housing Authority and obtain federal funds to build public housing. It was during this time that Atlanta's Techwood Homes and University Homes were built. Several other Georgia cities also began public housing programs.

During Rivers' second term, there were political scandals and charges of corruption. Some staff members did not follow proper procedures in awarding highway contracts. Some of them sold prison pardons. Many of Rivers' appointees and staff members were charged with corrupt practices, and the charges reflected poorly on the governor.

Governor E.D. "Ed" Rivers gives his first inaugural address. On the right is outgoing governor Eugene Talmadge.

Eugene Talmadge's stance, "I may surprise you, but I will never deceive you" led him to the campaign trail for the third time and voters continued to elect Georgia's friend to the farmer.

TALMADGE AGAIN

Following Rivers' second term, Talmadge ran for governor again and was elected. Talmadge had softened his anti-Roosevelt stand and began using modified versions of New Deal legislation. The state's economy was growing. Then, a series of events angered the voters and put Georgia in an unfavorable national position.

A Talmadge supporter was an instructor at the University of Georgia. He told the governor that one of the deans at the university and the president of the Teachers College in Statesboro (now known as Georgia Southern University) had plans to integrate the school. Talmadge convinced the board of regents to fire the two individuals. He also managed to get rid of several members of the board of regents who publicly opposed his interference in the university system.

There was a great deal of national publicity against the governor's stand. The situation so offended the Southern Association of Colleges and Schools that they voted to dismiss white Georgia colleges from the listing of accredited schools. Georgians were upset with both the association and the governor. Talmadge was not re-elected in 1942.

ELLIS ARNALL

Ellis Gibbs Arnall won the governor's race in 1942 and took office in 1943. Arnall was a native of Newnan and a lawyer who had served as the state's attorney general. A constitutional amendment passed during Talmadge's third term made Arnall the first Georgia governor to serve a four-year term.

Arnall soon took steps to correct the problems with accreditation. He removed the university system from the influence of the governor's office. Terms of regents were staggered so there would always be experienced members serving the board. Arnall won re-accreditation of Georgia's colleges and universities by the Southern Association of Colleges and Schools.

Arnall also removed the prison system from the political influence of the governor's office. He established a board of corrections to oversee state prisons and a pardon and parole board to handle requests for pardons and paroles. Arnall abolished the poll tax, and, under his leadership, a new state constitution was adopted in 1945.

Ellis Arnall, elected governor in 1942, was the first Georgia governor to serve a four-year term. Under his leadership, Georgia became the first state to grant the right to vote to eighteen-year-olds.

Governor Arnall is probably best known for leading Georgia to become the first state in the nation to grant eighteen-year-olds the right to vote. When young men were drafted into the armed forces during World War II, Arnall argued that youths old enough to fight for their country were old enough to vote for their country's leadership.

Do You Remember?

1. What senate position did Richard Russell, Jr., hold that put him in line for the presidency?
2. Who did Governor Talmadge call in to arrest striking textile workers?
3. Under which governor was Georgia's highway system expanded?
4. Which governor granted the right to vote to eighteen-year-olds?

AMERICA ENTERS THE WAR

Meanwhile, American-Japanese relations got worse. To protest Japanese aggression, the United States stopped exporting airplanes, metals, aircraft parts, and aviation gasoline to Japan. Roosevelt also revoked the trade treaty with Japan. After Japan invaded French Indochina in 1941, Roosevelt seized all Japanese property in the United States.

Badly needing the oil that Roosevelt had cut off, Japan decided to invade the Dutch East Indies (now Indonesia) in late 1941. The only force that could stop the Japanese was the U.S. Navy stationed in Hawaii. The Japanese made a surprise attack on the fleet at Pearl Harbor on December 7, 1941, causing great damage. On December 8, the United States declared war on Japan and entered World War II. A few days later, Germany and Italy declared war on the United States. Now it was a full-fledged war between the Allied Powers led by the United States and Great Britain and the Axis Powers of Germany, Japan, and Italy.

Japanese attacks continued into early 1942. Japan captured Burma, Hong Kong, Malaya, Thailand, and the Philippines. Japan threatened New Guinea and Australia before their assault in the Pacific was stopped.

THE ALLIES FIGHT BACK

Joining the Allies meant the United States had to fight on two fronts, facing Germany and Italy in Europe and Africa and Japan in the Pacific. British and American troops invaded North Africa in late 1942 and won control of the area by May 1943. From Africa, the Allied armies moved into Sicily and Italy. The Italian people overthrew

Within two hours, Japanese bombers destroyed 8 battleships, 14 smaller boats, and 200 aircraft at Pearl Harbor (above). Some 2,400 members of the armed forces were killed. The next day, President Roosevelt asked Congress to declare war (left).

THE TUSKEGEE AIRMEN

Bombs were a vital part of air attacks, and one group of men helped ensure successful air strikes. In World War I, Eugene Bullard had made history in France as the first African American to fly in combat. World War II did not represent much of an improvement in the area of discrimination in the military. However, one group of flyers made the Pentagon rethink its position on the role of African Americans in combat. The military referred to their flying as an "experiment" but the Germans, who faced the fighters, called them the "Black Bird Men."

Each flight crew was composed of six men. Working out of a training facility at Tuskegee Institute, these men were to make history as the "Tuskegee Airmen." After their training, the airmen were given the assignment as escorts for allied bombers. In the beginning, the bomber flight crews wanted nothing to do with their escorts, but quickly the reputation of the airmen spread and flyers clamored to have the Tuskegee Airmen by their side. In over two hundred missions, the flight squadron never lost a single bomber they were escorting.

It was never easy. Initially, funding of the training facility was a huge problem. Few gave the program any chance of succeeding, but the training continued, headed by Charles Anderson who, twelve years earlier, had taught himself to fly in a plane he purchased.

One day in May 1941, Eleanor Roosevelt arrived at Tuskegee to visit while the president rested at Warm Springs. She arrived at the airstrip, visited briefly, and told the small assembled group that she wanted to fly with Mr. Anderson. After the success-

ful and highly publicized flight, the training facility received money to continue its program.

By the end of the war, close to 1,000 young black men had completed the training. Their skills were demonstrated by shooting down or damaging over 4,000 enemy planes and flying over 1,500 missions, while losing only 98 pilots. One hundred fifty pilots were decorated with medals including Flying Crosses, Purple Hearts, and Silver Stars.

Many of these pilots' names are familiar today. Daniel "Chappie" James became America's first black four-star general. General Benjamin Davis became the Air Force's first black lieutenant general. Others included Coleman Young, who served as Detroit's mayor; cable television mogul Percy Sutton; and Roscoe Brown, president of Bronx Community College in New York.

The Tuskegee "experiment" was a success and led the way for the integration of the armed forces.

Above: The Tuskegee airmen flew over 200 escort missions without losing a bomber. The Germans called them the "Black Bird Men." ***Inset opposite:*** Colonel Benjamin O. Davis, Jr., became the first black general in the Air Force after the war.

Called Operation Overlord, on June 6, 1944, D-Day, Allied forces invaded the beaches of Normandy, France, to push back the German army. Future United States President Dwight Eisenhower led the assault that involved 4,000 ships, 11,000 planes, and 176,000 soldiers.

Mussolini and joined the Allies. Germany and Japan were the remaining Axis Powers.

World War II was fought differently from earlier wars. Tanks had become swift and powerful. Rockets and bazookas, or rocket launchers, were used for the first time. They allowed troops to fight each other from a distance rather than hand to hand. Airplanes, used mostly for observation in World War I, now carried bombs and machine guns. Air raids had become a major part of combat. Now it was also possible to drop paratroopers behind enemy lines or quickly move troops and heavy equipment great distances.

On the seas, giant aircraft carriers transported planes used to drop bombs on enemy ships and land targets. Radar (radio detection and ranging) and sonar (sound navigation ranging) tracked the movements of enemy aircraft, ships, and submarines.

On June 6, 1944, D-Day, Allied forces landed on Normandy beach in northern France. Involved were 4,000 landing craft, 600 warships, 176,000 soldiers, and 11,000 planes. By early 1945, the troops had pushed the German army out of France and across the Rhine River to Germany. At the same time, the Soviet Army recaptured four smaller countries that were part of the German alliance: Bulgaria, Finland, Hungary, and Romania.

THE WAR IN EUROPE ENDS

By February 1945, the war was almost over. President Roosevelt, British Prime Minister Winston Churchill, and Soviet dictator Joseph Stalin met at the Russian sea resort of Yalta. During the Yalta conference, the "Big Three" leaders discussed how to end the war in Germany and Japan; ways to reorganize Germany once victory was achieved in Europe; and how the United Nations, a peace keeping organization, should be set up. By the end of the eight-day, top secret meeting, it was agreed that the Soviet Union would be offered territory lost in an earlier war with Japan in exchange for entering the current conflict against that country. The Soviet Union would also be given eastern Poland, and, in exchange, Poland would receive part of Germany at the end of the war.

It was also agreed that Germany would be divided into four zones. Great Britain, the Soviet Union, France, and the United States would each occupy and govern a zone. Berlin, the capital of Germany, was in the Soviet zone, but each of the four countries would share in administering that city.

Finally, a charter for the establishment of the United Nations was accepted in principle by the three leaders. Europe was freed from Hitler's control in April 1945, when the Soviet and American troops

The "Big Three," Britain's Prime Minister Winston Churchill, United States President Franklin Roosevelt, and Soviet dictator Joseph Stalin, met on the grounds of Livadio Palace at Yalta in February, 1945. The three tried to agree on plans for the postwar world. Look at the picture carefully and you will notice how ill Roosevelt looked at that meeting. He died only a few weeks later.

Above: Located in Meriwether County, Warm Springs was the location of President Roosevelt's second home, the "Little White House." He first visited the area in 1921 seeking treatment of the hot springs for his crippling polio. *Right:* Shown here at Warm Springs is a stolen moment when the President simply became a man fishing with his dog beside him.

came together at the river Elbe in the interior of Germany. Adolph Hitler committed suicide on April 30, and the last German forces surrendered to the Allies in May.

GEORGIA LOSES A FRIEND

President Roosevelt had been a frequent visitor to Georgia, spending time at the "Little White House" in Warm Springs. He often played with the children who were there, bathed in the springs, or rested in the sunshine. With the help of friends, Roosevelt established the Warm Springs Foundation so children and adults crippled with polio could receive therapy. His effort led to the March of Dimes.

After the Yalta meeting with Churchill and Stalin in February 1945, the president returned to the Little White House. He planned to rest and work on a speech for the United Nations. On April 24, Roosevelt was sitting for a portrait, surrounded by his model ships. His Scottish terrier, Fala, was nearby. Suddenly, the president put his hand to his head and said, "I have a terrific headache."

At 5:48 p.m., a stunned nation was told that the man who led the country through recovery from the depression, the New Deal, and to the brink of victory in World War II, was dead. A massive stroke killed him while the artist was painting. FDR's wife, Eleanor Roosevelt, who was in Washington, sent messages to her sons, all of whom were in military service. She wrote, "He did his job to the end as he would want you to do. Bless you all and all our love. Mother." Vice President Harry S Truman became president on the death of Roosevelt and was the nation's commander-in-chief during the final months of World War II.

VICTORY AT LAST

While the nation mourned its lost leader and then celebrated the end of the war in Europe, the task of securing peace was not yet over. War continued to rage in the Pacific. The Japanese advance in the Pacific was ended in 1942 when Japan was defeated by the United

Four-time President Franklin Delano Roosevelt was taken ill on April 24, 1945, as he posed for this portrait by Elizabeth Shumatoff. With little warning the President, beloved by millions, died at the Little White House in Warm Springs. The painting was left unfinished.

States Navy in the battles of the Coral Sea and Midway. In early fall 1942, the Allies began to recapture Pacific islands from the Japanese. The Gilbert, Marshall, Caroline, and Mariana islands were retaken. Allied planes launched offensive bombing strikes against the Japanese mainland from bases in the Marianas. In the fall of 1944, the United States invaded the Philippines, and Great Britain invaded Burma. Allied forces moved through to China.

During the summer of 1945, successful daily air raids were made on Japan. On July 26, Allied leaders issued the Potsdam Agreement, demanding unconditional surrender. Emperor Hirohito was willing to surrender, but the foreign minister was not. To end the war and avoid the loss of life to Allied forces that would surely result from an invasion of Japan, President Truman authorized the use of a new weapon, one of enormous power. On August 6, the *Enola Gay,* a United States bomber, dropped an atomic bomb on Hiroshima. A fireball 650 feet wide scorched everything in its path. Shock waves destroyed brick buildings a mile from the blast, and wooden ones simply disappeared. A fire storm swept the city, followed by a muddy, chilling rain that poured radioactive materials over a wide area. By mid-afternoon, 80,000 were dead, and 120,000 more were dying. The city lay in ashes.

The Japanese still refused to surrender. A second atomic bomb was dropped on the city of Nagasaki on August 9. Japan surrendered on August 15, 1945. The bombings of Hiroshima and Nagasaki are the first and last times to date that atomic warfare has been used to settle differences between nations. At last, World War II was over.

GEORGIA IN WORLD WAR II

Following the United States' declaration of war, over 320,000 Georgians between the ages of 21 and 35 put on military uniforms. Of that number 7,388 died in battle. Eight Georgians received the Congressional Medal of Honor, the nation's highest military decoration. World War II brought prosperity to Georgia. Because of its climate and the influence of politicians like Senator Richard Russell, Jr., Senator Walter F. George, and Representative Carl Vinson, the state became the site of several military installations.

Millions of federal dollars poured into the state, strengthening the economy. Major military bases included Fort Benning in Columbus, Camp Gordon in Augusta, Fort Stewart and Hunter Air Field in Savannah, and Warner Robins Air Field near Macon. Airmen from

Aircraft mechanics work on the nose and cockpit of a B-52 bomber at Warner Robins Air Field near Macon in July, 1943.

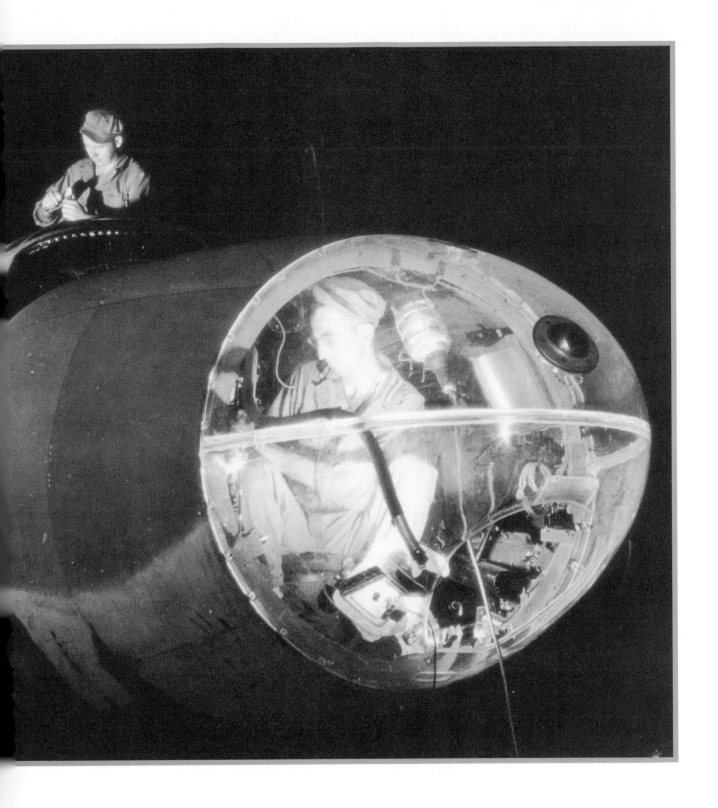

The Bell Bomber Plant, where World War II B-29s were manufactured, closed after the war. It reopened in the 1950s as Lockheed-Georgia. Today it is a 76-acre factory which produces many of America's military aircraft including the B-47 jet bomber and the C-130 Hercules transport.

Glynco Naval Air Station, near Brunswick, flew blimps along the southern Atlantic coast in search of German submarines. Several cities, including Americus and Augusta, were the sites of German prisoner of war camps.

Fort McPherson, in the Atlanta area, was a major induction center for newly drafted soldiers from all over the country. A military hospital, which had been used in World War I, was reopened in Atlanta. In nearby Clayton County, Fort Gillem, an army storage facility and railroad yard, began operation.

GEORGIANS SUPPORT THE WAR EFFORT

In Marietta, 30,000 men and women built B-29 bombers at the Bell Bomber Plant. Thousands of Georgians were also employed in automobile and textile plants that were being used to produce military vehicles and uniforms.

Women moved into the work force, filling jobs formerly held by men. They became welders and worked on assembly lines, helping to produce weapons, tanks, jeeps, and aircraft.

Left: Fort Benning, Georgia, near Columbus, covers 181,500 acres and serves as the United States Army Infantry Training School. It is the world's largest infantry camp.

With over 16 million men and women in the armed forces during World War II, thousands of women left at home were also called on to help. They performed an invaluable service by working to keep the country's factories producing the weapons, equipment, and supplies needed to support the war effort.

Georgia farmers planted peanuts for their oil, grew vegetables, and raised cotton and livestock to help feed the country and its allies. By 1944, the annual farm income was $454, over three times what it had been in 1940.

Volunteers watched the sky for enemy planes. Some prepared Red Cross kits for service men. They contained such items as soap, toothpaste, and sewing kits. Children helped grow "victory gardens" in their yards. Across the country, such gardens supplied over 40 percent of America's fresh vegetables during the war. Children also collected scrap metal to be melted down and reused in factories. Gasoline, shoes, and food items such as meat, butter, and sugar were **rationed** (had their consumption limited). Women used leg makeup because it was hard to get silk and nylon stockings. Georgia joined the rest of the nation in donating 13 million pints of blood for the war wounded.

During this time, two pieces of national legislation affected all citizens. The first was a tax on income, which was withheld from workers' pay and sent directly to the United States Treasury. The second, passed in 1944, was the Serviceman's Readjustment Act. The "G.I. Bill," as it was called, made low-cost loans to veterans who wanted to buy homes or start businesses. It also paid tuition and bought books for those who went back to school. Both programs, the withholding tax and the G.I. Bill, are still in effect today.

THE HOLOCAUST

One of the horrors of World War II was Hitler's effort to kill all the Jews in conquered Europe in what came to be known as the *Holocaust*. Before the war ended, six million Jewish men, women, and children had been murdered on Hitler's orders. They were rounded up by the thousands and packed into trains going to concentration camps like Auschwitz, Treblinka, Belsen, Dachau, and Buchenwald. Many died on the trains. Others died of starvation or disease in the camps. Millions were shot or gassed, their bodies burned in gigantic *crematoriums*. All this was part of Hitler's "final solution" to what he called the "Jewish problem," the elimination of an entire race of people.

The United States Holocaust Memorial Museum, established by an act of Congress, opened in Washington, D.C., in April 1993. The Museum was created as a living memorial to the six million Jews and millions of other victims of Nazi fanaticism who perished in the Holocaust.

The untold tragedies of war could not match the horror of the German concentration camps where six million Jews were murdered. A survivor of Gusen Camp in Austria is shown here. What does the face tell you? Could the "Holocaust," as the attempted destruction of the Jewish race was called, happen today? Why or why not?

Do You Remember?

1. Why did President Roosevelt feel so strongly about helping the British?
2. In what ways did the United States protest Japanese aggression in the Far East?
3. What event finally led the United States to enter the war?
4. What bombing raids led to the surrender of Japan?
5. Which military installation was located in Columbus?

SUMMARY

- The prosperity of the 1920s ended with the stock market crash.
- Failures of banks and businesses caused massive, widespread unemployment.
- After Roosevelt's election, a series of New Deal programs put people back to work, provided insurance and pensions for retirees, and delivered electrical power to the nation's rural areas.
- During this period, most Georgia governors supported New Deal legislation.
- Governor Talmadge at first did not support Roosevelt's economic policies, but he later softened his opposition.
- World War II broke out in Europe, and, after the Japanese attack on Pearl Harbor, America entered it.
- Germany surrendered in May 1945, and, following American atomic bomb attacks, Japan followed suit in August.
- During the war, the economies of the United States and Georgia prospered, and the Great Depression ended.

CHAPTER REVIEW

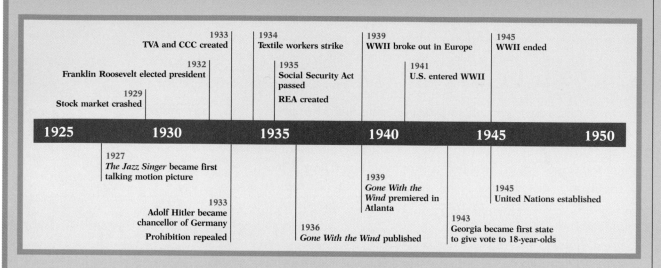

1925	1930	1935	1940	1945	1950

1933 TVA and CCC created

1932 Franklin Roosevelt elected president

1929 Stock market crashed

1934 Textile workers strike

1935 Social Security Act passed
REA created

1939 WWII broke out in Europe

1941 U.S. entered WWII

1945 WWII ended

1927 *The Jazz Singer* became first talking motion picture

1933 Adolf Hitler became chancellor of Germany
Prohibition repealed

1936 *Gone With the Wind* published

1939 *Gone With the Wind* premiered in Atlanta

1943 Georgia became first state to give vote to 18-year-olds

1945 United Nations established

Reviewing People, Places, and Terms

Use the following terms in a paragraph describing the United States during the Great Depression and World War II.

1. dictator
2. Great Depression
3. New Deal
4. relief
5. Social Security Act
6. stock market

Understanding the Facts

1. What were several indications that the 1920s was an age of abandon?
2. What natural disaster struck Georgia's cotton growers?
3. In what year did the great stock market "crash" occur?
4. What were two ways in which President Hoover tried to help the economy recover?
5. After President Roosevelt took office, what was his first act to prevent the nation's banks from failing?
6. What New Deal laws were intended to help the nation's workers?
7. Which Georgia governor refused to go along with New Deal programs?
8. What event occurred on December 7, 1941?
9. Where was the country's "Little White House" during Roosevelt's presidency?

Developing Critical Thinking

1. Do you believe that another "Great Depression" is possible in this country today? Why or why not?
2. Do you think a guaranteed minimum wage is a good thing? Why or why not?
3. What might have been the impact on history if the United States had not entered World War II?
4. Why do you think gasoline, shoes, and certain food items were rationed?

Applying Your Skills

1. The number of shares of stock traded on the New York Stock Exchange for certain years between 1920 and 1935 is as follows: 1920: 227,636,000; 1925: 459,717,623; 1929: 1,124,800,410; 1930: 810,632,546; and 1935: 381,635,752. Prepare a bar chart using this information. What does the chart suggest about the nation's attitude toward buying

stock after the stock market crash?

2. Prepare a short report on one of the New Deal agencies or laws. Include information on when the agency was created or when the law was passed, its purpose, and its effectiveness.

3. Using a world map, show the location of the following places and identify their importance to World War II: Berlin, Pearl Harbor, Normandy, Hiroshima, and Yalta.

Making Connections

1. Why were President Roosevelt's fireside chats so important to the American people?

2. Recent presidents have continued the practice of "fireside chats" with the American people. Listen to one radio broadcast by the president.

Prepare a short report that describes the topic, the president's presentation, and your reactions to the broadcast.

3. Ask someone you know who lived through the Great Depression what their most lingering memory of that period is. Share your findings with the class.

4. During the depression many people turned down help because they were asked to "take charity." Do you think the attitude toward accepting public help is different today? Why?

Did You Know?

• "The Star Spangled Banner" was written in 1814 but did not become our national anthem until 1931.

BUILDING SKILLS: DETECTING BIAS

Everyone has certain opinions or ideas about certain topics or subjects. For this reason, written material is not always objective (free from the writer's personal opinions). Even though a writer may try hard to be objective, what he or she writes or says may show *bias*, a highly personal, and sometimes unreasonable, opinion about something or someone. Bias can be either for or against an idea or individual.

To be a good and thoughtful citizen, you need to learn how to detect bias in both written and oral materials and in materials from both the past and the present. Asking the following questions may help you.

• When and why was the material written or the statement made?

• Did the writer or speaker use certain phrases for emotional impact or try to play on your emotions rather than present facts?

• Does the writer or speaker tend to show one group as good and the other group as evil?

Try This! In the early 1930s, over 15 million men were out of work. Many who had lost everything

took to the road in search of something better. Read the following statements, and identify any bias you believe exists.

Why, it's the best education in the world for those boys, that traveling around! They get more experience in a few months than they would in years at school.
(Henry Ford)

They are the people whom our post offices label "address unknown," and whom we call transients. Every group in society is represented in their ranks. . . .We think of nomads of the desert—now we have nomads of the Depression.
(Newton D. Baker, reporter for the *New York Times*)

Many of those who are most boisterous now in clamor for work have either struck on the jobs they had or don't want to work at all, and are utilizing the occasion to swell the communistic chorus.
(John E. Edggerton, National Association of Manufacturers)

UNIT VI

MODERN GEORGIA

No memorial or eulogy could more eloquently honor President Kennedy's memory than the earliest possible passage of the civil rights bill for which he fought. We have talked for one hundred years or more. Yes, it's time now to write the next chapter—and to write it in the book of law.

—Lyndon B. Johnson

THE FOUR CHAPTERS in this unit deal with happenings in Georgia and the United States from the end of World War II in 1945 until the present time. Each of the decades since then has been marked by events that serve to set it apart from those that preceded or followed it.

The forties saw the end of World War II and the beginning of the "Cold War." The fifties were marked with racial unrest and the Korean War. In the sixties, the feelings of the nation about the Vietnam conflict were sharply divided. The seventies marked the end of the Vietnam conflict and a political scandal that forced the resignation of the president.

During the 1980s, people were concerned about the stability of the economy. A "war" against drugs and disease was carried out, and there seemed no end to environmental problems.

As the 1990s end and the twenty-first century begins, many of the problems of the 1980s remained unsolved. However, the economy of the nation was stronger than it had been for many years, and amazing new technologies were available to apply to finding ways of dealing with our problems.

The period since World War II has been one of growth and prosperity for the state, and for Atlanta in particular. The skyscrapers of downtown Atlanta are symbolic of its current status as one of the most successful and prosperous American cities.

CHAPTER FIFTEEN

CHANGING TIMES

*All human beings are born free and equal in dignity and rights . . .
are endowed with reason and conscience and should act towards
one another in a spirit of brotherhood.*
— 1948 United Nations General Assembly
Declaration of Human Rights

*During the 1940s and 1950s,
cars became more than just a
means of transportation.
They became status symbols.*

THE YEARS IMMEDIATELY following World War II were for many a time remembered with much nostalgia and contentment. Many blacks and other minorities in the nation, however, still felt that they were unable to share fully in the American dream. Over the next several decades, the efforts of those who wanted rights that had long been denied to them would lead to extraordinary changes in the social fabric of the United States.

A NATION GROWING AND CHANGING

The 12,300,000 members of the armed forces returning home in 1945 and 1946 after World War II were welcomed as heroes. In the United States, life was good for many, especially after the bleak years of the Great Depression. Business was booming. City factories and office buildings were springing up in Georgia and across the nation. People were moving out of larger cities into the suburbs. As these new residential areas grew, shopping centers, schools, churches, and highways were built to serve them.

For many Americans, the period from the late 1940s through the 1950s were filled with enthusiasm, fun, and security. The austerity (harshness) of the depression and wartime had been followed by prosperity; neighborhood backyard barbecues were common, and front doors were rarely locked.

President Harry S Truman exemplified the ethical standards of the day. He was hard-working, responsible, and accountable. He expected those around him to show the same traits. His motto, reflected in a plaque on his oval office desk, was "The buck stops here."

If you asked most Americans to describe life in the years immediately following the war, they would probably use such terms as "satisfied," "comfortable," "fun," and "happy." A common theme of these years was family togetherness. School, church, and community events were designed for the entire family. On Sundays, families would get in their cars, and, free of the wartime restrictions on gasoline, take rides throughout the surrounding areas. Or they would stroll through their neighborhoods, stopping along the way to chat with their neighbors. Frequently, several families would spend their summer vacations together.

At the same time, these years were marked by the fear of the spread of communism, which gave rise to hysteria, bomb shelters, and half-truths. In addition, the civil liberties of some people were abused.

Especially for Americans of color, life was far different than the rosy scene pictured by many whites. Jim Crow was alive and flourishing in the South, and discrimination was the rule and not the exception throughout the nation. However, family life and society were beginning to change.

In 1947, the winds of social change slowly began to blow across the nation. The focus of this change was a young athlete from Cairo, Georgia. Jackie Robinson was signed by the Brooklyn Dodgers major league baseball team, thus becoming the first black player in a major professional sport. In the process, he changed major league baseball forever. Before that time, black baseball players had played in the all-black league. Although they sometimes played exhibition games against all-white teams, they never played on the same teams.

MUSIC OF THE TIMES

The period following World War II was also known for its **baby boom**, as millions of children were born during the postwar years. These babies, now in their fifties, grew up during a time of excitement and fun. The 1940s was the era of the big bands and bobby soxers. The bands of Glenn Miller and Tommy Dorsey played in theaters and dance halls throughout the country. Teenage girls, called *bobby soxers*, thronged to hear their favorite bands and singers—especially their idol, Frank Sinatra. In the 1950s and 1960s, rock and roll burst on the music scene. Elvis Presley and the Beatles joined hundreds of other rock stars as musical trends were set. In 1958, Berry Gordy, Jr., founded Motown Records in Detroit. Motown quickly made stars of musicians like the Supremes, Smokey Robinson and the Miracles, and Marvin Gaye.

Several Georgians made an impact on the music scene in the rock and roll era. In 1952, Gladys Knight was joined by her brother Bubba, her sister Brenda, and her cousins William and Eleanor Guest at the Phyllis Wheatley YWCA in Atlanta. The occasion was a birthday party, and eight-year-old Gladys and the "Pips" sang two songs for which they received $10. Nine years later, the group—which then consisted of Gladys, her brother, and her cousins William Guest and Edwin Patten—recorded the best-seller "With Every Beat of My Heart." From that million-dollar record, there was no stopping the versatile musical group.

The 1950s also saw the rise of Bill Lowery, who founded Lowery Music. Artists who have signed with Lowery Records include Billy Joe Royal, the Atlanta Rhythm Section, Ray Stevens, and Mac Davis.

In 1954, rock and roll quickly became a craze. In concerts, teenagers screamed, danced, and fainted over great performers like Chuck Berry and Elvis Presley. Augusta's "Godfather of Soul" James Brown and Macon's ever popular and flamboyant "Little Richard" actually set the stage for rock and roll. Songs such as Little Richard's "Tutti Frutti" and "Good Golly Miss Molly" continue to be classics today.

All of these musicians kept their musical styles, yet they were able to cross over to the music of the decade that followed. One of

Above: Augusta's "Godfather of Soul" James Brown helped set the stage for rock and roll in the 1950s. He remains a dynamic performer to this day. *Opposite page, below:* Jackie Robinson, born in Cairo, Georgia, became the first black player in major league baseball in 1947.

*Top: Born in Albany, Ray Charles' version of "Georgia on My Mind" was so successful it was made the state song. **Above:** Macon's flamboyant Little Richard recently performed at the Oscar ceremony.*

Georgia's best-known musicians saw his career soar in 1955 with the release of "I've Got a Woman." Albany-born Ray Charles lived in Georgia for several years before moving to Florida. At about age five or six, Charles was diagnosed with glaucoma, a disease of the eye. Shortly thereafter, he became blind. In no way, though, did the loss of his sight diminish Charles's talent or determination.

Another musical luminary was Otis Redding. Born in Dawson, Otis was the son of a Baptist preacher. He moved to Macon and, as was true of many musicians, got his start by singing in the church choir. Forced to leave school in order to help out the family after his father became ill, Redding is best known for his last song, "Sitting on the Dock of the Bay," which he was working on before his untimely death in a plane crash in 1967.

Georgia produced singers in other types of music besides rock and roll. Atlanta's Mattiwilda Dobbs had performed throughout Europe as an opera singer but not in the major opera houses in this country. Not until Marion Anderson sang at the Metropolitan Opera were the doors of opera houses in the United States opened for Mattiwilda Dobbs and other black performers.

Georgia also contributed to the world of gospel music. One group that achieved international fame was the "Singing Le Fevre Family" from Atlanta. And, as noted in an earlier chapter, Thomas Dorsey provided some of the country's best-loved gospel music.

TELEVISION CHANGES FAMILY LIFE

Teenagers in the 1950s grew up with television. At first, television programs ran only six or seven hours a day. Families gathered around the small black-and-white sets to watch such popular performers as Jackie Gleason in "The Honeymooners," Lucille Ball in "I Love Lucy," comics Sid Caesar and Milton Berle, and major productions such as the "Ed Sullivan Show." Television viewing began to replace family games and conversation as the evening entertainment of choice. Even food changed. Frozen TV dinners were developed to shorten the time spent in preparing evening meals.

Television also brought about a change in organized religion, which flourished in the 1950s. Evangelists such as Billy Graham and Oral Roberts developed national followings through their use of the television screen. Bishop Fulton J. Sheen, a nationally known Roman Catholic cleric, joined his Protestant counterparts in using the new medium to promote family values and fight against communism.

THE THEATER

On New York City's Broadway, elaborate musicals played to packed theaters. The team of Richard Rodgers and Oscar Hammerstein broke new ground in musical theater in the 1940s with *Oklahoma!*, and then followed with a series of hits including *Carousel*, *South Pacific*, *The King and I*, and *The Sound of Music*. Other musical theater classics of this era included *My Fair Lady* and *Camelot* by Alan J. Lerner and Fritz Loew and *West Side Story* by Leonard Bernstein, Arthur Laurents, and Steven Sondheim. *West Side Story* was one of the first musicals with a serious social theme. All of these stage plays were later turned into popular movies.

Much serious drama also was produced during this period. These included Tennessee Williams' *The Glass Menagerie* and *A Streetcar Named Desire*, Eugene O'Neill's *Long Day's Journey into Night*, Arthur Miller's *Death of a Salesman* and *All My Sons*, and William Inge's *Come Back Little Sheba* and *Picnic*.

PUBLISHING EVENTS

One of the most popular books for young adult readers of this period was J. D. Salinger's *Catcher in the Rye*. Another writer of this period was Georgia's Flannery O'Connor, who wrote two novels and about thirty short stories. O'Connor's work is ranked with other southern literary giants such as Eudora Welty, Robert Penn Warren, and

Top: One of the most enduringly popular television shows of the 50s was I Love Lucy. ***Above:*** *One of Georgia's best-known writers, Carson McCullers (left) is seen with southern playwright Tennessee Williams.*

Walker Percy. Her most famous short story, "A Good Man is Hard to Find," is included in most literature anthologies for today's classrooms.

An invalid for thirteen years as a result of lupus, O'Connor continued her habit of writing long and interesting letters to a wide group of friends and acquaintances. As her illness progressed, O'Connor moved into her mother's Milledgeville home, taking with her the peacocks, geese, and ducks she raised as pets. She continued to write three hours each day until her death in 1964 at the age of 39.

Carson McCullers was another of Georgia's great writers. Her popular novel *The Heart is a Lonely Hunter* was followed by the plays *A Member of the Wedding* and *Reflections in a Golden Eye*. The Atlanta writer Celestine Sibley is the author of more than fourteen books, including the delightful *Christmas in Georgia* and *Dear Store*. Sibley began her writing career in 1941 when she joined the staff of the *Atlanta Constitution* as a columnist. For many years, she worked with the newspaper's nationally known editor, Ralph McGill. McGill wrote probing and challenging columns for forty years. In the last twenty years of his life, his award-winning columns about the social changes in Georgia and other parts of the

Georgia's Flannery O'Connor, despite a tragically short life, wrote two novels and about thirty short stories that rank her with the literary giants of the South. Despite being an invalid for the last thirteen years of her life, she continued to write each day until her death in 1964.

South gained an audience in both Georgia and the rest of the country.

Among the nation's most popular magazines of this period was *The Saturday Evening Post*. While such periodicals as *Look*, *Life*, *Reader's Digest*, *Time*, and *Newsweek* were standard reading fare, it was the *Post* that made a unique American artist a household name. Norman Rockwell not only substantially increased the circulation of the magazine through his illustrations of everyday life in America, he also performed a vital role as social historian who depicted in his work the moods of the nation.

Another artist also has had a lasting impression on Americans. The comic strip "Peanuts" was introduced by Charles Schultz and caught America's fancy during this period. Even today, television shows featuring his characters are repeated each Halloween and Christmas.

Black America also had a powerful magazine voice. In 1942, using a $500 loan on his mother's furniture, John H. Johnson founded the Johnson Publishing Company. *The Negro Digest* and *Ebony* were periodicals with articles of special meaning to the black community. Later, the company expanded to include the publications *Jet* and *EM*.

ADVANCES IN MEDICINE

During this period, a whole array of new products was introduced to help fight various illnesses. For years, families in America and elsewhere had lived in fear of polio, or infantile paralysis. In the 1950s, the development of polio vaccines helped to almost eradicate the disease. In 1929, Sir Alexander Fleming discovered that a certain mold, which he called penicillin, had the ability to destroy bacteria. In the 1950s, scientists in Great Britain and America found a method of producing a synthetic version of penicillin, thus significantly lowering its cost. Almost immediately, a floodgate opened as laboratories throughout the world rushed to bring other **antibiotics** (antibacterial drugs) to the market.

Another breakthrough in medicine came when a young South African doctor, Christiaan Barnard, transplanted a heart in a human. Although the patient's body eventually rejected the transplant and died, Barnard's revolutionary surgical procedure paved the way for others. Today, heart transplants—as well as transplants of other organs—are commonplace and provide additional years to many who otherwise would not survive.

Do You Remember?

1. How did Jackie Robinson change major league baseball?
2. What is meant by "baby boom"?
3. How did television affect family life?
4. What did Sir Alexander Fleming discover?

Above: *After years of research, Dr. Jonas Salk developed a vaccine against poliomyelitis.* **Left:** *A San Diego boy receives a polio shot during the first mass inoculation following the approval of the vaccine in 1955. The boy's older sister, a polio victim, is looking on.*

CALLAWAY GARDENS

Above: A Canadian goose nests on a tiny island in the middle of one of Callaway Gardens' lakes. ***Opposite page, above and below:*** Callaway Gardens, near Pine Mountain, is justly famous for its spring display of azaleas and flowering trees.

On a sunny, warm day in 1921, Cason J. Callaway, a textile industrialist, and his wife, Virginia, were out for a leisurely drive. They were searching for a picnic site in an area south of LaGrange near Chipley and Hamilton. As they explored the area, they came upon a clear blue spring in a forested area outside Hamilton. The area became a favorite spot of the couple.

In 1930, Virginia, by then a self-taught wildflower expert, was walking through the area's woodlands and came across a wild plum-leaf azalea. She soon discovered that the rare flower bloomed only in a 100-mile radius. To protect the precious flower and other wildlife, the Callaways bought 3,000 acres, later expanding to 6,000 acres, and built a retreat cabin and lake that they called Blue Springs Farm.

In 1938, the still-young Cason, who suffered from heart problems, retired from Callaway Mills and began planting and crop experiments on the farm. His farming experiments helped other Georgia farmers of the area learn more about crop rotations and replenishing the soil. Because many friends visited the Callaways and enjoyed the area, the Callaways decided to expand their property into a recreation area. They built a golf course, a wildlife gardens area, eleven lakes, and a country store to sell products from the farm. Among visitors to Blue Springs was a neighbor from nearby Warm Springs at the Little White House, President Franklin Roosevelt, who used to sit and enjoy lively political debates with Cason.

The Callaways wanted to share their good fortune and the beauty of the area with other families. In 1952, they opened the area near Chipley and called their resort Callaway Gardens. The resort, which emphasized its natural wildlife setting, had native plantings with picnic areas overlooking them.

Callaway Gardens prospered as a popular family resort. In the mid-1960s, however, it was threatened when the state of Georgia and federal transportation officials made plans to build an interstate highway across Pine Mountain, close to the gardens. Virginia Callaway, by then a widow, believed the plans would ruin the beauty of the area. With the support of environmental groups and governmental friends, the gracious but feisty and determined Virginia Callaway fought and won her disagreement with the transportation officials. The interstate was moved about six miles away from the Callaway Gardens area.

Today, the one-time picnic spot is a resort covering over 14,000 acres. It includes both nature and biking trails, as well as other recreational areas. People come from all over to see its horticultural exhibit, which cover 5 acres with over 20,000 square feet of indoor floral display area and over 30,000 square feet of production greenhouse space. Callaway Gardens showcases the world's largest display of hollies, over 700 varieties of wildflowers, and over 400 different vegetables, herbs, and fruits. It also contains a model "Victory Garden" that is frequently seen on public television.

Cason Callaway thought some of the best ideas were those "conceived in superlatives, big in scope, impressive in appearance, and in some way connected with the improvement of mankind." According to his definition, Callaway Gardens is indeed a wonderful idea.

When the approximately 313,000 Georgia soldiers and sailors returned home after the war, they found their state in the midst of rapid change. Agriculture was no longer as dominant an industry as it had been. During the war years, many people had moved away from farms to work in wartime industries. After synthetic fabrics such as rayon and nylon were introduced, the demand for cotton fell. Trees and row crops such as peanuts, soybeans, and corn were planted in place of cotton. The use of farm machinery allowed fewer workers to produce higher yields per acre. This sent even more farm employees to cities in search of jobs.

INDUSTRIES MOVE INTO GEORGIA

After the war, industry continued to move into the state. Georgia's mild climate lured many northern industries that wanted to escape bitter cold winters, high heating costs, and transportation slowdowns caused by snow and ice. Georgia still had one weather drawback—the intense summer heat. Rich's Department Store had been the first air-conditioned building in Atlanta. Following the war, air conditioning was slowly introduced in other stores and office buildings. However, not until the 1960s were the climate controls we take for granted today installed in most businesses. And not until the 1970s and early 1980s did most homes and automobiles become air conditioned.

In addition to favorable weather, the state also had a favorable business climate. Georgia had low business and individual tax rates. In 1949, a typical Georgian paid only $38 in state taxes. Most importantly from a business owner's standpoint, Georgia was a non-union state. Workers could be hired at lower wages and with fewer labor demands than in states controlled by unions.

EDUCATION CONTINUES TO CHANGE

With more industry, larger cities, and fewer farms, education in Georgia changed. County and city school boards had been responsible for managing and financing elementary and secondary schools. A new state constitution extended schools to include grades one through twelve and, in 1949, the General Assembly passed the **Georgia Minimum Foundation Program for Education Act**. This act lengthened the school year to nine months and raised standards for buildings, equipment, transportation, and school curricula. A 3 percent sales tax was passed in 1951 to pay for these changes.

In 1946, Georgia Senator Richard B. Russell sponsored a bill in Congress that affected the entire nation. It was called the **National School Lunch Act**. The act outlined a program ensuring that school

Gainesville's Jesse Dixon Jewell was instrumental in developing Georgia's poultry industry. Today chickens and eggs rank as one of the state's most valuable commodities.

THE COLD WAR

The "Cold War" was the name given to the unfriendly relations between the United States and the Soviet Union after World War II. This Cold War was fought not with bullets but with words, diplomatic moves, and proxies.

The hostility arose for several reasons. At the end of the war, the United States and the Soviet Union were the two most powerful countries in the world. The United States expected the Soviet Union to permit free elections in the East European countries it occupied. Instead, the Soviets held them in an iron grip. Winston Churchill likened it to an "iron curtain."

The Soviets believed that communism would triumph over democracy and capitalism, and they supported communist revolutions in other nations. The United States thus feared for its security. The United States adopted a foreign policy called "containment," which was intended to prevent the Soviet Union from expanding its control over other nations. As part of this policy, the United States formed military alliances with nations on both sides of the Soviet Union. Containment led the United States into wars in Korea and Vietnam, a confrontation over nuclear weapons in Cuba, and the "arms race."

During this period, the economy of Georgia—like that of many other states—benefitted by the arms race and by the need for military preparedness. Businesses like Martin-Marietta employed thousands of workers. Military installations such as Dobbins, Warner-Robbins, and Fort Benning created employment for many other Georgians. Even textile firms were kept busy supplying clothing, sheets, and other items for the armed forces.

The Cold War ended with the breakup of the Soviet Union in the 1980s and Russia's movement toward democratic government. The fear of nuclear war has lessened, but regional conflicts are emerging all over the world.

Following World War II, Germany was partitioned by the victorious allies, with the United States, Great Britain, France and the U.S.S.R. each controlling a section. Berlin, the German capital, in the Soviet sector, was also partitioned among the four powers. In 1948, the U.S.S.R. set up a blockade of Berlin, refusing to allow trucks to drive across the Soviet sector to resupply the western sectors. The United States responded by airlifting supplies to Berlin (above). The fact that no actual fighting ever broke out is what made this a "cold" war.

children were provided nutritious lunches. It also encouraged school cafeterias to use government surplus food items such as cheese, flour, and peanut butter. Because of his work, Senator Russell is known as the "father of the school lunch program."

OTHER CHANGES IN GEORGIA

In the postwar years, other changes took place in Georgia. In 1940, less than half of Georgia's homes were wired for electricity, and only a fourth had refrigerators. After World War II, most Georgia home owners, even those in rural areas, could afford indoor plumbing and electric lights. Georgians earned more money in the 1950s and 1960s; purchasing power increased; and former luxuries, such as automatic washers and dryers, dishwashers, and televisions, became commonplace.

The introduction of inexpensive phonographs and 45 rpm records in the postwar period aided in the spread of popular culture (above), but nothing had the impact of television. This 1950s model living room (right) arranges the whole room around the television set.

GEORGIA POLITICS

Georgia politics during the early postwar years meant business as usual. But no political event in Georgia during this period got more publicity or caused greater confusion than the "Three Governors Episode."

In 1946, the successful terms of Governor Ellis Arnall were drawing to a close. Because he could not succeed himself, Georgians had to elect a new governor in 1946. The field of candidates in the Democratic primary included Arnall's arch rival, segregationist Eugene Talmadge; former Governor E. D. Rivers; and James Carmichael, who had headed the Marietta Bell bomber plant during the war. In the primary, Carmichael won the popular vote. His victory was due, in large part, to the fact that, for the first time since Reconstruction, black voters could take part in the primary election. However,

Above: *Little did the Georgia voters realize that when Eugene Talmadge paid his entry fee to run for an unprecedented fourth term as governor, the state would soon be embroiled in the "three governor episode."* **Left:** *Businessman James Carmichael campaigned hard before the 1946 election. Although he received 7,644 votes more than Talmadge, the county unit vote made "Gene" the Democratic nominee.*

Talmadge won the county unit vote, and he became the Democratic candidate.

The Republicans did not run a candidate, so the unopposed Talmadge could not lose in the November general election. Talmadge was sixty-two years old and in poor health. Because his close advisors were afraid he would not live long enough to begin his term in office, they made a secret plan.

It was decided that a few hundred selected supporters would write the name of Eugene Talmadge's son Herman on the ballot as the second gubernatorial choice. When the general election was over, Eugene Talmadge was elected governor, and Melvin Thompson was elected lieutenant governor. Shortly before Christmas, and before he was sworn in, Eugene Talmadge died, and the confusion began.

The legislature chose Herman Talmadge as governor, based on the size of the write-in votes for him—a good number of which were suddenly "found" after the election. Governor Arnall declared that Lieutenant Governor Thompson was the rightful successor. However, in the early morning hours of Wednesday, January 15, 1947, a group of Eugene Talmadge's men broke into the governor's office, changed the locks on the doors, and readied themselves to run the state.

Because he was locked out of his own office, Governor Ellis Arnall set up a temporary office at the Capitol information counter. Three days later, with news cameras flashing, Arnall officially resigned. In the meantime, Lieutenant Governor Thompson opened an office in downtown Atlanta and began legal proceedings to become governor. The government was in a state of total confusion.

Above: Herman Talmadge (center, to right of smiling woman), just after the state legislature put him in the governor's seat. ***Right:*** Herman Talmadge (left) and Melvin Thompson (right), could both answer "Yes"' when someone called out "Mr. Governor."

After Herman Talmadge forcibly took over the governor's office, Ellis Arnall set up his office at the information booth in the capitol rotunda (top). Three days later he resigned (above).

Secretary of State Ben Fortson refused to give the official state seal that is used for legalizing documents to either Talmadge or Thompson. As a result, no one was in a position to run the state. The national news media had a field day reporting Georgia's political chaos.

Finally, in March, the Georgia Supreme Court ruled that Thompson was the rightful head of state until a special election could be held in 1948 to fill the unexpired term of Governor-elect Eugene Talmadge. In that election, and again in 1950, Herman Talmadge was legally elected as Georgia's governor. Nevertheless, the "Three Governors Episode" would be remembered for years to come.

Do You Remember?

1. What caused the demand for cotton to fall after the war?
2. How much did the typical Georgian pay in state taxes in 1949?
3. Who was known as the "father of the school lunch program"?
4. Why was it thought that Eugene Talmadge would win the general election after the Democratic primary was over?

THE KOREAN WAR

At the end of World War II, Korea was divided along the thirty-eighth parallel of latitude. The United States supervised the government of South Korea, and the Soviet Union that of North Korea. On June 25, 1950, North Korea invaded South Korea, hoping to make one unified communist country.

Seventeen United Nations countries immediately sent troops to South Korea to stop the North Korean invasion forces. The U.N. troops, led by divisions of American soldiers that included 75,000 Georgians, pushed the North Korean troops back almost to the border of China. However, the United Nations forces were not prepared when China's huge army came to North Korea's aid. There seemed to be no way to avoid another world war.

After many attacks and counterattacks, a battle line was drawn between the two countries in July 1951. Truce talks between the United States and the Soviet Union began shortly afterward, but the war dragged on for two more years. Peace was declared in July 1953, with no clear victor.

The Korean War was a costly one, with 2,500,000 killed or wounded. Of those killed, 25,000 were Americans and over 500 were Georgians. Today, Korea still remains divided along the thirty-eighth parallel, and some United States troops are still in South Korea to help with its protection.

The stark contrast of a country faced with a liberating army on one side and fleeing refugees on the other is a literal picture shown here during the Korean War. What do you think were the feelings of both sides?

Do You Remember?

1. Which troops occupied North Korea?
2. Who sent troops into Korea after the invasion of South Korea?
3. How many Georgians fought in Korea?
4. Who won the Korean War?
5. What is the status of Korea today?

THE FIGHT FOR CIVIL RIGHTS

African-American military men found little change in attitudes toward blacks during World War II. Blacks had been placed in segregated military units. In southern training camps, black troops met much discrimination, both on and off base. As the nation prepared for war, most war industry jobs went to whites. To protest this treatment, A. Phillip Randolph, president of a black railway workers union, planned a march on Washington for June 1941. To head off the march, President Roosevelt agreed to form a Fair Employment Practices Committee. This committee encouraged war industries to hire blacks. By the end of the war, blacks were working in every war industry.

The president also helped blacks get better positions in the military. He approved the promotion of Benjamin O. Davis to general, the first black to reach that position. Roosevelt also ordered flying schools and officer training units established at a few black colleges.

Harry S Truman, who became president upon Roosevelt's death, was equally determined to protect civil rights. In 1946, he set up the President's Committee on Civil Rights to study the problem of discrimination. Two years later, in 1948, Truman signed an executive order that outlawed racial segregation in the armed forces. By the time of the Korean War, blacks and whites were serving in the same units. The **Federal Housing Act** was passed in 1949. It banned racial discrimination in federally financed housing. However, no matter how important these measures were to the cause of civil rights, it was in the field of education that the most far-reaching changes were to occur.

A year earlier, in 1948, **Dixiecrats** had walked out of the Democratic National Convention. This group of southerners, who were led by J. Strom Thurmond of South Carolina, were protesting the inclusion of a civil rights plank in the party's platform.

THE SUPREME COURT AND EDUCATION

You should recall from reading in an earlier chapter that in 1883, the United States Supreme Court ruled against the Civil Rights Act of 1875 and legalized the doctrine (principle) of "separate but equal." According to this doctrine, segregation was not against the law if blacks and whites were treated equally. In 1896, the Court upheld this decision in the case of *Plessy v. Ferguson*.

The period from 1945 to the present has been a time of racial unrest, but also of civil rights progress. This demonstration, in front of Atlanta City Hall in 1947, protested the lack of black policemen.

THE NAACP AND THE FOURTEENTH AMENDMENT

Jubilant attorneys capture a historical moment on the steps of the United States Supreme Court after the high court rules in their favor in Brown v. Board of Education, *ending school segregation. Left to right: George Hayes, Thurgood Marshall, and James Nabrit, Jr. Which attorney of this landmark case went on to become a Supreme Court Justice?*

The Fourteenth Amendment to the U.S. Constitution required states to treat people equally under the law. But in 1896, the U.S. Supreme Court ruled in *Plessy v. Ferguson* (see page 420) that separate facilities could be provided for African Americans if they were equal to those provided whites. In a 1938 case *(Gaines v. Missouri)*, the Court further ruled that states had to provide equal educational facilities for all citizens within the state.

By the late 1930s, the National Association for the Advancement of Colored People (NAACP) decided to use the Fourteenth Amendment to show that separate facilities were rarely equal. The NAACP determined that it would be easier to prove the inequality between all-black and all-white law schools. Thurgood Marshall led those efforts.

In 1950, the NAACP supported Herman Sweatt's application to the University of Texas law school. Texas had a separate law school for blacks, but the U.S. Supreme Court reasoned that the University of Texas law school had better facilities and a better faculty and would provide the opportunity for Sweatt to associate with influential whites. The Court ordered Sweatt admitted.

Similar reasoning was used to strike down segregated public schools. In the 1954 *Brown v. Board of Education* case, the Court ruled that segregated schools could never be equal. It reasoned that segregated schools caused black students to feel inferior, an argument advanced by NAACP lawyers. Thus did the NAACP use the courts to secure equal treatment in education for African Americans.

In 1935, the National Association for the Advancement of Colored People (NAACP) began the fight to end segregation in schools. Thurgood Marshall, who later became a U. S. Supreme Court justice, and Charles Houston, presented NAACP-supported cases in many of the twenty states where schools were still segregated.

In 1950, seven-year-old Linda Brown, a black student, tried to enroll in an all-white school in Topeka, Kansas. When entry was denied, the NAACP helped Brown's father sue the Topeka Board of Education. The case, referred to as **Brown v. Board of Education**, reached the Supreme Court in May 1954. After careful review, the Court said separate-but-equal schools were illegal. It ordered racial integration of schools "with all deliberate speed." After nearly sixty years of court-approved segregation, the ruling in the *Plessy* case was finally overturned. Although the Court had spoken, many states, however, were slow to carry out its orders.

FEDERAL TROOPS SENT TO LITTLE ROCK

On September 4, 1957, nine black students tried to enroll in an all-white high school in Little Rock, Arkansas. They were blocked by the Arkansas National Guard, which had been called out by Governor Orville Faubus. President Dwight D. Eisenhower responded by sending 10,000 federal troops to enforce the court-ordered desegregation for Little Rock's schools. On September 25, after several tense days with both federal and state troops present, the nine students were admitted to Central High School.

GEORGIA RESISTS SCHOOL DESEGREGATION

In Georgia, most of the state's school systems refused desegregation. Indeed, the opposition to desegregation was so deeply felt that the General Assembly voted in 1955 to cut off state funds to any system that integrated its schools.

Ernest Vandiver, who became governor in 1959, was elected, in part, on his promise to keep Georgia's schools segregated. However, in 1960, the Georgia General Assembly recognized change was at hand. It organized a fourteen-member commission, headed by Atlanta banker John Sibley, to study the problem of integration.

The Sibley Commission held hearings all over the state to learn how the public felt about integration. Reaction was swift and direct. By a three-to-two margin, Georgians said they would rather close schools than integrate them. The commission recommended that local school

Although segregation had been outlawed by the U.S. Supreme Court, integration was far from peaceful. What type of courage do you think it took for the nine African-American students to enroll in Little Rock, Arkansas' all-white Central High School?

Above right: Feelings in Georgia ran high during the mid 50s and early 60s. Pro-segregation rallies like the one seen here in 1959 in front of the governor's mansion were commonplace.
Above: Franklin county resident Samuel Ernest Vandiver was Georgia's governor from 1959-1963 during the most turbulent years of integration.

systems be allowed to decide if they would abide by a probable court order to integrate public schools or, instead, close them. In many communities, private schools were opened to avoid the issue.

GEORGIA BEGINS TO INTEGRATE SCHOOLS

Despite resistance from many states, including Georgia, the Supreme Court and United States district courts held their ground. On January 6, 1961, the University of Georgia, with the backing of Governor Vandiver, allowed its first two black students to be escorted into the school by state patrol officers. Although there were some student protests and the two had to walk to classes amid the cry, "two, four, six, eight—we don't want to integrate," they overcame the hostility facing them. One of these two black pioneers was Charlayne Hunter who graduated from the Henry W. Grady School of Journalism and later, as Charlayne Hunter-Gault, became a nationally known newspaper and public television reporter. The other was Hamilton Holmes, who was installed in Phi Beta Kappa, graduated with honors from the university, and later went on to practice medicine as an

Left: *Students Charlayne Hunter and Hamilton Holmes leave campus at the end of their first day. After leaving the University of Georgia, Charlayne Hunter Gault went on to become a respected journalist, and national correspondent on the McNeil-Lehrer Report news program. Hamilton Holmes became a doctor.*

Although the integration of Georgia schools was a slow process, it was, by and large, a peaceful process. Here you see counselor Dorothy Morrison showing Mary McMullen her new locker at Atlanta's Grady High School in 1961.

orthopedic surgeon in Atlanta until his death in 1995.

Many university alumni and Georgia politicians had pleaded with Governor Vandiver to close the university rather than allow the two students to enroll. Refusing to bend to pressure, the governor instructed the president of the university, Dr. O. C. Aderhold, to open the doors. This move by the governor shocked and angered many Georgians who had voted for the Lavonia resident based on his pledge to not integrate the state's schools.

During the heated discussions that followed, Vandiver admitted that he had been wrong in his pre-election speeches. After the two students were enrolled, he went even further. The governor went before the legislature and requested that other segregation laws in Georgia be repealed. Vandiver's actions were one of the main reasons that Georgia's subsequent efforts at desegregating schools were calmer and smoother than those in many others school systems in both the South and North.

Not only was the University of Georgia integrated in 1961, the state's largest school system also began token integration in that year. The Atlanta City School System allowed nine black students to enroll in a formerly all-white high school. The peaceful integration of four high schools by the end of the year prompted President John F. Kennedy to praise the system. During the next three years, the courts ordered all systems in the state to integrate schools. After the **Civil Rights Act of 1964** passed, the federal government refused federal funds to any system that did not end segregation. Some chose to take the cut in funding, but integration continued to come about across the state.

In 1969, the United States Department of Justice filed suit against the Georgia State Board of Education, demanding that the state withhold funds from systems that refused to follow court-ordered desegregation plans. Communities moved to comply with federal laws, and, by 1971, all Georgia's public schools were integrated. This made Georgia the first state with a sizable black population to have a statewide integrated school system.

Do You Remember?
1. When was racial segregation outlawed in the armed forces?
2. What Supreme Court case led to school integration?
3. Who were the first two black students to enroll in the University of Georgia?

THE MONTGOMERY BUS BOYCOTT

The successful desegregation of transportation systems in the South began at 5:30 p.m. on Thursday, December 1, 1955, and, along with it, a movement that would forever change race relations in America.

Rosa Parks, a middle-aged black seamstress was "bone weary" from a long day of work. She boarded a Montgomery, Alabama, public bus, paid her fare, and sat down in the first empty seat just behind the "whites only" section. At a stop by a theater, six white passengers got on the bus. There were no vacant seats in the "whites only" section, so the driver then ordered all blacks to move to the back. Three rose to move, but Mrs. Parks stayed where she was. The driver called for a policeman. Mrs. Parks was arrested, booked, fingerprinted, and briefly jailed. She had violated a city ordinance that gave bus drivers the right to decide where passengers sat. Her trial was set for December 5.

Frequently, reporters have asked Mrs. Rosa Parks the origin of her bravery when she refused to give up her seat on a Montgomery, Alabama, bus. She replied that she was just tired. However, her simple gesture of defiance, which led to the Montgomery Bus Boycott, would ultimately change the civil rights struggle forever. Here, Mrs. Parks and her attorney are seen on the way to the Montgomery courthouse.

Rosa Parks was a former officer in the Montgomery chapter of NAACP. News of her arrest quickly spread among the 50,000 members of the black community. A group of black ministers gathered to talk about ways to support her. They asked Atlanta-born Martin Luther King, Jr., to be their spokesperson and agreed to hold a one-day bus **boycott** (refuse to use) on the day of Mrs. Parks' trial.

On Sunday, December 4, black ministers and civic leaders asked that all blacks stay off the buses on Monday. Even though Rosa Parks was found guilty, the bus boycott was 90 percent successful. The black community was encouraged to continue the boycott until the following demands were met: Black passengers would be treated with courtesy; black drivers would be assigned to primarily black routes; and seating would be on a first-come, first-served basis. The protest organizers eventually were successful. Rosa Parks, who wanted only to be treated like a human being, won a place in history as well as a seat on the bus.

A NONVIOLENT MOVEMENT IS BORN

Dr. Martin Luther King, Jr., the leader of the bus boycott, began making speeches all over the city in support of peaceful protest. Car pools were formed in black neighborhoods, and black-owned taxi cabs charged only a dime for a ride to or from work. In a matter of weeks, the city's bus revenue fell by 65 percent.

In March 1956, three months after the boycott started, Dr. King and eighty-nine other black leaders were found guilty of violating an outdated 1921 antilabor law forbidding boycotts. They appealed their convictions. In November, the city went to court again, demanding an end to the car pools and asking to be paid for the money lost on bus service.

As the trial date approached, Dr. King was afraid a victory for the city would undo eleven months of progress made through peaceful protest. He entered the courtroom on November 13 to face the same judge who had found Rosa Parks guilty. About noon, a reporter handed Dr. King a teletyped message from one of the national news services. The United States Supreme Court had just upheld a district court ruling that made segregation on public transportation unconstitutional. When the Supreme Court decision officially reached Montgomery on December 21, 1956, Dr. King and a white minister boarded a city bus and rode through the streets without incident. The Montgomery bus boycott was over, but the movement for civil rights was just beginning.

Above: Today, visitors can return to 522 Auburn Avenue N.W. in Atlanta to see the childhood home of civil rights leader, Dr. Martin Luther King, Jr. Opposite page: This portrait of Dr. Martin Luther King, Jr., by George Mandus, hangs in the state capitol as a memorial to his civil rights leadership.

A TRADITION OF PROTEST

The success of the Montgomery bus boycott thrust Martin Luther King, Jr., into the national spotlight. Dr. King was a third-generation minister who had grown up with a tradition of protest. He was born on January 15, 1929, the second of three children. He lived in Atlanta and attended Booker T. Washington High School. The school was Atlanta's first black secondary school and had been built largely because of the protest efforts of Dr. King's grandfather, A. D. Williams, and other black leaders.

In 1944, when he was fifteen, Dr. King entered Morehouse College as a special student. Morehouse President Dr. Benjamin Mays was among the men who influenced the young man. King was ordained to the ministry at Ebenezer Baptist Church in 1947, after which he enrolled at Crozer Theological Seminary in Pennsylvania. After graduating with honors from Crozer in 1948, he earned a doctorate in theology from Boston University. While in Boston, he met and married Coretta Scott from Marion, Alabama, who was studying at the New England Conservatory of Music.

During his years of study, Dr. King developed a nonviolent approach to social change. He based his ideas on the writings of Henry David Thoreau, the author of *On Civil Disobedience*, and on the teachings of India's Hindu leader, Mahatma Gandhi. King first practiced nonviolence during the Montgomery bus boycott. He was aided by other ministers and civic leaders, including Edward Nixon and the Reverend Ralph Abernathy.

King called the boycott a conflict "between justice and injustice." He believed in a four-pronged approach for gaining civil rights for all Americans: direct, nonviolent actions; legal redress; ballots; and economic boycotts.

Encouraged by the success of the boycott, King carried his message of a nonviolent approach to social change to other parts of the South. He moved to Atlanta in January 1960 as head of the **Southern Christian Leadership Conference** (SCLC), a group he helped form the year before. Dr. King often traveled two or three thousand miles a week spreading the message of nonviolence.

During the early 1960s, King held lunch counter "sit-ins" to protest the segregation of department and chain-store lunch counters in the South. A **sit-in** is a type of demonstration where people enter a public building and refuse to leave until they are served. In 1952, Rich's Department Store had been the site of the first Georgia sit-in, where King was joined by Julian Bond, Lonnie King, and other students from Morehouse College. Fifty of the students were arrested. However, their efforts continued in spite of antitrespass laws passed by the Georgia General Assembly making sit-ins illegal.

Before the Civil Rights Bill of 1964 was passed, African-Americans frequently had to drive miles out of their way to find a motel or hotel that would accept them. Sometimes they were forced to sleep in their cars if accommodations were not available. In 1963, one of the many non-violent protest demonstrations took place at Atlanta's Grady Hotel.

ALBANY BECOMES CENTER OF CIVIL RIGHTS ACTIVITY

In 1961, Albany, Georgia, became a center of civil rights activity. This primarily farming community had a population that was about 40 percent black. Six years after *Brown v. Board of Education*, Albany schools were still segregated. Only a small number of African Americans were allowed to register to vote.

On November 1, 1961, the Interstate Commerce Commission backed the Supreme Court decision prohibiting segregation in interstate bus and train stations. Workers with the NAACP and **Student Nonviolent Coordinating Committee** (SNCC) decided to test the ruling by sitting in the "whites only" waiting room at the city's bus station. They were quickly arrested. This prompted the black community to unite and form the Albany Movement, which was led by Dr. William Anderson.

In December, black and white "freedom riders" arrived in Albany to support the Albany Movement. They were arrested at the Central Railway Terminal. The next day, SNCC organizer James Forman led a march of black high school students to the same train station. The students were arrested and jailed while members of the national press watched. At one point during the months of protest in Albany, five

Albany, Georgia, became the site of many demonstrations in the early 60s. Here police carry a protester down the steps of the Albany Public Library. However, arrest or threats of jail did little to dissuade those protesting to gain their civil rights. Today, Albany continues to progress in maintaining positive race relations in the city.

hundred people were either in jail or out on bond. Black leaders arrested included Dr. King and Reverend Abernathy, who had traveled to Albany to ask city officials for a meeting to resolve the dispute. Before the year's end, a biracial committee was formed to study concerns of the black community in Albany.

The United States District Court for the Northern District of Georgia heard the case of *Baker v. Carr* in May 1962. On May 25, the court ordered the state to redistrict and **reapportion** (redistribute) one house of the legislature on the basis of population. A called session of the Georgia General Assembly decided that the senate would be reapportioned. The state was divided into fifty-four districts. After the redistricting, Fulton County, where Atlanta is located, had seven senatorial districts. This change eliminated the county unit system.

It also gave predominantly black population areas an equal opportunity to elect legislative representatives. In a 1962 senatorial election, Atlanta attorney Leroy Johnson became the first African-American state senator in Georgia since Reconstruction.

PROTEST MOVES TO BIRMINGHAM, ALABAMA

In April 1963, Dr. Martin Luther King, Jr., began a campaign in Birmingham, Alabama, to end discrimination in all areas of that city's public life. For several nights, television news showed attempts to control demonstrators with attack dogs and high-pressure fire hoses. Over three thousand persons, including Dr. King, were arrested.

The bombing of the Sixteenth Street Baptist Church in Birmingham, Alabama, on September 15, 1963, shocked the nation. The racial rioting that followed the bombing led to two more deaths. The mayor appeared on television and appealed to the citizenry to end "this senseless reign of terror."

On September 15, 1963, during Sunday School at Birmingham's Sixteenth Street Baptist Church, a bomb killed four black children and injured fourteen others. Even though a riot followed the tragedy, many blacks and whites joined together to stop further violence. One of those individuals was Atlanta's Reverend Austin Ford, who ran Emmaus House, an inner-city mission. He was one of a small group who supported and encouraged the integration of churches in the 1960s. Other supporters, some lawyers, and even a few judges joined with white students from the North and South. In their own way, all did what they could to help the effort. Some died for their beliefs.

"I HAVE A DREAM"

President John F. Kennedy sent the strongest civil rights bill in history to Congress on June 19, 1963. It called for an end to discrimination in public facilities, assurance of fair employment and voter registration practices, withholding of federal funds from projects where discrimination was practiced, and the authority of the attorney general of the United States to file suit against school districts where desegregation had not been carried out.

Congress did not pass the bill quickly and, on August 28, 1963, over 250,000 people representing all races, creeds, and nationalities gathered before the Washington Monument to demonstrate for its passage. As they stood together, Martin Luther King, Jr., made one of the most remembered speeches of his career.

. . . I have a dream that one day this nation will rise up, live out the true meaning of its creed: "We hold these truths to be self-evident, that all men are created equal." I have a dream that one day on the red hills of Georgia sons of former slaves and the sons of former slaveowners will be able to sit down together at the table of brotherhood. I have a dream that one day even the state of Mississippi, a desert state sweltering with the heat of injustice, sweltering with the heat of oppression, will be transformed into an oasis of freedom and justice. I have a dream that my four little children will one day live in a nation where they will not be judged by the color of their skin, but by the content of their character. . . . Let freedom ring from Stone Mountain of Georgia. . . . Let freedom ring from every hill and molehill . . . from every mountainside. Let freedom ring. When we let freedom ring—when we let it ring from every village and every hamlet, from every state and every city, we will be able to speed up that day when all God's children, black men and white men, Jews and Gentiles, Protestants and Catholics, will be able to join hands and sing in the words of that old Negro spiritual, "Free at last! Free at last! Thank God almighty, We are free at last!"

On August 28, 1963, the largest crowd ever to assemble in front of the country's capitol came to demonstrate their commitment to the passage of the Civil Rights Bill. Dr. Martin Luther King, Jr., rewarded them with the greatest speech of his career.

Do You Remember?

1. Whose arrest led to the Montgomery bus boycott? Why was this person arrested?
2. What Indian leader influenced Dr. King's nonviolent approach to social change?
3. Who was the first black to become a Georgia state senator since Reconstruction?

THE ASSASSINATION OF JOHN F. KENNEDY

The morning of November 22, 1963, President and Mrs. Kennedy and Vice President and Mrs. Johnson attended a breakfast gathering in Fort Worth. Afterward, they flew to Dallas, an eight-minute plane flight, with the President and the Vice President, as was customary, flying in separate planes. At the Dallas Airport, President and Mrs. Kennedy joined Texas Governor John Connally, Jr., to begin the fateful drive into the city.

At 12:30 p.m. on November 22, 1963, President John F. Kennedy and his wife Jacqueline were riding in a motorcade through the streets of Dallas, Texas. Without warning, shots were fired. The forty-six-year-old president slumped down in the seat of the open limousine with a massive head wound. He was immediately taken to Parkland Hospital, but, thirty minutes later, President Kennedy died without regaining consciousness. A little over an hour and a half later, on the presidential jet that carried Kennedy's body back to the nation's capital, Vice President Lyndon B. Johnson was sworn in as the thirty-sixth president of the United States.

A stunned and shocked nation mourned its tragic loss. Several days later, as millions watched on television, alleged assassin Lee Harvey Oswald was being moved from one jail to another. Jack Ruby, a Kennedy supporter from Dallas, walked up to Oswald and shot him at point blank range. By this act, Ruby ended all chances of anyone knowing with certainty why the president had been killed.

PRESIDENT JOHNSON PUSHES CIVIL RIGHTS ACT

In a speech to Congress shortly after Kennedy's assassination, President Johnson vowed to continue fighting for the earliest possible passage of the civil rights bill that President Kennedy had supported. Under President Johnson's leadership, and with the political pressure of both black and white supporters, the Civil Rights Act of 1964 became law. This was the most far-reaching and important civil rights legislation since Reconstruction. Basically, the "equal protection of the laws" clause of the Fourteenth Amendment was given greater influence. It made segregation of all public facilities illegal. This included restaurants, theaters, hotels, public recreational areas, schools, and libraries. It also prohibited discrimination in businesses and labor unions.

In spite of the Civil Rights Act, blacks in many sections of the South still could not vote. Dr. Martin Luther King, Jr., who had been awarded the Nobel Peace Prize in 1964, began to turn his attention to voting rights.

Twenty-five people crowded into the cabin of the late President's jet as it stood on the runway of Love Field in Dallas ninety-nine minutes after President Kennedy was pronounced dead. The wife of the former President watched as Judge Sarah Hughes administered the oath of office to Vice President Lyndon B. Johnson, a former farm boy, teacher, and great-grandson of Georgian Jesse Johnson.

In the summer of 1964, "Freedom Summer," people from all over the country came to the South to help blacks register to vote. Much effort was made by SNCC, a group that included Georgia's Julian Bond as one of its founders and Georgian John Lewis as its national chairman. During the voter registration drive, three young men, two black and one white, were killed in Mississippi. This again drew national attention to the South.

In March 1965, Dr. King met with civil rights leaders in Selma, Alabama, to plan demonstrations and marches in support of voting rights. As he led marchers to the Dallas (Alabama) County courthouse, King and over five hundred students were arrested and jailed.

King planned a march from Selma to the state capital in Montgomery to call attention to the cause of voter's rights. On March 7, over six hundred marchers approached the Edmund Pettus Bridge that spans the Alabama River. There, they met about 200 state troopers armed with billy clubs and tear gas. The marchers fell back into Selma, followed by the county sheriff's mounted posse.

Dr. King went to Montgomery to request a march permit, which was granted by a United States district judge. President Johnson activated the Alabama National Guard and sent army troops, federal marshals, and FBI agents to Selma to protect the marchers.

Left: Georgia's John Lewis (seated center) leads a sit-in at the Mississippi state capitol in 1965. *Above:* Dr. King leads the Selma to Montgomery March in 1965. King told the group that, "We are on the move and no wave of racism will stop us."

On March 21, more than 4,000 Americans of different races, led by Dr. King and Rabbi Abraham Herchel, began the fifty-mile walk to Montgomery. About 25,000 others joined the group in Montgomery to complete the march to the Alabama state capitol in support of equal voting rights.

The march influenced Congress to pass the **Voting Rights Act of 1965**. Within a year and a half, a million southern blacks were added to the registers of voters.

In 1966, the Georgia House of Representatives votes to deny a seat to Julian Bond because of his criticism of the war in Vietnam and his association with SNCC. The United States Supreme Court later ordered that Bond be reinstated to his representative's seat in the Georgia General Assembly. Two years later, Bond's name was placed in nomination as a Democratic vice presidential candidate, but he had to refuse because he was not old enough to qualify as a candidate.

A SHIFT IN MOOD

After the march from Selma to Montgomery, the mood of many seeking equal civil rights changed. These people abandoned the moderate, nonviolent approach of Dr. King to follow much more aggressive activists such as Stokely Carmichael, H. Rap Brown, and Eldridge Cleaver. A militant (radical) group called the Black Panthers emerged. In the summer of 1967, riots and burnings of black communities began in places like Watts in Los Angeles, California; Detroit, Michigan; and Newark, New Jersey.

Dr. King and his supporters urged an end to violence. On April 3, 1968, King was in Memphis, Tennessee, to organize support for 1,300 striking sanitation workers. There had been threats on King's life, but he said,

It really doesn't matter what happens to me now because I've been to the mountain top . . . and I've looked over and seen the promised land. I may not get there with you. . . . But we, as a people, will get to the promised land. . . . Like anybody, I would like to live a long life. Longevity has its place . . . but I'm not concerned about that now.

The next day, Thursday, the 39-year-old King was on the balcony of a Memphis motel talking with Jesse Jackson, standing below. A shot from a high-powered rifle left Martin Luther King, Jr., dead at the hands of an assassin. His followers mourned the passing of their leader.

On March 11, 1969, James Earl Ray, a forty-year-old high school dropout, was tried and convicted for King's murder. He was sentenced to ninety-nine years in prison.

The movement toward civil rights for all Americans did not die with Martin Luther King, Jr. It continued through the work of many others, including Mrs. Coretta Scott King, Dr. Ralph Abernathy, Reverend Jesse Jackson, and Georgia political leaders Andrew Young, John Lewis, and Julian Bond. The movement for equality and fair treatment for all Americans continues today with new leaders and new participants, building on the contributions of those who came before.

Do You Remember?

1. When was John F. Kennedy assassinated?
2. What prize was awarded to Dr. Martin Luther King, Jr., in 1964?
3. What bill did the march from Selma to Montgomery influence Congress to pass?

SUMMARY

- Members of the armed forces returned home after World War II to a changing society.
- Life for most Americans was prosperous and contented.
- In Georgia, many left farms for work in the cities.
- Not all, however, shared in the prosperity.
- The continued struggle for civil rights for blacks led to the court-ordered integration of schools in Georgia and the rest of the nation.
- Nonviolent protests against discrimination, led by people such as Martin Luther King, Jr., included bus boycotts, marches, and sit-ins.
- President Kennedy was assassinated, and Lyndon B. Johnson carried out many advances in civil rights, including the Civil Rights Act of 1964 and the Voting Rights Act of 1965.
- Dr. King continued to work for civil rights until he, too, was assassinated.

On April 4, 1968, Martin Luther King, Jr., was shot to death on the balcony of the Lorraine Motel in Memphis. The motel is now a civil rights museum.

	1950 United States entered Korean War	**1955** Montgomery bus boycott	**1961** Black students enrolled in University of Georgia	**1963** President Kennedy assassinated

1947
Jackie Robinson
signed as first
black in major
league baseball

1954
*Brown v. Board
of Education*

1957
Federal troops sent
to Little Rock

1964
Civil Rights
Act passed

1945	**1950**	**1955**	**1960**	**1965**

1950
Senate McCarthy
hearings held

1954
U.S. sent first
advisors to Vietnam

1959
Alaska and
Hawaii
admitted as
states

1962
Lunch-counter sit-ins
staged throughout the
South

Reviewing People, Places, and Terms

Use the following in a paragraph or two describing the civil rights movements:

Brown v. Board of Education
Martin Luther King, Jr.
Rosa Parks
President's Committee on Civil Rights
sit-in
Student Nonviolent Coordinating
Committee

Understanding the Facts

1. What was Harry S Truman's motto?
2. Who wrote the short story "A Good Man is Hard to Find"?
3. Which doctor performed the first heart transplant in a human?
4. What 1949 act lengthened the school year in Georgia to nine months?
5. Who won the popular vote in the 1946 campaign for governor?
6. Who was the first black promoted to general?
7. What were the Dixiecrats protesting when they walked out of the 1948 Democratic National Convention?
8. Which man, who later became a U.S. Supreme Court justice, presented many of the NAACP-supported cases during this period?
9. What happened at Birmingham's Sixteenth Street Baptist Church on September 15, 1963?
10. In what city was Martin Luther King, Jr., assassinated?

Developing Critical Thinking

1. In what areas have you seen improvement in race relations during your lifetime?
2. What have been the positive effects of busing as a means of eliminating segregation in the schools?
3. Affirmative action programs have come under increasing criticism in recent years. Many white males claim they are victims of a form of "reverse discrimination." What is reverse discrimination? Do you agree or disagree with the criticism of affirmative action programs?

1. Many people and organizations important to the civil rights movements are mentioned in this chapter. Prepare a report on one group or person. Share your findings with the class.

2. Obtain a copy of the U.S. Constitution and the state constitution. Compile a list of the civil rights granted to citizens in each document. How do the two lists overlap? What are the differences?

3. Prepare a short report on one of the Georgia writers mentioned in this chapter.

Making Connections

1. Do you think the United States finally "won" the Cold War? Why or why not?

2. What problems have developed for the countries that once made up the Soviet Union?

3. Why was the decision in *Brown v. Board of Education* so important?

4. Why do you think that the doctrine of "separate but equal" facilities could never be fair?

Did You Know?

• For years in Atlanta and other towns throughout the South, blacks had a separate entrance to theaters and were seated in special sections such as the balcony.

• The "Pips" of the group Gladys Knight and the Pips were named after a relative who was nicknamed "Pip" because he was a "pip of a man," meaning he was dapper and stylish.

• Otis Redding wrote a song called "Respect" that Aretha Franklin reworked and called "R-E-S-P-E-C-T," which was one of her biggest hits.

• One of the Callaway's children, Howard H. "Bo" Callaway became Georgia's first Republican congressman since Reconstruction.

BUILDING SKILLS: READING NEWS ARTICLES

Newspapers are a good way for citizens to keep informed on a wide range of topics—local, national, or international. First, however, you must distinguish a news article from an editorial. Editorials mix facts and opinions and give a newspaper's opinion on an issue or event. A news article does not include opinions.

Newspaper articles usually follow a standard format. The *headline* is written in large, bold type with just a few key words. Its purpose is to capture the "heart" of the story and make you want to learn more. The size of the type often indicates the story's importance. The *byline* indicates who wrote the story, either an individual or a news service. The *dateline* includes the date and city where the story was filed. The *lead* is the first sentence of the article—the most important. It summarizes the main idea of the article and should tell you the five W's: *who, what, where, when,* and *why*. The *body* contains a more detailed account of the basic facts.

The body often contains quotations and background facts. As you read through the article, you will find less and less important details.

Look at any daily newspaper and select one of the major stories on the front page. Answer the following questions:

1. From reading just the headline, can you tell why the editors chose to put the article on the front page?

2. Who wrote the story and where was it filed?

3. What are the *who, what, where, when,* and *why* of the story?

4. After reading the article, do you think the headline accurately represented the information in the article?

Try This! Reread this chapter and choose an issue on which to write a news article. Write the article first, then the headline.

A grateful mother welcomes her son home from the 1991 Persian Gulf War, the first major, post-nuclear conflict in this century.

CHAPTER SIXTEEN

A FUTURE FILLED WITH PROMISE

We must adjust to changing times and still hold to unchanging principles.

—Plains School Teacher Julia Coleman,
quoted by President Jimmy Carter

THE ASSASSINATION OF MARTIN LUTHER KING, JR., may have temporarily slowed progress towards civil rights for people of color, but it certainly did not end it. Throughout the remaining years of the 1960s and the decades up to the present, major efforts were made to continue working toward the realization of Dr. King's dream.

The latter part of the 1960s and the early 1970s also saw the continuation and intensification of the struggle for women's rights and a wave of protests against a war in Vietnam. Subsequent decades also saw a major change in social behavior, a rise in terrorism, the collapse of the Soviet Union and its allies, and the threat of a new and terrifying disease. As Georgia and the rest of the nation enter the twenty-first century, many new challenges must be met with hope and with solutions.

A PERIOD OF PROTESTS AND CHANGES

The late 1960s and the early 1970s were periods of frequent demonstrations by young people against a variety of issues, ranging from the war in Vietnam to public morality. Many of these protests were fueled by singers like Bob Dylan and Joan Baez who mixed traditional ballads with antiwar and pro-civil-rights activist lyrics.

Hippies, young people who painted their vans in vivid colors, dressed in outrageous clothing, and often wore flowers in their hair (thus they were called "flower children") basically opposed any issue that the established system supported. At first, these antiestablishment

Terms: women's rights movement, affirmative action programs, National Organization for Women, National Women's Political Caucus, Equal Rights Amendment, credibility gap, terrorism, global warming, genes, Centers for Disease Control, cloning, gentrification, HOPE scholarship program

People: Betty Friedan, Gloria Steinem, Timothy McVeigh, Terry Nichols, Zell Miller

Places: Bay Street, Factor's Walk, Virginia Highland, Little Five Points, "Sweet Auburn," Underground Atlanta

and antiwar young people were an amusement to some and a bewilderment to most of their parents. But as their indulgences continued unchecked, this period marked the beginning of a widespread drug culture that was to plague the nation for decades to follow.

Music also began to change as new, loud rock bands such as the Byrds, the Rolling Stones, the Doors, and the Who became wildly popular. For three days in August 1969, close to a half million young people converged on a farm in New York called Woodstock, where for seventy-two hours they carried on a free-for-all party of nonstop music and celebration.

THE WOMEN'S RIGHTS MOVEMENT

Protests for expanded civil rights and against the war in Vietnam were not the only cause of dissension in the nation during the late sixties and early seventies. The rights of women and the roles they would play were rapidly changing. Women, who had always received less pay than men for the same jobs, began to demand equal pay for equal work. To raise people's consciousness of their situation, women pointed out how deep-rooted certain gender-biased practices were. For example, they called for changes in terminology that they felt reflected a male-dominated society. Soon a term such as *chairman* was replaced by such neutral terms as *chair* or *chairperson*. *Ms.* became a common form of address for single women, where an individual's marital status was unknown, or whenever a woman showed a preference for it. To get their message across, some women also pointedly refused to allow men to open doors for them, to stand aside so that women could precede them into an elevator, or to automatically reach for a check in a restaurant.

The real accomplishments of the women's rights movement, of course, were far more important than mere questions of etiquette and propriety. The **women's rights movement** reflected major changes in the way women viewed themselves and their contributions to society.

In colonial America, women worked beside men in social and economic activities and were considered equal partners. Yet men were the heads of the households and the political and religious leaders, and women were regarded as inferior to men.

As America changed from an agricultural to an industrial nation, the idea of separate "spheres" of activity for men and women developed. Men's sphere was working in industry, while women's sphere was in the home. Women were expected to be morally pure and to maintain the home as a haven for their husbands and children. Motherhood was considered the highest status that a woman could achieve or desire, and women were expected to pass on their "purity" to their children. These ideas were expressed in the phrase *true womanhood*.

By 1900, woman began to reject the idea of true womanhood. They wanted to help solve the many social problems that harmed homes and the family. Through their participation in clubs and organizations, women demanded better public education and health care, separate prisons for juvenile delinquents, prohibition, an end to child labor, and the right to vote. Men welcomed women's help in the effort to reform society, accepting them into a limited public sphere where home and family were affected. They helped women get the right to vote and get elected to office. This was the era of the "new woman" who began to take on limited public duties and worked outside the home in occupations considered to be "woman's work."

World War II was another major watershed in changing gender roles. Millions of men went off to war, and their civilian jobs were filled by women. Demonstrating their ability to do "man's work," women gained confidence that they could do many things besides clerk, type, nurse, teach, and tend house and children. When the war ended, many women wanted to continue to work outside the home. Some did, but others were expected to give up their war-time jobs and turn them over to men.

By the 1960s, many women were unhappy with their lot. The Civil Rights Act of 1964 made it illegal to discriminate against women in hiring practices. Federal **affirmative action programs**, designed to provide work opportunities for women and minorities, opened up some jobs to women. Still, most were not being treated fairly at work. They were discriminated against, and their pay was not equal to men's pay for the same work. Most women held traditional women's jobs. Leadership positions in business were generally closed to them.

Not only were women discriminated against in the workplace, they also were discriminated against in other places. Banks often refused to grant a woman credit without her husband's cosigning a loan. Single women, including widows, were often unable to obtain credit—no matter what their level of income. Many women, therefore, were unable to buy a home, lease an apartment, buy an automobile, or take out a credit card in their own names. When making major purchases or even taking the family car in for repairs, women

During the two World Wars, women proved they could do many different kinds of jobs, like these women in a World War I airplane factory (top). Now, women hold many jobs, in fields like construction, that in the past had been traditionally reserved for men.

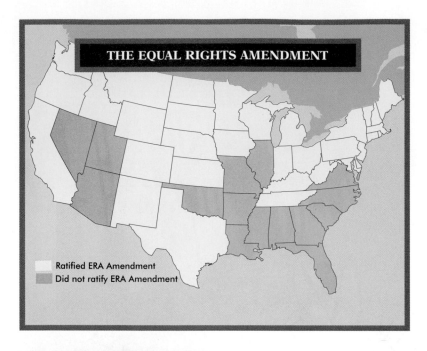

THE EQUAL RIGHTS AMENDMENT

☐ Ratified ERA Amendment
☐ Did not ratify ERA Amendment

were often asked for the approval of the "man of the house."

Women wanted equal acceptance into the American society, and they organized to secure the treatment they felt they deserved. Writers such as Betty Friedan and Gloria Steinem published books and magazine articles urging change. Some women joined the **National Organization for Women** (NOW), which worked for legal and institutional changes to benefit women. Some also joined the **National Women's Political Caucus** to get more women into political office. These organizations and others supported a drive to add an **Equal Rights Amendment** (ERA) to the U.S. Constitution. The proposed amendment read: "Equality of rights under the law shall not be denied or abridged by the United States or by any state on account of sex."

Not all women agreed with the goals and methods of the women's rights movement. While most women believed that the goals of equal pay and open career opportunities were just, they disagreed on how to best achieve these goals. Some women argued that extreme feminists looked down on all men and on women who elected to remain in their homes, raising their children while their husbands provided the family's finances. Many believed that the traditional differences between men and women should be respected and encouraged.

In 1970, Congress voted to send the proposed amendment to the states for ratification. Three-fourths of the state legislatures (or 38 of 50) had to approve the amendment before it became law. During the fight for ratification, both sides were loud and vocal. However, by June 30, 1983—the deadline for its ratification—the proposal still lacked the necessary approval. The ERA failed by three state votes.

Above: *Many rallies were held for and against the Equal Right Amendment. Ultimately, it fell three states short of ratification.* ***Opposite page:*** *As American soldiers slogged through the rice paddies of Vietnam, the nation was dividing over America's involvement in the war.*

THE WAR IN VIETNAM

Americans were deeply divided over the war in Vietnam. At first, America's involvement in the conflict was limited to providing money and a small group of advisors to help the government of South Vietnam withstand the invaders from North Vietnam. Within a few years, however, the United States stepped up its involvement. As fighting escalated, more and more American troops were sent until, by the end of 1965, there were 185,000 troops fighting there.

The initial philosophical differences which grew from the Vietnam War gave way to anger, violence, demonstrations, and the burning of draft cards and flags. On October 21, 1967, 50,000 antiwar demonstrators gathered around the Lincoln Memorial in Washington, D.C. Soon demonstrators stormed the Pentagon across the Potomac, clashing with military police.

Back home, hundreds of thousands of Americans—including key members of Congress and the administration—protested U.S. involvement in what they considered an "illegal" war. In November 1969, a protest demonstration was staged in Washington, D.C. On some college campuses, violent confrontations between National Guard troops and student protestors erupted. Negative news coverage of the war increased, as did the numbers of young people seeking to evade being drafted to fight a war in which they did not believe.

After his election in 1968, President Richard Nixon promised to bring American troops home. He tried to force the communists to negotiate by increasing bombings. As a result, thousands more were killed and injured. Sentiment against the war grew even stronger.

Finally, in January 1973, a cease-fire was declared, bringing America's involvement in the war to an end. More than 2,000,000 Vietnamese and 57,000 Americans had been killed. At least 1,200 Americans were missing. There was no clear victory, although the government of North Vietnam now occupied all of the country and continues to do so.

THE EFFCTS OF THE VIETNAM WAR

The Vietnam War was one of the most socially and politically divisive wars in American history. This was the first "televised" war. Americans could see what was happening on the evening news and compare that with what the government was telling them. The two were not always the same. Television helped increase opposition to the war and distrust of government.

This distrust increased in the late 1960s and early 1970s as American casualties rose and there were revelations of Americans killing Vietnamese civilians. The distrust fueled antiwar sentiment and led federal and state governments to use heavy-handed methods to suppress the war's opponents. Belief that the war was necessary to contain communism waned.

The war caused great problems for the military. Civilian leaders would not let the military invade North Vietnam or Laos. They feared that China would enter the war. Military leaders believed that they were fighting at a disadvantage. Disrespect for the military increased as young men burned draft cards or fled to Canada. In 1973, Congress found it necessary to end the draft and depend on volunteers. Returning veterans were met with scorn and hostility.

The war led to a reluctance to use military force. People feared being drawn into another long and divisive war. It was not until the Persian Gulf War of 1991 that the American people again supported large-scale military action.

One legacy of the Vietnam War was a reluctance to get involved in foreign wars. That changed in 1991, when Iraqi dictator Saddam Hussein's army invaded oil-rich Kuwait. Although some felt that the Gulf War was more about protecting America's oil supply than liberating Kuwait, these Georgia troops got a rousing welcome home.

Do You Remember?
1. What were affirmative action programs designed to do?
2. How many states were needed to approve the Equal Rights Amendment?
3. When was the cease-fire ending the war in Vietnam declared?

THE "CREDIBILITY GAP"

For most of this century, Americans were confident that the people who governed them were, more often than not, working for the greater good of all. Confidence was severely shaken after the war in Vietnam. It was further weakened when the investigation by Congress of the Watergate affair revealed illegal activity by members of President Nixon's staff and a subsequent cover-up involving the president himself. Many Americans, particularly the young, began to lose faith in their leaders and, unfortunately, to show distrust for authority of any kind. A new term, the **credibility gap**, was used to describe the difference between what many people believed to be true and what their leaders told them was true. As a result, the 1970s and the decades that followed were marked by a breakdown in traditional codes of behavior. Disrespect for authority—whether in the government, the school, the church, or the home—was flaunted. People of all ages felt free to say anything they wanted to anyone anywhere, no matter how offensive. Magazines, films, television, and songs directed to this young audience thrived and fed the discontent of the nation's youth.

President Nixon is beseiged by reporters seeking information about Watergate, the scandal that would eventually drive him from office. It was the first time in the nation's 198-year history that an American president had resigned from office.

Professional and career demands have caused many in America's work force to be more mobile, frequently moving to new job locations for short periods of time. Many young people, therefore, are separated geographically from their parents, grandparents, and other family members. The community family of relatives who traditionally shared in child-rearing tasks and who lived near one another became a thing of the past. In the 1990s the term *dysfunctional families* was used to describe a variety of family situations. Among these were families where parents are not available to rear and supervise children, families headed by separated or divorced parents, and families facing multiple and often conflicting job stresses and expectations.

DRUGS, VIOLENCE, AND CRIME

One unfortunate and continuing manifestation of the breakdown in morality and disrespect for authority has been the soaring rise in incidents of crime and violence, particularly those involving juveniles.

WATERGATE

In June 1972, police arrested a group of men for breaking into and "bugging" the Democratic National Committee offices at the Watergate building in Washington, D.C. Investigating newspaper reporters discovered that some of the burglars had worked for a committee to re-elect President Richard Nixon. Nixon denied any connection between the burglary and the White House. However, the newspaper investigative teams probed further and were able to uncover additional information that pointed to attempts at the highest level of government to cover up the incident.

When the burglars were tried in early 1973, one of them talked. What emerged was a story of the abuse of power by the White House. There were other burglaries, illegal wiretaps, reading of private mail, and illegal campaign contributions directed out of the White House.

During its investigations, the Senate committee headed by Senator Sam Ervin of North Carolina discovered that Nixon tape-recorded all of his Oval Office conversations. President Nixon continued to deny any involvement in Watergate and refused to give up the tapes. Eventually the Supreme Court ruled that the president had to turn over the tapes. When the tapes were reviewed, they showed that President Nixon knew of the Watergate burglary and had tried to cover it up. A number of people connected to the administration were convicted of Watergate-related crimes. The House of Representatives prepared to impeach President Nixon, but he resigned on August 8, 1974. The new president, Gerald Ford, pardoned Nixon rather than see him tried in criminal court.

The Watergate affair had a serious impact on Americans. It showed first and foremost that no person was above the law, not even the president. The affair also caused Americans to become more cynical about their government, a situation that continues today. And it popularized the practice of using investigative reporting teams to dig up and use all sorts of information to attract the eye of the reading and television viewing public. This practice has undoubtedly uncovered news items about which the public should be aware. However, it also has led to charges of the invasion of an individual's privacy and the trampling of his or her rights all in the cause of the public's "right to know."

Senator Sam Ervin of North Carolina was the chairman of the senate Watergate committee. The committee's televised hearings kept millions riveted to their T.V. sets during 1973.

JAMES EARL CARTER, JR.

Above: *With a population of less than 700, Plains, Georgia, was thrust into the national spotlight as the election headquarters and hometown of presidential candidate Jimmy Carter.* **Opposite page:** *The Plains peanut farmer who served as Georgia's governor and then as the 39th President of the United States is also known for his concern, interest, and work for those in need.*

James Earl "Jimmy" Carter was the first Georgian to become president of the United States. He was born in Plains on October 1, 1924, and grew up on his parents' southwest Georgia peanut farm. Carter attended Georgia Southwestern College and Georgia Tech before receiving an appointment to the U. S. Naval Academy. After graduation, he was assigned to the Pacific Fleet. Later, Carter went to Union College and studied physics.

Carter was elected governor in 1970 and, during his time in office, reorganized the state's executive branch, cutting government agencies from about 300 to 22. However, strife between Carter and Lt. Governor Lester Maddox made many of his efforts unsuccessful. By the end of his term, Carter's popularity had declined greatly. Many Georgians were surprised when he announced himself as a candidate for the 1976 Democratic presidential nomination, and won.

Americans upset by Watergate and President Gerald Ford's pardon of Richard Nixon were searching for a leader who was honorable, hard working, and earnest. Jimmy Carter fit that description. When the electoral votes were counted, Carter had defeated Ford 297 to 240. The unknown candidate reporters had dubbed "Jimmy Who?" was the first president from the Deep South since the Civil War.

As president, Carter will likely be best remembered for the Camp David Accords. This series of meetings was held at the presidential retreat, Camp David, between leaders of Israel and Egypt. These sessions, in which Carter acted as mediator, led to the first ever peace treaties between the two warring nations.

In addition, Carter developed a foreign policy emphasizing worldwide human rights. He appointed more women and minorities to federal judgeships and policy positions than any previous president.

Although some statistics indicate that in the late 1990s, certain types of crime were dropping off, crime and violence is still a major concern of people in both cities and rural areas. Throughout the United States, citizens are calling for speedier and stricter enforcement of laws as well as stronger punishment of those who commit crimes, especially repeat offenders.

Clearly related to the increase in crime and violence is the increase in the use of alcohol and other drugs. Sadly, the use of alcohol and other drugs is being found among all age groups, including those in elementary and middle schools. As more and more young people become involved in the use of alcohol and other drugs, they too become either the victims or provokers of crimes and violence.

Increasingly, however, communities are beginning to strike back. Many localities have established programs to reclaim their neighborhoods from drugs, violence, and crime. These programs include neighborhood watches, increased police surveillance, and—in some instances—the destruction of abandoned buildings known to attract criminal elements. Schools, of course, have played a major role in the fight against drugs, violence, and crime. In some districts, school hours have been extended to offer alternatives for students who might otherwise be unsupervised. Various courses at all levels, including those in health education, driver education, and science, provide information about the perils and pitfalls confronting today's youth. Cooperative efforts that involve schools, parents, and local law enforcement agencies have been successful in many communities. In addition, nationwide programs, such as Drug Abuse Resistance Education (D.A.R.E.), have also proven effective.

Because high rates of absenteeism and dropouts are often related to incidents of violence and crime, many feel that one way of reducing them is by increasing students' motivations to remain in school. In some particularly troubled areas, the creation of programs that tie student learning and skills to actual attainable jobs has led to dramatic outcomes. Because students know that their classroom instruction will help them secure employment within their community, their attendance rate has risen, and violence and crime have gone down.

General Barry McCaffery was appointed the nation's "Drug Czar" by President Bill Clinton. It is his job to direct the country's war against drugs.

Do You Remember?

1. After what two events was the confidence of many Americans in their leaders shaken?
2. What three types of programs have been established by localities to reclaim their neighborhoods from drugs, violence, and crime?
3. To what are high rates of school absenteeism and dropouts often related?

OTHER SOCIAL AND POLITICAL DEVELOPMENTS

The period from the 1970s to the present day has been marked by events that already have significantly changed our state and nation. Moreover, many of these events undoubtedly will continue to have a major effect on our lives in the years to come.

THE COLLAPSE OF THE SOVIET EMPIRE

Since the late 1940s, much of the nation and the world was under the cloud of threats to peace and stability from the Soviet Union and its allies. Most thought that the eastern bloc of nations would continue as a power for many years to come. Suddenly, in the later 1980s and early 1990s, the Soviet empire quickly and dramatically fell apart. The former Union of Soviet Socialist Republics broke up into a number of independent countries—including Russia, Belarus, Ukraine, Kazakhstan, and Georgia. Each in its own way attempted to deal with the novelties of freedom and democracy. Other members of the eastern bloc, such as Hungary, Poland, and Romania, also became independent and democratic. The people of Czechoslovakia and Yugoslavia chose to break up their countries and form "new" nations based on different ethnic groups and old boundaries. The wall between East and West Germany fell, and the two Germanies were united.

The breakup of the former eastern bloc was not without problems. Several of the republics of the old Soviet Union clashed, and some of these conflicts continue. At different times, troops from the United States as well as those from the United Nations have been called to maintain peace in the area.

The fall of the Soviet Union and the end of the Cold War had other effects on Americans, including those in Georgia. Vast amounts of

For almost thirty years, the Berlin wall was a symbol of the Cold War. In November 1989, East German citizens tore the wall down.

money were no longer needed to protect against the Soviet threat. As a result, many defense-related industries either closed or significantly trimmed personnel. In addition, many stateside military bases were closed or scheduled for closing, thus affecting the economy of the communities surrounding them.

THE RISE OF TERRORISM HERE AND ABROAD

As Cold War fears diminished, a new threat to peace and stability emerged: terrorism. The term **terrorism** refers to the actions of one group or individual designed to spread fear by committing acts of violence and destruction or by threatening to commit them. Overseas, international terrorists—many of whom are believed to be controlled by anti-American groups in the Middle East—have blown up planes, killed Olympic athletes, and bombed U.S. embassies and military installations. In this country, terrorists exploded a bomb in the basement of New York's World Trade Center, killing five and injuring over 1,000 people.

On April 19, 1995, 168 men, women, and children were killed when a truck bomb exploded at the Murrah Federal Building in Oklahoma City. It was the worst act of terrorism in the history of the United States.

Wanton destruction leading to the loss of innocent lives is not limited to international terrorists. On April 19, 1995, a truck bomb exploded at the Alfred P. Murrah Federal Building in Oklahoma City. Americans Timothy McVeigh and Terry Nichols were convicted of the act which killed 168 people, including children in a daycare center.

A single individual, Theodore Kaczynski, who over the years became known as the "Unabomber," was responsible for a series of deadly mail bombs. These bombs, which maimed and—on some occasions—killed those who opened the packages, were addressed to various people associated with organizations with which Kaczynski had a grievance of one kind or another. Violence in schools has become a major concern. Incidents such as the one in Littleton, Colorado, have resulted in student deaths.

The U. S. government has responded by making such threats a federal offense. In addition, federal, state, and local governments have had to implement security measures at the nation's airports and many public buildings.

ENVIRONMENTAL ISSUES

Concern for the environment has also been a major issue during the past several decades. Measures to improve air and water quality have in certain areas led to stark changes. Some polluted rivers and lakes have been reclaimed (returned to their original state), and in many communities throughout the nation smog has been greatly reduced. Global warming, however, worries many. **Global warming** is the overall increase in temperature as a result of various factors, including the discharge of carbon dioxide into the atmosphere. Legislation, including Clean Air acts passed in 1970 and 1990, has addressed ways of reducing air pollution. Among these methods are those that call for "cleaner" fuels, especially for automobiles; stricter controls on industries that discharge toxic wastes into the air; and the ban against certain refrigerants and aerosols.

Steps have also been taken to improve water quality. These include the passage of safe drinking water legislation; the reduction of the runoff of fertilizers into rivers, lakes, and streams; the cleaning up of our nation's shorelines; and the elimination of pollutants that have threatened our nation's supplies of finfish and shellfish.

SCIENCE AND MEDICINE

Significant advances were made in science and medicine during this time, advances that offer the promise of a longer, healthier life to many. Other advances, however, have led to new moral issues.

Medical researchers have discovered new ways of treating illnesses such as Alzheimer's and Parkinson's diseases. They have devised tests

Timothy McVeigh (above center), an anti-government extremist, was convicted and sentenced to death for the Oklahoma City bombing. McVeigh was arrested within hours of the explosion —for driving a car with expired license plates.

Atlanta's Centers for Disease Control is the nation's headquarters in the fight against communicable diseases like AIDS, which was unknown until the early 1980s.

for the early detection of certain forms of cancer. In some cases, they have found ways to reduce cancer fatalities. Researchers are also looking into the possibility that cancer, as well as many other disorders, result from defective **genes**, the body's building blocks. They believe that once they identify the specific genetic cause of a disease, methods can be developed to alter the gene or even "trick" it into behaving differently and prevent the disease.

Sometimes, however, the detection of a disease and the organized approach to dealing with it can be clouded by other, nonscientific issues. In the early 1980s, the public became aware of a new and terrifying disease that was attacking and, all too often, killing people in many of the nation's urban areas. Because at first many thought the disease was localized to a specific population and that it was not easily spread, organized efforts to control it were slow in coming. By the mid-1980s, however, it became apparent that the disease, now given the name Acquired Immune Deficiency Syndrome (AIDS), not only was contagious but was also affecting people of all ages throughout the nation and elsewhere.

Much of the early work on this disease was carried out in the **Centers for Disease Control** in Atlanta. Scientists there and in other laboratories in the United States and elsewhere were able to locate the source of the disease and its methods of transmission. As a result of their efforts, new medicines have been developed to control the disease. Equally important, programs have been established to educate the public about its dangers.

Recently, attempts at **cloning** (duplicating) animals have been successful. The success, however, has raised far-reaching religious, ethical, and scientific issues over the implications of genetic "tinkering."

Do You Remember?

1. What are five independent countries that were formed from the dissolved Soviet Union?
2. What groups are believed by many to be behind many international terrorist activities?
3. What three methods of reducing air pollution are among those addressed in the Clean Air acts of 1970 and 1990?

GEORGIA AT THE END OF THE TWENTIETH CENTURY

Georgia and its people also have experienced tremendous change in the past several decades. The state has become more urban and faces many of the same problems as other states with a large urban population. As people move into the state from other parts of the nation and world, they introduce new ideas and ways of looking at things. As a result, religion and politics have been transformed. And to keep pace with a changing world, Georgia's schools also are different from what they once were.

GROWTH OF THE STATE AND ITS CITIES

By the late 1990s, Georgia was the fourth fastest growing state in the nation. It had grown by 2 percent each year, and its population was conservatively estimated to reach 10 million by 2025. Because of the state's appealing quality of life, job opportunities, and support of education at all levels, more exact forecasts are difficult to come by.

A large percentage of Georgia's population is found in the metro-Atlanta area that includes Fulton, Gwinnett, DeKalb, Cobb, Rockdale, Clayton, and Douglas counties. Other metropolitan areas of the state are Chatham (Savannah), Richmond (Augusta), Bibb (Macon), and Muscogee (Columbus) counties. Altogether, these urban areas contain over 50 percent of the state's population.

The trend of movement away from inner cities to suburbs that began in the 1960s and 1970s has continued. As a result, the state's greatest expansion has been in suburban commercial and residential

Georgia's population is conservatively estimated to reach 10 million by 2025. A large percentage of Georgia's population is found in the metro-Atlanta area (above) that includes Fulton, Gwinnett, DeKalb, Cobb, Rockdale, Clayton, and Douglas counties. Georgia's urban areas contain over 50 percent of the state's population.

growth. At the same time, sections of cities that had once been virtually abandoned have been revived by people returning and upgrading neighborhoods through a process sometimes referred to as **gentrification**.

Georgia's growth in population is important for a number of reasons. Federal monies allocated to a state increases as the state's population increases. So, as Georgia grows, money from the federal government also grows. In addition, as the state grows, it gains additional seats in Congress. A more populous Georgia, therefore, translates into a state with greater political influence.

PROBLEMS OF CITIES

With the growth of cities, however, also came problems. As suburbs grew, traffic clogged the central city. Businesses moved to the suburbs, which among other things offered abundant free parking. As fewer people came into the downtown area, the central city declined and crime increased. People no longer felt safe and they, along with the businesses that had remained to serve them, also moved away. Streets and doorways were occupied by the homeless, many of whom in earlier days might have been institutionalized.

Once thriving and vital parts of the central city were largely abandoned to decay and crime. In many cities, this abandonment lasted

Downtown revitalization is an important priority in many cities. Underground Atlanta, a group of shops on three levels (only one of which is actually below ground) was an early success. The underground level was a Civil War marketplace.

for decades, with each succeeding year seeing more and more decline. Lately, however, some cities have tried to revitalize (give new life to) their downtown areas by building new convention centers in them, converting old warehouses and mills into sites for retail businesses, and urging people to relocate in them. Savannah, for example, has revived its historic waterfront by the renovation of warehouses along Bay Street and Factor's Walk. In Atlanta, restored neighborhoods such as Virginia Highland, Little Five Points, and "Sweet Auburn" draw many visitors and natives. Earlier, Atlanta had success with Underground Atlanta, a group of shops on three levels (only one of which is actually below ground). The underground level was a marketplace before the Civil War and was built over railroad tracks that met to form what was the heart of antebellum Atlanta.

EDUCATION

Each weekday morning, approximately 1 million students begin another day of classes in Georgia's schools. School population varies from an average daily attendance of 300 in some counties to over 70,000 in metropolitan Atlanta.

There are problems, however. Georgia still continues to rank high on the list of states with a large number of school dropouts. In addition to being at risk to the problems of drugs, crime, and violence discussed earlier in this chapter, these young adults are further handicapped. With minimal educational skills and job training, they enter a job market that increasingly calls for a fairly high level of skills.

These students at Spalding Elementary School in Sandy Springs are a few of the approximately one million students that go to school in Georgia.

Other areas of educational concern continue to be inadequate teaching salaries, funding for new programs, the acceptance of standardized testing scores as a method for evaluating schools, and the equality of educational opportunity in every part of the state. However, even in these areas there have been major improvements in recent years.

Perhaps the most significant changes in recent years have come about as a result of the efforts of Governor Zell Miller to implement a state lottery. Although many people disagree with the concept of a lottery, profits from it have been directed into education and school technology. Under Governor Miller's leadership, lottery funds went into a statewide preschool program. Now Georgia's schools serve

AND THE RAINS CAME DOWN

Some blamed it on *El Nino*. Others blamed *global warming* or the "hole in the ozone layer." In truth, it was the aftermath of a tropical depression from tropical storm *Alberto*. The national news media referred to it as "The Great Flood of '94," and it was a time of suffering, devastation, and shining example of neighbors helping neighbors.

On Monday, July 4, 1994, as Georgians prepared for parades, picnics, and fireworks to celebrate the nation's birthday, storm clouds gathered in Southeast Alabama. However, there was little to indicate that the forecast rains would be anything like the summer floods of 1993 in the Midwest that had killed 50 people and left over 70,000 homeless in states along the Mississippi River.

Tropical storm *Alberto* had not made hurricane status, for the winds were only about 54 miles per hour. From the Florida panhandle, the storm slowly meandered northward into Alabama and then into west-central Georgia. The stormfront stalled, and a rainy annoyance became a life-threatening situation. Rainfall measured over 10 inches in some areas like Irwinton and Buena Vista, and over 28 inches in Americus between July 1 and July 7. All across the state, cities and towns battled the rising waters and overflowing rivers.

Before the storm moved away, over 1200 roads and 600 bridges were out of operation. Some 55 Georgia counties were declared federal disaster areas. Albany and Americus were virtually under water. Newton and Montezuma were overrun as the Flint River rose above its banks. By the time the flood waters began to recede, 30 people had lost their lives; 40,000 had been evacuated from their homes; and over 400,000 acres of farmland were covered with water.

The combined losses in Georgia, Alabama, and Florida topped $1 billion. Perhaps one of the most painful losses from the floods was caused by sinkholes that formed in area cemeteries, unearthing over 900 coffins.

Citizens throughout the country joined those more fortunate Georgians in donating money, time, and resources for those suffering from the floods. Many helped by serving meals or taking in the homeless. Others rushed drinking water, food, and medicines to the victims. Cleanup efforts were made far easier with the help of federal agencies, the Red Cross, and Salvation Army volunteers. Neighbor helped neighbor, and no task was too small the year the rains came down.

The "Great Flood of '94" did more than $1 billion worth of damage in Georgia, Florida, and Alabama. This aerial view is of Montezuma, Georgia.

students at ages three, four, and up. The governor also allocated funds for improvements in technology to ensure that all schools throughout the state had adequate computer and satellite technology despite different levels of local funding support.

Governor Miller pushed for higher teacher salaries during each year of his term in office. As a result, Georgia, which was once near the bottom of the national salary scale, is now at the upper level of the scale for other southeastern states. He also supported higher education and worked with the Board of Regents in expanding the state's university system of community and technical colleges, four-year colleges, and research universities.

The **HOPE scholarship program** begun under Governor Miller provides scholarships to cover tuition and books for Georgia high school graduates. As long as students maintain minimum grade point standards, they can use these scholarships in any state college, technical school, or university. In addition to providing educational opportunities, the HOPE program enhances job preparation and training to support a stronger, better equipped work force to lead Georgia's economy.

Newt Gingrich served as Speaker of the House of Representatives from 1994 to 1998. One of eight Republican congressmen from Georgia, Gingrich resigned as speaker and as Representative in 1998.

POLITICS

Along with many other parts of the nation, Georgia's politics have changed over the past several decades. Once virtually a one-party state controlled by the Democratic party, the state has increasingly shifted to the Republican party. The state continued to elect a Democrat as governor as it has for over 125 years, and it elected a Democrat, Max Cleland, to succeed Sam Nunn. However, where once both of Georgia's two U.S. senators were Democratic, now only one is. And of the eleven members of the Georgia's delegation to the U.S. House of Representatives, eight are Republican. Moreover, much the same kind of shift in party allegiance has occurred at other levels throughout the state.

Do You Remember?

1. What percent of Georgia's population lives in urban areas?
2. Profits from what source of revenue have been directed to education and technology programs in Georgia's schools?
3. All of Georgia's governors for the past 125 years have been members of which political party?

Severely wounded in the Vietnam War, Democrat Max Cleland served as Director of Veterans Affairs in Washington, D.C., before winning Sam Nunn's senate seat in 1996.

SUMMARY

- The period from the late 1960s through much of the 1970s was marked by frequent, often violent, protests.
- Among the protestors were members of the women's rights movement, who called for long-overdue changes in the way their roles in society were viewed.
- The Vietnam war greatly divided the American people, many of whom believed that the war was illegal and that their leaders were not being forthright.
- In the wake of the war and the Watergate affair, a credibility gap arose between those in authority and the general public.
- As a result, many—especially young people—developed a distrust for authority that spilled over into a breakdown in the traditional codes of behavior.
- The soaring use of drugs, including alcohol, among people of all age groups intensified the split and led to a rise in crime and violence.
- On the international scene, however, things improved: the Soviet Union collapsed, and it and its former allies created new nations based on democratic principles.
- Terrorist acts, often claiming innocent victims, increased both internationally and within our country.
- As Georgia entered a new century, it and the rest of the country faced a whole new array of problems as well as a new set of hopes.

CHAPTER REVIEW

| 1973 Cease fire declared in Vietnam | 1974 Nixon resigned and Gerald Ford sworn in as president | 1981 First incidents of AIDS reported | 1989 Soviet empire collapsed | 1995 U.S. terrorists destroy federal building in Oklahoma City |

1976
Jimmy Carter
elected president

1970   1980   1990   2000

1988
George Bush
elected
president

1984
Reagan
re-elected

1996
Atlanta hosted Summer
Olympic Games

Clinton re-elected

1973
Vice President
Agnew resigned
amid charges of tax
evasion

1974
Ford named Nelson
Rockefeller as vice
president

1980
Ronald Reagan elected
president

1992
William Clinton
elected president

1994
Newt Gingrich named speaker of
the U.S. House of Representatives

Reviewing People, Places, and Terms

Define, identify, or explain the importance of each of the following.

1. affirmative action programs
2. cloning
3. credibility gap
4. Equal Rights Amendment
5. genes
6. gentrification
7. global warming
8. HOPE Scholarship Program
9. terrorism

Understanding the Facts

1. What 1969 event attracted close to a half million young people to a farm in upstate New York?
2. What major changes did the women's rights movement reflect?
3. What worldwide event is considered to be a watershed in the changing gender roles?
4. Why did the proposed Equal Rights Amendment fail to become part of the U.S. Constitution?
5. What was the result of President Nixon's plan to force an early peace in Vietnam by increased bombings?
6. What was one effect of the entry of women into the work force in relation to their school-age children?
7. What is global warming?
8. What kinds of issues have been raised over the implications of genetic "tinkering"?

Developing Critical Thinking

1. Do you believe the so-called credibility gap played a major role in the breakdown in morality and respect over the past several decades? Support your answer.
2. The schools in Georgia derive many benefits from the monies directed to them through lotteries. Nevertheless, many people believe that it is wrong to get money from an "immoral" act such as gambling. What do you believe? Share your answer with your classmates.
3. What do you consider to be the most critical social problem facing Georgia at this time?
4. What can individuals do to slow down the damage to the environment?

Applying Your Skills

1. Obtain recent statistics showing the incidents of specific crimes in the nation, Georgia, and your community over the past ten years. Choose three crimes such as auto theft, robbery, assaults, breaking and entering, and so on. Create a bar chart that compares the rate of each crime in the three areas, using a different color for each level of community.

2. Prepare a short report on the changes in the roles played by women in the 1950s and today. Do you think these changes would have come about without women's movements?

3. Research the major environmental problems in the state of Georgia. Choose one and tell what steps are being taken to solve this problem. What would you recommend? Share your findings with the class.

Making Connections

1. President Nixon resigned as a result of the Watergate affair. Prepare a report on what might have happened had he not resigned.

2. Interview someone who remembers the Watergate controversy. What did he or she believe was the most important outcome?

3. Survey five adults who lived through the Vietnam War. Ask them whether they believe America should have been involved in the war. Share your findings with your classmates.

4. Interview a Vietnam veteran. Find out how he or she felt about American reaction to our participation in the war.

Did You Know?

- At a student antiwar demonstration at Kent State University in Ohio, National Guardsmen brought in to control the crowd became nervous and fired into it—killing four and wounding eight.
- In 1981, Sandra Day O'Connor became the first woman to sit as a U.S. Supreme Court justice.
- In 1984, Geraldine Ferraro became the first woman to be nominated as a vice presidential candidate by a major political party.

BUILDING SKILLS: COMPARING COSTS AND BENEFITS

One of the responsibilities state and local governments have assumed is to provide essential services for the people. Examples of these services include education, environmental protection, road construction and repair, and health services. None of these services is, of course, free, and one of the ways to raise revenue to pay for the services is by levying taxes. The property tax and sales tax are two taxes used by state and local governments.

While citizens are usually willing to accept increased services, the decision to raise taxes is often met with resistance. Lawmakers are increasingly being forced to choose between services they can provide with limited revenues. One way to decide is to compare the costs and benefits of each service. Generally, the benefits that a community expects to receive from a particular service should outweigh the costs to provide that service.

This is not as easy as it sounds; not all benefits or costs can be measured in monetary terms.

Suppose you are a member of the governing body of your local community. Suppose too that your community provides the following services: police and fire protection; trash removal; schools; public libraries; parks and recreational facilities; road building, maintenance, and repairs; emergency management; licensing and inspection services. For this exercise, assume that the cost of each service is $1,000. Your community expects annual revenues to be $7,000 from the property tax this year. How would you deal with the shortage? You may wish to form a "committee" of several classmates to discuss your options.

Can you think of any services for which you would be willing to pay higher taxes? If so, list them and give your reasons.

CHAPTER SEVENTEEN

GEORGIA'S ECONOMY

An economist is an expert who will know tomorrow why the things he predicted yesterday didn't happen today.

—Laurence J. Peter

THE NATION and the state of Georgia have seen much economic growth and change since the end of World War II. Technology, particularly the introduction of computers, has spurred much of this economic growth. During the past decades, Georgia has moved from an agricultural to an industrial and service economy. With the help of state programs and various forms of aid, industry has also become more diversified, depending less on textiles and cotton. Moreover, jobs in the service sector—once a relatively small slice of the state's economic pie—have increased greatly.

GEORGIA'S DIVERSIFIED ECONOMY

In the 1800s and much of the first half of the 1900s, Georgia was mostly a one-crop agricultural state. Its present-day economic development is fairly recent. During World War II and for a period shortly afterward, there was a brief spurt of economic growth. Then the state experienced a slowdown that lasted until the late 1970s and early 1980s.

Today, Georgia has a strong, **diversified economy**—an economy with a variety of businesses or industries in which people work. Many of these businesses and industries are **interdependent**. In other words, they depend upon each other to succeed.

For example, on a given street a factory that makes parts for airplanes might be next to a fast-food restaurant. Across the street, there might be a bank, a flower shop, and a bookstore. Although their products and services are quite different, each of these places needs the others in order to succeed.

Factory workers might eat lunch at the restaurant or deposit their paychecks at the bank. On the way home from work, they might buy flowers for a friend or purchase a book at the bookstore.

In addition to handling checking accounts, the bank might lend money to the florist to enlarge its greenhouse. In return, the florist might pay the bank a fee, called *interest*, on the money it borrows.

Atlanta's Hartsfield Airport is the second busiest in the world. Every year more than 39 million people travel to or through Atlanta. Delta Airlines uses Atlanta as its southeastern hub. In addition, some 25 other airlines operate direct flights to 14 countries from Hartsfield.

ADVANTAGES OF A DIVERSIFIED ECONOMY

The advantages of a diversified economy are especially evident in times when certain businesses or industries experience trouble. If one industry faces problems, the overall economy may still be able to do fairly well. In earlier days, when the state was dominated by one industry, threats to that industry—such as the threat boll weevils posed to agriculture in the early 1900s—could bring about major economic problems statewide. Now things are quite different. With diversification, temporary setbacks in one **sector** (part) of the economy are offset by growth in another.

Georgia did not suffer as much from the recession of the early 1990s as did many other states. In large part, this was due to an increase in foreign investments in the state and to the selection of Atlanta as the site of the 1994 and 2000 Super Bowls and the 1996 Olympic Games. These two events pumped millions of dollars into the state's economy. Before the events took place, many workers were employed by all sorts of businesses to build the various facilities needed to host the events. Stadiums had to be built, roads improved, and additional hotels erected to accommodate the expected visitors. Visitors spent a great deal of money in the state, not only to attend the events, but also on hotels, food, and transportation. All of this added greatly to the state's economic well-being at a time when some other parts of the state's economy were not faring as well.

ECONOMIC INDICATORS

There are several ways of getting an economic picture of a nation or state. One way is to look at the number of people employed in different industries and the amount of income earned by the workers in these jobs. This method may provide an overall view of the different sectors of the economy at a given time. However, the number of people employed and the amount of income made changes every day. So a snapshot of the economy taken on one day may be vastly different from one taken on another day. For example, income from retail stores may be relatively high during holiday seasons and drop considerably in the following months.

Another way of measuring the economy of a nation or state is to look at its **per capita income** (the average annual income earned by a worker). Again, while this method may be useful for some purposes, it shows only part of the picture. A few people in the nation or state may have enormous incomes, while the majority of workers may be barely able to provide for themselves and their families on what they earn. When all the incomes are added together and divided by the total number of wage earners, a much rosier picture of the economy may emerge.

HELPING BUSINESSES DO BUSINESS THROUGHOUT THE WORLD

Since the beginning of modern history, the nations of the world have been trading with each other in one way or another. From its earliest days, America has been especially affected by international trade. Indeed, the discovery of America came about in a large measure because of the desire of Europeans to find shorter, more direct routes to the riches of the East. In colonial times, the craving of merchants in Britain, France, and other overseas nations for such New World products as cotton, tobacco, and forestry products, led to the establishment and growth of our major seaport cities. In the 1800s and 1900s, our country's amazing industrial output made the United States the leading supplier of a variety of goods and services to the world.

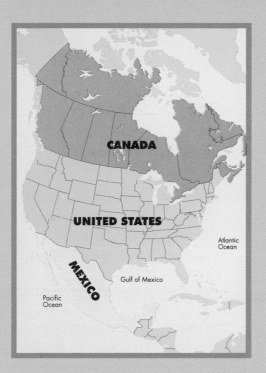

We are still the leading industrial power in the world and continue to offer the greatest variety of products. At the same time, many other nations offer products and services that compete with ours for a share in the global marketplace. Some of these products, while made by foreign companies, are actually produced in this country. And of course some products bearing the names of American companies are manufactured outside of our country. How does this come about? Who makes sure than our state and national interests are seen to? In recent years, both the federal government and most state governments have established agencies and practices to oversee international trade and foster its growth.

Foremost among the many federal agencies is the International Trade Administration (ITA), an arm of the Department of Commerce. The purpose of ITA is to help U.S. businesses compete in the global market. The ITA encourages and assists U.S. exports; ensures U.S. business has equal access to foreign markets— for example by implementing major trade agreements, such as the General Agreements on Tariffs and Trade (GATT) and the North American Free Trade Agreement (NAFTA—see map above); and enables businesses to compete against unfairly traded imports and to safeguard jobs and the competitive strength of American industry.

Through its International Trade Division, Georgia offers its manufacturers opportunities to increase sales and employment by means of exports, joint ventures, and licensing. The division offers special export assistance programs for manufacturers of a variety of products including consumer goods, technology products, and agri-tech equipment. The division assists companies in obtaining financing for their exports through a variety of state and federal agencies. It also offers companies market expertise and publishes *Made in Georgia USA*, a series of catalogs of Georgia products available for export.

THE AMERICAN ECONOMY AND COMPUTERS

Computers have become an integral part of the classroom. This first grader is learning to read at the same time that she learns to use a computer.

Suppose that one day all the computers stopped operating. How would this affect the American economy?

Our economy depends on communications, which depend on computers. Telephone companies use computers to route long-distance calls. Without microprocessors (simple computers), cellular phones would not send and receive signals. Practically all newspapers and magazines use computers to set type and control the presses. Television and radio stations use computers to handle the technical aspects of broadcasting. Even the post office uses computers to determine postage charges and to sort the mail.

Most transportation would stop cold without computers. Microprocessors in today's motor vehicles control their operation. Aircraft use computers to navigate and monitor engineering systems. Airline reservation systems are completely dependent on computers. Railroad signaling systems and switches are controlled by computers. Inside cities, traffic lights would not work without computer-controlled timing devices. Nor would subways operate without the computers that control train movements.

Money would flow at a snail's pace if governments, businesses, and banks had to write checks by hand. Banks use computers to keep tabs

The surest measure of a state's economy is its **gross state product** (GSP), which is the total amount of all goods and services provided. (A similar measure, gross domestic product, GDP is used to gauge the economy of a nation.) In 1990, Georgia's GSP was just under $137 billion. In 1994, it was approximately $183 billion. It has grown to over $200 billion, and economic forecasters predict it will continue to increase at a faster rate of growth than the national growth rate. Georgia's economy is expected to continue to be strong well into the next century.

Economic forecasters also predict that Georgia's population will continue to increase into the next century. In 1996, the state's population was 7.35 million. By the beginning of 1999, it was expected to be 7.7 million. In 1996, there were 3.7 million workers in the state's labor force. Its low unemployment rate of 4.9 percent reflected a on customers' accounts and generate monthly statements. Automatic teller machines and credit cards would not work without computers.

The buying and selling of goods would also be hindered. Modern cash registers are connected to computers that read bar codes and tally bills. These machines also keep records of a store's inventory and tell the store when to reorder.

Georgia, more than most states, uses computers in schools. During the administration of Governor Zell Miller, every school in the state received a satellite dish to use for distance learning and commercial broadcasting. "Peachnet" is available to every school, and the schools and the Georgia Department of Education are linked to allow schools access to special programs, to enable them to communicate with other schools in the state, and to permit interaction between students and teachers in classrooms throughout the state. In addition, special state technology grants have allowed schools to purchase computer labs and classroom computer workstations that would have been too expensive for local funding alone.

These are only a *few* of the ways computers keep our economy going. Without them, the economy would fall into chaos.

It would be difficult to find a business in Georgia that has not come to rely heavily on computers. Employment opportunities now and in the future will depend to a large degree on an applicant's computer skills.

growing economy. The cities with the fastest-growing economies in the state at the end of the 1990s are Savannah, Atlanta, and Athens. Savannah is expected to make the most gains as the state moves into the year 2000. Many industries contribute to Georgia's GSP. Among them are the service industry; manufacturing; and agriculture, forestry, and fisheries.

Do You Remember?

1. What are the advantages of a diversified economy?
2. What two events probably helped Georgia through the recession in the early 1960s?
3. What is the best measure of the state's economy?
4. What are the three fastest growing cities at the end of the century?

THE SERVICE INDUSTRY

For the past several decades, the service industry has been the fastest-growing sector of the American economy. This is also true in Georgia. About 75 percent of Georgia's GSP comes from such service-related industries as the retail and wholesale trade; finance, insurance, and real estate; transportation, communications, and utilities; professional and personal services; tourism; movie and television production; and government.

Examples of the service sector in Georgia: One of the biggest retail areas in Georgia is Lenox Square in Atlanta (above); good real estate sales can be an indicator of economic growth (opposite above); Citizens and Southern Bank, was one of the first chartered banks in the state (opposite below).

RETAIL AND WHOLESALE TRADE

Selling is the state's number one economic activity, employing over a half-million people. It includes everything from clothing, furniture, household appliances, and grocery stores to automobile and sports equipment dealerships. Almost anything a consumer wants can be bought somewhere in Georgia.

In a recent year, wholesale and retail trade accounted for about $26.5 billion a year, or an average of $4,850 per person. Increasingly, shopping malls are becoming the center of the retail industry. In the metropolitan Atlanta area alone, there are more than fifteen major shopping malls, with stores that appeal to all pocketbooks and all tastes.

FINANCE, INSURANCE, AND REAL ESTATE

The finance, insurance, and real estate industries employ about 150,000 Georgians. In 1887, the state's first bank, Citizens and Southern, was chartered in Savannah. In a recent year, over 383 banks held deposits of $31 million and **assets** (financial holdings) of over $40 million. Although four hundred Georgia banks closed in the 1920s due to the decline of "King Cotton," no state bank shut its doors during the Great Depression.

The state's real estate industry is thriving. In comparison to other parts of the nation, personal housing continues to be a good buy in Georgia. For example, in 1997, a 4-bedroom, 2-1/2 bath, 2,000-square-foot home cost about $370,100 in Honolulu; $254,400 in suburban Boston; and only $142,900 in suburban Atlanta.

As Georgia's population increases, the need for housing also grows larger. As new industries spring up in various parts of the state, additional housing is created to meet the needs of the new workers. Each day, single-family homes, apartment houses, condominiums, and other forms of housing are built and placed on an apparently bottomless real estate market.

Both banking and real estate influence the insurance industry. For example, to secure a loan for a house, the buyer must have insurance to cover the cost of the loan in case of fire or other loss. One must show "proof of insurance" on an automobile in order to buy a license tag in Georgia. In addition, most Georgians have medical and life insurance.

TRANSPORTATION, COMMUNICATIONS, AND UTILITIES

Together, transportation, communications, and utilities make up another major portion of the state's service industry. They employ over 200,000 persons. The state's outstanding transportation system is one of the main attractions for new businesses and industries. Atlanta's Hartsfield Airport is the second busiest in the world. Only Chicago's O'Hare Field handles more passengers. Hartsfield is the

Approximately 1200 miles of interstate highways connect Georgia with its neighboring states. The interchange at I-85 and I-285, shown here, is one of the busiest in the state.

southeastern hub for Delta Airlines, and over 39 million people a year change planes there for other destinations. Some 25 airlines operate many direct international flights to 14 countries from Hartsfield. In addition to Hartsfield, there are 121 other public, 142 private, and 6 military airports in the state.

Georgia has 1,200 miles of interstate highways, 17,800 miles of state highways, 87,000 miles of paved city and county roads, and 5,400 miles of railroad track. In Savannah and Brunswick, the state's two major seaports, millions of tons of soybeans, winter wheat, a clay product called kaolin, cherries, and forest products are exported each year. Ships bringing sugar, heavy equipment, and steel arrive daily at the two ports. In 1995, Savannah dredged (dug out and deepened) its harbor so that bigger ships could unload there rather than in Charleston, South Carolina, its major rival.

The communications industry includes publishing, radio, and television. The state has over 29 major daily newspapers with circulations ranging from some 5,000 in Cordele to over 400,000 in Atlanta. A total of 180 newspaper and 155 magazines were published in Georgia in a recent year.

Television began in the state in 1948 with the introduction in Atlanta of WSB-TV. Today, Georgia has over 25 commercial stations.

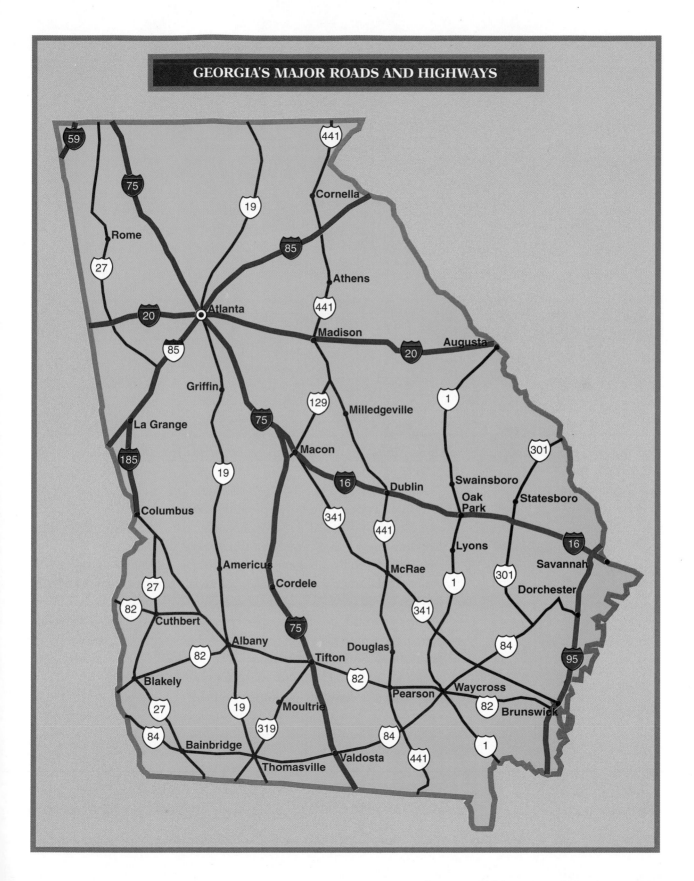

Dams around the state provide Georgia with hydroelectric power. This is Russell Dam on the Savannah River.

The state also has more than 300 radio stations that carry everything from hard rock music to twenty-four-hour news. Moreover, Atlanta is the home base to a vast complex of stations, including CNN and Headline News, that broadcast throughout the world.

Georgia's utilities, which include electrical and gas energy, are a vital part of the economy. Abundant electrical power—much of which is the result of New Deal programs such as TVA and REA—has been a major factor in the growth of Georgia's economy. Eighty-seven percent of the state's power is generated by plants that burn coal, oil, or natural gas. Seven percent comes from nuclear energy, and six percent from hydroelectric sources (water power). Plant Hatch at Baxley was Georgia's first nuclear-powered plant. Hydroelectric plants include Clark Hill and Hartwell dams on the Savannah River, Allatoona Dam on the Etowah River, and Buford and Walter F. George dams on the Chattahoochee River.

PROFESSIONAL AND PERSONAL SERVICES

Several hundred thousand doctors, attorneys, repair persons, garage attendants, barbers, beauticians, house cleaners, and theater employees form the part of the service industry related to professional

and personal services. The purpose of such businesses and professions is to make people's lives healthier, more secure, and more enjoyable.

One of the fastest-growing sectors of the economy in Georgia and the rest of the nation is health care. Hospitals, laboratories, medical equipment suppliers, medical research, and a variety of home health services have all expanded greatly in the past decades. As people continue to live longer because of improved medical care, businesses within this industry are expected to have significant growth.

GOVERNMENT

Government is a major link in the economic chain and one of the state's major employers. It regulates businesses, builds roads for transporting goods, educates workers, and provides other needed services, such as protecting the nation's security. Over 447,000 workers keep the state operating. Close to half that number are employed in the state's schools. Georgia is home to about 67,000 civilian employees of the federal government. The state's major military installations include Dobbins and Warner-Robbins air force bases and Forts Benning, Gordon, and McPherson. Naval bases and ports in Savannah, Brunswick, Kings Bay, and the lower coastal area continue to expand.

Paratrooper training takes place at Fort Benning in Columbus, one of eleven military installations in Georgia.

TOURISM

Tourism is now the second largest sector of the service industry in Georgia. It employs over 250,000 people in hotels, motels, restaurants, entertainment centers, amusement parks, airlines, rental car agencies, and other services related to attracting visitors to the state and making their stays in Georgia pleasant. Each year, tourism generates over $10 billion within the state. Although the center of tourism in Georgia is metropolitan Atlanta, which draws a good deal of convention business, the economies of other parts of the state also benefit from the money earned from tourism.

After Atlanta, the biggest tourist attraction is Savannah, the state's historic seaport city. Although Savannah has always been a popular tourist destination, the extraordinary success of John Berendt's book, *Midnight in the Garden of Good and Evil*, published in the mid-1990s, has brought additional thousands of visitors to its storied squares.

Georgia's many state parks, including Black Rock Mountain, Cloudland Canyon, Crooked River, Fort Mountain, Franklin D. Roosevelt, and Skidaway Island, are major tourist attractions. Other areas, such as the Chattahoochee and Oconee National Forest and the

Cumberland Island National Seashore, are also popular vacation spots. Each year, thousands journey to Stone Mountain, Helen, Six Flags Over Georgia, Callaway Gardens, and the Martin Luther King, Jr., National Historic Site.

MOVIE AND TELEVISION PRODUCTION

Another growing part of the state's economy is the production of movies and television programs. In the early 1970s, the movie *Deliverance*, based on the novel by James Dickey, was filmed around Tallulah Falls in north Georgia. Since that time, such successful movies as *Roots, Smokey and the Bandit,* and *Midnight in the Garden of Good and Evil* have been partly or totally filmed in Georgia. A number of television series, including "In the Heat of the Night," have been filmed here. Today, Georgia ranks third, behind California and New York, as a site for motion picture and television filming.

Do You Remember?
1. About what percent of Georgia's GSP comes from service-related industries?
2. What was Georgia's first nuclear-powered plant?
3. How does the federal government affect the state's economy?
4. Why is tourism important to Georgia?

Visitors to Georgia can enjoy a buggy ride around Savannah (opposite above), a country store in Helen (opposite below), boating on St. Simons Island (top), and Providence Canyon (above).

MANUFACTURING

Manufacturing is another important industry in Georgia. It accounts for over 550,000 jobs and 20 percent of the GSP. There are numerous industries associated with manufacturing, including textiles, clothing, food products, and transportation equipment. Other businesses include those that manufacture chemical products, electrical equipment, and pianos.

TRANSPORTATION EQUIPMENT

Over 50,000 Georgians work to produce transportation vehicles and equipment. Lockheed-Georgia, which merged with the Martin Marietta Company to become Lockheed Martin, is the state's top aircraft manufacturing employer with over 15,000 workers. This company builds the C130 Hercules, a cargo carrier, and the C5A Galaxy, world's largest airplane.

The automotive industry is also an important part of Georgia's economy. In recent years, Atlanta has been called "little Detroit" because of the number of vehicles built in the area. Ford's Taurus, which was the best-selling car in America for much of the 1990s, is built in Hapeville. There are other automotive ties in the metro area. General Motors builds minivans in Dora-ville. Genuine Parts, a major distributor of auto parts, has its NAPA headquarters in Cobb County. And the Swedish car maker, Saab, has its U.S. corporate offices in Norcross.

The Blue Bird Body Company in Fort Valley is another major manufacturer of transportation vehicles. Blue Bird sells one out of every three school buses bought in the United States. It also makes the Wanderlodge, a luxury camper home that sells for about $200,000.

Formerly the Bell Bomber factory in World War II (see pages 486-487), Lockheed-Martin in Marietta is essential to the national economy and defense. The 76-acre facility is one of the largest in the world.

TEXTILES

The manufacture of carpets, rugs, fabric, yarn, and thread makes Georgia a leader in the textile industry. The industry employs over 100,000 people in cities like Dalton, Griffin, Columbus, Thomaston, and Dublin. Georgia produces a third of the world's carpets. Dalton, where more carpet is made than in any other United States city, is known as the "Carpet Capital of the World."

West Point Pepperell is Georgia's textile pioneer. Another textile giant is the Bibb Company, whose headquarters are in Macon. This company, which was founded in 1876, employs 5,600 people in 9 Georgia plants. Its principal products include yarns for carpet and clothes and items such as sheets, comforters, blankets, bedspreads, and draperies. The company is probably best known for juvenile lines such as Strawberry Shortcake, Annie, and the Dukes of Hazard.

Above: The textile industry in Georgia accounts for well over one billion dollars a year in revenues and employs more than 100,000 workers. ***Opposite page, above and below:*** *Over fifteen percent of the nation's poultry comes from Georgia, and the state is second only to California in the number of eggs it produces each day.*

APPAREL

Like the textile industry, Georgia's apparel (clothing) industry is big business. Although figures vary from year to year, the manufacturing of apparel is carried out in 122 of Georgia's 159 counties and employs over 80,000 workers. This represents almost 10 percent of all workers employed in manufacturing. In a recent year there were over 458 firms making wearing apparel ranging from T shirts to men's suits. The industry continues to expand as more plants, some of them owned by foreign firms, are built in the state.

FOOD PRODUCTS

The wholesale and retail sectors of the food industry contribute more than $2.1 billion to Georgia's economy and employ about 90,000 workers. Food and fiber processing companies that turn the raw farm products into the goods sold in grocery stores contribute about $27 billion to the state's economy and provide jobs for about 170,000 workers. Food in Georgia is big business, whether it is poultry, eggs, soft drinks, canned fruit, bread and pastries, peanut butter, fruitcakes, pickles, barbecue, candy, or seafood. From Claxton, which is known for fruitcakes, to Gainesville, noted for poultry and

eggs, to Brunswick, famous for seafood, food production is important to Georgia's strong economy.

Probably the most famous Georgia food production company is the Atlanta-based Coca-Cola Bottling Company. Coca-Cola is a worldwide, multinational company. Its "refreshing taste" can be bought from bottlers in Mozambique, Romania, or Sri Lanka. Coca-Cola does business in more than 200 countries, and its products account for more than 48 percent of the world's soft drink market.

The poultry industry is a vital part of the state's economy. In an average week, the poultry farms in 92 of Georgia's counties process over 21 million pounds of chicken. Over 15 percent of the nation's chicken fryers comes from Georgia. The state ranks second in the nation in the production of broilers and eggs.

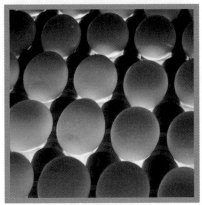

Castleberry Foods cans such items as barbecue, chili, corned beef hash, and beef stew. The company produces over 450,000 pounds of food each day. Harris Foods, headquartered in Marietta, oversees Wendy's franchises. Marietta is also home to Georgia Mountain Water, which distributes spring water. For a sweet tooth, Bob's Candies in Albany is well known for its peppermint candy canes, particularly popular around the Christmas holidays.

One Georgia company, Tom's, is based in Columbus. It first packaged Tom's Roasted Peanuts for five cents a bag. Today, the company has some 360 snack products and, with over 150,000 machines, ranks first in national vending sales.

In the early 1950s, Pennsylvanian Nick Pascarella and his wife were driving north from Florida, where they had tried to find a suitable place for a steak house restaurant. A tire blew out on their car, and Pascarella was advised to go to a store on Walton Way in Augusta for a replacement.

While in the store, he told of his failure to find a suitable restaurant site in Florida. The manager encouraged him to consider Augusta. A year later, Pascarella opened his first Western Sizzlin' down the street from the tire store. It was an immediate success. One of the early visitors to the restaurant was Athenian Jim Maupin. He was so impressed with the quality of food and service that, in 1965, he purchased a franchise to open an Athens Western Sizzlin'. Today, there are over 650 Western Sizzlin' steak houses in the United States.

Below: The specialized skills of Georgia's 15,000 construction workers are essential to a growing state. **Opposite page, above:** *More granite monuments and markers are made in a twenty-mile radius of Elberton than any other location in the nation.* **Opposite page, below:** *Georgia granite on the docks at Savannah waits for shipment overseas.*

One of the newest successes on Georgia's food scene is La-Van Hawkins. His company, Inner City Foods, opened the first Checkers restaurant in 1991 on Decatur's Lawrenceville Highway. Today, over twenty-two Checkers restaurants are located in the metro Atlanta area, and others are being built throughout the state.

OTHER MANUFACTURING-RELATED INDUSTRIES

Over 25,000 Georgians are employed in the chemical industry. There are some 380 chemical plants in Georgia. Most are located in Fulton and DeKalb counties. These chemicals are used in medications, polishes, soaps, and detergents.

Electrical equipment companies like Scientific-Atlanta and General Electric employ 25,000 Georgians. These workers make such items as household appliances, batteries, communication cables, transformers, and video games.

Georgia's construction industry accounts for only 5 percent of the GSP. Without it, however, other industries could not build or expand. Close to 150,000 workers are employed, including contractors, carpenters, electricians, painters, and people with other related skills.

MINING

Mining is the state's smallest manufacturing employer with 8,000 workers. However, it is important to larger industries. Georgia ranks first in the nation in the mining of granite and marble. It is also first in the world in the production of kaolin.

Crushed granite, used mainly for highway construction, is produced in forty quarries located in the Piedmont and Eastern Highlands areas of the state. Elberton is known as the "Granite Capital of the World." Here, 1,800 persons make over 150,000 granite monuments, markers, and mausoleums each year.

Marble is located in small areas around Tate in southeast Pickens County. There is enough marble at Tate to last for the next 3,000 years. Large blocks are used for carvings like the Lincoln Memorial. Crushed marble is put in roofing and agricultural lime. It is also a filler for over two thousand products, including toothpaste and poultry feed.

Kaolin, called "white gold," is found in a narrow band from Macon to Augusta. It is a fine white clay used mainly as a coating for paper. It gives magazines and books a shiny look. Kaolin is also used in making china, paint, rubber, plastic, cement, detergents,

There is a strong likelihood that the page you are touching and reading right now was coated with kaolin, a fine white clay mined in Georgia. The industry is worth over 500 million dollars a year to the economy.

and fertilizer. The China Clay Producers Association, with six companies and over a hundred mines, is the major supplier of kaolin. In all, Georgia has 60 percent of the world's purest deposits of kaolin.

Georgia also has the largest deposits of fuller's earth, most of which is found in the southwestern part of the state. Once it is processed, this soft, clay-like mineral is an excellent filter and drying agent. Fuller's earth is used in cat litter. Other uses include additives to cement and fillers for a variety of products such as cosmetics, toothpaste, and pills.

Georgia also has rich deposits of bauxite, manganese, limestone, and phosphate. Until 1849, when large amounts of gold were discovered in California, Georgia was the leading gold-producing state. There were mines throughout north Georgia, particularly near Dahlonega. Today, gold is scarce and the cost of mining it is high. It is now found by panning, running water through a trough to separate the gold from sand, or in dredging operations. In Lumpkin County, tourists sometimes pan for gold.

Do You Remember?

1. What city is called the "Carpet Capital of the World?
2. In which two counties are most of the state's chemical plants located?
3. What percent of the world's purest deposits of kaolin are found in Georgia?

AGRICULTURE

Until recently, the agriculture industry, which includes farming, fishing, and forestry, was the leading industry in the state. Although it is no longer as dominant as it once was, the industry still contributes over $38 billion annually to Georgia's economy. One in six Georgians works in agriculture-related jobs, and almost half of the state's manufacturing jobs are in agribusiness. Clearly, agriculture is still a major component of Georgia's economy.

FARMING

Before World War II, Georgia was primarily an agrarian state. Today, mechanization and electrification have helped make farmers more efficient. However, the improved techniques meant that fewer farmers were needed. There are also many fewer farms than before because technology allows fewer farmers to tend more land. In addition, large businesses bought thousands of acres of land, thus increasing the average farm size.

Although the number of farms and farmers has declined, farming is still important to Georgia's economy. The state ranks first in the nation in the production of peanuts, pecans, and rye. It ranks second in the production of broilers and eggs, third in peaches, fifth in fresh tomatoes, sixth in tobacco, and seventh in cotton.

Grains are important crops in Georgia's agricultural economy. The state is second in the nation in the production of rye.

Cotton continues to be a major crop, although it is no longer as important as it once was. During the 1980s, cotton production in the state plummeted, partly because of bad weather, the boll weevil, and changing styles in fabrics. Prior to 1995, peanuts had been Georgia's number one farm crop. But in 1995, cotton production rebounded with over 21 million bales produced. The following year, cotton was responsible for over 35,000 jobs in the state and added $3.1 billion to Georgia's economy. Cotton and peanuts may swap places again as a leading industry in the state, but in 1997, cotton was once more "King" in Georgia's economy.

Each year almost one-half of the total U.S. production of pecans is grown in Georgia. Pecans are grown primarily in the red, gray, and brown soils of Georgia's Piedmont and Coastal Plains regions. Over 300 species of pecans are grown on 180,000 acres in the state.

Apples, tobacco, peaches, watermelons, and soybeans are other important crops. Georgia's farmers raise over twenty types of vegetables, and corn is grown on nearly every farm. Two of the state's most valuable crops are sweet potatoes and Vidalia onions, which are quickly gaining the reputation of being the best on the market.

Georgia has long been called the "Peach State," and each year bushels of peaches are still shipped throughout the country. Recently a new type of peach was introduced to the market. The Java peach, also called the Peento, is something of a novelty fruit. It is white-fleshed and juicy and—this is what sets it apart from other peaches—totally flat.

One of Georgia's newest cash crops is called **kenaf**, a tall, multi-leafed plant growing on a fairly narrow twelve-foot-high stalk. The plant, which may be seen in fields near Americus, is related to other members of the hemp family such as cotton and okra. Although relatively new to this area, kenaf has been grown in other parts of the world for over six thousand years. After a six-month cultivation season, the fibrous plant is gathered and processed into various products including paper pulp, industrial absorbents, drapes, fiberboard, and rope. Kenaf stalks are also crushed into a lightweight, biodegradable kitty litter product. Because kitty litter is an $800-million-a-year market nationally, Georgia's farmers now have another new cash crop.

There are few areas in Georgia that are not involved in some type of agriculture. The chart on the opposite page shows farm production by leading counties.

Top: *Third nationally in the production of peaches, Georgia first started cultivating this delicious fruit in 1899.* **Above:** *The sweet, "no tears" Vidalia onion is shipped throughout the country.* **Opposite page, above:** *Many residents in the picturesque community of Darien depend on the shrimp industry for their livelihood.*

FISHING

Commercial fishing continues to be a major industry in Georgia. Among its most important catches from the sea are shrimp, which ranks first; crab, second; and fin-fish, third. Darien, Savannah, and Brunswick are the leading commercial fishing ports.

A fairly new fishing enterprise is **aquaculture**, in which ponds are built to raise trout or catfish. The fish are fed until they are large enough to harvest and sell commercially. Although Texas leads the nation in the amount of commercially grown catfish sold each year, Georgia has increased its annual production to well over 8 million pounds. One indicator of the growth of aquaculture can be seen in the Atlanta public schools. In addition to courses of study in urban forestry, agribusiness, and biotechnology, Carver High School has added aquaculture to its curriculum.

Conch is another sea product offered up by Georgia's waters. The state is one of the leading suppliers of these mollusks, which are often harvested by shrimpers during the off season. The "meat" of the conch is sold all over the country, but it is particularly popular in the New England area. Conch is used in soups, chowders, Italian dishes, or just fried conch fritters.

Shad is another seafood harvested by the state's fishing industry. This popular delicacy is a seasonal catch off the Atlantic coastline from the ports of Darien, Savannah, and Brunswick.

FOREST PRODUCTS

Forest-related industries are important to Georgia's economy because of the large number of products used daily that are made from trees. Forests cover 70 percent of Georgia with 250 types of trees. When cut, they would make a 569-foot-high stack across all four lanes of Interstate 75 from Tennessee to Florida. The forest products industry is Georgia's largest and oldest industry, and it brings in over $17 billion each year. From the settlers who cut logs from Oglethorpe's settlement to the giant timber companies that turn the state's bounty of trees into all sorts of products, Georgia's forests have always been a big business in the state. One of the state's most heralded businessmen is Howard Gilman. The family immigrated to Vermont in the 1880s with $100 to start a business. Today, the Gilman Paper Company in St. Marys is part of the largest privately held group of paper mills in the nation.

The state's 24 million commercial forest acres rank it first in the country. Georgia has many forest-related industries, which employ about 80,000 people.

Georgia had a long history of producing naval stores or pitch (resin) from slash or longleaf pines. This resin is used to fill the seams of

FARM PRODUCTS BY COUNTY	
Product	**County**
apples	Gilmer
broilers	Barrow
cattle	Mitchell
corn	Grady
cotton	Dooly
dairy	Morgan
hogs	Morgan
peaches	Peach
peanuts	Worth
pecans	Dougherty
soybeans	Burke
tobacco	Colquitt
turkeys	Oconee
vegetables	Decatur
wheat	Sumter

Since it takes from 15 to 45 years for a tree to grow from a seedling to harvest size, attempts are being made to carefully supervise the hardwood logging industry to avoid stripping the land of its most valuable renewable resource.

wooden ships. Tar, also produced as a by-product, is used to coat the wood in ships to prevent rotting. Today, "gum naval stores" include turpentine, which is used as a paint thinner or solvent, and rosin. Rosin is the yellowish to dark brown resin used on violin bows. Gum naval stores are no longer a major industry in Georgia. In fact, Baxley is the nation's last distiller of pine gum. About 80 workers there combine their efforts to produce turpentine for paint and rosin for printers' ink.

Eight out of every ten trees harvested in Georgia are southern yellow pines. Much of the success of Georgia's forest industry is due to the efforts of Milledgeville native Dr. Charles Herty. He showed that pine pulp could be processed and bleached easily for a variety of uses. Today, Georgia leads the nation in the production of pulp. Each time you read a newspaper or magazine or book, load groceries in a paper bag, or write a letter, there is a strong possibility that the paper came from a Georgia pulp mill. Union Camp, located in Savannah, is the world's largest pulp and paper mill. Each day the mill manufactures 2,850 tons of paper. Plants in areas around Savannah produce an average of 4 million boxes a year.

Lumber and plywood are also important forest products. Related industries employ about 16,000 workers. Such items as houses, cabinets, and flooring are made from Georgia's pine and hardwood trees. Furniture and mobile home industries employ over 9,000 Georgians.

Another major forest industry is firewood production, valued at $136 million a year. Trees used for firewood are usually hardwoods, such as oak, birch, or hickory.

Forests are a renewable resource. Each time a tree is cut, another can be planted. Depending on its type, it takes fifteen to forty-five years for a tree to grow from a seedling to a size for harvesting.

Do You Remember?

1. In what three farm products does Georgia rank first nationally?
2. What are Georgia's three leading commercial fishing ports?
3. How much money does the state's forest products industry bring in each year?

SUMMARY

- Today, Georgia has a strong, diversified economy.
- One of the surest measures of a state's economy is its gross state product (GSP). Georgia's GSP is growing at a faster pace than the national average. Various industries contribute to the state's GSP.
- The service industry has been the fastest-growing industry, both in Georgia and in the nation.
- About 75 percent of the state's GSP comes from such service-re-

THE LEGACY OF THE 1996 SUMMER OLYMPICS

At 7:45 p.m. on Tuesday, September 18, 1990, several million Georgians simultaneously cheered as Atlanta was named the host city for the 1996 Summer Olympic Games. Immediately, jobs were created, construction began, and money started to flow into the state. Between 1991 and 1996, an estimated $4 billion was infused into the state and local economy. Atlanta's downtown area received a $78 million grant for beautification, inner-city improvements, and additions to the cultural centers.

When the Olympic flag lowered for the last time, most Georgians were extremely proud of the games that had brought visitors from every corner of the world. The Olympics left a legacy of good feelings about Atlanta and the other venues scattered throughout the state. The games also left a significant economic legacy. Many of the streets and bridges in Atlanta were repaired, and major basic structural changes were made in preparation for the Olympics. These improvements remain to serve the city and its inhabitants for years to come. A permanent Centennial Olympic Park continues to draw tourists to Atlanta, and the Olympic Stadium has been renovated to serve as the new home for the Atlanta Braves.

Other benefits include apartment and dormitory facilities for Georgia State University and Georgia Tech. In addition, $500 million was spent on permanent competition sites and upgrades of other venues.

It may be difficult to estimate the good will benefits to the state from the 1996 Summer Olympics, but the economic benefits will continue for years to come.

Atlanta Olympic Organizing Committee members (left to right) mayor Maynard Jackson, former mayor Andrew Young and chairman Billy Payne, jubilantly returned to the city after Atlanta had been named the site of the 1996 Summer Olympics. Atlanta, and Georgia, will feel the benefits of hosting the Games for many years.

lated industries as the retail and wholesale trade; transportation, communications, and utilities; personal and professional services; tourism; movies and television production; and government.

- Another Georgia industry is manufacturing, which includes textiles, clothing, food products, and transportation equipment.
- Although agriculture is no longer the dominant industry it once was, its various sectors—which include farming, fishing, and forest products—still contribute a great deal to the state's economy.

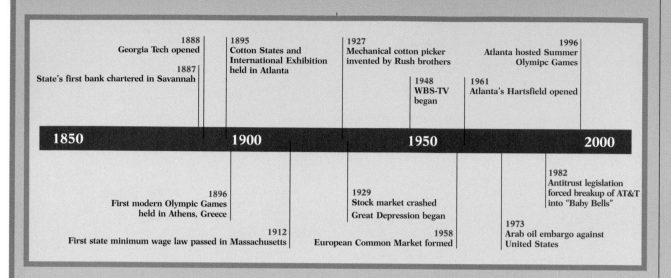

Timeline:

1888
Georgia Tech opened

1887
State's first bank chartered in Savannah

1895
Cotton States and
International Exhibition
held in Atlanta

1927
Mechanical cotton picker
invented by Rush brothers

1948
WBS-TV
began

1996
Atlanta hosted Summer
Olymipc Games

1961
Atlanta's Hartsfield opened

1850   **1900**   **1950**   **2000**

1896
First modern Olympic Games
held in Athens, Greece

1912
First state minimum wage law passed in Massachusetts

1929
Stock market crashed

Great Depression began

1958
European Common Market formed

1982
Antitrust legislation
forced breakup of AT&T
into "Baby Bells"

1973
Arab oil embargo against
United States

Reviewing People, Places, and Terms

Use the following terms in a paragraph describing Georgia's economy at this time.

aquaculture
diversified economy
gross state product
interdependent
per capita income
sector

Understanding the Facts

1. What three cities in Georgia had the fastest-growing economies in the state at the end of the 1990s?
2. Where are approximately one-half of the state's government workers employed?
3. What company is considered to be Georgia's textile pioneer?
4. What Georgia company ranks first in the nation in vending machine sales?
5. What community is known as the "Granite Capital of the World"?
6. In which two of the state's regions are pecans primarily grown?

7. What is the world's largest pulp and paper mill?

Developing Critical Thinking

1. In what ways did Atlanta and its neighboring areas benefit from the 1996 Summer Olympics?
2. Contact a local radio or television station. Find out when the station began operation and what type of programming it broadcasts. Share the information with your classmates.
3. In what ways would you, your family, and your friends be affected if a new company employing four thousand workers relocated to your community? What do you think would happen if a company that size moved *out* of your community?

Applying Your Skills

1. Economic maps can indicate where products are grown in a given area. Using an outline map of Georgia, mark in the areas noted for the production of these major crops: peanuts, pecans, poultry, peaches, apples, Vidalia onions, and cotton.

2. Using a blank map of Georgia, mark the location of fifteen of the state's major tourist attractions, including the state and national parks.
3. From the information provided in your school or public library (or from the Internet, if you have access to it), prepare a pie chart showing the percent of Georgia's Gross State Product contributed in a given year by each of these economic sectors: service industries; manufacturing; and agriculture, forestry, and fisheries.

Making Connections

1. Make a list of ten of your daily activities that are affected in some way by the computer. Compare your list with the lists of your classmates.
2. Write a one-page story entitled "The Day the Computers Shut Down." Share your story with your classmates.

3. Do you think the United States finally "won" the Cold War? Why or why not?
4. What problems have developed for the countries that once made up the Soviet Union? Why do you think these problems developed?

Did You Know?

- Georgia's pecans were first raised in Baconton as the result of a gift to little girls in the Bacon family. Today, both Albany and Baconton lay claim to being the "Pecan Capital of the World."
- Peanuts are not really nuts. They belong to the pea family and are called legumes.
- One of Georgia's best-known restaurants is the Varsity, with branches located both in Athens and Atlanta. The sixty-year-old drive-ins sell two miles of frankfurters, a ton of onions, and 2,500 pounds of potatoes each day.
- During the 1996 Olympics, the athletes' dining hall served over 2 million soft drinks, 70,000 gallons of milk, and over 950,000 apples.

BUILDING SKILLS: TRAVELING THROUGH TIME

You have the following task: For your vacation you want to visit as many of the state historic sites as you possibly can. You have two important limits on your plans: time and money. As a result, you can travel no more than 550 miles round-trip on your vacation. On your trip, you cannot go over your mileage limit. You may wish to choose a traveling companion to keep you company and to help in planning.

Use a list of state historic sites and a state highway map to help you design your route. A student living in Rome, for instance, might begin the trip as follows:

Take U.S. 27 north through Mount Berry, Summerville, and Linwood to the Chickamauga and Chattanooga National Military Park. Then go south on I-75 to Dalton, take U.S. 76 to Ellijay, and connect with Georgia Hwy. 52, and so on.

Begin your trip from your starting point (your town or school). Visit as many sites as possible until you have used your allotted mileage. Remember, the mileage to return home must be included in your plans.

Present your vacation trip to the class by marking your route on a map. After completing your plan, consider the following questions.

1. What parts of Georgia history will you visit on your trip?
2. Will you see all the sites you want to see?
3. How did your starting point limit the number of sites you could include?
4. Why do you think the state chose to make the sites you visited historic sites?
5. Is there a local site that you would like to nominate as a historic site? Why do you think it would make a good site?

CHAPTER EIGHTEEN

THE PROCESS OF GOVERNMENT

Let us say this much to ourselves, not only with our lips but in our hearts. Let us say this: I myself am a part of democracy—I myself must accept responsibilities. Democracy is not merely a privilege to be enjoyed—it is a trust to keep and maintain.

—Stephen Vincent Benet

IDEAS ABOUT GEORGIA GOVERNMENT have changed greatly over the centuries. When the generation of Georgians who formed the state's earliest government first met, they believed that government existed to protect life, liberty, and property. Today's generation, however, believes that government should do that and much more. It should also provide education, build roads, relieve poverty, protect health, and make the economy grow. These activities require much larger state and local governments. Although government has grown and done different things, several basic principles have remained the same as they were in 1776.

PRINCIPLES OF GOVERNMENT

One of the most basic principles of American government is the idea of **sovereignty**, the supreme power or source of authority. Before 1776, Georgia was a British colony. In theory, the British king was the "sovereign," and all governmental power came from him. When the United States gained its freedom, the source of power shifted from the king to the people. The people of the United States, thus, are now sovereign. That is, the people are the source of authority in government. The people elect representatives to make the laws. This practice results in a *democratic* form of government.

Constitutionalism is another basic principle of American government. This means that a written constitution describes the rights of the people and the framework of government. By describing the framework of state government, the constitution *limits* government's powers. Since it was written in 1787, the United States Constitution has been amended more than twenty-five times, but

The State Capitol in Atlanta houses the General Assembly, the governor's office, the State Museum of Service and Industry, and the Hall of Flags.

the basic document remains as it was over two hundred years ago. On the other hand, our state constitution changes periodically. In Georgia, there have been ten state constitutions, all designed to reflect the needs of our citizens as long as there is no conflict with the U.S. Constitution.

Under our state constitution, the **electorate** (voters) choose the individuals who will be a part of government and represent us. Thus, our state also has a democratic form of government. The state constitution also provides for a government made up of three branches: an executive branch, a legislative branch, and a judicial branch. This division of responsibilities is called the **separation of powers**, which is another principle of our government. This type of divided governmental duties and responsibilities echoes that of the federal government. It ensures that we are not denied our just rights under the constitution. Such a government is called a "limited government," because it limits the power of any single part of the state government to take away basic rights that are listed in the U.S. Constitution. These basic rights—often referred to as the **"Five Freedoms"**—are included in the first amendment to the original Constitution, which reads:

> *Congress shall make no law respecting an establishment of religion, or prohibiting the free exercise thereof; or abridging the freedom of speech, or of the press; or the right of the people peaceably to assemble, and to petition the Government for a redress of grievances.*

Federalism is another guiding principle of American government. When the United States Constitution was ratified in 1788, it established a **federal system** of government. A federal system is a form of government in which the national government and state government exercise authority over the same territory and the same people. Georgians are state citizens, but they also are United States citizens. They are subject to both state and national laws. If there is a conflict between these laws, the national law takes precedence. State officials must swear or affirm that they will uphold the United States Constitution and national laws over the state constitution and state laws when they are in conflict. Both the United States and the Georgia constitutions are written in such a way that the individual citizens are protected by law.

Do You Remember?

1. What are the basic principles of government in the United States?
2. What are the Five Freedoms?
3. When was the U.S. Constitution ratified?
4. By whom are members of the Supreme Court appointed?

LEVELS OF GOVERNMENT

POLITICAL MANAGEMENT BY LEVEL OF GOVERNMENT

Government is carried out at three levels: federal, state, and local. Each level is separate, but the functions of the three levels often overlap. This chart provides an overview of our political management system.

Level/Branch	Elected By	Functions
FEDERAL		
Legislative Senate House of Representatives	Popular vote in each state	Makes laws for the nation
Executive President Vice President	Electoral vote	Approves law; Commander in Chief of armed forces Makes treaties
Judicial Supreme Court Court of Appeals District courts	Appointed by president	Interprets laws and U.S. Constitution
STATE		
Legislative* Senate House of Representatives	Popular vote in state districts	Makes laws for state Can veto state legislative bills
Executive Governor Lieutenant governor	Statewide popular vote	Heads state militia
Judicial State supreme court Superior court State court	Generally elected by popular vote	Interprets state laws Passes sentences
COUNTY / CITY		
County commissioners	Popular vote in county districts	Provides services to county residents (police, fire, sanitation, schools, etc.)
Mayor and city council	Popular vote of residents of city (Mayor sometimes elected by city council or commissioners)	Provides services to residents (police, sanitation, schools, etc.)
City council and city manager	Council elected by popular vote of residents of city, city manager appointed by council	Provides services to residents (police, sanitation, schools, etc.)

*Collectively the senate and the house of representatives are called the Georgia General Assembly.

The state of Georgia can boast of nine national parks and eight national wildlife refuges. One of the most famous is the largest national wildlife refuge in the eastern United States, the Okefenokee Swamp. Why is it important for the government to offer a refuge area to endangered and threatened species?

GEORGIA AND THE FEDERAL GOVERNMENT

Like all other states, Georgia both gives to and receives from the federal government. Each year, Georgians pay out millions of dollars in income tax and receive millions back from the federal government in various forms of social programs. And citizens of the state also serve in the nation's armed forces and different branches of the federal government.

HOW THE FEDERAL GOVERNMENT HELPS GEORGIA

Georgians, like other Americans, pay taxes to the federal government. In turn, the federal government uses part of this money to help the state. Georgia receives millions in federal dollars each year. Even though some states receive larger amounts, Georgia gets more federal dollars than its citizens pay in income taxes.

How does federal money come back into the state? The federal government builds and keeps up the interstate road system and all other federal highways in the state. Well over millions of dollars come into Georgia each year as social security benefits and federal and

THE NATION'S GREAT SEAL

Georgians can be proud that our state is one of the thirteen represented as part of the nation's Great Seal. The next time you see the president of the United States make a public speech, notice the large emblem placed on the front of the speaker's lectern (stand). It is a reproduction of the Great Seal. This seal, utilized on all important government documents, has been in use since 1782. The seal consists of the following elements.

Crest   There are two parts to the crest. The first part contains thirteen stars representing the original colonies. The outer circle has nineteen clouds with "rays of glory" showing through them. Together these two parts symbolize a new country taking its rightful place among the other great nations of the world.

Bald Eagle   The bald eagle is the national bird of the United States. It was chosen by the first Congress to represent freedom and power.

Shield   The shield covering the eagle was meant to symbolize the self-reliance of the new nation. The blue bar represented Congress in 1782, but since 1789 has been interpreted to stand for the three branches of government. The red, white, and blue colors are designed to symbolize valor (red), purity (white), and vigilance and justice (blue).

Olive Branch   The olive branch represents the nation's hope for peace. There are thirteen leaves and thirteen olives to represent the original thirteen colonies.

Arrows   The thirteen arrows are additional symbols of the original colonies and signal the nation's willingness to use military force when necessary to defend the nation.

Scroll   The scroll contains Latin words meaning "from many, one." This refers to the creation of one nation from thirteen colonies.

The Great Seal of the United States of America has been in use since 1782. Each element of the seal represents something different about our country.

military retirement payments. The federal government makes sure we have postal service and the service of federal courts. It takes care of the national forests and parks, such as Oconee National Forest and Chattahoochee National Forest. Your own school may receive some federal money. About 10 percent of what is spent by most public school systems comes from the federal government.

The military presence in Georgia takes a large number of federal dollars. Georgia is home to eleven military bases. They employ over 120,000 civilian and military personnel who are paid over $2 billion a year. The state's newest military facility is the Naval Submarine Base at Kings Bay in Camden County. It cost over $1.5 billion to build, making it the most expensive peacetime building project in Navy history. Industries in Georgia receive close to $4 billion a year for military contracts, mostly to build aircraft. Because of the defense dollars, Georgia ranks tenth in the nation in federal money received.

Several of the major tourist attractions in the state are maintained by the federal government. Visitors can drive through the 396-acre Okefenokee National Wildlife Refuge and Wilderness Area watching for wood ducks, storks, alligators, and hundreds of flowering plants and trees. They can wander along the beaches and marshes of Cumberland Island National Seashore and photograph a bald eagle or picnic in the maritime live oak forest.

Tourists interested in military history can visit the sites of Civil War battles at Chickamauga-Chattanooga National Military Park in northeast Georgia. They can also visit Kennesaw Mountain National Battlefield Park north of Atlanta. Along the state's coastline, visitors can tour the site of James Oglethorpe's fortified town, Fort Frederica, or touch cannon fired during the Civil War at Fort Pulaski on Tybee Island.

Those interested in the Georgia Indians who lived eight thousand years ago can view artifacts at Ocmulgee National Monument in Macon. There are over forty-two national historic landmarks in the state. One of Georgia's newest national historic sites is the home of Dr. Martin Luther King, Jr., in Atlanta. Visitors can tour the twenty-three acres that include Dr. King's birthplace, his boyhood home, church, and memorial grave site. Nearby is another tourist highlight that fills Georgia's residents with pride: the Jimmy Carter Presidential Library. The presidential library contains historical documents, writings, and mementos of Jimmy Carter's years in the White House.

WHAT GEORGIA GIVES TO THE FEDERAL GOVERNMENT

In addition to the revenue the federal government gets from Georgians through income taxes, the federal government also receives a far more important commodity. In the various wars throughout this century, men and women from Georgia have served in various capacities. Many have given their lives for their country.

Over the years, Georgians have served in different branches of the federal government. Senators from Georgia in this century include such leaders as Walter George, Richard Russell, Sam Nunn, and Max Cleland. Among its members of the U.S. House of Representatives are Newt Gingrich (who served as speaker of the house), John Lewis, and Carl Vinson. And, of course, Georgia also provided the nation with a president, Jimmy Carter, whose contributions to world peace and humanity continued long after he left the White House.

Four ways that Georgia receives money back from the Federal government are shown here (clockwise from opposite page below): I-16, part of Georgia's 1200 miles of interstate highways; wild horses on Cumberland Island National Seashore; Civil War artillery damage at Fort Pulaski; Ocmulgee National Monument in Macon.

POLITICAL CARTOONS

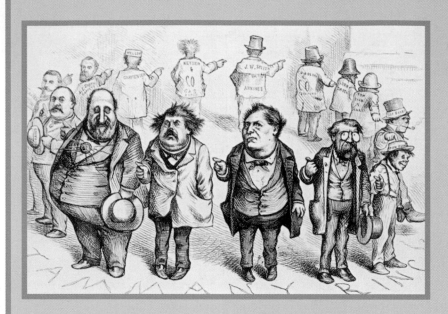

Thomas Nast created this cartoon entitled "Who stole the money? Do tell. Twas he," criticizing political corruption in New York under William M. "Boss" Tweed, the fat man on the left (see page 334). Nast is also given the credit for creating the image of Santa Claus as we know him today.

A *political cartoon* is a drawing that makes a statement about a subject of public interest. It can be about a person, an event, or an important problem. Good cartoons deal with emotions and are a form of protest. They get their message across in a simple and humorous way, usually with few words.

Thomas Nast was one of the earliest and best-known American political cartoonists. His cartoons were very dramatic and supportive of the Union during the Civil War. Abraham Lincoln called him the Union's best recruiting sergeant. Nast created several symbols that are used by political cartoonists today — the Republican elephant and the Democratic donkey.

In 1884, Joseph Pulitzer's New York *World* became the first newspaper to hire a political cartoonist, Walt McDougall. One of McDougall's cartoons so increased the *World's* circulation that Pulitzer hired him full time. Political cartooning as a profession was born.

One of the best-known recent cartoonists is Herbert Block. A New Deal liberal supporting the newly rising middle class, Block used humor to lampoon or mock conservatives. He did not regard them as mean, but as daffy and dim-witted.

In recent years, the political cartoon has found able practitioners in people like Pat Oliphant, Jeff MacNelly, Bill Mauldin, and Bill Sanders. They deftly use humor to present a political point of view.

Do You Remember?
1. About how much money comes into the state each year through social security benefits and federal and military pensions?
2. Where does Georgia rank among states in terms of federal dollars received?
3. Whose boyhood home in Atlanta in a national historic site?

GEORGIA STATE GOVERNMENT

Georgia was one of the thirteen colonies that became a state after the American Revolution. Georgia adopted its first state constitution in 1777. In 1983, Georgians approved the state's tenth constitution. Even though there have been changes in the bodies of these various constitutions, their purpose has remained the same. The state constitution declares:

> *To perpetuate the principles of free government, insure justice to all, preserve peace, promote the interest and happiness of the citizens and of the family, and transmit to posterity the enjoyment of liberty, we the people of Georgia, relying upon the protection and guidance of Almighty God, do ordain and establish this Constitution.*

Georgia's constitution claims, "All government, of right, originates with the people, is founded upon their will only, and is instituted for the good of the whole. Public officers are the trustees and servants of the people and are at all times amenable to them." In other words, any power the government has is given by the citizens and is for the good of everyone. Persons elected to public office in state government work for the people and are accountable to the voters for their actions.

The dome of the Georgia State Capitol in Atlanta is covered with gold leaf from Dahlonega. Among the statues on the grounds of the capitol is a replica of the Statue of Liberty.

The constitution further states: "The people of this state have the inherent right of regulating their internal government. Government is instituted for the protection, security and benefit of the people; and at all times they have the right to alter or reform the same whenever the public good may require it." Therefore, Georgia's government is meant to serve the people, and the constitution allows the people to change the government when it fails to serve their needs.

The constitution gives voters the right to control state government by electing state officials. Citizens also may suggest laws that might improve the way the state is governed.

Georgia, like the nation, has three branches of government: executive, legislative, and judicial. The tasks of these branches are, in many ways, like those of the federal branches.

Sworn in as Georgia's 79th governor in 1991, Zell Miller served as Georgia's lieutenant governor longer than anyone in the state's history—from 1974 until his election as governor. He was reelected in 1994.

THE EXECUTIVE BRANCH OF GOVERNMENT

The largest branch of state government is the **executive branch**. The executive branch of Georgia's government employs approximately 67,000 people. They fill jobs ranging from teaching in one of the state's colleges to protecting state-maintained roads or forests. The governor is the chief executive officer of the state. Since the end of Reconstruction, Georgia's governors have been members of the Democratic party.

The governor is elected by a majority of the popular vote for a four-year term. The law allows governors to serve two consecutive terms, so it is possible for one person to be the state's chief executive officer for eight years in a row. After a second term, an individual has to wait four or more years before being eligible to run again.

Formal Powers of the Governor

The Georgia constitution describes the governor's formal powers. They can be classified as executive powers, legislative powers, and judicial powers.

Executive powers include the right to appoint state officials and the right to see that civil and criminal laws are enforced.

Legislative powers include the right to send requests and messages to the legislature and the right to veto a **bill** (draft of a proposed law) so it does not become a law. The governor may also call special sessions of the legislature.

Judicial powers include the right to pardon persons convicted of crimes and the right to appoint state justices in the event of unexpired terms.

Other formal powers include the following:
• managing the state's budget

Top: *The governor's mansion in Atlanta serves as the official residence of the governor and for public functions such as state dinners and receptions.*
Above: *Roy E. Barnes was elected governor in 1998.*

Governor Joe Frank Harris served from 1983 to 1990. Major changes in Georgia's education system were made during his terms in office.

- directing the attorney general to act as a representative of the state in lower court cases involving state law
- presenting annual "State of the State" address to the legislature
- preparing budget bills for consideration by the Georgia house of representatives
- acting as commander-in-chief of the Georgia National Guard
- heading the state's civil defense units
- sending Georgia Highway Patrol officers and the Georgia Bureau of Investigation into communities in times of danger

Informal Powers of the Governor

In addition to formal powers, Georgia's governor has many informal powers. Some are the result of tradition and custom. Others are necessary to enforce formal powers. The informal powers of the chief executive include the following:

- communicating to the public a personal position on issues of interest to all Georgians
- acting as honorary head of the political party that elected him or her to office
- issuing proclamations to honor individuals, holidays, or special events and, with the legislature's approval, adding new state symbols
- representing the state in meetings with other state officials, federal officers, or foreign dignitaries
- meeting with business and industry leaders from other states or nations to encourage them to expand their businesses into Georgia
- working with members of the legislature to get laws passed
- guiding state agencies

Sometimes, the informal powers of a governor may seem more important than the formal powers. However, a governor's greatest influence is gotten through the use of the power to appoint individuals to boards and executive offices. For example, Governor Joe Frank Harris, who served from 1983 to 1990, appointed all fifteen members of the board of regents (the board that controls the University System of Georgia and all public colleges and universities). He named all ten members of the state board of education (the board that controls public elementary and secondary schools of the state). He also selected a state superintendent of schools needed to complete an unexpired term of office.

Governor Harris appointed a panel of business leaders, legislators, and citizens to write a legislative package called Quality Basic Education (QBE). When this package became law in 1985, it affected all public school students in Georgia. For example, an eighth-grade student in Ocilla has the same study objectives as an eighth-grade student in Columbus. Today, this standard state curriculum is called **Quality Core Curriculum.**

In several grades, all students take a state-prepared test during the spring. First-time teachers in the state of Georgia must pass tests during their first three years of teaching to show they are able to instruct students. This legislation also changed the way school systems are funded. In these ways, Governor Harris made an effort to improve education all over the state.

One of the primary duties of the lieutenant governor is to preside over the state senate. Here, Lt. Governor Pierre Howard (third from left) discusses the 1991 state budget with (left to right) Speaker of the Georgia House of Representatives Tom Murphy, Senator Don Johnston and Representative Terry Coleman. First elected in 1990, Lt. Governor Howard was elected to a second term in 1994.

Office of Lieutenant Governor

The executive branch of state government also includes the office of lieutenant governor. The lieutenant governor is elected by popular vote. However, unlike the governor, this official can serve an unlimited number of consecutive terms in office.

The lieutenant governor is the presiding officer of the senate. The lieutenant governor makes senate committee appointments, assigns senate bills to committees, and recognizes members of the senate who wish to speak. Because of these powers, the lieutenant governor may affect the passage or failure of some senate bills.

In the event of a governor's death, resignation, or impeachment, the lieutenant governor becomes the state's chief executive. The lieutenant governor also serves as the chief executive officer when the governor is out of the state.

Do You Remember?

1. How many consecutive terms can a Georgia governor serve?
2. What are the three classifications of the governor's formal powers?
3. How is the lieutenant governor elected?
4. How does the lieutenant governor affect senate legislation?

THE LEGISLATIVE BRANCH OF GOVERNMENT

The Tenth Amendment to the United States Constitution states that "The powers not delegated to the United States by the Constitution, nor prohibited by it to the States, are reserved to the States, respectively, or to the people."

State constitutions grant the reserved law-making power to the legislatures. An exception has to do with amending the constitution. The legislature may propose an amendment, but the amendment must be approved by the voters before it becomes law.

The **legislative branch**, or law-making body, of Georgia's government is officially known as the Georgia General Assembly. It was formed in 1777 as a one-house legislative body and is older than the Congress of the United States. In 1789, the Georgia General Assembly was reorganized as a two-house, or bicameral, legislature, with a senate and a house of representatives.

The house of representatives and the senate operate in similar fashion except for two major differences. Only the house of representatives can write appropriations (spending) bills. Only the senate can confirm appointments of the governor to executive offices. Either group can propose and pass bills, and all bills must be approved by both houses before being sent to the governor.

Members of the legislature are elected by popular vote to two-year terms of office. There is no limit to the number of terms a representative or senator can serve. There are 180 members of the house of representatives and 56 members of the senate. Each of these members is elected by voters in a house or senate election district. Equally important, each house election district contains approximately the same number of people as the other house districts. And each senate district contains approximately the number of people as other senate districts.

The Georgia General Assembly meets each year for a forty-day session, beginning on the second Monday in January. Breaks and recesses do not count as part of the forty days, so the sessions usually last until the middle of March.

The lieutenant governor presides over the senate. The representatives elect a speaker as their presiding officer. The speaker, like the lieutenant governor, appoints committees and their chairs, and assigns bills to those committees. A presiding officer has the power to do the following:
• determine the order of business
• control debate
• rule out proposed amendments to bills
• enforce rules of procedure for the General Assembly
• control meeting times and recesses of the General Assembly
• order a roll call vote on any issue

On the second Monday of each January, 180 members of the house of representatives join together in the house chamber for the start of the 40-day legislative session.

Legislative committee meetings are an integral part of serving as a member of the Georgia General Assembly. Here you see the House Industry Committee discussing one of the Governor's most controversial bills of the mid-1990s—the inclusion of the lottery. How would you have voted?

The lieutenant governor does not have a vote in the senate, but the speaker of the house votes when it is necessary to break a tie.

Members of the house and senate are organized into **committees** (small working groups). Some committees are permanent, lasting during a session and from one session to the next. Others are appointed for a special task and last only until their work is completed. All proposed legislation is reviewed by a house or senate committee before being presented for a vote to the whole body. Some of the standing committees include the Ways and Means Committee, which handles bills involving taxes; the Appropriations Committee, which works on the budget; and the Judiciary Committee, which deals with bills concerning the state's laws and court system.

A member of the Georgia General Assembly may serve on several committees. Committee chairs decide when their committees will meet. They choose the order in which assigned bills will be discussed and when they will be voted on. The committee system makes it possible for proposed bills to be studied closely. There would not be time for such study if each bill were discussed only by the entire house.

After a committee studies a proposed bill, it may take one of three actions. It can decide to pass the bill as written to the house or senate for a vote. It can make changes in the wording of the bill before sending it to the legislature. Or it may choose to keep the bill in committee, thus killing the bill. When presenting a bill to the full body, both house and senate committees may recommend either a favorable or unfavorable vote. In the house, a bill can also be presented with no committee recommendation.

One kind of special committee is an **interim committee**, one that works on assigned issues and concerns between sessions of the legislature. Another special committee is the **conference committee**, which is appointed when the house and senate pass different versions of a bill. The conference committee takes the two bills and tries to write one that can be passed in both houses. Another special committee, called a **joint committee**, is made up of members of both houses and works on an assigned topic or issue.

Types of Legislation

The Georgia General Assembly can pass laws on any matter not denied it by the United States Constitution. It can amend state laws or do away with them. The General Assembly can pass legislation on such matters as taxation, educational improvement, contracts, and real and personal property. Other subjects it deals with include inheritances, mortgages, corporations, and marriage and divorce. The legislature makes laws concerning fines, imprisonment, or death in criminal matters. It also considers **public regulation**, such as morals, public health, business or professional regulations, or any general welfare rule that restricts personal property.

Pages to serve both the Georgia House of Representatives and the Georgia Senate come from all areas of the state. Their job is to deliver messages, distribute bills, and perform other errands for the members of the Georgia General Assembly. The job provides invaluable experience and insight into the workings of government.

How State Laws Are Made

Any citizen may suggest an idea for a law, and any senator or representative can propose a bill for consideration. All bills that affect how the state raises or spends money must come from the house of representatives. Bills about anything else may begin in either house.

Bills in the Georgia General Assembly go through almost the same steps as those in the United States Congress before they become law. These are as follows:

During a regular legislative session, thousands of bills can run from one or two pages in length to the size of a small book. It is the role of men and women like Jimmy Vining at the Capitol Print Shop to see that the bills are printed and put together correctly for house or senate members to read and study before making final votes.

1. A proposal is written in legal language and turned in to the clerk's office. There it is given a name and number. For example, the twelfth proposal turned in to the house of representatives' clerk during a given session will be H.R. 12. After the proposal is given a number, it is called a bill.

2. Copies of the bill are made for members of the house that is to consider it. The bill is assigned to a committee.

3. The committee to which the bill is assigned may hold public hearings so that interested persons may speak for or against the bill. The committee may also ask legislative staff members to gather information about the bill. The committee studies the bill and discusses its good and bad points.

4. The committee assigned to handle the bill can do several things: (a) it can hold the bill and not release it to the house or to the senate; (b) it can vote the bill out of committee and recommend that it be passed; (c) it can vote the bill out of committee and recommend that it not be passed; (d) it can make changes in the bill and vote the new version out for consideration by the house or senate; and (e) in the house only, the bill can be voted out of

committee with no recommendation. If a bill is not voted out of committee, it is "killed" unless the full house votes to take the bill from the committee and assign it to another committee.

5. A bill sent to the full house or senate can be discussed, debated, and amended. A majority vote is required to pass a bill.

6. When a bill is "certified," or passed, by one house of the General Assembly, it is carried by messenger to the other house for consideration.

7. Again, the bill is assigned to a committee. As before, the bill may be kept in committee, changed, or voted out without change to be handled by the entire house.

8. If both houses pass a bill, it is signed by their presiding officers and clerks before being sent to the governor.

9. The governor can handle a bill in one of three ways. He or she can sign it into law. He or she can take no action, thus letting it become law automatically. He or she can veto it and return it to the house where it originated. If a bill is vetoed, the General Assembly can override the veto by a two-thirds vote of both houses. The bill then becomes law.

A bill passed by the state legislature finally becomes law when it is signed by the governor. Here, Governor Joe Frank Harris signs a bill in the rotunda of the state capitol.

When the House and Senate Disagree

Remember that for a bill to become a law, the exact same version of the bill must be passed by both the house of representatives and the senate. Many times, one house will pass a slightly different version of a bill than the one adopted by other house. When this happens, the amended bill must be sent back to the other house to be reconsidered for a vote there. If the two legislative groups cannot agree to pass, or adopt, identical versions of a bill, a conference committee is appointed. The conference committee is made up of three senators and three representatives. Their job is to work out a compromise bill that both houses might accept. The compromise bill must be passed by both the senate and the house of representatives before it is sent to the governor.

Do You Remember?

1. Which house can propose a bill concerning how the state spends money?

2. What happens when the governor takes no action on a bill passed by both houses?

3. Who makes up the conference committee?

"FIAT JUSTITIA, RUAT CAELUM"

Justices of the Georgia Supreme Court frequently deliberate for hours in committee, debating the pros and cons of a law as it applies to an individual or to the state. What are some of the characteristics which a person would need to become a Georgia Supreme Court Justice?

THE JUDICIAL BRANCH OF GOVERNMENT

The **judicial branch** of government consists of the courts. The highest-ranking court in the Georgia court system is the state's **supreme court**. The seven supreme court justices are elected by a majority of the popular vote to six-year terms. If a supreme court justice resigns or dies before the end of a term, the governor may appoint a justice to complete that term of office.

Supreme court justices elect the chief justice from among the seven members. The supreme court is an appellate court, which means it only reviews cases on appeal from lower-ranking courts. There are no witnesses and juries as in lower-ranking trial courts.

Another responsibility of the supreme court is to interpret both the state and federal constitutions. It may review cases involving treaties, the constitutionality of laws, titles to land, equity, wills, capital felonies, habeas corpus, extraordinary remedies, divorce, and alimony. It may outline a code of judicial conduct for the judges of the state, and regulate the admission of attorneys to practice law in Georgia. The supreme court automatically reviews all Georgia cases involving the death penalty.

Decisions of the supreme court are binding. This means they have the final authority in matters of law at the state level.

The second highest ranking state court is the **court of appeals.** Nine judges serve on this court, and they elect one of their members to serve as the chief judge. The judges are elected to six-year terms.

The court of appeals, like the supreme court, is an appellate court. It hears cases appealed from lower-ranking courts.

Below the appellate courts are the trial courts of Georgia. The **trial courts** hear original cases, such as civil cases involving disputes between private parties, and criminal cases involving violations of laws or commission of crimes. Trial courts include the state superior courts, state courts, probate courts, juvenile courts, magistrate courts, municipal courts, and justice of the peace courts.

Each court has a special **jurisdiction** (the range of actions over which the court has control or influence). For example, the juvenile court handles cases involving persons under the age of seventeen. The probate court deals with the wills and estates of deceased persons. Magistrate courts can only hear cases involving sums under $3,000.

The role of the judicial branch of Georgia's government is to protect citizens from abuses of government by providing each citizen with "due process of law." The U.S. Constitution says no state can deprive any citizen of life, liberty, or property without "due process of law." This means persons arrested for a crime have the right to have a lawyer present during questioning. Individuals must be given a speedy, public trial before a fair judge and jury. They may face and question witnesses, or they can remain silent so as not to incriminate (blame) themselves.

The courts also protect citizens from each other by handling civil cases (disputes that are not crimes), and criminal cases.

The offices and courtroom of the Georgia Supreme Court are in the Judicial Building, next to the State Capitol in Atlanta.

SEPARATION OF POWERS AMONG THE BRANCHES OF GOVERNMENT

The Georgia constitution, like that of the United States, provides separate powers for each branch of government. It also provides for **checks and balances** so each branch of government can prevent the other branches from having too much power.

- The executive branch can veto bills passed by the legislature and can call special sessions of the legislature. It also has some appointment powers when officers of the court resign or die.
- The legislative branch can impeach government officials. It can override a governor's veto of bills to make them into law. It must confirm appointments made by the governor. It can also propose constitutional changes.
- The judicial branch determines whether or not laws are constitutional.

Each branch of government is responsive to the citizens of Georgia because most officials are directly elected by the voters.

LOCAL GOVERNMENT IN GEORGIA

Local governments are the most numerous of all governments in the United States. Georgia has 159 counties, and each of these counties has a governmental organization. In addition to the counties, there are many cities in Georgia. Each of them also has a government.

Not only are local governments the most numerous forms of governance, they are also the closest to the people and the most likely to affect people directly. Local governments get their powers and their right to exist from the Georgia state constitution.

COUNTY GOVERNMENT

Counties are set up by the state government to carry on certain governmental functions. In Georgia, county powers are limited by the purposes for which the counties may tax. These purposes are listed in the state constitution. They include the power to tax to cover the cost of county administration; police (sheriff) and legal systems; construction and maintenance of roads and bridges; public health; medical care for people who cannot afford to pay; assistance to dependent children; parks and libraries; and public education.

County governments are required by the state constitution to be uniform except for the following instances: The Georgia General Assembly may, in any county, establish commissioners of roads and revenues; consolidate the offices of tax receiver and tax collector into the office of tax commissioner; and abolish the office of treasurer. Because all county governments are similar, the governmental structure of one county, Fulton County, can serve to show both how a county operates and how cities and counties cooperate in sharing services.

Fulton County is the most populous county in Georgia. It was originally created in 1853 by the Georgia General Assembly. Fulton County was enlarged in 1931 when Milton and Campbell counties merged with it. Fulton County covers 523 square miles. Atlanta occupies about 117 square miles, or 22 percent, of Fulton County. Nine other incorporated cities are also located within Fulton County: Alpharetta, College Park, East Point, Fairburn, Hapeville, Mountain Park, Palmetto, Roswell, and Union City.

A board of commissioners governs Fulton County. The board consists of seven members elected to four-year terms. Four commissioners are elected from geographic districts and three are elected from the county at large. The chair of the board was elected by a majority of its members until 1990 when, for the first time, the office was filled through election by the voters. The board of commissioners sets levels of services to be provided by each department of county government when it approves each annual departmental budget.

The county courthouse is the seat of government for a county. This is the Taliaferro County Courthouse in Crawfordville.

In Fulton County, the board of commissioners appoints a county manager as its chief executive officer. The county manager, with the commission's approval, appoints all department heads except those department heads who are elected officials or whose appointments are specifically provided for in the law. The county manager's chief function is to carry out policies set by the county commission.

Through contract agreements, the county provides financial support to shared ventures, such as the Fulton-DeKalb Hospital Authority. Public hospital facilities are administered by the Fulton-DeKalb Hospital Authority, which operates Grady Memorial Hospital. Property zoning is a joint function of the county and Atlanta. Library services to residents of Fulton County are provided by Atlanta in a contract between the two governments.

The school system for the county, including all nine incorporated areas outside the city limits of Atlanta, is operated by the Fulton County Board of Education, which is elected by the voters and which appoints a superintendent of schools. The elected Atlanta Board of Education appoints a superintendent of schools for the city.

Atlanta operates with an elected city council and an elected mayor form of government. Municipal court judges, city traffic court judges, and the chief solicitor of city court are elected. All other officials or department heads are appointed.

Top: *The Wilkes County Courthouse is located in Washington.* **Above:** *This is the impressive granite county courthouse in Elberton, Georgia. At one time, the town was actually called Elbert Court House.* **Right:** *Charlton County Courthouse in Folkston.*

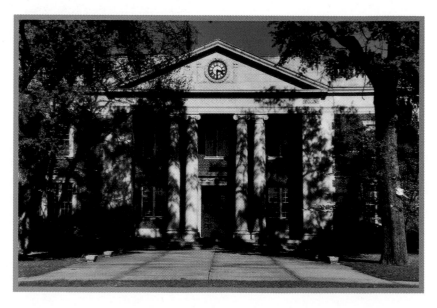

THE CITY AS A POLITICAL UNIT

A city with its own government is called a municipality. The city can exist as a political unit when it is given a charter by the state legislature. A city government can do only what the charter authorizes it to do. For example, most city charters allow cities to provide police protection, license businesses, maintain streets and sidewalks, control traffic, and provide water and sewerage services. Other services to the citizens may be provided if they are included specifically in a city's charter. Atlanta and some other cities in the state, for example, operate their own school systems because that power is granted in their charters from the state.

City Government

The most common forms of city government are called the mayor-council form, the council-manager form, and the commissioner form. In the mayor-council style of government, the elected city council is responsible for making the laws. An elected mayor acts as the city's chief executive officer with the responsibility for seeing that the laws are carried out and that city agencies do their jobs. The role of mayor in such a form of government may be a weak position or a strong position, depending upon the amount of power and authority given to the mayor's job.

In the council-manager style of government, the voters elect a city council that appoints a city manager. The council establishes laws and policies, and the city manager is responsible for appointing the heads of city governments and for seeing that they carry out their jobs.

In cities with a commissioner form of government, the voters elect commissioners. Each commissioner is the head of a department within the city government, and the mayor is elected by the commissioners from among themselves.

The Atlanta City Hall was built in 1929, at a cost of more than one million dollars. The multi-storied terra cotta (a hard waterproof ceramic clay) exterior is an impressive sight to the many visitors who conduct their city business there each day.

City-County Government

Some counties also provide services outside of incorporated municipalities for things such as water, sewage, sanitation, and fire protection. As long as city and county governments provide distinctive types of services in the same area, they do not get in each other's way in providing good services to the people. However, as a county becomes more urban, city and county governments may provide the same services to the same people.

One way to avoid this duplication is for city and county governments to form a single government. Two such mergers have taken place to date. The city of Columbus and Muscogee County merged in 1971. Athens and Clarke County formed a single government unit in 1990.

A school system is one example of a special district. Georgia has 159 county school systems and 28 independent school systems.

SPECIAL-PURPOSE DISTRICTS

In addition to states, counties, and cities, many people have to interact with various other special-purpose districts. Each of these districts provides a service and has its own set of regulations governing it. A school system is one example of a special district. The law says you must attend school, but much of the control of that school is left up to a local board of education and the school district office. Within the guidelines set by state law, local school systems can establish starting and stopping times for the school day, spell out standards of behavior and punishment, determine dress codes, and schedule students' time during the school day.

Within the metropolitan area of Atlanta, **Metropolitan Atlanta Rapid Transit Authority** (MARTA) is another special-purpose district. MARTA runs a bus and rail system, determines the cost of fares, selects routes, and schedules public transportation times.

Generally, a special-purpose district is created for a single job or single group of tasks. Most such districts govern themselves. Special-purpose districts include the Public Housing Authority, which provides services such as determining the location of public housing, constructing and maintaining the buildings, renting the units, and drawing up tenants' rules and regulations.

Other special-purpose districts include community fire departments, parks and recreation authorities, and airport and port authorities. No matter what individual special-purpose districts are called, they all have one thing in common: they exist to provide for the public's welfare.

THE VOTER'S ROLE IN GOVERNMENT

Georgia citizens take an active part in state government by voting. Voters select persons to fill some government offices and decide major questions and issues.

To register to vote in Georgia, a person must be at least eighteen years old and a citizen of the United States. An individual must also be a legal resident of Georgia and the county in which the registration takes place.

Voting in national, state, and county elections is managed according to the Georgia Election Code. The secretary of state is the chief election official. The secretary of state makes sure candidates meet the qualifications to run for office. This official also schedules elections, prints ballots, and provides all election materials to Georgia's counties. After an election, the secretary of state checks the results in each county and publishes them.

A **general election** is held in November, at least every even-numbered year. This is when major federal and state officials are selected. Other elections are held as needed to select public officials at all levels of government: national, state, county, or city.

Voters select the most important state officials. These officials, in turn, appoint others who work for and with them. Therefore, a citizen can, by voting, influence all of state government.

Two of the many people who cast their votes during the 1990 primary in Marietta are shown here. They joined thousands of voters throughout the state in exercising the most fundamental right of any Georgian or American citizen—the right to vote to choose those who will represent them. However, only about forty percent of those Georgians who were eligible to vote took advantage of that right. Why do you think it is important to vote? Will you take the time to vote?

CAMPAIGN FINANCE REFORM

In the three-quarters of a century since candidate Warren G. Harding (above, making an early voice recording during the 1920 campaign) was able to run his presidential campaign from the front porch of his home in Marion, Ohio. Campaign financing has become a multi-million dollar affair.

Lately, there has been growing concern about the costs of political campaigns. Millions of dollars are spent by individuals running for offices at all levels of government. For example, a recent U.S. Senate hopeful spent over $35 million of his own money during his run for office—and he lost! This is a far cry from the days in the 1920s when presidential candidate Warren G. Harding was able to run his campaign from the front porch of his home in Marion, Ohio. In those days, reporters and others simply gathered on Harding's lawn and listened as the candidate spoke of the issues of the day.

At various times, government has tried to limit the amount certain individuals and groups could give to federal campaigns or political parties. In 1907, the Tillman Act barred direct contributions from corporations. In 1943, this prohibition was extended to include labor unions. The Congress of Industrial Organizations (CIO), however, overcame this obstacle by forming the first political action committee. The rationale behind a political action committee, or PAC, was that campaign money was coming not from the union's treasury but, rather, from members' voluntary contributions. Soon other unions, along with corporations and other groups, formed PACs of their own.

Although the PACs were not authorized by the federal government, neither were they strictly illegal. After Watergate, when cries for political reform of all sorts were popular, Congress approved amendments to the Federal Election Campaign Act that officially approved the creation of PACs. This paved the way for creation of thousands of PACs. The Federal Election Commission (FEC) has set limits on how much can be contributed to federal campaigns. But there are no limits to how much congressional candidates can spend or whether the money comes from supporters or from their own savings. In addition, there is no control over so-called soft money. "Soft money" refers to contributions not covered by federal regulation. For example, money that is used to support a political party—not a specific candidate—falls under the accepted definition of soft money. In the past several decades, the use of soft money for purposes other than those

for which it was originally intended has become one of the major abuses of federal campaign finance legislation. Soft money can be given by anyone, even those banned from giving to political parties or candidates running for federal offices. It allows people who have already contributed the maximum under federal election laws a way to give much more. And it enables unions and corporations to directly support presidential candidates.

Of course, this is not the 1920s, and today's election campaigns use methods of spreading their messages far differently from those used by President Harding. For most candidates, the single largest expense is for television ads. Office seekers, particularly those in the largest—and thus, most expensive—markets face extraordinarily large fees to compete. And this is especially true of those running for a national office.

Most suggestions for campaign reform center on tightening up the loophole that soft money provides. And most also suggest that television stations and networks have an obligation to provide free air time to qualified candidates. Many feel that if some major changes are not made in the way campaigns are financed and run, soon only the very wealthy will be able to afford to run. Or, people who should be attending to the duties of their offices will continue to scramble for dollars no matter what the source.

Zell Miller's eighteen years as lieutenant governor gave him high name recognition with voters when he ran for governor in 1990. Here, he makes a campaign appearance with Lt. Governor candidate Pierre Howard (left) and out-going governor Joe Frank Harris (right). Zell Miller was elected to a second term in 1994.

Voters also have the right and responsibility to decide some issues. Because it requires a vote of the people to change the state constitution, proposed amendments sometimes appear on the ballot. Voters are also asked to decide **bond issues**, in which some level of government asks permission to raise money for a public project. For example, some schools, libraries, and hospitals have been built with public money approved by the voters on a bond issue.

No matter what the purpose of an election, low voter turnout is a matter of serious concern. Many people fear that democratic government will not last if so few people are concerned enough about the issues and individuals to vote. Some fear that government will be taken over by wealthy, well-organized interests that have only their self-interest at heart. Effective, democratic government needs voters who are interested in the common good of all citizens of the nation, state, or community.

GEORGIA'S CAPITAL AND CAPITOL

Atlanta, once a crossroads for Creek and Cherokee Indians, is now home to over half a million people. It is also the **capital**, or seat of government, of the state of Georgia. Each January, several hundred legislators arrive from all over the state to open the annual session of the Georgia General Assembly. Senators and representatives work in the gold-domed **capitol,** the building that also houses offices for the governor, lieutenant governor, and other state officials.

Building the capitol took five years. Its exterior walls are Indiana limestone. Inside, the walls, floors, and stairs are polished Georgia marble. When the capitol was dedicated in 1889, it was the state's tallest building. Today, its 75-foot round dome is highly visible on the Atlanta skyline. The dome is covered with 60 ounces of gold mined in Dahlonega. A statue called "Miss Freedom" stands on top of it with her arm stretched skyward holding a torch of liberty and freedom.

Over nine thousand employees work in the government office buildings located near the capitol. These buildings range from three-story marble structures to the twenty-story brick- and-glass twin tow-

"Miss Freedom" sits atop the gold-plated dome of Georgia's state capitol in Atlanta, welcoming Georgia's citizens and visitors.

ers of the James H. Floyd Veteran Memorial Building. With the exception of the State Forestry Commission, which is located in Macon, every state department is headquartered in Atlanta.

Do You Remember?

1. What court handles cases involving persons under seventeen years of age?
2. Who is the chief election officer of the state?
3. What is the difference between the state's *capital* and the state's *capitol*?

SUMMARY

- Because the activities people expect governments at all levels to perform have increased, the size of these governments has also increased.
- However, these basic principles of government remain: sovereignty, constitutionalism, separation of powers, and federalism.
- In the United States, government is carried out at three levels: federal, state, and local.
- Like most other states, Georgia gets more from the federal government in services and benefits than its citizens pay out in income taxes.
- The three branches of government in Georgia are the executive, the legislative, and the judicial.
- Georgia's governor has both formal and informal powers.
- The state's legislative body, called the General Assembly, consists of two houses: the house of representatives and the senate.
- Before they are enacted into laws, bills in the state's legislative bodies follow almost the same paths as those in the federal legislature.
- The state's judicial system consists of various levels of courts, including its supreme court, courts of appeals, and trial courts.
- The most numerous governments in the nation are those at the local level, including county, city, and special-purpose governments.
- Effective government needs voters interested in the common good of all and who turn out to participate in elections at all levels.

No longer the tallest building in Atlanta, the Georgia State Capitol is still impressive among modern skyscrapers.

1998 Elections for house of representatives, senate, and local offices	2000 Elections for governor, house of representatives, senate, superior courts, appellate courts, and local offices	2002 Elections for house of representatives, senate, and local offices	2004 Elections for governor, house of representatives, senate, superior courts, appellate courts, and local offices
1998	**2000**	**2002**	**2004**
1998 Elections for U.S. House of Representatives and U.S. Senate	2000 Federal census and elections for president, U.S. House of Representatives, and U.S. Senate	2002 Elections for U.S. House of Representatives and U.S. Senate	2004 Elections for president and U.S. House of Representatives

Reviewing People, Places, and Terms

Use the following terms in a paragraph describing the basic principles of democratic government.

constitutionalism
executive branch
federal system
judicial branch
legislative branch
separation of powers
sovereignty

Use the following terms in a paragraph that describes how laws are made in Georgia.

bill
committee
conference committee

Understanding the Facts

1. If there is a conflict between a national and a state law, which law has precedence?
2. What are the three branches of state government?
3. Who is the head of the executive branch of the state government?
4. What are the two houses of Georgia's General Assembly?
5. Which body of the General Assembly can write appropriation bills?

6. Why are committees so important to the legislative process?
7. What kind of committee is appointed when the two legislative groups cannot agree on a bill?
8. Who elects the chief justice of the Georgia supreme court?
9. What is the difference between the mayor-council form of government and the council-manager form?
10. What are the qualifications needed for a person to register to vote in Georgia?

Developing Critical Thinking

1. Why is a constitution so valuable?
2. Why is it important in a democratic society to have a separation of powers in government?
3. Why is it important for each house or senate district in the state to have approximately the same number of people?
4. Why do you think that for most of the twentieth century people said that the real election in Georgia was the Democratic primary? Do you think this still holds true?

Applying Your Skills

1. Prepare a chart that shows (a) the current elected officials in the state's executive branch (governor, lieutenant governor, and so on), (b)

your state senate district and your current state senator, and (c) your state house district and your current state representative.

2. Get a copy of the most recent state budget. Determine the major sources of revenue for that year and the percentage each was of the original amount received.

3. Research your county or community. Find information about its history as well as its current officials. Determine its main sources of revenue and its major expenditures.

4. Interview a county commisioner to find out what services the county provides to residents.

5. Monitor the local newspaper for articles pertaining to city and county government. Create a bulletin board for your classroom.

Making Connections

1. Collect three political cartoons from the newspaper. Write a brief interpretation of each cartoon.

2. Draw a political cartoon about a leading community, state, or national politician or a political issue. Share the cartoon with classmates.

3. Prepare a report on the current campaign finance laws, as well as proposed legislation to reform these laws. From your research, what do you believe are the greatest abuses of the current laws? How would you change them?

4. The media, especially television, now earns a significant amount of money from political campaign ads. Try to determine what suggestions the media in your community might make for improving this situation by posing questions either in person, on the phone, or by either regular or electronic mail. Share your results with the class.

Did You Know?

• The symbol for the Republican party came about when cartoonist Thomas Nast drew an elephant in 1874 to symbolize the size of the party.

• The first head of our national government was Maryland's John Hanson, not George Washington. Hanson was chosen as "President of the United States in Congress Assembled," under the Articles of Confederation on November 5, 1781.

• When electric lights were installed in the White House in 1889, President Benjamin Harrison was so afraid to touch the switch that aides had to turn the lights on and off for him.

• In 1997, Georgia appointed its first black state attorney general, Thurbet E. Baker.

BUILDING SKILLS: ANALYZING STATE INTERESTS

A *state* is a group of people living in the same area, under the same government. Each state is unique; for example, there is no other state like Georgia.

Just as individuals look at things from their own personal viewpoint, a state tends to look at events and issues from its own viewpoint. A state has concerns about its political and economic well-being as well as the personal well-being of its citizens. And each state acts to promote its own interests. Those state interests may vary from year to year as circumstances within the state change from year to year. Do the following:

1. Read a newspaper or listen to a news broadcast to identify current issues in Georgia. Make a list of these issues.

2. Talk to family members, friends, and neighbors to find out what issues they believe are important in the state. Add these to the list you made in #1.

3. Compile a list of laws passed by a recent session of Georgia's General Assembly.

4. Compare your two lists. How many of the laws address the issues you identified in #1 and #2?

APPENDIX I

GEORGIA STATE SYMBOLS

You can learn much about where you live by examining the symbols selected to represent the state.

The term *symbol* is defined as something that represents another thing. For example, a ring can be a symbol of love or friendship. An anniversary symbolizes an important event such as a wedding or birthday. States also have symbols to remind us of important events, valuable resources, or significant ideals. The Georgia legislature by majority vote officially names a state symbol to identify something representative of the state. Each time you see one of Georgia's state symbols, it can be a reminder of your home and heritage.

The State Flag

The present-day Georgia flag was adopted in 1956, replacing the original state flag that had been adopted in 1879. The state pledge of allegiance bears the words *Wisdom, Justice, and Moderation.* These three words are also the state motto.

The State Bird

The brown thrasher (opposite page, top) officially became Georgia's state bird in 1970, although Governor Eugene Talmadge had issued a proclamation naming the brown and white songster a symbol of the state in 1935. Farmers, in particular, like to see the long-beaked bird nesting in low bushes on their land, because the thrasher diet includes grasshoppers, worms, and caterpillars that can be destructive to crops.

Also in 1970, the Georgia House of Representatives selected a second bird, the bobwhite quail, as the official game bird of the state. This quail is best known for its distinctive "bob-bob-white" call and as a sports bird for game hunters. Georgia is known as the "Quail Capital of the World" and has several plants that process and ship the delicacy throughout the country.

The State Flower

The Cherokee rose, Georgia's state flower, was adopted by the Georgia Federation of Women's Clubs and confirmed by the state legislature as a state symbol in 1916. The rose originally came from China and was introduced into the New World by Spanish settlers who brought it to Florida. Its American name came about because the rose was a favorite of the Cherokee Indians, who spread it throughout Georgia. The plant is high-climbing, is excessively thorny, and has vivid green leaves. The flower has waxy-white petals with a velvet texture and a large golden center. Because of its hardy nature, the plant was once used as a hedge throughout the state. It is not seen as often now due to the ever-expanding highways and housing developments.

The State Tree

The live oak (below) was adopted as the state tree of Georgia in 1937. It is found primarily along the coastal plains and on the islands where

settlers first made their homes. The majestic tree sometimes has a trunk twenty-five feet in diameter. It can grow more than forty feet high and have a limb span of more than a hundred feet in diameter. A live oak tree often lives for several hundred years and is a host for clinging Spanish moss which, during the early settlement days, was used for stuffing mattresses and chairs.

Other State Symbols

The state fish, the largemouth bass (see page 39), is found mostly in warm-water streams and lakes. Georgia boasts one of the world's records for the biggest largemouth bass ever caught. The bass was adopted as a state symbol by the Georgia House of Representatives in 1970.

The state insect is the honey bee. It is highly valued by agriculture and is responsible for the cross pollination of more than fifty different crops. Honey produced by the bees is also a valuable commodity in Georgia's economy.

In 1976, the Georgia House of Representatives recognized three other state symbols: the official state mineral, state gem, and state fossil. Staurolite, found in old crystalline rocks, was designated the official state mineral. The popular names for staurolite crystals are "Fairy Crosses" or "Fairy Stones." These minerals are abundant in north Georgia and have been collected for generations as good luck charms.

The state gem—quartz—is the second-most abundant mineral on earth. It can be seen in a wide variety of colors in Georgia. Quartz is most commonly recognized as the amethyst, often used in jewelry, and the clear quartz which resembles a diamond when it is faceted with many small flat surfaces.

The shark tooth, Georgia's state fossil, is a common fossil in the coastal plan region. In fossil form, the shark tooth can be traced back 375 million years. Fossilized shark teeth are found in a variety of colors ranging from the common black and gray to white, brown, blue, and reddish brown.

In 1989, the gopher tortoise became the newest state symbol of Georgia. It is the official state reptile.

Each of these symbols is a reminder of the wealth of natural resources found throughout the state of Georgia.

APPENDIX II

GEORGIA COUNTIES

County	Date Founded	County Seat	Named For
Appling	1818	Baxley	Col. Daniel Appling
Atkinson	1917	Pearson	William Yates Atkinson
Bacon	1914	Alma	Augustus Octavius Bacon
Baker	1825	Newton	Col. John Baker
Baldwin	1803	Milledgeville	Abraham Baldwin
Banks	1858	Homer	Dr. Richard E. Banks
Barrow	1914	Winder	David Crenshaw Barrow
Bartow	1832	Cartersville	Gen. Francis Stebbins Bartow
Ben Hill	1906	Fitzgerald	Benjamin Harvey Hill
Berrien	1856	Nashville	John MacPherson Berrien
Bibb	1822	Macon	William Wyatt Bibb, M.D.
Bleckley	1912	Cochran	Logan Edward Bleckley
Brantley	1920	Nahunta	William G. Brantley
Brooks	1858	Quitman	Preston Smith Brooks
Bryan	1793	Pembroke	Jonathan Bryan
Bulloch	1796	Statesboro	Gov. Archibald Bulloch
Burke	1777	Waynesboro	Edmund Burke
Butts	1825	Jackson	Capt. Samuel Butts
Calhoun	1854	Morgan	John Caldwell Calhoun
Camden	1777	Woodbine	Sir Charles Pratt, Earl of Camden
Candler	1914	Metter	Gov. Allen Daniel Candler
Carroll	1826	Carrollton	Charles Carroll
Catoosa	1853	Ringgold	Cherokee Indian Word

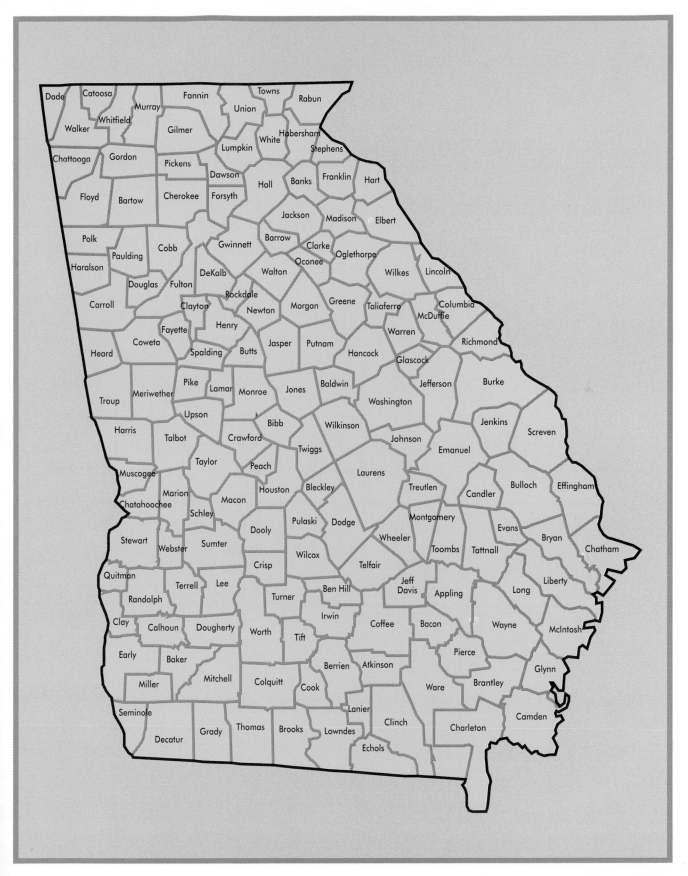

Charlton	1854	Folkston	Robert Charlton
Chatham	1777	Savannah	William Pitt, Earl of Chatham
Chattahoochee	1854	Cusseta	Chattahoochee River
Chattooga	1838	Summerville	Chattooga River
Cherokee	1831	Canton	Cherokee Indians
Clarke	1805	Athens	Elijah Clarke
Clay	1854	Fort Gaines	Henry Clay
Clayton	1858	Jonesboro	Augustin Smith Clayton
Clinch	1850	Homerville	Gen. Duncan Lamont Clinch
Cobb	1832	Marietta	Thomas Willis Cobb
Coffee	1854	Douglas	Gen. John E. Coffee
Colquitt	1856	Moultrie	Walter Terry Colquitt
Columbia	1790	Appling	Christopher Columbus
Cook	1918	Adel	Gen. Phillip Cook
Coweta	1826	Newnan	Coweta Indians
Crawford	1822	Knoxville	William Harris Crawford
Crisp	1905	Cordele	Charles Frederick Crisp
Dade	1837	Trenton	Maj. Francis Langhorne Dade
Dawson	1857	Dawsonville	William Crosby Dawson
Decatur	1823	Bainbridge	Commodore Stephen Decatur
DeKalb	1822	Decatur	Johann DeKalb
Dodge	1870	Eastman	William Earl Dodge
Dooly	1821	Vienna	Col. John Dooly
Dougherty	1853	Albany	Charles Dougherty
Douglas	1870	Douglasville	Stephen Arnold Douglas
Early	1818	Blakely	Gov. Peter Early
Echols	1858	Statenville	Gen. Robert M. Echols
Effingham	1777	Springfield	Francis Howard, Earl of Effingham
Elbert	1790	Elberton	Gov. Samuel Elbert

Emanuel	1812	Swainsboro	Col. David Emanuel
Evans	1914	Claxton	Gen. Clement Anselm Evans
Fannin	1854	Blue Ridge	Col. James Walker Fannin
Fayette	1821	Fayetteville	Marquis De Lafayette
Floyd	1832	Rome	John Floyd
Forsyth	1832	Cumming	Gov. John Forsyth
Franklin	1784	Carnesville	Benjamin Franklin
Fulton	1853	Atlanta	Robert Fulton
Gilmer	1832	Ellijay	Gov. George Gilmer
Glascock	1857	Gibson	Thomas Glascock
Glynn	1777	Brunswick	John Glynn
Gordon	1850	Calhoun	William Washington Gordon
Grady	1905	Cairo	Henry Woodfin Grady
Greene	1786	Greensboro	Nathaniel Greene
Gwinnett	1818	Lawrenceville	Gov. Button Gwinnett
Habersham	1818	Clarkesville	Joseph Habersham
Hall	1818	Gainesville	Gov. Lyman Hall
Hancock	1793	Sparta	John Hancock
Haralson	1856	Buchanan	Gen. Hugh Anderson Haralson
Harris	1827	Hamilton	Charles Harris
Hart	1853	Hartwell	Nancy Morgan Hart
Heard	1830	Franklin	Gov. Stephen Heard
Henry	1821	McDonough	Patrick Henry
Houston	1821	Perry	Gov. John Houstoun
Irwin	1818	Ocilla	Gov. Jared Irwin
Jackson	1796	Jefferson	Gov. James Jackson
Jasper	1807	Monticello	William Jasper
Jeff Davis	1905	Hazelhurst	Jefferson Davis
Jefferson	1796	Louisville	President Thomas Jefferson

Jenkins	1905	Millen	Gov. Charles Jones Jenkins
Johnson	1858	Wrightsville	Gov. Herschel V. Johnson
Jones	1807	Gray	James Jones
Lamar	1920	Barnesville	Lucius Q. C. Lamar
Lanier	1920	Lakeland	Sidney Clapton Lanier
Laurens	1807	Dublin	Col. John Laurens
Lee	1826	Leesburg	Gen. Richard Henry Lee
Liberty	1777	Hinesville	concept of freedom and liberty
Lincoln	1796	Lincolnton	Gen. Benjamin Lincoln
Long	1920	Ludowici	Dr. Crawford Williamson Long
Lowndes	1825	Valdosta	William Jones Lowndes
Lumpkin	1832	Dahlonega	Gov. Wilson Lumpkin
Macon	1837	Oglethorpe	Gen. Nathaniel Macon
Madison	1811	Danielsville	James Madison
Marion	1827	Buena Vista	Gen. Francis Marion
McDuffie	1870	Thomson	George McDuffie
McIntosh	1793	Darien	William McIntosh, Creek Chief
Meriwether	1827	Greenville	Gen. David Meriwether
Miller	1856	Colquitt	Andrew Jackson Miller
Mitchell	1857	Camilla	Gen. Henry Mitchell
Monroe	1821	Forsyth	President James Monroe
Montgomery	1793	Mount Vernon	Maj. Gen. Richard Montgomery
Morgan	1807	Madison	Gen. Daniel Morgan
Murray	1832	Chatsworth	Thomas W. Murray
Muscogee	1826	Columbus	Muscogee Indians
Newton	1821	Covington	Sergeant John Newton
Oconee	1875	Watkinsville	Oconee River
Oglethorpe	1793	Lexington	James Edward Oglethorpe
Paulding	1832	Dallas	John Paulding

Peach	1924	Fort Valley	Georgia Peach
Pickens	1853	Jasper	Gen. Andrew Pickens
Pierce	1857	Blackshear	President Franklin Pierce
Pike	1822	Zebulon	Gen. Zebulon Montgomery Pike
Polk	1851	Cedartown	President James K. Polk
Pulaski	1808	Hawkinsville	Count Casimir Pulaski
Putnam	1807	Eatonton	Gen. Israel Putnam
Quitman	1858	Georgetown	Gen. John Anthony Quitman
Rabun	1819	Clayton	Gov. William Rabun
Randolph	1828	Cuthbert	John Randolph
Richmond	1777	Augusta	Charles Lennox, Duke of Richmond
Rockdale	1870	Conyers	Rockdale Church
Schley	1857	Ellaville	Gov. William Schley
Screven	1793	Sylvania	Gen. James Screven
Seminole	1920	Donalsonville	Seminole Indians
Spalding	1851	Griffin	Thomas Spalding
Stephens	1905	Toccoa	Gov. Alexander H. Stephens
Stewart	1830	Lumpkin	Gen. Daniel Stewart
Sumter	1831	Americus	Gen. Thomas Sumter
Talbot	1827	Talbotton	Gov. Mathew Talbot
Taliaferro	1825	Crawfordville	Col. Benjamin Taliaferro
Tattnall	1801	Reidsville	Gov. Josiah Tattnall
Taylor	1852	Butler	President Zachary Taylor
Telfair	1807	McRae	Gov. Edward Telfair
Terrell	1856	Dawson	Dr. William Terrell
Thomas	1825	Thomasville	Gen. Jett Thomas
Tift	1905	Tifton	Col. Nelson Tift
Toombs	1905	Lyons	Robert Toombs
Towns	1856	Hiawassee	Gov. George Washington Towns

County	Year	Seat	Named for
Treutlen	1917	Soperton	Gov. John Adam Treutlen
Troup	1825	LaGrange	Gov. George Michael Troup
Turner	1905	Ashburn	Captain Henry Gray Turner
Twiggs	1809	Jeffersonville	Gen. John Twiggs
Union	1832	Blairsville	Union loyalty
Upson	1824	Thomaston	Stephen Upson
Walker	1833	LaFayette	Maj. Freeman Walker
Walton	1818	Monroe	Gov. George Walton
Ware	1824	Waycross	Nicholas Ware
Warren	1793	Warrenton	Gen. Joseph Warren
Washington	1784	Sandersville	President George Washington
Wayne	1803	Jesup	Gen. Anthony Wayne
Webster	1853	Preston	Daniel Webster
Wheeler	1912	Alamo	Gen. Joseph Wheeler
White	1857	Cleveland	David Thomas White
Whitfield	1851	Dalton	Reverend George Whitfield
Wilcox	1857	Abbeville	Maj. Gen. Mark Wilcox
Wilkes	1777	Washington	John Wilkes
Wilkinson	1803	Irwinton	Gen. James Marion Wilkinson
Worth	1853	Sylvester	Gen. William James Worth

APPENDIX III

GOVERNORS OF GEORGIA

TRUSTEE

James Edward Oglethorpe, Trustee 1733-1743

William Stephens, President 1743-1751

Henry Parker, President 1751-1752

Patrick Graham, President 1752-1754

ROYAL GOVERNORS

John Reynolds 1754-1757

Henry Ellis 1757-1760

James Wright 1760-1776

PROVISIONAL GOVERNORS

Archibald Bulloch (President, Safety Council) 1776-1777

Button Gwinnett (President, Safety Council) 1777-1777

STATE GOVERNORS

John Adam Treutlen 1777-1778

John Houstoun 1778-1779

John Wereat (President, Executive Council) 1779-1780

George Walton 1779-1780

Richard Howley 1780-1780

Stephen Heard (President, Executive Council) 1780-1781

Nathan Brownson 1781-1782

John Martin	1782-1783
Lyman Hall	1783-1784
John Houstoun	1784-1785
Samuel Elbert	1785-1786
Edward Telfair	1786-1787
George Mathews	1787-1788
George Handley	1788-1789
George Walton	1789-1789
Edward Telfair	1789-1793
George Mathews	1793-1796
Jared Irwin	1796-1798
James Jackson	1798-1801
David Emanuel (President, State Senate)	1801-1801
Josiah Tattnall, Jr.	1801-1802
John Milledge	1802-1806
Jared Irwin (President, State Senate)	1806-1809
David Brydie Mitchell	1809-1813
Peter Early	1813-1815
David Brydie Mitchell	1815-1817
William Raburn (President, State Senate)	1817-1819
Matthew Talbot (President, State Senate)	1819-1819
John Clark	1819-1823
George Michael Troup	1823-1827
John Forsyth	1827-1829
George Rockingham Gilmer	1829-1831
Wilson Lumpkin	1831-1835
William Schley	1835-1837
George Rockingham Gilmer	1837-1839
Charles James McDonald	1839-1843

George Walter Crawford 1843-1847

George Washington Towns 1847-1851

Howell Cobb 1851-1852

Herschel Vespasian Johnson 1852-1857

Joseph Emerson Brown 1857-1865

James Johnson (Provisional) 1865-1865

Charles Jones Jenkins 1865-1868

Thomas Howard Ruger 1868-1868

Rufus Brown Bullock 1868-1871

Benjamin Conley 1871-1872

James Milton Smith 1872-1877

Alfred Holt Colquitt 1877-1882

Alexander Hamilton Stephens 1882-1883

James Stoddard Boynton (President, State Senate) 1883-1883

Henry Dickerson McDaniel 1883-1886

John Brown Gordon 1886-1890

William Jonathan Northen 1890-1894

William Yates Atkinson 1894-1898

Allen Daniel Candler 1898-1902

Joseph Meriwether Terrell 1902-1907

Hoke Smith 1907-1909

Joseph Mackey Brown 1909-1911

Hoke Smith 1911-1911

John Marshall Slaton (President, State Senate) 1911-1912

Joseph Mackey Brown 1912-1913

John Marshall Slaton 1913-1915

Nathaniel Edwin Harris 1915-1917

Hugh Manson Dorsey 1917-1921

Thomas William Hardwick 1921-1923

Clifford Walker 1923-1927

Lamartine Griffin Hardman 1927-1931

Richard Brevard Russell, Jr. 1931-1933

Eugene Talmadge 1933-1937

Eurith Dickinson Rivers 1937-1941

Eugene Talmadge 1941-1943

Ellis Gibbs Arnall 1943-1947

Melvin E. Thompson 1947-1948

Herman E. Talmadge 1948-1955

S. Marvin Griffin 1955-1959

Samuel Ernest Vandiver, Jr. 1959-1963

Carl E. Sanders 1963-1967

Lester Maddox 1967-1971

Jimmy Carter 1971-1975

George Busbee 1975-1983

Joe Frank Harris 1983-1991

Zell Miller 1991-1999

Roy Barnes 1999-

GLOSSARY

This glossary contains those terms that are **bold-faced** in the textbook. The chapter in which the term appears is shown in parentheses following the definition. Correct pronunciation of selected terms is provided.

PRONUNCIATION KEY

ǀ	pat	Đ	t**o**e, h**oa**rse
~	p**a**y	ô	c**au**ght, p**aw**, f**or**
â	**a**re	oi	n**oi**se
ä	f**a**ther	ö	t**oo**k
b	**b**i**b**	ü	b**oo**t
ch	**ch**ur**ch**	ou	**ou**t
d	**d**ee**d**, mille**d**	p	**p**o**p**
"	p**e**t	r	**r**oa**r**
—	b**ee**	s	**s**au**ce**
f	**f**i**f**e, **ph**ase, rou**gh**	sh	**sh**ip, di**sh**
g	**g**a**g**	t	**t**igh**t**, stopp**ed**
h	**h**at	th	**th**in
hw	**wh**ich	th	**th**is
°	p**i**t	è	c**u**t
°	p**i**e. b**y**	û	**ur**ge. t**er**m, f**ir**m
îr	p**ier**		w**or**d, h**ear**d
j	**j**u**dg**e	v	**v**al**v**e
k	**k**i**ck**, **c**at, pi**q**ue	w	**w**ith
l	**l**id, need**l**e	z	**z**ebra, **x**ylem,
m	**m**u**m**		vi**s**ion, plea**s**ure
n	**n**o, sudde**n**	-	**a**bout, it**e**m, edibl**e**,
ng	thi**ng**		gall**o**p, circ**u**s
Đ	**p**ot	-r	butt**er**

A

abolitionists (ǀb'- - l°sh'-n - °st) many northern whites and free blacks who worked to get rid of slavery. (7)

affirmative action programs federal programs designed to provide employment opportunities for women and minorities. (16)

Agricultural Extension Service created by the Smith-Lever Act of 1914, this service gave matching federal funds to states that spent money to teach young people better farming methods. (12)

ally (ǀl' °) one who shares a common cause. (10)

amend to change. (5)

American Federation of Labor a labor organization begun in 1886 with Samuel Gompers as president that worked to bring about collective bargaining, higher wages, shorter working hours, and better working conditions. (12)

anarchist (ǀn'-r - k°st) an anti-government terrorist. (12)

annals (ǀn'-lz) records. (10)

antebellum (ǀn' t— - b"l'-m) before the war. (7)

anthropologist (ǀn' thr- - pĐl'- - j°st) one who studies how human culture began and developed. (2)

antibiotics (ǀn' t— - b°' Đt - °ks) antibacterial drugs. (15)

anti-Semitic (ǀn' t°- s- - m°'- t°k) anti-Jewish. (13)

appropriate to budget. (10)

aquaculture a fairly new fishing enterprise where ponds are built to raise trout or catfish that are fed until they are large enough to harvest and sell commercially. (17)

archaeologist (är' k— - Đl'- - j°st) one who studies artifacts to learn about the life, people, and customs of early times. (2)

armistice (är' m- - st°s) an agreement to stop fighting. (12)

arsenal (är' s- - n-l) an arms storehouse. (7)

Articles of Confederation a set of rules that formed the first constitution of the United States of America. (4)

artifacts items such as pottery, tools, or weapons that were made by humans. (2)

artisan (är' t- - z-n) a craftsperson. (3)

assets financial holdings. (17)

Atlanta Compromise speech a speech given by Booker T. Washington that proposed that blacks and whites should agree to benefit from each other. (13)

Australian ballot a ballot printed by the government rather than by a political party, distributed at the voting places, and collected there in sealed boxes so that the votes would be kept secret. (10)

B

baby boom the period following World War II when millions of children were born during the postwar years. (15)

Back-to-Africa movement popular in the 1890s, this movement promised cheap transportation to Liberia for the purpose of establishing colonies. (13)

bauxite (bôk' s°t) a mineral used in the manufacture of aluminum. (11)

bill a draft of a proposed law. (18)

Black Codes laws passed that were designed to restrict the rights of freedmen. (9)

blockade to obstruct a port from incoming or outgoing vessels. (8)

blockade runner one who attempts to steal past the port blockades. (8)

boll the place where the fibers are formed on the cotton plant. (14)

boll weevil a small, grayish, long-snouted beetle that hatches in the yellow flower of the cotton plant and feeds on the white, fluffy cotton, making it useless. (14)

bond issue the method of some level of government to raise money for a public project. (18)

Bourbon Triumvirate (bür' b-n tr° - èm' v- - °t) three Georgia political leaders in the period right after Reconstruction. (10)

boycott the refusal to buy, sell, or use an item or service in order to force a change. (15)

brain trust a group of advisers to President Franklin Roosevelt who helped Congress pass a series of laws that came to be known as the New Deal. (14)

Brown v. Board of Education the judgment of a lawsuit brought by the father of Linda Brown against the Topeka Board of Education to allow her enrollment in an all-white school in Topeka, Kansas; it declared that "separate but equal" schools were illegal and ordered the racial integration of schools "with all deliberate speed." (15)

C

capital the seat of government. (18)

capitol a building that houses offices for the governor, lieutenant governor, and other state officials. (18)

carpetbaggers northerners, attempting to help carry out Congress's Reconstruction plan, who arrived in the South with all their belongings packed in cheap luggage made from carpets. (9)

cavalry troops mounted on horseback. (8)

celluloid (s"l' y- - loid') a hard plastic-like material that was produced commercially for the first time in 1872. (11)

Centers for Disease Control laboratories where scientists are able to locate the source and methods of transmission of diseases. (16)

chain gangs a method of handling prisoners in which they were chained by their wrists and ankles so they could not escape. (12)

charter a legal document that grants special rights and privileges. (3)

checks and balances a system providing separate powers for each branch of government which prevents any one branch having too much power. (18)

Cherokee Phoenix the first Indian newspaper, edited by Elias Boudinot, and printed in both Cherokee and English. (6)

civil rights the rights of citizens of a country. (13)

Civil Rights Act of 1875 a law enacted by the U.S. Congress that provided for equal accommodations for blacks and whites and said that blacks must be allowed to serve on juries. (13)

Civil Rights Act of 1964 a law passed by Congress which resulted in the federal government refusing federal funds to any school system that did not end segregation. (15)

clan a group of people who believed themselves related by blood to other groups of people. (2)

class structure the position one group has in relation to others. (7)

climate the kind of weather a region has over a period of time. (1)

cloning (klÐ' n°ng) duplicating. (16)

collective bargaining discussions between a union and an employer regarding working conditions and workers' wages and benefits. (14)

committee a small working group. (18)

compromise a way to settle disagreements in which each side gives way a little in its demands. (5)

Compromise of 1850 a bill that allowed California to enter the Union as a free state, ended slave trading in the District of Columbia, and kept Texas from annexing New Mexico and thereby becoming part of a slave state. (7)

Confederate States of America the name given to the new nation formed by seceding states. (7)

conference committee a committee appointed when the house and senate pass different versions of a bill and need to reach a compromise. (18)

Congress of Augusta the meeting between the governors of Georgia, South Carolina, North Carolina, and Virginia and representatives of the Indian nations of the Chickasaw, Choctaw, Creek, and Cherokee that resulted in peace in the southern colonies and the transfer of 2.5 million acres of Georgia land from the Creek to the state of Georgia. (6)

conservation the management of a natural resource to prevent its destruction. (14)

constitutionalism a government that has a written constitution that describes the rights of the people and the framework of government. (18)

contracted a service for an agreed-upon price (10)

convict-lease system an attempted method to deal with high prison population where prisoners were leased to people who provided them with housing and food in exchange for labor. (10)

co-ops (kÐ′ Ðps) cooperative buying stores that purchased goods and equipment directly from producers and sold to farmers at wholesale prices. (10)

court of appeals the second highest ranking court in a state or national government. (18)

county unit system a system established for political primaries by the 1917 Neill Primary Act. (12)

Crackers a group of what plantation owners called "undesirable people" who moved from Virginia and the Carolinas to settle in the middle and western parts of the colony. (4)

credibility gap the term used to describe the difference between what many people believe to be true and what their leaders tell them is true. (16)

Crédit Mobilier scandal (kr~ - d—′ mÐ - b—l - y~′) a scandal where railroads misused funds and gave some congressmen shares of stock to influence votes on construction of a transcontinental (cross continental) railroad. (10)

culture the beliefs, traditions, music, art, and social institutions of a group of people. (2)

D

Declaration of Independence a document signed on August 2, 1776 by the colonists seeking independence from England. (4)

dictator a ruler who has complete control. (14)

discrimination the denial of a person's rights because of prejudice. (7)

disfranchised (d°s - fr|n′ ch°zd) having voting rights taken away. (9)

diversified economy an economy with a variety of businesses or industries in which people work. (17)

Dixiecrats a group of southerners led by J. Strom Thurmond of South Carolina who protested the inclusion of a civil rights plank in the Democratic party's platform. (15)

driver one, usually an older slave who was loyal to the owner, who could manage the other slaves. (7)

drought (drout) an extended period of extreme dryness from the lack of rain. (14)

E

Eighteenth Amendment a U.S. Constitutional amendment which prohibited the manufacture, sale, and transportation of intoxicating beverages. (12)

electorate (° - l"k′ t-r - °t) voters. (18)

electric street trolley an electric railway invented in 1888 by Frank Sprague in Richmond, Virginia. (11)

Emancipation Proclamation a document that stated that unless the South surrendered by January 1, 1863, all their slaves would be forever free. (8)

embargo stopping all trade with a foreign country. (5)

emigrated moved to another place. (6)

Equal Rights Amendment an attempted amendment to the U.S. Constitution which would prohibit denial or abridging a person's equal rights under the law because of his or her sex. (16)

estate possessions. (13)

exhibition large meetings, like the International Cotton Exhibition, that showed progress in agriculture or business. (11)

executive branch the largest branch of state government which is led by the governor, the chief executive officer of the state, or the president, the chief executive officer of the nation. (18)

F

Farmers' Alliance began as a social organization, this group formed cooperative buying stores to help farmers buy goods at wholesale prices. (10)

fauna (fô′ n-) the animal life of a particular area. (1)

Federal Housing Act passed in 1949, this act banned racial discrimination in federally financed housing. (15)

federal system a form of government in which the national government and the state government exercise authority over the same territory and the same people. (18)

Fifteenth Amendment an amendment to the U. S. Constitution that stated that the rights of a citizen to vote should not be denied because of race, color, or previous condition of servitude. (9)

Five Freedoms the five basic rights described in the first amendment to the U. S. Constitution. (18)

flora (flô′ r-) the natural vegetation of the land. (1)

Force Act of 1870 one of the laws enacted by the U. S. Congress that ended the activities of the Ku Klux Klan in the South. (9)

Fourteenth Amendment an amendment to the U. S. Constitution that forbade any state from making laws that would limit the rights and privileges of any citizen. (9)

free soilers a group who were against slavery and wanted land to be given to western settlers for farming. (7)

free states states that permitted slavery. (7)

freedmen (fr—d' m-n) former slaves. (9)

Freedmen's Bureau an agency established after the Civil War by the U. S. government to help both blacks and whites cope with their everyday problems by offering them clothing, food, and other necessities. (9)

French and Indian War a 1756-1763 war in which the British fought the French and the American Indians for control of land. (4)

G

garrison military force. (8)

General Assembly the Georgia bicameral legislature that includes a senate and a house of representatives. (5)

general election an election held in November at least every even-numbered year when major federal and state officials are selected. (18)

genes the body's building blocks. (16)

gentrification (j°n' tr° - f° - k~' sh-n) the return to and upgrading of older neighborhoods by people. (16)

geography the science of studying the earth as the home of humans. (1)

Georgia Act a law passed by the federal government which placed the state of Georgia under military rule. (9)

Georgia Minimum Foundation for Education Act passed by the Georgia General Assembly in 1949, this act lengthened the school year to nine months and raised standards for buildings, equipment, transportation, and school curricula. (15)

Gettysburg Address a speech made by President Abraham Lincoln that dedicated a cemetery for those who died in the Battle of Gettysburg. (8)

Girl Scouts of America established in 1915 by Juliette Gordon Low and first known as Girl Guides, this organization was for girls to experience the fun of scouting. (12)

global warming the overall increase in temperature on the planet as a result of various factors including the discharge of carbon dioxide into the atmosphere. (16)

grandfather clause A clause in a law enacted in 1908 by the Georgia General Assembly that stated that only those men whose fathers or grandfathers had been eligible to vote in 1867 were now eligible to vote. (13)

Grange (the) the name used for the "Patrons of Husbandry," a group organized to allow social gatherings where farmers could talk about common problems. (10)

Great Depression the period of economic depression after the 1929 stock market crash. (14)

Great Migration the movement in 1910 of many rural South blacks to cities in the North. (13)

Gross State Product (GSP) the total amount of all goods and services provided in a state and the surest measure of that state's economy. (17)

H

headright system a system of giving land that once belonged to the Indians to male settlers, counting each white male as a "head" and able to receive 1,000 acres. (5)

Hope scholarship program a Georgia program begun in Governor Zell Miller's term of office that provides scholarships to cover college, technical school, or university tuition and books for Georgia high school graduates. (16)

hurricane A destructive storm that is spawned when waters of 80°F or more transform the heat energy of tropical waters into strong winds and heavy waves. (1)

I

impeachment the process in which charges are brought to seek removal of a person from office. (9)

incandescent (°n' k|n - d"s' -nt) a lamp that glows by carbonizing a filament of cotton. (11)

indentured servants people from other countries who agree to work for someone for a set period of time, usually from 4 to 7 years, in return for passage to the new world. (3)

independence political or economic freedom. (4)

interdependent dependence upon others in order to ensure success of both. (17)

interim committee a special committee which works on assigned issues and concerns between sessions of the legislature. (18)

International Ladies Garment Workers Union an organization formed in 1900 to work toward improving local building codes and labor laws that would make work places safer. (12)

J

Jim Crow laws laws in the South that resulted in separate restrooms, water fountains, railroad cars, waiting rooms, dining areas, and schools. (13)

joint committee a special committee made up of members of both houses that works on an assigned topic or issue. (18)

judicial branch the branch of government that consists of th courts (18)

judiciary (jì - d°sh' — - "r' —) the court system. (5)

jurisdiction the range of actions over which a court has control or influence. (18)

K

Kansas-Nebraska Act act creating territories of Kansas and Nebraska. (7)

kaolin (k~' Ð - l°n) a white clay used in the manufacture of paper and other products. (11)

kenaf one of Georgia's newest cash crops, this tall, multi-leafed plant is used in various products such as paper pulp, industrial absorbents, drapes, fiberboard, rope, and kitty litter. (17)

King Cotton Diplomacy the name of the Confederacy's political strategy in the Civil War in which the South believed that the British and French textile mills needed the South's cotton to keep running and would be forced to help the South break the blockades and win the war. (8)

Know Nothing party political party against citizenship for immigrants or political office for anyone not born in the United States. (7)

Ku Klux Klan secret organization that tried to keep blacks from using their newly granted civil rights during the early Reconstruction period. (9)

L

latitude the distance north or south of the equator. (1)

legislation (l"j' °s - l~' sh-n) laws passed by a government. (9)

legislative branch known as the Georgia General Assembly, this branch of state government makes the laws for the state. (18)

levy (l"v' —) to impose taxes. (5)

Liberty Boys a group of Georgians who came together to oppose the Stamp act. (4)

linotype machine (l°' Ð - t°p') a mechanical type-setting device invented in 1885 by Ottmar Merganthaler. (11)

litigation (l°t' ° - g~' sh-n) suing in a court of law. (6)

longitude a measure of the distance east or west of the prime meridian. (1)

Louisiana Purchase a transaction in which the United States bought all the land from the Mississippi River west to the Rocky Mountains from France for $15 million, doubling the size of the country. (5)

lynchings (l°nch' °ngs) illegal hangings, usually by mobs. (13)

M

magnanimity (m|g' n- -n°m' ° - t—) generosity. (6)

martial law military rule. (12)

mercantilism (mûr' k-n - t—l' °z'-m) England's trade policy that it should export more than it imported. (3)

Metropolitan Atlanta Rapid Transit Authority (MARTA) a special-purpose district that runs a bus and rail system, determines the cost of fares, selects routes, and schedules public transportation times. (18)

middlemen traders who buy goods from producers and sell them to other traders and consumers. (3)

militia (m- - l°sh' -) a citizen army that defends a town or area. (3)

minimum wage the least amount an employer can pay an employee for a certain number of hours worked. (14)

Missouri Compromise admitted Maine into the Union as a free state and Missouri as a slave statc. (7)

monarchs kings and queens. (3)

motels motor hotels provided for the convenience of the traveling public. (14)

N

National Association for the Advancement of Colored People a group formed in 1909 consisting of white liberals and the black Niagara Movement to help blacks in their struggle for equality. (13)

National Congress of Colored Parents and Teachers a group organized in 1926 through the work of Selena Sloan Butler that was dedicated to protecting the rights of all children, regardless of their race. (13)

National Organization for Women a woman's organization that works for legal and institutional change that benefits women. (16)

National School Lunch Act passed in 1946, this bill ensured that school children were provided nutritious lunches through the use of government surplus food items such as cheese, flour, and peanut butter. (15)

National Urban League an interracial organization begun in 1910 that worked to solve social problems facing blacks who lived in the cities. (13)

National Women's Political Caucus an organization that attempts to get more women into political office. (16)

naval stores a raw material from forests such as turpentine, rosin, tar, and pitch used in shipbuilding. (11)

Navigation Act a law requiring the colonies to use only British vessels to ship their goods. (4)

Neil Primary Act an act passed that established a county unit system for political primaries. (12)

neutral not taking sides. (12)

New Deal a series of laws passed by the United States Congress during the presidency of Franklin D. Roosevelt to fight the effects of the depression. (14)

New South a term coined by Henry W. Grady and used to describe southern progress in the late 1800s. (10)

Niagara Movement a group of black educators and professional men formed in 1905 by W. E. B. DuBois and William Trotter that drew up a list of demands that included the abolition of discrimination based on race or color. (13)

Nineteenth Amendment an amendment to the U. S. Constitution giving women the right to vote. (12)

normal school a training school for teachers. (11)

Northwest Passage an all-water route to Asia through the North American continent. (3)

O

ocean current water in the oceans that move constantly and form rivers in the ocean. (1)

Oconee War war along the Oconee River between the Creek tribes led by Chief Alexander McGillivray and the pioneer settlers. (6)

ordinance a bill introduced into a legislative body. (7)

overseer a person hired to manage slaves on a day-to-day basis. (7)

P

parish a section of land that was both a church and a British government district. (4)

pasteurization (p|s' ch-r - - - z~' sh-n) the process of heating milk, cider, and other products to a high temperature to kill the bacteria before transferring the products into sterilized bottles with sealed tops. (11)

patronage (p~' tr- - n°j) a system where officeholders promise favors and jobs in return for support. (10)

Pendleton Civil Service Act of 1883 an act of Congress in which a series of competitive civil service examinations are used to fill job vacancies, ensuring that the person best suited for the job would be chosen for it. (10)

per capita income the average income earned by each worker. (17)

philanthropic (f°l' -n - thrÐp' °k) charitable. (10)

platform a statement of the principles and policies a political party supports. (7)

Plessy v. ***Ferguson*** a U. S. Supreme Court case decision that created the separate-but-equal concept which allowed states to pass laws to segregate facilities for blacks and whites. (13)

plurality (plü -r|l' - - t—) a majority. (12)

poll tax a tax imposed to be able to vote. (13)

polls voting places. (10)

popular sovereignty the right of people to decide an issue. (7)

Populist party a "People's party" formed by combining the Farmer's Alliance and members of labor organizations whose purpose was to protest unfair practices. (10)

precipitation rain, hail, sleet, or snow. (1)

price supports guaranteed higher prices to farmers who agreed to cut back their cotton, tobacco, and other crops. (14)

prime meridian an imaginary line beginning at Greenwich, England, encircling the globe. (1)

Proclamation of 1763 Britain's plan for establishing certain boundaries in an attempt to manage two million colonists and maintain peace between the colonists and the Indians. (6)

progressive movement a movement by the Progressives in the late 1800s and early 1900s that was fueled by the belief that government—local, state, and national—was best equipped to correct the ills of society. (12)

prohibition the banning of alcoholic beverages. (12)

proprietary colony (pr- - pr°' - - t"r' —) a colony that is directed by those to whom a charter has been granted. (4)

provisional temporary. (9)

public regulation laws made by the legislature governing the morals, public health, business or professional dealings, or any general welfare rule which restricts personal property. (18)

Puritans a group of people who had broken away from the Church of England because of religious differences. (4)

Q

Quality Core Curriculum a standard state curriculum that ensures similar study objectives for each grade throughout the state. (18)

Quartering Act a law of England that forced all citizens of the colonies to house and feed British soldiers at their own expense. (4)

R

ratified approved. (4)

rationed the limiting of the consumption of certain items. (14)

rations portions of food. (8)

reapportion (r—' - - pôr' sh-n) to redistribute. (15)

Reconstruction the process developed to restore the southern states to the Union as quickly and easily as possible after the Civil War. (9)

Red Sticks Indians that wanted war. (6)

Redemption Era the term used to describe the period right after Reconstruction. (10)

regulation government orders used instead of laws. (3)

relief money or goods given to people in special need. (14)

Republican party a new political party created in 1854 as a result of the issue of slavery. (7)

royal colony a colony that was directly governed by the king. (4)

rural electrification a New Deal program in which power companies ran electric power lines to rural areas. (14)

Rural Free Delivery (RFD) bill a bill introduced into Congress that required the U. S. postmaster general to spend $10,000 to find a way to deliver mail to rural homes free of charge. (10)

S

scalawags a term used to describe southerners who supported the radical Republicans in 1867. (9)

scrip paper money that is not legal currency. (11)

secession (s° - s°sh' -n) the act of pulling out of the Union. (7)

Second Continental Congress a meeting of the colonists asking King George II to not take further unfriendly steps against the colonies and to create an army which was to be led by George Washington of Virginia. (4)

sectionalism a concept in which people in an area believe their ideas and interests are more important than those of people in other areas. (7)

sector a part of the economy. (17)

segregation separation of races. (13)

separate-but-equal concept a concept created by the *Plessy v. Ferguson* ruling that allowed states to pass laws to segregate facilities for blacks and whites. (13)

separation of powers a division of responsibilities within government. (18)

sharecropping a system of farming in which the land owner provided the land, a house, farming tools, animals, seed, and fertilizers in exchange for the farmer's labor and a share of the crops. (9)

sit-in a type of demonstration in which people enter a public building and refuse to leave until they are served. (15)

slave a person who has few rights and who spends his or her entire life in involuntary service to others. (3)

slave codes laws that took away nearly all the rights of slaves. (7)

slave states states that permitted slavery. (7)

Smith-Hughes Act an act that helped establish vocational programs in public schools across the nation. (12)

Smith-Lever Act an act that created the Agricultural Extension Service which gave matching federal funds to states who spent money to teach young people better farming methods. (12)

Social Security Act a law passed by the United States Congress that protects workers against unemployment. (14)

Southern Christian Leadership Conference a group formed with the help of Rev. Martin Luther King, Jr., that advocated the non-violent approach for social change throughout the South. (15)

sovereignty (sÐv' -r - -n - t—) the supreme power or source of authority. (18)

Stamp Act a law passed by England to tax newspapers, legal documents, and licenses in the colony to raise enough money to pay for the French and Indian War. (4)

states' rights the idea that any power not clearly given to the United States Congress belonged to the states. (5)

stock market the place where shares of stock in corporations is bought and sold. (14)

strategies plans laid down. (8)

stretch out the practice that required workers to do the same amount of work in a shorter period of time. (14)

Student Nonviolent Coordinating Committee a student organization that worked with the NAACP to test the ruling prohibiting segregation in interstate bus and train stations. (15)

suburbs communities on the outskirts of cities. (11)

suffrage the right to vote, particlarly for women. (10)

suffragettes (sèf - r- - j"ts') a name given to those fighting for women's rights.(12)

supreme court the highest-ranking court in a state or national government. (18)

sutler wagons non-military wagons that followed behind the troops that were packed with food, razors, writing papers, pens, sewing needles, and other goods. (8)

sweatshop a business that employs young children to work long hours at often dangerous duties for low pay. (12)

syllabary (s°l' - - b"r' —) a group of symbols that stand for whole syllables. (6)

T

tariffs taxes on imported items. (5)

temperance anti-alcohol. (10)

tenant farming a system of farming where tenants worked the owner's land using their own equipment and supplies and paid the land owner a set amount of cash or an agreed-upon share of the crop. (9)

Tennessee Valley Authority an improvement project by the United States Congress that created a number of dams on the Tennessee River and its tributaries to provide cheap electricity to states, improve navigation on the rivers, attract industry, control flooding, improve farming, and create recreational areas. (14)

terrorism action of a group or individual to spread fear by actually committing acts of destruction or by threatening to commit them. (16)

textiles woven materials. (11)

Thirteenth Amendment an amendment to the U. S. Constitution that ended slavery. (9)

three-month school year a school term of three months. (11)

tilling plowing the soil. (11)

Tories colonists who remained loyal to England. (4)

tornado severe thunderstorm that forms when warm moist air mixes with a rapidly moving cold front. (1)

Townshend Acts a law of England that placed import taxes on tea, paper, glass, and coloring for paints. (4)

Trail of Tears (The) the forced removal of the Cherokee Indians west to reservations in Oklahoma. (6)

transcontinental across the continent. (10)

Treaty of Ghent a peace agreement which was signed in 1814 and ended the War of 1812. (5)

Treaty of Indian Springs an agreement that the U.S. would pay $200,000 for the Lower Creeks to cede the last of Creek lands in Georgia to the federal government. (6)

Treaty of New York an agreement to settle the Oconee War. (6)

Treaty of Paris (1763) an agreement ending the French and Indian War. (6)

Treaty of Paris (1783) an agreement signed by England, France, and the United States acknowledging the colonies' independence. (6)

trial court courts that hear original cases. (18)

tribe a group of people who share a common ancestry, name, and way of living. (2)

U

U.S. Constitution the document that set up our current framework for government; written in 1787 and ratified by the thirteen states. (5)

underground railroad a chain of homes, farms, and churches where runaway slaves could rest and hide from slave catchers. (7)

urban (ûr' b-n) city-like. (10)

V

Voting Rights Bill of 1965 an act passed by Congress in 1965 that enforced equal voting rights among all races. (15)

W

weather the day-to-day changes in temperature, rain or snow fall, wind, and so on. (1)

Whigs (hw°gs) a group of Georgians who joined others in the colonies to seek freedom from British rule. (4)

White Sticks Indians that wanted peace. (6)

white supremacist (s- - pr"m' - s°st) someone who believes the white race is superior to the black race or to any other race. (12)

wind current a continuous movement or flow of air. (1)

Women's Christian Temperance Union a temperance organization led by Frances Willard. (12)

women's rights movement an effort by women to bring about major changes in the way society viewed women and their contributions to society. (16)

World War I the war "to make the world safe for democracy" fought between 1914 and 1918 between the Central Powers led by Germany and Austria-Hungary and the Allied Powers led by France, Great Britain, and Russia, and the United States. (12)

World War II the 1939-1945 war between the Axis powers of Japan, Germany, and Italy and the Allied powers led by Great Britain and, in 1941, America. (14)

Y

Yamasee War skirmishes in which the Yamasee, a Creek tribe, attacked plantations along the South Carolina coast and killed traders in Creek and Choctaw towns. (6)

Yazoo Land Fraud sale of land to four land companies after the governor and members of the general assembly had accepted bribes. (5)

yeoman farmers (yÐ' m-n) farmers who owned less than 500 acres of land. (7)

INDEX

Miller, Arthur, 499
Miller, Glenn, 497
Miller, Governor Zell, 553, 556, p598-599, p617
Miller, H. V. M., 298
Miller, Mrs. Catherine Greene, 164
Milliken's Bend, Mississippi, 266
Minimum wage, 459
Minnesota, 158
Mississippi, 160, p161, 190, 196, 242, p241, 242, 264, 265, m265
  River, 58, p82-83, 88, 99, 125, 158, 160, 188, 189, 199, 253, 254, 554
  state capitol, p528
  Territory, 192
Mississippian Indians, 49, m56, 58, p58, 59, 60
Mississippian Period, 58, p58
Missouri, 218, 221, 222
  Compromise, (1820), 218, p218, 221, 238
  Territory of, 218
Mitchell, General (Union), 261
Model T Ford, 398, 409, p409
Mohawk Indians, 131, p131
Monongahela River, 188
Monroe Advertiser, 377
Monroe Doctrine, 193
Monroe, Georgia, 171
Monroe, President James, 158, 184, 193, p193
Montezuma, Georgia, 87, 353, 554, p554-555
Montgomery, Alabama, 242, 247, 248, 375, 519, p519, 520, 528, 529
  Bus Boycott, 519, p519, 520, 522
Montgomery, Sir Robert, 96, p96, 100
Montgomery Ward, 398, 446, 449
Monticello, Georgia, 171
Moore, Henry P., 283
Morehouse College, 312, 432, 433, 522
Morris Brown College, 433
Morrison, Dorothy, p518
Morse, Samuel F. B., 276
Morton, Dr. William, 174
Morton, "Jelly Roll," 374
Motown Records, 497
Mott, Lucretia, 219, 393
Mountain Park, Georgia, 610

Mozambique, 577
Mrs. Wiggs of the Cabbage Patch, 396
muckrakers, 386
Mulberry Grove Plantation, 164
Murphy, Representative Tom, p601
Murrah Federal Building, see Alfred P. Murrah Federal Building
Muscogee Indians, 62
Musgrove, John, 102
Musgrove, Mary, 102
Mussolini, Benito, 473, 480
My Fair Lady, 499

N

Nabrit, James Jr., p514
Nagasaki, Japan, 484
Nahunta, Georgia, 79
Nairne, Thomas, 186
Naismith, Dr. James, 396
Nantahala Mountains, 79
Nashville, Tennessee, 372, 426, 432
Nast, Thomas, 596, p595
Nat Turner Rebellion, p216, 217
Nation, Carrie, 390, p391, 392
National Archives, 136
National Association for the Advancement of Colored People (NAACP), 429, 433, 438, p464-465, 514, p515, 520, 523
National Association of Teachers of Colored Schools, 433
National Congress of Colored Parents and Teachers (NCCPT), 434
National Education Association, 422
National Industrial Recovery Act (NIRA), 458, 460
National League, 380
National Organization for Women (NOW), 538
National Origins Act, 1924, 333
National Pencil Company, 440
National School Lunch Act, 504
National Union of Textile Workers, 388
National Urban League, 430
National Woman Suffrage Association Convention, 394

National Women's Political Caucus, 538
National Youth Administration (NYA), 461, p464
Navigation Act (1763), 128
Nazis, 473
Nebraska, 221
Negro Soldier Law, 267
Neighborhood Union, 433, p433
Neill Primary Act, 1917, 404
New Deal, 445, 458, p458, 462, 464, p464, 465, 468, p468, 470, 483, 570, 596
New Ebenezer, 107
New Echota, 183, p183, 198, 199
New England, 95, 118, 120, 312, 583
  Conservatory of Music, 522
New Guinea, 476
New Hampshire, 117
New Hope, Georgia, 270
New Jersey, 117, 122, 294
  Plan, 154, 155
New Mexico, 220, 221
New Orleans, Louisiana, 125, 158, 189, 209, 280, 354, 377, 421, p429
New South, p348-349, 356, p359, 360, p368-369, 369, 374, 377, p381, 419, p421
New York City, 22, 117, 119, 190, 218, 226, 249, 277, 282, 297, 299, p300-301, 302, 303, 312, 331, 334, 350, 355, 374, 386, 389, 390, 395, 398, 408, 411, 429, 433, 436, p449, 479, 499, 536, 548, p596
New York state, 573
New Zealand, 474
Newark, New Jersey, 530
Newfoundland, 86
Newnan, Georgia, p338-339
Newsweek Magazine, 500
Newton, Georgia, 554
Niagara Falls, New York, 427
Niagara Movement, 427, p427, 428, 429, 432, 436
Nichols, Terry, 549
Nisbet, Eugenius, 241
Nitti, Frank "the Enforcer," 446
Nixon, Edward, 5622
Nixon, President Richard M., 540, 542, p542, 543, 544
Nob Hill, San Francisco, 395
Nobel Peace Prize, 403

Thirteenth Amendment, 291, 292
Corps of Engineers, 29, p29
Department of Commerce, 563
Department of Justice, 437, 518
District Court for Northern District of Georgia, 524
Government Bill of Rights, 156
executive branch, 156, 598-601
judicial branch, 156
Great Seal, 592, p592
House of Representatives, 155, 156, 218, 234, 334, 342, 459, 505, 543, 556, p556
legislative branch, 156, 603-607
National Guard, 540
Naval Academy, 544
Navy, 256, 475, 476, 484
Patent Office, 349
Revenue Cutter Service, see U.S., Coast Guard
Senate, 155, 218, p221, 324, 326, 327, p330, 334, 404, 407, 466, 468, 543, p543
Supreme Court, 198, 220, 222, p222, 334, 419, 420, 421, 448, 460, 513, p514, 515, p515, 520, 523, p531, 543, 591
Treasury, 488
White House, 159, 543
Conference on Child and Health Protection, 434
United States Holocaust Memorial Museum, 489
United States Steel, 449
United Textile Workers of America, 459
University Homes, Atlanta, 469
University of Berlin, Germany, 426
University of Georgia, 169, 171, 175, 322, 324, 331, 381, 470, 516, p517, 518, 600
Board of Regents, 466, 556
University of Texas Law School, 514
Upper Creek Indians, See Creek Indians
Utah, 221, 394

V

Valdosta, Georgia, 309
Van Buren, President Martin, 200

Vanderbilt University, 377
Vanderbilt, William, 395
Vanderbilts, 395
Vandiver, Governor Samuel Ernest, p516, 518
Vann, Chief James, 179, 184, p184-185
Veazy, Georgia, p450
Venable, Willis, 365, 367
Venerable, James, 441
Venezuela, 437
Venice, Italy, 85
Vermont, 583
Verrazano, Giovanni, 87
Vesey, Denmark, 217
Vespucci, Amerigo, 87, p87
Vicksburg, Mississippi, 266
Vidalia onions, 582, p582
Vietnam, 505
North, 538, 540, 541
South, 538
Vietnam War, 493, p531, 535, 538, p538-539, 540, p540, 541, p541, p542, p557
Villa Rica, Georgia, p365, 366, 439
Villard, Oswald Garrison, 429
Vinson, Representative Carl, 484, 595
Virgin Islands, 86, p464-465
Virginia, 91, p91, 94, 117, 126, 128, 129, 134, 139, 142, 143, 152, 154, p154, 166, 181, 188, 189, 209, p216, 217, 222, 233, 248, 255, p255, 258, 259, 264, 269, 274, 290, p322
Army of Northern, 250
Plan, 154
Voting Rights Act of 1965, 529

W

Wagner Act (1935), 460
Walker, Governor Clifford, p444-445
Wall Street, New York, p449
Walter F. George Reservoir, 25, 29, 570
Walton, George, 133, p133
Wanamaker, General John, 344
War Hawks, 159
War of 1812, 159, p159, 160, 191, 266
War of Jenkins' Ear, 110
Warm Springs Foundation, 483

Warm Springs, Georgia, 458, 478, 482, 483, p483, 502
Warner Robins Air Field, Macon, 484, p484-485, 505, 571
Warren, Robert Penn, 499
Warrenton, Georgia 20
Washington, Booker Taliaferro., 360, 422, p422-423, 424, p424, 425, p425, 426, p426. 427,428, p428,429, 430, 432, 437
Atlanta compromise speech, 425, p425, 427, 432
Washington, D.C., 136, p148-149, 159, 199, 226, 239, p257, 258, 264, 275, 289, 335, 344, 390, 402, 437, p464-465, 489, 513, 540, p540, D.C., 543, D.C., p557
Washington, Georgia, p612
Washington Monument, 525
Washington, President George, p125, 134, 139, 143, p153, 154, 156, p173, 188, p188, p189, 190, p207
Watergate, 542, p542, 543, p543, 544, 616
Waterman, Lewis, 350
Watson, Thomas Edward, 331, 342, p342, p345, 404, p404-405, p406, 428, 440, 466
Watson's Jeffersonian, 344
Watts riots, 530
Waycross, Georgia, 16
WCTU, 391
Weatherford, Chief William, p192
Weaver, James B., 341
Weaver, Robert, p464-465, 465
Webb-Kenyon Bill, 392
Webster, Daniel, 199
Webster, Noah, 172, p172
Webster's dictionary, 172
Wells, Ida, 435, 436
Welty, Eudora, 499
Wesley, Charles, 108, 112
Wesley, John, 108, 112, p113
Wesleyan College, 173, 174, 372, p372
West Germany, see Germany
West Indies, 124
West Point, Georgia, 27
West Point Lake, 25, 29
West Point Military Academy, 259, 437, p437
West Point Pepperell, 576

ACKNOWLEDGEMENTS

PICTURE CREDITS: The following abbreviations are used for sources from which several illustrations were obtained.

ADAH	Alabama Department of Archives and History
AMNH	Alabama Museum of Natural History
AHS	Atlanta Historical Society
AJ&C	*Atlanta Journal & Constitution*
AUSC	Atlanta University Special Collections
GDITT	Georgia Department of Industry, Trade, and Tourism
GHS	Georgia Historical Society
GSA	Georgia State Archives
LC	Library of Congress
NA	National Archives
NCDAH	North Carolina Division of Archives and History
OHS	Oklahoma Historical Society
TSM	Tennessee State Museum
UASC	William S. Hoole Special Collections Library, University of Alabama

FRONT MATTER: Front Cover Robin McDonald. i Robin McDonald. ii-iii Robin McDonald. iv-v Robin McDonald. vii Robin McDonald. viii (both) Bruce Roberts ix (top) Bruce Roberts; (above) Robin McDonald. **UNIT ONE:** x-1 Robin McDonald. **CHAPTER ONE:** 2-3 (all) Robin McDonald. 6 Robin McDonald. 8-9 Robin McDonald. 9 (below) GDITT. 10 (below) GDITT. 10-11 Robin McDonald. 11 GDITT. 12-13 Robin McDonald. 13 (above) Bruce Roberts 14 GDITT. 15 Robin McDonald. 16 GDITT. 16-17 Robin McDonald. 17 (below) Robin McDonald. 18 Robin McDonald. 18-19 Robin McDonald. 20 Robin McDonald. 21 (both) Robin McDonald. 23 (both) Robin McDonald. 24-25 (both) Robin McDonald. 26-27 (all) Robin McDonald. 28 (below) GDITT. 28-29 Robin McDonald. 31 GDITT. 32 GDITT. 35 Corbis/Bettmann. 36-37 (all) Robin McDonald. 38 (both) Robin McDonald. 39 Kentucky Department of Travel and Tourism. 40-41 Robin McDonald. 42 Peter Bergh. 43 Robin McDonald. **CHAPTER TWO:** 46-47: GSA. 49 Patrick Brady. 50 Pinson Mounds State Archeological Area, TN. 51 (above) AMNH; (right) Tennessee State Museum. 52 Pinson Mounds State Archeological Area, TN. 53 (below) AMNH; (right) TSM. 54 (top and above) Red Mountain Museum, drawings by Harrison Prince; (right) AMNH. 55 Pinson Mounds State Archeological Area, TN. 56-57 GDITT. 58-59 Robin McDonald; 59 (below) GDITT. 60 GDITT. 61 GDITT. 62-63 (both) Birmingham Public Library. 64 NCDAH. 64-65 Billy Barnes. 66 Smithsonian Institution. 67 Robin McDonald. 68 NCDAH. 69 North Carolina Department of Travel and Tourism. 70-71 TSM. 72 Robin McDonald. 73 Robin McDonald. 74-75 (both) UASC. 76 Cherokee Historical Association. 77 (above) Billy Barnes; (below) Cherokee Historical Association. 78 North Carolina Department of Travel and Tourism. 79 Robin McDonald. **UNIT TWO** 82-83 Architect of the Capitol. **CHAPTER THREE:** 84-85 Architect of the Capitol. 85 Corbis/Bettmann. 87 (both) Corbis/Bettmann. 88 (left) Tennessee State Library and Archives; (below) GSA. 90 LC. 91 LC. 92 University of North Carolina Press. 93 Corbis/Bettmann. 94 National Park Service 95 Public Domain 96 GHS. 97 GSA. 98 GSA. 99 (right) GSA; (above) Corbis/Bettmann. 100 GSA. 101 GSA. 102 GHS. 103 Smithsonian Institution. 104 Special Collections, University of Georgia. 105 GSA. 106 (above) GHS. 106-107 Winterthur Museum. 108 GHS. 109 GHS. 110 (top) Robin McDonald; (above) GHS. 111 GSA. 112 GSA. 113 GHS. **CHAPTER FOUR:** 116-117 Painting by David Wright. 118 GDITT. 119 TSM. 120 Robin McDonald. 121 Kentucky Historical Society 122 AUSC. 123 GSA. 124 (both) GSA. 125 Washington and Lee University. 126 Robin McDonald. 127 Robin McDonald. 128 GSA. 129 LC. 130 GSA. 131 LC. 132-133 Corbis/Bettmann. 134 (both) GSA. 135 GSA. 136-137 Architect of the Capitol. 138 GSA. 139 (top) S; (above) GSA. 140 Robin McDonald. 141 GSA. 142 GSA. 144-145 Architect of the Capitol. **UNIT THREE:** 148-149 Architect of the Capitol. **CHAPTER FIVE:** 150 Corbis/Bettmann. 151 GSA. 153 (left) GSA; (top) LC; (above) Corbis/Bettmann. 154 Library of Virginia. 155 GSA. 156 GSA. 157 LC. 159 Corbis/Bettmann. 160 (both) GSA. 161 GSA. 162 (both) GSA. 163 ADAH. 164 ADAH. 165 GHS. 166 GSA. 167 Public Domain 168-169 UASC. 170 Robin McDonald. 171 LC. 172 LC. 173 GSA. 174 AHS. 175 GSA. **CHAPTER SIX:** 178-179 Woolaroc Museum, Bartlesville, OK. 180 OHS. 181 New Echota State Historic Site. 182-183 Robin McDonald. 183 (above) GDITT. 184 GDITT. 184-185 Robin McDonald. 186-187 Wisconsin Historical Society. 188 Library of Virginia. 189 Corbis/Bettmann. 190 Museum of the City of Mobile. 191 ADAH. 192 Horseshoe Bend National Military Park. 193 Corbis/Bettmann. 194 OHS. 195 LC. 196 TSM. 197 Robin McDonald. 198 OHS. 199 OHS. 200-201 OHS. **UNIT FOUR:** 204-205 GDITT. **CHAPTER SEVEN:** 206-207 GDITT. 209 Corbis/Bettmann. 210 GSA. 211 GSA. 212 NCDAH. 213 GSA. 214 NCDAH. 215 Corbis/Bettmann. 216 TSM. 217 Corbis/Bettmann. 219 LC. 220 LC. 221 LC. 222 Corbis/Bettmann. 223 West Virginia State Archives. 224 Robin McDonald. 225 LC. 226 AHS. 227 GSA. 228-229 AHS. 230 Robin McDonald. 231 (above) G; (below, left and right) Robin McDonald. 232 Robin McDonald. 233 Robin McDonald. 234 Robin McDonald. 235 (both) GSA. 236 GSA. 237 Robin McDonald. 238 (top) TSM; (above) Filson Club. 239 LC. 242 UASC 243 UASC. **CHAPTER EIGHT:** 246-247 Robin McDonald. 249 AHS. 250 *Battles and Leaders of the Civil War.* 251 AHS. 252 Bruce Roberts. 253 LC. 254 LC. 255 LC. 256 ADAH. 257 LC. 259 LC. 260-261 (all) *Battles and Leaders of the Civil War.* 262-263 GDITT. 264 LC. 266 LC. 267 AHS. 268 LC. 269 LC. 270 LC. 271 LC. 272-273 AHS. 274-275 AHS. 275 (above) LC; (below) *Battles and Leaders of the Civil War.* 276 (above) LC; (below) Corbis/Bettmann. 277 Corbis/Bettmann. 278-279 LC. 280 NCDAH 281 AHS. 283 LC. **CHAPTER NINE:** 286-287 GSA. 288 Corbis/Bettmann. 289 NCDAH. 290 LC. 291 NCDAH 292 GSA. 293 GSA. 295 Corbis/Bettmann. 296 (above) GSA; (right) LC. 297 GHS. 298 GSA. 299 GSA. 300-301 GDITT. 302-303 AHS. 304-305 (both) AHS. 306-307 (both) AHS. 308 AHS. 309 Arizona Historical Society. 310 AHS. 311 GSA. 312 GSA. 313 AHS. 315 LC. **UNIT FIVE:** 316-317 Robin McDonald. **CHAPTER TEN:** 319 AHS. 320 GSA. 321 GSA. 322 GSA. 323 GSA. 324 Robin McDonald. 325 GSA. 326-327 Robin McDonald. 327 GSA 328 (top) GSA; (above) AHS 329 AHS. 330 AHS 331 *AJ&C* 332 LC. 333 LC. 334 LC. 335 LC. 336 Corbis/Bettmann. 337 LC. 338-339 GSA. 339 LC. 340 AHS 341 LC. 342 GSA. 343 GSA. 345 Robin McDonald. **CHAPTER ELEVEN:** 348-349 AHS. 350 LC. 351 LC. 352 LC. 353 LC. 354 ADAH. 355 LC. 356-357 LC. 358 (top and above right) AHS; (above left) Robin McDonald. 359 GHS. 360 GSA. 361 GSA. 362 *AJ&C.* 363 (both) AHS. 364-367 (all) Coca-Cola Company Archives. 368-369 AHS. 370 GSA. 371 AHS. 372 GSA. 373 GSA. 374 LC. 375 AHS. 376 GSA. 377 AHS. 378 AHS. 379 LC. 380 LC. 381 LC. **CHAPTER TWELVE:** 384-385 AHS. 387 NA. 388 Corbis/Bettmann. 389 Corbis/Bettmann. 390 LC. 391. (left) AHS; (right) Corbis/Bettmann. 392 GSA. 393 AHS. 394 AHS. 395 LC. 396-397 AHS. 398 (above left and right) AHS, (below) LC. 399 (top) GHS; (above) Corbis/Bettmann. 400 (left) GDITT; (below) GSA. 401 GDITT. 402 (both) Girl Scouts of the U.S.A. 403 LC. 404 GSA. 405 GSA. 406 AHS. 407 (both) Robin McDonald. 408 LC. 409 LC. 410 (top) Corbis/Bettmann. 417 NCDAH. 411 LC. 412 LC 413 AHS. 414 GSA. 415 (both) GSA. **CHAPTER THIRTEEN:** 418 GSA 419 GSA. 420 AHS. 422 ADAH. 423 Corbis/Bettmann. 424 LC. 425 LC. 426 Corbis/Bettmann. 427 AUSC. 428 AUSC. 429 AUSC. 430 AUSC. 431 Corbis/Bettmann. 432 AUSC. 433 AUSC. 434 AUSC. 435 AUSC. 436 AUSC. 437 AUSC. 438 (both) AUSC. 440 *AJ&C.* 441 *AJ&C.* **CHAPTER FOURTEEN:** 444-445 AHS. 446 AHS. 447 LC. 448 GHS. 449 UPI/Corbis/Bettmann. 450-451 (all) LC. 452-453 (both) LC. 454 LC. 455 LC. 456-457 AHS. 458 LC. 459 UPI/Corbis/Bettmann. 460 Birmingham Public Library. 461 LC. 462 AHS. 463 Alabama Department of Travel and Tourism. 464 (top) AUSC; (left) LC. 465 AUSC. 466 GSA. 467 GSA. 468 *AJ&C.* 469 *AJ&C.* 470 *AJ&C.* 471 GSA. 472-473 LC. 474 UPI/Corbis/Bettmann. 475 UPI/Corbis/Bettmann. 476 LC. 476-477 UPI/Corbis/Bettmann. 478 LC. 478-479 LC. 480 LC. 481 LC. 482 (top) LC; (right) *AJ&C.* 483 GDITT. 484-485 LC. 486-487 AHS. 487 (below) GSA. 488 GHS. 489 LC. **UNIT SIX:** 492-493 Robin McDonald. **CHAPTER FIFTEEN:** 494-495 AHS. 496 UPI/Corbis/Bettmann. 497 UPI/Corbis/Bettmann. 498-499 (all) UPI/Corbis/Bettmann. 500 UPI/Corbis/Bettmann. 501 (both) UPI/Corbis/Bettmann. 502-503 (all) Robin McDonald. 504 *AJ&C.* 505 UPI/Corbis/Bettmann. 506 (both) LC. 507 (both) *AJ&C.* 508-509 (both) *AJ&C.* 510 (top) AHS. (right) *AJ&C.* 512-513 *AJ&C.* 514 UPI/Corbis/Bettmann. 515 UPI/Corbis/Bettmann. 516 GSA. 516-517 *AJ&C.* 517 (below) *AJ&C.* 518 AHS 519 UPI/Corbis/Bettmann. 520 AHS. 521 GSA. 522 *AJ&C.* 523 UPI/Corbis/Bettmann. 524 *Birmingham News.* 525 UPI/Corbis/Bettmann. 526 UPI/Corbis/Bettmann. 527 UPI/Corbis/Bettmann. 528-529 (both) UPI/Corbis/Bettmann. 530 *AJ&C.* 531 Robin McDonald. **CHAPTER SIXTEEN:** 534-535 *AJ&C.* 537 (top) LC; (above) Billy Barnes. 538 Billy Barnes. 539 UPI/Corbis/Bettmann. 540 LC. 541 *AJ&C.* 542 LC. 543 LC. 544 GDITT. 545 GSA. 546 UPI/Corbis/Bettmann. 547 UPI/Corbis/Bettmann. 548 UPI/Corbis/Bettmann. 549 UPI/Corbis/Bettmann. 550 Robin McDonald. 551 GDITT. 552 Bruce Roberts. 553 *AJ&C.* 554-555 UPI/Corbis/Bettmann. 556 *AJ&C.* 557 UPI/Corbis/Bettmann. **CHAPTER SEVENTEEN:** 560-561 Bruce Roberts. 564 Billy Barnes. 565 GDITT. 566-567 (all) GDITT. 568 GDITT. 570 GDITT. 571 GDITT. 572 (both) Bruce Roberts. 573 (both) Robin McDonald. 574-575 GDITT. 576-577 (all) GDITT. 578 (both) GDITT. 579 (above) Robin McDonald; (below) GDITT. 580 GDITT. 581 Bruce Roberts. 582 (both) GDITT. 583 Robin McDonald. 584 GDITT. 585 *AJ&C.* **CHAPTER EIGHTEEN:** 588-589 Robin McDonald. 590 Robin McDonald. 591 U.S. Bureau of Engraving. 592 (top) B; (above) Robin McDonald. 593 (top) Bruce Roberts; (above) Robin McDonald. 596 LC. 597 Bruce Roberts. 598 *AJ&C.* 599 GDITT. 600 *AJ&C.* 601 *AJ&C.* 602-603 GDITT. 604 *AJ&C.* 605 *AJ&C.* 606 *AJ&C.* 607 *AJ&C.* 608 Supreme Court of Georgia. 609 Robin McDonald. 610-611 Robin McDonald. 612-613 (all) Robin McDonald. 614 GDITT. 615 *AJ&C.* 616 LC. 617 *AJ&C.* 618 Robin McDonald. 619 GDITT. **BACK MATTER:** 622-623 (all) Robin McDonald. Back Cover: Robin McDonald.